Modern Architecture and Other Essays

Vincent Scully

Selected and with introductions by Neil Levine

Princeton University Press
Princeton and Oxford

Chandler House (cloth edition only)

Racquet and Tennis Club, and Lever House (cloth edition only)

Larkin Building

Seaside

Temple of Athena

Vanna Venturi House

Front cover: *(spine):* Andres Duany and Elizabeth Plater-Zyberk (master planners), Seaside, Florida, begun 1979–82; *(left edge):* Frank Lloyd Wright, Larkin Building, Buffalo, 1902–6; *(middle):* Temple of Athena, Paestum, c. 510 B.C.; *(lower right):* Venturi and Short, Vanna Venturi House, Chestnut Hill, Pennsylvania, 1959–64

Back cover *(cloth edition only): (left):* Bruce Price, Chandler House, Tuxedo Park, New York, 1885–86; *(right):* Park Avenue, New York: Racquet and Tennis Club (left; McKim, Mead and White, 1916–19) and Lever House (right; Skidmore, Owings and Merrill, 1950–52)

Frontispiece: Louis I. Kahn, Library, Phillips Exeter Academy, Exeter, New Hampshire, 1965–72

Published by Princeton University Press,
41 William Street, Princeton, New Jersey 08540
In the United Kingdom: Princeton University Press,
3 Market Place, Woodstock, Oxfordshire OX20 1SY
www.pupress.princeton.edu

Publication of this volume has been supported by grants from Furthermore, a program of the J. M. Kaplan Fund, and from the Graham Foundation for Advanced Studies in the Fine Arts.

Designed by Worksight
Typeset by Sam Potts
Printed by South China Printing, Hong Kong

Manufactured in China
(Cloth) 10 9 8 7 6 5 4 3 2 1
(Paper) 10 9 8 7 6 5 4 3 2 1

Library of Congress Cataloging-in-Publication Data
Scully, Vincent Joseph, 1920–
Modern architecture and other essays/
Vincent Scully; selected and with introductions by Neil Levine.
p. cm.
Includes bibliographical references and index.
ISBN 0-691-07441-0 (cloth : alk. paper)—
ISBN 0-691-07442-9 (pbk. : alk. paper)
1. Architecture. 2. Architecture—United States —20th century. I. Levine, Neil, 1941– II. Title.
NA27 .S38 2002
724'.6—dc21 2002019005

Contents

Acknowledgments

One of the most pleasurable aspects of producing this book was the chance to spend time with Vincent Scully learning about his life and career and, especially, about the circumstances surrounding the writing of the essays selected for this book. Though never interfering with any of my choices, he willingly submitted to hours and hours of questions and prodding for vital bits of information. Amazingly, I cannot think of a single instance in which his memory was proven wrong by someone else's. His wife, Catherine Lynn, was of equal assistance in providing information as well as hospitality.

I originally presented the idea for this book to Elizabeth Powers, who was then the art history editor at Princeton University Press. Her enthusiasm for the project was crucial in getting it launched. Deborah Malamud, then editor of American studies at Princeton, took over the book when Elizabeth retired and before a replacement could be found for her, and provided the intellectual energy that gave the book shape. Patricia Fidler, Elizabeth's successor, inherited the project from Deborah once it became clear that this was truly a book that needed an art history editorial and production staff. Her critical judgment and enthusiasm proved crucial. Nancy Grubb, who replaced Patricia, has been unwavering in her commitment to see this project through. Nancy's staff is also deserving of my most sincere thanks: Sarah Henry, Devra K. Nelson, Ken Wong, and Kate Zanzucchi.

The process of reading and selecting Scully's writings began with a seminar I offered in the Department of History of Art and Architecture at Harvard University in the fall term of 1997–98. The students who participated in the course were enormously helpful, and I should therefore like to thank Fernando Alvarez, Claudia Bancalari, David Celis, Elen Deming, Ada Polla, Scott Rothkopf, and Geoffrey Taylor for their contributions. Robert A. M. Stern was an astute and extraordinarily careful reader who made many valuable suggestions—not to mention catching numerous mistakes and errors. Nancy Gruskin agreed to compile the bibliography and did a marvelous service for us all. Helen Chillman, at Yale, proved as usual to be a valuable resource for locating visual materials; Jennifer Hock helped complete the job.

Many others provided information and help that was critical to the production of this book. My thanks go to David Brownlee, Joan Chan, David Daschiell, Michelle Elligott, Ron Evitts, Deborah Fausch, Peter Katz, Alex Krieger, Ellen McCulloch-Lovell, David Mohney, Jeff Speck, John Thorpe, Robert Venturi, Keith Walker, and the White House staff.

I also wish to acknowledge the original publishers of the essays included in this volume for graciously providing reprint permission. For reference, the introduction to each essay opens with a full bibliographic citation to the original publication. The texts of the essays appear exactly as they were originally published, except for minor editorial changes made for the purpose of consistency or clarification. In the case of essays that were originally illustrated, not all of the images have been reproduced in the present volume, and those that have are generally, though not always, precisely the same view. On the other hand, some images have been added in the present volume to essays that were not originally illustrated. Finally, although dates of buildings, projects, and other works of art have not been changed in the essays, they have, when necessary, been altered in the captions, either for consistency or to conform with recent scholarship.

Rowley, Massachusetts
August 1999 / June 2001

Introduction

NEIL LEVINE

When I was beginning the research for my college senior thesis on late-nineteenth- and early-twentieth-century American architecture, I came across an article by Vincent Scully in a relatively obscure academic journal that made a deep impression on me. The article was "The Nature of the Classical in Art" in the 1958 double-issue of *Yale French Studies.* The author was not unknown to me. I had read his book *The Shingle Style,* which had appeared three years earlier. But "The Nature of the Classical in Art" was different—from his book as well as from almost every other scholarly publication to which I had been exposed. It was provocatively broad ranging in scope, yet precise in detail and observation. The language was riveting and passionately engaged with its subject. With references to Winckelmann, Wölfflin, Panofsky, Ingres, Delacroix, Le Corbusier, and Picasso, the article made sense of a large and complex issue in clear and pregnant terms. Over the years, I have mentioned this essay to many friends and colleagues, but I cannot recall a single one of them having read it or even having known of its existence. This is just one of the reasons why I thought a volume of Vincent Scully's collected writings was a necessary and valuable undertaking.

It is, in fact, difficult to believe that no such publication already exists. As an author, as well as a teacher and lecturer of charismatic force, Vincent Scully has been a major voice in the history of modern architecture for almost half a century. His writings, which include more than fifteen books and over one hundred and twenty articles—not counting such miscellanea as reviews, introductions, and forewords—have significantly shaped not only how we view the evolution of architecture in the twentieth century but also the actual course of that evolution itself. Combining the modes of historian and critic in unique and compelling ways, with an audience that reaches across the spectrum from student and scholar to professional and layperson, Scully has profoundly influenced the way architecture is thought about and made. One can only assume that the ready availability of his many books, not to speak of the frequency with which he has lectured throughout this country and abroad, has made it seem as if there is nothing lacking in what we know of him and his work. Clearly, this is not the case—and the contents of this book are meant to reveal and fill the gaps.

The twenty essays collected here have been chosen for their unique contribution to our understanding of modern architecture together with their relative inaccessibility to the average reader. The selection, which was finalized in 1999 and thus includes nothing after that date, has been limited to articles that appeared in magazines, journals, publications of symposia, collections of essays, and books to which Scully was asked to contribute an introduction or afterword. No excerpts from his own books have been included, nor any articles that were published separately but eventually incorporated in a later edition of one of his books. Since the intention was to bring together into a single volume writings dealing in one way or another with the subject of modern architecture, important pieces related specifically to other fields have been excluded. Almost all the major themes and issues of modern architecture with which Scully has been concerned are represented in this collection, although comprehensiveness was not a primary criterion for selection. Nor was it considered essential to include writings from all periods of the author's career. And finally, since this book's purpose was not to document Scully's trajectory but rather to make readily available his most significant works, articles and essays that were important at the time they originally appeared but were superseded by later writings on the same subject have reluctantly also been eliminated. They will, however, be referred to and discussed in my brief biography of the author as well as in the introductions to the relevant individual pieces.

From the beginning, Scully's writings have been concerned with the definition of what constitutes the modern experience in architecture and how that has found expression in forms peculiar to the modern age. The special role played by America in the formation and evolution of modern architecture has been central to his thought as has been the work of some of its leading practitioners, notably Frank Lloyd Wright, Louis Kahn, Robert Venturi, and most recently, Andres Duany and Elizabeth Plater-Zyberk. Profoundly committed to the ideals of modernism, Scully has, at the same time, never ceased to reevaluate and revise his views on how those ideals can and should be achieved. Throughout his career he has been interested in the way history and memory intersect with the modernist demand for invention and originality. The importance of the classical tradition and its changing relation to the vernacular and the academic have preoccupied him since his days as a graduate student in art history at Yale. The tension between freedom and order, initially perceived in terms of architectural design per se, soon expanded into a larger conception of the relationship between the individual and the community that saw its field of operation, and influence, as the entire physical and cultural environment. The urban whole, at one extreme, and the natural landscape, at the other, replaced the isolated building as Scully's frame of reference and established the broad contextualist approach to architectural history and criticism that has sustained his writing over the years and given it its unique perspective.

Many of the essays reprinted here began as slide lectures and preserve the traces of a direct confrontation with the subject in the immediacy of the critical climate of that moment. They also reveal how willing and able Scully has been to change his opinions and revise his approach despite the constancy of certain fundamental preoccupations. His historical investigations are invariably grounded in and inflected by the critical present just as his criticism of contemporary events is guided and enriched by the historian's longer view of things. Crucial to his method is a belief in the importance of history as a process of development and change over time, a process that reveals certain universal patterns at the same time that it makes itself manifest through the discrete and ineluctably individuated expressions that are works of art. All art, in this view, owes its existence to previous works of art and thus can truly be understood and evaluated only within a historical frame of reference. The process is a dynamic one, as T. S. Eliot and Henri Focillon both pointed out in their different ways. As contemporary works build on the past and bring new meanings to its conventions and imagery, the perception of the past itself is radically altered. Reinforcing this quintessentially modern combination of aesthetic idealism and historical relativism is Scully's conviction that art is a "mysterious being," with a "constantly complicated, ambiguous, inexhaustible character of meaning."[1]

At the core of Scully's writing is the primacy of the experience of the work of art. There is, in his view, a "particular way of perceiving reality through plastic experience," and it is the special knowledge and understanding gained from this that the art historian or critic must be able to convey through precise and resonant verbal equivalents.[2] With something akin to "Dada blindness," the art historian attempts to see each new work of art afresh—for what it is and represents—without preconceptions of any sort. Scully likes to think of this as a way of "breaking the model," and his ability to "see"—and make others "see"—Kahn and Venturi very early on, despite the obvious impossibility of such a completely ideology-free mode of perception, is testimony to the powerful visual effort and effect of his writings. The psycho-philosophical concept of empathy underwrites this direct physical confrontation with the work of art and provides an explanation for the combined intellectual and emotional response that Scully holds to be the basis for any significant value judgment. Being moved by a building, painting, or piece of sculpture is one thing, but being able to induce others to have a similar experience is another. Scully has worked as hard at this as at almost anything else, and it should come as no surprise that more than one reviewer has compared the poetic sensitivity and rhetorical power of his prose to that of John Ruskin.

Recalling the writings of John Ruskin also reminds us that Scully's modernist faith in the idea of "pure visibility" should in no way be taken as a sign of mere formalism. Scully's profound investment in the means of verbal expression is an integral aspect of his activist approach to the role of architectural historian. He has always taken strong positions on issues having to do with the built environment and has often gone out on a limb to support architects and others who would help bring about desired change. As with Ruskin, a heightened visual sensibility is marshaled for moral and ethical purposes. Scully has long held the belief that "art . . . [is] as close to religion as we've got. It engages our richest, deepest, most loving and involved feelings" in what can only be described as "an ennobling experience."[3] The role of the architectural historian as critic, or the critic as architectural historian, is ultimately to bring to bear on the reader's mind the social vision that gives value and meaning to the work of art. For Scully, this vision has consistently been architecture's place in helping to shape a community where all citizens have equal opportunity and where the environment thus created respects and pays tribute to the physical conditions and cultural traditions out of which it has developed. The vision is a classically liberal one, which Scully has willingly and forthrightly defended against those to the right as well as those farther to the left. Addressing what Norman Mailer had called the "totalitarianism" of establishment modern architecture, Scully outlined his position, and political faith, in the Annual Discourse to the Royal Institute of British Architects in 1969, at the height of his involvement with redevelopment, the Vietnam War, and the Civil Rights movement:

> If heroic attitudinizing goes, what is left? Why, everything: the town with its people, . . . the country, and the road; all of it, all of architecture that is, made possible by good Government: decent policy, the consent of the governed, justice, and peace. It is that principle which emerges, and remains. In the end, when all the perceptions are in, it is that principle which the architectural historian and critic must serve, and for which he must fight in every way he can: at Tewa Tesuque under Lake Peak no less than in New Haven, under its own sacred mountain, with the monument to our Revolution and our Civil War upon it.[4]

Echoes of these sentiments can be heard throughout the writings collected here, whether they be in defense of Le Corbusier's architecture at Chandigarh, Karl Ehn's Karl Marx Hof in Vienna, Robert Venturi's Guild House in Philadelphia, the United States federal government's World War I emergency housing at Bridgeport, Connecticut, or Duany and Plater-Zyberk's town of Seaside, in Florida.

Notes

1 Vincent Scully, "Interview with Vincent Scully," 21 Oct. 1980, interview by Patricia Leighten and William B. Stargard, *The Rutgers Art Review: The Journal of Graduate Research in Art History* 2 (Jan. 1981): 96–97.

2 Vincent Scully, Letter to the Editor, *Art Bulletin* 46 (Mar. 1964): 120.

3 James Stevenson, "Profiles: What Seas What Shores," *New Yorker*, 18 Feb. 1980, 63.

4 Vincent Scully, "RIBA Discourse 1969: A Search for Principle between Two Wars," *RIBA Journal: The Journal of the Royal Institute of British Architects* 76 (June 1969): 247.

Vincent Scully: A Biographical Sketch

NEIL LEVINE

Vincent Scully is a member of the second generation of historians and critics of modern architecture, the one that followed on the heels of the pioneering work of Sigfried Giedion, Henry-Russell Hitchcock, Nikolaus Pevsner, and John Summerson and that also includes Reyner Banham, William Jordy, Colin Rowe, Peter Collins, Bruno Zevi, Leonardo Benevolo, and Christian Norberg-Schulz. He was born on 21 August 1920 to a family of relatively modest means in New Haven, Connecticut, a city that he never really left and to which his entire professional life has been intimately connected. After graduating from public high school at the age of fifteen, he entered Yale University as a scholarship student in the fall of 1936. As an English major, he fell under the sway of Chauncey Brewster Tinker, the esteemed scholar of eighteenth- and nineteenth-century British poetry, who gave the Charles Eliot Norton Lectures at Harvard University during Scully's sophomore year—the year before Giedion lectured on the subject that would become his seminal book *Space, Time and Architecture*, published in 1941. Scully was also interested in French literature and took the introductory course in the history of art in his senior year, but apparently could not quite yet find an intellectual direction. Although he was accepted by the English department to do graduate work, he was seriously put off by the increasing theoretical hegemony of the New Criticism and quit after only one class. After washing out of the Army Flying Cadets within two months, he joined the Marine Corps in 1941 and served in both the Mediterranean and Pacific theaters.

Following his discharge in January 1946, Scully entered the graduate program in the history of art at Yale, later saying that he "discovered that I had been waiting for the subject all my life. It was something I could talk and write about in words that wasn't words itself. It somehow gave me a subject, or perhaps I should say an object."[1] (His first wife, the former Nancy Keith, also of New Haven, whom he married in 1942, had majored in art history at Wellesley.) The Yale department was among the most distinguished in the country, including on its faculty George Hamilton in modern art, George Kubler in Hispanic and Pre-Columbian art and architecture, Carroll Meeks in modern architecture, and Sumner Crosby in medieval architecture. It was also unusual in being dominated by a French tradition of scholarship, stemming mainly from the presence there during the war of Henri Focillon and Marcel Aubert, rather than the German one that would become much more widespread in America under the impact of such émigré scholars as Erwin Panofsky, Kurt Weitzmann, Richard Krautheimer, Karl Lehmann, George Hanfmann, Jakob Rosenberg, Julius Held, and Rudolf Wittkower at places like the Institute of Fine Arts, Princeton, Harvard, and Columbia. Scully was deeply influenced by Focillon, whose *La Vie des formes* (1934; translated as *The Life of Forms in Art* by Kubler and Charles Beecher Hogan in 1942) was required reading for graduate students at Yale. Its emphasis on the changing meanings of forms over time and their relation to the viewer's direct visual experience would remain a guiding principle of Scully's mature thought. Aside from Focillon, Scully was also significantly affected at the time by the writings of Giedion, Hitchcock, D. H. Lawrence, Geoffrey Scott, Jean Bony, Emil Kaufmann, Le Corbusier, and Frank Lloyd Wright.

Scully took a mere three and a half years to earn his Ph.D., completing the program with a dissertation that became an award-winning book and a classic in its field. But he did much else during that brief time that presaged his quick rise to prominence. He spent the accelerated summer term of 1947 taking a course in architectural design in the architecture department. This brought him into close contact with architects and established the basis for a close relationship with the professional world that has continued to the present. The more immediate purpose of this effort, however, was to prepare him to teach Meeks's course on architectural history when the latter went on sabbatical leave in 1947–48. Scully was also hired, in the spring term of that year, to teach in the large Introduction to the History of Art course. (James Ackerman, who graduated from Yale College a year after Scully, taught with him.) During this first year of nearly full-time teaching, he published his first article, "Architecture as a Science: Is the Scientific Method Applicable to Architectural Design?"—a critique of the Giedion position, in the *Yale Scientific Magazine* (May 1948). And just a few months prior to that, he was invited to be a panel member, along with such distinguished figures as Marcel Breuer, Walter Gropius, Lewis Mumford, Hitchcock, Philip Johnson, Alfred Barr, George Nelson, and Eero Saarinen, at the very important symposium "What Is Happening to Modern Architecture?" at New York's Museum of Modern Art. Scully's comments, which were not published in the issue of the Museum's *Bulletin* devoted to the event, were critical of Breuer and Gropius for leaving Wright out of consideration. This was the first of many public statements of animus toward the neo-Bauhaus of Harvard.

Scully began a lifelong friendship with Louis Kahn in 1947, when the somewhat older Philadelphia architect came to teach at Yale. Around that time, Scully also met Philip Johnson, with whom he would maintain a mutually respectful and cordial relationship over the years. The introduction to Johnson, which took place in New Canaan while the architect's Glass House was being laid out, came through Henry-Russell Hitchcock, who would soon serve as Scully's dissertation advisor. Hitchcock—by then the dean of modern architectural historians in America and author of *In the Nature of Materials: The Buildings of Frank Lloyd Wright, 1887–1941* (1942), the definitive book on the architect—also served as Scully's introduction to Wright. In the late spring or summer of 1947, Scully and his wife visited Taliesin, in Wisconsin, for the sole purpose of seeing the major work of the architect he most admired. During the following year, as he began thinking about building a house for his own family, the idea came to him of commissioning Wright. Scully returned to Taliesin and convinced Wright to take the job. But the plans, originally designed for a lot just over the New Haven town line in Hamden and then adapted for a site in the suburb of Woodbridge, turned out to be significantly over the young couple's $20,000 budget. In the end, Scully abandoned the Wright project and designed the house himself. This he did in 1950—in a woodsy, part-Johnson, part-Breuer International Style box—and published it in *Architectural Forum* in a three-page spread with comments by the designer, in June 1951.

All this, or at least the first stages of this house-building episode, was taking place while Scully was researching and writing his doctoral dissertation. His original advisor was George Hamilton, who had encouraged him to work on the Hudson River School painter Frederick Edwin Church. An American subject seemed most appropriate since, except for his time in military service, Scully had never visited Europe and had no funds to do so. But he clearly preferred an architectural topic. Scully recalls that a photograph of McKim, Mead and White's Low House in Bristol, Rhode Island, which he saw probably late in 1947 in Hitchcock's book *Rhode Island Architecture* (1939), directed him toward an investigation of American domestic architecture in the second half of the nineteenth century.[2] Hamilton put Scully in touch with the author, who was then teaching at Wesleyan University, not far from New Haven, and Hitchcock agreed to act as Scully's advisor. No one could have been better qualified or more appropriate. Hitchcock had written about H. H. Richardson's domestic architecture, which played a central role in the creation of what Scully was to call the Shingle Style, in his 1936 book *The Architecture of H. H. Richardson and His Times.* In addition, Hitchcock's book *In the Nature of Materials* and his article "Frank Lloyd Wright and the 'Academic Tradition,'" published in the *Journal of the Warburg and Courtauld Institutes* in 1944, showed how many of the ideas developed on the East Coast by the mid-1880s had found their way into Wright's early work.

According to Scully, he began researching his dissertation in the summer of 1948 and by the following spring completed the writing of "The Cottage Style: An Organic Development in Later Nineteenth-Century Wooden Domestic Architecture in the Eastern United States."[3] This is an extraordinary feat when one considers the amount and precision of the research that went into it, and, even more, the fact that the dissertation organizes what was fundamentally raw and disregarded material into an entirely new and ultimately definitive explanation for the evolution of premodern architecture in the United States from its earliest phases in the late 1840s to its culmination in the work of Frank Lloyd Wright at the turn of the century. (The dissertation was published with no significant theoretical or methodological revisions, although reduced in length and with a different title, in 1955.) Working mainly from contemporaneous architectural periodicals and pattern books, Scully painstakingly pieced together a historical narrative that fully integrated the theoretical and practical concerns of the period. Taking issue with Giedion's perception of the balloon frame as the source for an American development of the "plain wall" that predicted 1920s modernism, Scully systematically analyzed and fully documented the much more complex process of how the obsession with structural expression beginning with Andrew Jackson Downing, whose importance Scully was the first to signal, was gradually undone by a new awareness of the spatial characteristics of architecture and how this eventually led to a demand for a new kind of spatial order and discipline. Although tied to a conception of architectural history grounded in the idea of style, Scully was able to go beyond the eclectic notion of a nineteenth-century "battle of the styles" to forge a more modern, and abstract, definition based on material expression through form. His terms, the Stick Style, responding to the earlier emphasis on structure, and the Shingled (later amended to Shingle) Style, responding to the material surfacing of the new space, were so apt and transparent as to become normative within less than a decade.

The dissertation owed much to Hitchcock, which Scully clearly acknowledged by dedicating the work to him. One could also certainly ascribe Scully's sensitivity to the concern for materiality and structure to his contact with Eugene Nalle, a teacher in the architecture department, and the focus on the concept of order to his discussions with Louis Kahn. But, as a whole, "The Cottage Style" remains a remarkably original and pregnant work of scholarship. Though ostensibly, and even quite unrelentingly, about the architecture of the previous century, it was also very much in tune with the current state of architectural politics and production, a fact that helped give it a significant afterlife. The choice of domestic architecture, rather than monumental or commercial buildings, was one that ran against the grain of recent historical studies of the nineteenth century but was very much in keeping with the interest in domestic architecture that was central to the modern movement in the 1940s and 1950s, when so many of the opportunities to build were restricted to that area. At the same time, the distinction Scully set up between the prerogatives of structure and of space was one that was to prove crucial in the discussions of design theory of the period. In fact, the debate over what Mumford called the "Bay Region Style" and what Hitchcock and Barr both referred to as the "Cottage Style," which had occasioned the Museum of Modern Art symposium "What Is Happening to Modern Architecture?" was in essence a debate about the revival of certain aspects of the Stick Style.

Scully, who was appointed a full-time member of the History of Art faculty at Yale in 1949, wasted little time before publishing the results of his research, which was of interest to many different constituencies. The first of these publications was a joint effort with Antoinette Downing, a preservationist and historian of colonial architecture, who asked Scully in 1949 to contribute the section on the nineteenth century as coauthor of the book *The Architectural Heritage of Newport, Rhode Island, 1640–1915.* His two chapters were entitled "The Stick Style" and "The Shingle Style." The book, published in 1952, won the Society of Architectural Historians' Annual Book Award. The following year, a slightly revised version of the first chapter of his dissertation appeared in the *Art Bulletin,* with the title "Romantic-Rationalism and the Expression of Structure in Wood: Downing, Wheeler, Gardner, and the 'Stick Style,' 1840–1876." George Kubler—who was then editor of the History of Art series at Yale University Press, which was in the process of publishing the dissertation—thought that the manuscript was too long and should include only the Shingle Style material.

Indeed, the book was published in 1955 as *The Shingle Style: Architectural Theory and Design from Richardson to the Origins of Wright.* (In the second edition, which came out in 1971, Scully reintegrated the chapter on the Stick Style and altered the title of the book to reflect the addition.) In early 1954, a year prior to the book's appearance, Scully published the article "American Villas: Inventiveness in the American Suburb from Downing to Wright" in the prestigious British *Architectural Review*, a monthly magazine that was read both by practicing architects and by academics of all sorts. The piece was a concise presentation of Scully's thesis and the professional reading public's first exposure to its major ideas. For these reasons, it is included here (see chap. 1).

The Shingle Style was extremely well received. It won the annual Art Historical Award of the College Art Association, with praise for how it "brings new life to aspects of the past . . . in a way few historians of art in our day are able to do." One might have thought that it would serve as the basis for further work in the field, but that was not what Scully had in mind; and not until many years later did he come back to the subject matter he had so firmly controlled and established as his own. Having completed the dissertation, he felt the need to broaden and deepen his understanding of art, which, for an art historian at the time, meant going to Europe. He was awarded a Fulbright Fellowship in 1950 to study Gothic architecture in France—a legacy of the Focillon-Aubert-Bony tradition—but had to defer due to the teaching needs of his department. When he took up the fellowship the following year, however, he changed his program and instead went to Italy to study the relationship of the city to the natural environment. This change of venue proved to be crucial, ultimately becoming for Scully "the central event of my intellectual life."[4] By this he meant the experience not just of Italian art and architecture but also of the Greek architecture he saw in Italy that year.

Scully and his wife and their three young sons rented an apartment just outside Florence, in Bellosguardo, on the *piano nobile* of the villa formerly owned by the German sculptor and theoretician Adolf von Hildebrandt. Much time was spent looking at paintings and sculpture in museums and public buildings in Florence as well as in Rome, Paris, and elsewhere. Scully had read Geoffrey Scott's *The Architecture of Humanism* in graduate school and now tried to work out Scott's concept of empathy in relation to his own sense of how one experiences art and writes about that experience. The methodology would remain central to Scully's development as an architectural historian. A preliminary instance was the article he wrote on Michelangelo's fortification drawings, which he saw in the Casa Buonarroti in Florence and published that summer (1952) in the first volume of *Perspecta: The Yale Architectural Journal* (it was republished in an expanded version in the *Actes du XVIIème Congrès International d'Histoire de l'Art* in 1955). Scully visited and studied the ancient Roman sites, like Hadrian's Villa; the medieval Italian cities, like Siena; and the smaller hilltowns, like San Gimignano, and came to share with Louis Kahn and other contemporary architects a passion for the hilltowns. It was at this time that the Ambrogio Lorenzetti frescoes, most notably the so-called *Allegory of Good Government,* in the Palazzo Pubblico of Siena impressed Scully with the vision of how a town, as a communal place, should work and relate to its natural setting. But by far the most significant event of the year was a trip to southern Italy in the spring to see the Greek temples at Paestum. The manifestly animate forms of the buildings amply justified an empathic response while the relation of the buildings to the landscape seemed so integral to their meaning that Scully apparently decided there and then that this would be the subject of his future research.

When he returned to Yale, he began to teach courses on Greek and Roman art and architecture in addition to those on modern architecture. Frank Brown, the Roman archaeologist who came back from the American Academy in Rome (where Scully first met him) to take over as head of the classics department in 1953, became one of his closest friends and strongest supporters. Scully spent the summer of 1955 in Greece, looking at the major sites and museums. The following summer, he returned to southern Italy and also traveled to Sicily, studying the sites of Magna Graecia. Finally, with a grant from the Bollingen Foundation, he was able to spend the entire academic year of 1957–58 in Greece where, as an associate of the American School of Classical Studies at Athens, he completed the research and the bulk of the writing for his book *The Earth, the Temple, and the Gods: Greek Sacred Architecture* (1962). During the nearly ten-year period of gestation and elaboration of his ideas on ancient Greek architecture and religion, Scully also produced some of his most significant books and articles on modern architecture, four of the latter of which are included here. These reveal a set of new interests and influences that intersects with his work on Greece, creating an unusual and vital synergy between his activities as historian and as critic.

Having gotten into print all that he had done on late-nineteenth-century domestic architecture, Scully first broadened his interpretation of Wright's work by considering its entire development in relation to the modern movement in Europe in the article "Wright vs. the International Style," published in *Art News* in early 1954 (see chap. 2). His continued interest in Wright led him to investigate Jungian writing on art and literature as a way of explaining, or rather describing, certain characteristic aspects and qualities of the experience of a Wright building, such as the movement from dark to light or from a constricted to an expansive space. Maud Bodkin's writings on poetry, in particular, impressed him. The Jungian term "archetype" first made its appearance in Scully's work in an article published in *Art in America* later that year, entitled "Archetype and Order in Recent American Architecture" (see chap. 3; these terms would also be paired in the title of the culminating chapter of *The Shingle Style*, as it was revised for publication in 1955). "Archetype and Order" represents Scully's first venture into contemporary criticism as well as his first attempt to deal with the issue of urbanism. Both Philip Johnson and Louis Kahn figure prominently in it, as does Mies van der Rohe's seminal work in the United States. Scully was one of the first to note the importance of Mies's "Neoclassicism" and its relationship to Rudolf Wittkower's book *Architectural Principles in the Age of Humanism* (1949).

Scully's interest in Mies and Wright was soon overshadowed by an intense involvement in the postwar work of Le Corbusier that profoundly affected his reading of contemporary architecture as well as ancient classical architecture. The massive masonry forms of the Unité d'Habitation at Marseilles (1946–52), the Chapel of Ronchamp (1950–55), the Maisons Jaoul outside Paris (1952–55), and the High Court at Chandigarh (1951–56) reinterpreted, in his view, the lithic structure of the Greek temple to induce a powerful empathic response in the observer. The modernity of this architecture of active sculptural force was underwritten by the existentialist philosophy of Sartre and Camus, which Scully now seriously engaged. "The Nature of the Classical in Art" (see chap. 5), initially given as a talk in December 1956 and published two years later, provides the earliest indication of the synthesis of these different strains of thought and can be seen as the basis for Scully's major works of the next few years in both the ancient and modern fields. The article "Modern Architecture: Toward a Redefinition of Style" (see chap. 4), which appeared in the 1957 volume of *Perspecta,* was the most immediate and significant expression of the synthesis in terms of Scully's work in the modern field; it became the book *Modern Architecture: The Architecture of Democracy*, published in 1961 by Braziller, and remains one of the standard texts on the development of modern architecture. *The Earth, the Temple, and the Gods: Greek Sacred Architecture*, written mainly in 1957–58 and published in 1962, derives its impetus from the same system of thought but expands its sphere of influence to take into account the entire natural environment, of which the building is just one part. It is arguably the most important, and certainly the most absorbing, scholarly work Scully has ever undertaken.

The elements in the title *The Earth, the Temple, and the Gods* refer to the three inseparable components of what Scully describes in the book as "the 'architecture' of any given site."

> All Greek sacred architecture explores and praises the character of a god or a group of gods in a specific place. That place itself is holy and, before the temple was built upon it, embodied the whole of the deity as a recognized natural force. With the coming of the temple, housing its image within it and itself developed as a sculptural embodiment of the god's presence and character, the meaning becomes double, both of the deity as in nature and the god as imagined by men. Therefore, the formal elements of any Greek sanctuary are, first, the specifically sacred landscape in which it is set and, second, the buildings that are placed within it.
>
> The landscape and the temples together form the architectural whole, were intended by the Greeks to do so, and must therefore be seen in relation to each other.[5]

Many writers and scholars played a part in helping Scully to arrive at this highly original argument; the list would include Auguste Choisy, Edith Hamilton, Constantinos Doxiadis, and, especially, Guido Freiherr von Kaschnitz. But no one had as great an impact as Le Corbusier, whose description, in *Vers une architecture* (1923), of the Athenian acropolis with its "axis . . . [that] runs from the sea to the mountain" and whose sculptural forms of the postwar years were acknowledged by the author, and pointed out by reviewers like Peter Smithson, as his primary inspiration.[6] Only the buildings and sites themselves had a greater impact.

The Earth, the Temple, and the Gods begins with the act of perception and is more thoroughgoing in its reliance on what one might call a visual empiricism than anything

Scully had written before. Its major innovation, which was revolutionary for classical studies, was to reconstitute the way ancient temples were seen and experienced, as integral parts of their natural settings, using the physical evidence before one's eyes. Unlike the typical classical scholar, Scully did not resort to reconstruction drawings to provide an image of what a ruined structure might have looked like or what the plan of its precinct might indicate. Rather, he focused on everything that still exists—meaning the surrounding landscape—to give body, as it were, to the temple remains. The move from object to context proved crucial for Scully's future thinking while at the same time predicting, and in certain ways underpinning, later developments in architecture as well as sculpture. In her book *Overlay* (1983), which documents the phenomenon of site-specific sculpture and Earthworks, the art critic Lucy Lippard singled out *The Earth, the Temple, and the Gods* for providing an "eye-opening" understanding of how meaning can be attributed to and drawn from the interaction of man-made forms and the natural environment. In the field of architecture in the early 1980s, the emphasis on the study of the landscape would join with a concern for contextualism to produce one of the major shifts in the evolution of twentieth-century architecture, a development in which Scully, as a critic, would play a major role.

Vincent Scully was tenured at Yale in 1956 and promoted to the rank of full professor five years later. By 1959 his reputation in the professional world of architecture was such that he was the subject of an article in *Architectural Forum* entitled "Architectural Spellbinder." Written by David McCullough, the piece focused on the "phenomenal success" of Scully's teaching but also stressed his contributions to criticism and scholarship. The article began with a quote from Philip Johnson, who had concluded a guest lecture he gave in Scully's modern architecture course the previous year by saying: "Hurrah for History! Thank God for Hadrian, for Bernini, for Le Corbusier, and for Vince Scully!"; and ended with the following prediction: "It seems inevitable that [Scully's] influence will expand beyond the Yale campus. It also follows that he will become increasingly important not only for students of architecture, and students in general, but for architects as well. . . . His potential is great, but the pattern is refreshingly unpredictable."[7] How correct McCullough proved to be is borne out by events of the following decade.

The 1960s began for Scully with a series of publications that seemed to be logical extensions of his thinking about modern architecture during the mid- to late 1950s. A monograph on Frank Lloyd Wright was the first of three short books he wrote for George Braziller between 1960 and 1962, all intended to provide a basic introduction to the subject at a reasonable price. The essay on Wright, which appeared in the Masters of World Architecture series one year after the architect's death, is the first English-language publication to deal with his entire career, and it remains one of the most insightful and provocative. The discussion of Wright's later work, in particular, is marked by ideas developed in the author's study of Greek and Minoan sites. The second book, *Modern Architecture: The Architecture of Democracy*, came out in 1961 as part of Braziller's Great Ages of World Architecture series. It is, as already noted, an expanded version of the earlier essay "Modern Architecture: Toward a Redefinition of Style" (see chap. 4). The third work, included in

Braziller's Makers of Contemporary World Architecture series, was a monograph on Louis Kahn. Written in the spring of 1962, soon after the completion of the initial phase of Kahn's Richards Medical Research Building at the University of Pennsylvania and while the First Unitarian Church at Rochester was in construction, but before any of the mature works like the Salk Institute at La Jolla or the National Capital of Bangladesh at Dhaka were off the drawing boards, Scully's essay is a seminal and authoritative study about the architect's work at a crucial moment of transition. In the fall of 1961, just prior to the publication of the Kahn book, Scully gave a talk at the Twentieth International Congress of the History of Art in which he related Kahn's work to Wright's, at a comparable stage in the latter's career, as a way of explaining certain larger patterns in the evolution of modern architecture. Initially published in 1962 in condensed form as "Wright, International Style, and Kahn," the content of the talk appeared in full in 1963 as "Frank Lloyd Wright and Twentieth-Century Style" and is included here in that version (see chap. 6).

Scully returned to Greece in 1962–63 with the purpose of writing a book on the site at Olympia. A number of articles resulted from this stay, dealing both with ancient and with modern Greek architecture. However, the Olympia project was aborted (the material was later incorporated in *Architecture: The Natural and the Manmade* [1991]). It is difficult to say whether the termination was due to the critical reception of *The Earth, the Temple, and the Gods*, although there is little doubt that Scully was deeply wounded by the way the book was attacked in the classical archaeology community. The review by Homer A. Thompson, of the Institute for Advanced Study at Princeton, for instance, described Scully's approach as "mystical" and his overall "hypothesis" of a correlation between buildings and landscape as "the fabrication of a modern mind to suit a modern interpretation of a given set of ancient phenomena." Discounting the almost overwhelming visual evidence adduced by Scully, he maintained, as a good classicist well might, that there was no "ancient literary evidence" to prove that "very great importance was attached by the Greeks to the natural setting of man's activities."[8] In any event, the classicists' critique of his Greek book was just the first in a series of experiences that effected a significant shift in Scully's interests and way of thinking over the next four to five years. To it must be added a confrontation with Norman Mailer in the pages of *Architectural Forum* over the value of modern architecture and urbanism; contact with the work of Robert Venturi and the writing of an introduction to his book *Complexity and Contradiction in Architecture*; and finally, the struggle against redevelopment and the involvement with the preservation movement in New Haven.

Despite his longstanding aversion to the neo-Bauhaus teaching at Harvard, Scully could never have been thought of, before the mid-1960s, as anything other than a solid supporter of the ideals of the modern movement. Prompted by the specter of the Pan Am Building blocking the view down New York's Park Avenue, his article "The Death of the Street," published in *Perspecta* in 1963 (see chap. 7), gives the first indication of a disenchantment with the effects of commercial modern building on the fabric of the city. But it is more a critique of what happens to architecture when "the architecture of genius," as Hitchcock put it, gives way to "the architecture of bureaucracy."[9] It also probably did not hurt that one of the main players in the design of the Pan Am Building was Walter Gropius. The concern over the future of Park Avenue, along with the impending destruction of McKim, Mead and White's Pennsylvania Station, arguably New York's grandest Beaux-Arts building, raised in Norman Mailer an even more profound ire, accompanied by an all-consuming condemnation of modern architecture. Writing in his column "The Big Bite" in the May and August 1963 issues of *Esquire* magazine, Mailer launched a diatribe against "the plague of modern architecture, a plague which sits like a plastic embodiment of cancer over our suburbs, office buildings, schools, prisons, factories, churches, hotels, motels and airline terminals." Mailer located the cause of the disease in the "totalitarianism [that] has slipped into America with no specific political face" and that "proliferates in that new architecture which rests like an incubus upon the American landscape." Bemoaning the fact that all "our buildings . . . [have] come to look like one another and to cease to function with the art, beauty, and sometimes mysterious proportions of the past," Mailer noted, with a certain wistfulness, that "the Gothic knots and Romanesque oppressions which entered his psyche through the schoolhouses of his youth have now been excised. . . . This new architecture," he railed, "this totalitarian architecture, destroys the past," leaving us "isolated in the empty landscapes of psychosis, precisely that inner landscape of void and dread which we flee by turning to totalitarian styles of life."[10]

The editors of *Architectural Forum* could hardly resist the temptation to reprint these remarks. They secured Mailer's permission to include excerpts in their April 1964 issue as part of a debate. Scully was chosen to present the other side. In a confrontation entitled "Mailer vs. Scully," which included photographs of the two combatants, the *Forum* published a "rebuttal" from Scully followed by "a few final words" from Mailer. Criticizing the novelist's "lazy, pot-boiling paragraphs" as "representationalist in bias" and smacking of nineteenth-century romanticism and eclecticism, Scully characterized Mailer as "generally uninformed about the great modern architects" and opining with "pure indifference" to their achievements. He agreed that, "indeed, as we ream out the centers of our cities for redevelopment and more or less leave them as scaleless open spaces inhabited largely by parked automobiles, it may be that we are in fact imaging that 'inner landscape of void and dread' to which Mailer refers," but he countered that this was only the result of the commercial buildings "generally to be seen around us" that had co-opted the ideas and look of modern architecture. On the other hand, "the work of Wright, Le Corbusier, and Aalto—not surely, to mention that of Lou Kahn—flatly contradicts everything, absolutely everything, Mr. Mailer has to say . . . especially that bit about destroying the past." Thinking that he had hit upon the weakest point in Mailer's argument, Scully asserted that "to equate modern architecture, which was banned by all the most totalitarian of the totalitarian countries, with totalitarianism, is historically speaking, the Big Lie at its most majestic."[11]

In his final remarks, Mailer admonished Scully for having "all but deliberately missed the point" of what he meant by totalitarianism and then quickly disabused him of any comfort one might find in distinguishing between "the architecture of genius" and "the architecture of bureaucracy." It is the "lack of ornamentation, complexity, and mystery" in modern buildings, Mailer says, that "I choose to call totalitarian. . . . It should be obvious," he goes on, "that in 30 years an esthetic movement can shift from a force which opens possibilities to one which closes them. Once totalitarianism is seen as a social process which deadens human possibilities, . . . it is not too great a jump to declare that the Guggenheim Museum may be a totalitarian work of art. . . . That museum shatters the mood of the neighborhood. More completely, wantonly, barbarically than the Pan Am building kills the sense of vista on Park Avenue." He then concluded with the following resounding remarks:

> It is too cheap to separate Mafia [read commercial] architects with their Mussolini Modern . . . from serious modern architects. No, I think Le Corbusier and Wright, and all the particular giants of the Bauhaus are the true villains; the Mafia architects are their proper sons; modern architecture at its best is even more anomalous than at its worst, for it tends to excite the Faustian and empty appetites of the architect's ego rather than reveal an artist's vision of our collective desire for shelter which is pleasurable, substantial, intricate, intimate, delicate, detailed, foibled, rich in gargoyle, guignol, false closet, secret stair, witch's hearth, attic, grandeur, kitsch, a world of buildings as diverse as the need within the eye for stimulus and variation. For beware: the ultimate promise of modern architecture is collective sightlessness for the species. Blindness is the fruit of your design.[12]

The debate was clearly of international interest, and the British *Architectural Review* published a detailed and critical summary of it in July 1964. New York's *Village Voice* also reprinted excerpts of Scully's comments on 16 April of that year and the full text of Mailer's final remarks on 18 June. Scully was asked if he would like to have "the last word," since Mailer was afforded that opportunity in the previous round. Scully declined the offer, saying, "I feel that I have had the last word already."[13] Indeed, it was probably impossible for him at that time to add anything that might bridge the gulf between his position and Mailer's. And it is also fair to say that he would never be able to agree fully with Mailer's contention that the "serious modern architects," like Le Corbusier and Wright, were no different in certain important respects from their commercial counterparts. Scully restated and amplified his position in a lecture given in the 1964 Modern Architecture Symposium, held at Columbia University in May and published with the provocatively gloomy title "Doldrums in the Suburbs" the following year (see chap. 8). But quite soon after that, he would not only adopt a tone quite similar to Mailer's when talking about the contemporary urban situation, he would also edge closer to Mailer's categorical view of the "Faustian," ego-driven modern hero-architect as he came to appreciate the work of Robert Venturi and to write about its historically based, contextually driven critique of "establishment Modern architecture."[14]

Scully became aware of Venturi as early as 1961, when he presciently chose the young architect for the "New Talent USA" issue of *Art in America*.[15] At that time, Venturi's only completed work was the relatively insignificant renovation of the James B. Duke House, in New York, for the Institute of Fine Arts. What had really caught Scully's eye, however, was the architect's 1959 Beach House project. It was based, in large part, on McKim, Mead and White's Shingle Style Low House, which had originally inspired Scully's dissertation and about which Venturi had learned in *The Shingle Style.* But it was not for another three years or so that Scully focused his attention on Venturi. Robert Stern, then a student in the architecture school at Yale, convinced his teacher to go to Philadelphia to see the work after his own initial exposure to it (through Helen Searing, a fellow graduate student at Yale) in the early part of 1964. Scully was overwhelmed by the Guild House (1960–66), then still in construction, and equally impressed with the Vanna Venturi House, in Chestnut Hill (1959–64). His first attempt to put some of his thoughts and reactions into print came when he wrote, at Venturi's request, the introduction to *Complexity and Contradiction in Architecture*, the book that upset the world of architecture when it came out in 1966 and not only made its author's reputation but also played a large part in remaking Scully's.[16]

As Venturi stated in his preface, *Complexity and Contradiction* was an attack on "the limitations of orthodox Modern architecture and city planning."[17] The opening section, "Nonstraightforward Architecture: A Gentle Manifesto," could be read, in certain ways, as reflecting the position articulated by Mailer in his concluding list of desiderata. Venturi advocated "elements which are hybrid rather than 'pure,' . . . distorted rather than 'straightforward,' . . . perverse as well as impersonal, . . . accommodating rather than excluding, redundant rather than simple, vestigial as well as innovating, inconsistent and equivocal rather than direct and clear"; in sum, a "messy vitality" with a "richness of meaning"—including even "the non sequitur" and "honky-tonk elements"—rather than the "easy unity of exclusion" characteristic of most modern architecture.[18] Even the methodology was in large part derived from literary theory and criticism. Concepts such as ambiguity, double-functioning elements, juxtaposition, and inflection toward the "difficult whole" undergird the fundamentally formal and compositional procedures and strategies that Venturi proposed as a way of returning a greater degree of "complexity and contradiction" to modern architecture. But the author never went so far as to condemn the efforts of its leading practitioners like Le Corbusier, Wright, Aalto, and Kahn; on the contrary, he highlighted, whenever possible, their achievement of "the difficult unity of inclusion." Nor did he characterize the pioneering generation of modern architects as a *heroic* one—with all the implications of Faustian tragedy someone like Mailer might attach to the term.

In many ways, Scully's introduction to *Complexity and Contradiction* made the book seem more radical than it appeared to be on the surface; or rather, it drew out ideas that were still in the process of formation to their logical conclusion. Scully claimed much more for the book than its author did, which infuriated many readers at the time yet has proven to be an accurate assessment of its significance. He asserted that *Complexity and Contradiction* was "probably the most important writing on the making of architecture since Le Corbusier's *Vers une Architecture*, of 1923" and maintained that "the future will value it among the few basic texts of our time." To understand it requires "a serious reorientation in all our thinking," for Venturi, like Le Corbusier before him, has been "able to free himself from the fixed patterns of thought and the fashions of his contemporaries." Scully commented little on Venturi's formal or compositional categories, emphasizing instead his "flexibly function-directed method," his ease with "the particular" and his ability to deal with the "common artifacts of mass culture," and the "renewed connection with the whole of the past" that the work embodies. But what was most radical and important about the book, in Scully's view, and most apt to stir resentment in the establishment, was what he characterized as the "consistently antiheroic" tenor of Venturi's argument. "His proposals," Scully noted, "in their recognition of complexity and their respect for what exists, create the most necessary antidote to that cataclysmic purism of contemporary urban renewal which has presently brought so many cities to the brink of catastrophe, and in which Le Corbusier's ideas have now found terrifying vulgarization." In opposition to "a hero's dreams applied en masse," Venturi provided, in Scully's estimation, "this generation's answer to grandiose pretensions which have shown themselves in practice to be destructive or overblown" by "qualifying his recommendations with an implied irony at every turn."[19]

The introduction to *Complexity and Contradiction* established Scully as Venturi's interlocutor and champion, a role that he continued to play over the succeeding decades. In 1971, he wrote the short text for the exhibition catalogue *The Work of Venturi and Rauch, Architects and Planners* for the Whitney Museum of American Art in New York; and in 1977, he added a note to the second edition of *Complexity and Contradiction*. Although he featured the firm's work in all his publications that dealt with the evolution of contemporary architecture from the late 1960s on, it was only in the 1980s and 1990s that Scully wrote major articles entirely devoted to the architect. "Robert Venturi's Gentle Architecture," originally given as a talk in 1985 and published four years later, and "Everybody Needs Everything," a discussion of the house Venturi built for his mother that appeared in 1992, represent Scully's most important and extensive treatments of the architect's thought and work. Both are included in this volume (see chaps. 15 and 18).

Scully's focus on the deleterious effects of urban renewal in the introduction to *Complexity and Contradiction* paralleled his growing questioning of redevelopment as it manifested itself in his own city of New Haven in the mid- to late 1960s. Aside from the earlier discussion of the Pan Am Building and Park Avenue in "The Death of the Street," and an article entitled "The Athens Hilton: A Study in Vandalism" published in the same year (1963) in *Architectural Forum*, Scully had never taken a proactive stance on issues of preservation. But with the impact of new highway building on the existing city fabric of New Haven and the planned demolition of important public buildings, including the post office and the public library, to make way for a new government center on the Green opposite Yale's Old Campus, he was galvanized into action and played a significant role in preserving the historic buildings that define the city's main square. Following the 1967 riots in the black areas of New Haven most affected by urban renewal, Scully expanded his critique to include the social issues of housing for the poor and maintenance of neighborhood integrity. "America's Architectural Nightmare: The Motorized Megalopolis," which first appeared in *Holiday* magazine in 1966, and "The Threat and Promise of Urban Redevelopment in New Haven," which was published, along with the *Holiday* piece, in the Italian journal *Zodiac* in 1967, preceded the more pointed and extended treatment of the subject as a defining aspect of modern city planning in the Annual Discourse Scully was invited to give at the Royal Institute of British Architects in the early spring of 1969. Published as "RIBA Discourse 1969: A Search for Principle between Two Wars" (see chap. 9), this autobiographically based historical-critical account of postwar developments contains in germ the main conclusions of Scully's book *American Architecture and Urbanism,* which came out in the same year.

American Architecture and Urbanism was, in effect, a rewriting of *Modern Architecture* in light of the events of the 1960s. Aside from an expansion of specifically American material, the most important additions were a new and, for the most part, quite positive emphasis on traditional Beaux-Arts architecture of the earlier part of the twentieth century; an analysis of Kahn's mature work; plus major sections about Venturi, his contemporaries, and the impact of redevelopment on the American city. Most unexpected to those who had not attended Scully's classes at Yale or heard him lecture on the subject was his introduction to the history of American architecture not through the British colonial architecture of the eighteenth century but rather through the Pre-Columbian, Amerindian architecture of the Southwest and its continuity in the Spanish succession in the region. This represented the first appearance in print of an entirely new campaign of research that Scully had begun in 1964.

Following the adverse critical reaction of classical scholars to *The Earth, the Temple, and the Gods* and a trip to the Southwest in the summer of 1964, Scully became convinced that a study of the ancient architecture of that region would not only complement his Greek work but would add another dimension to it, enabling him to reach more general conclusions regarding the relationship between manmade structures and the natural environment. The pueblos of the Southwest became, in Scully's view, the antitype of the Greek temple, a human construct designed to echo the forms of the surrounding landscape rather than to contrast with them. It was an architecture of accommodation, not of confrontation, and thus responded to Scully's newfound appreciation for the antiheroic, anti-Hellenic aspects of Venturi's work as well. Scully immersed himself in the archaeological, anthropological, and mythological literature of the area. As with his work on Greek architecture, Scully's effort concentrated on close observation and description of the buildings in their landscape settings. Unique to this project, however, was the fact that many of the sites were still home to ritual dances and ceremonies. Scully attended as many of these as he could and incorporated them into his analysis. All this represented a significant departure from his art-historical training, not to speak of his cultural upbringing, and Scully labored over the manuscript far longer than was his custom. Research was completed by 1969, but the text for the book, *Pueblo: Mountain, Village, Dance,* took more than three years to complete, and it was not published until 1975. The introduction appeared earlier as "Man and Nature in Pueblo Architecture" in the exhibition catalogue *American Indian Art: Form and Tradition* published by the Walker Art Center in the fall of 1972. The main thesis of the sympathetic relationship between building and landscape in Amerindian culture was eventually incorporated into the overall argument of *Architecture: The Natural and the Manmade* (1991), of which a much-condensed and preliminary version appeared as an essay with the same title (see chap. 16) in the Museum of Modern Art's *Denatured Visions: Landscape and Culture in the Twentieth Century* (1991).

The latter half of the 1960s marked an important shift in Scully's thinking. It ushered in a period of reconsideration that endured throughout the following decade and coincided with major changes in his personal life. In 1965, soon after divorcing his first wife, he married Marian LaFollette Wohl; but that marriage also came unstuck and lasted only until 1978. During the 1970s, there were significant books, like *The Shingle Style Today, or, The Historian's Revenge* (1974) and *Pueblo* (1975), as well as sizable additions to new editions of earlier books, including *Modern Architecture* (1974). Nonetheless, the momentum that had previously characterized Scully's publishing career was waning, with much of his energy being given over to fulfilling his role as Master of Morse College at Yale, a position he held from 1969 through 1975. A lull occurred particularly in the publication of major journal articles or essays with significantly new material or new approaches. For this reason, nothing from the decade of the 1970s is included in this volume. Some pieces, like the *New York Times* article "The Case for Preservation" (1977), though historically important, are not substantial enough for inclusion. Others, like the *Architecture and Urbanism* article "Works of Louis Kahn and His Method" (1975) and the introduction to the exhibition catalogue *The Travel Sketches of Louis I. Kahn* (1978), were revisited and reworked by Scully and are included in their later iterations.

Scully's single most important publication of the 1970s relating to contemporary architecture was the short, essay-like book entitled *The Shingle Style Today, or, The Historian's Revenge* (1974).[20] Responding to the appearance in 1972 of *Five Architects*—the volume that first grouped together and brought to public attention the work of Peter Eisenman, Michael Graves, Charles Gwathmey, John Hejduk, and Richard Meier—Scully countered their revival of Le Corbusier's purist forms of the 1920s with an argument for the greater historical relevance, in terms of the establishment of an American vernacular tradition, of the revival of the Shingle Style that was inspired by his own writings and that began with Venturi's Beach House project of 1959. Further making the case that it was Venturi, Charles Moore, and their students and followers—rather than any one of the New York Five—who should be credited with building upon and developing Le Corbusier's legacy, *The Shingle Style Today* inserted itself into a debate about the use of history and the critique of modernism that Venturi himself was responsible for bringing out into the open with his book *Complexity and Contradiction.* In the professional journals, and even the popular press, the two opposing sides in the battle were dubbed the "Whites" (for their purist exclusiveness) and the "Grays" (for their eclectic inclusiveness), with Colin Rowe generally accepted as the critical standard-bearer for the former and Scully for the latter.

Although very much a product of the moment and deeply embedded in its cultural politics, *The Shingle Style Today* is also interesting for reasons related to Scully's career and development as a critic and historian. The book's argument is very much based on Scully's own personal involvement as a historian in the unfolding of events and thus, by his own account, he becomes not only the interpreter but an agent in the process (even exacting "revenge" for the refusal of most architects to acknowledge the influence of history). He had pointed out, as early as 1967 in the introduction to the second edition of *The Architectural Heritage of Newport, Rhode Island*, that his construction of the Shingle Style was not only a "reinterpretation . . . of the art of the past" but that it "played . . . [a] part in the art of the present," noting specifically that "Venturi has himself been critically influenced by the Shingle Style."[21] Though he must have known it by then, he did not state that his later book *The Shingle Style* actually served as Venturi's source for images such as McKim, Mead and White's Low House, the building that Scully establishes in *The Shingle Style Today* as fundamental for the creation of the "New Shingle Style." The self-consciousness apparent in Scully's writing of history here is matched by a new psychoanalytic interpretation of the way history works on the creative mind. This Scully owed to Harold Bloom, his colleague in the English department at Yale. Bloom's provocative study *The Anxiety of Influence: A Theory of Poetry* (1973), provided Scully with a Freudian framework for theorizing the difference between the "strong" architect and the "weak" architect as seen in the choice of historical model each makes and how, in grappling with it, the former intentionally "misreads" it, or "swerves" from it, to produce the new. The effects of both his insertion of the self into the construction of modern architecture's history and the reliance on Freud rather than Jung as an aid in explaining certain aspects of the creative act made important and lasting contributions to his writings of the 1980s and 1990s.

It was also in the 1970s that Scully embarked on his third major campaign of research in a field other than modern architecture. In 1972–73, with a National Endowment for the Humanities Senior Fellowship, he spent a sabbatical year in Europe studying the Gothic architecture of France, an area that had fascinated him since his graduate student days. Living in Switzerland with his second wife (who had edited *The Earth, the Temple, and the Gods* as well as Venturi's *Complexity and Contradiction)* and their young daughter, Scully traveled back and forth to France. During his trips there he also began to visit and study, in addition to the major Gothic cathedrals, the classical gardens of the seventeenth century, notably those by André Le Nôtre at Versailles, Vaux-le-Vicomte, and elsewhere. This interest soon overtook the Gothic and became the main focus of his research beginning in 1975 and lasting well into the following decade. Once again, it was a subject involving the relationship between the manmade and the natural, which complemented and extended his earlier work on Greece and the American Southwest. And just as each of those historical investigations reflected certain preoccupations with contemporary architecture, the engagement with the classical landscapes of Louis XIV's France coincided with the revival of interest in the architectural theory and practice of the Ecole des Beaux-Arts, a phenomenon that was given major impetus by the exhibition of drawings from the Ecole held at the Museum of Modern Art in the winter of 1975–76. The French classical garden was seen by Scully, as it was by a number of others, as a valuable model for contemporary urban planning and design, marking the beginning of a tradition extending from L'Enfant's Washington, D.C., and Haussmann's Paris through the American City Beautiful movement of the first half of the twentieth century.

The confrontation between the Whites and the Grays, on the one hand, and the promotion of Beaux-Arts classicism by the Museum of Modern Art, on the other, were only two obvious signs of the profound changes in architectural culture that occurred in the 1970s. Both can now be seen as part of a larger development toward an emphasis on theory and history in the discourse of architecture. The term *postmodernism*, which at first referred almost exclusively to the use of historicizing elements for contextual or decorative purposes, became part of the common vocabulary with the publication of Charles Jencks's *The Language of Post-Modern Architecture* in 1977. The journal *Oppositions*, which began publication in 1973 with Peter Eisenman as its directing force, established itself almost immediately as the mouthpiece, in America at least, for the application of structuralist, poststructuralist, Marxist, and semiotic theory to architecture. Scully, who only published one very short piece in that journal (on Venturi's Mathematics Building project for Yale), was never comfortable with the importance that theory began to gain in critical circles. In an interview in 1980, he acknowledged "wrestling . . . agonizingly for about ten years" with "the semiotic model" but, in the end, decided it was "much too restricted to its sign structure to be able to deal with the physical embodiment, which is the function of a work of art."[22] Having to confront the issue, however, had a significant outcome, for it forced Scully to articulate, as he never had before, his own position. In his case, this meant a reconsideration of the concept of empathy and its distinction from that of associationism in the perception and reception of works of art. Scully explained that he "wanted some ground to stand on because he could feel everything shifting underneath his feet."[23] The article "Architecture, Sculpture, and Painting: Environment, Act, and Illusion," published in 1981 (see chap. 12), is a richly rewarding expression of this self-analysis and just one of the many important articles that Scully published in a renewed burst of critical and historical writing beginning in the early 1980s.

The decade of the eighties opened with a feature on Scully in the *New Yorker*, a testimony to the singular position he had achieved in the academic/critical world of architecture.[24] He had been recognized in 1966 by *Time* magazine as one of the ten "Great Teachers" in the United States, and was voted one of the "12 Great U.S. Professors" by *People* magazine in 1975. He had also been made an honorary member of the American Institute of Architects in 1976 and awarded an AIA Medal for his teaching, scholarship, and preservation efforts in that same year.[25] Honors of all sorts multiplied in the 1980s: he was awarded the University of Virginia's Thomas Jefferson Medal and was asked to present the Mellon Lectures at the National Gallery of Art in Washington, D.C., in 1982; he was named the Sterling Professor of the History of Art at Yale in 1983; he won the Associated Collegiate Schools of Architecture/American Institute of Architects "Topaz" Award for Excellence in Architectural Education in 1986; and he was made an Honorary Fellow of the Royal Institute of British Architects in addition to receiving an honorary degree from the New School for Social Research and the Margaret Flint Award from the New Haven Preservation Trust—all in 1988. He also participated as a professional consultant to juries for competitions for the Alaska State Office Building in Anchorage (1982–83), the Public Park in Bellevue, Washington (1984), and the Harold Washington Public Library in Chicago (1988–89).

Scully's production of journal articles and essays soared and, for the first time in his career, far outweighed in significance the publication of books. He wrote short pieces on many of the important architects of the period, including Aldo Rossi, Michael Graves,

Robert Stern, Philip Johnson, and Charles Gwathmey, as well as some dealing specifically with key buildings, like the competition for the Humana Building in Louisville, Kentucky, and Peter Eisenman's Wexner Center for the Visual Arts in Columbus, Ohio. Between 1983 and 1988, he was a fairly regular contributor to *Architectural Digest.* At the same time, he produced a number of essays revisiting and rethinking the careers of architects about whom he had written much in the past. Four of these are included in this volume. "Frank Lloyd Wright and the Stuff of Dreams," which appeared in *Perspecta* in 1980, marshaled Freudian psychoanalytic theory in a completely original way, opening up new avenues of approach to Wright's earlier work (see chap. 11). The introductions to *The Le Corbusier Archive* (1983) and *The Louis I. Kahn Archive: Personal Drawings* (1987) gave Scully the opportunity to review their careers with a greater historical perspective (see chaps. 13 and 14). Finally, "Robert Venturi's Gentle Architecture," which was presented as the keynote lecture in a symposium on the architect in 1985 and published four years later, represents the most in-depth study Scully has yet published on the architect with whom his own career has often been associated (see chap. 15).

His most interesting and thorough analysis of the state of affairs—at the moment when postmodernism was emerging as the key critical term—is contained in an article Scully wrote in the spring of 1980 for the new Japanese journal *GA Document.* Tellingly entitled "Where Is Modern Architecture Going?" (see chap. 10), it was a response to the exhibition *Transformations in Modern Architecture* that Arthur Drexler had mounted at the Museum of Modern Art the previous year. The exhibition itself was viewed by most critics as a fairly deliberate effort by Drexler to demonstrate the formal reductiveness and expressive inadequacies of late modern architecture, a reaction that Scully shared. But whereas Drexler, MoMA's director of Architecture and Design, seemed to remain undecided as to how the situation might resolve itself, Scully provided a clear idea of the direction he thought architecture should take if it was to succeed in reviving itself. The key, in his view, was a return to the vernacular, understood not simply in historical terms but in all its contemporary manifestations. Scully cited two lines of development already in place, one American, established by Venturi, and the other European, at the head of which was the Neorationalist Aldo Rossi. Scully had visited Rossi's Gallaratese housing project in the summer of 1979 and was greatly impressed by it, as he was also by Leon Krier's classically inspired urban designs. He characterized the two different approaches to the vernacular as more or less antithetical to one another, the American version being concerned with the suburb and the European with the city. How to resolve the distinction and create a viable pattern for urban planning at a scale adaptable to both was a question to which he had no answer—and would not until he started looking closely at the earliest results of the New Urbanism at the beginning of the following decade.

Scully's life changed dramatically when he was forced to retire from full-time teaching at Yale at the end of the spring term of 1990–91. His final lecture, attended by many of the architects he had befriended and influenced, such as Philip Johnson, Kevin Roche, Robert Stern, Cesar Pelli, Maya Lin, and Leon Krier, was considered an event of such significance that it was the subject of a front-page story in the following Sunday's *New York Times.*[26] Although he continued to teach his modern architecture course every fall term as an emeritus professor, in the spring of 1992 he began to spend the second half of the academic year at the University of Miami as Distinguished Visiting Professor in the architecture school. Andres Duany and Elizabeth Plater-Zyberk, who had been students of his in the early 1970s at Yale and were now teaching and practicing in Miami, were instrumental in attracting both Scully and his third wife, the art historian Catherine Lynn, whom he had married in 1980, to join the faculty. It was a move that brought Scully into close contact with the work of the firm that was quickly establishing itself as the leader of what would soon be called the New Urbanism.

Scully's first visit to Seaside, the planned Florida Gulf Coast town that brought Duany and Plater-Zyberk to national attention soon after building began there in 1981, came in the spring of 1990, following the ceremony at the University of Miami in which he was awarded an honorary degree. Later that fall he wrote a short piece for the *New York Times*, "Back to the Future, With a Detour through Miami," which appeared in January 1991. In it he described Duany and Plater-Zyberk as "by far the most interesting young architects practicing today," whose work "is coming close to bringing to fruition the most important contemporary movement in architecture . . . , the revival of the vernacular and classical traditions and their reintegration into the mainstream of modern architecture in its fundamental aspect: the structure of communities, the building of towns." Realizing from their work that one could no longer separate general planning ideas from specific historical types and forms of building, Scully now linked the vernacular and the classical in a unifying program that finally provided an answer, in architectural as well as urban terms, to "the disoriented abstractions that modernism proposed." Sounding almost as categorical as Mailer once had, Scully lambasted modernism's "pioneers, Gropius, Mies van der Rohe, Le Corbusier"—not just their followers—for "despising the structure of the traditional city" and being "determined to outrage it as much as possible in their individual buildings and to rebuild the whole thing according to their own impatient dogmas." By contrast, he applauded the effort in Seaside to establish architectural and urban codes, based on the traditional architecture of the region, as a way to discipline "egotistical architects" and to challenge them to "work together as an inspired group rather than anarchically alone."[27] Scully's promotion of Duany and Plater-Zyberk's ideas and principles soon made him a chief spokesperson for the New Urbanism. He was asked to give the opening lecture at the First Congress for the New Urbanism in the fall of 1993 and wrote the critical afterword to Peter Katz's *The New Urbanism: Toward an Architecture of Community*, which was published in 1994 (see chap. 19).

In Scully's mind, the integration of building and town plan to form a community was but a subset of the necessary relationship between architecture and the natural environment that had been the subject of most of his life's research since his initial visit to the Greek site of Paestum in 1952. Building on his subsequent study of the pueblos of the Southwest and the classical gardens of seventeenth-century France, Scully spent much of the late 1980s working toward a grand historical synthesis of these ideas, which finally came together in his book *Architecture: The Natural and the Manmade*, published in 1991. Dealing with the natural and built environments from ancient Egypt, Mesopotamia, and Pre-Columbian Mexico through the twentieth century in a way that reminds one, if only tangentially, of Sigfried Giedion's synoptic late work *The Eternal Present*, the book provides an insight into Scully's fundamental understanding of architecture's meaning and purpose. While he was preparing the manuscript, he was asked to give the opening lecture at the symposium "Landscape and Architecture in the Twentieth Century" at the Museum of Modern Art in 1988. Published three years later, just prior to the book, his essay based on that lecture, "Architecture: The Natural and the Manmade" (see chap. 16), epitomizes the main argument of the book and directly connects it to the problems of the present.

An important aspect of Scully's embrace of the New Urbanism—which, by the way, he had hoped would be called the Architecture of Community—was his increasing sense of the "failure of the hero architect."[28] Duany and Plater-Zyberk's institution of codes, allowing them to recuse themselves from the actual design of buildings, provided a clear alternative to the modernist prescription for constant individual invention and originality. Yet Scully never seems to have been able to shake off completely his own need to identify the new, which invariably turns out to be the invention of particularly creative and thoughtful individuals. Throughout his career, he has perceived the significance of general movements and trends through the work of their most inventive individual architects, beginning with Frank Lloyd Wright, Le Corbusier, and Louis Kahn, and later including Robert Venturi, Aldo Rossi, and, finally, Andres Duany and Elizabeth Plater-Zyberk themselves. This paradox, which lies at the very core of Scully's thinking and no doubt stems from its original existentialist impetus, is just one manifestation of the acute tension in his writing between the opposing poles of subjectivity and objectivity. And so it should come as no surprise that two of his most moving and deeply probing articles on individual architects, "Louis I. Kahn and the Ruins of Rome" and one on Venturi's Vanna Venturi House, entitled "Everybody Needs Everything," were both written while he was considering the anti-authorial implications of Seaside's codes. Both essays were published in 1992 (see chaps. 17 and 18).

Scully's advocacy of the New Urbanism was, nonetheless, the main thrust of his lecturing and writing during the 1990s. And he used the prominent position he attained in the world of scholarship and criticism to promote its principles at the highest levels. In 1992 he was appointed to the Board of Trustees of the National Trust for Historic Preservation and won the New York Public Library's Literary Lions Award the same year; he was given the Governor's Arts Award Medal by the State of Connecticut in 1993 and the Lucy G. Moses Preservation Leadership Award from the New York Landmarks Conservancy in 1994. In 1995 he was chosen by the National Endowment for the Humanities to give the Jefferson Lecture in the Humanities at the Kennedy Center for the Performing Arts in Washington, D.C., a lectureship that is the highest honor the government can bestow on a scholar in the humanities. The audience was composed of not only academics and interested laypeople but also included senators and representatives, as well as various other government officials and workers. The subject he chose was "The Architecture of Community," and the lecture traced the path taken in the United States from the realizations of the City Beautiful movement at the beginning of the twentieth century through the overturning of its ideals in the redevelopment schemes of the 1950s–70s to the emergence of the New Urbanism in the 1980s, with its provision of hope for the future. When he was asked three years later to speak at the White House on the occasion of the twentieth-anniversary celebration of the awarding of the Pritzker Architecture Prize, Scully reworked the Jefferson lecture into a tightly woven and concise statement of its central theme of the balance between freedom and order, or the individual and the law, which in his view was necessary for the creation of a humane living environment. Published in the following year as "America at the Millennium: Architecture and Community," it is included here (see chap. 20) as the final selection from Scully's prodigious, sustained, and ongoing literary output during a professional career that has most recently been recognized by Yale University's creation in 1997 of an endowed chair in his name, as well as by the establishment of the Vincent Scully Prize, an award to be given annually at the National Building Museum in Washington, D.C., in recognition of "exemplary practice, scholarship, or criticism in architecture, landscape design, historic preservation, planning, or urban design." Scully himself was its first recipient in the fall of 1999.

Notes

1 Vincent Scully, "Yale and After," typescript, 3.

2 Vincent Scully, interview by Neil Levine, audiocassette, 18 Oct. 1998. See also "Robert Venturi's Gentle Architecture" (chap. 15); and Vincent Scully, "Henry-Russell Hitchcock and the New Tradition," introduction to *In Search of Modern Architecture: A Tribute to Henry-Russell Hitchcock,* ed. Helen Searing (New York: Architectural History Foundation; Cambridge, Mass.: MIT Press, 1982), 11.

3 One of the readers of the dissertation was William Jordy, who had received his Ph.D. degree from Yale the previous year and taught there from 1948 to 1955, before moving on to Brown. Although the term "Cottage Style" surely refers to such nineteenth-century publications as Andrew Jackson Downing's *Cottage Residences* (1842), it was used by Hitchcock in his 1936 book *The Architecture of H. H. Richardson and His Times* to refer specifically to Richardson's shingled seaside houses and was later used by him and Alfred Barr in the February 1948 MoMA symposium "What Is Happening to Modern Architecture?" to refer to the contemporary work of William Wurster and others on the West Coast.

4 Scully, "Yale and After," 11.

5 Vincent Scully, *The Earth, the Temple, and the Gods: Greek Sacred Architecture* (New Haven, Conn., and London: Yale University Press, 1962), 3, 1–2.

6 Peter Smithson, review of *The Earth, the Temple, and the Gods,* by Vincent Scully, *Architectural Review* 133 (Apr. 1963): 237. For Scully's acknowledgment, see his *The Earth, the Temple, and the Gods,* 235n53; and "RIBA Discourse 1969: A Search for Principle between Two Wars," *RIBA Journal: The Journal of the Royal Institute of British Architects* 76 (June 1969): 244.

7 David McCullough, "Architectural Spellbinder," *Architectural Forum* 111 (Sept. 1959): 136, 202.

8 Homer A. Thompson, review of *The Earth, the Temple, and the Gods: Greek Sacred Architecture,* by Vincent Scully, *Art Bulletin* 45 (Sept. 1963): 277, 280. Scully responded to the review in a letter to the editor (*Art Bulletin* 46 [Mar. 1964]: 120). It should be pointed out, however, that the reviews from modern observers were in general full of praise. Peter Collins, for example, wrote: "It is probably fair to say that this is the most distinguished book of its kind in the English language since the publication of Ruskin's *Stones of Venice.* . . . This book is a delight to read. . . . But more important than this, his book will also be highly valued as a completely new and refreshing interpretation of Greek architectural ideals by everyone called upon to study the subject. . . . [O]ne cannot but marvel that it has taken two centuries of staring at ruins and rummaging amongst fallen stones for an architectural historian to raise his eyes at last to the horizon and see the Greek temple in its totality, that is to say, as forming with its environment, an inseparable whole." (Peter Collins, review of *The Earth, the Temple, and the Gods,* by Vincent Scully, *Journal of the Society of Architectural Historians* 22 [Mar. 1963]: 45–46.)

9 Henry-Russell Hitchcock, "The Architecture of Bureaucracy and the Architecture of Genius," *Architectural Record* 101 (Jan. 1947): 3–6.

10 Norman Mailer, "The Big Bite," *Esquire* 60 (Aug. 1963): 16, 18, 21, 24. The first article, with the same title, had been published in *Esquire* 59 (May 1963): 37, 40.

11 "Mailer vs. Scully," *Architectural Forum* 120 (Apr. 1964): 96–97. A summary of the debate was printed in *Architectural Review* 136 (July 1964): 2–3.

12 "Mailer vs. Scully," 97.

13 *Village Voice*, 18 June 1964, 5.

14 Robert Venturi, *Complexity and Contradiction in Architecture*, The Museum of Modern Art Papers on Architecture, no. 1 (New York: Museum of Modern Art; Chicago: Graham Foundation for Advanced Studies in The Fine Arts, 1966), 103.

15 "New Talent USA: Architecture," chosen by Vincent J. Scully Jr., *Art in America* 49, no. 1 (1961): 63.

16 This is the central theme in A. Krista Sykes, "Vincent Scully and Robert Venturi: The Strategic Alliance of Historian and Architect" (senior thesis, Princeton University, 1997). I am grateful to the author for providing me with a copy of the thesis.

17 Venturi, *Complexity and Contradiction*, 21.

18 Ibid., 22–23, 52.

19 Ibid., 11–16. Venturi only adopted the notion of the "heroic and original" as a pejorative category in *Learning from Las Vegas*, which was published in 1972. See Robert Venturi, Denise Scott Brown, and Steven Izenour, *Learning from Las Vegas* (Cambridge, Mass.: MIT Press, 1972), 70–109.

20 Excerpts from the book were published in Japanese in *A+U: A Monthly Journal of World Architecture and Urbanism*, no. 52 (Apr. 1975): 97–106, in an issue entitled "White and Gray."

21 Antoinette F. Downing and Vincent J. Scully Jr., *The Architectural Heritage of Newport, Rhode Island, 1640–1915*, 2nd rev. ed. (New York: Bramhall House, 1967), 126. The introduction is dated 1965 and was written at about the same time Scully was writing the introduction to *Complexity and Contradiction*, which he mentions as "forthcoming."

22 Vincent Scully, "Interview with Vincent Scully," 21 Oct. 1980, interview by Patricia Leighten and William B. Stargard, *The Rutgers Art Review: The Journal of Graduate Research in Art History* 2 (Jan. 1981): 95.

23 Vincent Scully, interview by Neil Levine, audiocassette, 18 Oct. 1998.

24 James Stevenson, "Profiles: What Seas What Shores," *New Yorker*, 18 Feb. 1980, 43–48, 53–54, 57–58, 63–64, 69.

25 He declined to accept either award at the annual May meeting in protest against the failure of the national organization to award fellow status to Venturi after the local Philadelphia chapter had proposed it.

26 John Tierney, "Mr. Scully's Architecture Class Is Dismissed," *New York Times*, 28 Apr. 1991.

27 Vincent Scully, "Architecture View: Back to the Future, With a Detour through Miami," *New York Times*, 27 Jan. 1991.

28 See, e.g., Vincent Scully, "The Failure of the Hero Architect," *Metropolitan Home* 20 (Nov. 1988): 81–83, 200.

"American Villas: Inventiveness in the American Suburb from Downing to Wright." *Architectural Review* 115 (March 1954): 168–79.

By the late 1940s, when Scully wrote his dissertation at Yale on the subject of late-nineteenth-century American domestic architecture, the single-family suburban or country house had become the main site for the proliferation of modern ideas in architecture in the United States as well as many places abroad. Completed in 1949, Scully's "The Cottage Style: An Organic Development in Later Nineteenth-Century Wooden Domestic Architecture in the Eastern United States" provided the first documentary history of the earliest phases of this process and the first clear evidence for its origins in the previous century. The interest in what Lewis Mumford had recently hailed as the Bay Region Style, with its roots in the turn-of-the-century work of Greene and Greene, made Scully's analysis relevant not only to an art-historical audience but to a professional one as well.

Although the dissertation (minus its first chapter) was not published until 1955, as *The Shingle Style: Architectural Theory and Design from Richardson to the Origins of Wright*, many of the ideas contained in it had appeared somewhat earlier. The chapters entitled "The Stick Style" and "The Shingle Style" constituted Scully's contribution to *The Architectural Heritage of Newport, Rhode Island, 1640–1915*, coauthored with Antoinette Downing (1952). This was followed in quick succession by two important articles. "Romantic-Rationalism and the Expression of Structure in Wood: Downing, Wheeler, Gardner, and the 'Stick Style,' 1840–1876," based on the first chapter of the dissertation, appeared in the scholarly journal *Art Bulletin* (1953). The second article, reprinted here for

1

American Villas: Inventiveness in the American Suburb from Downing to Wright

VINCENT SCULLY

Within the last generation, critics and historians of modern architecture have turned their eyes more and more towards America. They have seen there whatever architectural qualities might serve best to bolster their own particular view of the direction which architecture should follow in the twentieth century. Le Corbusier in the twenties saw skyscrapers, factories, and grain elevators, the last two types especially indicating to him the mechanistic excitement of harsh geometries and the power of industrial forms. Giedion in the late thirties, impelled by an aesthetic formulated by Gropius and Le Corbusier, investigated as well some aspects of American domestic architecture and found what he was looking for, that is: simple structural techniques, "plain walls," and an early apotheosis of the "functional." Bruno Zevi, reacting against Giedion, sees an "organic" development in Wright and in the "Bay Region Style" of the San Francisco area. Zevi's analysis of nineteenth-century American domestic architecture is, however, bounded basically by the researches of Giedion, and, in consequence, the foundations of the American "organic" perhaps tend to elude him. The profound discipline of Wright's

the first time, is an abridgment of the dissertation that highlights the polemical thrust of its main argument for the broader audience of professionals who read Britain's *Architectural Review*, which, under the coeditorship of Nikolaus Pevsner, was the only English-language architectural journal then seriously interested in history and criticism.

Focusing on the evolution of the suburban house (the use of the anglicism "villa" in the title was apparently an editorial decision), Scully constructs a coherent history of progressive developments in America leading from European-derived midcentury theories of the picturesque and structural rationalism to the novel and, in his view, wholly indigenous spatial innovations of the 1880s by McKim, Mead and White, among others, that culminated in the turn-of-the-century designs of Frank Lloyd Wright. This pathbreaking thesis —which goes well beyond the conventional interpretation of the nineteenth century as a sequence of revival styles and gives to American architecture a uniquely instrumental role in the prehistory of modernism—incorporates important suggestions made previously by Scully's mentor Henry-Russell Hitchcock while it convincingly critiques and amends earlier accounts of the American contribution by Sigfried Giedion and Pevsner.

A fascinating though no doubt unintended by-product of Scully's correlation of the increasing discipline and order in the work of McKim, Mead and White and the origins of Wright's interwoven spaces was the reevaluation of the academic tradition by a later generation of architects and scholars. More to the point for Scully, and undoubtedly something very much on his mind, was the appearance in the recent work of Mies van der Rohe and Louis Kahn of a renewed tendency toward symmetry and clear geometric forms. But Scully is still very wary here of anything that smacks of eclecticism or academicism. Space, not structure, is the sign of creativity. The ideal architect is an artist, who freely invents out of his own experience, rather than a professional member of a large firm, who loses touch with the vernacular and learns how to design in school. Such strongly defended positions have remained operative in one way or another throughout Scully's career, but the relations between the material and the ideal, the creative and the academic, the universal and the vernacular, have shifted and realigned over time.

design is understressed, and European criticism of American architecture thus makes a rather exclusive sweep from the extreme of the concrete grain elevator to that of the redwood cottage—with, in some quarters, an exaggerated attention to forms of urban blight by no means restricted to America.

Actually, a study of American domestic architecture in the nineteenth century reveals a richly complex range of activity. For an American it brings into focus his formative century and thereby helps him to know himself. To a European it can illuminate the growing tensions of a culture almost but not quite the same as his own. It can do this because into its comparatively modest domestic building activities were poured cultural energies reserved in earlier centuries for projects of larger scale. On it, too, the American yearning for epic expression began to work itself out, as with Melville and Whitman, in the only materials ready to hand, in this case the freestanding house of moderate size. These houses provided the vehicle for an intense program of invention which was to culminate in the architectural epic of Wright's career.

The architects who carried out this development were peculiarly free for a long time from academicism of any kind, and the vigorous growth which ensued was brought to a partial close in the nineties by some of the factors which harass architecture today: large-office practice, the division of activity, the closing of minds, and the imposition of formulae of design. Thus the story of American domestic architecture in the nineteenth century is that of a freely developing way of building, and one which moved by 1885 towards its own large architectural order. This free, spatial, and disciplined design was consciously imbibed by Wright from the eastern architects, and he continues its tradition. Elsewhere I have been able to indicate, through a consideration of building in Newport, Rhode Island, that such a coherent development in American domestic architecture actually took place.[1] In this article I shall attempt briefly to isolate its main thread of invention in structure, space, and massing and to show, parenthetically, that it was not confined to Newport and that Frank Lloyd Wright's work did in fact grow out of it.

We shall be concerned here mainly with a few of the cottages and suburban buildings of the early eighties, but we must first look briefly at some of the earlier aspects of the tradition out of which they grew. To say that the philosophical roots of the nineteenth-century single-family rural or suburban house in America are Jeffersonian and Jacksonian is not to stretch a point too far. Jefferson's insistence upon the individual ownership of land, his abolition in the Virginia House of Burgesses in 1776 of the English system of entail, his preoccupation, following that of Locke, with the "natural" superiority of agrarian over urban living, all entered deeply into the consciousness of early-nineteenth-century America, and were in accord with the basically agrarian organization of its culture. These, coupled with a similarly Jeffersonian concern for labor and space-saving devices, formed a durable philosophy which had as its basis democratic, agrarian, and utilitarian values. Jefferson's own attempt to create a new American architecture through classic geometries and the forms of antiquity proved much less durable, and the capacities for further growth of the American phase of the classical revival—called generally in America the Greek Revival—were exhausted by the 1840s.

At this point, however, the principles of picturesque design, developing in England since the mid-eighteenth century, were introduced into America by Andrew Jackson Downing, a landscape gardener and the spiritual heir of Capability Brown, Repton, and Loudon, the last of whom he indicated as his master. Downing produced the first and most important of those pattern books which were to be the main vehicle of the American development until 1876. These were *A Treatise on the Theory and Practice of Landscape Gardening Adapted to North America . . . With Remarks on Rural Architecture*, New York and London, 1841; *Cottage Residences . . .* , New York and London, 1842; and *The Architecture of Country Houses . . .* , New York, 1850. In these books Downing, working with his friend and collaborator the architect Alexander Jackson Davis,[2] presented

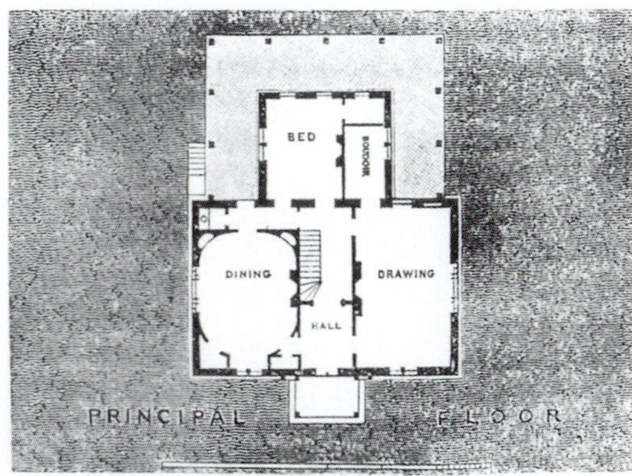

1.1 ABOVE: Richard Upjohn. Kingscote, Newport, Rhode Island, 1841. Exterior

1.2 RIGHT: Andrew Jackson Downing. "A Cottage Villa in the Bracketed Mode," wooden version of Design V, 1842. Exterior perspective and plan. From *Cottage Residences* (New York and London, 1842)

Italian villas and *cottages ornées* types which had been familiar in England since 1800, as in John Nash's Cronkhill of c. 1802 and his Blaise Hamlet group of 1811. Asymmetrical, both in plan and massing, and manipulating natural light in a richly pictorial manner, these broke out of the late Georgian box and developed a new sense of three-dimensional design. The King House at Newport by Richard Upjohn, built in 1845, is an excellent example of the more massive Italian villa type introduced to America by Notman and
popularized by Downing, while his Kingscote of 1841, also at Newport, is a typical *cot-* 1.1
tage ornée, with an articulated plan, jagged massing, the void of a veranda, and eave carvings which enhance the picturesque development of shadow.

Downing then went beyond the purely picturesque, concerned himself with the very smallest type of house and with the realities of wooden construction, the cheapest method of building in most of the United States. He presented his Design V, in *Cottage Residences*, as the prototype of an "American cottage style." One version is of masonry,
but the other is of frame construction, sided vertically with battens over the joints. The 1.2
windows are set in panels formed by continuous vertical stripping and become visually not holes cut into a wall but voids between vertically continuous structural studs. The

plank and beam roof then overhangs deeply and casts a shadow upon the wall, which emphasizes the vertical strips of the battens, and the basic expression of the house becomes not planar—not the "plain wall" of Giedion—but instead skeletal and articulated like its frame within. Moreover, this expression of the frame is exactly Downing's reason for the use of vertical board and batten siding, and in his *Country Houses*, of 1850, he states:

> We greatly prefer the vertical to the horizontal boarding, not only because it is more durable, but because it has an expression of strength and truthfulness which the other has not. The main timbers which enter into the frame of a wooden house and support the structure, are vertical, and hence the vertical boarding properly signifies to the eye a wooden house.

Downing then presents as his first design in *Country Houses* a "Laborer's Cottage" where not only is the boldly wooden skeletal expression of the new American "cottage style" very evident, but which also in the nature of its program reveals a concern for the dwelling of the poorest which is at least symptomatic of the Jacksonian egalitarian democracy of the America of the 1840s. Moreover, the orientation in this social project is still Jeffersonian in its essentials. It is toward the single-family house on its own plot of ground in an agrarian setting, or in that which will less and less successfully evoke the agrarian, the suburban setting.

It will not be feasible here to discuss in detail all the aspects of this agrarian or suburban cottage style up to 1876,[3] but its architectural expression should be clear. Picturesque in its soft and darkening colors and in its rough textures—which revolted against what were to Downing the abstract white surfaces of the Greek Revival—it was most of all wooden building, dominated by a sense of its structural studs. The vertical continuity of its battens echoed visually the technical invention of the vertically continuous thin studs of the balloon frame, which was developing in the West at the same moment—although many of the eastern houses were never actually built in the balloon frame method. It was, in sum, a skeletally articulated "stick style" in wood.

Such houses were built all over the United States, especially many in California during gold-rush days and afterwards, and much of the work of the Bay Region architects at the present time reveals the strong influence exerted upon them by these buildings. Wurster, Esherick, Belluschi, Dailey, and others have all used vertically boarded and battened walls with overhanging plank and beam roofs, much as did Downing in the 1840s. Downing's picturesque looseness and suburban orientation have also been basic in much of their domestic design.

Carried by the pattern books, the stick style itself developed widely till 1876, and into it were poured increments of the Swiss chalet, of medieval half-timber, of Japanese frame construction, and, indeed, of whatever types might be assimilated to enhance the expression of the skeleton frame. A strong reaction against it, carried first by

1.3 Dudley Newton. Cram (later Sturtevant) House, Newport, Rhode Island, 1872. Exterior

the massive Italian villa types in the forties and fifties and then by sculpturally mansarded Second Empire types in the fifties and sixties, was generally played out by the early seventies, and the articulated stick style clearly emerged at this period as the exuberant and expressive carrier of the American vernacular in wood. The Jacob Cram, now 1.3
Sturtevant, House, at Middletown, near Newport, Rhode Island, built in 1872, presumably by a local architect named Dudley Newton, may stand as an excellent example of this moment. Structure, utility, and the picturesque all combine in it to achieve a strong, masculine, and "real" expression. Such "reality" is to be equated in England with the philosophy of the *Ecclesiologist* and Street and with the work of Butterfield. As an expression of technique and social purpose it represents in wood an application of the principles of Philip Webb and William Morris as exhibited in brick in their Red House of 1859. The old cry, then, against the so-called "eclecticism" of the midcentury is not strictly true, and the stick style of 1840–76 was an inventive and coherent method of achieving expression with indigenous techniques for an especially American building program. Such writers as Eugene Clarence Gardner of Springfield, whose own work was pure stick style, stated their case very clearly. They themselves never used the word "style." Gardner, in his books, *Homes and How to Make Them*, 1874, and *Illustrated Homes . . . Real Houses and Real People*, Boston, 1875, was concerned with the country and the suburb rather than with the city, produced multitudinously varied plan types for different family programs, and in general developed in an even more clear-cut manner the point of view initiated by Downing.

Beginning roughly in 1876 the wooden domestic style underwent a profound change, amplified its expressive means, developed a new kind of space, created a new order, and eventually lost momentum in the East and subsided into semi-academicism by the late eighties. This phase from the mid-seventies on was carried by architects

ABOVE, LEFT: Henry Hobson Richardson. Watts Sherman House, Newport, Rhode Island, 1874–76. Exterior 1.4

ABOVE, RIGHT: Charles Follen McKim. Dennis House (orig. built 1760), Newport, Rhode Island. Remodeled living hall, 1876 1.5

rather than by pattern books and was disseminated by architectural periodicals, of which the most important was the *American Architect and Building News*, founded in 1876. The social milieu of this phase was still suburban, with one aspect of suburbia, the summer resort, becoming more and more important. The program was still the single-family house, with the "casino" or clubhouse as social center of suburb and resort. However, by this time the suburb and the summer resort were apparently turning snobbish, and though the suburb may be said still to have been functioning as a creative social organism in the early eighties, the high point of this phase, it tended to function less well by the later eighties. Consequently, the eventual collapse of original invention in the East may be partially explained by the rise of an at once more pretentious and more conformist attitude in the social milieu which had supported the integrally democratic and individualistic architectural development throughout the midcentury.

In 1874, Henry Hobson Richardson, assisted by the young designer Stanford
1.4 White, built the Watts Sherman House at Newport, Rhode Island, the hub of suburban summer resort activity. Richardson here continued his experiments in the creation of a new kind of interior space which he had been carrying on since his Richard Codman project of 1869–71. In these he was clearly influenced by the English late medieval and early Renaissance living halls which were published by Robert Kerr in *The English Gentleman's House*, London, 1864. More particularly, however, Richardson was moved by the living halls used by Norman Shaw in his "Old English" manor houses of the late sixties and early seventies. The publication of the tile-hung Leyes Wood by Shaw in the *Building News* of 1872 coincides with Richardson's first use of shingles as surface covering, in his F. W. Andrews House, at Newport, also of that year. In the Watts Sherman House, following closely upon the photo-lithographic reproduction of Shaw's seductive pen and ink rendering of Hopedene, Surrey, in 1874, Richardson built his closest adaptation of a Shavian manor house.

This antiquarian influence, sometimes called in America "Queen Anne," was supplemented from the first by another, that of the American "Colonial." Resort developments in eighteenth-century towns, a depression, and a general feeling of the over-

complication of modern life had driven both architects and the public, by 1874, into a growing enthusiasm for the picturesque wrecks of seventeenth- and early-eighteenth-century houses, often shingled, which were in various states of pleasing decay in the colonial centers most visited—Newport, Portsmouth, Newburyport, and so on. In 1872, Charles Follen McKim, a young architect, educated at Harvard, the Beaux-Arts, and in Richardson's office, added a purposefully colonial room to the eighteenth-century Robinson House on Washington Street in Newport. Here two characteristics which the Queen Anne also possessed are apparent: a large fireplace and a lower ceiling height, emphasizing horizontality rather than verticality. In 1876, at the enormously influential Centennial Exposition at Philadelphia, the majority of the wooden buildings were of the fully developed stick style, but the most heavily attended architectural attractions were the half-timbered British buildings, by Thomas Harris, and the "New England kitchen of 1776," set up at full scale and stocked with colonial housewives in complete regalia. Colonial and Queen Anne influences now began to merge, and when McKim remodeled
the Dennis House in Newport in 1876 he created what amounted to a Queen Anne living 1.5
hall. Taking the stairs from their position near the front door, he added them to the old kitchen in the rear, increased the size of the fireplace, and extended the room by means of a bay window. All the elements are brought together: colonial enthusiasm, a few semi-eighteenth-century details, fireplace, stairs, and window wall. The space is inventive; the antiquarian preoccupations might be considered full of future dangers.

Thus, the new phase of the domestic development rested upon rather shaky and certainly antiquarian foundations. The element of escape, hardly a real factor in the mid-century, also became a cottage-style component. Yet the sense of experiment was still dominant, and by 1880, when renewed prosperity again made a good deal of building possible, American architects had generally assimilated the new influences and created from them what may be called an original "shingle style." Best known, almost solely known, of these houses of the early eighties are those designed by Richardson. The Stoughton House of 1882 has been published innumerable times, with its living-hall plan, its rough shingle surfaces enclosing its interior volumes, and its banks of windows. So commonly has this period been associated with Richardson's work that Hitchcock coined the phrase, "Suburban Richardsonian," to describe the general run of shingled houses. However, this phrase is misleading, as Professor Hitchcock would now be the first to admit. Richardson contributed to this architecture that same largeness of simpler and fewer shapes which was his gift as well to the other architectural programs with which he worked. But other architects played a greater part than Richardson in formulating and developing the shingle style, and other architects indeed carried it much further than did Richardson along those lines of spatial invention which led toward the work of Wright.

William Ralph Emerson of Boston, for instance—only distantly related to Ralph Waldo Emerson—appears to have been the first architect to dispense with the Queen
Anne practice of shingling only the upper stories. In his house of 1879 at Mt. Desert, an 1.6
island summer resort off the coast of Maine, he extends the shingles over the whole surface, brings his windows to the corner with a small overhang, and thus expresses the wall

ABOVE, LEFT: William Ralph Emerson. Morrill House, Bar Harbor, Mount Desert, Maine, 1879. Exterior perspectives and plan 1.6

ABOVE, RIGHT: Peabody and Stearns. Black House (Kragsyde), Manchester-by-the-Sea, Massachusetts, 1882–84. Exterior and interior perspectives and plan 1.7

as a thin and continuous shingled skin over profoundly plastic interior volumes. The living hall is raised a quarter flight from the entrance level and opens above through a wide staircase well. From the hall one may look back down into the living room through a large aperture or may move outside under the shelter of a porch to an open pavilion. Space is freed in this design, within the limits of an enclosing shell which the architect organizes loosely and penetrates with deep voids. The debt to Shaw is clear, with the window seat, the sketchy half-timber, and the Shavian chimney, but an essentially stud-frame lightness and flexibility are also apparent, and the house represents to all intents and purposes a complete Americanization of Shaw. Emerson's method in this kind of design is extremely interesting, since it is at once picturesque and personal, difficult to develop in large-office practice. It is a painterly method whereby all areas and intersections are studied in richly pictorial little sketches, and the house grows and changes constantly in both space and massing. The sketches by E. Eldon Deane, renderer for the *American Architect and Building News*, illustrating another of Emerson's houses, the Loring House, can demonstrate not only the contemporary method of seeing but also Emerson's design approach as described by his pupils. These sketches break through the convention of plan and elevation as well as the tyranny of the formal perspective, and in consequence they allow a real freedom of formal invention as well as an intense feeling for the sensuous qualities of shingles, glass, and rough stone. Their power lies in plastic invention, most weak today, but their own weakness is a tendency toward the quaint, the inadequately organized, and the purely pictorial. At any rate, this picturesque method was one which required study and the total commitment of one man's sensitivity and intelligence. It possessed freedom; if it could acquire its own geometric discipline it could become a really flexible tool for architectural invention. Best of all, Emerson's design, like that of the other architects of this period, was peculiarly spatial in its basic sensitivities and as such was capable of continued architectural growth. Its sense of space generally saved it from quaintness and from the finicky fanfaronade of a purely "cottage" style. In a real sense, spatial control was the architectural discipline into which this design proved itself capable of growing.

1.8 Arthur Little. Little House (Shingleside), Swampscott, Massachusetts, 1880–81. Exterior and interior perspectives and plans

With this building technique, this sense of space, and this picturesque method free to their hands, the American architects of the early eighties embarked upon spatial experiments of several kinds. First was the space of volume, the large cave of space. This
can be seen in the G. N. Black House (called Kragsyde!) at Manchester-by-the-Sea, 1.7
Massachusetts, another summer resort. The Black House was built by the firm of Robert Swain Peabody and John Goddard Stearns, of Boston. Peabody had been one of the most enthusiastic early admirers of colonial architecture, and his two articles on the "Georgian Homes of New England" had appeared in the *American Architect and Building News* in 1877 and 1878. From such a colonial example as the Fairbanks House at Dedham, Massachusetts, of which he was very fond, and which was reproduced photographically in the *American Architect and Building News* in 1881, Peabody had acquired a feeling for the modeling of spaces through the sculptural planes of the gambrel roof, common in late-seventeenth- and early-eighteenth-century colonial work in New England. To this he added a feeling, certainly Richardsonian in its origin, for large and simple geometries in rough materials.

Spatially even more interesting is Shingleside, a house built in 1880–81 at 1.8
Swampscott, Massachusetts, by the Boston architect Arthur Little. This was published in England in the *Architect and Building News* in 1881. Here one enters at the middle level, walks across an open gallery, goes either to the living room, from which an open balcony projects into the space of the hall, or else descends through the open space to the floor of the hall itself, lighted by a two-storied wall of glass on the ocean side. Off this again a low inglenook around the fire offers spatial relief. The enclosed volume, utterly open within its
containing skin, is to be compared here with Le Corbusier's Citrohan houses of the early 4.8
twenties, which also make use of enclosed volumes, two stories high, with projecting

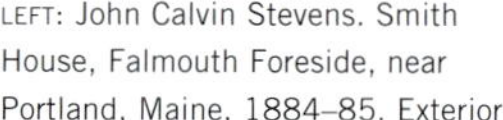

LEFT: John Calvin Stevens. Smith House, Falmouth Foreside, near Portland, Maine, 1884–85. Exterior 1.9

BELOW: John Calvin Stevens. House by the Sea project, 1885. Exterior perspective. From John C. Stevens and Albert W. Cobb, *Examples of American Domestic Architecture* (New York, 1889) 1.10

balconies and a wall of glass. Le Corbusier was probably influenced by Adolf Loos in his destruction of interior floor divisions, and, since Loos spent several years in America in the late eighties, one may at least be allowed the tentative observation that the line of development between houses such as Shingleside of 1880–81 and Le Corbusier's work of the twenties may be more direct than is usually supposed.

The American architects of the early eighties, however, were not content merely with space as volume, however open within its shell. They apparently desired two other things as well, that is, interpenetration of spaces, both interior and exterior, and, most of all, a sense of continuity in that interpenetration. Such objectives can be seen in the work of John Calvin Stevens, of Portland, Maine, who in the mid-eighties took as his partner Albert Winslow Cobb, one of Emerson's pupils. Together Stevens and Cobb produced a book of domestic designs, *Examples of American Domestic Architecture*, New York, 1889. In this they extolled Emerson and continued as well that preoccupation with the importance of domestic architecture as a cultural program which Downing had initiated in the forties and which E. C. Gardner had carried on in the early seventies. Stevens's
1.9 James Hopkins Smith House, at Falmouth Foreside, near Portland, Maine, dating from 1884–85, can illustrate the development of spatial interpenetration. The house is a gambrel-roofed volume intersected by the void of a deep terrace veranda. The roof of the upper stories folds over the lower void so that one can feel them pass through each other,

and the penetration becomes actual below by the ranges of glass doors which open from living room to terrace. It will be perceived that the colonial-inspired gambrel is not an antiquarian domination of the design, but is a plastic shape at the service of a spatial intent, with window and intersection detailing which is original and not eclectic. Rough stone, big arches, heavy piers, and weathering shingle walls are also evidence of a builder's sensitivity to materials—a vernacular sensitivity, stoutly developed and totally at the service of the architect, not in competition with his intent.

The desire to extend such spatial penetration into a long horizontal continuity can be observed in a sketch for a country house by Stevens, dating from about 1885. 1.10
Here the long axis of the house stretches away across the site and is extended by its integral veranda. The voids and solids of the house all move plastically within a dominant horizontal sweep.

Continuity in spatial organization was the dominant discipline which the shingle style imposed upon itself by 1885.[4] It was a discipline generated from within rather than from without the architectural envelope—a kind of classic phase in this design where coherence arrived by means which were integral to its own nature and not imposed upon it by an academic canon. The houses of Wilson Eyre, of Philadelphia, can show this most clearly. The plan of his Potter House, at Chestnut Hill, Pennsylvania, of 1881–82, 1.11
one of the many houses he built in the Main Line suburbs of Philadelphia, develops a long axis within which the room spaces are organized as one volume. Short interior diagonals vitalize the space, but the discipline of single extension, continued by the veranda, organizes the whole. All rooms are lighted from opposite sides, with one set of windows being shaded by the porch ceiling. The stairs are set back behind the fireplace,

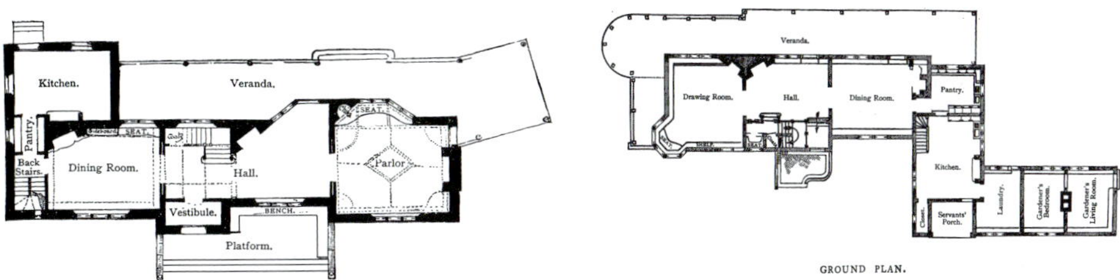

1.11 ABOVE, LEFT: Wilson Eyre. Potter House, Chestnut Hill, Pennsylvania, 1881–82. Plan

1.12 ABOVE, RIGHT: Wilson Eyre. Ashurst House. Plan

1.13 RIGHT: Wilson Eyre. Ashurst House, Overbrook, Pennsylvania, 1884–85. Exterior

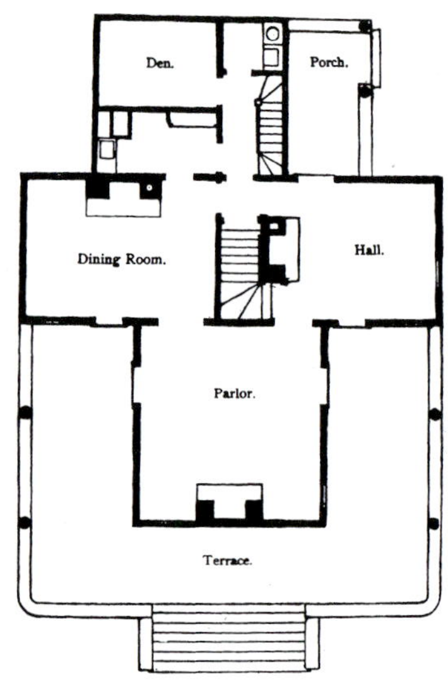

as if consciously being got out of the way so as not to disturb with their vertical movement the horizontal continuity of the ceiling planes. This is even more apparent in Eyre's
1.12, 1.13 Ashurst House, at Overbrook, Pennsylvania, of 1884–85, where the stairs are heavily masked by newels and where one's diagonal movement upward is interrupted and partially screened. Wright's staircases are later screened and broken in this way. Horizontal continuity thus ensured, the rooms stretch out along the ground plane, widely open to each other and, indeed, part of the same continuous space. The veranda again extends the interior space and actually penetrates the house, as can be observed in the photograph of the exterior. Spaces pass through each other, and their continuity is emphasized by the long range of windows which pass around the corner of the house, although the
1.28 total continuity of plane above plane, as Wright would later develop it, is still incomplete here because of the gabled volume above the second floor. The scale is brought down in order to intensify one's experience of the horizontal extension, and the balcony over the entrance is very low overhead. To enter under it and to take the few steps down the hall is to be seized by the impress of the space and forced thereby to experience its long, sheltering continuities. Wright later was to develop extensively exactly this device of forcing the scale.

ABOVE, LEFT: Bruce Price. Kent House, Tuxedo Park, New York, 1885–86. Exterior. From George W. Sheldon, *Artistic Country Seats* (New York, 1886–87) 1.14

ABOVE, RIGHT: Bruce Price. Kent House. Plan. From George W. Sheldon, *Artistic Country Seats* (New York, 1886–87) 1.15

By 1885 the principle of the interpenetration of volumes and of clarity in their organization was well established, and Bruce Price of New York extended this principle to the design of very small houses, as demonstrated in his small "Honeymoon Cottages" at the new suburban development of Tuxedo Park, New York, founded in 1885 by Pierre Lorillard. Price's design was generally coarse, in contrast to the more delicately scaled work of Emerson, Eyre, and others. His heavier scale was in accord with his feeling, later important in Wright, for monumentally powerful architectural shapes, even in small

houses. Certainly, his coarseness was the expression of vitality, and the kind of discipline to which he was able to subject himself by 1885 was probably more creative than the later antiquarian disciplines into which he and his contemporaries fell. Unworried by "good" taste, as yet unrevived, Price piled up rock, studs, and shingles with a kind of animistic energy hardly in keeping with the apparent tastes of his daughter, Mrs. Emily Post, who brought out in the thirties a volume entitled *The Personality of a House, The Blue Book of Home Design*. This work expressed, though with some charm, the prevalent antiquarian-ism and desire for conformity which was typical of that epoch in American domestic
architecture. Price's William Kent House of 1885–86, is remarkable in its plan, too. The 1.14, 1.15
crossing of the two axes is very similar to that in some early Wright houses, for instance
the Ward Willits House of 1902. Wright may well have known the Kent House, since it 1.28
was published in George William Sheldon's *Artistic Country Seats*, 2 vols., New York, 1886–87. This book was probably owned by Joseph Lyman Silsbee, as by almost all other eastern domestic architects, and was possibly in his office in Chicago when Wright worked there in 1887. Wright may have owned it himself, since he certainly seems to have used material from it in his own early experiments. Such seems clear in this case, where the Willits House develops a crossed-axial discipline along lines already indicated by Price.
Moreover, Wright's own first house, built for himself in Oak Park, in 1889, while he was 1.16
working for Louis Sullivan, shows a very close elevational similarity to Bruce Price's Kent
House. It is even closer in its exterior organization to Price's Chandler cottage at Tuxedo, 1.17
dating from 1885–86, and published in 1886.[5] The designs were therefore available to Wright, who clearly adopted them for his own house. The similarity of projecting gable

1.16 Frank Lloyd Wright. Wright House, Oak Park, Illinois, 1889. Exterior

over bay windows and of bands of windows in the gable, surmounted by a semi-Palladian arched motif, are striking. It is from this basis and at this time that Wright begins his own experiments and embarks upon the well-known if inadequately understood course of his own growth.

ABOVE, LEFT: Bruce Price. Chandler House, Tuxedo Park, New York, 1885–86. Exterior. From *Building: A Journal of Architecture* (1886) 1.17

ABOVE, TOP RIGHT: McKim, Mead and White. Casino, Newport, Rhode Island, 1879–81. Exterior 1.18

ABOVE, BOTTOM RIGHT: McKim, Mead and White. Casino. Interior 1.19

However, Wright begins from a richer synthesis of the tradition of American building than has as yet been indicated here, for in the early eighties by far the most advanced and distinguished work in domestic design was being done by the young firm of McKim, Mead and White. When this firm became perhaps too big and too successful in the mid-eighties—when it became preoccupied at once with the correct, the grandiose, and, because of its compartmentalized and profitable activity, with that which would be easy to produce or reproduce—from that moment dates the beginning of real eclecticism in the East and the collapse of the development in domestic architecture which has been traced so far. Yet in the early eighties the work of McKim, Mead and White was of supreme diversity and quality. Much of this early quality must be assigned to the design sensitivity of the young Stanford White. The library of the Watts Sherman House, finally decorated by him in 1879, shows a slightly "aesthetic" preciousness, a little like that of Godwin. But beyond this the room has delicacy of scale and precision of material and detail. The green woodwork is organized rhythmically into panels picked out with gold paint in a detailing which is at once semi-colonial and semi-Oriental. Over the doorways as well appear plant tendrils against a sunburst ground which exhibit the typical whip lash curve of Art Nouveau.

When Charles Follen McKim, William Rutherford Mead, and Stanford White
1.18, 1.19 organized as a firm in 1879, one of their first commissions was the Casino at Newport, Rhode Island, a large complex of restaurant, tennis courts, a theater, and shops, the

1.20 ABOVE, LEFT: Stanford White. Kingscote, new dining room, 1881

1.21 ABOVE, RIGHT: McKim, Mead and White. McCormick House, Richfield Springs, New York, 1881–82. Exterior

social center for the summer community. This building combines both discipline and plastic invention. The facade is symmetrical, although rich in the play of solid and of void. Plastic shingled volumes, with dark brown, painterly surfaces, are poised above smooth brick piers. The delicate scale, the play of light, the color of the flapping awnings are all important elements in this eminently suburban, resort, and holiday kind of design. The curving piazzas of the courtyard represent a strong synthesis of the pavilion space created by wood-frame elements which, as we have seen, had been so much a part of the whole American porch sensitivity since the midcentury. Spindle and lattice screens, carefully differentiated in scale from the structural posts, plates, and braces, form patterns of light and shade and play changes upon the sense of enclosure and exposure. Japanese influence, strong also after the Philadelphia Centennial of 1876, can be detected as well in this play of skeleton and screen, especially in the long thin rectangular area under the plate which the eighties called an "open-work fascia" and assigned to the Japanese. Something of the Japanese also plays a part in the interweaving not only of structural but of spatial areas which the firm, probably largely through the sensitivity of White, was able to produce at this period. McKim and White experimented in this
direction in the Victor Newcomb House, Elberon, New Jersey, 1880–81, but their most 11.1
successful attempt occurred in the dining room which White added in the same year
to Upjohn's Kingscote of 1841. This distinguished room is an interwoven organization 1.20
of articulated elements in which the space is created not by planes so much as by a basketry which weaves the pattern of an area.

As this weaving of spatial elements takes place, so also McKim, Mead and White create the impression of a real weaving together of the fabric of the house as
a whole. Their Cyrus McCormick House of 1881–82, at Richfield Springs, New York, 1.21
presents the volume of a roughly textured gable-shape. The gable is then penetrated deeply by a porch which cuts in under the volume and sweeps voluminously around the corner into a large pavilion. The vertical posts of the porch are scaled to a semi-bamboo section; some appear to penetrate the plates below them, and the whole architectural expression becomes that of an organized basketry. Solid and void interpenetrate, and

ABOVE, LEFT: McKim, Mead and White. Tilton House, Newport, Rhode Island, 1882–83. Stair hall 1.22

ABOVE, RIGHT: Frank Lloyd Wright. Martin House, Buffalo, 1903–4. Living room 1.23

spatial volumes pass through each other in a more ample and assured manner than in the work of either Stevens or Eyre.

Such creation of space through the interweaving of structural elements and of
1.22 light values should be noted especially in the hall of McKim, Mead and White's Tilton House of 1882–83, where it calls for comparison with, say, the living room of Wright's
1.23 Martin House, Buffalo, 1904. Wright intensifies, extends, and clarifies the basically similar experience. He also interweaves spatial areas, and this interweaving eventually extends itself to his whole design, as it was also an important element in Sullivan's skyscraper organization. Wright's advance perhaps over the Tilton hall is one of greater discipline, clearer geometry, and a more total order which eliminates the adventitious, however pleasant in itself, such as the light-splintering spindle work screen of the Tilton House. The sensitivities of the shingle style to form, as seen here in the work of White, are parallel to those of the Impressionist painters; Wright's to those of Seurat and Cézanne. Wright's scale is more intense, the feeling of a strictly architectural fabric in operation more insistent. By contrast, one aspect of Wright's genius should be clear, and that is the power to organize totally—sometimes implacably—the ability to study the elements of design in their basic aspects. With Wright, precise geometries organize a peculiarly biological experience. The virtuosity with light and space with which he has done so much is partially an inheritance from his tradition.

The power of that American suburban tradition to make works of art in the early
1.24 eighties is revealed in the living room of the Tilton House, as in an early painting by John
1.25 Singer Sargent, such as *The Daughters of Edward Boit*, painted in 1883. In both a slightly precious, very delicate feeling for the shapes and textures of objects is organized by a creation of space which has clarity, definition, and a sense of the real tension between things. In both, too, a kind of proto–Art Nouveau delicacy of scale is very apparent, as is also the atmosphere of suburban ease and satisfaction, of an adequately rich life without too much necessity for pretension.

For a variety of reasons, much of this tended to disappear in the arts of the East
1.26 after 1890, and the interior of the dining room in the Breakers by Richard Morris Hunt,

1.24 ABOVE, LEFT: McKim, Mead and White. Tilton House. Living room

1.25 ABOVE, RIGHT: John Singer Sargent, *The Daughters of Edward Boit,* 1883

1892–95, as well as *The Daughters of Asher Wertheimer* by Sargent, painted in 1901, 1.27
can possibly show why. A rather obvious grandeur has overwhelmed life in both, and in both the sense of real space is drowned by a windy expansion of grandiose forms. Sargent is now slick, fashionable, and cynical rather than spatial. Hunt is pillowy, sickly rich, and flatulent. The suburb has turned palatial, and rather snobbish, and has thereby lost the general cultural creativity which it had previously possessed. Although the situation is complicated, a further observation might be made concerning the feminization of taste and the resultant rise of interior decoration. Certainly at this time the American suburb began to adapt the forms of older and grander civilizations without being able to absorb them. Plastic invention and spatial sensitivity, evidences of cultural health, temporarily succumbed to representational and apparently artificial pretenses. Thus, although the shingled style continued in one form or another in the East for some twenty years longer, it no longer represented the main stream of architectural development.

In this movement McKim, Mead and White played their part, mainly as they continued their own success story as a firm. Creative design demands probably as many failures as successes, as Wright's work, for instance, most courageously shows. McKim, Mead and White produced some of these architectural aberrations in the early eighties, such as the Metcalfe House, Buffalo, 1883–84, where the plan was tortured, where nothing hung together, all materials oozed nastily into each other, and everything went just a little out of scale. The necessity for a formula to safeguard against such failures was certainly felt by the firm—just as most architectural firms of the present day, operating upon a large professional scale, similarly attempt to stay as much as possible upon "safe" ground. In the mid-eighties Joseph Morrill Wells found for the firm its formula in the Renaissance and the pseudo-classic and thus led the way for other American firms to follow into academicism. These factors, coupled with the growing domination of architectural education in America by the Beaux-Arts system, all resulted in the gradual decay of the indigenous tradition in the eastern United States. The vernacular became a quasi–eighteenth century semi-Palladianism of which the first and probably the best example was McKim, Mead and White's H. A. C. Taylor House, Newport, of 1885–86. In

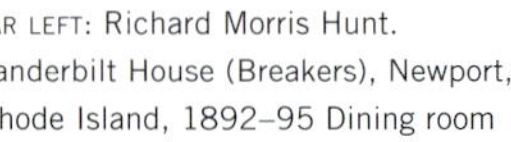
FAR LEFT: Richard Morris Hunt. Vanderbilt House (Breakers), Newport, Rhode Island, 1892–95 Dining room 1.26

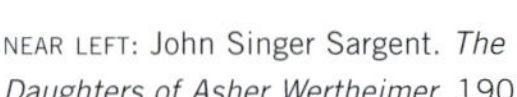

NEAR LEFT: John Singer Sargent. *The Daughters of Asher Wertheimer,* 1901 1.27

these designs space eventually retreats again into separate rooms, the cube takes over once more, and the spatial invention of the nineteenth century enters into a lingering decline. The feeling for materials as design components also tends to disappear, as does, tragically, the native sensibility of the vernacular builder, and all surfaces become covered with that light—usually white—paint which has now become once again, as Downing claimed it to be, a dominant feature of the American landscape and a restricting factor in the sensitivity to architectural color of two generations of Americans.

Some of the later work of McKim, Mead and White and others may have had qualities of its own. These qualities cannot be explored here, since they were the outcome of objectives and methods rather different from those which produced the architectural invention with which we have been concerned. Yet even the phase of reaction had its positive aspects, since in part it also grew out of that whole movement toward discipline, clarity, and order which we noted in the creative work of Stevens, Eyre, and Price as well. Clear planes of wall, now clapboarded or rendered in stucco instead of shingled, an insistence upon geometric discipline, all these might be positive design elements, however burlesqued and turned into formulae by the eclectics who used them in a representational fashion to imitate the Renaissance or the colonial. Hitchcock, in his article "Frank Lloyd Wright and the 'Academic Tradition,'" *Journal of the Warburg and Courtauld Institutes*, vol. 7, 1944, has pointed out how Wright absorbed from the academic reaction these positive elements, concerned mainly with discipline in design. Consequently, we need not labor the point here. It should be noted, however, that Wright was enabled to begin his work under social conditions which were exactly those we have seen as the support of the original nineteenth-century development as a whole. Oak Park, where he worked in the nineties, was at that time an idealistic suburb, suffused, like much of the rest of the Chicago area, with the agrarian radicalism which was the core in America of the Populist Party of that period. While the eastern suburbs were going conformist and antiquarian, Wright, dug into the last memory of the agrarian tradition in suburban Oak Park, was able to find clients who were capable of continuing to embrace the nineteenth-

1.28 Frank Lloyd Wright. Willits House, Highland Park, Illinois, 1902–3. Exterior

century tradition of invention and who would allow him to go on under the compulsion of his own vision. As he read his Ruskin, Owen Jones, Whitman, and Viollet-le-Duc, and as he slowly grew in his search for that "reality" which the men of the mid-nineteenth century had also sought, it was a suburban milieu whose aspirations at least were both democratic and agrarian which sheltered him. In it he evoked with epic power the experiments of those romantic realists who had preceded him, as the rich interweavings of his Ward Willits House orchestrate, for instance, not only Japanese influences but also such 1.28, 2.4
stick style projects as those of E. C. Gardner. And from these early houses by Wright directly formative influences can be traced—through the Wasmuth publications of 1910 and 1911—upon De Stijl designers and Gropius in the teens, and from them to the Bauhaus and Le Corbusier in the twenties.

Consequently, the tradition which threads its way from the agrarian dream of Jefferson to Broadacre City is one which burgeons in the American suburb of the nineteenth century and which is presented by it, as a kind of unforeseen gift, to the twentieth-century world. Its limitations and its strengths are part of the whole, and, if it fell into temporary decline, it at least envisages in Wright, and in those who now come after Wright, a social and architectural invention which may be more coherent but no less free.

Notes

1 See Vincent J. Scully Jr., "Nineteenth-Century Architecture," pt. 4 of *The Architectural Heritage of Newport, Rhode Island, 1670–1915,* by Antionette F. Downing and Vincent J. Scully Jr. (Cambridge, Mass.: Harvard University Press, 1952), 117–63.

2 See Wayne Andrews, "Alexander Jackson Davis," *Architectural Review* 109 (May 1951): 307–8.

3 This has been done by the author in a paper on the "Stick Style" in *Art Bulletin* 35 (June 1953): 121–42.

4 Such continuity and discipline were noted by Pickens among buildings in Detroit during this period. See Buford L. Pickens, "Treasure Hunting at Detroit," *Architectural Review* 96 (Dec. 1944): 169.

5 *Building: A Journal of Architecture* 5, no. 12 (18 Sept. 1886).

"Wright vs. the International Style." *Art News* 53 (March 1954): 32–35, 64–66.

For Scully the graduate student and young assistant professor at Yale, Frank Lloyd Wright represented the true beginning and richest expression of modern architecture. After a tour of recent Wright buildings, especially the Usonian houses, and an initial visit to Taliesin in 1947, he commissioned Wright to design a house for his family. Although it was never constructed, Scully remained so associated with Wright, as a historian and a critic, that when he was introduced to Eero Saarinen around 1952, Saarinen placed him by saying, "You're the Frank Lloyd Wright fanatic." But within a year or two of that, things began to change as Scully's opinion of Wright's ideological position, though not of his architecture, took on a sharper critical edge. This article, published in the art journal most associated with the New York School and Abstract Expressionist painting, set forth many of the crucial ideas that would determine this reappraisal.

"Wright vs. the International Style" is ostensibly a discussion of influence, a common art-historical preoccupation of the time. Scully defines the relationship between Wright and the younger generation of European modernists as a complex give-and-take: first Wright gives the idea of an architecture of shifting planes and interpenetrating spaces to the Europeans via publications like the Wasmuth portfolio and book of 1910–11; and then, in turn, he takes from them a more fluid and open sense of composition gleaned from publications of their work in the late 1920s and early 1930s. The final outcome is Wright's resurgence in the later 1930s, epitomized by the powerful synthesis of Fallingwater.

2

Wright vs. the International Style

Frank Lloyd Wright's relationship to the "International Style" of modern European architecture is simple and intense. It has two phases, separated by approximately twenty years:

1. Wright, more than any other architect, had, by about 1910, set in train the series of experiments in form which were eventually to make the International Style possible.

2. The second phase reverses the process. By about 1929, European architects of the International Style, notably Le Corbusier and Mies van der Rohe, had published buildings and projects which were available to Wright at this period, itself a critical moment in his development. From their work, Wright apparently received direct influences in the late twenties; and he used elements from their design in important projects of his own during the next decade. In fact, the stimulus which these influences provided would seem to have been one of the several factors which made possible Frank Lloyd Wright's renewed burst of achievement during the later 1930s.

This double relationship transcends the romantic or nationalistic notions of the aloneness of the individual artist or of the individual state. It demonstrates instead a

Nikolaus Pevsner, Henry-Russell Hitchcock, and others had already written convincingly of Wright's impact in Europe. The originality of Scully's argument was in seeing, and describing, the counterinfluence of the younger Europeans on Wright, an idea that had been suggested only in passing by Alfred Barr in the Museum of Modern Art's 1948 symposium "What Is Happening to Modern Architecture?" In this, Scully established what would become a commonplace of modern architectural history.

But the influence of Mies van der Rohe and Le Corbusier on Wright is not what the article is ultimately about, nor what Scully had in mind in writing it. If that were the case, the title probably would have been "Wright *and* the International Style." The *vs.* indicates a combativeness on Wright's part and signals the reader to pay close attention to the political subtext. Indeed, the essay is framed by a discussion of the contemporary polemics of nationalism and internationalism which, though never referring directly to either Senator Joseph McCarthy or his journalistic avatar Elizabeth Gordon, does indict Wright for castigating the International Style as "something 'un-American.'" Gordon, the editor of *House Beautiful*, had published a scathing attack on Mies's Farnsworth House in April 1953, entitled "The Threat to the Next America." Wright added his voice in two articles published in July and October, calling the International Style "totalitarian," "collectivist," and "communistic," and claiming that only his idea of organic architecture was "truly American" in its celebration of "freedom" and "individualism." Scully bridled at such jingoism, saying it was "unworthy" of

meaningful process of creation and mutual exchange which links together the whole of European civilization and the Western world.

Therefore it is most unhappy that some of the architects of the International Style have at times belittled Wright in their teaching, occasionally in obtuse and petulant words. That Wright should never have acknowledged the influences he received from them was perhaps only to be expected and can probably be overlooked in the curious father-and-son relationship between generations which is involved here. That he should continually have attacked over a period of years those elements in their design which seemed to him to demand attack is a professional matter and can also be understood. On the other hand, that Wright should have recently added his voice to that of the clangorous pack which has been decrying the International Style as something "un-American" seems doubly unworthy of him. Many of those writers who second him now, for dubious purposes of their own, were calling his own work "International Style," or even "Secession," only a few years ago. Some of them, primarily New Yorkers and Bostonians, are also engaged in attempting to revive the doubtful splendors of Richard Morris Hunt and of the later work of McKim, Mead and White, thereby suggesting a pattern of architectural nationalism leading toward a return to eclectic classicism which has already had full development in two modern states: Nazi Germany and Soviet Russia. One thing is

Wright and demeaning of his work. He countered the latter-day America Firsters with a humanist appeal to those very values of Western civilization he saw embodied in Wright's architecture, namely an inclusiveness and a receptiveness to any and all influences.

The article elicited a strong reaction from those who would defend Wright. Letters from Edgar Kaufmann Jr., Director of the Good Design Project in MoMA's Department of Architecture and Design and son of the client of Fallingwater; T. H. Robsjohn-Gibbings, furniture and interior designer; and Elizabeth Gordon were published in the September issue of *Art News.* None made reference to the larger cultural and political issues most important to Scully; all stressed how inconceivable it was to think of Wright as having been influenced by the younger Europeans. As in a chorus, they criticized Scully for making purely formal comparisons based on the use of photographs. Scully wrote a rejoinder not merely to justify his art-historical methodology, which he did, but also to remind his critics of his main point, which was the ennobling universality of the modern artistic experience: "As we recognize the large order of civilization which our architectural interchanges indicate that we possess, so we ought the more to be capable of rising to the grandeur of our time by a civilized comprehension of its diversity."

clear. At bottom, such people can have no more real understanding of, or sympathy for, Wright's work than they have for that of their present quarry, the architects of the International Style. In supporting their febrile clamors, Wright puts himself into a place where those who have always admired him and his work have no wish to see him. Indeed, by so doing he in part denies himself and some of his most glowing accomplishments.

The first phase of Wright's relationship with the style he now derides began with the well-known publication of his work by the German, Ernst Wasmuth. In 1910 Wasmuth published a large volume of Wright's drawings, including plans and perspectives, entitled: *Ausgeführte Bauten und Entwürfe von Frank Lloyd Wright.* It was accompanied by a large exhibition of his work, shown in Berlin in 1910, and by a visit from the architect himself. In 1911 Wasmuth published a second volume, this one consisting mainly of plans and photographs and entitled, rather lamely, *Frank Lloyd Wright, Ausgeführte Bauten.* From this time on the American's works were often published in Europe, culminating in the large but—so far as the International Style is concerned—probably not too influential Wendingen edition of 1925.

The effect of the Wasmuth publications was, however, immense. They appeared exactly at the moment when the young architects of Europe apparently required a kind of formal catalyst to fuse their deeply felt, but as yet undirected, aspirations. The impact of Wright's work has been described with eloquent sincerity by Mies van der Rohe. Writing in 1940 apropos of the Wright show at the Museum of Modern Art, Mies alludes to the early years of the century, to Behrens, Van de Velde, and Berlage. He then goes on:

> Nevertheless we young architects found ourselves in painful inner discord. Our enthusiastic hearts demanded the unqualified, and we were ready to pledge ourselves to an idea. But the potential vitality of the architectural idea of the period had by that time been lost.
>
> This then was approximately the situation in 1910.
>
> At this moment, so critical for us, the exhibition of the work of Frank Lloyd Wright came to Berlin. This comprehensive display and the exhaustive publication of his works enabled us to become really acquainted with the achievements of this architect. The encounter was destined to prove of great significance to the European development.
>
> The work of this great master presented an architectural world of unexpected force, clarity of language and disconcerting richness of form. Here, finally, was a master-builder drawing upon the veritable fountainhead of architecture; who with true originality lifted his creations into the light. Here again, at long last, genuine organic architecture flowered. The more we were absorbed in the study of these creations, the greater became our admiration for his incomparable talent, the boldness of his conceptions and the independence of his thought and action. The dynamic impulse emanating from his work invigorated a whole generation. His influence was strongly felt even when it was not actually visible.

But Wright's influence upon Europe is actually visible, and is sometimes to be
found in unexpected places, as, for example, in the Fabrik designed by Walter Gropius
for the Werkbund Exhibition at Cologne of 1914. In this building Gropius created a bal- 2.1
ance between two pavilions, each with a wide overhang played off against a lower central
area with a strong horizontal element sliding across at second story level. This design so
closely resembles Wright's perspective of his Mason City (Iowa) Hotel of 1908, that it is 2.2
difficult to believe that direct influences were not at work, even though the Gropius
building is more linear, more planar, and uses glass in a different manner. If there is a
direct relationship between the two buildings, it has never been acknowledged.

However, acknowledged influences are not difficult to find. In Mies's work they
seem particularly clear. The plan of his Brick Country House project of 1923 continues 2.3
a line of experiment towards the extension of crossed axes out into space which should
be referred back to the sweeping crossed axes of Wright's Ward Willits House of 1902. 2.4
Also in Mies's use of thick and thin planes as space definers is a sensitivity which may be
related to such projects as Wright's Walter Gerts House, Glencoe, Illinois, 1906.
Similarly, Mies's Barcelona Pavilion of 1929, a precise organization of planes placed 2.5
upon a firm, raised platform, recalls the most important characteristics of Wright's
Yahara Boat Club, 1902. All of these Wright projects were published in the 1910 2.6
Wasmuth edition.

In relating these works by Mies to designs by Wright, one may perhaps be accused of ignoring the obvious relationship between Mies's work of the 1920s and the

LEFT: Walter Gropius and Adolf Meyer. Model Factory, Werkbund Exhibition, Cologne, 1914. Exterior 2.1

BELOW: Frank Lloyd Wright. Hotel, Mason City, Iowa, 1909–10. Perspective. From *Ausgeführte Bauten und Entwürfe von Frank Lloyd Wright* (Berlin, 1910) 2.2

earlier experiments in form carried out during the teens and the early twenties by the architects, sculptors, and painters of the Dutch De Stijl group: van Doesburg, Vantongerloo, Mondrian. Yet here again the figure of Wright must intervene. No one who saw the exhibition of early De Stijl work at the Biennale in Venice in the summer of 1952, or later at the Museum of Modern Art in New York in the winter of that year, could have failed to be struck by the similarity between its forms and those of Wright's earlier work. To explain this similarity as something deriving from common stimulus in Japanese architecture and prints is not convincing. It would seem unlikely that the refining process upon original Japanese inspiration which is shown by the side elevation of the Willits House of 1902 could have been carried on in the same way and independently by the De Stijl group, especially after the publication in Europe of the Willits House and of many similar Wright designs of this period. Wright's influence upon other aspects of Dutch architecture was tremendous, as the streets of Amsterdam testify; but his effect upon the developing De Stijl movement and, through it, upon the later aesthetic of the German Bauhaus, must be considered as equally decisive. Even a late and fully developed
2.7 Mondrian of the twenties, compared to the Willits exterior, shows the vibrating proportional relationships which are common to both, as well as the linear and asymmetrical
2.8 compositions, the occult balance, and the shifting planes. The Willits house exterior, published by Wasmuth in 1911, may also be compared to designs by van Doesburg and Vantongerloo, as well as to the Mies Country House plan itself.

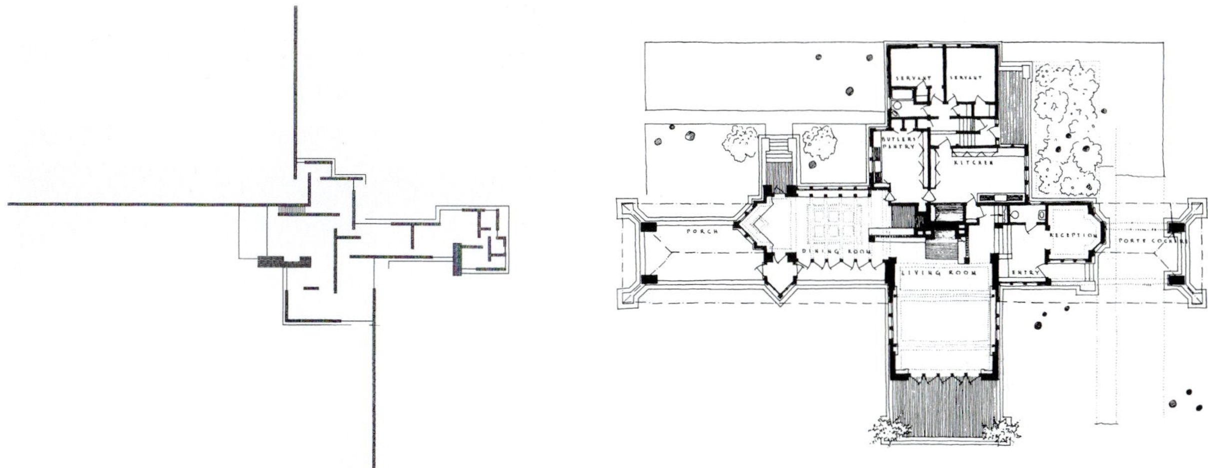

2.3 ABOVE, LEFT: Ludwig Mies van der Rohe. Brick Country House project, 1923/1924. Plan

2.4 ABOVE, RIGHT: Frank Lloyd Wright. Willits House, Highland Park, Illinois, 1902–3. Plan

2.5 RIGHT: Mies van der Rohe. German (Barcelona) Pavilion, International Exposition, Barcelona, 1928–29. Exterior

2.6 BELOW: Frank Lloyd Wright. Yahara Boat Club project, Madison, Wisconsin, 1902. Exterior perspective. From *Ausgeführte Bauten und Entwürfe von Frank Lloyd Wright* (Berlin, 1910)

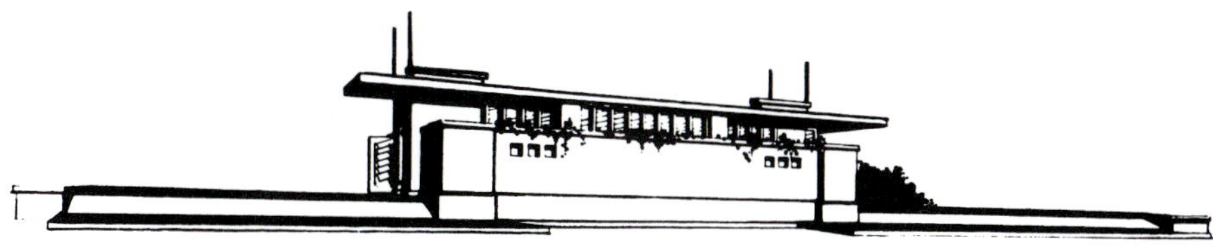

ABOVE, LEFT: Piet Mondrian. *Composition with Red, Yellow, and Blue,* 1930 2.7 

ABOVE, RIGHT: Frank Lloyd Wright. Willits House. Exterior. From *Frank Lloyd Wright: Ausgeführte Bauten* (Berlin, 1911) 2.8 

By 1910, therefore, Wright had created patterns of form and had opened avenues for experiment which were of vital importance in the formation, ten years later, of what has come to be known as the International Style. Yet Wright himself during the teens and twenties had experienced a long crisis in his attitude toward design. The rupture with his suburban environment in 1910 was followed by extended work in Japan, where, at the Imperial Hotel, he experimented with heavy visual masses and richly sculptured ornament. Following this line of development in the twenties, he certainly sought inspiration (as Tselos has shown) among the published examples of the similarly massive, sculptural Maya architecture of Pre-Columbian Central America. From the pyramidal, typically Maya-mansarded Barnsdall house in Hollywood, of 1920—which closely resembles such published Maya temples as those which had appeared in such folios as Alfred B. Maudslay's section on archaeology in *Biologia Centralia Americana* (London, 1899–1901)—Wright moved toward a more organic interpretation of Maya mass and surface in his concrete block houses of the later twenties. However, by 1929, with the
2.9 Lloyd Jones House at Tulsa, Oklahoma, Wright would seem to have reached an impasse in this development and to be searching for something new. In the Jones House his scale becomes very strange, his massing powerful but unresolved. At the same time, its cubical blockiness seems rather different from Wright's earlier work but very like similar compositions by Mies during the twenties, such as the Brick Country House project of 1923 or the Wolf House at Guben, Germany, 1926. One can probably assume direct influence here. Both of these important works by Mies were published and were available to Wright. He would certainly seem to have been aware of them in his massing, if not in his planning, of the Jones House. Most unhappily, Wright's great projects of these years, the Elizabeth Noble apartment house and St. Mark's Tower, were never built; and Wright entered the 1930s further hampered and frustrated in building by the Depression.

2.10 In 1932 there came a fuller change in his design. His House on the Mesa, done for the Museum of Modern Art exhibition of the same year, clearly resembles in massing

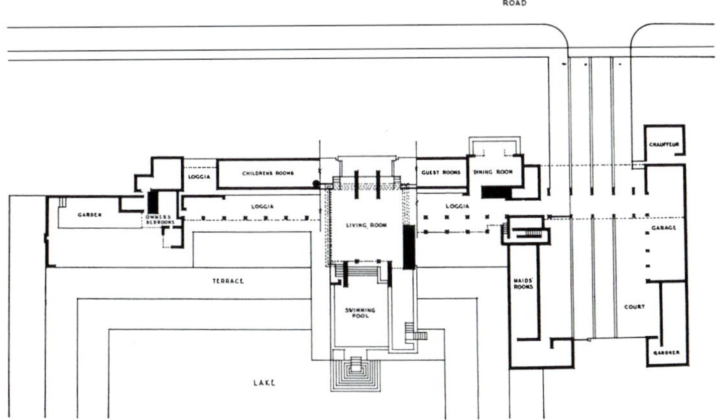

2.9 RIGHT, TOP: Frank Lloyd Wright. Jones House, Tulsa, Oklahoma, 1928–31. Exterior

2.10 RIGHT, BOTTOM: Frank Lloyd Wright. House on the Mesa project, Denver, 1931–32. Plan

the spread-out cubes of Vantongerloo and of the De Stijl group. More specifically, it seems to relate again to the massing of Mies's Country House project of 1923. Here the respective plans also become important in the relationship, and Wright's organization of thin planes moving out to make space around a few pivotal solid masses takes on here an almost Miesian simplicity of means. Therefore, if the Mies design itself may be said to have continued experiments in space organization which can be traced back to Wright, so the plan of the House on the Mesa, by Wright, begins to make use of loose and subtle relationships of solids and of voids which should, one feels, be referred back to Mies, as should the spread-out blocks in space which develop the design in three dimensions. In the plan of the Willits House the volumes had been contained longitudinally by definite wall boundaries; but in the House on the Mesa, as in Mies's project, the boundaries of the space are becoming fluid and releasing, suggested rather than fixed by the interplay of planes.

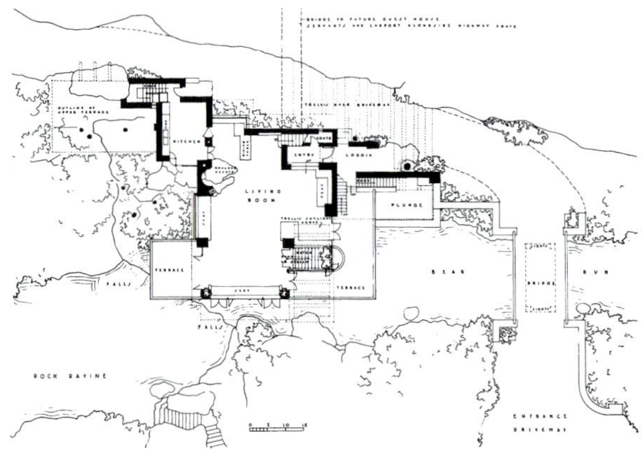

ABOVE, LEFT: Frank Lloyd Wright. Kaufmann House (Fallingwater), Mill Run, Pennsylvania, 1934–37. Exterior 2.11

ABOVE, RIGHT: Frank Lloyd Wright. Kaufmann House. Plan 2.12

A more developed phase in this kind of planning is to be found in Wright's
2.11, 2.12 next great work—perhaps his masterpiece of these years—the Kaufmann House, Fallingwater, at Bear Run, Pennsylvania, 1936. The boundaries in plan are ordered in subtler and more shifting definitions than had been characteristic of Wright's pre-1932 design. It is a plan which has been more than touched by the gentle, open rhythms of Mies's designs of the twenties. Also, unlike Wright's work of the late twenties, the massing of the Kaufmann House is an open and fully defined play of solid and of void, the planes clean and precise in the light, the deep shadows between them defining their advance and recession in space. Again one feels De Stijl. Much of the decision of the earlier prairie houses also returns in this design, which somewhat recalls—except that it is richer, more asymmetrical, and fuller—the Gale House at Oak Park, of 1909. The influence of another International Style architect can also be felt in the Kaufmann House. The clean planes, the dark window voids with their metal details, and, most of all, the spatial play of curved against rectangular planes—very rare in Wright's work up
18.7 to this time—most decisively recall Le Corbusier's Villa Savoye, of 1929–30, and other
18.2 of Le Corbusier's published designs.

A full assimilation of International Style influences would seem, therefore, to play a large part in Fallingwater. To say this is by no means to attack its value or its originality. It has both to an absolute degree. As a matter of fact, it represents the assimilation of the earlier Maya-like experiments as well. Its massing is pyramidal, like a Maya temple base; but its planes, unlike those of the Barnsdall House, now move freely in the space of a twentieth-century world. Structurally, spatially, and in its derivations, the Kaufmann House is one of the mightiest syntheses in the modern will toward form.

In sum, through a culmination of personal work over two generations and through the creative assimilation of a host of influences—some of them originally made possible by himself—Wright came by the late thirties into one of the richest and most serene phases in his rich career. If Wright's work means anything, and it means a great deal, then one of its meanings is its assertion of the power of Western civilization in the modern world to receive freely and to be stimulated rather than destroyed by influences from all cultures and from all periods. Wright's architecture gives the lie every day to those timid men who are afraid to receive influences from without. It seems also to cast doubt upon the theory of Toynbee that a receptivity to exotic influences indicates the decay of a culture and its loss of creative power. So it is in Wright's relationship with those proud young men who took from him in the teens and the twenties what they could use themselves and from whom he himself then took what he could use when he had need of it.

In 1929 Le Corbusier designed a museum in which one mounted to the top by elevator and came down slowly on foot along a descending ramp. This fact does not make Wright's projected Guggenheim Museum any less an original and inventive work of art. It creates again a synthesis of structural and spatial continuities not imagined in the earlier project. From this, one thing more is clear: that there is plenty of room in the world for all its noble spirits. Each one is needed, and they are yet too few. In this materialistic and half-brutalized age, it is still the faith of great architects that noble men can be formed and made by noble buildings. Wright, Le Corbusier, and Mies van der Rohe all have this faith in common, and they must all know in their hearts that the differences between them do not really matter; their meanings vary widely but are still the same. To this profound truth the buildings of Wright bear—and will bear across the centuries—the grandest testimony, a grander testimony than do his words.

Original editor's note: Due to exigencies of space, the author's footnotes—specifying references to primary sources, specific plates, and previously published critical comment on Wright's architecture—have had to be omitted. —Ed.

"Archetype and Order in Recent American Architecture." *Art in America* 42 (December 1954): 250–61.

This is Scully's first critical essay dealing with contemporary architecture. Appearing in a special issue of *Art in America* devoted to "Trends 1954," it was described by guest editor S. Lane Faison in his introduction as "so provocative" that he made it the lead article. It remains a landmark in the postwar critique of the "modern movement" and a fundamental contribution to the prehistory of postmodernism.

Scully identifies a move toward generically classical forms, proportions, and systems of composition in concert with a renewed interest in historical precedent as the underlying factors giving interest and promise to the recent work of Eero Saarinen, Paul Rudolph, Louis Kahn, Paul Schweikher, and, especially, Philip Johnson—all architects associated in one way or another with the Yale School of Architecture. The *éminence grise* behind this turn from mainstream modernism is Mies van der Rohe, who had now replaced Wright, in Scully's view, as the most influential figure of the moment. In contrast to the structural order and spatial clarity that Mies effected in his work in America, the neo-Bauhaus methods of Harvard are seen as regressive and repressive, a view that would only intensify in Scully's writing and teaching over time. While the new work's openness to history allows it to appeal to a sense of "memory" through the use of "metaphor"—two terms that would become increasingly common in the discourse of architectural criticism—its reliance on blocklike shapes, symmetrical composition, and regular patterns of order laid the foundations for a restorative urbanism.

3

Archetype and Order in Recent American Architecture

The most significant development in American architecture during the last few years would seem to be the trend, evident in the work of many architects, toward order and clarity in design. This trend brings with it a renewed sense of large simple volumes of space, of clear structural articulation, of high, dignified proportions, and of unity in the whole. With it has come, like a dam breaking, a release from many of the curious academicisms and clichés of the recent past. Unnecessary asymmetries have disappeared; obsessively "functional" planning no longer shreds the building mass; space no longer necessarily "flows." Instead, with the renewed sensibility toward volumetric space, vaults and domes have reappeared to model volumes plastically with the continuity of their surfaces. Along with these have come precise pavilions, defined by the metrical beat of high colonnades. Both dome and pavilion insist upon the unity of the spaces which their structural systems create. Consequently, a desire for that unity is causing architects to investigate various kinds of space frames, in which the overall spanning structure is essentially unified and cellular rather than simply additive in a bay system.

Many of the ideas developed in this essay can be attributed to the year Scully spent in Italy in 1951–52. Living mainly in Florence, he was able to experience firsthand the dense fabric of Italian cities and hilltowns such as San Gimignano, so different in almost every way from his own typically suburban community of Woodbridge, Connecticut. He was profoundly impressed by the Greek temples at Paestum as well as by the ruins of ancient Rome. In his villa at Tivoli, Hadrian seemed to have created a world of imaginative retrospection that Scully could analogize to his own. Frank Brown, of the American Academy in Rome, was instrumental in guiding Scully through the Etruscan and Roman past. And Rudolf Wittkower's *Architectural Principles in the Age of Humanism* (1949) opened up for him, as it did for others like Colin Rowe, a way of looking at the classicism of Renaissance architecture that made its basic principles of geometric order seem applicable to the present.

The image of a renewed classicism presented by Scully is of an abstract and generic order—the term "order" itself probably deriving from Kahn's use of it. The abstraction, however, does not depend upon or result from mere formalism. This is where the second term, "archetype," comes in and why it is foregrounded in the title. The Jungian concept referring to the paradigmatic patterns and forms of a collective unconscious had become common parlance in the art world of the 1940s and 1950s. Impressed, in particular, by the literary criticism of Maud Bodkin, Scully here was one of the first to apply psychoanalytical theory to architecture. He does so in an original and subtly directed way. Temples, domes, courtyards, or colonnades are understood as metaphors of the essential, ur-forms of building that embody deeply ingrained experiences of nature and of place. Seizing on them in their primitive clarity and simplicity ensures an expression of modern abstraction at the same time that it endows the modern memory with access to the universal. Moreover, the psychological reaction to such primal conditions as confinement, release, darkness, or light provides the sensational core for an empathic relation to buildings that Scully would later always hold to be at the basis of architectural meaning.

The large open spaces formed by all these means are hospitable to painting and sculpture, either as autonomous objects or complementary details. Most of the architects here considered conceive of their buildings as great shelters within which the other arts—not necessarily executed by themselves or by their protégés—can live full lives and exert their maximum effect upon the lives of men. Therefore they have little fear that painting and sculpture from the present or the past will "spoil" their work, and many of them are better prepared than most architects of recent times to recognize quality in those arts when they see it.

The present movement is far removed from the eclectic classicism of the early twentieth century and from its later, official or antiquarian manifestations. Yet so earnestly does it seek for integrity and order in the parts and in the whole that one is tempted to call it truly "classic" in its aspirations. Certainly the architects who participate in it have

begun to create an abstract, anti-romantic, classic order without recourse to antique details. But the movement is not purely a classic one; there are elements in it, as there are in the art of our time in general, which evoke both archaic and baroque values. The desire for a few strongly contrasted shapes with decisive details, for the direct impact of fixed and very "formal" forms, is essentially an archaic one, as in much contemporary painting and sculpture. It reveals the yearning of a complex age for direct and simple experience, deeply felt and presented as general truth, without rhetoric. At the same time, the technical possibilities of vaults, domes, and space frames also give rise to forms which have certain "baroque" qualities of curvilinearity or of spatial continuity. Where such occur
3.4 they are at present clearly differentiated from contrasting cubical volumes, either hung
3.6 within them, used as vestibules, or set apart as separate structures. In these ways each
form remains clearly itself; nothing flows together. The whole scheme remains at each point clear in its parts.

These qualities tend to recall other moments in the history of architecture, and the architects concerned with them are by no means unaware of the past. One may thus be forgiven for beginning a discussion of the present movement through an analogy with the past, in this instance with Rome of the Hadrianic period, 117–138 A.D. Grappling with complex problems of belief and power, and having available the accumulated philosophical and aesthetic experiences of centuries, the age of Hadrian, in the person of its emperor, yearned like ours for vanished simplicities and lost clarities. Like this generation, it consciously sought to employ ancient and basic forms in its creation of the new. Technically proficient in building, with concrete vaults and domes as well as stone trabeation available to it, the age produced probably its most memorable monuments in the Pantheon at Rome and in the Emperor's own villa near Tivoli. I should like to use a plan
3.1 of the so-called Piazza d'Oro from that villa, as a kind of prelude to the work of this gen-
eration of architects. Several elements in it will be referred to again as analogies to the modern work: the lobed, "melon" dome, with oculus, which creates a kind of vestibule and recalls, as Lehmann has shown, the windswept tent pavilions depicted on Etruscan mirrors; the columned rectangle of the court, which is both Greek stoa and peristyle; the terminal nymphaeum with its curvilinear colonnade carrying a continuous beam, perhaps domed, certainly with light coming from above and from the sides. These elements, taken as a directed experience in space, made a design full at once of invention and of memory. With precise differentiation of part from part, and with a decisive direction of technical possibilities toward spatial expression, the architect of the Piazza d'Oro, probably Hadrian himself, evoked Greek, Etruscan, and Roman archetypes in the service of his own longing. One may feel that basic archetypes of human experiences of the world are here, as well, created by the metaphors of architecture. That is: the defined plain of the courtyard, the forest of the colonnade, the cave of the dome, the light that bursts through the cave, and the sound of water.

It is the primary characteristic of the architects of the present movement that they appear to express, with a similar sense of memory and of the uses of metaphor, the same clear archetypes of plain, pavilion, and cave. Behind them all, in varying degrees,

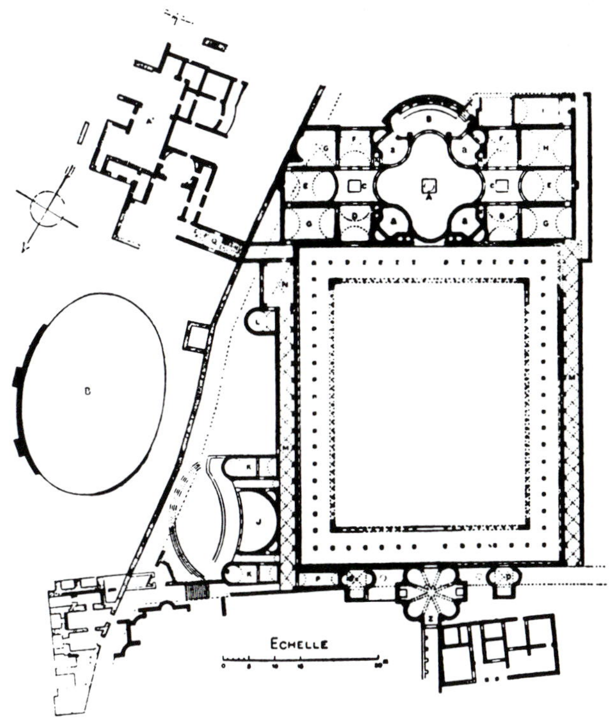

3.1 Piazza d'Oro, Hadrian's Villa, near Tivoli, c. A.D. 117–138. Plan

stands the work of one master: in this case, Mies van der Rohe. Eight or ten years ago one might have felt that the architecture of Frank Lloyd Wright would by the present time be exerting a more important influence upon creative architects than that of Mies. Such, however, has not generally been the case. It is true that Wright's work, certainly rich in archetypal metaphor, is now enjoying a considerable amount of popular success. The youngest generation of architects, with whose work we cannot as yet be adequately familiar, has also been brought during recent years into increasing contact with Wright's architecture and its principles—although these latter have often been obscured rather than clarified by the statements of Wright himself and of many of his admirers. Yet the generation with which we are concerned has turned for the time being from the richly interwoven, structurally complex, spatially fluid buildings of Wright toward the simpler, more static, precisely controlled and detailed work of Mies. Taking the productions of Wright's imitators as a sign that only Wright himself can meaningfully control his kind of design, it has sought to base its own development upon something most desired in our time, something clear, integral, known, and capable of being fully, not partially, controlled.

Mies van der Rohe's more recent buildings—the Illinois Institute of Technology, 8.21
the Farnsworth House at Plano, Illinois, and the Lakeshore Apartments in Chicago—have
had the most direct effect upon recent developments. His Barcelona Pavilion, of 1929, 2.5
with the flowing space which was influential in the thirties and forties, has been less of an influence in the contemporary movement than have his later, more precisely volumetric and structurally articulated buildings. These are put together with a craftsmanship in steel

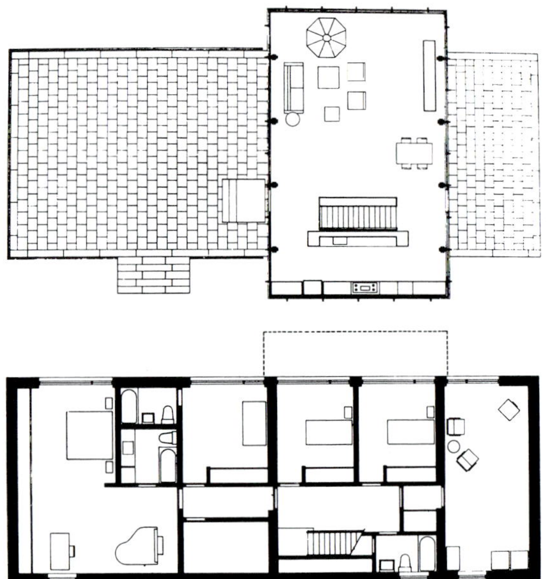

and brick which evokes the craftsmanship in stone of the Greek temple. Like the temple they attempt only what they can fully accomplish, one clear volume of space, a few simple shapes, the clear integrity of part to part in proportion and detail. As unashamed works of art they break with the positivistic functionalism of the late-Bauhaus school, and they demonstrate, as does the work of Wright, that the basic function of architecture in any society is a spiritual one—not least in our own. They break also with the painting-inspired play of planes of earlier "International Style" architecture and insist again upon the direct rhythm of the structural skeleton. Frame and cladding are precisely differentiated, and each element is clear.

ABOVE, LEFT: Philip Johnson. Wiley House, New Canaan, Connecticut, 1952–53. Plans 3.2

ABOVE, RIGHT: Philip Johnson. Wiley House. Exterior 3.3

Contrary to what might normally have been expected, the effect of such buildings upon this generation of architects has not been a purely academic one. Eero Saarinen, whose work has been of considerable importance in defining the present trend, at first appeared to follow Mies rather closely in his General Motors Research Center, but then went on to his advanced domical structure at the Massachusetts Institute of Technology. In Florida, Paul Rudolph has followed a similar pattern. His first, more precisely Miesian buildings have been followed by continued invention and by a similar movement toward vaults and domes. The reason for such continued growth from a beginning of Miesian principles was stated unmistakably by both Saarinen and Rudolph at a recent convention of the American Institute of Architects. Each of them felt "the uses of history" to be both the liberating and the solidifying factor in his growth. Imbued with the sense of pure form and precise control which the work of Mies possesses, these architects felt in a sense liberated from the clichés of the "modern movement," from the psychological blocks concerning the "past" which had been one of the Bauhaus legacies, and, consequently, from the expedients of fashionable change.

The anti-historical attitude of the thirties has thus given way to a more civilized awareness of the unity of all architecture, as of all human experience. Like Wright and Le Corbusier, and unlike the Bauhaus group, the present generation is prepared to learn from the architecture of all periods and places; like Le Corbusier, but unlike Wright and the romantics, it is also prepared to admit what it has learned from its forebears.

Of all those who admit their debt both to Mies and to history, few architects have been more influential than Philip Johnson, working out of his office in New Canaan, Connecticut. Johnson's debt to Mies was apparent in his first house, at Cambridge,
Massachusetts, and in his second house, at New Canaan, of 1949. In the latter, how- 19.2
ever, the division of the building into two separate blocks, one of steel frame and entirely glazed, the other of brick with only three round windows, indicated his own more original and dramatically opposed expression of the archetypal sensations of enclosure and
exposure. His Wiley House, at New Canaan, completed in 1953, can show a further 3.2, 3.3
stage in that development. Upon the hill slope is set a clearly defined platform of masonry. Within the platform are the bedrooms, facing down the slope. Upon the platform, at a cross axis to it, is a high open pavilion of heavy timber structure. This contains living room and kitchen. Monumental timber columns support the roof beams. Their intersection is plastically expressed, and they have a decisively different scale from that of the smaller window mullions and stiffening fins. Entrance to the living pavilion follows a measured and ceremonial path from the stairs across the open platform. To reverse the movement and to climb from the enclosed, fairly dim spaces below to the living area above is to experience a poetic and meaningful contrast between enclosure and release. To this end the living area is, as it were, double-scaled. Its high, wide, classically "abstract" proportions are in direct contrast to the more intensely scaled, low-ceilinged effects of Wright. In most of Wright's houses the effects of pressure and of release are even more fully developed, but they are made to flow together into a continuous experience which usually finds its fulfillment back out again in the space of nature. In the Wiley House these effects do not flow but are kept separate from each other and clearly apart from, though open to, nature as well. The house is a small, contained temple in the landscape. In such a temple-pavilion, sculpture also could function with its traditional power, as in Hadrian's Villa or in Johnson's own house, to people the space with its own magical presence.

From the precise rectangles of the Wiley House, with its contrasting circular pool, Johnson's design has moved toward an increased use of curvilinear forms, of the
circle and the ellipse in plan and the vault in section. His synagogue for Port Chester, 3.4
New York, now under construction, is again set upon a decisive base, before which is an elliptical vestibule with a fairly low dome, lit by an oculus. One is reminded of the
vestibule at the Piazza d'Oro and, in point of fact, a direct experience of Hadrian's Villa, 3.1
as of Palladio and of the Baroque, has played a large part in Johnson's recent growth. Behind the vestibule rises the high, trabeated pavilion which is the main body of the building. From the beams of the ceiling penetrated vaults are frankly suspended. They move—again like a wind-blown canopy—toward the altar, and are echoed by the altar

Philip Johnson. Kneses Tifereth Israel Synagogue, Port Chester, New York, 1954–56. Interior 3.4

shape itself. A play of rectangular and curvilinear volumes is set up, lit in the vestibule from above, in the body of the synagogue by slots in the side walls.

Johnson's vaults of the synagogue are plainly expressed as non-structural, but their curvilinear forms are poetic evocations of some of the vaults and slabs now being designed by the most advanced European engineers. Torroja's sweeping vaults, and Nervi's vaults and shell slabs all demonstrate the basically curvilinear pattern of the moment of bending which modern reinforced concrete, given adequate form work, can so beautifully attain. The spreading structural canopy which another kind of space frame
12.35 can become was at least envisaged in the addition to the Yale Art Gallery, designed by Louis I. Kahn, with the collaboration of Douglas Orr and Henry Pfisterer, and completed in 1953. Building code difficulties caused a revision of the system to the point where it was no longer a true space frame, but it still creates a strong and flexible setting for human activity and for works of art, and it can be taken as symptomatic of the new direction in design. Each open volume of floor, enclosed by the quadrangular building block, is defined overhead by the powerful tetrahedrons of the reinforced concrete slab. These exert a cellular principle of growth which the exterior shape of the Art Gallery does not express but which Kahn's later projects are beginning to demonstrate. Their shapes (*Perspecta* 11, 1953), based upon the tetrahedron principle and the space frame, are part of the new movement as a whole in its search for the integral, complete, and generalized form. In this case it would grow as a totality—columns, slabs, and spaces—from a reproductive principle inherent in the structural unit. Here again is a desire for intrinsic order in which Kahn is transposing the researches of engineers like Samuely, Le Ricolais, and Buckminster Fuller into the terms of human experience which make architecture.

The recent work of Paul Schweikher demonstrates a certain amalgamation of these influences toward geometric order, volumetric control, and space frame structure. It is especially interesting because Schweikher was, in the thirties, one of the most

3.5 Schweikher and Elting. Maryville College Chapel and Theater, Knoxville, Tennessee, 1953–54. Aerial view

informed and disciplined of those architects who attempted to base their personal growth upon principles which were close to those of Frank Lloyd Wright. Schweikher's movement in the fifties toward a kind of design which seems at first more Miesian than Wrightian is thus important as indicative of a trend. Beyond the superficial level, however, it becomes clear that Schweikher's present work represents a more integrated stage of the kind of design toward which he had apparently always been moving. His experiments with plank and beam construction in wood during the thirties—experiments strongly influenced by Japanese architecture—were concerned in essence with values rather apart from those of Wright, although many of his houses certainly owed much to Wright's example. Yet the plank and beam system's skeletal insistence, like that of the mid-nineteenth-century "Stick Style," is basically different from the "flesh-covered" continuities of most of Wright's work. The beat of its columns and beams tends intrinsically to invoke the simple pavilion rather than a complex and poetically modulated series
of shapes. Thus Schweikher's recently completed Maryville College Chapel and Theater, 3.5
near Knoxville, Tennessee, is not in essence so different from his work in wood of the thirties as it might at first appear to be. Chapel at one end and theater at the other are separated by an open court and connected by a high colonnade of noble proportions. The reinforced concrete columns continue to be expressed where the brick cladding occurs. The chapel is lighted from above through the ends of shell concrete vaults which also add structural rigidity. A variety of functions are consequently pulled together into one building, as the vaults, the court, and the stage house are unified by the continuous rhythm of the structural system, and the basic system of proportions is fixed by it. The building becomes a large pavilion within which several shapes are set. This is its order. Once again we are reminded of temple, stoa, and the Piazza d'Oro.

Schweikher's projected church for Park Forest, Illinois, is also one large shape, recalling buildings by Mies and Johnson but different from theirs in scale. Side walls of

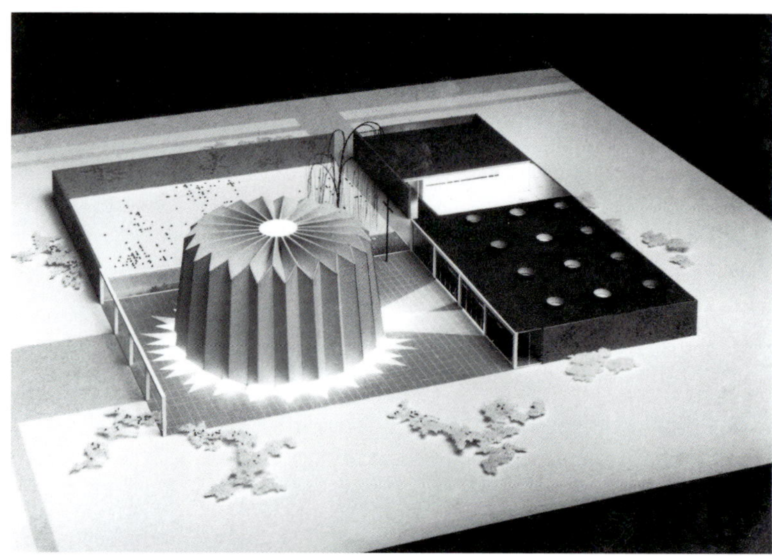

Schweikher and Elting. Methodist Church project, Pocahontas, Iowa, 1954. Model 3.6

stone-concrete, like those used by Wright at Taliesin West and by Schweikher afterward in several buildings, support a true space frame made of light steel struts in pyramidal form. Here again, as in Kahn's Gallery, the space frame is intended to create one open volume of space which can then be partitioned as desired.

3.6 It is probably in Schweikher's projected Methodist Church for Pocahontas, Iowa, that many of the elements of the movement we have been considering can be seen most clearly. Two decisively different shapes are set within an area defined by platform and by wall. The blocks of sunday school and pastorate are separated by an enclosed court. Next to these is an open space where the church itself is set. This building is intended to contrast decisively with the carefully studied rectangles of its site. In the architect's description for the building committee, it is of: "'folded' or 'space-frame' construction. It is proposed to build the framework of steel ribs and mesh, covering this inside and out with 'Gunnite' concrete applied under pressure." An oculus above and trigonal windows below supply the illumination, which thus recalls that of Hadrian's melon dome and nymphaeum at the Piazza d'Oro—as the "folded" shape of Schweikher's dome also recalls that of Hadrian's.

Perhaps the few buildings which have been discussed are enough to base some tentative conclusions upon. The nature of the movement toward geometric order, structural expressiveness, and volumetric plasticity should be clear. The relation of this to a renewed and creative sense of historical precedent should also not be underestimated. It tends to demonstrate an important mode of vision and design among contemporary architects, open once more to the fullest kind of architectural experience but profoundly determined to create those experiences by forms which can be thoroughly controlled and integrally detailed in all their parts, and which may be developed into primary standards of design. From this concern derives a renewed interest in Renaissance and antique systems of proportion and of columnar and vaulted structures. In these characteristics

resides also the main relationship between the American architects and Le Corbusier. Their concern for standards, proportion, number, and geometry echoes in a sense his *Modulor*, as the rough surfaces of Kahn's and Schweikher's concrete recall his Unité 5.3
d'Habitation at Marseilles. Most of the American buildings tend to lack the powerfully sculptural quality of Le Corbusier's forms. Still, their vaults, monumental columns, and articulated intersections relate them more to his work than to the structurally enigmatic, polished slab effects of American buildings of a few years ago, such as Lever House and 7.2
the United Nations Secretariat.

Nor should we believe that the present movement will finally represent such a direct rejection of Wright's objectives as it may now appear to do. Its conscious limitation of itself to a few geometric shapes may be taken as a kind of instructed humility, prepared to grow integrally, with elements it can handle, into powers of expression which may in the end become not less than Wright's own. Yet in one important respect the present movement breaks sharply with some aspects of Wright's philosophy, especially from that of his followers. The forms created by this generation are urban forms, contained, generalized, civil in their relationship to other forms. As such they indicate a turning away from romantic isolation, from the modern suburb, and from the decentralization of Broadacre City. They seek instead the qualities of the city, or, as in the case of the Wiley House, of urbanity in the country. All of them recall, in one sense or another, the great tradition of European urban design; they are conceived in high-ceilinged blocks, as palazzo architecture. Such an attitude is a most poignant and meaningful one at the present time, when the city—until industrialism, the carrier of the primary values which formed Western civilization—seems, after its nineteenth-century industrial decay, to be threatened with complete destruction. In that tradition of civilization, too, painting and sculpture, starved for worthy programs in the materialism of the modern world, are beginning once more to be sought for intelligently and with keen desire by the architects involved.

The attitude of these architects is thus rooted in optimistic and ancient principles. It rejects the undignified, materialistic formlessness to be found in the Real Estate section of any Sunday newspaper. The order which it seeks is based upon human dignity, spiritual awareness, discipline, and pride. One can observe that the majority of the illustrated projects have had religious programs. It is no attack upon the spirituality of those buildings to note that their basic forms could be used for factories, office buildings, apartment houses, and individual homes as well. What this generation is seeking is a standard for generalized answers upon a noble plane. Like the architects of the Greek Revival, but without their restriction to "classicizing" forms, this generation would have all its buildings function like temples, on the hills, within the cities, and upon the hearts of men.

"Modern Architecture: Toward a Redefinition of Style." *Perspecta: The Yale Architectural Journal* 4 (1957): 4–10 (originally unillustrated).

"Modern Architecture: Toward a Redefinition of Style" represents the first major synthesis of Scully's ideas on how modern architecture developed over the course of its two-hundred-year history since its origins in the eighteenth century. First presented in January 1957 at the annual joint meeting of the College Art Association and the Society of Architectural Historians in a session called "Redefinitions of Style," which was chaired by Richard Krautheimer and included Frank Brown, Bates Lowry, and Wolfgang Lotz, it was reprinted twice in 1958 (in the *College Art Journal* and in Suzanne Langer's *Reflections on Art*) after its initial publication in *Perspecta*, the standard-setting journal of architectural theory, criticism, and history produced by the students of what was then the Department of Architecture of the Yale School of Art and Architecture. In 1961, it was revised and expanded into the book *Modern Architecture: The Architecture of Democracy*, which is still in print after nearly forty years and remains one of the fundamental treatments of the subject.

The origin of the essay is even more fascinating than its publication history and predicts something of the role it was destined to play in the historiography of modern architecture. Scully had become quite close to Henry-Russell Hitchcock by the late 1940s and through him met Philip Johnson. Sometime between 1950 and 1952 they apparently convinced Alfred Barr, then director of the Museum of Modern Art, that their young protégé should be commissioned to write a history of modern architecture for the Museum of Modern Art as a sequel to *The International Style*, which they had published in 1932 in con-

4

Modern Architecture: Toward a Redefinition of Style

In a talk of this length it will be less valuable, I think, to begin by attacking the admittedly ambiguous concept of style than to accept the word in broadest terms as meaning a body of work exhibiting family resemblances. In dealing with the modern world it is especially necessary to do this, since we need an eye for resemblances to guide us as we seek an elusive image which is essentially of ourselves. All of us who engage in this search owe a debt to work which has gone before, especially to Hitchcock's pioneering researches: embodied in his *Modern Architecture* of 1929 and in his and Johnson's *International Style* of 1932. Yet by far the most influential book which has dealt with this problem has been Giedion's *Space, Time and Architecture*, published in 1941 and now in its third enlarged edition. Giedion's view of nineteenth- and twentieth-century architectural development has been especially influential among architects, who—through an iconoclasm they have imbibed from some of their pedagogical masters—have otherwise tended to be suspicious of historical investigation in any form. Their approval of *Space, Time and Architecture* would seem to have arisen from the fact that it gave them

junction with the museum's celebrated exhibition of recent architecture. Barr scotched the idea when he found the draft Scully submitted not to his liking. Reworked and brought up to date, it became the lecture and essay reproduced here.

Scully's tone now, for the first time, is magisterial, even becoming at moments rhetorical. The scale of the enterprise is grand in relation to the actual length of the piece. The goal is nothing less than a rewriting of Sigfried Giedion's *Space, Time and Architecture* (1941), which Scully characterizes as a kind of "court history," a sloganeering, mythmaking operation supported by a scientistic discourse. To this is opposed a historical schema ontologically grounded in the modern idea of democracy as the underlying social force of the era. The "architecture of democracy," which is a phrase Scully borrows from Frank Lloyd Wright's London Lectures of 1939, thus begins in the later eighteenth century, as Emil Kaufmann had proposed, rather than in the Baroque period, as Giedion suggested. Its three main phases—fragmentation, continuity, and a new humanism—describe the breakup of what Kaufmann called the "Renaissance-Baroque system," its reformulation through the concept of continuous space in the architecture of Wright and the International Style, and its recent evolution from the crypto-classicism of late Mies van der Rohe and his followers to the imagistic, bodily form of expression found in the postwar work of Le Corbusier. Two unexpected theorists are brought in to help make the case: the classicist Guido Freiherr von Kaschnitz-Weinberg provides the basis for the distinction between an Italic space-positive, engulfing architecture and a Hellenic mass-positive, liberating one; while Geoffrey Scott offers a definition of humanism rooted in the psycho-physiological theory of empathy.

Scully would eventually question a number of the conclusions proposed in this essay, most notably the appropriateness of Le Corbusier's monumental forms for the urban problems of the later twentieth century. But the general outline of modern architecture's history, the spatial-sculptural dialectic underpinning it, and the empathic understanding of the human response to built form as a physical, bodily one are never disputed. But what is perhaps most prophetic about this essay is the stirring quality of its prose—the ability Scully displays, as in his descriptions of Taliesin West and Ronchamp, to capture in words the emotional meaning of the visual experience and, through that, to make the architectural image singularly memorable.

what they wanted: a strong technological determinism, a sense of their lonely, rational heroism in the face of an unintegrated world. But it gave them more: myths and martyrs, and a new past all their own. It presented them with a historical mirror, so adjusted as to reflect only their own images in its glass. What they did not want was to be told that they were working in a style. That is, they wished to be recognized but not identified, and for this there were many reasons, some superficial and some profound. *Space, Time and Architecture* brilliantly avoided the difficulty of identification by producing instead a formula, that is, "Space-Time." This cabalistic conjunction (or collision) had both the qualities necessary for an acceptable architectural slogan: at once a spurious relation to science and a certain incomprehensibility except in terms of faith. Like all the best slogans it could mean anything because, even as one shouted it, one might entertain the comfortable suspicion that it need not, in fact, mean anything at all. It is, on the other hand, a phrase which one can all too easily avoid using when seeking definition. For example, the events of the years around 1910, which do in fact culminate a long development, may be described in simpler and more generally applicable words, such as fragmentation and continuity: fragmentation of objects into their components and the redirection of these elements into a continuous movement in space.

Yet *Space, Time and Architecture* has had considerable effect upon us all, and conclusions as influential as those presented by it cannot be challenged without alternative conclusions being offered at some length. Therefore I feel compelled to attempt what perhaps should not be attempted at this restricted historical distance: that is, not only to isolate if possible the primary characteristics of the architecture of our era but also to name it. I should like to call it what Wright calls his own work but with, I hope, a more historically based and objective use of the term: The Architecture of Democracy. Out of modern mass democracy's program this architecture has grown, and the character of that democracy it demonstrates. I see it as having developed in two great phases, with a third phase just beginning. The first may be called the phase of fragmentation, the second the phase of continuity, and the third the opening phase of a new humanism. (And this last word also I would hope to define in precise architectural terms.) The development between phases is chronological but overlapping, and none of the phases, not even the first, has wholly ended. Under them all, and usually in tension with them, has run a counter instinct toward what I think we must call "classic" or, more correctly, "classicizing" values, and this instinct is probably stronger at present than it was a generation ago.

Giedion's early researches into the Romantic-Classicism of the later eighteenth century had convinced him that the effects of this period were largely negative so far as the development of contemporary architecture was concerned. Thus he tended to look back beyond it to his own view of the Baroque for historical precedent, and to see later creative architecture as developing despite the events of those revolutionary years. Yet if we seek an image of ourselves it is precisely at the beginning of the age of industrialism and mass democracy that we first find it, in terms of fragmentation, mass scale, and a
17.29 new, unfocused continuity. In Piranesi's prophetic *Carceri* etchings of 1745, the Baroque harmonies of subordination, scale, climax, and release are fragmented and exploded into a vast new world of violence. The orbits of movement come into collision, and the objectives of the new journey are as yet unknown. Man is small in a challenging but crushing ambient which seems to work according to its own laws and from which the elements, such as columns, to which the individual had been accustomed to orient himself, have been removed. Through this new world the engineers, released by nineteenth-century positivism and materialism from the burden of humanist tradition, have moved freely. The Galerie des Machines of 1889 creates the new scaleless ambient in steel, to serve a typical program of mass industrialism: the housing of vast batteries of machines, symbolized

4.1 ABOVE: Max Berg. Centennial Hall, Breslau, Germany, 1913. Interior

4.2 RIGHT: Claude-Nicolas Ledoux. *From top to bottom:* Workshop of the Charcoal Burners project; House of the Agricultural Guards of Maupertuis project; and Panaréthéon project, all c. 1793–1802. Exterior perspectives

by Henry Adams's Dynamo. In Max Berg's reinforced concrete Centennial Hall of 1913 at 4.1
Breslau, the world of Piranesi is housing mass man, almost as Piranesi himself had imagined it. Vast scale, the smallness of the individual, and violent continuity are its themes. In the Livestock Judging Pavilion at Raleigh, in an advanced structure of continuous parabolic arches from which a canopy in tension is slung, men and animals are small together in a disoriented universe of flight and movement—one which creaks and groans as the structure moves like the rigging of the *Pequod*, wind-driven on a quest one cannot name. Here that vision which Focillon recognized in Piranesi is realized: of "une architecture à la fois impossible et réelle."

Returning to the later eighteenth century, we find a further fragmentation of the Baroque synthesis of freedom and order in terms of two movements: one an impatient revolutionary search for harsh, pure, geometric order alone and the other for an apparently total freedom from geometry. Each of these movements continues in a sense to the present day. The first, which may loosely be called Romantic-Classicism, can be seen
alike in the projects of Ledoux and in the earlier work of Le Corbusier. This relationship 4.2, 4.8
is ignored by Giedion but was pointed out by the late Emil Kaufmann in his book of

ABOVE, LEFT: Adler and Sullivan. Guaranty Building, Buffalo, 1894–96. Exterior 4.3

ABOVE, RIGHT: Louis Sullivan. Carson-Pirie-Scott (originally Schlesinger and Mayer) Store, Chicago, 1898–1904. Exterior 4.4

1933, *Von Ledoux bis Le Corbusier*. The other movement, exactly contemporary, may loosely be called Romantic-Naturalism, and its asymmetry and nostalgic naturalism in siting and materials are demonstrated alike by Marie-Antoinette's Hameau of 1783 and by much present suburban architecture, especially on the West Coast of the United States. Critics such as Bruno Zevi have held the later phases of this movement to be of overriding interest and importance.

Yet to accept "classicism," so-called, and "romanticism," so-called, as polarities which are typologically irreconcilable, as the nineteenth century tended to do, is to accept as a natural state that fragmentation of human experience of the whole which the nineteenth century for a time created. To believe that variety and change (the "picturesque" of the nineteenth century) should be necessarily antithetical to order and clarity, is not only to see the past in fragments, as a part of nineteenth-century thought did, but probably also to encourage that desire for restricted identifications—such as national ones—which has been a counterirritant in, though hardly a solution for, modern mass society.

When the dubious polarities are brought into resolution toward the close of the nineteenth century they are resolved in terms of an even more insistent nineteenth-century belief: that in the dynamism of morphological continuity. Scientifically oriented, such confidence embodies—as Egbert has pointed out—a kind of Darwinian optimism in the emergence of species and types through the process of development itself. In America, characteristically, the most typical offspring of the new age, Sullivan—himself enthusiastic about "morphology"—produces out of the materials of mass industry the types for the new, mass metropolis: vertical continuity for the freestanding tower, ideally to be set in a square or a park; horizontal continuity for a space-bounding building, to
4.3 define a street or a square. Thus in the Guaranty Building, in a plastically plaited system,
4.4 the vertical supports are stressed and visually doubled; in the Carson-Pirie-Scott Store
they are withdrawn behind the surface (except at the corner) and especially masked by ornament on the lower floors so as not to interrupt the horizontal continuity of the window

bands and of the volume of the building above. Sullivan's ornament carries continuity out into more fluid forms, and in Europe during the same period—in Art Nouveau and its related movements—such fluidity is intensified. In Horta and Gaudí the images evoked are those of the forces that move through nature, as seen especially in water, plant life, and lava flow. One feels oneself in a Bergsonian world of flux and becoming, in an endless continuity which recalls, at the end of the scientifically confident nineteenth century, the intuitions of the first scientists of all in Western civilization: of those Ionian philosophers who themselves embraced the concept of continuity and who, in Thales, saw water as its essential element. Once more, with Herakleitos, we "cannot step twice into the same river, because fresh waters are continually flowing in upon" us.

During the early twentieth century, however, we encounter in Europe a reaction against these images of continuity on grounds both technological and classicizing. In Perret, in 1905, the union of a kind of Cartesian rigor of thought with a technological determinism like that of Viollet-le-Duc produces in reinforced concrete a closed and visually discontinuous rectangular skeleton which is in the tradition of French classicizing design. Similarly, in the work of Behrens and Gropius in Germany, the determining factors are a rigid technological *sachlichkeit* and an aesthetic preference—justified by Gropius on moral grounds—for clear, sharp-edged forms of German Neoclassic design. 2.1
In a sense Romantic-Classicism and a new romanticism of the machine coalesce here. Both represent—despite Gropius's glazed corners—a reaction against continuity in favor of a machined permanence of classicizing.

In America, however, the compulsion toward continuity was strong. In a development out of the nineteenth-century resort houses by the sea or in the suburb, Wright develops, by 1902, his cross-axial plan and his interwoven building fabric of continuous 1.28, 2.4
roof planes and defining screens. He attacks the concept of the skeleton frame, and says, "Have no posts, no columns," again, "In my work the idea of plasticity may now be seen as the element of continuity," and again, "Classic architecture was all fixation . . . now . . . let walls, ceiling, floors become *seen* as component parts of each other, their surfaces flowing into each other." He goes on, "Here . . . principle . . . entered into buildings as the new aesthetic, continuity," and he acclaims "the new reality is *space* instead of matter." He calls this new reality of continuous space "The Architecture of Democracy," and hails Whitman as its prophet. The analogy here is in fact profound. D. H. Lawrence, for example, has made us aware of the deep compulsion toward movement—toward "getting away"—which has played so large a part in American symbolism. In Cooper, Dana, Melville, and Mark Twain the symbols evoked are those of the seas or the river. In Whitman they focus upon the "Open Road," along which—in terms of a democratic mass compulsion which would have been understood by Tocqueville—*everyone* must travel and for which there is no goal but forward. The cities of men are to be left behind, as Jefferson would have had them left, and the infinitely extending axes of movement cross like country roads in a boundless prairie. In the low ceilings—"I broadened the mass out . . . to bring it down into spaciousness," wrote Wright—there is compulsion forward and flow like Mark Twain's river carrying us along. The compulsion is to get away:

away from the traditions of Western civilization, farther west to Japan and the Orient, if possible, as Tselos and others have pointed out.

There is no need to dwell here upon Wright's direct influence, through the Wasmuth publications in 1910 and 1911, upon Gropius and other Europeans in the teens, since this has already been indicated elsewhere. But one should point out that in
4.5 a Mondrian of 1915, touched by this spirit, there rises a deep bloom like the sea which then resolves itself into crossing currents like those of the Wright plan. This profound impulse toward continuity is then "classically" stabilized by Mondrian in clear rectangles sliding and moving around an armature of interwoven lines: which it is just possible may owe something to drawings and stripping details by Wright, reproduced by Wasmuth. These lines Mondrian himself writes of as being "continuous" beyond the painting frame. Mondrian's synthesis then forms the basis for a compromise in design in the work of Gropius and the Bauhaus. The continuous armature—which would be the building frame—is discarded, but the planes are used as thin sheets which enclose or define spatial volumes. Continuity in the form of a sliding relationship between elements is brought into a kind of union with the fragmentation of building mass and with picturesque composition, and the separate functions are enclosed in those same sharply defined boxes which are at once machined and Neoclassic. This amalgamation or synthesis becomes the "International Style" as isolated for us by Hitchcock and Johnson and as influential upon the work of many architects ever since.

However, it was another pupil and collaborator of Behrens—and the most Romantic-Classic of all the German architects of the twenties—who still most fully developed in Europe the examples toward continuity which had been offered by Wright and De
2.3 Stijl. In Mies van der Rohe's project of 1923 a cubical massing is stretched in plan by the continuous directional lines of Mondrian. The discipline is that of crossed spatial axes which recall Wright's cross-axis plans of many years before. Now, however, the movement is less compulsive and even more flowing, loosened and syncopated like a dance pattern and certainly owing much to the researches into continuity and its interruptions which
6.4 had been carried on by such De Stijl artists as van Doesburg.

2.5 By 1929 Mies has found a way to bring opposites into harmony. His Barcelona Pavilion is a masterpiece of the "International Style" precisely because it brings together as a harmony—and in a clearly separated structural and screening system—the American compulsion toward that Open Road which allows of no conclusion and the deeply seated European instinct for defined permanence and enclosure. Present, too, in the gleamingly polished surfaces, is the European romanticism of the machine. In a way the Barcelona Pavilion represents a new system of freedom and order but within a rather restricted emotional range, and, unlike the Baroque synthesis, without a single focus or a fixed conclusion. Nor is it a plastic and pictorial system like that of the Baroque, but a skeletal, planar, and "Constructivist" one.

For a period during the thirties this international synthesis of the nomadic and the permanent was apparently sympathetic to Wright, at least in compositional if not in structural (or polemical) terms. A comparison between the Barcelona Pavilion and a Wright

4.5 OPPOSITE: Piet Mondrian. *The Sea,* 1914

4.6 RIGHT: Frank Lloyd Wright. Goetsch-Winckler House, Okemos, Michigan, 1939–40. Exterior

house of ten years later should make this fact clear; and the adjustments expressed here 4.6
have also continued to direct the work of many architects.

But Wright, unlike Mies but like Picasso, is mighty; and he thinks like him in terms of compelling force. The monumental stability which both Wright and Picasso achieve in the later thirties out of the most violent oppositions and movements makes
both Fallingwater and the *Guernica* "classics," as it were, of the continuous phase in 2.11, 5.4
modern form.

Yet Wright is driven by his compulsion toward movement. Only the complete continuities of the circle can answer his need, and his poetic imagery remains close to the great nineteenth-century symbols of the road, the sea, and the river. The human observer is pulled inexorably into a current. This sweeps him under water into a cave which opens up into a pool. He is compelled to undergo the rite, as of immersion and purification. The building solids, whether structural or screening, are treated even more than before as purely space defining elements: they enclose it like a shell or they grow in it. Truly space, not matter, is the "reality" here. This fact raises certain questions concerning the position of man. As he is compelled into the ultimate continuities where all is done for him, against what does he judge himself? Where does he define his stand? How, on the one hand, can he be released from compulsion in order to know himself; how, on the other, can he be challenged not in terms of changing ambients but in unmistakably human terms?

Wright's answer is that of a westering pioneer, that one need not ask the question but go on. He will not provide humanity with references to itself in building mass. When, in the teens and twenties he had sought a monumental weight to answer human needs for ceremony more deeply than his suburban tradition had been able to, it was to the compact, hill- or mound-evoking masses of Maya architecture that he had turned (as in the Barnsdall House of 1920). Again: it is outside of classic humanism. Similarly, at
Taliesin West, it is the Mexican dance platform which has been compacted here; above 4.7
is spread its opposite in the tent of the nomad. All the forms have reference to those of

Frank Lloyd Wright. Taliesin West, Scottsdale, Arizona, begun 1938. Exterior 4.7

nature, not of man, and the building fabric as a whole, however massive or interwoven, is still expressed not as a sculptural body but as a flexible and opening sheath which defines a channel of continuous space. Along this dry river the viewer is compelled—through a building which is pure ambient—to carry out that journey which culminates the myth. He must move forward, beyond the places of men, until he comes at last to the pure emptiness of the desert and the beckoning hills beyond.

Since 1937, however, when Mies van der Rohe came to the United States, a movement has been growing in this country itself to reject such compulsive continuity and its concomitant asymmetry and to create instead a more fixed and symmetrical kind of
8.21 design. Mies's early classicism thus serves him well at the Illinois Institute of Technology, where he lets what continuity there is expand naturally from a symmetrically conceived central space. In this way his cubical buildings are in modular harmony with the rectangular spaces created by them, and he is released from the compulsion—as the Harvard Graduate Center is not—of forcing closed blocks to define a continuous and fluid space which is out of harmony with them and which properly belongs to another mode of buildings.

Mies thus rejects the old International Style compromise and insists, with a new compulsion, upon the skeleton cage of the steel frame. This is the classicizing "fixation" against which Wright had inveighed. It is also the lines rather than (or as well as) the planes of Mondrian. It involves a classicizing sense of types, where the vertical and horizontal solutions of Sullivan are further clarified and frozen. Mies's recent design, in its modularity and urbanity, has often been compared with that of the Renaissance. Certainly, in contrast to Wright's Broadacre City and its images of the Open Road, Mies now offers the images of the Renaissance townscape and the permanent order of the urban piazza. But Mies's forms in steel frame are thinner, less sculptural, than those of Renaissance buildings, and they have also the sharply willed linearity which seems typical in all ages of classicizing or Neoclassic work.

In the buildings of those distinguished architects like Philip Johnson and Eero Saarinen who have acknowledged their debt to Mies, such classicizing or, in their case,

more markedly Romantic-Classic quality is intensified. For example, the release from a compulsion to make space flow asymmetrically and the acceptance of fixed discipline and order often give rise in their work to a rather Palladian *parti* of closed corners and central openings. It also produces the separate forms of vaults and domes once more—where men are no longer directed along flowing routes but are left alone in a clear and single volume—and the buildings themselves are seen as sharp and abstractly scaled entities which recall those of Boullée and Ledoux. At the same time, while architects humanely react against the narrow expediency of much contemporary building, still their buildings would not yet seem to be fully humanist ones. Saarinen's Auditorium at M.I.T.
and Johnson's Synagogue at Port Chester are certainly the result of a humanist search for 3.4
clear, permanent, and man-centered forms, but—though bright in color and luminously conceived—they are still curiously lunar and remote. Eloquent but detached, the buildings of these architects sometimes seem to embody, perhaps most appropriately at the necessarily machine-like General Motors Technical Center, a certain quality of modern mass anonymity—at its best releasing, at its worst inadequately cognizant of the vital pressures and tensions which make human life. Their thinness and weightlessness also arise from another fact, however, which is that, in their design, space is still the "reality" over matter, and the solids are either simply a frame or a thinly stretched membrane which encloses a volume. Thus the buildings are not bodies but containers, and there is good reason to believe that Johnson and Saarinen are aware of the limitation. Certainly Saarinen's Chapel at M.I.T. would seem to be seeking more "physical" values.

This brings us to a central problem. It has been accepted by most critics of recent times that space is in fact the "reality" of a building. Indeed, our generation has talked of little else. Yet, whether or not we accept Kaschnitz-Weinberg's conclusions in his book *Die Mittelmeerischen Grundlagen der Antiken Kunst*, we still find that there is imbedded in the mind of Western man the memory of two opposing architectural traditions. One tradition, which becomes Italic, is indeed concerned with the dominance of interior space and with what Wright has termed the "great Peace" of such space, since it is associated with the protection and hope of rebirth offered by the female deities of the earth and—in the Neolithic period, as in Malta—may indeed be a constructed hollow cave, in the shape of the goddess herself. One is reminded of Wright's obsessive business with the water glass. Le Corbusier, attempting like most modern men to reconstruct a usable past for himself, has studied such architecture in its Roman phase, as at Hadrian's Villa, where Hadrian himself would seem to have been evoking the images of this tradition (which brings to mind, for example, the modern cult of the house). Le Corbusier, like Hadrian, understood perfectly what this was all about. "Un trou de mystère," he writes, and we are shown his cave-sanctuary project for Mary Magdalen, commissioned by the possessed Trouin at Sainte-Baume. But there is in antiquity, according to Kaschnitz, and obviously, another tradition, having to do not with the female engulfment of interior space but with a sculptural, challenging evocation of the gods of the outside and of the sky. Thus the megaron cella is surrounded by the peripteral colonnade. This produces an architecture which is upright and which supports weight, and which has at once a purely sculptural scale and a curious analogy, felt empathetically, to the standing bodies of men. Le Corbusier writes in 1923 of the Parthenon columns: "nothing . . . left but these closely knit and violent elements, sounding clear and tragic like brazen trumpets." He speaks of the space as swinging clear from them to the horizon verge. And we should remember that Le Corbusier's comments were published in a book entitled *Towards a New Architecture* (Vers une architecture).

The problem of the volume as interior and having essentially no exterior—unless one allows the space to be the whole "reality," as Wright would do—has concerned all architectural ages which have cared for the image of man. The Romans masked the volume with the column until a dwindling of classical tradition made it seem no longer so necessary to do so. The Gothic architect, on the other hand, organized his vaults so ethat the whole system became an integument like the column system itself, though on rather dematerialized and scholastic terms. The Renaissance engaged the columns in the wall or built up its window details as aggressive solids.

Le Corbusier grapples with this problem from the very beginning of his design.
4.8 His Citrohan Houses of 1922 are pure megaron volumes, with an open end and closed sides, though with an interior space which, one should point out, seeks the tumultuous and challenging qualities of Cubism rather than the flow of Wright and De Stijl or the "great Peace" of feminine protection. On the exterior Le Corbusier finally supports his volume upon his columns, but both are thin and tight in the manner of the twenties, and the space is still the "reality," with the solids affecting us only as poles or membranes. By 1930, in his Swiss pavilion, Le Corbusier has gone a step further. Two opposites are joined. Some of the *pilotis* have the muscular mass of weight supporting elements, but the box of rooms above is still pure skin around a space.

5.3 By 1946, however, in the Unité d'Habitation at Marseilles—in a housing program which attempts to answer one of the typical challenges of mass democracy—Le Corbusier has arrived at a more integrated system. The mighty *pilotis* support a framework in which the megaron-like apartments are set. Each of these has its pronaos or porch integrated with a *brise-soleil* which makes it impossible for the eye to read the building as merely a skin around a volume. Similarly, use-scale elements, which also cause us to see a building as simply a hollow, are suppressed. On the other hand, the Unité cannot be read as a solid, like an early Maya building, nor as a frame, like a Japanese one. Instead its solids appear to be in an almost one to one relationship with its voids. Since, therefore, the building in fact seems to have only that space which is integral to the articulated system of its mass it can no longer be seen as an ambient or a box or a hill but only as a sculptural body: a quality which has been noted by many critics. Since, however, we empathetically experience upright bodies in terms of our own, the building becomes a humanist one. I define architectural humanism here in the terms used by Geoffrey Scott in his book *The Architecture of Humanism*, of 1914. Of the humanist architecture of antiquity and the Renaissance, Scott wrote, "The centre of that architecture was the human body; its method, to transcribe in stone the body's favourable states; and the moods of the spirit took visible shape along its borders, power

4.8 ABOVE, LEFT: Le Corbusier. Citrohan House project, 1922. Model

4.9 ABOVE, RIGHT: Le Corbusier. High Court, Chandigarh, India, 1951–56. Exterior perspective

and laughter, strength and terror and calm." Such humanism, as it has meaning in the present, does not yearn weakly toward an Edwardian sediment of worn-out details, as a small and rather mauve group of critics now does. Instead it seizes and challenges the present, makes especially the alternately cyclopean and airborne world of the engineers comprehensible in human terms, and seeks its fellowship in the deepest patterns of the human past.

Scott then went on as follows: "Ancient architecture excels in its perfect definition; Renaissance architecture in the width and courage of its choice." In these terms it would appear that the Unité d'Habitation—in the modern material of reinforced concrete—is more like Hellenic architecture even than it is like that of the Renaissance to which it bears certain resemblances. It would seem to have passed beyond choice toward a new definition of space and body and to have brought the modern age, finally, to the frontiers of a new humanism. As the impatient nineteenth century discovered the joys of spatial continuity, the beleaguered twentieth seeks a new image of man.

Now, as at Chandigarh, the human being returns to the landscape; he no longer 4.9
dissolves into it as he may do in the lonely dream of Wright. Nor is he an intruder there who simply interrupts the land—as a classicizing cube might do—instead, as in the Greek temple, his architecture is one which, through its purely sculptural scale and its implied perspectives, can at once leave the major landscape elements alone to be themselves and can at the same time bring the whole visible landscape into human focus. It deals now with a double reverence, both for the beloved earth and man.

But it does more than this. Like classic Greek architecture itself it stretches us with the challenge it presents in terms of our capacity to grasp the whole of things afresh, and the images it evokes are multiple. Like the Parthenon to the Virgin Athena—whose attributes were alike of mind and force, of female sympathy and male power, and which was, of course, during the middle ages a church to the Virgin, first as Sophia, then as Theotokos, "God-Bearing"—like the Parthenon, Nôtre-Dame-du-Haut at Ronchamp 4.10
is active, but instead of rising tensely upward toward its center, as the Parthenon does, it splits out of the Euclidean envelope in a weight-shifting lunge to the southeast corner. Its architect tells us that the form, as a "vessel" on a "high place," is intended to respond to a "psycho-physiologie de la sensation," which is Scott's "empathy," and to

Le Corbusier. Nôtre-Dame-du-Haut, Ronchamp, France, 1950–55. Exterior 4.10

"une acoustique paysagiste, prenant les quatre horizons à témoin." Indeed the outside pulpit is like the clapper in the great bell. But Ronchamp is other things as well. Its hooded chapels (the hidden one behind the lectern, blood-red) are apsidal megara which recall in plan and elevation not only Le Corbusier's drawings of the Serapeion in Hadrian's Villa but also certain Neolithic earth sanctuaries in Sardinia which are related
4.11 in shape to the Serapeion. Rising and turning from its chapels, the main body of the church, instead of bulging with its contained volume—which would cause it to be seen simply as a shell—instead presses in both walls and catenary slab upon its interior space until, within, one is conscious of enclosure in a positive body and, outside, the whole becomes one pier which thrusts upward as a material force. Cave and column—in the words of the Litany: "Spiritual Vessel . . . Tower of David . . . House of Gold . . . Tower of Ivory" become one.

Thus we cannot look at Ronchamp without considering the capacity of architecture to function as sculptural presence, as a Greek temple does. Perhaps among modern buildings Le Corbusier's church deserved the Acropolis, and, in the mind of its architect, indeed swings upward from it into a splendid sound, itself a "brazen trumpet," an acoustic bell.

It is clear that we have come to a challenging moment. The "problem of monumentality," which is the problem of commitment both to the absolutes of completeness and to the present, now solves itself. Now the image of the river—along which we float like Huck and Jim, fugitives and spectators in a dreamlike time—is arrested by the image of the demanding presence on the high place: in the fixed temenos, rooted in the caverns of earth, but turning toward the open sky. It may not be fortuitous that we are also driven here away from Henry Adams's symbol of the Dynamo toward his counter symbols of the Virgin and St. Michael, where the Archangel, too, "loved the heights." We are informed

4.11 Le Corbusier. Nôtre-Dame-du-Haut. Interior

now that our fate in the present remains more wholly human than we had recently been led to believe and that the world as we can know it is made up not only of nature, nor of machines, nor only of an engulfing female security, but of the blazing ardor of men. It may be that in the face of total challenge the values of humanist civilization, as yet not dead, call to us, and we take our stand.

But a further observation should be made, and an obvious one. Ronchamp is not the Parthenon which, though brilliant, is cool, though intellectually clear-eyed, is still in touch with a purely tribal reverence. Ronchamp is at once more complicated, more primitive, and more impatient, like modern humanity. Its megara chapels are both glaring fetishes and archaeological demonstrations. Its architect is aware of many symbols, and he juggles them with irony: the pierced fortress wall which is no fortress, the roof that breaks apart, the threatened door. At the limit of the realm of consciousness Ronchamp seems to seek, with a violence like a burst of engines, the double quality of unique existence and of memory which can be used. Its forms, laden with old images, still find their life in action. And at their climax the cutting prow pierces space like Camus's image of a remade humanity: "a shaft which is inflexible and free." This may not appear to be a definition of architectural style, but it offers, I think, the only method through which we can seek definition. Slogans, tags, and verbal formulas are useful, but in the end they cannot define modern architecture or any art. At their worst, when dealing with the present, they may limit it. True definition, for any period, can only come when the nature and objectives of the self—with its present, its hopes, and its memory—are truly identified and humanly defined. Out of such definition arises that sense of identity which is style.

NEIL LEVINE

"The Nature of the Classical in Art." *Yale French Studies* ("Contemporary Art" Issue), nos. 19–20 (Spring 1957–Winter 1958): 107–24.

By the end of the 1930s, any serious discussion of the relevance of the classical tradition to the development of modern architecture had been rendered suspect by its association with the totalitarian regimes of Europe and the reactionary cultural policies of the New Deal in America. Yet within just a few years, the symmetrical planning, modular organization, and hierarchical composition of Mies van der Rohe's campus for Chicago's Illinois Institute of Technology (begun 1942–43) reopened the issue. Between 1949, when Rudolf Wittkower published his *Architectural Principles in the Age of Humanism*, and 1963, when John Summerson published *The Classical Language of Architecture*, a revisionist history began to emerge. Scully's essay "The Nature of the Classical in Art" is one of the very significant yet least well-known of these early attempts to recover the classical ground. Originally delivered as a talk in December 1956 at a symposium called "The Nature of the Classical" at the annual joint meeting of the Archaeological Institute of America and the American Philological Association, it provides evidence of the growing interest in all fields in defining the meaning of the classical, both for the past and for the present. The other talks in the symposium were given by Harry Levin ("The Nature of the Classical in Literature"), John Moore ("The Classical in Greek Literature"), Phyllis Lehmann ("The Classical in Greek Art"), Inez Ryberg ("The Classical in Roman Art"), and Ronald Syme ("The Classical in Roman History").

Scully's interest in the classical or, rather, the "classic," as he prefers to call it here, stemmed from an intense involvement with ancient art that began during the year he spent

5

The Nature of the Classical in Art

VINCENT SCULLY

An essay upon this tormented subject can, unhappily, begin only with a definition, and with a definition of the word "classic" rather than of "classical." In modern English usage, "classical" is a rather ambiguous term. It is synonymous neither with "classic" nor with "classicizing." As presently used in relation to the art of Greece and Rome, it is intended to characterize, rather loosely, all Greek and Roman art. The word "classic," on the other hand, is normally used to describe what is generally considered to be the central phenomenon in the formation of the fully "classical," and is usually identified with the art of fifth-century and sometimes fourth-century Greece. The term "classicizing" is used to describe an art which consciously attempts to imitate or re-create the classic, as occurs at times during the Hellenistic period, during the Augustan age, and later. It is acutely necessary that we clearly draw this distinction between the "classic" itself and that "classicism" which is the product of the classicizing process and whose art may be called "classicistic."

We are fortunate that the English language is supple (or barbarous) enough to deal with the semantics of this problem. The French language cannot do so, since the

in Italy in 1951–52. His visit to the Magna Graecia site of Paestum ultimately led to the publication of *The Earth, the Temple, and the Gods: Greek Sacred Architecture* (1962), arguably Scully's most important intellectual achievement. As the initial step in researching and writing that book, he spent the summer of 1955 in Greece. "The Nature of the Classical in Art" follows directly from that experience. It is one of the most revealing and heartfelt of Scully's writings, capturing well the sense of his very moving lecture style. It is at once an exploration of a theme of profound personal importance, an analysis and explanation of art-historical methodology, and a vision of art's higher purpose. The essay begins by disputing the appropriateness of the term "classical"—used in the title in deference to the topic of the archeological symposium in which the talk was first delivered—in order to substitute for its narrow referencing of certain historical periods or styles the more generic, valuative, and meaning-laden term "classic," which in turn is also contrasted to the merely imitative "classicizing" forms of "classicism." The "classic" for Scully, though initially made manifest and uniquely embodied in fifth-century Greek art, becomes a metaphor for art's expression of the human condition and a measure of its wholeness.

The "fragmentation" that began in the art of the eighteenth century, already pointed to in the essay "Modern Architecture: Toward a Redefinition of Style" (see chap. 4), is now seen as having produced an art-historical dead end in which the choice between formalism and iconography (represented by Heinrich Wölfflin and Erwin Panofsky) simply reinscribes the divisions within modern art itself. To overcome this dualism and restore the form-content/mind-body connection—in art as in the writing about art—Scully proposes a model of perception based on the existential philosophy of Jean-Paul Sartre and Albert Camus. Le Corbusier's postwar work at Marseilles and Ronchamp and Picasso's painting of *Guernica* exemplify such an art of existential struggle and confrontation. In focusing on the powerful sculptural forms and significant social themes of these works, Scully associates his interpretation of the classical tradition with contemporary interest in a new humanism and a new monumentality. But in emphasizing the need to recapture a primitive, almost barbaric sense of the physicality of artistic expression to achieve the "classic," Scully distances himself from the more abstract and academic interpretations of classicism, be it Palladian or Beaux-Arts, then being offered by Colin Rowe and Reyner Banham. Fully aware of the ironic dimensions of his approach, Scully acknowledges that a new "myth of the classic" can only arise in the existential absurdity of "fresh eyes of astounded barbarians" viewing it "across the battered early-morning suburbs of our souls."

adjective "classicistique" does not exist, and the word "classiciste," like the English, "classicist," means merely one who works with the "classics." The noun, "classicisme," is therefore applied to a state of being which can be described only by the adjective, "classique," rather than by a weaker and more limiting word. "Classique" thus loses something of its capacity to denote a more special and intense state of consciousness and becomes inextricably bound up with "classicisme." No one would claim that because of this restriction French critics have been unable to distinguish between "classic" and classicizing works and states of mind, but one can claim that it has caused the meaning of the classic to be blunted and the word itself to be directed toward areas which are not entirely appropriate to it—as to seventeenth-century French art, for example. Peyre, in his brilliant book upon the subject (*Qu'est-ce que le classicisme?*), is careful to distinguish his intentions but must use the adjective, "classique," to describe the specific works cited from his chosen period, which is that of *Le Classicisme Français*. An increasing respectability for the term "classicisant" might, like the use of "classicizing" in English, help to clarify the problem.

It becomes apparent that we must concern ourselves here directly with the concept of the "classic," because it is upon that central concept that the related concepts depend. I should like to define the classic as that art which is concerned with a total exploration and grasp of the large meanings which are involved in the inner and outer life of man—in his individual life and in his group life—and which deals with such meanings in terms both intellectual and physical, embodied in forms at once abstract and organic, tactile and optical, and compacting the real and the ideal into a dynamic but stable whole which appears on its own terms to be both clear and complete, instantaneous and permanent.

The "restraint" and "proportion" of the classic, its "measure" in the later Aristotelian sense, are built into it; they are not applied, and if the classic seems to later ages to supply "ideal" types for art it does so because it deals with the whole of life, and many types are thus implicit in it. Consequently, the classic age becomes one in which the oldest past and, in a certain sense, the farthest future, come together as tensions in a keenly lived present and are resolved there in terms of experience. Such experience is not safe but daring. Because the classic age is ignited by a love for the challenge of life as a whole it will try almost anything that comes to mind. It is thus released alike from the more restricting aspects of those older patterns which parochial or tribal traditions may have enforced before its time and from those which its own radiant sense of wholeness may suggest to later ages.

Whether one can find all the qualities of the classic wholly present in any art other than that of fifth-century Greece is a question. They may certainly exist in varying degrees during the late twelfth and thirteenth centuries in the Ile de France, and it clearly seemed to the men of the sixteenth century that Raphael had in fact accomplished these things in his painting, as in his *School of Athens* and his *Exposition of the Sacrament* in the Stanza della Segnatura in the Vatican. A total world of past and present is set up here, complete on its own terms and formed within an embracing ambient which is based upon the domed and apsed architecture of Bramante—as in his contemporary project for St. Peter's and his Cortile del Belvedere, in which these forms are echoed in space directly outside the windows of this room. Explicit in this art also is a view of antiquity as having created an excellence which must be rivaled by modern life and brought into union with it.

This view sees antiquity as a whole; it does not seek for a perfect "classic" within antiquity, nor does it seem to use the term "classic" in this sense. Therefore the

High Renaissance creates an art which is widely open to the richness of both antiquity and the present. It is exclusive only in its own sense at once of its modernity and of its brotherhood with the far past as it rejects the more recent past of the middle ages which lay between. Thus antiquity was a spur, not a bridle, to High Renaissance invention, and antiquity itself was judged in terms of present experience. What the High Renaissance knew of antiquity it used according to its own needs: primarily Roman works, some Greek. In Raphael we recognize the embracing solemnity of an Italic tradition; in Michelangelo, forever breaking out of later conceptions of High Renaissance order, we often recognize the solid thrust of the Hellenic of whatever period—as behind his Sistine Chapel frescoes of 1510 we perceive such Greek works as the Belvedere Hercules, discovered a few years before.

As, however, the later sixteenth century lost a certain confidence in its own capacity for accomplishment in the present, it seems to have looked back upon the High Renaissance as an ideal period and to have sought, both in the High Renaissance and in antiquity, for a set of laws and a theory which might restore that lost ideal. A certain split between theory and practice began to arise. The real and the ideal began to diverge, and the ideal was held to be higher, because conceived in the mind. When in sixteenth-century French usage, for example, the term "classique" appeared (as in Sébillet's *Art poétique*, of 1548: "bons et classiques écrivains français"), it had about it much of its old aura of intellectual approval, as of something worthy to be a model because past and known, a "classic" in other words. About such a concept could gather the view of the highest art as an "ideal" art, rational and intellectual, restrained by rule. Such insistence upon the ideal mirrored that of later antique classicizing theory itself, where the classic had been seen as primarily an intellectual art of distance and permanence which rejected of necessity those aspects of form having to do with the violent, the instantaneous, and the sensational. In the similarly classicizing view of the seventeenth century the wholeness of the classic as such was partly lost once more, and human experience both of the past and in the present began to be fragmented into polarities.

The seventeenth-century controversies between the Poussinistes and the Rubénistes in the French Academy essentially accepted as polarities two ways of figuring reality: that of Rubens as coloristic and optical, full of the violence of illusion and the momentary and without the serenity, clarity, and permanence to be found in the linear, strict, and calm forms of Poussin. The latter was seen as related to Raphael and the antique in terms of antique sculpture, and Rubens was held to be "modern" and thus not so related. In this way past and present, the classic as model and the present as sensation, tended to be split apart as they had not been during the Renaissance. At the same time antiquity was still viewed more or less as a whole—as made up of classics—and no specifically "classic" or high moment was factored out of it. Yet in the successfully balanced classicism of Poussin certain strong formal predilections can be found which are related to specific periods in ancient art. For example, it is obvious today that pictorial and dramatic effects, like those of Rubens, existed in some monuments of Hellenistic antiquity, as in the Pergamene altar—and that both tactile or linear, and optical or pictorial, effects are to be found in the art of fifth-century Athens itself.

The predilection of Poussin and after him of the Academy—though its members were never able to carry it out in practice as he had been—is actually toward classicizing works from antiquity. These tend to tone down from the classic its more advanced and movemented, that is pictorial, aspects and to concentrate upon its more conservative, linear, solid, and sculptural qualities. One may go further and say that classicism, whether in antiquity or in the seventeenth century, was in fact reaching backward toward earlier—early classic or archaic—values of a conservative character and that classicism itself would seem to represent in part a deeply felt, regressive side of human nature as it longs for the most ancient and unchanging ways of certainty for experience.

With Winckelmann—at the moment when the whole structure of Baroque society was beginning to break up—such concentration upon the archetype of the permanent was intensified and given a moral basis. "The good and the beautiful are the same," said Winckelmann, "and only one path leads to them, while many go to the evil and the ugly." In his *History of Ancient Art*, published in 1764, Winckelmann insisted upon the purely Greek quality of good and beautiful art and in effect denied an art to the Romans at all. He also discovered what he called a "high" period, a "golden age" in Greek art and explained that phenomenon in terms of development. He saw this development as one to which a biological, or botanical, analogy of "bloom and decay" might be applied and he found "four stages of style, namely the straight and hard, the grand and square, the beautiful and flowing, and the imitative." He goes on: "The first probably lasted for the most part until the age of Pheidias; the second until Praxiteles, Lysippus, and Apelles; the third probably ceased with the school of the three later artists; and the fourth continued until the downfall of art."

Out of such a view arose not only a further exclusiveness in theories of value but also a fixed belief, morally justified, in cultural progress and decay. From this point of view Winckelmann explained art since the Renaissance in historical terms, with his own period in that art described as a period of decay. During the Renaissance itself the present had called to the past because it felt itself to be great, like the past, but with Winckelmann, at the beginning of the modern age, the present feels itself to be weak and impermanent and calls to the past for permanence and strength. Thus, through Winckelmann, in terms of theory and history, the detached but moralizing view of a biological development of growth, flowering, and decay in cultures was made possible, and, in art, its opposite, a consciously "classic" revival. This took several forms. While Winckelmann distinguished between the "square and grand" and the "beautiful and flowing" in the art of antiquity, it may be felt that his own peculiar physiological qualifications—those which had apparently enabled him to distinguish some essential characteristic of Greek sculpture even through the veil of copies—led him in practice to prefer a rather emasculated version of the "beautiful," out of which may be said to grow the rather androgynous classicism of Canova, who was praised by Winckelmann's follower, Cicognara, as the highest and most antique of modern sculptors. Yet we find in

5.1 West pediment sculpture, Temple of Zeus, Olympia, c. 460 B.C.

Winckelmann not only great learning and discrimination but also intense intuitions, as when he writes that he would have liked to excavate at Elis because there, he said, "I am assured that the yield...would be abundant beyond conception, and that a great light would shoot up from this soil of art, if it should be thoroughly searched."

What Winckelmann would have made in fact of the sculptures from Olympia it is 5.1
difficult to say. In all likelihood he would have included them in his earlier phase of "straight and hard" rather than in his more developed one of "square and grand." Yet he had always insisted, in a way like the Academy, upon what he called "drawing" (that is, linearity and purity in form), and the more intense and creative aspects of the Neo-classicism, which Winckelmann had played a part in unleashing, actually did move toward much the same kind of hardness, density, and geometric purity that are to be found in the Olympic forms. The reconstruction drawings of Stuart and Revett, and the projects of Ledoux, Boullée, and Jefferson have this character, as do the most "classic" paintings of David—directed to all of these into an empathetic comprehension of the new, violent, modern world in terms of harsh linear clarity and uncompromisingly solid forms.

Yet the fragmentation of human experience which we have noted as a progressive development in theory since the Renaissance now burst forth more intensely in practice than it ever had before. While Winckelmann had been concentrating a part of European attention upon the sculptural clarity of antiquity, another part was being directed with equal intensity and sense of loss toward the pictorial obscurity of the middle ages and the exotic. In a painting by Constable, for example, the values of light and shade and shifting color which are evoked are consciously the opposite of those desired by Stuart and Revett and David. Two complementary ways of experience—that through reason and clarity and that through feeling and intuition—are seen as opposites. The word "classic" is now used more commonly and with a meaning at once more intense and more restricted: as the opposite of "romantic." In this way the false polarities of "classic" vs. "romantic" are set up. The polarities are false, first, because both are present in the classic itself and, second, because the impetus behind both Neoclassicism and romanticism in the later eighteenth century was essentially—and in terms of their own semantics—a romantic one, emotionally concentrated upon a restricted idea. Yet, from this period, a sense of dichotomy between "classic" and "romantic" becomes firmly imbedded in the modern mind—to its great psychic disadvantage.

To the disadvantage especially of classic values, because, as the polemic developed in the nineteenth century—recalling but refocusing the old Poussinistes-Rubénistes controversy of the seventeenth—the classic began more and more to be defended on terms which avoided experience as known in modern life and saw the classic as something which could be found only through rejection of the present. It did no good for Delacroix, who understood this problem rather well, to insist that he was as classic as Ingres (to our eyes he may sometimes appear more classic). He must be shouted down by the critics who knew, they believed, that these ways of making art were truly different. Whole ranges of human experience were thus, at last, fully forced out of the nineteenth-century view of the classic—especially those ranges dealing with action and involvement—and the classic was described in terms of a sentimental academic classicism, both "sweetened and dried" (as Peyre put it) in comparison alike with the classicism of the seventeenth century and with its own Neoclassic beginnings.

Such academic classicism became a grab bag of culture, superficially invoking antique forms but profoundly uninvolved in the classic disciplines of structural geometry and the tensions of organic beings. Nor was it involved very much with the most pressing preoccupations of its age; thus it was hardly classic. Through it, in the nineteenth century, the classic in fact became profoundly lost, and with it, in a way, antiquity itself. (A comparison between Ingres's *Apotheosis of Homer* and Raphael's *School of Athens* can make the fact of this loss all too apparent.) At the same time, however, in a development out of these movements called "romanticism" and "realism" rather than "classicism," a number of much more "classic" works than those of the Academy were being produced by later-nineteenth-century artists. Both Sullivan and Seurat compact a kind of classic order in terms of life as lived: an order disciplined therefore by the classic rather than the classicizing method and deriving out of this process the largely conceived but active forms which seem best to embody the meaning of the whole. Yet there are elements in the art of Sullivan and Seurat which cannot truly be counted as classic. From the point of view of the inner and outer life of man and of the ceremonies whereby he articulates the meanings of his individual and group life there is too much left out in both, as in a sense the nineteenth century as a whole left too much out.

At the same time, from the point of view of classic permanence, there is in Sullivan a continuously movemented interweaving of elements and in Seurat a constantly shifting kaleidoscope of figures which seem more completely involved in an inherently nineteenth-century confidence in physical change and continuity. Perhaps the nineteenth century, scientifically absorbed, had not yet been required by circumstances to search deeply enough into the self to unearth the permanent qualities beneath a changing present which seemed always to be opening up the world for its enjoyment. Certainly continuity and change are the essence of late-nineteenth- and early-twentieth-century art. Both Wright and Cézanne feel deeply for the classic solidity of objects, but these they then bring into a movement of flux and becoming, in which physical forces pull them along. There is the problem too of the dwindling of classic themes, though these are profoundly wished for by Cézanne. Through a study of Poussin and nature in tension he struggles with the human form and the culminating pyramidal shape but is somehow compelled to draw both into the oscillating ribbons of physical continuity. Yet in the attempt to resolve these counter forces there is much that is classic, and to this point we shall be obliged to return. Similarly, while the Cubism which developed by 1910 out of the work of Cézanne and others has sometimes been called a classic art, one cannot entirely accept it as such. The classic sense of discovery is there, but the large themes of the classic and its completeness are not. In a sense Cubism beautifully culminates and synthesizes the most important developments of the nineteenth century: fragmentation, confidence only in the material process of matter, the dwindling of human allusions, most of all a rejection of the classic faith in the permanence of the instantaneous in favor of a Bergsonian becoming and the time not of moments but of continuity. Therefore, for many reasons, the classic as viewed or as created, indeed, the need for it, may be felt to have largely disappeared from the early-twentieth-century world.

At this point we should turn briefly toward twentieth-century art history and criticism in order to demonstrate the loss of the classic more fully. By 1900 the characteristic nineteenth-century confidence in change and continuity had produced an art history which, while it tended to accept the developmental philosophy of Winckelmann, had, except among the unenlightened, subtracted value judgments from the process. Thus the rehabilitation of the Baroque led to Wickhoff's rehabilitation of Roman art in its more pictorial and illusionistic aspects. Indeed, the subtracting of judgments of value concerning quality and meaning led to a curious new judgment concerning fullness of development, a rather Darwinian view in which Mrs. Strong, for example, though still paying service—as all since Winckelmann had been obliged to do—to fifth-century Greek art, was constrained to point out that Roman illusionism, dealing as it did with optical rather than with tactile values, represented in fact a higher level of human intellectual development than was to be found in less developed Greek art.

Similarly, Heinrich Wölfflin, in a series of books published between 1889 and 1915, set up new polarities between what he called "classic" and "baroque" as different kinds of art. The classic becomes more isolated as a moment and is seen as restricted in form. Wölfflin's distinguishing terms have been persistent in art history ever since and have certainly been heard in this talk: linear vs. painterly, plane vs. recession, closed vs. open form, multiplicity vs. unity, clearness vs. unclearness. Though Wölfflin thought of these arts as polarities it was obvious to him that the Baroque represented a development in time out of the classic, and he also recognized an archaic or experimental period as preceding the classic. Shortly thereafter other scholars isolated a phase of sixteenth-century European art as existing between the "classic" of the early sixteenth century and the Baroque of the seventeenth and entertaining objectives and producing forms which were clearly different from those of either the classic or the Baroque. To this art the title "mannerist" was given, not only because it seemed to mannerize and refine the forms of Raphael and Michelangelo (and indeed the word "mannerist" had been used in this way during the sixteenth century itself), but also because it was in large part preoccupied with shock effects, contrasts, and ambiguities in form and meaning. These have proved extraordinarily sympathetic to the twentieth-century world.

With such identification of experimental, classic, mannerist or refined, and baroque phases in art, the way was now open for twentieth-century morphologists to turn the whole business into the characteristically desired flux of growth and development and to handle any art, anywhere, upon these fluid terms. We can be spared here a demonstration of this method upon arts, such as those of India and China, about which I know almost nothing, although one might point out that the method works most convincingly with arts about which one knows nothing at all. A brief demonstration with Greek art may be allowed: that is, with the archaic as experimental, with the mid-fifth century as classic or the culmination of those experiments, the fourth century as refining and mannerizing the balance of the classic, and the Hellenistic as producing a baroque which coils outward into space, re-creates classic release in more explosive terms, and otherwise demonstrates most of the characteristics defined by Wölfflin. One will note that the four stages of Winckelmann are back, but without the exclusive value judgments and—in all fairness to the morphologists—without the biological cultural analogies which, along with judgments of value, have been incorporated into this method by some contemporary historians such as Spengler and Toynbee and which, partly through their influence, have found their way into various textbooks on world art.

When intelligently applied, the morphological method has the great virtue of making many kinds of art available for systematic, if rather detached, analysis, but it has one paramount weakness so far as we here are concerned: namely, that through it the classic is irrevocably lost. The moment of balance is harder and harder to find; it is eaten into on one side by the experimental and even more on the other by the mannerist or refined, until we come at last upon the trauma of the graduate student whose eye has become so acute to disequilibrium that he has lost the classic forever and can never work again.

One reason morphology loses the classic is because it is inadequately concerned with meaning as embodied in form. It is here that the iconologist, reacting against the morphologist, might have been expected to serve us well. The iconologist's preoccupation with the themes of art, and especially—through the influence of such universal intellects as Erwin Panofsky—with the rich humanist tradition of classical themes which run through the art of the Western world from antiquity to the present, might have aided us in rediscovering that complexity of meaning which is an essential of the classic and which makes it so much more than merely a moment of balance or equilibrium. Indeed, the method of the iconologist has helped us to value the density of allusion which is involved, for example, in the organization of the various cult centers on the Acropolis in Athens or in the identification of the figures in Raphael's *School of Athens*. The iconologists have attempted as well to widen our concept of the classic in all periods by bringing into it, as in the middle ages, such a figure, considered refined by the morphologists, as Pierre de Montreuil, or as in the Renaissance, such a titan as Michelangelo.

Yet in the end, the effect of the work of the iconologists has been to lead us not toward the classic but away from it along a river of change which seems not so different from the one which is furrowed by the canoes of the morphologists. This would seem to occur because the iconologist has become preoccupied not with a classic resolution of complexity but with complexity itself. He is most happy, it seems, when traveling through the labyrinth of humanist allusion, following a new thread of Ariadne which leads us to many curious and forgotten culs-de-sac of knowledge along the way but which this time never brings us forth from the splendid labyrinth into the vulgar light of day. Thus iconology would seem, like morphology, to be essentially concerned with the process of becoming, and it too loses the classic for us, accomplishing a certain fragmentation of our view of the whole. It seems obvious that we must bring form, as in the morphologists, and meaning, as in the iconologists, back together again in terms of experience, as the classic does. (One should point out that a rather similar desire to bring all relevant aspects of human experience together would seem to have motivated the symposium on the classic held at Naumburg in 1930, cf. Werner Jaeger, ed., *Das Problem des Klassischen und die Antike*, Leipzig, 1931.)

Yet if the classic can be lost through a modern desire for continuous complexity it can also be lost through a counter modern yearning for maximum directness and shock impact in form. Here the iconologist is countered by the modern artist and critic who renounces humanism in favor of primitive clarity and violent sensation. This predilection for the abstract has served us well by making the archaic comprehensible and desirable to our eyes. It has done the same—despite Mr. Berenson's violent objections—for late antique art, at the other end of Greek and Roman civilization. But with critics such as Seltman it would deny us the Hellenistic, as less abstract and too pictorial, and it would deprecate the Parthenon sculptures because certain pictorial, modeled values are apparent in them. In effect, it is the classic's love for the forms of nature to which this attitude objects. It would leave us Olympia for what is archaic or (in a peculiar terminology borrowed from Roger Fry) "formal" in Olympia, but beyond that it will not value the classic, which is thus lost to us once more. We should note that the aesthetic criteria involved here are not so different from those of the old classicizing academy, insofar as they both are based upon profoundly conservative—one might say hieratic rather than natural—ways of seeing.

Through similar criteria the Parthenon itself is also lost to us. Martienssen sees 5.2
its octostyle facade as less easily grasped at once than the usual hexastyle facades of archaic or of other fifth-century temples. Again the criterion is one which values direct impact rather than that stretching of vision and comprehension which the Parthenon, as

Ictinos and Callicrates. Parthenon, Athens, 447–32 B.C. Exterior 5.2

a classic monument, certainly demands. Valuing the archaic, the criterion is still a classicizing one, like that of Vitruvius who insisted that Doric temples were, by nature, hexastyle.

If we have lost the classic in all these different ways, how are we to find it again? Here we should return to our definition of the classic as that art which is of highest class because it is involved in presenting the variety of human experience and the tensions of actual life in forms which resolve but do not deny that variety and those tensions. By this I do not mean exactly what Proust meant when he said, "Only romantics know how to read classic works, because they read them as they were written, romantically." I do not believe in the distinction, but I am in sympathy with Proust's intention here—which is to make us realize the classic as the result both of a profoundly searching creative struggle and of a sense of positive human release. Therefore, we should attempt to experience the nature of that struggle to compact opposites into resolution, to adjust tensions into stable forms, to create indeed that harmony of tensions, "as of the bow and the lyre," of which Herakleitos had spoken. We should try above all to see the classic as it is involved, most optimistically, in creative acts—in discovery, invention, and the expansion of experience. We must, in other words, try to go forward to the classic positively as it came to itself, through creation, rather than negatively as the "classicizers" have gone back to it in search of the finished, the perfect, and the ruled.

For example, in architecture the Nashville Parthenon can help us little to recover the Parthenon in Athens; it remains a curiosity since its exterior sculptural form

5.3 Le Corbusier. Unité d'Habitation, Marseilles, 1946–52. Exterior

in the Hellenic manner is not in tension with the meaning of modern buildings, which is in their interior use as space containers as well as in their exterior presence. Jefferson's Pantheon Library can, however, help us more because here, using an Italic tradition related to space enclosure, Jefferson shows us still the nature of the building as used in tension with the form as applied. This too has undergone more of the creative process in variation from its model than has the other building.

If we wish, however, to see an architecture which attempts integrally to resolve the Italic tradition of interior space with the Hellenic one of the articulated sculptural integument in terms of new discovery, we must turn to the work of a contemporary architect. In Le Corbusier's Unité d'Habitation at Marseilles, the building contains its interior 5.3
of megaron-like apartments within a plastic system which appears from the outside to be related only to its own laws and which achieves in this way something of the purely sculptural scale of the Greek temple. We can now experience it in terms of the classic metaphor of the temple as a human-evoking, upright and weight-supporting, but purely abstract order in the natural world. Thus Le Corbusier extracts the maximum sculptural quality from his supports, and—as a Greek temple, by direction and contrast, brings the

whole visible landscape into human focus—so Le Corbusier seeks a similar classic ten- 4.9 sion and focus in his buildings, like that which houses the High Court of Chandigarh in India. Such combination of opposites relating to man and nature is no less daring than many of the unlikely combinations brought into resolution by classic art itself. For a man like Le Corbusier, who desires classic values above all things, the method of finding them has been one of unremitting search and struggle. He has been obliged, like most of us, to reconstruct a usable past for himself, because the academy had withdrawn the past from human meaning in the twentieth century. For interior space he seeks the meaning of Hadrian's Villa in his drawings. Like Hadrian himself he digs into the hollows of swelling cave types for the nature of interior experience. For exterior sculptural challenge which can state the splendor of the human will he travels to the Acropolis in Athens, and writes of classic art among the ruins, "nothing . . . left but these closely knit and violent elements, sounding clear and tragic like brazen trumpets."

When Le Corbusier builds a church out of the elements of interior body and exterior challenge he will stretch us as Ictinos apparently stretches the comprehension of the critics still. The plan may be like the whole Acropolis brought inside. As we follow Pausanias's route from shrine to shrine without—through all the complexity of forms— 4.10, 4.11 so within Nôtre-Dame-du-Haut at Ronchamp we journey from hairpin megaron to megaron. These are the cavelike chapels, recalling to us Le Corbusier's drawings of Hadrian's Villa, and beyond those the horned earth sanctuaries of Sardinia, Brittany, and Ireland—female sanctuaries which Le Corbusier was also consciously evoking in his Mary Magdalen cave for the obsessed Trouin at Sainte Baume. The exterior of Ronchamp shows a double intent: to hood the chapel spaces as interior volumes but to bring up the main form as an exterior sculptural shape, an acoustic bell, rising in a curve to the southeast corner: a presence stretching challengingly upward like an airfoil about to take flight. Since both walls and vault press inward, the building cannot be seen simply as a hollow shell, like most buildings. Instead, one feels inside the reality of engulfment in a positive body, while outside the whole becomes one pier which thrusts upward as a material force. Cave and column become one. Ronchamp, in the lived present, challenges our capacity for experience until we remember that the Greek temple was involved in a rather similar intent, that is, to clothe its inner cella shrine in the exterior forms of sculptural force. We remember, too, that the Parthenon itself, though closed within its Euclidean envelope, is also stretching upward. It, too, challenges us: a purely compression system which is, nevertheless, apparently rising upward as a colonnade held down in tension at its corners—which it pulls with it—stretching upward and with all its life wholly being the unlikely, complex, but present fact of Athena, purely flesh and purely spirit.

Both the Parthenon, and (I think we must say) Ronchamp, are classic buildings because they both deal with the whole of things—in this case relating to the Virgin Goddess—as presently existing fact. One notes that the carefully chosen, archetypal words of the Litany apply to both: "Spiritual Vessel . . . Tower of David . . . House of Gold . . . Tower of Ivory." These opposites are not carefully balanced in the Parthenon and Ronchamp but are fused in the heat of the experience of them. It is little wonder that classicizers, such as Perret, have been among Le Corbusier's most persistent detractors, since it is not the living heat of the classic which the classicistic desires but instead its apparently reproducible order. Yet neither the Parthenon nor Ronchamp is reproducible, and they give further the curious impression, intrinsic to the classic, of being, despite their obvious prototypes, undeniably unique of their kind. They deal not with the comfort of the purely relative but with the challenge of that absolute which culminates relativity. Thus they do not mesmerize the viewer's self but simply confront him with themselves—existing presences counter to his own. In this way that freedom which Sartre saw in the work of art calls to the freedom in those individuals who can recognize it. The Parthenon and Ronchamp are therefore not for the timid, nor is the classic, which seems to be a terrible freedom most of all. Perhaps, though hidden and therefore unidentified behind the semantic mask of "classicisme," it has always been the classic that modern existentialists have in fact sought, since the Law of the classic—as in Plato's dialogue on this theme—is intrinsic to it and neither outrages the individual nor denies the group; it need not be stolen, as in Camus's *La Chute*, like the panel of the Just Judges from its proper place. If Sartre's stated goal, "the absolute at the heart of relativity," means an absolute which grows out of the full acceptance of relativity rather than one which is insulated against it, then perhaps the Parthenon, not Communism, is the true object of the existentialist's search. We can believe that this may be the case when Sartre writes, "dans l'oeuvre d'art nous avons découvert la présence de l'humanité entière." Certainly, with Le Corbusier, whose culture is wholly French, the French search for meaning now passes beyond its traditional "classicisme"—which is order imposed upon anarchy—toward the organic awe and terror of the classic, which is the inseparable wholeness of life.

If I now seem to see the classic over much in terms of active violence and struggle—in almost existentialist terms—it may be because a desire to discover the truth of classic values once again has been a consistent and poignant factor in the work of some of the greatest artists of our time. Again, they have been French artists or artists who have worked in France. There was, it is true, a moment at the end of the last century when there blossomed a curiously haunting classic as of those who had never left home. Maillol on the shores of the Mediterranean made his solid but radiant images, and Picasso in his father's house on that same littoral grew up to a kind of classic which, like that of Maillol, recalls the severity of Olympia. But it is in the nature of the modern world that a man must leave his father's house and come in contact with a world which is as wide as mass civilization and history have made it. Picasso in 1901, in the metropolis of Paris, becomes a part of a sophisticated and elegant milieu, refined and fluid like the Minoan civilization whose forms were being excavated and published by Evans at precisely that time. But for every modern man who is brought into a fully formed environment, there seems to operate—if he is to become a full man—the peculiar necessity to begin again from the beginning, to relive as personal experience the creation of those values out of which the world is truly made. Thus Picasso consciously primitivizes himself: a painting of 1907, a Bakota guardian of the dead, and the Great Mother from a

Boeotian amphora of the late geometric period seem all to belong together. What are the forces underneath, the artist asks. What are the images and the geometry? Then in full tide of joy and strength and in full command of his material Picasso makes his richly mature Cubist forms, like archaic Greek art but without that art's clearly fixed tribal and ceremonial pattern to base his meaning upon—without the image of humanity as a constant in his search. He is a normally uprooted man of the modern technological and mass world. But he desires a tradition, or a past, passionately and searches for it in antiquity. And when his human beings emerge after the first world war, it is as if they, like the Kouros by Kritios, were the first human beings to move upright in the world and to shift their weight.

But Picasso, as a modern man, cannot find confidence or excitement in the deeply organic character of that movement. His figures create the effect, found also in the characters of Cocteau, Anouilh, and Gide, of knowing that they are playing a Hellenic part—engaged in the archetypal act because they know they are expected to do so. It is a moment of ironic classicism, fusing wit and longing. Thus Picasso's men are here not radiant like the Greek; instead they have a heavy, earth-bound mass, which reminds us a little of Italic art, and a kind of reflective sadness which recalls late antiquity. Here Picasso searches too and other groupings suggest themselves: a third-century Roman bust, withdrawn and strange; a Picasso head with the same great eyes and the strong forms of nose and hair; then, finally, the same motifs arranged into a whole new set of reverberations where the original form has been pondered until its essential elements have been found. The form which results may not be a classic one, but it reveals a kind of classic process: that is, the attempt to rearrange the past in terms of present meaning. It is the opposite of the classicizing process.

Yet Picasso cannot focus these attempts until he is faced with an event which pulls him into contact with public as well as private life. For him this event can hardly be a great victory over barbaric forms, like Salamis, Plataea, or the Himera. Instead it is one of the characteristic twentieth-century defeats—in this case the bombing of the town of Guernica. Nevertheless, under the pressure of a need to find an adequate form for a personally valid and generally true statement about that event he now comes closest to a
5.4 classic method and a classic form. His *Guernica*, of 1937, is organized by severe shapes and limited colors into a pyramidal composition like that of a Greek pediment. Picasso avoids reporting the event. There are no bombing planes. He is interested in the large meanings involved in the destruction of a town. Therefore a few figures, in terms of the unities of classic drama, stand for the whole; it is complex meaning resolved in forms which are clear and complete, instantaneous and permanent. Cubist geometry is resolved with the organic; movement with stability. As at Olympia, the time of continuity becomes the time of *now*.

The forms themselves are pushed farther than forms had been pushed before, and like the figures from the west pediment of the Temple of Zeus at Olympia they are pushed for one reason only, to make the meaning more direct and clear. They are forms which express as intensely as possible the agony which is the meaning of the event, and

5.4 Pablo Picasso, *Guernica,* 1937

they move within and as part of the basic order of the shape which controls the dynamic unity of the whole. The meaning is a classic one. It takes an attitude; it describes barbarism and defines civilization. It is the rape of decency which is its theme. But there is no radiant young god to state the triumph of human truce and order. Instead the hero is broken and a hollow man, and the beast totem rises triumphant once again and watches.

In this there is a profoundly classic reference. As on a stage the whole is being regarded and illuminated. On the eastern pediment from Olympia the crime and countercrime of human beings is watched by the river god as nature which is outside humanity and which fixes a cold, unwinking stare upon the terribly exposed ranks of men. In the *Guernica,* nature as the beast observes and approves human self-destruction. For Picasso the indifferent watcher, outside man, created by him, but now destroying him, is technology. This illuminates the scene and pins humanity, as upon a dissecting table, under the unwinking light of an unshaded bulb. Whatever the result we see it whole. It is not a fragment any more but a concentrated image of ourselves, and perhaps it tells us that our problem now is to bring horse and rider back to life once more—as they are alive on the Parthenon frieze—in terms of commitment, devotion, and joy. There is also ritual to be understood, and its harmony of the ideal and the real. There is above all life, since it has been precisely with a living harmony of real and ideal that great classic works of art have dealt. In the *Guernica,* the violence of the event in our time is still too white hot, but by reference of imagery and form the implications of classic meaning are present, and the need for a resolution, as the classic would have it, is asserted.

Yet we may ask ourselves whether such resolution, if it should ever come again, could produce once more a truly classic art. There was a freshness in the Greek awakening to the whole of life, for example, which has never been possible with quite the same newness for those later ages which have had that example already fixed before their eyes. Thus, perhaps the definition of the classic which I have offered throughout this talk has been—because it has inevitably had exemplars of the classic in mind—partly a classicizing one despite itself. Perhaps a classic art can arise only in a certain way, as a certain kind of people awake to individuality out of a tribal situation, with which, for a period, their new freedom exists in vital tension. Perhaps, therefore, some might hold the view that there can never be another fully classic art until an adequate set of disasters forces the human race to lose everything—even its present stock of memories—and to start again from the beginning. Some aspects of the existentialism to which I referred earlier have seemed to demonstrate at least a partial sympathy toward such an eventuality. A barbarianization even more complete than that which separated antiquity from the High Middle Ages might be conceived.

Our imagination revolts at the possibility. It is the one which Shelley embraced in exacerbated form in his poem, *Hellas*, when he consigned civilization as it had become to the destruction he felt it deserved:

> Heaven smiles, and faiths and empires gleam,
> Like wrecks of a dissolving dream.

Then all might begin again. The great decisions could be made afresh.

> A new Ulysses leaves once more
> Calypso for his native shore.

Then the new heroic acts and climactic victories might create the new fund of memories, out of which comes the new awakening:

> Another Athens shall arise,
> And to remoter time
> Bequeath, like sunset to the skies,
> The splendor of its prime;

But Shelley knew that this dream too would be fated to impermanence by the very nature of human life. Why, therefore, should the world begin again? He cries:

> The world is weary of the past,
> Oh, might it die or rest at last!

Yet this last cry seems nihilistic and even sentimental. It is L'Homme Révolté among the broken images, choosing death in the impasse. In all likelihood the world of human values can wish for neither death nor rest and remain human. The world must use the memories it has; it cannot discard them. Picasso and Le Corbusier, both sensing the necessity to begin anew in the face of the new challenges of the modern age—and Picasso especially seeming to relive the development of experience from its beginning—

have still recognized this fact instinctively. They have understood that men cannot put away what they have once discovered and that the challenge of the present is to see the classic as it is and to create a fresh life for it on our own terms if we can. They have realized also that the classic itself essentially demands of us that we look not backward, but forward, to find it. It is the concentrated image of a whole humanity which we must seek—Sartre's "humanité entière"—and in our time not a classicizing order but a classic awakening. As we commit ourselves to this, classic art regains its meaning for us. It can no longer be viewed from a distance, as merely a moment of balance in a world of eternal flux; nor as a pure creation of the mind; nor as one of two polarities.

Perhaps this may mean that we already are awakening—indeed out of the shadows of that revolution which Shelley envisaged and which has largely come to pass. "Faiths and empires" have gleamed "like wrecks of a dissolving dream." Perhaps the Athens we see now, as we view it across the battered early-morning suburbs of our souls, is in fact a new city, perceived through the fresh eyes of astounded barbarians. And if we, no less than earlier ages, make our own myth of the classic, we at least know now that it deals with thought and sensation, with a keenly lived present, a challenged future, and a liberated memory: creating forms of permanent humanity out of the utter impermanence of the human situation but blazing, not gently, with the hope and ardor of searching men. They seek nothing less than the whole.

NEIL LEVINE

"Frank Lloyd Wright and Twentieth-Century Style." In *Problems of the Nineteenth and Twentieth Centuries*. Vol. 4 of *Studies in Western Art: Acts of the Twentieth International Congress of the History of Art*. Princeton: Princeton University Press, 1963 (originally unillustrated).

The title of this essay, which comes from a lecture given in the fall of 1961 at the Twentieth International Congress of the History of Art, is somewhat opaque, even misleading. It gives little indication of the main argument of the text, which proposes a radically abstract reading of the history of twentieth-century architecture in terms of the symbolism of space and, through that, a dialectical evolution in which Frank Lloyd Wright states the initial thesis and opens the first cycle while Louis Kahn responds to the waning force of the International Style with a new synthesis paralleling Wright's. A condensed version of the essay—published in *Arts* magazine in March 1962 on the occasion of the opening of the major exhibition of Wright drawings organized by Arthur Drexler at New York's Museum of Modern Art—was more transparently entitled "Wright, International Style, and Kahn."

Scully's fascination with Wright culminated in the publication of a monograph on him in 1960, the year after Wright died. With the critical world still in the process of evaluating Wright's legacy, Henry-Russell Hitchcock, dean of Wright scholars, chose "Frank Lloyd Wright and Architecture around 1900" as the subject of the session he chaired at the International Congress held the following year in New York. All the participants other than Scully spoke about Wright's contemporaries and limited their remarks to the period in question: H. Allen Brooks dealt with the Prairie School; Stephen Jacobs with the California scene; Carroll Meeks with the East Coast; G. C. Argan with Italy; and John Summerson with Great Britain. Scully's talk served, in Hitchcock's words, as the "keynote of the session" by setting

6

Frank Lloyd Wright and Twentieth-Century Style

VINCENT SCULLY

Some years ago a student asked Frank Lloyd Wright how he could make his own work wholly original. Wright replied, in effect, "You can't. I invented a new architecture . . . about 1900, and all you can do is learn its principles and work with them." At the time, this answer seemed to me to be one of unparalleled, if delightful, arrogance. Now I am not so sure that it was far from being the simple truth. And the period of Wright's work upon which the scholar must concentrate, in order to seek out that truth, is the period cited by Wright himself, that which spanned the two centuries and came to a close at about the fateful date of 1914.

In this distinguished company I make no pretense of being prepared to produce fresh data about Wright. Nor can all the many qualities of his work be discussed or illustrated here. Instead, despite the risk of repeating what I, or others, have written elsewhere, I should like to present a thesis for argument, developed as follows: first, that Wright not only created a style of architecture but also, through his long life span, carried that style through all its possible phases; second, that Wright's early work, of the period noted

forth Wright's work of the Oak Park years as the foundation for the subsequent development of modern architecture as a whole. In this, Scully mainly followed the argument already laid out in "Wright vs. the International Style" (see chap. 2). A significant difference, however, lies in the isolation of the formal elements of structure and space as the fundamental principles in Wright's creation of a modern style untainted by eclecticism. And where the full integration of these two principles in Wright's early architecture was upset by a focus on the continuity of space in the International Style as well as in his own work indebted to it, the revival of a concern for structural integrity in concert with Louis Kahn's novel conception of spatial modulation is now put forth as the basis for a new cycle of developments.

It was an extremely bold, not to say perceptive, move to single out Kahn as the Brunelleschi of the second half of the twentieth century. His first important building, the Yale University Art Gallery, had been finished only eight years before, while the Unitarian Church in Rochester was still in construction and plans for the Salk Institute at La Jolla were just being developed. Scully, who met and befriended Kahn as early as 1947 when the latter began a ten-year teaching stint at Yale, was the first art historian to discuss his work in print ("Archetype and Order in Recent American Architecture," 1954; see chap. 3). Reyner Banham referred to it the following year in his article "The New Brutalism" in *Architectural Review*, and more relevantly, perhaps, Hitchcock himself wrote a piece for the Italian journal *Zodiac* in 1960 comparing the recent work of Wright and Kahn. But it was

above, was more solely his own than the work of the later periods normally was, and more fully embodied a balance between his two major principles of design than the later work usually did; third, that out of one of those principles the International Style of the following decades took form, and out of another the new architecture of the second half of the century—the architecture which may succeed that of Wright—would now seem to be making its beginning.

This thesis as a whole implies that Wright's work indeed had two major separable aspects and sought two distinct objectives which he himself was able to merge only when at his most complete. Both these objectives were built into Wright's life by the circumstances of his birth. One was the creation of building form through a totally integrated structural system; the other was the creation of spaces which were, in his own term, "continuous." The first objective derived from the Gothic Revival theory of the middle of the nineteenth century, and into the Gothic Revival Wright was, literally, born. As we all know, his mother determined before his birth in 1869 that he should be an architect and, to that end, hung nineteenth-century engravings of English cathedrals in the room she had prepared for him. Her impulse may be taken to have been picturesque, transcendental, possibly partly Ruskinian in tone. Some of these attitudes were to cling to Wright all his life, and he read Ruskin later. But, as he himself tells us, the book that most affected him

only with the exhibition of the University of Pennsylvania's Richards Medical Research Building at the Museum of Modern Art in 1961 that more serious attention began to be given to Kahn's work. Scully's monograph *Louis I. Kahn* (1962), for a long time the only book on the architect, was written soon after the paper reprinted here was delivered and incorporates its dialectical thesis.

One can read "Frank Lloyd Wright and Twentieth-Century Style" as a legitimation of Kahn; one can also read it as a vindication of Wright. In either case Scully establishes, by what he calls the "familial" relationship of descendance, a purely American origin for the two major phases that he outlines in the development of modern architecture. The later work of Mies van der Rohe is disregarded, while the postwar efforts of Le Corbusier, representing the continuing Hellenic tradition of active sculptural form, are referred to only in passing and given no teleological power. The thoroughly nationalist account of history is played off against, and supported by, the radical abstraction of the principles of modern architectural history. Echoing to some degree Sigfried Giedion's idea of the successive dominance of different "space-conceptions," and sharing Suzanne Langer's interpretation of the expressive nature of art as cultural "symbol," Scully proposes that the work of both Wright and Kahn embodies the "fundamental spatial symbol" of its time and thus expresses, through the structurally integral environment it creates, the modern, and particularly American, urge to find permanence in a world of change. The ongoing contest between "environment" and "act" in Scully's thought here clearly favors the former and, with that, a preference for a kind of traditional monumentality at odds with typical modernist practices.

and which, in his own words, "was the only really sensible book on architecture in the world," was Viollet-le-Duc's *Dictionnaire raisonné*. Here the attitude was a tough and mechanistic one, expressive of nineteenth-century positivism and scientism and insisting that the forms of Gothic architecture derived purely from the logical demands of its skeletal structural system. In this way the later nineteenth century was able to see Gothic architecture according to its own pragmatic and materialistic image of reality and to embody such, as Banham has otherwise shown, in its own architectural theory.[1]

But Wright was also born into another engrossing nineteenth-century attitude, one which achieved its greatest symbolic force in America. This was the sense of continuous expansion, of the endless opening up of the environment. The print of 1868 by Palmer and Ives, comprehensively entitled *Across the Continent: "Westward the Course of Empire Makes Its Way,"* makes this point. All was to flow on endlessly, boundlessly, in the unity that comes with flow. Physical space, biological evolution, and the democratic future were alike regarded in terms of such unified progress forward.

Here, then, were two concepts, structural and spatial, and both directly expressive of the major goals and symbols of their time. Wright was to set himself the task of integrating the two through the chemistry of his art, and of weaving them into single organisms at once unified and serene. Before his birth and in his childhood the way was

already being prepared for him. During the midcentury the American Stick Style, carried
by the Pattern Books which began with those of Andrew Jackson Downing, had attempted 1.2
to apply Gothic Revival principles of structural expression to American domestic programs and wood frame techniques. And Wright tells us that when, as a beginning
architect, he first settled in Oak Park in 1887, it was not the new houses but Mr. Austin's
"old barn vertically boarded and battened," that he loved. But by this time, when he himself was about to build, the other image, that of spatial continuity, had become dominant
in American work. It had begun in England during the sixties, with Richard Norman
Shaw's tile-hung "old English" houses planned around living halls, and later in the
United States to be associated with American colonial work and called Queen Anne. This
mode was introduced into America by Henry Hobson Richardson in his shingled Watts 1.4
Sherman House of 1874, where the horizontal continuity of the surface, expressive of
the new continuities of interior space, was made even more decisive. By the mid-eighties
such spatial continuity reached a point in America never approached by the English
houses. Wilson Eyre's Ashurst House of 1885, with its horizontally extended and open 1.13
interior, its projecting porches, and its bands of windows, is an excellent example. By
1886, another architect of this Shingle Style, Bruce Price, had organized the new open 1.14, 1.15
interior space into that cross-axial type which had been popular in North America since
Jefferson's time; and Wright's own house in Oak Park, of 1889, was closely derived from 1.16
the houses of Price, although the cross-axial plan was not yet employed in it. Around 1.17
1900, however, when Wright came into his first maturity, as in the Ward Willits House, he 1.28, 2.4
used Price's cross-axis to create a set of horizontal continuities which recall those of Eyre
but are infinitely more decisive and are extended with low-ceilinged compulsiveness.
Indeed, the house as a whole seems to have passed beyond the underlying picturesque
eclecticism of the Shingle Style into a new style that is entirely its own. It is true, as many
critics have pointed out, that other sources of inspiration can be seen here, such as
the Japanese Ho-o-den at the World's Fair of 1893. The stripping, the cross-axis, and
the projecting roofs are common to both, but Wright has so woven together the structural
and cladding elements, reminiscent of those of the Stick Style, that the building
fabric as a whole is now completely in accord with the continuously expanding spaces
it defines.

With these wooden houses of the beginning of the century, therefore, Wright's
integration of continuous space with frame structure was already complete. Instantly, in
1902, he turned to the same problem in masonry, where his image of continuity could be
given permanent, monumental form. Here I must apologize for recalling a sequence of
development that is familiar to us all, but the need to do so will, I hope, be apparent at the
end of this talk. In the Heurtley House the direct influence of Richardson's eminently per- 11.4
manent masonry can be felt, as from the Glessner House in Chicago, which Wright knew 11.3
at first hand, or from the Quincy Library, which was well published. But Wright divides
Richardson's engrossing shell, with its volumetric gable roof, into separate planes, across
which the wooden spanning elements stretch with the running continuity of bridges.
Spatial movement and sculptural mass were in this sense combined. Immediately, having

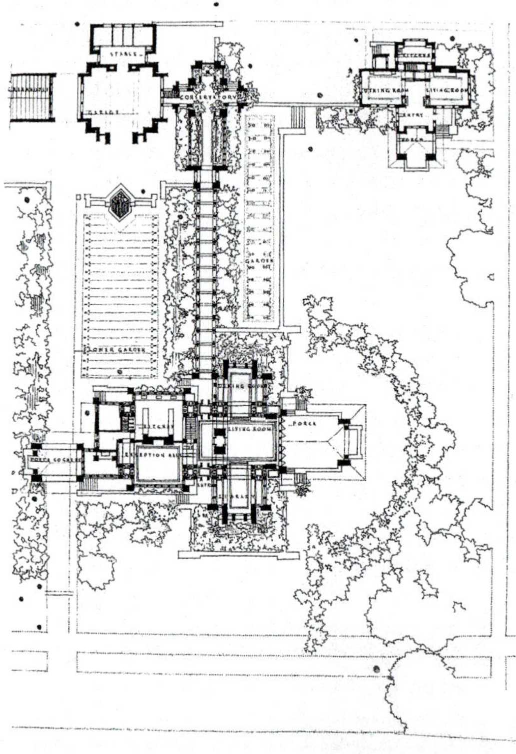

ABOVE, LEFT: Frank Lloyd Wright. Hillside Home School addition, Hillside, Wisconsin, 1902–3. Exterior 6.1

ABOVE, RIGHT: Frank Lloyd Wright. Martin House, Buffalo, 1903–4. Plan 6.2

developed his masonry as plane, Wright turned to masonry as pier. Perceiving the vertical
demands of such, he also sensed the volumetric bay which the pier somehow wants to
6.1 bound. So, in the Hillside Home School, also of 1902, the four piers support a symmetrically placed hip roof, defining a volume of space which is fundamentally static but which
is brought into the cross-axes of spatial expansion through projected window bays and
cantilevered ceiling planes.

1.23, 6.2 In 1904 a further step was taken in the Martin House, where the piers were
exploited to the full as space definers, marching outward in companies to form the major
spaces and, where the axes cross, grouping in fours to create smaller service spaces for
heating and lighting equipment. Thus the unification of spatial desires with structural
and mechanical demands is so complete that the house approaches the integration of a
working machine. The only exception to this is the widely overhanging roof, where the
desire for horizontal spatial extension causes steel beams to be concealed in the wooden
structure and so introduces an element lacking the inner structural rationale of the other
11.10, 11.15 forms. But in the Larkin Building—also of 1904 and now tragically demolished—the
spatial continuity was contained by the building fabric, and the integration of space with
structure was complete. Concrete beams supported brick parapets, threaded horizontally through the vertically continuous piers, and capped them above. The whole was a
tensile unity in which major and minor volumes were structurally formed through the
bay system into an industrial cathedral that should have delighted Viollet-le-Duc.

6.3 Adler and Sullivan. Wainwright Building, St. Louis, 1890–91. Exterior

The mechanics never faltered. The thickness of the piers received the filing cabinets; vertical circulation was clearly separated into corner towers, and all these major, minor, and service spaces worked together to create the building's exterior form. The only captious elements, the globes and putti, seem related to European developments of the period, as perhaps to Olbrich's Secession Building in Vienna, of 1898–99, whose 11.13
Romantic-Classic, geometric severity Wright's building also shared.

Yet it is clear that this industrial form could not have been built as it was without the example of Louis Sullivan, and its vertical piers and interwoven horizontal spandrels recall those of Sullivan's first great skyscraper, the Wainwright Building of 6.3
1890–91. Wright has recorded his emotion when Sullivan laid the first sketches for the Wainwright Building on his drawing board. But Wright himself was attempting something fundamentally different from the master's work. Sullivan's building was integrated facade design, at most a schematic description of the character of the spaces it contained, but Wright's was an integral embodiment of those spaces. Sullivan's building was conceived as a standing body, with a base, a middle, and an end, and can therefore be described, as Sullivan described it, in terms of the classic column. But Wright's solids, though supremely strong, expressed the volume of space they defined. Thus the exterior of his building was that of a container of spaces and is to be read not as a column but as a galleried cavern.

This difference, which I have discussed elsewhere, is important because of the fundamental polarity in attitude it reveals. When Sullivan looked at Richardson's work, as for example at the Marshall Field Warehouse, of 1885, he saw it not in terms of spatial definition, but in anthropomorphic and humanistic terms with which Wright had nothing to do. So, in his *Kindergarten Chats*, Sullivan wrote of this building, "Here is a man for you to look at. A man that walks on two legs instead of four, has active muscles . . . lives
4.3 and breathes . . . in a world of barren pettiness, a male."[2] Therefore, in his own Guaranty Building of 1895, designed after Wright had left the office, Sullivan developed Richardson's forms further in terms of skeletal skyscraper construction and caused the building truly to stand upon its legs, stretch, and stir. In these ways it became primarily the expression of a physical presence rather than of a spatial environment. Indeed, the Guaranty Building, with its doubled piers and its calculated drama of compression and tension, purposely overrode its description of its space and structure in favor of the sculptural unity of its body. Such intentions have ultimately Hellenic rather than medieval backgrounds; they seem related to the Greek rather than the medieval revival of the early nineteenth century and, in part, to the general classicizing reaction of its close. They have become central to some mid-twentieth-century architecture other than Wright's. So the late skyscrapers of Mies van der Rohe stand upon exposed columns and multiply their vertical mullions in order to achieve bodily unity in terms which, though now rather frozen, are still Sullivan's figural rather than spatial ones. More forcefully, the late buildings of Le Corbusier culminate this modern expression of the human presence and its act. They stand as muscular forces, and mask, where necessary, both their interior spaces and their actual structure in order to appear to be the sculptural embodiments of powers with which men can identify their own.

But Wright's way was the opposite. Perhaps no less sculptural, it yet sought a sculpture that was Constructivist and environmental, rather than figurally active, in
11.14 effect. Unity Temple, of 1906, culminated its integration. Here, as Wright most lucidly describes in his *Autobiography*, square hollow piers, flat planes, crossed beams, and projecting slabs in poured concrete all worked together to create the kinds of space desired, and the building's plastic solids wholly revealed both the shape of those spaces and the structural process whereby they were formed.

If Unity Temple may be regarded as a culmination of Wright's integration, the
11.8, 11.9 Robie House documents his movement beyond it toward a more arbitrary state. Now the desire for continuous space most movingly dominates the fabric. The heavy masses of brick are lifted by that compulsion, and the steel-concealing, low-hipped roofs take wing. In that sense the solids burst apart, like—as so many critics have pointed out—those of contemporary Cubist painting. At the same time, the Robie House, designed as if in exaltation, sums up several hundred years of American imagery. The containing, protective box of colonial architecture, which had exerted considerable influence upon the architects of the Shingle Style and thus upon Wright himself, now splits around the central fireplace mass and embodies to the full the nineteenth-century feeling for spatial expansion and flight.

With this house Wright summed up his earlier intentions and burst their boundaries. Its completion in 1909 coincided with a decisive break in his own personal life. Thereafter he had no fixed place in the American nineteenth-century suburban culture—and especially middle-western suburban culture—that had nourished him. Indeed that culture itself, as a creative milieu, began to break up by the time of World War I. The reasons for this are still in dispute and cannot be developed here, but the fact remains that the middle-western suburb had been prepared to support the idealistic radicalism of its architects: it then became, and has generally remained, carefully conservative. It is as if Wright, having lost his functional place—and never again to have around him so mature and productive a group of followers, associates, and sympathetic but free and equal critics as the other architects of the Prairie School had been—was now forced to seek out only the most grandly personal and mythic of objectives. So, at the Midway Gardens of 1914 12.32
he forced his earlier forms into vast spatial continuities, like those of some nineteenth-century American landscapes, where the solid shapes, however symmetrically framed, are eaten through by space and slide forward and out continuously under the empty sky.

After 1914, now personally involved in the tragic flux of American culture and totally uprooted from his past, Wright seems to have felt a need to begin again upon cultural foundations more wholly permanent. His overt dependence upon precedent, here on Maya forms, became much more marked than it had been in any of the work done between 1900 and 1914. A wish for overwhelmingly stable mass dominates, spatially appropriate perhaps in the A. D. German Warehouse of 1915, less so in the Barnsdall House of 1920. There, too, the desire for structural integrity was entirely given up in order to achieve the Maya mansarded roof profile in lath and plaster. And even when, in his splendid block houses of the twenties and his inspired 1929 project for St. Mark's Tower, Wright achieved once again a complete integration of structure and space, the Mayoid inspiration was still seen as much to the fore.

Yet, through these decades so difficult for him, the influence of Wright's work had acted more strongly than any other single force to give form to the new architecture of modern Europe, and the special way it had acted is of critical importance. Wright's work had become generally known through the great Wasmuth publications in 1910 and 1911. From such publications Berlage, whose Amsterdam Bourse of 1903 had also been a brick structure with an enclosed court, saw the Larkin Building as an eminently machine architecture, as Banham has shown. We may assume that Berlage understood, in other words, its complete integration of function and structure. The formal influence of Wright upon other Dutch architects and upon Gropius in the teens need not be discussed here. But the Dutch De Stijl group of the late teens and early twenties, whose members also admired Wright, must be considered. This group appears to have seen Wright's work not in terms of integration but through its own predilections for line and plane, classicizing severity, and the abstract manipulation of space. This is important because it was clearly through De Stijl that the International Style of the twenties found its characteristic shapes. The process, whatever it also owed to both Cubism and Futurism, can be traced almost step by step from the illustrations in Wasmuth. If we take a photograph of

2.8 the side of the Ward Willits House from the 1911 volume and concentrate upon the running, asymmetrical pattern of dark stripping, we can derive from it a painting by van
6.4 Doesburg of 1918. Ignoring the lines and focusing upon the advanced and recessed masses, we arrive at a construction, a Constructivist sculpture, by Vantongerloo, of 1919. Hollowing out the masses and seeing the surfaces as thin, sharp-edged planes defining volumes of space, we approach a house project by van Doesburg, of 1922. Finally, stretching the whole out once more into an asymmetrical organization of inter-
8.11 locked, thin-surfaced boxes, we come to Gropius's Bauhaus of 1925–26, and to the full International Style. The bounding solids are now merely planes which exist to define volumes. There is no structural mass and no question of structural and spatial integration; in fact the space definers and the supporting members are normally kept separate, one from the other. The relation to the machine, which was of persistent importance in European theory, and of which Banham has brilliantly made so much, is now not, as in the Larkin Building, primarily in how the building functions as a working machine, but how, industrially glazed and brightly stuccoed, it looks.

The fullest understanding of Wright's continuity of space was shown during the
6.5 twenties by Mies van der Rohe, as a comparison between a plan of 1906 by Wright and
2.3, 2.5 one of 1923 by Mies clearly shows. And Mies's Barcelona Pavilion of 1929, itself a piece of Constructivist sculpture, is a synthesis between Wright's fluid, American planning, as reinterpreted by De Stijl, and the classicizing containment that was also desired by European sensibility. At the same time the planes are everywhere detached from the structural columns and therefore act purely as arbitrary space definers. Such separation is to be contrasted with the integration of space and structure in a somewhat similar
2.6 project by Wright, the Yahara Boat Club, of 1902, published by Wasmuth in 1910. If, however, we step forward instead of back in Wright's work, we find that the influence of Mies and, very secondarily, of other European architects of the International Style, has, by the thirties, come to exert a direct and indeed regenerating influence upon Wright's

ABOVE: Theo van Doesburg. *Rhythm of a Russian Dance,* 1918 6.4

BELOW: Frank Lloyd Wright. Gerts House project, Glencoe, Illinois, 1906. Plan 6.5

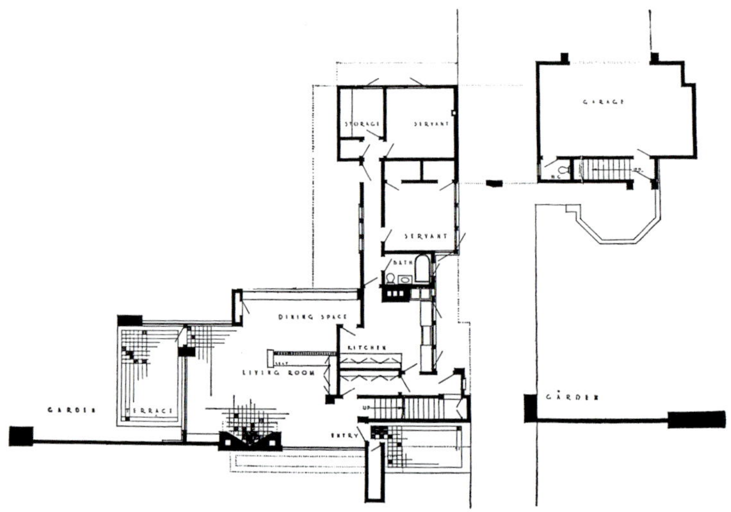

own design. The *parti* of the entrance side of the Goetsch-Winckler House of 1939, for 4.6
example, shows the relationship very clearly. Wright's earlier influence upon Europe now
bore fruit for him, but, as indicated, a certain metamorphosis had taken place in the
process. Now, for example, Wright creates his space almost entirely by flat planes rather
than by an interwoven skeletal fabric. In wood in the Usonian Houses (though steel
flitches were often inserted between their joists) and in reinforced concrete in such
a great masterpiece as the Kaufmann House, Wright found various ways to make those 2.11
planes structural, but the dominance of International Style intentions seems clear.
So the Kaufmann House, though creating a splendidly complex and serene spatial
ambient, and being itself a structure of much daring, is also a kind of mature Constructivist sculpture, recalling types developed by the Europeans out of Wright's earlier work.

Finally, when he attempted to escape from the International Style through the
continuously curvilinear forms of his last decades—which themselves (like those of the
Johnson Wax Building) reveal other immediate sources of inspiration that need not con- 11.18
cern us here—Wright often manipulated the solids, whether as walls or columns, so that
all structural demands and expressions were, visually, denied by them and it was truly, in
his own words, "space, not matter," that became the reality. Similarly, it is clear, as the
researches of Folds have shown, that Wright was never entirely sure how the continuous
spiral of the Guggenheim Museum was to be constructed, so that, in the final version, the
vertical piers, which do much of the actual work, are in conflict with the helical conception
of the space, and injure it. All this sharply contrasts with the balance between solid and
void in the similarly top-lighted and galleried Larkin Building, where the members, fully
creating the space and expressive of it, were structurally convincing as well.

Wright may therefore be said to have pushed his style to its ultimate, space-dominant, solid-denying phase—to what may perhaps be referred to as its late baroque phase. That is to say, if Brunelleschi stated a clear principle of the relation of solid to void, and of structure to space, and Alberti and others developed the system into a balance between mass and space, in which solid and void were sculpturally interdependent, so the Late Baroque may be said to have dissolved the solids in favor of the space, bending them entirely to the service of the total environment they created. If a similar course can be traced in Wright, it can also be perceived in the International Style as a whole. Because that style had begun, by Wright's last years, to exhibit characteristics that were almost rococo. The lacy fragmentation of mass in Yamasaki's recent work is one example among many, while Stone's fluttery elegance in his project for a National Cultural Center is even more striking. Many recent Russian works, most of them apparently inspired by Stone, show the same characteristics. So Stone's project of 1961 closely resembles one of the schemes submitted in the new competition for a Palace of the Soviets, of 1959, which in turn seems to have taken as its point of departure Stone's American Pavilion at Brussels, of the year before. The new rococo is thus strikingly international.

If, therefore, the International Style saw Wright purely in terms of defined space, and if it and he seem to have reached concluding phases together, we are compelled to ask how the fresh architecture of the second half of the century is to take shape. Where is it to begin? That question is significant for this paper because the answer would appear to be that the new architecture is now beginning not where Wright ended but where Wright began, and, as indicated earlier, is apparently developing according to one of his principles, the structural one. Several names might be associated with this movement, but the one which most architects would, I think, now advance as essential is that of Louis I. Kahn, and it is Kahn whose influence upon architectural students, at least in the United States, is presently greater than that of any other architect. This is not the place to describe Kahn's unusual career or to analyze his theory and design in detail. I should only like to point out that, from about 1955 to the present, his development has paralleled that of Wright between 1902 and 1906 in almost every significant detail. I do not say that this relation to Wright was necessarily conscious on Kahn's part; indeed, the fact that it was probably unconscious makes it doubly significant. Clearly enough it has followed a course laid down in Kahn's own theory, which is itself ultimately based upon Viollet-le-Duc and Choisy: functional ("What," as Kahn puts it, "does the building want to be?"); integrational, as he insists, like Wright, that architecture is the "making of spaces" and that those spaces should be defined by structure. At the same time, considerable influence from some of Le Corbusier's later buildings in brick and concrete, such as the Maisons Jaoul, has obviously played an important part.

Yet the parallel with Wright seems central, since Kahn's fully mature projects
6.6 can be said to have begun with his archaic Trenton Bathhouse of 1955. Here hollow
piers support hipped roofs to create structurally conceived bays of space which closely
6.7 recall Wright's Hillside Home School, of 1902. To go further, the plan of the bathhouse

Louis I. Kahn. Bathhouse, Trenton Jewish Community Center, Trenton, New Jersey, 1955. Interior 6.6

6.7 RIGHT: Louis I. Kahn. Bathhouse. Plan

6.8 BELOW: Louis I. Kahn. Community Building project, Trenton Jewish Community Center, 1956–58. Model

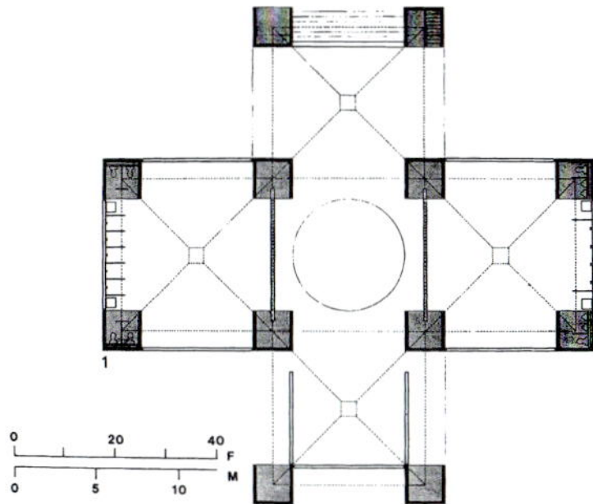

is cross-axial, defined by the piers. In this it of course strikingly recalls Wright's work, like the plan of the Gale House of 1902. But here a difference is apparent. Wright's squares interlock, and the axes penetrate each other, creating the kind of continuously
fluid space that was so expansively extended in the Ward Willits plan. Kahn's spaces are 2.4
not continuous, but separate. The squares do not interlock; each volume has its own roof cap with oculus, and in the central unroofed square the opposite geometric shape, a circle, is inscribed. The Kahn plan is thus intended to be static and fixed; Vitruvian and Renaissance conceptions, and indeed the cubes and spheres of Brunelleschi, are recalled. Where, however, Brunelleschi could define his spatial areas with slender, solid columns, Kahn's piers are hollow, containing those services which are essential to most modern buildings and which, therefore, Kahn now integrates into the structural and spatial concept as a whole. We have, of course, seen this before and in exactly this
sequence. Wright's Martin plan, of 1904, with its grouped columns containing heating 6.2
and lighting elements, comes to mind, as do the hollow piers of Unity Temple. So, too, in 11.16
sequence, comes Kahn's project for the Trenton Community Center as a whole, now 6.8
recalling the columnar groupings of the Martin House and making both major and service spaces with them. But again Kahn caps each bay with its own precast, hipped roof, even where the demands of the spaces below require that the column system be interrupted. In this way Kahn again rejects the nineteenth-century image of expansive continuity in favor of the separateness of parts, but, as with Wright, it is the structure that makes the space and the two together which produce a convincingly fresh and powerful form.

The same holds true in Kahn's Medical Research Laboratories for the University 17.12
of Pennsylvania, completed in 1960, when the next step in the sequence, that to the

11.10 Larkin Building, is taken. Again, vertical service towers, clad in brick, house stairways and, here, ventilating ducts, while the floor levels are defined by horizontal spandrels plaited, as by Wright, through vertical piers. At the same time, Kahn's cantilevering of the floor levels off exposed columns recalls the system used in the Philadelphia Savings Fund Society Building of 1930–32, designed by George Howe, later one of Kahn's closest associates and mentors, and William Lescaze, while the stepped diminution of the cantilevered precast trusses was prefigured in the similar beam treatment of one of the buildings in Richard Neutra's Rush City Reformed Project of the twenties. Now, however, Kahn makes the space through an interweaving of the toughly scaled armature of the reinforced concrete skeleton, as Wright had done, but the space itself differs once more. The functions are surely less integrated with the structure—here in Kahn a cross-axial structure—than Wright's admittedly simpler program permitted, but there is a difference of intention as well. Wright's spaces pull the observer in, enclose, release, soothe him, drawing all finally together into an expansive harmony; but Kahn's spaces are exposed, pushed out by the structural members, not sequential but fundamentally separate, while the scheme of the complex as a whole avoids Wright's embracing envelope to insist upon the separateness of each structurally conceived, eight-columned tower.

The larger differences between Wright and Kahn can now be determined. Wright develops fluid spatial sequences, Kahn units of space. Wright will, if choice be necessary, override the structure in favor of the space; Kahn, if necessary, the space in favor of the structure. Wright emphasizes the continuous plastic unity of parts, Kahn their jointed separateness. Wright insists upon the expansiveness and serenity of the environment, Kahn upon its pressures, difficulties, and demands. Both earnestly attempt to balance human desires against the intrinsic physical requirements of the thing made. Wright will normally, and with lyric fervor, opt for the former; Kahn, with a kind of tragic intensity, for the latter. The first set of attitudes adds up to a late-nineteenth-century view of human possibility, the second to a mid-twentieth-century perception of human fate. So each of these buildings belongs to the best thought of its own generation, but that they also belong to the same family is clear. And it seems most important for the future of American architecture that the relationship should be a familial one, because Kahn, for the first time among those Americans whose work has consistently recalled Wright's, seems not a follower but a descendant.

Their mutual sequence is by no means concluded. Kahn's project of 1960–61
17.13–16, for the First Unitarian Church in Rochester recalls Wright's Unity Temple of 1906. Their
11.14, 11.17 exteriors are strongly fortified masses, lighted primarily from above and expressive of the deeply enclosed volumes they contain. Kahn, however, avoids Wright's projected roof slabs, expressive of spatial interlocking and horizontal continuities. So, too, a plan for church and school resembling Wright's was considered but rejected by Kahn on spatial and functional grounds. And again, though in the final plan the units are brought into a closer grouping by Kahn, they still retain their spatial, structural, and formal separateness and discontinuity, and are not woven into interlocking echoes of each other as Wright, with his concern for rhythmic unity, has them. At the same time, a system of

precast bent slabs, supported on crossed beams, forms Kahn's top-lighted roof, and recalls in this way Wright's system in the temple.

The church at Rochester is now under construction, and many other projects by Kahn are developing the creative sequence further. Some, like that for the Salk Center in California, seem to show evidence of influences from sources that were also important to Wright in his later years. What this may foretell cannot be determined at present. (It is discussed in detail in my recent book on Kahn.)

It is now apparent, however, that a family of principle, of complicated ancestry but brought to form by Wright, produced, comparatively late in his own life, a new champion, who may, perhaps most significantly, be creating another indigenously American school. The forms of that family rise across the general picturesque eclecticism of much of the century and indeed across the International Style of the intervening years. The two generations differ in the fundamental spatial symbol to which each adheres, but they are alike in the governing desire for spatial and structural integration that binds them. Each, though considerably more concerned with the mechanics of function than the International Style usually was, still belongs to the tenacious Western tradition of solid, monumental building in common materials, as the International Style had not always seemed to do. Their specific ancestry lies in that large segment of Western experience which has been primarily concerned with the construction of interior spaces. Their opposite, equally important today, is eventually Hellenic in ancestry, and seeks, with subjective idealism, to embody the human act in architectural form. They, however, seek to image not the human body but the objectively realistic force of the settings constructed for it.

There is clearly room and need for both symbols in the modern world, and indeed both have been sought by it in one way or another since its beginnings. Wright's and Kahn's principle, whatever its backgrounds, has been especially sympathetic to Americans, since, under the prod of anarchic change, it passionately insists upon the need to produce a permanent environment that shall be abstractly moral, insofar as it embodies fixed principle and law. Ironically enough, the fluid instability of modern times destroyed Wright's building. But it now comes to life once more through the revival of an intention that was most succinctly stated by its builder many years ago, when he wrote, "Above all, integrity."[3]

Notes

1. Reyner Banham, *Theory and Design in the First Machine Age* (New York, 1960).
2. Louis Henry Sullivan, *Kindergarten Chats* (Lawrence, Kans., 1934).
3. Since this talk was intended to reappraise and realign material already well known, it is presented here as given, without footnotes.

NEIL LEVINE

"The Death of the Street." *Perspecta: The Yale Architectural Journal* 8 (1963): 91–96.

Although the outcome of the "battle for modern architecture" was a foregone conclusion by the late 1940s, examples of victory in the daily life of the American city were few and far between until Park Avenue, in New York, began to feel the pressures of commercial real-estate development. Within a decade, Skidmore, Owings and Merrill's Lever House (1951–52) and Union Carbide Building (1957–60), Mies van der Rohe's Seagram Building (1954–58), and Walter Gropius, Pietro Belluschi, and Emery Roth's Pan Am Building (1958–63), along with a number of speculative office towers, had changed the visible face of Manhattan's most dignified, boulevard-like street. While many architects and critics simply focused on the relative quality of the buildings themselves, others were quick to perceive the larger urban issues at stake. Scully was one of the most urgent and articulate to enter the fray.

In the fall of 1961, while the controversial Pan Am Building was beginning to be built, the Architectural League of New York and the Museum of Modern Art jointly organized a series of forums called "The Building Boom—Architecture in Decline," moderated by Peter Blake, editor of *Architectural Forum*. The first of these was, significantly, "The Transformation of Park Avenue." Scully was asked to be the lead-off speaker (he was followed by Richard Roth, a principal of Emery Roth and Sons, and James Felt, chairman of the New York City Planning Commission). Scully's talk, entitled "The Death of a Street," was, in the words of one reporter, "a moving analysis of the nature of Park Avenue's grandeur" and a scathing critique of the buildings now destroying it. It was Scully's first public engagement

7

The Death of the Street

VINCENT SCULLY

I should like to start with a word about how Park Avenue got to be what it once was. It and the surrounding blocks at its southern end were once a great hole in the ground that stretched as far as 59th Street, filled with acres of railroad tracks and steam engines belching smoke. This expressive but perhaps rather satanic urban feature was finally filled in when Reed and Stem built the new Grand Central Station at the beginning of this century. The blocks were then built up and a new avenue, the present one, left open between them. But the width of this avenue was in function with its length, so that it never seemed overly wide. Instead, its long axis always had a kind of velocity in accord with the scale of the city and its automobile traffic. It came swooping down from the northern highlands with the rush of a great river, until it branched around Grand Central in the channels Reed and Stem had imagined for it. Like a river, it could move with that velocity because it was contained by banks or, like a rapids, by walls. These were formed by the buildings which defined it on both sides. Perhaps no one of them (with the possible exception of McKim, Mead and White's Racquet Club) was overly distinguished itself, but they all had two things in common: they were built side by side in one plane,

with the issue of urbanism and his first statement of the idea of what would come to be called contextualism.

When the talk was revised for publication in *Perspecta* a little over a year later, the substitution of the definite for the indefinite article in the title signaled Scully's desire to broaden the focus from the specific concern for *a* street to a general one for the fate of *the* street. This also highlighted the parodistic reference to Le Corbusier's prediction in 1929 that, with the advent of modern architecture and city planning, "the street as we know it will cease to exist." Where Le Corbusier decried the traditional street, bounded by the continuous masonry facades of buildings, as a "joyless," "murky canyon" that oppresses and constricts the individual, proposing in its stead glass-clad skyscrapers set in wide green plazas, Scully defends the solid, space-defining character of Park Avenue's eclectic architecture as providing a "civil" framework for urban life. The Avenue receives praise for its containment of movement, its axial focus, and its coherent shape, all ideas that depend more on Beaux-Arts than on modernist principles of urban design and ones that Scully certainly owed in part to discussions over the years with Louis Kahn, Paul Rudolph, and Philip Johnson. Though he was fully aware of the uncompromising traditionalism championed since the early 1950s by Henry Hope Reed and Yale's own Christopher Tunnard, there is no evidence that Scully was influenced by their reactionary point of view.

"The Death of the Street" is both a lament and a plea, marking a decisive moment in the questioning of modernism with the profound ambiguity of anxiety. The modernist glass skyscraper is seen as a blind destructive force eroding the very street fabric it needs as a foil for its own individual and commercial ends. The self-centered display of power offers no pattern for social activity to match what it has undermined and displaced. And although Scully expresses a certain wistfulness about the disappearance of the Park Avenue of the 1920s ("too bad it all had to happen there"), there is no sentimental call for remaking the street in that earlier image. Instead, he appeals to the architect to think outside, and beyond, the Corbusian paradigm of modernist urbanism while at the same time relying on the forms and principles of modernist architecture. The separation of the historical models of modernist architecture and urbanism outlined here in this initial attempt by Scully to come to terms with the urban problematic would have profound repercussions in the development of critical thought on the subject over the coming two decades.

most of them contiguous, and they had solid, opaque facades, pierced by windows but sustaining the barrier plane. They were also high enough to control the street's width, but not generally so high as to deny it. Therefore, they were true walls for the street; they defined and directed its flow. At the same time, they were all fairly weighty and static, with a certain plastic depth and variety of scale, creating appropriate points of subsidiary focus on the river's banks. Thus they did not rush themselves, but allowed the street to do so between them. Though varying in height, they still struck a kind of norm, so that

the Avenue was formed in three dimensions and became a single long space, whose
7.1 shape as a whole can still best be seen from the military crest at 68th Street.

By the twenties, the axis of that space received a visual focus in the tower of Whitney Warren's New York Central Building at the end of the Avenue. This was a vertical point-marker. Though fairly broad, it was not a full barrier, so that the eye went past it at the sides, exactly as the ramps carried traffic around the terminal below. The Avenue's flow was thus enhanced, not blocked, and its continuity beyond Grand Central was underscored.

Such direction of a clearly defined axis toward and beyond a fixed point was of course characteristic of Beaux-Arts planning; but it would be a mistake to call it only Beaux-Arts. Its specific background was in the European Baroque, and its general background lay in all preindustrial architectures, where the defined river of the street, the essential complement to the wide lake of the square, was a fundamental factor in the life of the city. Park Avenue, by covering over its trains, which had up till then never been anything but an urban nightmare, extended that tradition to the era of the motor car and of megalopolitan scale. In so doing, it formed one of the few convincingly imperial avenues in the world.

Park Avenue, New York, looking south from 68th Street, c. 1940 7.1

7.2 Park Avenue, looking northwest from plaza of Seagram Building to Racquet and Tennis Club (left; McKim, Mead and White, 1916–19) and Lever House (right; Skidmore, Owings and Merrill, 1950–52)

Some of the buildings built on it in the following decades did little to sustain that concept of the Avenue, but it was in the 1950s that its lower reaches began to be destroyed. The process got under way with Lever Brothers. When that building was designed, it was hailed as a humane step away from the crowding of the building line characteristic of most large New York buildings. But such crowding may sometimes be essential rather than deplorable and so it had been here. True enough, Lever's attempted to acknowledge the Avenue's direction with its first two floors, which were themselves almost as high as the building it replaced. But in turning its tower and leaving much of its
defined air-space free, it cut a hole in the wall that defined the Avenue. Instead of being 7.2
trapped by a facade which wholly respected the street—like that created by the Racquet Club next door—the eye was now purposefully led out of the Avenue above the second floor to fall upon the undesigned side walls of the buildings on the cross street to the west. So Lever's broke up the street by breaking its facade, and, in so doing, questioned the validity of the concept of the street facade. It is true that, seen against the incoherent masses westward or against the older solid buildings to the north, Lever's was an elegant, pristine object, and might have been considered a special adornment to the Avenue, the

breaking of whose continuity might thus have been condoned. But when the building to the north of it was reclad in a glass and plastic skin imitating Lever's, it became apparent that Lever's itself had owed everything to the preexisting civility of the street. No longer seen against the contrasting solid backdrop which the older buildings had made, Lever's cool cube instantly lost something of its elegance and most of its point.

Much of the same is true of the Seagram Building, perhaps the outstanding monument on the Avenue. Here the original attitude of its architects toward the street seems to have been less ambivalent than had been the case with the designers of Lever House. And since the whole block was now developed, Seagram's could be set behind its own plaza, which opened a decisive cross-axis. The building became a purely freestanding presence, while, by flattening its slab, it attempted to echo the Avenue's north-south direction. But Seagram's, too, owed much to preexisting structures. That is to say, if visual chaos rather than the arches of the Racquet Club had been mirrored in its entrance doors, it would have been a much less successful building itself.

Perhaps, even more than with Lever's, if Seagram's had been allowed to stand alone, its rupture of the street's facade might have been permissible. But it was not allowed to do so, and why should it have been? If it was intended to be a striking monument, we can hardly be surprised that, in the present building boom, other buildings have hastened, thus far never with quite the same success, to emulate it. As they have done so, Seagram's has perhaps not lost in intrinsic quality, but it has disastrously lost its urban point and its setting. That is to say, the aggressive tower which has now risen to the north of it, using similar cladding elements in different materials, does not enhance Seagram's but, itself fluffed up in size and shaky in details, casts visual doubt upon the integrity of the former's dense armature and splendid scale. The two buildings fight each other—to the detriment, again, of the directional unity of the Avenue as a whole and of its coherent definition.

Here another point arises. It has been claimed by some critics that Mies van der Rohe's work is potentially the ideal background architecture of its time. But Seagram's, like most other buildings by Mies, casts doubt upon the correctness of that view. His buildings have never yet succeeded in being backgrounds for anything. They are monumental assertions on their own. They are separate, and, above all, cannot back each other up, as the glass facade of the apartment slab behind Mies's row houses in Detroit all too clearly shows. The monumentality of Mies's buildings arises from their union of a tense skeleton with visual transparency and reflectiveness. If towers, they tend at their best to be bony bodies; if low, tightly stretched containers or airy pavilions. They require, if set in close proximity to other buildings, that the latter be solider, chunkier than they. The best setting a Mies building ever had was the square, defined by solid masses of small, crotchety, *echt* German houses, in which he chose to display the taut glass planes of his skyscraper project of 1920–21.

Seagram's, no less than Lever's, was conceived as a freestanding monument on its own, an aggressive statement of the special talent of its architects, dependent upon the preexisting civil design of the Avenue but taking a step toward its destruction.

Since that time each additional building on the Avenue, even when it keeps to the facade plane, has further shown us that we cannot define a civil space with glass screens and banks of fluorescent fixtures. This seems the fundamental point in its simplest terms: space must in one way or another be defined by solids. This is equally true of exterior urban space, the most important kind of space for the popular life of the city as a whole. Undefined, such space becomes a commercial funfair, appropriate in some places, but not here. It therefore follows that concern for the exteriors of city buildings is hardly a kind of aristocratic frippery, as some architects would apparently like to imply. Instead, it should be obvious that the exterior is such a building's most democratic aspect, since it is the one that all the people of the city use. It creates the architectural space common to them all; and on Park Avenue, in the area under discussion, space no longer exists.

It received its fatal blow from the fat, wide slab of the Pan American Building, 7.3
which now balloons like a cloud beyond Whitney Warren's tower. Unlike that earlier solid point-marker, which allowed the eye to go beyond it at the sides, the new building blocks the view. It visually denies the continuity of the Avenue beyond Grand Central, deprecates the length of the Avenue's axis of movement, and smothers its scale. In any terms other than those of brute expediency it should not be there at all. Bulging grossly above Grand Central, it can only remind us of the Vittorio Emanuele Monument hunching over the Capitoline.

But now that it is there, joining Lever's, Seagram's, and their followers to the north, we should ask ourselves what, in their self-centered aggressiveness, these buildings now portend. That answer is easy to guess; it was given by Le Corbusier many years ago when he described the destiny of the skyscraper as he envisaged it. That is, these buildings portend what he called for: the death of the street, the destruction of the *rue corridor.* "The skyscrapers are too many," Le Corbusier said when he visited New York in the thirties, "and they are too small." And he stated as a general principle that if skyscrapers were to become the basic building-type for the city, and he thought that they should be, they would have to be spaced far apart and the street would have to go.

So, on Park Avenue, the street is going, but not quite as Le Corbusier imagined its passing, since the new skyscrapers are being placed close to each other according to the principle of who owns what lot, not of who should control the entire area, for whose good. The skyscrapers fight each other: their own worst enemies, but the Avenue's most of all.

At the same time, it seems clear that, with a certain juggling, a new pattern can be conceived as emerging from the present wreck of Park Avenue. That pattern could be of some significance for the future. But it was a good street, one of the few splendid ones in America, in its own way noble and unique: too bad it all had to happen there.

The further point must be made that there is nothing intrinsic to the way we build today which demands the present outcome. There is no reason why the street must always be destroyed: there is nothing to prevent us from building solid street-facades of considerable height and defining the axial direction of an avenue. Open courts on a street are not always desirable; far from it. On the other hand, to keep separate things

separate and thus alive, there is no reason why we cannot open up from such streets to frame, as Mies had originally intended, the reflecting prisms of glass towers by solidly defined squares. Nor, conversely, is there any reason why facades largely of glass, if properly designed in some shadowed depth, may not frame spaces in which more massive and actively sculptural buildings may deploy. There should be no reason, finally, why the decisions taken by elected authority cannot be larger ones, disciplining anarchy in order to make the city what it has always been, the ultimate work of human art: making possible the effective action not only of the group but of the individual citizen, so liberating what Sophocles called "the feelings that make the town." The times do not make us, but we the times. To think in smaller or more cynically positivistic terms is neither practical nor realistic.

7.3 Park Avenue, looking south from 50th Street to New York Central Building (Warren and Wetmore, 1929) with Pan Am Building (Walter Gropius, Pietro Belluschi, and Emery Roth and Sons, 1958–63) behind it

NEIL LEVINE

"Doldrums in the Suburbs." *Journal of the Society of Architectural Historians* 24 (March 1965): 36–47.

As the heroic period of modern architecture appeared to be coming to a close in the early 1960s, Henry-Russell Hitchcock organized a series of three symposia devoted to a broad reconsideration of the history of the movement prior to World War II. The first of these was "Frank Lloyd Wright and Architecture around 1900," held at the Twentieth International Congress of the History of Art (see chap. 6). The following two, sponsored by Columbia University, were each devoted to a single decade—the one in May 1962 to the period 1918–28, and the one in May 1964 to the period 1929–39. Scully did not participate in the former. His paper "Doldrums in the Suburbs" from the final meeting, officially called Modern Architecture Symposium 1964, was published along with the rest of the proceedings in the March 1965 volume of the *Journal of the Society of Architectural Historians.* It was republished later that year in the now celebrated double-issue of *Perspecta* (nos. 9/10), which was edited by Scully's student Robert Stern, and which also contained preview selections from Robert Venturi's *Complexity and Contradiction in Architecture*, Philip Johnson's "Whence & Whither: The Processional Element in Architecture," Louis Kahn's "Remarks" along with studies and descriptions of recent projects (including Dhaka, Mikveh Israel Synagogue, the Indian Institute of Management, and the Salk Institute), plus Charles Moore's "You Have to Pay for the Public Life."

Compared to the tightly focused and clear-cut issues that presented themselves for the first two symposia, the third seemed to Hitchcock to be more diffuse and to lack any

8

Doldrums in the Suburbs

VINCENT SCULLY

I must apologize for the fact that my talk is not written out, as those of many of my colleagues seem to be; it will therefore not be as smooth as I should like. Fortunately, the theme of my topic is a childishly simple one. It is as follows: that during the 1930s in America architectural theory suburbanized itself up to the point where it became almost nonexistent; and where, indeed, architecture itself, or architecture as a topic of general urbanistic meaning, almost ceased to exist.

I personally came in contact with this phenomenon at a symposium at the Museum of Modern Art in 1948. At that symposium two points of view, or what we were told were two points of view, were presented. One was supposed to be that of the International Style and was upheld largely by Alfred Barr. In his description of work like
8.1 that of Gropius's house in Lincoln, Massachusetts, of 1938, Barr fundamentally confined himself to the arguments of Hitchcock and Johnson in 1932 and enunciated once more the ringing words of that earlier decade: "We have an architecture still." On the other side was Lewis Mumford, who told us that there was, in fact, another kind of architecture, that this architecture was not inorganic like that of Gropius but was, in fact,

single unifying theme. For this reason, the more than fifteen invited speakers were assigned topics covering a broad range of subjects tailored to their individual interests and areas of expertise. William Jordy, for instance, spoke on the evolution of the International Style during the 1930s; Peter Serenyi and Edgar Kaufmann Jr., on Le Corbusier and Frank Lloyd Wright, respectively; George Collins, Eduard Sekler, Christian Otto, and Henry Millon, on the reactions to modernism in Spain, Austria, Nazi Germany, and Fascist Italy; James Marston Fitch on new developments in technology; and Paul Norton on world's fairs. The talks were all essentially descriptive and documentary. Only Sibyl Moholy-Nagy, Catherine Bauer Wurster, and Scully offered critical polemics. Moholy-Nagy, speaking on "The Diaspora," condemned the reductiveness in the transplantation of Bauhaus ideas to America; Wurster described the complete failure of the "International Stylists," as she called them, to affect the development of social housing during the period; while Scully, refusing to confine his remarks either to the suburban single-family house, which was his topic, or to the cutoff date of 1939, seized the opportunity to launch a general critique of the impact of modernist ideas, and especially Bauhaus pedagogy, on what Aldo Rossi was about to call "the architecture of the city."

Instead of considering the suburb simply as a neutral ground for certain architectural developments, Scully used the concept of suburbanization in an ideological sense to define the architectural mind-set of the period from the late 1920s through the late 1940s. By this he meant a specifically anti-urban, anti-monumental attitude that results in a small-scale, asymmetrical, two-dimensional type of design that is inimical to existing patterns of city building and, as he previously claimed in the case of New York's Park Avenue, destructive of them. Building on the argument for a New Urbanism adumbrated as early as

organic and was best seen in the work of the Bay Region architects. Figure 8.2 is a house 8.2
of 1949, not from the Bay Region but more or less of that type, a house in Los Angeles, the Johnson House by Harwell Hamilton Harris. And these two *modes* of buildings were held up to us in 1948 as what architecture was; and between these two, apparently, the polemic was to take place. That polemic had already been developed a little bit by Walter Curt Behrendt in his *Modern Building* of 1937 and was to be carried further by Bruno Zevi in his book, *Towards an Organic Architecture*, of 1950. Zevi, picking up many of Behrendt's concepts, said that between these two kinds of architecture there was indeed a very great difference. You had, on the one hand, an organic architecture and, on the other hand, an inorganic architecture. We were told that organic architecture was a native art, like the Harris house. We were told that the inorganic was a fine art, presumably like the Gropius House. We were told that organic architecture had to do with intuitive sensation and that inorganic architecture was a product of thought, and so on and so on, making it perfectly clear that what we were being shown once more was the old false polemic between classic and romantic, which had served so long as an excuse

1954 in "Archetype and Order in Recent American Architecture," Scully once again pointed to Mies's Illinois Institute of Technology as the first step in rejecting International Style principles in favor of more monumental, classicizing ones. The revival of an expression of monumentality, which had been disparaged by modernists and subjected to intense debate in the noted symposium "The Need for a New Monumentality" in the pages of *Architectural Review* in 1948, was now seen by Scully as reaching some form of fulfillment in the recent designs of Louis Kahn.

"Doldrums in the Suburbs" reflects the profound disenchantment in the liberal intellectual community with the unchecked growth of the suburb in America after World War II that led, in part, to the creation of the Department of Housing and Urban Development in Lyndon Johnson's Great Society of the mid-1960s. William Whyte's *The Organization Man* (1956), David Riesman's *The Lonely Crowd* (1958), and Robert Woods's *Suburbia: Its People and Their Problems* (1958) are only the most well-known studies preceding Morton and Lucia White's *The Intellectual versus the City* (1962). On the other hand, the resurgence of interest in making the city work, in part by rejecting modern ideas of city planning, can be dated to the publication, in 1959, of Herbert Gans's *The Urban Villagers* and, in 1961, of Jane Jacobs's *The Death and Life of Great American Cities*—both works that Scully knew well. But Scully's critique of the suburban mentality remains distinct from most of these in its promotion of the monumental rather than the social as a solution to the problem of re-creating a meaningful urban environment.

to escape from thought in the criticism of much of the art of the past 150 years. We were more or less being told that Gropius's art was classic or classicizing and that the art of the Bay Region School was romantic.

Now I would suggest that the polemic was false, and that the reason we got nowhere with it was that there was basically no difference between these architectures at all: no important difference between Gropius's house at Lincoln and Harris's house at Los Angeles. Both are small, single-family suburban houses. Both of them are built of wood; both of them are light in weight; neither of them has anything whatever to do with the problem of urbanism. In fact, both of them, in the suburbs, embody an attempted escape from the larger questions of monumental architecture and city building as a whole. Now it may be argued that the Harris House, dating from 1949, is outside the period stated for the symposium. But, in fact, like Robert Stern earlier, I find the stated period not too useful. I would suggest that the suburbanization which took place in the 1930s continued, largely because of the war, until 1949. It was only in 1949, for a number of reasons, that a significant shift began to be apparent—away from it to something new. Thus the Harris House of 1949 was continuing a development which in the 1930s had been carried on in California especially by the work of William Wilson Wurster, such
8.3 as the house of 1938 in figure 8.3. Here a traditional construction of vertical board-and-

8.1 NEAR RIGHT: Walter Gropius and Marcel Breuer. Gropius House, Lincoln, Massachusetts, 1937–38. Exterior

8.2 FAR RIGHT: Harwell Hamilton Harris. Johnson House, Los Angeles, 1947–49. Exterior

8.3 BELOW: William Wilson Wurster. Campbell House, Stockton, California, 1938. Exterior

batten siding is employed, showing a conscious attempt to reconstruct local traditions of wooden small-scale building. Hence the Harris House of 1949 grows out of developments of the 1930s and can therefore be considered there.

To get back to the main point, these are both suburban architecture, they are small in scale and anti-monumental, and they have nothing to do with the larger architectural problem of urbanism with which, in its own way, the International Style as a whole also had a rather curious record. That is to say, figure 8.4 is an "ideal" scheme for 8.4
New York. It is typical of the city-planning fantasies of this decade. They are fantasies which hate the city and all preexisting urban architecture. In them the city—indeed the whole past—is conceived of as something which simply needs to be destroyed. The town is to be spread out across the landscape, in a Garden-City sense, or to be built up thoughtlessly in the towers of the Ville Radieuse in a Corbusian sense. This is a project from Yale of 1940 by a very important critic there at the time, Richard Bennett, in which New York is destroyed. There is a project for Philadelphia by Louis Kahn of almost the same period and of exactly the same kind. I think it might be noted that the great Stonehenge down at the end of Manhattan in Bennett's scheme was supposed to be the regional-planning center. The planners give themselves the cult place. The city is gone.

I would suggest therefore that modern architecture as it had developed and was being taught in America by the late 1930s was small in scale, anti-monumental, and urbanistically destructive. Despite the sociological pronouncements of its pedagogues it was in fact neither functional nor structural in its methods and in its forms. Instead, it

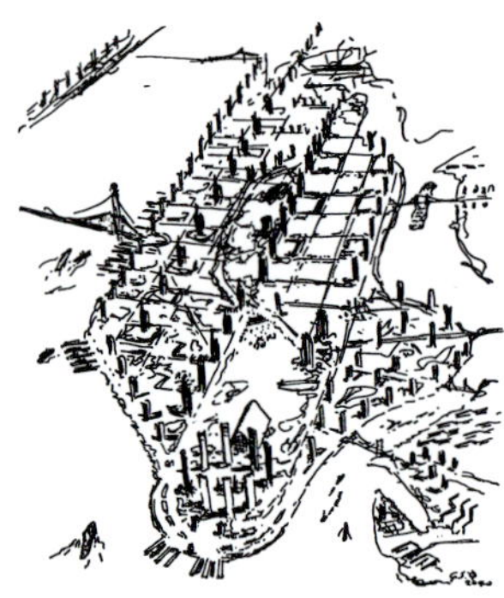

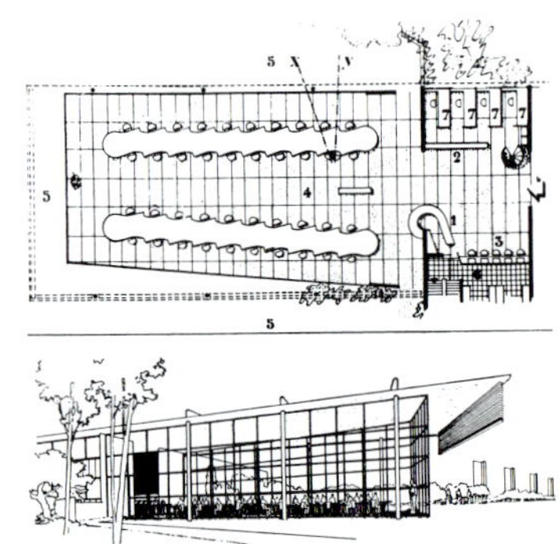

ABOVE, LEFT: Richard M. Bennett and G. Hicks. New York in the Future project, 1940. Aerial perspective 8.4

ABOVE, CENTER: F. S. Culbertson. Monument to J. S. Bach project, 1933. Plan and elevation 8.5

ABOVE, RIGHT: Richard M. Bennett. Microfilm Library project, 1940. Plan and perspective 8.6

was pictorial. That can be seen I think in these two projects, one from Yale and one from
8.5 Penn: figure 8.5 is a project of 1933 for a memorial for Johann Sebastian Bach. It looks to us today a little bit like a building by Philip Johnson. But in 1940 when this project
8.6 for a microfilm library, or something of the sort, was designed, the architecture of the Bach memorial was seen as the enemy. It was the Beaux-Arts enemy. It was the enemy for two reasons: first, because it was heavy, which meant probably that it was Fascist; and secondly, because it was symmetrical, which probably meant the same thing—or even worse, that it had some relationship possibly to Renaissance rather than to Gothic design. So the one architecture was seen by Mr. Bennett and the other architects and critics of the time as something too heavy and too symmetrical to be modern architecture. Bennett's building is maximally light. All its solids are made as evanescent as possible, and in the drafting technique those solids are made even lighter than they would in fact have been structurally able to be. Therefore I submit as follows: that both
8.5 of these architectures are pictorial, the one of figure 8.5 is developed with a kind of baroque sense of modeling of forms by chiaroscuro in light and shade. The method of fig-
8.6 ure 8.6 I think you will recognize as essentially a Bauhaus one of graphic devices: thin lines, planes behind, transparency, passage of planes, movement and flux of light, and so on. It is no less pictorial than the other; it simply deals with different pictorial devices. Therefore I would suggest that in the America of 1940 architecture was still as fundamentally pictorial as it had been earlier in the American Beaux-Arts.

Now I think you can see all that very quickly in a drawing from Yale of 1946
8.7 which shows the whole thing. It is by a critic named Eugene Nalle, who later becomes extremely important at Yale in the middle 1950s; here he is in his late-Bauhaus phase. His architecture is as light as possible. Indeed it is exaggeratedly so: his perspective—as he himself used often to point out later—is distorted to give a sense of the passage and float of planes. The space is constructed purely by graphic tricks: a line, a little bit of shadow up above, and the *snap* of the black plane down below. Passage, transparency, flux, flow, no weight, no symmetry, and in front, demonstrating, I think, a good deal of the distrust with which Western civilization as a whole was held by the practitioners of this period, what is apparently the head of a Fiji Islander heaves into sight—so introducing in the project the necessary purity of primitive art. Now it seems to me that the

fundamental prototypes for all these visions of form are the constructions painted by Laszlo Moholy-Nagy in the early 1920s at the Bauhaus, such as the one now in the 8.8
Collection of the Société Anonyme at Yale. The passage of planes, the graphic creation of space in terms of transparency, flux, flow, light and dark, forward and back, is already developed, and Nalle's rendering of the mid-1940s represents no visual advance beyond its image.

The same is true in the architecture of the Bay Region Style, as shown in a house of this period from Lafayette, California, by Clarence Mayhew. This photo 8.9
appeared in 1946 in a book by Elizabeth Mock of the Museum of Modern Art—a book poignantly entitled: *If You Want to Build a House.* This was the end of everyone's desire in 1946. The preoccupation is on the house, but again you will see that the passage of planes, the maximum thinness, the lightness, the asymmetry, and so on, is that of Moholy-Nagy. Ergo: Bauhaus and Bay Region all in one. The same is true of the Graduate Center at Harvard by Walter Gropius and The Architects' Collaborative of 1949–50. The 8.10
changes of plane, the small lally columns as against the larger columns, the shadow, the

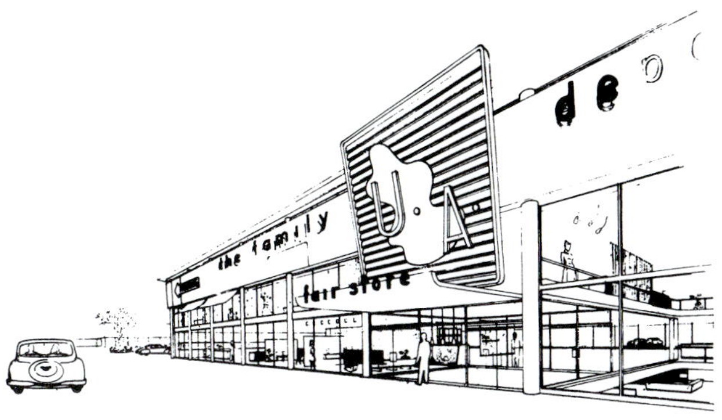

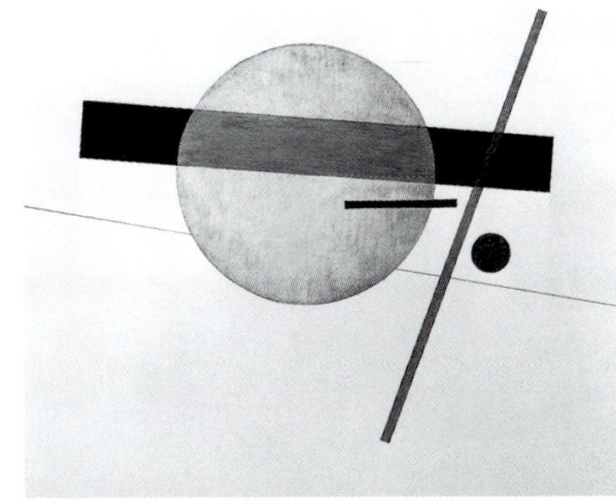

8.7 ABOVE, LEFT: Eugene Nalle. Department Store project, 1946. Perspective

8.8 ABOVE, RIGHT: Laszlo Moholy-Nagy. *Light Display Machine,* 1923–26

8.9 BOTTOM, LEFT: Clarence Mayhew. Manor House, Soule Tract, Lafayette, California, 1937. Interior

8.10 BOTTOM, RIGHT: Walter Gropius and the Architects' Collaborative. Graduate Center, Harvard University, Cambridge, Massachusetts, 1949–50. Exterior

light—even the way the photographer has been instinctively trained to take the picture—are all part of the pictorial method, whose prototypes can be seen in Moholy-Nagy's constructions.

I think it should be pointed out that the relationship of the International Style to a pictorial sensibility goes back to 1929 at least. It certainly goes back before that in practice, but in historical perception it can clearly be traced to that point. We owe that perception to Henry-Russell Hitchcock, who in his great book of 1929, called *Modern Architecture: Romanticism and Reintegration*, decided that the difference between those architects whom he called "of the New Tradition" and those whom he called "the New Pioneers" was precisely that "the New Pioneers" were aware of the aesthetic inventions and experiments of the painters of the early twentieth century and of the teens. The difference for him between the "heavy" architecture of early Wright or Behrens, or of the Scandinavians, and that of Le Corbusier, Oud, Gropius, and so on, was that the latter architects had been aware of the experiments of De Stijl and so on and their buildings participated in its pictorial perception. Now, in 1932, when the *International Style* by Hitchcock and Johnson appeared, the pictorial side, while still mentioned, was played down a little bit. And I feel—if I may comment within this talk on some of the comments made earlier here by Mr. Hitchcock—I feel that their comments were perhaps not quite candid. That is to say, it seems to me that Hitchcock's book of 1929 was a work of pure history and one of the most beautiful works of history we have seen in this century; one in which he tried to bring together all the disparate happenings of the past two hundred years and to state gropingly what *was* in fact the development which had occurred. But the book of 1932 was, I think, under the influence of Mr. Johnson, primarily a polemic. It was a statement of what architecture ought to be, and I think this is important because I do believe, as was suggested earlier, that a good deal of the character of the architecture of the 1930s in America, does, in fact, derive from the statements of what architecture ought to be which Mr. Hitchcock and Mr. Johnson made in 1932.

8.11 I think the point is this: that certainly the great Bauhaus by Gropius of 1925–26 is stronger than its prototypes, even its pictorial prototypes. It lays its elements out strongly and stiffly and proudly in space, and you feel that it is as tough as a set of gears. But Gropius's house in Lincoln of 1938–39 is weaker than the prototypes, it seems to me; it is more compromised than the prototypes, and the set of pictorial elements with which it is involved are those which are more concerned with the subtle transparencies, the diminution of scale, the play of very thin planes—in a word, with flow, change, and ambiguity which the stronger, much more monumental Bauhaus does not have. Now again I think that we find all these elements—the slide, the movement, the transparency, the flow, the ambiguities of form—in Bauhaus pedagogical experiments like those of Laszlo Moholy-Nagy.

It seems to me that Marcel Breuer—who has been cited as a sort of archetypical modern architect by Professor Jordy—that Marcel Breuer is the perfect expression of this period, the outgrowth, the archetypal outgrowth of Bauhaus education, its prime expres-
8.12 sion, and its victim. That is to say, in Breuer's own house in Lincoln of 1939, it should be

8.11 ABOVE: Walter Gropius. Bauhaus, Dessau, Germany, 1925–26. Aerial view

8.12 RIGHT: Marcel Breuer and Walter Gropius. Breuer House, Lincoln, Massachusetts, 1939. Interior

perfectly clear that the space is made by light and decorative planes. The stone becomes a mosaic much thinner than the mosaics of Le Corbusier upon which it is based; indeed, it becomes almost wallpaper—a weightless plane back there in space—behind a set of transparencies derived from Moholy's experiments. Now Breuer keeps right on after this decade, right into the 1940s with basically the same pictorial, small-scale, designer's sensitivity. And it seems to me that he does it splendidly for a time. He does it with all the attention to work at very small scale and with all the strangeness and ambiguity that Klee himself had been able to develop at the Bauhaus; so it seems to me that the pointing arrow, odd in scale and utterly without weight, in the house in Williamstown of
the 1940s by Marcel Breuer is very close to Klee's *Precious Container for Stars* in the 8.13
Société Anonyme Collection at Yale. It seems to me Breuer's great quality here is that of an insectile tension, a positive development of the characteristics of small-scale,

anti-monumentality, asymmetry, tension of line, and so on, which had been characteris-
8.14 tic of his pictorial education. And it seems to me his house in New Canaan of 1948 is a perfect expression of that, suspended like a little insect, like a little creature, off the ground with all the old stabilities of architecture overset; now everything is utterly light, held together by wires, and so on. But when Breuer came into the 1950s and received large projects, it seems to me that the continuation of his small-scale graphic sensibility made it impossible for him to build a monumental building—a properly scaled urban building—and has so far continued to make it impossible for him to do so. This point is not an attack on Breuer, but only an expression of what the character of the 1930s *was*

ABOVE, TOP LEFT: Marcel Breuer. Robinson House, Williamstown, Massachusetts, 1946–48. Exterior 8.13

ABOVE, TOP RIGHT: Marcel Breuer. Breuer House, New Canaan, Connecticut, 1947–48. Exterior 8.14

ABOVE, BOTTOM LEFT: Marcel Breuer. Church, Saint John's Abbey, Collegeville, Minnesota, 1953–61. Exterior 8.15

ABOVE, BOTTOM RIGHT: Le Corbusier. High Court, Chandigarh, India, 1951–56. Main entrance 8.16

and after them of the 1940s (Breuer continuing it into the 1950s) toward small-scale and anti-monumentality with an avoidance of monumental mass, a lack of structural weight, and a preoccupation with small-scale graphic effects. It is all these things that turn Breuer's bell tower at Collegeville into a little plywood object. I think the point is 8.15
clear. If we compare it with the development which is characteristic of the 1950s, as in the late work of Le Corbusier, we see the difference between a graphic sensibility and a sensibility which is concerned with monumental architecture. One would say, looking at 8.16
the work by Le Corbusier, that the force that Chandigarh has derives from the fact that it elevates to heroic scale the standing figures of men; whereas in the Breuer there is *no* possibility to associate oneself empathetically with the form lifted. The relationships are insectile, small-scale, and related to furniture design. The same thing is true of the *brise-soleil* in both buildings. In each the *brise-soleil* is essential. It is essential so that the eye will believe the sculptural lift of the other parts. If there were only the thin plane of glass we could not physically believe that one building could be both a thin container and an active sculptural force. Therefore the box must be masked. But the difference is that Le Corbusier, when he masks his glass wall, makes his *brise-soleil* plastically active itself, precisely because he relates it architecturally to human scale, whereas Breuer is thinking only in terms of graphic textures, scaleless repetitions. I think you can see the difference—Le Corbusier's magically makes you read it both as an abstract structural force and as something which also indicates the sizes of men and the building's use by them, because the basic unit is the door height, and moreover he lets you see where each floor is. But then he breaks it across so as to confuse all that for the eye and to make the thing move in and of itself. He does not cheat one bit; it is all there; whereas in Breuer's screen, with the simple repetition of the element which is that of graphic design, what is created is a radio cabinet much like the radio cabinets of the late 1930s or the early 1940s. Again I cite Bauhaus methods. It is industrial design, not monumental architecture; it is abstractly graphic, not humanistically active in space.

I only want to point out that this change begins at the end of the 1940s. Indeed, it begins in 1948 when Le Corbusier begins to construct his Unité d'Habitation 5.3
at Marseilles. And the difference between it and the *pilotis* of Breuer's recent IBM build- 8.17
ing is again the same one. In Le Corbusier's swelling shapes we can read muscular force. At IBM we have not only an overscaling in relation to the height of the building but also a set of graphic devices which do not convince us that they relate to the noble sense of lifting a great weight which we can feel in our own bodies as men. And this seems to me the basic shift.

Now if that is the case with the "inorganic" International Style by the late 1930s, what is the case with what was supposed to be its "organic" alternative—with the Bay Region wing? Was that capable of developing into a monumental urban architecture? Again I would suggest, "No"—here again largely because of that mode's preoccupation with the single-family house, but also because of its special preoccupation with wood and also with a conscious desire to make architecture as shack-like as possible. I would suggest, by the way, that these limitations were not confined to

ABOVE, LEFT: Marcel Breuer. IBM Research Center, La Gaude, France, 1960–63. Aerial view 8.17

ABOVE, RIGHT: Stick Style house, Newport, Rhode Island, 1845. Exterior 8.18

architects at this period. My own first work, carried on under the direction of Professor Hitchcock in 1948–49, was with American domestic architecture, with what I came to
8.18 call the Stick Style and the Shingle Style, of which an early Stick Style house at Newport (1845) is an example. Between the two, with what I was able to conceive of as being architecture and what seemed an appropriate subject for historical investigation in the late 1940s on the one hand, and with what Harwell Harris was doing then, there is an exact concordance—just as, in fact, Mrs. Harris was at this time studying the work of Greene and Greene, which is part of the whole tradition. The limitations are the same: what architects do and what historians study are of course intimately bound up with each other.

Now so far as the California group or the West Coast group is concerned, how far could they go with this articulated Stick Style of architecture? Well, about as far as a
8.19 small church. And I think you can see that in the work of Pietro Belluschi in his Lutheran church at Portland of about 1950. This was apparently as far as it could be pushed, because when, in 1949, Belluschi built the Equitable Building in Portland he totally left this mode; he completely abandoned whatever might have been a development out of the articulated skeleton structure of the stick and instead sheathed the whole thing over in a kind of screen wall, a cellophane envelope which had nothing whatever to do with his smaller-scale works. Therefore, the Bay Region School, too, was not capable of creating a monumental architecture. It could not deal with large city buildings.

So I come back to the same thing: a California house of 1949 that goes perfectly
8.20 with a house of 1938–39, for example Gropius and Breuer's Hagerty House at Cohasset of the late 1930s. The composition is almost the same, the light, pictorial elements are similar, and the anti-monumental suburbanization of architecture seems complete. When does all this change? It begins to change in 1939. It begins to change with the late work
8.21 of Mies at IIT; however, as already pointed out, it was still going on in a fairly late example

in the Harvard Graduate Center of 1949. Here all the shapes are, as it were, purposely tentative in their organization of space, purposely asymmetrical, weakly curved, loosely connected with each other, interpenetrating, sliding; indeed laden with all those qualities that we found characteristic of the pictorial devices we have looked at already. Whereas Mies's first project of 1939 for IIT is symmetrical, with a strong cross-axis formed by big separate shapes, hollowed out inside as clear building blocks which define a large, confident volume of space, here is a return to a simple projection of architectural symmetry, mass, and space which had been regarded as anathema during the 1930s.[1] I remember a very good student at Yale, Duncan Buell; about 1952 he was working on a space frame and suddenly he said, "I can't make it asymmetrical—it won't *become* asymmetrical, so what am I to do?" And then he said, "Why, a great many great buildings have been symmetrical!" and his project was published by Mr. Meeks in his book on railroad stations. Buell is now working for Louis I. Kahn.

Mies therefore was the beginning, and, it seems to me, the return. I would suggest also that late Mies was not begun to be understood until about 1949. And I would suggest also, as I have done elsewhere, that the publication of Professor Wittkower's *Architectural Principles in the Age of Humanism* was of considerable relevance here. This book, whose influence has been amply acknowledged by English architects such as Peter and Alison Smithson, who have also related its principles to those of Mies at IIT, indicated a return to all those things that were considered useless or even harmful by the American Bauhaus—for which the Renaissance was evil because it was symmetrical; it was bad because it was not made by happy craftsmen but was instead laid out in a strong, symmetrical urban sense. And it was Mies's strong shapes—shapes indeed related to those of Sullivan himself—that began to make us feel once more the possibilities for city building. He began to get us out of the suburbs, back into the city to make monumental architecture once more. True enough, it has turned out that Mies's method cannot solve everything, and that a truly urban architecture demands more than he had to give. The point here is that by 1939 his work began to point out a reasonable direction for us.

8.19 BELOW, LEFT: Pietro Belluschi. Central Lutheran Church, Portland, Oregon, 1948–50. Exterior

8.20 BELOW, RIGHT: Walter Gropius and Marcel Breuer. Hagerty House, Cohasset, Massachusetts, 1938. Exterior

ABOVE: Ludwig Mies van der Rohe. Illinois Institute of Technology, Chicago, begun 1939. Aerial perspective of final scheme, photomontage 8.21

LEFT: Alvar Aalto. Baker House Dormitory, Massachusetts Institute of Technology, Cambridge, Massachusetts, 1946–49. Aerial view 8.22

And of course by 1950, following Dr. Wittkower's lead, we had the *Architectural Forum* putting together a picture of Vignola's urban facades with one of Mies's constructions at IIT and indicating concordance between them. Now it seems to me again that *1949* is the critical date here. It is the date when Philip Johnson began to give his splendid talks which those of us who first heard them regarded almost as the pronouncements of the Devil. He stood on the platform at Yale University, and he said to a shocked hush across the room, "I would rather sleep in the nave of Chartres Cathedral with the nearest john two blocks down the street than I would in a Harvard house with back-to-back bathrooms!" This terrible and even rather frightening pronouncement was the one after which, for the first time, I remember students saying to me, "He's talking about architecture as an art!" And suddenly I realized that that is what it was all the time.

In this way began in 1949 that particular classicizing mode of monumentality in the 1950s which Mr. Johnson knows that I feel to possess very strong limitations. I do think that there are many limitations in it, growing more apparent all the time. That is something we might discuss later. But it seems to me that in 1949 the complement and the antidote of that classicism had already been stated, indeed constructed in America,
especially as seen in the dormitory at the Massachusetts Institute of Technology by Alvar 8.22
Aalto. Here we had an architecture which was massive and solid, which, most of all, physically released functions to make forms and went far beyond simple symmetry to a noble generosity in the fullness of its shapes. Strong, big, masculine, and powerful, it outstepped the small, hermetic, pictorial world of the late 1930s in America and reached toward the possible grandeurs of architectural form. And if I may not seem overly chauvinistic, it seems to me that in these two things together—Johnson's order and Aalto's generosity—you have the beginning. You have by the early 1950s such a combination of
the two as that which resides in the Yale Art Gallery by Louis I. Kahn. Therefore, it seems 12.35
to me that if, in 1948, the statement, "We have an architecture still," was the correct one, by 1951 we should have said, "We have an architecture again."

Note 1 To call such symmetry "Nazi," as was oddly done by a participant during the Sunday discussion, because the Nazis preferred symmetrical architecture, is like calling "Peace" communist because the Communists continually use the word.

NEIL LEVINE

"RIBA Discourse 1969: A Search for Principle between Two Wars." *RIBA Journal: The Journal of the Royal Institute of British Architects* 76 (June 1969): 240–47.

In 1957 the Royal Institute of British Architects, England's venerable professional organization, established a lecture to be given on a yearly basis by "distinguished designers or scholars of worldwide reputation." Called the Annual Discourse, it was intended to "involve not merely statements" by the speaker, but, as Leslie Martin noted, "it should also be an assessment" of the current state of affairs. As a result, many of those invited chose to be quite critical and even rather personal in their observations. Most of the speakers in the 1950s and 1960s were architects, planners, engineers, or some other type of design professional. These included Alvar Aalto (1957), Buckminster Fuller (1958), Charles Eames (1959), Constantinos Doxiadis (1960), Louis Kahn (1962), José Luis Sert (1963), Ralph Erskine (1964), Gino Valle (1965), Myron Goldsmith (1966), and Ray Affleck (1968). In 1961 the journalist Alistair Cooke spoke on the suburbanization of America and the prospect for the same in Britain, and in 1967 the theorist Christian Norberg-Schulz offered a methodological inquiry into the subject of "Pluralism in Architecture."

Scully was the first art historian to be invited, and his talk stands out from the others of the period in the way that it interweaves issues of history, criticism, and autobiography around a core of profound moral and ethical significance. In the course of a narrative highlighted by references to the negative impact of urban renewal on the American city and to the value of moderation to be learned from the study of the Native American architecture and culture of the Southwest, Scully takes the auditor/reader

9

RIBA Discourse 1969: A Search for Principle between Two Wars

VINCENT SCULLY

Some years ago an American painter of the 1950s, the late Franz Kline, was talking about a teacher who he felt had done him a great deal of good. He said, "She can make you see the difference between the side of the vase and the plane of the table, and that's not much, but it's Heaven, too, and England." I have only the vaguest idea what he meant by that, but I sense from it an England indescribably reasonable and kind. I will need even more of your kindness than of your reason as I come out from behind the mask which all historians wear and, in accordance with the terms of this discourse, attempt to define what I mean by architecture, to characterize contemporary American architecture, and to describe what I have tried to do about it over the years.

The general definition can be very embracing and brief. It seems to me that the human act of architecture is the construction of the whole human environment, and that the entire constructed environment is architecture. Therefore, the first element of architecture is the natural world, and the second element is everything manmade. In that relationship between the manmade and the natural, the metaphysical wholeness of

through a personal history of postwar architecture and urbanism in America that filters events through the screen of his own evolving research interests. The fast-paced *bildungsroman* moves from an analogy between his own work on the Shingle and Stick Styles and the focus of architects in the late 1940s and 1950s on small-scale suburban domestic architecture, through the development of Brutalism seen in relation to his involvement with Greek architecture in the later 1950s and early 1960s, finally to the reaction against the sterile, "classicizing" urbanism of late modernism that finds its parallel in his current interest in the work of Robert Venturi and the architecture of the Pueblos. The review of his own thinking in light of recent developments in architecture reveals a number of important reversals and reassessments, the most notable of which are the critique of Miesian classicism (see "Archetype and Order in Recent American Architecture," chap. 3) and the almost total acquiescence to Norman Mailer's jaundiced view of the present state of things (see "Vincent Scully: A Biographical Sketch," this volume).

"The Death of the Street" and "Doldrums in the Suburbs" (see chaps. 7 and 8) predicted some of the critical positions adopted here, but the sense of angst and despair about the future as well as the heightened level of social consciousness is new. Scully's derision of downtown urban renewal efforts, their disregard for the historical fabric of the city, and their lack of provision for housing the poor had been discussed in earlier articles published in 1966 ("America's Architectural Nightmare: The Motorized Megalopolis," *Holiday*) and 1967 ("The Threat and Promise of Urban Redevelopment in New Haven," *Zodiac*), but "A Search for Principle between Two Wars," like the concluding section of his book *American Architecture and Urbanism*, also published in 1969, takes the argument much further. It is deeply marked by the political and social unrest of the later 1960s in America—what Scully refers to as a "crisis in the national life of the United States"—and must be read as a direct reaction to events that literally hit home. Touted as a "model city" in the mid-1960s, when it became a showcase for the urban renewal and anti-poverty programs sponsored by its longtime liberal Democratic mayor Richard C. Lee, New Haven was the scene of serious riots in its African-American community during the summer of 1967.

architecture is always seen. The Greek temple, a closed and single shape riding its sacred landscape, shows us one kind of connection. The Italian town, existing in a complex ecological relationship with its terraced slopes, shows another. Here too are infinite complexities of interaction between manmade forms, and every town like San Gimignano is a record of the pressures of those relationships from generation to generation. So in any city, architecture builds an environment which normally takes shape and changes across time, and everything (as Ian Nairn and the *Architectural Review* showed us long ago) plays a part in it: buildings with interior functions and exterior responsibilities, streets, sidewalks, lights, signs, and automobiles. Hence all of the constructed environment is architecture, and we may follow that logic to the concentrated science-fiction dreams of

Many, like Scully, believed that the riots were directly attributable to the disruption of poor neighborhoods and the dislocation of their inhabitants by a business-oriented, white middle-class redevelopment agency.

Scully's reaction in this essay to the situation in New Haven does not remain a localized phenomenon but is elaborated into a general critique of American militarism that finds a parallel between the barbarism and brutality of the Vietnam War and the destructive designs of "cataclysmic Redevelopment." Pervading all forms of modern society, in his view, is a heroic, confrontational model of action that finds its philosophical roots, however degraded, in the existentialism Scully himself had formerly embraced. Venturi, the Native American pueblo dwellers, and Pop culture all offer alternatives for seeing reality in a non-confrontational way. Scully does not yet envisage, nor does he pretend to predict, what forms such an approach may finally take in terms of restoring the wholeness of the environment and the integrity of neighborhoods, but he is adamant in maintaining that the solution will not be found in the autonomous world of architectural practices and principles (à la Wittkower), but must find its source in the realm of the social and the political. The "principle which emerges" from this historico-autobiographical analysis, and for which "the architectural historian and critic must fight in every way he can," is the sense of moderation, of accommodation, and of "common humanity" that provides the political and social framework for a decent and humane architecture.

the Archigrammists or to the American strip, where the city is strewn out along the road like the contents of an affluent wastebasket. It is all architecture. It always grows out of us, forms us, and shows us what we are.

From that point of view, the general pattern of American architecture as it is practiced at the bureaucratic level at the present moment is a rather frightening one. The center of Dayton, Ohio, as it stands today has buildings, streets, people of various colors, trees, multiple uses of business and living, and so on. Dayton, Ohio, as its Redevelopment Agency would like to see it as bombed out, with no streets, no people, nothing left but a kind of amusement park for suburbanites on wheels. Cataclysmic, automotive, and suburban, such are the principles which have formed the architectural conception here.

How did it get this way? What can be done about it? A long story and a hard answer. Let me concentrate tonight upon the intellectual and professional aspects of the problem, leaving the general sociological situation to reveal itself as it may.

Since 1945, American architecture has reflected two diverse movements in American thought, and both of them have been central to my own work in history. First has been a compulsion to explore the American continent in a physical sense and the American experience in a psychic sense. It is that persistent problem of identity which is apparently felt by all peoples who have recently been colonials. Out of it, when we look at ourselves hard, we have generally derived principles of mobility and flight, exactly as D. H. Lawrence most brilliantly said we would in his *Studies in Classic American Literature* of 1922. Second has been a passionate desire to make contact with the European homeland once again. That yearning has been recurrent in colonial America; there is some reason to believe that we have now made the attempt for the last time.

One of many indications to that effect is the growing rejection by American artists and intellectuals, and most of all by the young, of several central aspects of the Hellenic tradition, among them especially the heroic, or confrontational, view of human life—or what those who make that rejection would call the "uptight" attitude toward experience. (The Temple of Athena at Paestum is as "uptight" as it can be.) That rejec- 16.8
tion seeks instead what those who make it would call the "with it" attitude, like the more relaxed Indian stance, wherein the building at Taos pueblo dances its sacred mountain 16.3
in its forms. Of course, Hellenic civilization itself had been complete enough to harbor both attitudes in it, and some Pueblo sites look much like Greek sites in which the chorus of Dionysos has once again been reborn.

My own research of the past five years has followed this course from Europe to America, from Greek to Pueblo, perhaps from more individualistic to more communal, and to a concern for the future of all non-European Americans, whose total liberation is a fundamental part of the "with it" movement as a whole. Taos danced when it came to believe—prematurely as it turned out—that its sacred Blue Lake up on Taos Mountain was to be returned to it. Among blacks, as for centuries among the Pueblos, culture is taking on the primary aspect of resistance to the pressure of the white world. In that resistance the Pueblos have been remarkably successful. Tesuque, in the heart of a heavily urbanized valley, still dances under Lake Peak, the Tewa Sacred Mountain of the East, which rises above Santa Fe's ski resort. Black resistance on the cultural level makes less obvious sense, of course, than such does among the Pueblos, in view of the fact that their African culture was broken up by slavery long ago. But it is understandable enough, because the dream world which (colonial) American society has persistently tried to create has never in the past had other than a servile place for non-white peoples in it.

Indeed, American architecture of the twentieth century can be understood only
in terms of dream experience: Wright's Minoan pool of space at Racine, of 1936, no 11.18
less than McKim, Mead and White's Beaux-Arts splendors in Pennsylvania Station, of 1906 (now foolishly and ignobly destroyed, while the equally fine Grand Central Station is also threatened).

To someone who began graduate work as I did, in 1945, it became apparent that the toughest and most realistic days of the dream were to be found in the past,
before the First World War, exactly as Wright's Larkin Building of 1904 was tougher, 11.10
harder, and more realistic than his Johnson Wax Building of thirty years later. So I tried to trace the thread of American mythology backward in time, as along that continuity of the Open Road I mentioned earlier. It led back through the spatial continuities of Wright to those of what I called the "Shingle Style" of the 1870s and 1880s, and finally to the vertical boards and battens and the open porches of what I called the "Stick Style,"

derived in part from the English picturesque, and beginning in the 1840s. Focusing as a historian upon small-scale, suburban, domestic building in wood, I was in accord with the scale and focus of American architecture itself in those years directly after the Second World War. The so-called "Bay Region School" of the West Coast, basking in a suburban dream, used vertical boards and battens and plank and beam structure. We were told that the neo-Bauhaus architecture of the East Coast was exactly the opposite, but in all essentials it was the same: suburban, small in scale, asymmetrical, and built of wood.

Therefore when I came to design and build my own house in 1950, it was like a combination of the two, with plank and beam structure like the West Coast and diagonal sheathing like Breuer down the road. I refer to it here only as a record of intention, and as such it differed from both the Bay Region and the Bauhaus in aspiring to be a single more or less symmetrical shape, entirely open around a central core, and with the walls set as panels within a frame. Here the direct influence was from Philip Johnson's Glass House of 1949 and beyond that from Mies's work of the 1940s at the Illinois Institute of Technology. And the totally unconscious congruence was with Alison and Peter Smithson's Hunstanton School, designed in 1949, wherein the Smithsons said that they wanted to create a "compact, disciplined architecture" once again. So, with all respect, did I. Hunstanton was also intended to be a socially direct and anti-genteel kind of building, where the space was created by exposed structure, and so (if I may continue this comparison between the almost sublime and the faintly ridiculous) was my house. I therefore claim a ground-floor Brutalist position which, in terms of contemporary architecture as a whole, I have never entirely abandoned. The rough materials and heavy beams in my own house show my predisposition to admire Le Corbusier's Maisons Jaoul when they were published, but before that a much more direct relative had appeared in
12.35 New Haven. This was Louis I. Kahn's Art Gallery of 1951–53. Here, not only in the exposed structure, but also in the central service core with open loft space around it, is the similarity of intention apparent—with, in Kahn's case, a related space-frame influence from Buckminster Fuller as well.

But Kahn's tetrahedrons are, as it were, trapped in the Miesian envelope, and he had to break out of that box, exactly as Wright had done, if he was to advance the cause of architecture further in his own way. It is therefore probably no accident, though somehow eerie enough, that Kahn next came, wholly on his own, to employ exactly the same strategy Wright had used: the cross-axis of space, articulated by service clusters.
6.2 In Wright's Martin House of 1904, groups of piers contain heating and lighting. In
6.6 Kahn's bathhouse at Trenton, of 1955, a Renaissance reference may be felt as well. Next these articulated served and serving spatial units rose up in a grand, bony structure for
6.8 Trenton, of 1957, which was then integrated as a Fuller-like space-frame in the concrete
9.1 skyscraper project of the same year. This is Kahn at his best, I think. The building braces itself against lateral forces as people do, and it stands as a major feature of City Center, ringed with parking towers in one of Kahn's most beautiful urban fantasies of the immediately succeeding years.

9.1 Louis I. Kahn. City Tower project, Philadelphia, 1956–57. Model

Yet once raised in America, the question of urbanity has always in the past led us rushing to Europe, and it did so with special urgency during the postwar years. Fulbright grants led us to the Italian Renaissance. Here, like the Smithsons in their demonstration of a "compact, disciplined architecture," we were not unaffected by Wittkower's *Architectural Principles in the Age of Humanism*, of 1949. Geometric discipline and the Renaissance together seemed especially necessary to us in America in 1950, because of the fact that the iconoclastic wing of the European modern movement which had taken root on our shores had so conspicuously failed to produce a compact,
disciplined architecture at that time. Indeed the Harvard Graduate Center was weakly 8.10
strung together and flaccidly pictorial in contrast to the sharp-edged Bauhaus itself of 8.11
twenty-five years before. (The situation was analogous to that in Wright's design.)

Once more we turned to Mies as an image of urban clarity and order, and we
associated his lucid, cubical volumes at IIT with those of the Renaissance. But here 8.21
considerable violence had to be done, because IIT was not massive, heavily scaled, or densely grouped like the High Renaissance buildings with which it was compared, but light, linear, and smaller in scale. It was an architecture not of the center of the city but of the two- or three-storied zone, like South Chicago itself, which spreads out around the denser centers of cities to this day. And Mies wanted it planted like a garden. Out of this amalgam the American corporate dream world took shape: the urbane suburb of nice company guys, with Mies's architecture stretched out by bureaucratic American architects as thin as a Dacron suit and as depersonalized, creating the fundamental Nowheresville of the contemporary corporation world.

Skidmore, Owings and Merrill. Beinecke Rare Book and Manuscript Library, Yale University, New Haven, Connecticut, 1962–63. Exterior 9.2

But it was when American architects tried to be solidly Renaissance and monumentally urban that the truly spectacular disasters occurred. If we start with the hard, eloquent Farnese, with string-courses, windows, cornice, entrance, Roman bathtub and
9.2 all, and turn from it to the Beinecke Library, of 1962–63, we find humanity with its eyes put out, and mum. It reflects a technology not of process but of packaging. It creates a world without human reference points, wherein no contact with things is possible. Indeed it is the true "empty landscape of psychosis" about which Norman Mailer warned us in 1963.

As the Renaissance turned to salt sterility in the hands of our most bureaucratic designers, other American architects turned away from it toward medieval architecture—generally not, as in the nineteenth century, to the structure of the French cathedrals, but to what seemed to them to be the expressive flexibility and the lively urban *scenografia* of the hilltowns of Italy. Kahn, Saarinen, and many others, including myself, visited San Gimignano in the early fifties, and its effect upon us paralleled that of the work of Alvar Aalto as we saw it in what was then its newest form at Säynätsalo. And if we put San Gimignano and Säynätsalo together, with perhaps a touch of pueblo
9.3 adobe, we have Saarinen's Stiles and Morse Colleges at Yale. These formed a purely picturesque but fairly well-functioning stage-set which attempted to enhance the older architecture on the site and to engage in an urban dialogue with it. A pictorial re-use of European forms, sometimes for wildly different functions, has been characteristic of American architecture from its colonial beginnings, and it was not lacking in Kahn's
17.12 Medical Research Building at the University of Pennsylvania, of 1958–60. Still, the housing of ducts and stairways in San Gimignano's towers here was partly the result of economic and procedural pressures, or so Kahn tells us. Originally he had stepped out the ducts and perforated the stair bases, so that the towers avoided the false structurally dominant look which they now have, and which once aroused Reyner Banham's mar-

9.3 Eero Saarinen. Stiles and Morse Colleges, Yale University, New Haven, Connecticut, 1958–62. Exterior

velously English ethical ire. The functioning of the building also leaves much to be desired, but its undeniable force, its somber rectitude despite everything, perhaps derive as much from its darkly towered silhouette and its urban cluster of laboratories as from the tense, precast skeleton which is its most intrinsic glory, and which was the fruit of those structural projects we looked at before. Here structure at least lifts Kahn beyond the American trap in the picturesque, and soon function was to do so as well and was to complete Kahn's liberation into the undeniable formal invention of his work of the past nine years. So at Rochester all the shapes in massing derive from the lighting of the interior spaces: from the bayed window seats and sun hoods of the classrooms around the periphery to the great monitors over the central meeting hall, which flood its Brutalist structure and common materials with a marvelously cool and silver light. As always in Brutalism, the ethic and the methods of the nineteenth-century Gothic Revival (here of the French structuralist Viollet-le-Duc, no less than of English ecclesiologists like William Butterfield) are alike recalled.

Yet Kahn pushes the American exploration of Europe farther back in time. Like all of us in the early fifties, he was overwhelmed by the spatial grandeur of Imperial Roman architecture, especially of Hadrian's Villa, to which most of us were led by that most perceptive of classicists, Frank E. Brown, of the American Academy in Rome. Like so many architects from Soane to Le Corbusier, Kahn tried to put the villa to use, and decided that its pure voids in solid walls could be used as garden definers and sun shields in his project for the Community Center (not yet constructed) at the Salk 17.20

Institute in La Jolla, California. "Wrapping ruins around buildings," Kahn called it. He has since made these shapes a much more integral part of buildings and projects from
17.7, 12.36 Dhaka to Ahmedabad and Fort Wayne. And in part out of this phase of Kahn comes the
15.14 early work of Robert Venturi, as in his Guild House, in Philadelphia, of 1960–63, where Venturi flattens out Kahn's hollow Roman walls into a street facade.

Yet there is a fundamental difference between Kahn and Venturi, a difference which has proved critical for the advanced American architecture of the past few years. That is to say, Kahn's work professes to be special and heroic; there is nothing ironic about it; it is Rome in concrete, Olympian in intention. But Venturi peels back his wall to show us the structural skeleton, lets his windowed masses step back on both sides with an ease approaching Aalto's, stamps a huge column, recalling one of De Klerk's, down in the center, and gestures generously upward from it to a television aerial in gold which culminates his building just as it does the lives of the old people in the common room below. That television aerial obsessively infuriates Kahn. He is of the older, "uptight" generation, its most heroic figure; Venturi is the most intelligent spokesman and best architect of the new "with it" world, in which a number of other distinguished architects, such as Charles Moore, also function.

But Venturi, like Kahn, starts from the beginning. Again that beginning recalls Wright's, and in Venturi's case also derives (I am pleased to say) from the Shingle Style.
1.16 Wright started in 1889 with a simple gabled house, as a child might draw a house but with a kind of vestigial Palladian motif in the gable. I made a great deal in *The Shingle*
1.14, 1.17 *Style* of Wright's dependence upon two houses by Bruce Price in this design. So Venturi:
18.1 he presents an ur-house with a Palladian gesture literally drawn on it. Irony enters in: the gable splits, space escapes, protection dissolves and, while all this exactly reflects the curving lift of the space inside, it also turns the facade to cardboard, like an ironic comment on one of Kahn's cardboard models or on the whole American *rêve à deux millions* itself, surely on everything that is conjured up when real-estate operators refer to a house as a "home."

Still, I do not wish to give the impression that Venturi's irony has unfitted him for large, straightforward projects. The opposite is true. It connects him with reality,
15.17 with things as they really are. A housing project of his faced the sea, gave each apartment a view of the water, handled the cars easily below, and would have done the whole job very cheaply in terms of vernacular American construction if it had won the competition. The outcome indicates a good deal of what is wrong with American architecture at the moment: an inability to focus on function, a genteel and derivative pretension, a platitudinous abstraction. The lack of all those qualities in Venturi's
15.18, 15.19 Transportation Square Office Building for Washington caused it to be denied a building permit by the Washington Fine Arts Commission. That gratuitously unpleasant body also repeatedly denied a permit to Romaldo Giurgola for his competition-winning headquarters for the American Institute of Architects. Having ruined his building as far as he felt he could go in order to bring it into line with the commission's ponderously classicizing demands (and I mean Bauhaus classicizing, not Beaux-Arts ditto),

Giurgola finally resigned from the project. Venturi, in the shadow of the Capitol, is still struggling along.

But in order to give Venturi his proper due in relation to American architecture as a whole, it is necessary for me to digress for a moment to my own work and, alas, related topics. From 1955 until 1963, despite publication in the modern field, I worked almost entirely on Greek architecture and was obsessed by it. Here, as Peter Smithson once correctly said, was the burning in me of a long fuse which had been lit by *Vers une architecture*, when Le Corbusier wrote of the Acropolis "nothing . . . left but these closely knit and violent elements, sounding clear and tragic like brazen trumpets." And of the Parthenon: "This creates a fact as reasonable to our understanding as the fact 'sea' or the fact 'mountain.'" And of the landscape: "The axis of the Acropolis runs . . . from the sea to the mountain." Upon these three concepts all my own work on Greek temples in landscape might be said to have had its inception. But it had another beginning too, when Alvar Aalto lectured at Yale in 1947, and in his 250 words of basic English gave the most moving lecture about architecture that I have ever heard. His topic was the reconstruction of Finland, and he drew the Acropolis and its setting on the blackboard, talking about the Periclean buildings as the reconstruction projects they were. Then he said, "In Finland in the reconstruction we will build no temporary buildings, because not by temporary building comes Parthenon on Acropolis."

Perhaps that was the moment when I learned that the ages are all linked together. Or perhaps I was merely acting out the latest, perhaps the last, phase of the recurrent American Greek Revival, a little like Thomas Cole in his painting of 1840, called *The Architect's Dream*. Whatever the case, arriving in Greece was more like coming home than any other experience I have ever had: appropriately enough at the Temple 12.6
of Hera at Paestum where the goddess reminds the Greeks of Argos and holds the land for this colonial city as its fair share. At the same time, the experience of Greece opened me to a philosophical and social view more intense than the rather empirical New Deal optimism I had professed before. Here the basic text, for me as for many others of my generation and, I am glad to say, for many young Americans since that time, was Albert Camus's *The Rebel*, of 1951. I would show a slide of this in class (the first I ever took of a Greek temple) and read from Camus something like, "We shall choose Ithaca, the faithful land, frugal and audacious thought, lucid action, and the generosity of the man who understands. In the light, the earth remains our first and our last love. Our brothers are breathing under the same sky as we; justice is a living thing."

It seemed to me marvelous and true beyond words that Le Corbusier said the
same thing at Chandigarh, and in the same way, balancing the embodiment of the human 4.9
act with the open landscape against which it is judged and with which it creates that image of the existential reality of the human position in the world with which I began this
talk. It seemed to me right beyond all hope that, on the one hand, the Temple of Athena at 16.8
Paestum should have omitted its horizontal cornice and lifted the center of visual gravity in its columns so that her embodiment of civic force should rise victoriously upward against the Italian hills and that, on the other, Le Corbusier should have done exactly the

same thing in his embodiment of human law in the High Court at Chandigarh. And I concluded my book on *Modern Architecture*, of 1961, with a photograph (from the *Illustrated*
8.16 *London News*) and the last lines from *The Rebel*: "At this moment when at last a man is born, it is time to forsake our age and its adolescent furies. The bow bends; the wood complains. At the moment of supreme tension, there will leap into flight an unswerving arrow, a shaft that is inflexible and free." All this seemed to me to make a monumental structure of everything I could feel to be true about the essential fact of human life in action, as Le Corbusier had shown it to us in *Le Modulor* and as our greatest American painters of the fifties, such as Franz Kline, had embodied it in their forms. Yet I suppose that this was the rub: the word "essential," because the classic Greek passion has always focused upon the essential statement and let everything else go hang.

In the long run it is not an entirely satisfactory premise in dealing with the multiple and varied kinds of architecture we have to build today. At any rate, by the early sixties its limitations had become apparent. I would not be so pretentious or foolish as to claim any part whatever in Paul Rudolph's Art and Architecture Building at Yale, of 1961–63. Rudolph's work is his own, but it reflects interests similar to mine at the time. A sculptural lift is desired, like that of Le Corbusier's La Tourette; and a lift requires a weight to be lifted lest it look absurd. Hence the upper floor had to be designed as a beam. But where Le Corbusier could use monks' cells at that level, so creating a visually dense element without either disguising or restricting its actual spatial requirements, Rudolph had to deal with painters' studios there, and therefore squeezed them in area and impoverished them in light. Hence one of the most determined efforts to make a classically sculptural embodiment of action in America ended in at least partial architectural failure.

Worse than this, by the middle sixties it had become apparent that Le Corbusier's images of human power had become bureaucratized into something repellently arid and inhuman, so merging with the classicizing design which produced the Beinecke Library. The proposed government center for New Haven, which was blocked by citizen action, turned the High Court at Chandigarh into something out of Mussolini's EUR, another of those "empty landscapes of psychosis" we noted earlier. The lift of Le Corbusier's piers was now intended to go on for forty stories in a government-subsidized, privately-owned speculative office building which beat its breast in a vast open space formed by its new plaza (for which a fine old post office was to have been demolished) and by New Haven's historic central square, called the Green, whose scale would have been ground down by it. Such placement was clearly a further bureaucratization of the Corbusian model, where, in 1925, we are shown the skyscrapers of the Voisin plan standing free in superblock *jardins anglais*, which destroyed what were to Le Corbusier the dark *rues corridor* of the existing city, while the *autostrade* leaped through and over it all.

Here was cataclysmic redevelopment at its inception. There can be no doubt but that it would have brought sun, air, and space to the tubercular crannies of old Paris, and it surely created the archetypal modern image of mass man housed in his millions, overriding all previous forms with his might. Humanized by a true park, it could produce

9.4 Oak Street Connector, New Haven, Connecticut. Aerial view, c. 1968

Roehampton and some reasonable housing elsewhere, but when perverted as a model for redevelopment in America it has proved an unmitigated disaster. The process normally began with a low-income neighborhood, called a slum, like the Oak Street area in New
Haven. Into that, by the late fifties, was rammed Le Corbusier's *autostrade*, now the Oak 9.4
Street Connector, by which cars were to be encouraged to drive at a mad pace into the center of town. With sloping sides, frontage roads, and so on, the whole thing was designed like that Open Road I mentioned earlier, as if it were being laid out in the center of Nebraska rather than in a crowded city. Indeed the great gulf which was created is still intended to be pushed brutally and at even greater width through the rest of the low-income area beyond it, so permitting suburbanites to drive into the shopping center of the city, rather than to a suburban shopping center, without, in the process, being obliged to look at the urban poor along the way. The form created is exactly that of a
drawing by Le Corbusier of 1922, but only superficially so. Because here again was a 9.5
gross distortion of a European program in which the housing built was not for the poor who had originally lived on the site, but is instead luxury housing for the really quite rich. (Crummy, but luxury.) The only exception is Rudolph's old-people's tower, stuck up like an obelisk above the freeway.

Where did the poor go? "To Bridgeport," is the waggish reply in New Haven. Some were rehoused (though not in low-income housing, of which only twelve units have been built in fifteen years as against five thousand or so dwellings of the poor destroyed). In any event, the neighborhoods were broken up, and true slums began to be created as new neighborhoods crowded and sickened under redevelopment's threat. Some of the

Le Corbusier. Contemporary City for Three Million Inhabitants project, 1922. Perspective 9.5

poor, especially the coloreds, to whom the suburbs were normally closed, were forced to move before redevelopment's bulldozers two or three times. Many ended up in an area known as the Hill where, by 1966, redevelopment threatened once more. We cannot be surprised that New Haven's riot of 1967 occurred there. The scheme originally proposed for the area by the Redevelopment Agency was based, curiously enough, upon exactly the same classicizing model as that for the government center I mentioned a moment ago. A freestanding tower of old folks rose above a vast open area surrounded by space-defining buildings to be used as middle-income housing. The open space was intended to be justified by two schools set at the busiest intersection in the area. The process might be described as escalation on the home front: bomb it, clean it up, rehouse fewer people than were there before, and different people, because the projected rents were not at all within a low-income range. Again, it can be no surprise that citizen pressure of all kinds brought the scheme to a halt and forced the agency to hire a presumably responsible architect, in this case Louis I. Kahn, to make sense out of the mess. This Kahn has manifestly not yet done. True enough, he has thrown out the tower and requested the resiting of one of the schools in order to reduce the open area and to make possible the addition of more housing. But the people of the neighborhood, black and white alike, trust neither him nor the agency any more. They would like to control their own destinies, as rich people do. They would like to design their own neighborhood, but they don't know how to do it. The impasse is total, and it is symbolic of that general crisis in the national life of the United States of which you can hardly be unaware. Some awesome birth is impending, but who the fathers may eventually turn out to be is still a matter of dispute. The heroic pretensions of the last decade have turned to tragic war, and the old confrontational models of action, in politics as in urbanism, have shown themselves to be unrealistic and out of date, brutalized by time. For these reasons a disgust with action has begun to creep over all of those who think. This is true in architectural schools as elsewhere, because our architecture of this kind has come to be

9.6 Roche and Dinkeloo. Knights of Columbus Buildling, New Haven, Connecticut, 1965–69. Elevation

seen by American students as an all too obvious symbol of the larger horrors of our time. Camus said all this too. "Our purpose," he wrote, "is to find out whether innocence, the moment it becomes involved in action, can avoid committing murder. . . . In that every action today leads to murder, direct or indirect, we cannot act until we know whether or not we have the right to kill."

From that point of view, much of the architecture now being produced in the United States according to the outworn classicizing model does exhibit disquieting qualities. The Knights of Columbus Office Building, now rising above the Oak Street 9.6
Connector, is presented by its designers as an image of paramilitary dandyism, jack-booted, stagy, and disoriented. It stands above the wasteland of the Connector like the last victor, a bemused mastodon, severely savaged somewhere below the belt. Across from it rises its complement, which I had great trouble making Jim Stirling believe was a school. (It is named after the mayor.) In fact it looks like a pillbox, set to sweep the Connector if necessary, and sited in unusable space in order to be visible from it. It is set directly against the "Hill" we just discussed, an indication of the "uptight" attitude par excellence. How different is Taos under its hill, where things happen naturally and as if they belonged there. How meager and wrong the architectural models of the past decades now look to us by comparison. How blinded by vulgarly genteel taste and how insensitive to fundamental human values we surely were. But some of us have tried to change. Jane Jacobs, for example, did a great deal to make us recognize the architectural superiority of the traditional street to a redeveloped street where everything rushes in one direction, devoid of multiple uses. Robert Venturi also played a critical part in his book, *Complexity and Contradiction in Architecture*, when he said, "Main Street [is] almost all right." As indeed it is, with its variety of scales and functions, its civil false fronts, its

embrace but command of the automobile. Because of this we have also come in America to revaluate our past, to see in Sullivan, for example, not only a creator of proto-Miesian skyscrapers but also a consummate artist of Main Street who made a generous permanence out of its shifting forms. So Venturi, in the Guild House we looked at before, comes up to the street, defines it, and expands the false front upward toward the sky. He connects us as well with the life in our popular culture, from which that movement which our historians tended to call the International Style, had, no less than the Beaux-Arts, previously divided us. So the supergraphics of the Guild House are a Pop Art phenomenon and remind us of the painting by Robert Indiana in which the message of the American Dream is reduced to its essentials. Now we reverse the process—and see Rome in our own terms, as supergraphics and informational theory.

Or, more truly, we merge what we are in vulgar fact with what we would like to be more fully than we have ever been able to do before. So the Pantheon with its billboard in front and its dream world behind becomes Venturi's competition entry for a weirdly
15.15 necrophiliac monument called the Football Hall of Fame, with an electronic football field flashing frontally away while running backs and goal-line stands flicker in interminable victory across the rounded surfaces inside. We see the same principles at work in Las Vegas, to which critics like your Reyner Banham and our Tom Wolfe have also directed our attention. The electric signs lift, expand in scale, and carry on against the sky like Roman arches or Etruscan pediments. Some even genteelly invoke their ancestry. In this new focus the "uptight" nerves relax (some think too much so) and the cultural worm turns. My son, for example, is going to Rome next year to study it according to principles he and his classmates worked out under the direction of Robert and Denise Venturi for the analysis of Las Vegas. So almost everything we were once told was messy (the "mess that is man-made America," the *Architectural Review* called it in 1950) many of us now regard as great. But there is a clear danger here that we will see these forms in purely picturesque terms—which, in our affluent, permissive world, has always been our tendency with everything. Our elms, for example, were once our finest urban forms—indeed in many towns our largest ones—and when they die, as they are doing everywhere, it often turns out there is no urban definition left at all. The signs of the strip are much the same, larger than their buildings; another easy way out of more complex urban problems if we consider them only visually and by themselves. But if we look at them and at their related automobilized experiences both sadly and ironically, for what they are, the products of crime and the children of ignorance, the embodiments of adolescent mobility and geriatric self-indulgence, of technical virtuosity and philosophical innocence, we are starting to face ourselves as we are, and to cast our illusions aside. That is why the students trust
12.39 Venturi when he designs buildings like this one, models perhaps of what we knew was true when we were children, before a fouled-up modern society put guns in our hands and gave us strange objectives, and twisted justifications in our brains. Far beyond systems analysis, buildings like this seem at the moment to touch our basic problem; it lies in the soul, which needs to be liberated into common humanity. Claes Oldenburg says it, too: better and truer than the Pan Am Building, Venturi says, is a Popsicle turned upside

down. And he is right. You will recall his lipsticks for Piccadilly Circus, his lavatory floats like suns for the Thames, and his teddy bear for Central Park.

If heroic attitudinizing goes, what is left? Why, everything: the town with its people, as Lorenzetti shows us, the town, the country, and the road; all of it, all of architecture that is, made possible by good Government: decent policy, the consent of the governed, justice, and peace. It is that principle which emerges, and remains. In the end, when all the perceptions are in, it is that principle which the architectural historian and critic must serve, and for which he must fight in every way he can: at Tewa Tesuque under Lake Peak no less than in New Haven, under its own sacred mountain, with the monument to our Revolution and our Civil War upon it. How well a large Oldenburg lipstick would look up there.

Camus wrote this too: "When revolution in the name of power and of history becomes a murderous and immoderate mechanism, a new rebellion is consecrated in the name of moderation and of life. We are at that extremity now. At the end of this tunnel of darkness, however, there is inevitably a light, which we already divine and for which we only have to fight to ensure its coming. All of us, among the ruins, are preparing a renaissance beyond the limits of nihilism. But few of us know it."

NEIL LEVINE

"Where Is Modern Architecture Going?" *GA (Global Architecture) Document* 1 (Summer 1980): 6–11.

The critique of modern architecture that had been slowly developing since the mid-1950s reached a point of sharpness and clarity in the latter half of the 1970s when the term post-modernism began to be used to describe the new initiatives. The exhibition *The Architecture of the Ecole des Beaux-Arts*—organized by Arthur Drexler and held in the fall and winter of 1975–76 at New York's Museum of Modern Art, the very bastion of modernism—was one of the first of a number of public manifestations of the changed way of thinking. It was followed in quick succession by the publication of Charles Jencks's *The Language of Post-Modern Architecture* (1977), the second editions of Robert Venturi's precedent-setting *Complexity and Contradiction in Architecture* and his and Denise Scott Brown's and Steven Izenour's *Learning from Las Vegas* (both 1977), Rem Koolhaas's *Delirious New York* (1978), Colin Rowe and Fred Koetter's *Collage City* (1978), the Archives d'Architecture Moderne's *Rational Architecture: The Reconstruction of the European City* (1978), and Paolo Portoghesi's *After Modern Architecture* (1980). Two exhibitions at the end of the decade, Drexler's follow-up to the Beaux-Arts, *Transformations in Modern Architecture*, held at MoMA in the early part of 1979, and Portoghesi's *The Presence of the Past*, held in the summer of 1980 at the Venice Biennale, presented striking visual documentation of what had led up to the current crisis and where things might be heading.

10

Planned to coincide with the opening of the Venice Biennale, a new quarterly called *GA Document* was launched in mid-1980 by Yukio Futagawa, publisher and chief

Where Is Modern Architecture Going?

VINCENT SCULLY

In order to answer that question I went to Arthur Drexler's show at the Museum of Modern Art. It suggested the following to me:

Modern architecture is an environmentally destructive mass of junk, dominated by curtain-wall corporate structures which will continue to be built so long as modern bureaucracy exists. Marxist critics might rather disingenuously say, while modern capitalism exists. But that, alas, would be inaccurate, because modern socialism has its bureaucracy too, and it shows no sign of withering away either. So while vast numbers of unhappy human beings herd themselves into towers and slabs in order to move papers from one tray to another, and while that activity is regarded as essential to modern life, and while the primary criterion for housing it remains simple economic determinism, the towers and slabs will continue to be built much as they are—surely the dreariest archetype for an urban architecture that human history has so far recorded. How sad that statement is, considering the pure excitement the skyscraper generated in the years of its birth. Those years coincided with the birth of the "modern" consciousness; the two grew up together, and the skyscraper became the major modern symbol. But now, alas

editor of *Global Architecture.* A number of critics, including Scully, Christian Norberg-Schulz, Bruno Zevi, and Paul Goldberger were asked to respond to the question "Where Is Modern Architecture Going?" Scully's answer was the first to be published and was the lead-off piece in the first regular volume of the journal. He took as his point of departure the *Transformations* show at MoMA, in which Drexler had set out to survey the architecture of the 1960s and 1970s. Scully, like most observers, was profoundly disturbed by what he saw. In the catalogue accompanying the exhibition, Drexler gave a sense of the despair he himself felt by quoting Mies van der Rohe describing a typical working day at the very beginning of the period in question: "I get up. I sit on the bed. I think 'what the hell went wrong? We showed them what to do.'" The exhibition, which was composed of a little over four hundred relatively small-scale photographs depicting nearly that many buildings, appeared to reduce late modern architecture to a blur of visual noise. The effect was intentional. Drexler believed that current practice had lost early modernism's idealistic social and ethical purpose and had become "impoverished" in the process, merely a game of formal manipulations often parodying its own sources. Among individuals, only Louis Kahn, James Stirling, and Robert Venturi were singled out for providing any sense of direction; and among movements or trends, only the revival of interest in the vernacular with its logical extension into historicism was seen to offer any new approach, albeit one that gave serious cause for concern. Drexler's overall assessment of modern architecture's future could be said to lie somewhere between inconclusive and dire.

The *Transformations* show gave Scully a perfect foil for articulating his more forthright answer to the question "Where Is Modern Architecture Going?" Although he initially seems to take umbrage at Drexler's apparent trashing of modern architecture, Scully

for Sullivan and his ornament, and for Le Corbusier and his armies of Cartesian towers; alas even for Mies who worked out the details that made it all a far-flung, computer-controlled reality.

Drexler's show puts the case plainly. It enshrines the curtain-wall slabs at the center of the exhibition, within a kind of womb in the middle of the space. Around its inner walls the glassy towers all wink in color, a vacuous paradise of stiff but ectoplasmic forms. The rest of the exhibition is in black and white. Its hundreds of photographs are dumped en masse around the periphery of the main exhibition area and spill over into a couple of adjacent rooms. They are mostly organized into purposely non-intellectual and logically inconsistent groupings, such as "slant roofs," "structural exhibitionism," and so on, so that, with one exception, they do not develop thematically. The general impression, surely an intended one, is of mindless profusion, of a grab-bag of aggressively maladjusted, primitive, and crippled forms. What Drexler is doing is directly in line with the attack on modern architecture which he has been mounting for several years, and it is an effective continuation of that destructive campaign. Here, in his hands, it all looks like

in the end agrees with the basic premise that, in the process of its universalization and institutionalization, the modern movement lost the ideals and values that had once made it what it was. But unlike Drexler, who neither historicized nor defined his own critical position, Scully immediately points out that the very reason why one has been able to see the situation for what it is, namely, postmodernism's "reversal of vision and belief," should be looked to as the basis for renewal. With almost none of Drexler's reservations, Scully maintains that the answer to present-day problems lies in a return to the vernacular, understood here in a very broad sense as encompassing historical and contemporary, urban and suburban patterns of environmental design. Two different though interrelated approaches are highlighted—the first, essentially American and suburban, stemming from Venturi and engaged with pop culture and literary symbolism; the second, predominantly European and urban, deriving from the Neorationalism of Aldo Rossi and embodying more abstract, authoritarian, and typological predilections. Although Scully admits he prefers the former for its sense of realism and irony, he predicts (correctly, in retrospect) that the latter would be more acceptable to the academic establishment. He also predicts, though with less reason and conviction, that the interest in energy-conscious design sparked by the recent oil crisis could add an important functional rationale for formal invention.

The essay reprinted here was published in a somewhat different and expanded form in the catalogue for the Venice Biennale exhibition in which Scully, along with Jencks,

junk. One wouldn't care if every bit of it disappeared off the face of the earth tomorrow. It begins to seem wholly unworthy of a complex civilization: brutally underconsidered and detailed, mindlessly "inventive" but lumpishly inarticulate, all wrong in material and scale, and wrong in intention most of all. Is it really so, or does it only appear so in the glare of the criminal line-up?

The question answers itself. Nobody, however hostile, could have made this mass of material look so shoddy a few years ago. Now things have changed. The model has broken. It might be said that Jencks, Stern, and the other postmodernists have gone a long way toward completing the reversal of vision and belief which was begun by Venturi about twenty years ago. But if we look back as far as the early 1950s we can see that the job had already begun by that time. When it finally became possible to build modern buildings in large numbers after World War II, so that modern architecture became a reality rather than largely a dream, its limitations rapidly became apparent—especially its inability to create an environment either adequately articulated or properly unified. That is to say, in the thirties there were only a few masterpieces of modern architecture to see, and they were truly masterpieces, borne up by the still solid vernacular architecture in which most of the world was built and which set them off as precious objects. By the fifties, however, when they became numerous enough to begin to destroy the subtle and complex urban structure of the vernacular and so began to create much of the urban envi-

Norberg-Schulz, Udo Kultermann, Roberto Mazzariol, and Robert Stern, served as an advisor (Kenneth Frampton, originally a member of the committee, resigned in protest). *The Presence of the Past* was intended, in its organizer Portoghesi's words, to document "the return of architecture to the womb of history and its recycling in new syntactic contexts of traditional forms . . . [as] understood by some critics in the ambiguous but efficacious category of Post-Modern." The central feature of the show was the Strada Novissima, a model street defined by facades designed by the likes of Robert Venturi, Robert Stern, Michael Graves, Frank Gehry, Allan Greenberg, Charles Moore, Leon Krier, and Rem Koolhaas to demonstrate "the return of the street" as "a formative element of the city." Although Scully was not responsible for this idea, it certainly owed something to the prescient criticism of modernist urbanism he had launched in the early sixties in "The Death of the Street."

ronment themselves, their effect was cancerous. They ate out the world, emptying it of definition and meaning, reducing its capacity to speak or to nourish. After a generation of that our eyes have learned to rebel. They are at last ready to see architecture in a new way. They have lost their most recent set of scales. Before they grow new ones they may see clearly for a while. And what they see around us seems by and large to be the worst architecture the world has ever produced. Is that opinion only a matter of changing taste? (A charmingly antiquarian phrase for that enormous phenomenon when the brain turns around and loves what it hated and hates what it loved.) I think it is more than that. There is some recognition of objective reality in it. Consider an empty site. Today we are perfectly sure that it will be better empty than with a new building on it. Consider an old building. We shudder when a new building is projected to replace it because we have good reason to suspect that it will be worse than the old. The whole activity is becoming uneconomic anyway. It all costs so much that only profiteers of one kind or another can build anything. Every new triumph on the Houston skyline reads like a new victory for reaction, another monument to the terminal illness of liberal America. Government money goes not into correcting that situation but into armaments which make it worse. Nobody will build low-income housing, especially in the city where it is needed. The excuse is that it will be vandalized, which closes a vicious circle and makes it unnecessary to do anything for anybody until it is too late, which it just about is right now.

What are the ways out of all this? How to make architecture respectable again so that decent people can take joy in it and let it resume its ancient role of building (gently, bit by bit) a decent world? I think, as a matter of fact, that a few enormously intelligent and talented architects have been proposing two different answers to that question. As is so often the case in such situations, each of those answers seems the exact reverse of the other, and indeed one appears to have arisen in part as a kind of reaction to the first. Yet in the end they have a good deal in common. I refer, first, to that movement toward the revival of the vernacular which was begun by Robert Venturi and to which Drexler's show briefly refers (and we should remember that it was Drexler who published *Complexity and Contradiction* in 1966), and second, to that movement called Neorationalism which was apparently initiated by Aldo Rossi and which involves, among others, Leon and Robert Krier and, by extension and in part, Isozaki and Stirling. The influence of Ungers and, more indirectly, of Kahn, can also be pervasively felt. The objectives and achievements of the two movements may be rather crudely put as follows: The first broke the hermetic grip of the International Style and tried to plug architecture back into the power that vernacular architecture has always possessed. Hence Venturi's distinguished oeuvre has embodied suggestions from the late-nineteenth-century Shingle Style on the one hand and from the contemporary American automobile strip on the other. It has especially sought out the multiple symbols that are involved in modern culture and has tried to conceptualize and form architecture in the simplest possible way as an affair of "decorated sheds" of well-proportioned buildings shaped very simply around their functions and decorated with some device which will physically and associatively embody their meaning, tell us what they are about. (This is, for example, precisely the way Palladio designed his villas.) So all the elaborately "inventive" contortions of modern architecture, which make such a brutal effect in Drexler's show, are thrown out in favor of the timeless essentials of function and symbol, embedded in a living vernacular matrix. In Venturi's view what he is doing is still modern architecture, because he wants to adapt, clarify, and generally to abstract the basic vernacular forms. He changes their scale, imbues them with gestural power, and sometimes parodies them with wicked precision. Most of all, though contrary perhaps to some opinion, what he is fundamentally doing is simplifying everything. His system is an utterly rational one and is in that sense very "modern" even in the canonical, International Style meaning of the word. It is true that Venturi has been followed—and now in some cases disowned as a reactionary—by a number of architects and critics who would like to regard modern architecture as just another style among many and who want to go much farther than Venturi does in the use of all kinds of vernacular and historical forms. Jencks and Stern, whom I mentioned earlier, are among them, as are, I suppose, Charles Moore and many of the young architects who have been taught by him. Some are doing colonial architecture of a sort; one at least is basing his buildings on the shapes of various kinds of vehicles. Most outrageous of all is Allan Greenberg, though I understand that there are others somewhat like him in England. Greenberg quotes the good old aphorism that the architect should decorate construction, never construct decoration, and would affirm, I am sure, that much modern

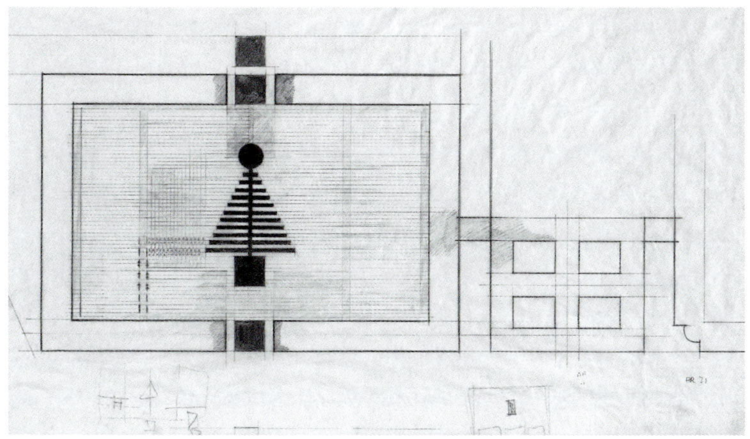

10.1 ABOVE, LEFT: Aldo Rossi. Cemetery extension, Modena, Italy, 1971–80. Plan

10.2 ABOVE, RIGHT: Aldo Rossi. Apartment Block, Gallaratese District, Milan, 1968–76. Exterior

architecture of the kind to be found in Drexler's show is in fact decoration constructed at a building's scale and hence a disaster in every significant way. He believes that classic architecture knew how to build an urban environment correctly—by having all buildings much the same in massing but differently decorated. To that end he has painstakingly taught himself how to do literally classic design, in his hands a kind of marvelously scaled Lutyens-Baroque.

From these phenomena the Neorationalists turn in pious Marxist horror. While they regard the whole scene as a self-evident expression of American decadence, it is for Venturi that they reserve their choicest invective. They profess to regard much of his work as non-architectural because of its use of "signs," supergraphics, and patterned surfaces, of tacked-on, representational, vernacular elements, of electronic projection, and so on. They object to his theoretical distinction between the "shed" and the "decoration," and they especially dislike his adaptation of forms derived from capitalist popular culture which, to the very depths of their stern souls, they regard as degraded. And stern is, I think, the most appropriate adjective with which to characterize their
work. Aldo Rossi's project for a cemetery in Modena and his housing slab in the 10.1, 10.2
Gallaratese project in Milan are its archetypal monuments so far. In them the forms of the International Style of the twenties (in Italy called Rationalist) are revived, simplified, clarified, made stiff and static. Architecture is reduced to its geometric essentials in the
typical Neoclassic way, recalling that of Ledoux. It is very Italian: the conception is on 4.2
the one hand utterly immaterial and Neoplatonic, all pure Idea and primary shapes in the ancient tradition of Renaissance humanist theory. But, as is also typical of Italian architecture, the forms are also very physical. They are heavy—in which they differ most from their Rational predecessors—solemn, and insistently repetitive, casting ominous shadows like those painted by de Chirico so long ago. In all this they strongly recall the forms of Italian Fascist architecture, especially those of Fascism's swan song, the EUR exhibition grounds outside Rome. In them one can almost hear the young black-shirted idealists of the 1920s calling for discipline, order, courage, and self-denial—for all of

those qualities and states of being which Fascism so vilely perverted but which are by no means necessarily wrong in themselves and which are, as a matter of fact, distinctly lacking in most of the modern world and its architecture. Neorationalist architecture is unashamedly attempting to bring them back. And much of its appeal lies precisely in that. It calls up simple and rather heroic emotions and avoids the relaxed, civilized ironies which are so central to Venturi's work, no less than the multiple layers of complex and contradictory meanings which Venturi first suggested and which Jencks and other semiologists now hail. Where Venturi's design is realist and materialist, Neorationalism is idealist in method. Where is Marxist materialism now, one asks, but that is really an unfair question because art, where free, remains true only to its own hopelessly irrational laws, whoever the artist and whatever he names his art. The Neorationalists regard themselves as ideologically directed, but like all art their own is effective because of its form. Neorationalism is in fact peculiarly formalistic, wedded to pure form. But it is also ideological and authoritarian, much as the International Style before it was. Leon Krier's
10.3 stunning project for the quarter called La Villette in Paris is an excellent example of that. His perspective of the quarter is one of the great modern drawings, greater even than
9.5 Le Corbusier's famous perspectives of his Ideal City, of 1922. Krier's love-hate relationship with Le Corbusier is obvious. The drawing recalls the Master (though the airplanes are closer to Melnikov, as we can now see him in Frederick Starr's fine book), but the urbanism is totally different. It throws out the automobile as destructive to the urban life of the quarter and designs solid blocks of housing respecting the traditional street. Down the center, on a wonderful axis toward the Seine, where the Corbusian throughway would normally have been found, Krier substitutes a fine garden and a long *bassin*, stretching out into the heart of Paris. Like Le Corbusier's, Krier's urban model funda-

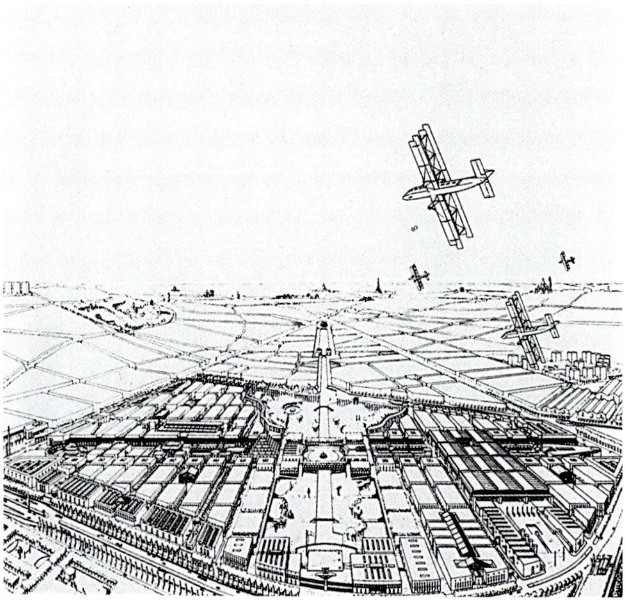

Leon Krier. La Villette District project, Paris, 1976. Aerial perspective 10.3

mentally derives from the planning of Louis XIV. Here the grand *bassin* recalls Versailles, while the curvilinear garden which opens out to it from the quarter itself has the same mitre-like shape that Le Nôtre designed for Bossuet's garden in Meaux, when that eloquent prelate became bishop there. A monumental city center occupies a cross-axis, and here the shapes give the impression of having been conceived by Le Corbusier and then stiffened and made more strictly geometric by Louis I. Kahn. It is odd and touching that Kahn should apparently have played such a large part in creating the forms used in both camps—by Venturi no less than here. Kahn himself would have preferred the Neorationalists, I think. He was an idealist, as they are, and distrusted Venturi's realism and irony, as well as, most of all, his semiological liveliness, his genius for gestural communication, and his linguistic virtuosity. Kahn, too, was formed by Rome, and some
of his beautiful pastels of 1951–52 prefigure the quality of Krier's de Chirico–like 17.5
perspective of the Place de la Mairie at La Villette. The reminiscences of Fascist monumentalism are also common to both.

Krier's great project also calls up the question of authoritarianism in directly programmatic terms. That is, what about no cars? The only ways in which a modern worker can be prevented from owning an automobile are a) to keep him so poor that he can't afford one, or b) to forbid the economy to produce them for him. Theoretically, and the Neorationalists surely hope for this, the city might be made so attractive and public transportation throughout it and the countryside so cheap and efficient that nobody wanted an automobile. But I don't believe it. If so, only authoritarian solutions remain. The Neorationalists quite rightly believe that the destruction of the traditional city by the automobile has been one of capitalism's worst crimes. A number of us were saying exactly that in America fifteen or more years ago, at a time when the big planners of the modern movement were still calling for the throughways to be rammed right through the center of the town. We fought them then, along with their urban zoos, the parking garages, which began to take over what was left of the city. Krier won't permit any of those either. So the inhabitants of his quarter will either never own automobiles or will park them three deep in the street. Splendid: a fine reaction. But is it realistic? Is there not a reasonable balance that could be found which would take account of the facts as we know them? We can and should design against the automobile in many instances, but we can hardly exclude it. In other words, is not Neorationalist urbanism exactly as idealist and authoritarian as Le Corbusier's was, except that some of the ground rules have changed, no doubt for the better? Yet some of Venturi's most expressive and historically important designs have directly grappled with the problem of the automobile on its own turf, along the urban strip and in the enormous parking lot. Before the great "Bill-Ding-
Board" of his project for the Football Hall of Fame, the automobiles were brought up in 15.15
two great waves, parking in vast reflex diagonals before the triangular reflecting pool with the broad electronic facade rising behind it. Venturi made architecture out of the automobile. Perhaps he will be able to do as much for Westway if that problematical project ever goes through. But the Neorationalists throw it out. Their happy workmen had better behave like traditional happy workmen or else.

Venturi and Rauch. Tucker House, Katonah, New York, 1974–76. Exterior 10.4

Beyond all that, the hauntingly beautiful artists' studios with which Krier so picturesquely defines Bossuet's garden can also, despite their Corbusian parentage,
10.4 remind us of a number of buildings by Venturi, such as the Tucker House or the Brant House in Aspen. They all share a wonderful lift, a heartwarming expansion of scale in the upper stories. They rise up singing together because their creators are both splendid architects. So, I hope I have indicated above, is Rossi. This is what they all share. This, and the fact that each side apparently wants to simplify architecture in its own way—not to impoverish but to solidify it and to reassert its fundamental character as that seems to them to be. So there is in fact much tragic irony in the heroic postures of the Neorationalists, while Venturi's design is no less geometric and considerably more pointed as a criticism of capitalism than theirs.

Yet, further consideration suggests that the Neorationalists have as strong links to the vernacular tradition as Venturi does. Rossi's work is luminously haunted by archetypally Italian forms (he revives the tradition that Fascism compromised), while Krier and Culot are deeply involved in the pervasive patterns of European urbanism. But again, Venturi's special contribution to a fresh conceptual and physical structure has grown out of his ability to draw viable architectural suggestions from the new and specifically modern vernaculars of strip and suburb no less than from traditional vernacular building types.

Which if either of these directions will finally save architecture in the end? Both have already had an enormous effect on young architects, and various combinations of both will continue to exert considerable influence and give rise to new forms and ideas. We may have preferences between them. I personally prefer realism to idealism; it has generally been less destructive of human life over the centuries. Still, Neorationalism is sweeping the architectural schools. Its geometric abstraction, suggestive of Spartan simplicity, seems to have a perennial appeal to the young, and has in fact been constantly renewed in every succeeding modern generation. Most germane here is the fact that

Neorationalist forms (leaving aside Krier's exquisite talent) are very easy to draw: nothing easier than undecorated hard-edged cubes and cylinders in isometric projection. The vernacular is much harder: those complicated Stick Style turned posts, for example. Beyond that, the stripped formalism of Neorationalism is ideal for academies, where design takes place under more or less hermetic conditions and needs to encourage easy comparative judgments. The overall environmental questions with which realistic vernacular building has to be concerned make it much more difficult for academies to deal with, as do its resultant forms, which are normally at once less spectacular, more qualified, and more complex in detail.

Indeed, much of Neorationalism as yet exists only in graphic form. The present boom in architectural drawings sold as paintings is in part related to its rise and to the influence of some of its mentors in drawings, such as Walter Pichler. The graphic work of Rem Koolhaas is an excellent example, and it spans both the Neorationalist and the vernacular schools. Indeed, it perfectly expresses and celebrates that love for those various kinds of architecture which the modern movement had bypassed that is affecting everyone now. So, in Koolhaas's drawings, and in those of his brilliant collaborators of the 10.5
OMA, the Russian Constructivist students of the twenties finally sail their floating swimming pool into New York harbor, and the Beaux-Arts skyscrapers which Le Corbusier despised rise up as persons and walk around and go to bed together and fall into the Hudson and swim about. The dreary slabs with which this article began fall back, and the Woolworth Building and Rockefeller Center step modestly forward. We all applaud. It surely is a lot of fun, so maybe there's hope after all.

Hope, maybe. But there is a larger problem, that of power. The question of political power is cogent enough, but I refer here to energy. Oil is failing, and will eventually, perhaps surprisingly soon, cease to exist. This constitutes, among other things, the most serious problem that architecture has faced during the entire modern period, but it also offers opportunities for architecture of a kind unmatched since the elevator and central heating got together to make skyscrapers possible. Once again, the creative solutions seem to be up to individuals, since government has persistently done all the wrong things so far. It has up to now permitted the oil companies to profiteer beyond all reason, so enabling them to spend a fraction of their profits on paid ads in all the media which tell the public how tenderly they hold its interests at heart. Government has moreover put almost no pressure on the automobile industry to explore power sources other than pure gasoline; it has put its money on the chancy horror of nuclear power, and in the United States it has unbelievably permitted the building, administration, and exploitation of nuclear plants to remain in private hands; it has persistently played down solar energy, perhaps because its favorite private utilities corporations have not yet been able to determine how to make money out of it; and where government has encouraged solar experiment at all it has for much too long opted for enormously complicated mechanical systems rather than for the simpler passive systems whereby energy is really saved.

But passive energy systems such as those developed by architects like David Sellers or the Total Environmental Action group, when used in conjunction with energy

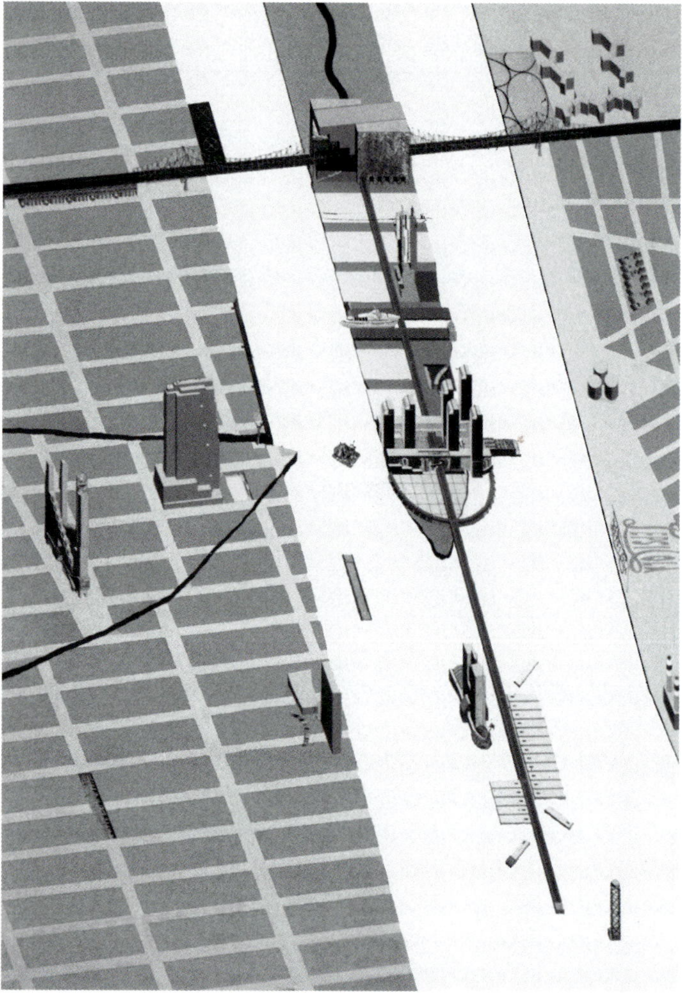

Rem Koolhaas and OMA. New Welfare Island project, New York, 1975–76. Axonometric 10.5

conservation techniques, are capable of handling about two-thirds of a normal house's requirements for energy anywhere in the United States right now. Passive solar energy should therefore be encouraged by government in every conceivable way. Incentives of a type long granted to other kinds of utilities should make it possible, perhaps mandatory, for every new building to be designed and built with a maximum passive energy system, including conservation measures, solar collectors, greenhouses, and all the many simple devices which are now available to recycle wastes and, where applicable, to harness the wind. Beyond that, all old structures, whether urban or rural, and of whatever size, should be fitted with whatever set of passive systems and conservation devices their conformation and setting permit, and concentrated urban groupings should be served by special facilities capable of distributing solar- and wind-derived energy to them in varying degrees.

In all these categories the opportunities for architecture are enormous. Growth is step by step, from the individual unit outward, from the general to the particular, the unit to the whole. The shapes of houses change in fundamental, if not necessarily spectacular ways; the street changes but gains new kinds of definition. Great new urban structures, worthy of Venturi, Krier, or Koolhaas, come into being; enormous solar collectors open to the sun; windmills rise up in massed batteries on the heights, deploy along the ridge lines, and string out in great files across the plains. Everything begins to adjust itself to working with nature rather than against it. Everything opens like plants to the light and closes in the darkness like flowers rather than like fists. The whole feeling of the environment changes as does, in consequence, the character of the life which is lived within it.

It could, soberly considered, be a wonderful world. It could go very far toward freeing modern life from the polluting tyranny of oil and the corroding terror of nuclear disaster. Its architectural forms could be richer, more varied, and more fantastic than those of any of the utopian visions we have seen so far. They would also be much more reasonable, logical, and easy to bring about, shaping modern urbanism's last hope, architecture's frontier.

NEIL LEVINE

"Frank Lloyd Wright and the Stuff of Dreams." *Perspecta: The Yale Architectural Journal* 16 (1980): 8–31.

This essay is as exceptional in Scully's writings as it is in the historiography of Frank Lloyd Wright. Using the structure of Freudian psychology as set forth in *The Interpretation of Dreams* (1900) to explain the formation and meaning of the architect's early work, it is at once a study in the history of ideas, an analysis of the creative process, a theorizing of abstraction, and an investigation of the nature of the modern experience. It shows us how Scully rethought the themes of his earlier work on Wright and reconsidered them in the light of new and more complex approaches to the study of the history of art.

"Frank Lloyd Wright and the Stuff of Dreams" is based on a lecture given in 1977, most appropriately, at the Nineteenth Century Woman's Club in Oak Park, an organization of which Wright's mother was a founding member and to which his first wife, Catherine, and the woman for whom he left her, Mamah Borthwick Cheney, both belonged. The talk was co-sponsored by the Yale Club of Chicago and the Frank Lloyd Wright Home and Studio. Almost twenty years had passed since Scully had written his book *Frank Lloyd Wright* (1960), during which time Wright scholarship had entered a new phase marked by sociological and psychological concerns. The two most important books of the period, Norris Kelly Smith's *Frank Lloyd Wright: A Study in Architectural Content* (1966) and Robert Twombly's *Frank Lloyd Wright: An Interpretive Biography* (1973), explain Wright's architecture of the Oak Park years in terms of the institution of family life it was meant to embody and the tension that resulted, both in the work itself and in his own personal life, from the

11

Frank Lloyd Wright and the Stuff of Dreams

VINCENT SCULLY

It should be said at the outset that this article is about Wright and Freud. The fact that it backs into that topic and at intervals backs away from it is due in part to its original conception, which was as a general talk about Wright's early work to be given in Oak Park, and for which the central theme emerged only during its preparation. For this reason some extraneous material still adheres to it, and what now seems to me to be the most important point of all—the monumental fact of abstraction—comes through almost parenthetically, almost unconsciously, itself. Yet abstraction, created separately by Wright and Cubism in strikingly similar ways, should now, I think, be seen as quintessentially, indeed "unconsciously," Freudian in its method—infinitely more so than the overtly "Freudian" symbolism employed by the Surrealists later.

Wright came first. It is therefore about his work that the fundamental questions must be asked. What does it mean? How do we experience it? What was in Wright's mind when he made it, and by what alchemy did he bring his intentions to physical form? These questions lie at the heart of the mystery of all art—and they seem especially urgent when we have to deal with forms like those of Unity Temple, for example: so

emphasis Wright placed on individual freedom. Scully refers to both authors in the text reprinted here and builds on some of the same ideas about architecture in the service of turn-of-the-century, middle-class ideals of the family. The crucial difference—in method—is his correlation of Wright and Freud and—in intention—his focus on the creation of symbolic form.

Scully proposes a parallelism between Freud's analysis of dreams and Wright's formulation of the Prairie House that is grounded in a shared ethos of familial sanctity and well-being. The very terms Freud used to explain how the dreamwork functions, namely, condensation, displacement, abstraction, and dramatization, are shown to be precisely the ones that best describe how Wright achieved the unique spatial effects of his buildings. As house and dream are motivated by the same wish-fulfilling desires, the architect's process of form-making instantiates a feeling of serenity in its occupants recalling the maternal calm of the world of childhood and, by extension, the underlying sexual references of the Oedipal stage. In this way, Scully is able to give new meaning to Wright's education in the Froebel system of gifts and to integrate it with a definition of abstraction that goes beyond the formal and the geometric to engage universal ideas of emotional content and symbolism. It is no longer to tradition or to history that the architect looks for inspiration but rather to his own memories and sense of self.

Scully's appropriation of the principles and vocabulary of Freudian thought was extremely unusual and prescient, especially in the context of architectural history, where such considerations of gendered spaces and sexual symbolism really appear only a decade or so later (the analysis of the statue of the *Flower in the Crannied Wall* is a perfect example). His close friendship with the literary critic Harold Bloom, a colleague at Yale whose psychoanalytically driven book *The Anxiety of Influence* (1973) is referred to at some length in the text, may have exerted some influence on him, but Scully clearly chose to use the psychological framework not as a general-purpose methodology but for a very specific case that seemed to him to be culturally and historically relevant. Since the 1920s, when the Dutch architect J. J. P. Oud described Wright's designs as appearing not to involve "any mental exertions to produce" and its "process . . . a perfect mystery," notions of the magical, the inimitable, the inexplicable, even the irrational have plagued our understanding of Wright's work. Though never specifically referring to Oud, Scully alludes to these ideas more than once in the text. The choice of Freud's *Interpretation of Dreams* as the structure on which to map Wright's design thinking was an exceedingly apt one that provided a powerful means for the following generation of Wright scholars to rethink the architect's creative process.

unique and complete, rich and confident, sheltering and bold, stripped and symphonic, worthy of Wright's beloved music of Bach and Beethoven, which he called "an edifice of sound." They are forms, most of all, which are so releasing to the human spirit that when we enter them we are at once brought close to our fellow human beings and, together with them, turned into giants. How can we approach those forms and the deep question behind them—the question of how they were imagined and brought into being?

Interesting recent studies like those of Wright's life and social philosophy by Smith and Twombly and about the character of his clients by Eaton help us to know Wright and his environment, but that essential question of the complex process of the mind's making is never asked by them, so that their analysis of Wright's method of design tends to remain in the realm of program and intention, which is not that, or not yet that, of art.

One assumption which is made in all these studies, as in Manson's informative book before them, is that Wright's work has to be regarded as absolutely original, "creative" in a kind of "ur" sense, as if it owed nothing to what had gone before it during the nineteenth century. This is, of course, the view that Wright himself sedulously fostered—and which he even bolstered by his pious invocations of his Lieber Meister, Louis Sullivan—but it is not a true one, and it represents a concealment on Wright's part of one of the foundations of his work. He is not alone in such concealment: all artists are engaged in covering up their tracks—for reasons which are perhaps profound ones and which I think this study will show were indeed essential to Wright. But the fact is that if we are to get somewhere near the truth about Wright we must find out where he stood when he began to design buildings. What was there for him to see? How did he use it?

In 1889, when, at the age of twenty-two or so (if we accept Hines's conclusions
1.16 about Wright's birthdate, as I think we must), he designed his own house in Oak Park,
Wright had the whole rich tradition of the American Shingle Style of the 1880s available to him. A late Shingle Style house at Tuxedo Park, New York, by Bruce Price, the
1.17 Chandler House, was published in 1886: it slips two bay windows under an impressive
1.14 gable with an arched window at attic level. Another house by Price at Tuxedo, the Kent
House of 1885–86, was published in *Building* in the latter year. The Kent House presents its gable frontally and has, like the other, a little semi-Palladian arched window at the top. Wright adopts this design almost in toto but changes it in the following significant way: he condenses it, combines the arched window with the windows of the second floor, and makes the gable sharper and more dramatic. He also condenses two designs into one by sliding the twin bays from the side elevation of Price's other design under his frontal gable.

He does the same kind of thing as he begins to work out his revolutionary plans.
1.15 Price's Kent House had used a cross-axial plan, recurrent in American houses since
Jefferson's time. It breaks out of the old English box by projecting rooms into space and
by drawing exterior space into the open volume, as the porch does here. Other plans of
1.12 the Shingle Style of the 1880s, like the Richard L. Ashurst House by Wilson Eyre, stretch
out in long horizontals, each room widely open to the next, lighted on two sides, and
1.28. 2.4 extended by porches. Wright, by about 1900, as in the Ward Willits House, had condensed the two types, clarified the openness of the space, and stressed its unity: he displaces the entrance so that it is discovered at the side, and the interior space then unfolds mysteriously in a new perspective beyond it. The fireplace is set firmly in the middle, so making the whole a highly dramatic representation of the idea of house: focused on fire, unity, oneness. Its clarity derives from its formal abstraction, through which, so Wright tells us, its power as symbol is firmly embodied and can be physically grasped.

Conventional household emblems, such as mantelpieces, for example, are to be eliminated, so that worn-out associations will be revitalized by an intensely empathetic experience of what Wright called plastic form. Here Wright combines the pervasive nineteenth-century concept of physical empathy with the new concept of abstraction (as do Roger Fry and Wilhelm Worringer at about the same time), through which traditional images can now be represented indirectly by visual equivalents or surrogates. This is one of the essential conceptual bases for modern abstract art. The artist's "creation" becomes a new unity in which the meaning is built into the form, based upon a condensation, displacement, and abstraction of preexistent materials now thoroughly reworked in terms of basic meanings physically conveyed.

The same holds true for the three-dimensional organization of the space. In a Shingle Style interior of 1880–81 by McKim, Mead and White, the space is open and 11.1 horizontally extensive. The *kamoi* and *ramma* of Japanese practice, with which the American architects had become familiar at the Philadelphia Centennial of 1876, lead the eye along the horizontal and weave the solids together in a continuous spatial movement. The fireplace moves asymmetrically into the fabric as a whole. The same words apply: he condenses, displaces, dramatizes, abstracts, and intensifies the plastic form so that it presents its basic symbol of fire with fresh intelligibility and new unity. And that will for unity controls the entire environment. The axes are crossed with great power; the spaces interpenetrate and are thus seen simultaneously and as a composite unity. The older Japanese details have become strong, beam-scaled elements carrying our vision deeply into space; the furniture is built-in or scaled to the whole. The environmental order is total. But the height of the scale-making beam, though always quite low and generally judged by Wright according to his moderate height of 5 feet 8½ inches, is appreciably varied in each case, apparently according to the height of the client.

11.1 McKim, Mead and White. Newcomb House, Elberon, New Jersey, 1880–81. Living hall

Hence the new environment is non-classic; it is realist and individual, exactly as Wright claimed it to be. The family has been brought into a specific but expansive place of total protection, permanence, and peace. That peace is also a condensation and dramatization, though Wright doesn't tell us so, of deep old cultural memories, especially of the colonial house, its furniture stern and sculptural and scaled to it, its ceiling low and defined by beams. A revival of that folk memory had been important, along with
1.23 the influences from Japan, in the Shingle Style itself. Wright inherits that memory but opens it out to new spatial release. The ceiling is lowered, so that the protective, stable environment also rushes continuously out and away. Wright tells us that he both brought the house down and broadened it out into spaciousness, saying too that continuity of space was the major principle he had in mind. But he also condensed and displaced in that process. In the Horner House the stairs fall down toward the entrance, causing the plane of the living room floor, lifted well above ground level, to detach itself and to float forward with the ceiling just barely overhead; our eyes are carried, as Wright said they would be, by the continuous velocity of the stripping, to the ribbon of light of the continuous window voids with the raised terrace beyond them.

At last the problem of the exterior is posed: last because Wright is careful to tell
1.13 us that his design develops from within to without. A Shingle Style house by Wilson Eyre, of which we have already considered the plan, stretches out in a long horizontal, overhangs the second floor with a decided shadow line, is extended by a porch, uses ribbon windows going around the corner, but employs gambrel and gable roofs which are
1.28 expressive of contained volumes of interior space. Once more, as in the Ward Willits House, Wright condenses, displaces, and focuses with abstract power. The gambrel goes; the roofs are the lowest hips he can get away with, so that while they are still expressive of shelter they can also seem to interpenetrate like flat horizontal planes expressive of those long, low, interior spaces and extending them out in porches and porte-cochères to control the broad, squarish, middle-western suburban lot as a whole. On the exterior, as within, Wright needs little or no secondary revision of his design. It derives logically, so he tells us, from his analytical process: here from his plan and his space. There is essentially no facade, and the associational elements of the Shingle Style, whether colonial details or half-timbering, have all been eliminated, abstracted out, while the Japanese associations are muted and more remote.

How different this all is from, for example, the average nineteenth- and early-twentieth-century house on its narrow city lot, exemplified by any number of two-family
11.2 houses in New Haven, Connecticut. Here is a tough verticality (which the nineteenth century called masculine), with a strong gable end. The gable gathers and points, a physical symbol of the family unit, proud and rather defiant, but it is also very good for defining the streets, with their complementary elms, and it thus functions as an effective urban facade. Each unit is semiologically aggressive, but each works in the larger architectural order. The frontal gables were part of a long tradition in America, one which ran through the Stick and Shingle Styles alike. It was with a condensed version of such a
1.16 gable (see Frank Lloyd Wright House) that Wright started, and from which he made his

11.2 Orange Street, New Haven, Connecticut, c. 1900

great swerve, throwing out the arrowhead with its sharp-pointed frontal gesture, and with it the concept of the street facade, in order to express and extend the continuity of the interior space across a broad building lot. (If the lot is narrower, as are some of those in Oak Park, Wright will often employ the alternate tactic of turning the house sideways to the street to control it all.) So the mass of the house fragments and recombines in planes, sliding out and away and seeming, like this view of the Willits House as it was 2.8
published in Germany, as if it had in fact no urbanistic context at all, had indeed broken free from its whole middle class environment and spun out into a new, abstract, revolutionary situation.

That was in fact the situation which the International Style of the teens to the sixties designed and fostered, and which illustrations of Wright's work, like the Ward Willits House, did so much to bring into being. This is not our concern here, but it should be noted that one of the major challenges to the International Style, that mounted by Robert Venturi, came in America toward 1960 and started right back where Wright had started, with a single-family house, a frontal gable, and an arched Palladian motif. 18.1
Venturi's house is also very much a facade, but it moves in the opposite direction from Wright: it pulls apart horizontally along one frontal plane and opens vertically up the middle, the space rising up through that aperture like smoke up a flue. Finally, on Nantucket, where so much of the old Shingle Style had found its inspiration, Venturi's 12.38
building stands up like the nineteenth-century houses and fills out its gable with the arched window, so containing the expanding volume in the pointing arrow under the Atlantic sky and keeping itself above all a taut facade and a flat sign, much like those of the nineteenth-century house.

But that is not at all what Wright was after out in the Midwest in 1900. It is interior space, flowing out, floating out, but firmly defined, which he intends to have dominate the whole expression of the house, which will therefore present no "masculine" signal to the street but will instead embody a deep, expansive, pervading calm, which, deep back in shadows suggestive of sleep, will come home at last to the maternal hearth, Hestia's fire.

If we can trace Wright to this point by suggesting his relationship to his artistic past, is there any method by which we can penetrate more deeply into the meaning of his forms and the way they may have come into being? The words *condensation, displacement, dramatization, indirect representation involving simultaneity and composite figures*, and *a new unity* which I have already used to describe Wright's method of design were indeed chosen with this question in mind. They are the words which were employed by Sigmund Freud in 1900 in his major work, *The Interpretation of Dreams*, as he attempted to describe for the first time the mysterious process whereby what he called the dreamwork brought dream thoughts into dream content, or, we might say, into dream form. Freud called that process the *Vorstellung*, the setting forth. One of the phases which he sometimes included in it but later excluded from it, however, that of "secondary revision," played little part in Wright's way of working, as we have already had occasion to observe.[1] But that fact, too, seems especially interesting, because "secondary revision" was the only phase for which Freud proposed an architectural analogy; he suggested that it might sometimes have constructed, at the very end of the process, an acceptable "facade" for the dream. And it was precisely the concept of facade that Wright specifically discarded.

But are these words so important? Others could well have been used, and I have no intention of "reducing" the complexity of Wright's work by pretending that these words wholly or solely describe it. Yet, beyond that, can a consideration of a historical parallel between Wright and Freud help us to understand Wright's work better? Perhaps it can. Freud and Wright were contemporaries who, despite their geographical distance and cultural differences, still shared certain pervasive aspects of nineteenth-century culture and dealt with problems involving in many ways similar kinds of people: people formed by late-nineteenth-century middle-class family units, consisting of mothers and fathers and suffering children. It is therefore no wonder that the family was the basic concern of both men, Freud unraveling its secrets to heal its members, Wright moving from the opposite direction to construct what seemed to him the ideal, sane environment for it, and especially for its young.[2]

I am not competent to pass judgment on the merits of Freud's reading of those problems, but I believe that I do not have to do so here. I wish only to point out that Freud, in the major literary and scientific work of the beginning of the century—as Wright's houses of these Oak Park years were the major architectural works—used sequences of words to describe that most central of creative processes: how the mind makes those forms which embody the meanings that are most essential to it, which can be applied (and I think we can agree without strain of any kind) to the process whereby Wright made his houses. And I prefer those words, in their curious physicality so appropriate to architecture and so finally incomplete, to the infinitely more articulated combination of psychoanalytical and rhetorical terms which Harold Bloom, for example, employs as he explores the problem of the making and reading of poetry. So Wright with the Shingle Style: he condensed, displaced, and so on—not on unconscious material at first, but on preexisting architectural forms which he singled out for his attention. Literary critics like Bloom would insist that conscious repression, "willed falsification," is involved in the artist's "misreading" of such predecessors. We may accept that phenomenon as obvious enough and go on to say that in Wright's case at least he worked down beyond them until he brought forth the depths and powers of his own mind—until, we might say, he at once trained his instincts and gained confidence in them—and could then work upon them by this same process. The artist, therefore, "learns" how to construct out his so-called "unconscious" by first developing that process on conscious material, i.e., on existing works of art.

Freud, as scientist and artist, did the same. In any event, he proves to have been an excellent critic; his terms, along with others, can be valuably used to analyze the way in which many of the most critically important monuments in the history of art came to be made.[3] Yet I do not have to claim that this is the way that all works of art are made. I think that in large measure they are made somewhat differently in different historical periods, just as Freud's book would have been different if it had been written at a different time. Still, Freud, and all psychoanalysis after him, had a deep conviction that his discoveries were universal ones, and attempts by his followers, especially those of Carl Jung, disavowed by Freud, to simplify the problem into large collective patterns of symbolism, which Jung called archetypes, have often been regarded as useful for the criticism of works of art and will be referred to later here.

Yet the most important issue seems to me to be that of the structure of form which, beyond Freud's own aesthetic limitations, the structure of *The Interpretation of Dreams* itself inevitably suggests and heroically approaches. Because all such questions must in the end come down to the problem of how form is made, since without form, as Freud shows, no symbol can be embodied. Form *is* content; content *is* form. Jacques Lacan has, of course, been concerned with exactly this in his linguistic analysis of Freud's dream-structure, *The Language of the Self*, which, however, in its characteristic psychoanalytical focus upon the verbal discourse, upon the Word as the carrier of meaning (which Freud shares), does not deal with visual problems. And later semiologists from Eco to Jencks who have dealt with architecture invariably leap as fast as possible past the physical form to the associated verbal sign, while modern iconographers in the history of art itself, with the notable exception of Panofsky at his best, have generally been more concerned with the simple identification of symbols than with the way they are embodied in form. But it is precisely in this, as we have seen, that the *Vorstellung* is of major artistic interest—of greater potential relevance, we art historians might now boldly claim, to the visual arts than to literature—and the parallels between Freud and Wright are close and rich in meaning. Each brings inexhaustible intellectual energy to the problem posed: Freud to the infinitely individual complexity of the analytical narrative, Wright to the multiple possibilities suggested by every detail of his design, perhaps most obvious and varied in the absolute particularity of the spatial stripping in every one of his houses. Hence, the forms made by Wright and those developed by Freud, no less than those identified by him, suggest each other, and since both are dealing with the family, their contents tend to merge.

What motivated the building of Wright's houses, after all, was what Freud said motivated the production of dreams: "wish-fulfillment." Surely that is exactly what Wright's houses were for the people who built them, and that is what Wright gave his clients far beyond their identification of it: not simple associative references as, say, to Romanesque halls and colonial kitchens, but something deeper in, the very stuff of their dreams. And how American it was at that period to day-dream of "better things." Is that one major reason why there was nothing like these spaces by Wright produced in Europe? The "dream house" is an American concept after all. In any event, we recognize the national phenomenon, which is why we are so moved when Dreiser, who later knew Freud's work well, wrote of (and to) Sister Carrie in 1900: "Know, then, that for you is neither surfeit nor content. In your rocking chair, by your window dreaming, shall you dream such happiness as you may never feel." Wright's clients were not poor Carrie, but they clearly had their dream-wishes, perhaps not easily discernible in their waking lives. But that was no problem for Wright; he simply let them share his own, which were, in this artistic process, accessible to him—especially as he was creating in his houses what was so much a comforting child's world. Oak Park itself shares that character; just in sight of the towers of Chicago along the magical elevated railroad line, but wholly silent, flat, and somnolent, an utter dream world, too.

What is the function of dreams? asked Freud, and he replied, "The dream is the guardian of sleep." It censors out, he claimed, the upsetting material that is clamoring for recognition in the mind, and when that censor fails, anxiety and nightmare will ensue. Hence for Freud the "disguised fulfillments of repressed wishes," and "one of the detours by which repression can be evaded." Are Wright's forms this? Perhaps all the forms of art in some measure are; they disguise so that our minds can deal with whatever lies in there, can begin to handle it somehow on these terms, which are those of the "new unity" of art's "setting forth." Like dreams, they at once probe our hopes and anxieties and protect us from them. Again, in previous ages there were more or less fixed iconographical systems which, as it were, ticketed and screened such problems through a battery of symbols; but the new modern man of the late nineteenth century began to be obliged to disentangle them for himself. So, in art, Wright eventually made his own—by, I think Freud would have said, his especially strong capacity to "regress" to the unconscious material of dreams. In doing so, he, the modern man, cut adrift from the past, found a new past within himself, which, as Thomas Mann later wrote, was the greatest gift of Freud's work to the modern world.

This is where the study of Freud can most help us to appreciate the greatness of Wright because it points out that, in an age when the old classic traditions and institutions were breaking down and the first glow of romanticism had long gone out, the individual was forced to construct all his works out of his childhood memories, out of whatever direct personal experiences had made him whatever he was. If they had made him ill, Freud set out "to unravel what the dream work has woven" in order to make him well. But Wright was strong (as he often tells us) and an artist, and he set out to put whatever he was, whatever he could "remember," to use. Freud discovered that the experiences of childhood were of supreme importance to the individual, were never really forgotten, and produced dream shapes in later years. Wright made art out of these experiences and constantly evoked the dream that might recall them. At the end of a night conversation with himself he cries, "Yes, it seems to me, that is what it means to be an artist . . . to seize this essence brooding just behind aspect." So he brings dream thoughts to consciousness at once intensified and concealed by his beloved abstraction (Freud's "pictorial arrangement"), so that his work of art is a waking dream. Indeed, Wright's interior spaces, with the fire glowing in the dark under the low ceiling with its hypnotic stripping leading us to other mysterious spaces beyond, go far toward dream states themselves. This can hardly be said of Brunelleschi, Ictinos, or the International Style, for example. They do other things. So, while the process of form-making which Freud distinguished may be widespread in time, the dream content, for which we alternatively read dream form, is not necessarily so. And here, as I have indicated, Freud and Wright are close, and the point can be made stronger.

For example, Freud came increasingly, and reluctantly, to the view that the major symbols of the dream content dealt with problems of human sexuality (arising, one might say, from the structure of the modern family but tending to universality for Freud), and he invented the great concept of the Oedipus complex to describe what he felt lay at the heart of most of those problems, which was the boy's wish to kill the father in order to possess the mother. Again you will realize that I am not competent to comment upon the validity of Freud's views, and I am certainly no more anxious than Freud was to be accused of sexual sensationalism. Nor do I wish to fall or be accused of falling into the reductiveness of the "Freudian symbol," as employed by some would-be Freudians, assassins of the multiplicity of art. Nevertheless, I will claim that Wright's houses are deeply familial in quality and that their symbolism seems to be a rich interweaving of the male and female with the male strong but the female, the wife and mother, enclosing all. So the houses are caverns which engulf us and give us peace as we submit to their laws. They pull us in, and they do so according to the same principles of condensation, displacement, and abstraction which we have noted all along; but now that process is acting not only upon previous architecture but also upon fundamental symbols deep underneath it as well. That is why, one supposes, Wright had to have confidence in his "originality" and so insisted upon it throughout his life. Most of all, his principle of abstraction is fundamental here, since it permits Freud's "indirect representation" of physical images which would have been unacceptable otherwise to Wright or his clients.

Behind the intense brooding little fireplace in the Martin House, of 1904, stand the deep Romanesque arches of Henry Hobson Richardson, images of physical engulfment into the hollow within. But Wright goes far beyond Richardson in pulling us into that hollow. Richardson's Glessner House in Chicago, of 1885–87, is what Wright 11.3

called a "box" of space with an arched opening pushed up to the frontal plane. It is a
11.4 closed box; we must push our way in. Wright's Heurtley House, of 1902, has opened up the box (Wright's proudest accomplishment) so that it draws us into it. It is at once secret, dark, and concealing, profoundly primitive and brooding in aspect but also inviting, leading us by tortuous ways into its enfolding body: cavern, pavilion, and castle all at once.

There can be no doubt that Wright is dealing, through the necessary order and concealment of abstraction, with deep symbols of life and fertility in his houses and that their major image is of the female who encloses all. They are indeed temples to that idea.
11.5 The arch of the Dana House is abstracted into a vibrant entrance; deep in the shadows

ABOVE, LEFT: Henry Hobson Richardson. Glessner House, Chicago, 1885–87. Exterior 11.3

ABOVE, RIGHT: Frank Lloyd Wright. Heurtley House, Oak Park, Illinois, 1902. Exterior 11.4

BELOW: Frank Lloyd Wright. Dana House, Springfield, Illinois, 1902–4. Entrance 11.5

OPPOSITE: Frank Lloyd Wright and Richard Bock. *The Flower in the Crannied Wall*, Dana House 11.6

within it stands a white column; it is a piece of sculpture designed by Wright and executed by his friend Richard Bock, shaped like a phallus and reminiscent, as a matter of fact, of contemporary, highly sexed work in Vienna, such as the paintings of Klimt. It was called *The Flower in the Crannied Wall,* and I think that Freud would suggest that both 11.6
those words represented perfect symbolic displacements. The point is important. It reminds us to ask once more whether Wright no less than Bock was not now working with unconscious, i.e., "repressed,"[4] material; he was surely not using the words "womb" or "phallus" to describe to himself the forms he employed and would in all likelihood have indignantly rejected them if they had been suggested to him. The point is underlined: "abstraction" was essential. Of course, each one of the forms involved can take on any number of symbolic meanings. But the column standing in the female body to make a composite image of fertility, birth, and indeed, resurrection, is a very old and quite specific motif.

In his late work Wright was overtly to adapt rounded shapes like those of the Neolithic temples on Malta (as in the Martin Spence project, the Guggenheim Museum, and so on) which were built like hollow goddesses with the column standing in the center of fancy, which is the head.[5] The entrance to those temples suggested at once a labyrinth and that of a body itself. But even closer in noble form and familial meaning to Wright's combination of shapes in the Dana House is Giotto's meeting of Joachim and Anna, one pure united cone, before Jerusalem's Golden Gate. In all these instances the column is at the service of the female principle and is framed by it.

But Freud claimed that such symbols, like all the products of the mind's condensation of experience, usually had multiple meanings. The fireplace and the chimney are a case in point. We have already noted Wright's female hearths with the colonial memory behind them. But what of the chimney? The tall chimneys of colonial houses ran as massive solids up through the hollow of the house and protruded boldly above the roof. Herman Melville recognized this quality when he wrote his strange and witty story "I and My Chimney." In it the owner of a colonial house is forced to defend its (by him) beloved chimney from the attacks of his wife and daughters who insist that it takes up too much room in the center of the house and is, besides, faulty in structure and might fall down at any moment. ("I and my chimney, we will never surrender," says Melville.) With Wright there is no contest. The chimney has plenty of space around it and protrudes above the roof only enough to satisfy whatever fire laws existed at the time. The principle remains that of enclosure. In that sense one might say that Venturi's madly aggressive chimney in his important project of 1959 is the first free chimney in American houses since 15.2
before Wright's time, an expression of male liberation, one supposes—but in reality a purposeful exaggeration of the active sign. When Wright, for example, builds vertical piers other than chimneys he not only has them stand very free and strong but also—with only one significant exception which we will consider later—caps them off and encloses them in the overhanging roof. The family is kept together as one unity—one might say, calmly, stably, maturely—making, above all, a dignified spatial environment for the child. In this way what Smith correctly identifies as Wright's compelling interest in a

strong, conservative family structure finds its formal embodiment, its symbolic vocabulary, and becomes art. Wright *builds* the family. It was what had formed him, what he knew, and what his architectural programs were. Later, when he himself breaks away from its suburban mode and conservative structure, his forms change in considerable degree but not, I think, in kind. And our experience of them always remains empathetic, physical. If we permit them to do so they comfort us by their close physical presence: they the family, we the child. This is one major reason, I think, why so many people have obdurately resisted the appeal of Wright's work and so many others given way to it wholly.

If, then, a consideration of Freud's proposed dream structure and its symbolic content helps in some measure to value Wright's artistic achievement, what of Jung's symbolic archetypes in that regard? It seems that they can be at least superficially applied, and it is what Maud Bodkin, in her book *Archetypal Patterns in Poetry*, was later to describe as the archetype of the Image of Woman which first suggests itself for transposition into architectural terms to describe Wright's work. That image may be regarded as dominant over the male images in Wright's houses, but it clearly poses no threat to his view of male sexuality. Instead, it completes it. He, who so much in his own personality embodied (like his father) another Jungian archetype—that of Devil, Hero, God—was somehow able to achieve complete artistic expression by weaving that image into the maternal body. He condenses the archetypes; he "marries" them.

It is, as so often with Wright, a matter of scale, of our empathetic response to the size of things in relation to ourselves. For example, in a Colonial Revival room with
1.5 fireplace of 1876 by Charles Follen McKim, the ceiling is low and the mantel high so that the occupant feels himself dominated by it. He is small in a small space. In Wright's
11.7 Coonley House, the ceiling is low, so that the occupant towers over it, dominates the space, and is also led out by it to enormous physical release and triumph. It is like an illustration of one of Freud's most beautiful dreams, in which he is sitting on a terrace in a chair firmly fixed in place but also rushing forward at enormous velocity. Stability and movement, protection and release, fulfill several sets of wishes all together. The conden-
11.8 sation is of multiple and contradictory symbols. The Robie House is at once an airplane and another of Jung's archetypes, a sacred mountain: heavy, hollowed, massive, and rising on wings. Death-and-Resurrection, Hell-to-Heaven, these other archetypes are also
11.9 embodied here. One must go on an ancient labyrinthine journey, seeking the secret entrance, finding it finally concealed in a low, dark, restricted place through which one moves up and around the fireplace mass toward the light until the long horizontal release of the upper floor takes wing. The pilgrim has grown in stature. His head almost reaches the soffit; the fireplace is pushed down very low. Looming over it, he is a giant, a child become Oedipal hero, most specifically a Titan of earth, strong so long as he remains in touch with the mother, as he does here. The scale is everything.

This constant and wearisome use of the pronoun "he" is essential for the material and in relation to the nineteenth-century psychology and education out of which it grew. Wright himself was a triumphant product of that psychology and that education, and we should now consider the relevance of those nineteenth-century phenomena to an

11.7 RIGHT: Frank Lloyd Wright. Coonley House, Riverside, Illinois, 1906–9. Living room

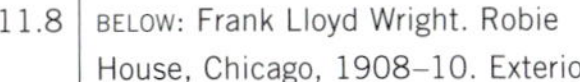

11.8 BELOW: Frank Lloyd Wright. Robie House, Chicago, 1908–10. Exterior

Frank Lloyd Wright. Robie House. Living room 11.9

understanding of his genius. We are told, first of all, that when his mother, who was a teacher, became pregnant, she determined (a) that it would be a boy and (b) that he would be an architect, and to that end she hung engravings of the great Gothic cathedrals in her room. So the process began for Wright while he was still in the womb. When he finally appeared the engravings were placed in his room. So he was from the very first the builder, the victor, and during his adolescence, just before he left home to go to work in Chicago, his father was thrown out of the house and conveniently disappeared, so that Wright could sally forth as an Oedipus unrivalled, conqueror of the city, singing his song of work and manhood, cited by Smith: "I'll live as I work as I am / No work for fashion or sham / . . . My work as befitteth a man," etc. How entranced poor Freud, with his neurotic Viennese, might have been with it all.[6]

11.10 Therefore, it is probably no accident that the Larkin Building—where, almost uniquely in Wright's early work, the piers rise up uncapped by roofs and overhangs—is strongly reminiscent of Gothic cathedrals in its twin towers and its spatial interweaving of vertical and horizontal, solid and void. But its hard-edged, abstract shapes also have another very cogent source in the Froebel kindergarten blocks with which Wright was encouraged to play as a child. And who encouraged him? His mother, of course, whose "intense interest in the Froebel system was," he tells us, "awakened at the Philadelphia Centennial of 1876." Indeed, the mother and what he most usually called "the boy" were the two basic human units in Froebel's educational system. Friedrich Froebel was the inventor of the kindergarten, and he wrote his greatest book, *The Education of Man*, in 1826. Interest in his work and his pedagogical methods grew throughout the century and continued at a peak rate of republication, translation, and critique from the 1850s

11.10 Frank Lloyd Wright. Larkin Building, Buffalo, 1902–6. Exterior

until about 1914. And I might add that women rather heroically broke a way for themselves into his system in various publications of the 1880s and 1890s. Froebel's theories were especially popular in America, perhaps because in them the child was to be trained through the practical use of his hands toward a way of grasping reality that would transcend previous human limitations and so connect him with the fundamental rhythm of the universe as a whole.

Wright passionately believed in all this throughout his life and repeatedly stressed the fact that the abstraction which evolved out of the Froebel system was the fundamental tool of his design, and it was emphatically essential, as we have noted, to the indirect representation of its symbolic content. Speaking about his play as a child with the Froebel elements, Wright wrote: "The virtue of all this lay in the awakening of the child mind to rhythmic structure in Nature—giving the child a sense of innate cause-and-effect otherwise far beyond child comprehension. I soon became susceptible to constructive pattern evolving in everything I saw. I learned to 'see' this way and when I did, I did not care to draw casual incidentals of Nature. I wanted to design." It all sounds very godlike, but what is especially interesting, I think, is that Wright later had to work his way back to Froebel too. Though there may be a kind of preconditioned Froebelism in early buildings like the Charnley House, there are apparently no overtly Froebelian details until they appear in Wright's remodeling of his own house and his building of its vaulted playroom for his children in 1895. His sympathetic association with their dreams and play, to which they all were later to attest, clearly helped him find his way back to his own childhood as well, and to a structural perception of that child's dream world which his mature houses were to embody.

Froebel's system is also based upon a symbolic imagery which is sexual in part. As he refined his ideas from 1826 onward, Froebel planned that the mother would give the child (usually, as I said, read as "boy") a series of what Froebel called "gifts," starting from his first year and running through his seventh. Various other of what Froebel called "occupations" were also involved and were to follow. Wright was already nine—again, if we accept Hines's date of 1867 for his birth—when his mother discovered this system, but that hardly seems to have blunted its effect.[7] The first gift was a soft ball of yarn—in later refinements six balls. For Froebel the sphere of the ball was specifically intended to acquaint the child with the link between the mother's breast and the unity of the world. A psychologist, Denton J. Snider, of the Chicago Kindergarten College, writing on *The Psychology of Froebel's Play-Gifts* in 1900, described (presumably) his own sensation of playing with the ball in profoundly sexual terms, although he does not identify them as such. "You cannot blame your hand," he burbles, "if it soon closes more passionately upon that Ball, with an eager embrace, to which the latter replies by a stronger and warmer osculation imparted to your palm and fingers. . . . You nestle it, you coddle it, you rock it and swing it with both hands, you toss it up into the air like a baby and catch it coming down with a smile. It has all sorts of domestic suggestions—that of a nest with its birdling; you can house it between your palms in a cosy little home." This is all heady stuff, especially so because in the end the boy puts the ball back in the box and says, in this English version of 1871, "He sinks deep. Look for him." And there you are.

Wright—claiming, perhaps falsely, to have started all this later—discusses only the subsequent, tougher, hard-edged gifts: the wooden cylinder and cube which join the ball in the second, the hard-edged patterns that can be made with the cubes of the third.
11.11 Finally, as here with the fourth gift, the child builds structures labeled "Triumphal Arch," recalling Leo von Klenze's Neoclassic Propylaea in Munich whose name figured in one of Freud's most famous dreams. The shapes are classicizing ones, as befits Froebel's publication date of 1826: strictly geometric, symmetrical, and hard. Finally, and this is
11.12 the sixth gift, the boy builds the box and is presumably on his way. Perhaps most of all, he also builds a good clear European urbane facade for himself, a public face to carry off to school—like the facade of the Berggasse in Vienna behind which Freud and his family, like the other members of the Viennese middle class, lived their private lives.

In the context of this discussion, we obviously have to divert for a moment to ask ourselves whether Freud was interested in Froebel. We know that Froebel's system was well known in Vienna by the latter decades of the century, but I can safely state that his name does not occur in any of the literature by or about Freud. We know, however,

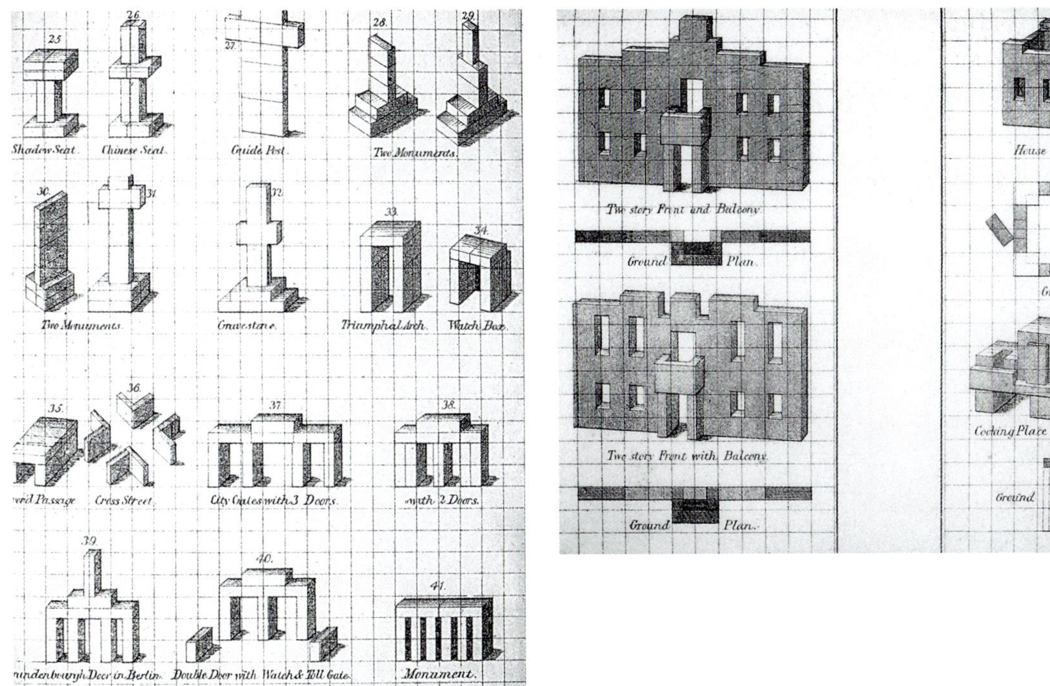

11.11 ABOVE, LEFT: Froebel system, fourth gift

11.12 ABOVE, RIGHT: Froebel system, sixth gift

that Freud too suppressed some early biographical data about himself and that information about his earliest education is especially scanty right up to the moment when at the age of seven, he began to read Philippson's Jewish Bible and to be taught by his father. Many years later his father sent him a copy of that book and recalled the event. Thus Freud's education, so far as we know it, was wholly verbal, exactly the opposite of Wright's. Yet, might not Freud have had contact with some variation of a Froebel system (gifts of the mother) in his earliest years? The Oedipal guilts which he describes in himself especially make us wonder if this might not have been so, but there is no evidence whatever for it. And it seems in the end that the mature Freud was truly not interested in Froebel, who had followed lines of investigation different from his own. They were Protestant and pedagogical, cultural worlds apart from Freud's Patriarchal Word and the gifts of the father. So even the concept of empathy is not valued by Freud, though known to him as *Einfühlung* through the writings of Lipps. Yet in later years he sometimes referred to the mother's breast as the primal form, which his follower, Rank, associated with the "maternal vessel."

The speculations to which all this gives rise cannot be pursued here, but one can hardly be blamed for being unable to resist suggesting them, especially in this context, because what is in some ways the most Froebel-like building of all is not by Wright
but by Josef Maria Olbrich, and it is in Vienna. It is called the Secession Building and 11.13
was built in 1896–99, not far from the Ring, as a headquarters, exhibition, and work center for a new anti-establishment art. It is still flanked by a charmingly subversive bronze group of a Roman emperor in a chariot with coil springs drawn by lions (Vienna's

Josef Maria Olbrich. Secession Building, Vienna, 1897–99. Exterior 11.13

own Marcus Aurelius but looking more like Nero). The building itself looks like Froebel blocks piled up. Was Olbrich, like Wright, trained in the Froebel system? That question remains to be answered, but I think we may safely bet that he was, because there it is, finally, the ball in the box—primal symbol of the beginning of a new, individualistic art—the sphere of open metalwork construction but, in contrast to the hard blocks that contain it, looking soft and compressible like Froebel's yarn. And those piers and that ball, no less than the avoidance of the usual deep roof slab, suggest that Wright was influenced by Olbrich when he designed the Larkin Building in 1904. The world globes (which are, one should point out, lifted by the piers and buttressed by babies), represent one of the very few times that Wright permitted himself quite this kind of what he normally characterized as rather overly literary representational form.

But if we go back to the Secession Building and look again at its closed blocky
11.14 shape enclosing one major room we cannot help but realize that Unity Temple of 1904–6 is even closer to it than the Larkin Building was. Again, there are condensations and major displacements; the entrance is brought around to the side in order to leave the meeting room closed and inviolate on the street where, so Wright tells us, the noisy trolley tracks were laid. But there are many similarities. The advanced and recessed planes which, as Wright handles them, are clearly expressive of the spaces they contain, are at least suggested in the Secession Building, as is the detail of the cornice in both, striated in fine horizontal lines. But while Olbrich breaks out of a Froebel system by permitting Art Nouveau figural ornament to grow like lovely vines along his surfaces, Wright characteristically disciplines it all out into pure Froebel abstractions.

Yet can it be that Wright was drawn to Olbrich precisely because of his Froebel-like qualities? Contemporary Europeans recognized the fraternal relationship between the two architects, and Wright tells us that when he visited Germany in 1909 he was

11.14 Frank Lloyd Wright. Unity Temple, Oak Park, Illinois, 1905–8. Exterior

called "the American Olbrich," and so went to visit that architect in Darmstadt, where he had then been working. But when Wright arrived Olbrich was already dead. (This episode recalls Dürer's famous story of himself and Schongauer, who died before Dürer could reach him.) It is especially touching because some of the buildings which Olbrich built for the Art School at Darmstadt during the first decade of the twentieth century strongly suggest not only earlier American forms but also a few designs made by Wright while he was still in Europe and shortly after his return. Wright of course says nothing about all this, but there was clearly some deep affinity at work between the two men.

On the other hand, Wright's buildings are more complex, more integrated, and I think we must say more multiple in meaning than Olbrich's are. They are in that sense much more Freudian in structure. But we should perhaps try to read them at first in the driest and most straightforward of functional and structural ways, as expressions of a typically American passion, strong in the late nineteenth century, for practical organization and rationalized order. They can sustain even this supremely well. The Larkin Building 11.15
can be read—indeed was read by the Dutch architect Berlage—as a great machine,

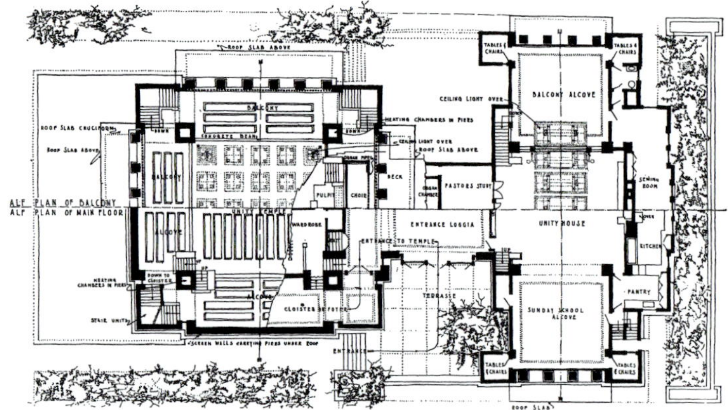

ABOVE, LEFT: Frank Lloyd Wright. Larkin Building. Interior 11.15

ABOVE, TOP RIGHT: Frank Lloyd Wright. Unity Temple. Plan 11.16

ABOVE, BOTTOM RIGHT: Frank Lloyd Wright. Unity Temple. Interior of sanctuary 11.17

perfectly organized to carry out machine-age tasks. And Reyner Banham, claiming rather inaccurately that no one had done so before him, later praised it as a perfectly integrated environment. It is certainly all that and must be seen as it fulfills its primary function as an agreeable place to work. The desks of the office workers are set (were set) on spacious balconies around a central open space lighted from above. The employees had ample restroom and locker facilities and safe fire stairs enclosed in the corner towers. There was a roof garden. The noise and distractions of the neighborhood outside, near the railroad tracks, were filtered out by keeping the windows high so that the whole lift inside was to the sky, beautifully carried by the vertical piers of the structure, through which the horizontal floor slabs rode and in whose depth the filing cabinets were fitted. They, like all the furniture, were designed by the architect and adjusted to the entire structure. It was a great accomplishment: an uplifting place to work in, and Wright shows us on the outside that this is what the building is for, with its stairs, balcony levels, high windows, and noble central space reaching up at last to light and ornament and the symbolic sphere.

In his own extremely lucid descriptions of how he designed Unity Temple, Wright takes a similarly rational, clear, and hardheaded line. Now he will have no symbol at all, he says, by which he means no steeple. Instead it must be one great meeting room with a sub- 11.16, 11.17
sidiary space for parish activities on the other side. Entrance will be between the two with the pastor's headquarters bridging between them. These functions will be housed by concrete walls, laid up in wooden forms and with the pebble aggregate brought forward to the surface so that no painting or plastering will be required on the outside. For economy the construction forms should be reusable; hence walls of the same size are suggested by them—so forming a Froebel cube, "a noble form," Wright says. With all that figured out beforehand, the architect then draws the scheme up through one long night, so that the plan, abstract as it seems, grows directly in a "new unity" out of the logic of the functional requirements and the structural facts, with little "secondary revision" involved. One will enter the great room from below, primarily from cloisters at the sides, so as not to disturb the rest of the congregation, and the crowds will flow down and out again past the minister in the pulpit who will thus be able, so Wright tells us, to greet them all as they leave. Otherwise, everyone has a fine view of the speaker, is indeed intimately connected with him, and hears him well, protected from outside distractions and lighted no less peacefully than inspiringly from above. Though one is inside a solid mass, no mass is felt. The stripping conceals the piers and carries the eye upward and around them so that only a weightless space-defining character is felt in the surrounding planes. (Something of the sort was worked out at much greater scale in Hagia Sophia.) But here the space is small enough so that it is all one's own and the transparent simultaneities and interwoven compositions enlarge it around the self.[8] One tends to climb to the top and look down into the center, protected and enclosed but also liberated and irradiated by the light coming down from above. Here is another of Wright's greatest displacements and intensifications of a model source, which is the traditional meeting house of New England, whose spire, we remember he had eschewed. Now the walls at once solidify and dissolve; the roof parts around its beams, and the heavenly light of Froebel's system shines through.

It is therefore obvious that Unity Temple and the Larkin Building, the two major buildings where Wright brings his family-formed individuals into the community environment of work and worship, fulfill their functions supremely well and are integrated in structure, space, and massing in ways undreamed of since the days of those Gothic cathedrals from which Wright had received his primary training. But there is surely much more to say about them than this, and it has to do with the symbols which are built into their forms. Let us begin by using, for simplicity if not for the whole truth, the Jungian Death-and-Resurrection and Hell-and-Heaven archetypes I mentioned earlier. On the outside of the Larkin Building we are shown what the interior is like, but we cannot enter 11.10
it at the front. An arched entrance was originally proposed here but was discarded; so once more we have to look for an entrance at the side. There it is, tucked away. But it is guarded by some rather threatening objects. Down comes the fountain slab with a crack

Frank Lloyd Wright. Johnson Wax Administration Building, Racine, Wisconsin, 1936–39. Interior 11.18

and cuts something off: water, a metal sheet. Anyway, watch out, especially as the monster is spouting formidably paternalistic slogans at the same time. Beyond it, if we make it, a dark narrow pathway between high threatening masses leads up into the building through doors of clear glass. Not really inviting, it is a heroic passage, but it pulls us in, where we find ourselves in a low, dark place, compressed by weighty struc-
11.15 tural masses, but if we follow forward: Hallelujah! Death and Resurrection, Hell to Heaven, mounting in "the heavenly ascent" like Dante guided by Beatrice toward the "supersensuous light".

The plan itself, read this way, sings through all its abstraction of such tension and release, of what Jung called "frustration and transcendence." It embodies, if we return to Freud's more sober and clinical terms, the fact that "any given process originates in an unpleasant state of tension and thereupon determines for itself such a path that its ultimate issue coincides with a relaxation of this tension." And we can also recall Freud's own touching description of the course of a successful analysis, passing, so he says, through a wood, into a defile, and out into the open at last. The Jungian concept of the archetype is useful here, too, I think, in the Heaven to which we are at last introduced. So religious was the atmosphere that the management, as we know, introduced an organ for the appropriate "edifice of sound." It was their recognition of what can only be called, with Wallace Stevens, an American Sublime. And that environment created for the typists takes on further dimension when we remember Melville's sadistic story called "The Tartarus of Maids," about starved women working in a freezing cold horror factory somewhere in the North. Melville contrasted their state, in a fine perverted nineteenth-century polarity, with that of young men reading law in warm lodgings in London, in what he called "A Paradise of Bachelors." There was clearly plenty of sadism and guilt bound up in men's treatment of women throughout the earlier industrial period. Now, beset by paternalistic slogans, the typists can be regarded as saved, transported to Paradise themselves. In the Larkin Soap Company's house publication Wright called it all "a family gathering."

Wright did all this once again in the Johnson Wax Building of 1936, there in 11.18
even more oceanic, and female, terms. We are pulled into the current, drowned, resurrected, and floated up to a watery heaven with the supersensuous light flooding down. A philosopher in a horrid interdepartmental seminar many years ago once remarked of this, "Isn't it rather excessive for typists?" Fortunately one could recall that other early modern prophet, Marx, and ask, I think correctly, "If not for workers, for whom?" The natural corollary to the tapping of the individual unconscious has to be the disappearance of a hierarchy of programs. As Wallace Stevens said, "The sublime comes down to the spirit and space." The modern human being must take it where he can find it, and if everyone can get it, so much the better. Certainly Wright was extremely proud of his achievement in the Larkin Building, which may be another reason why he for once gave his vertical piers free rein. Such a shout of triumph it is—the father victorious in the place of work—while Unity Temple, a concrete monolith, can be seen as the sacred mountain of the goddess with her cavern deep within it, her previous heavy box with its secret room inside. So we follow the labyrinth around the side, under the low, dark entrance into the gentle shadows, then forward again toward the light, all opening before us until we come up into the transcendent meeting space where the lifting shapes sing together in their chorus. They indeed transcend their archetype and are in fact Unitarian and Universalist, united and free, a brand-new structure of modern symbolic form. Here, as in the Larkin Building, Wright's own utopianism, his evangelically American democratic optimism give his work a special flavor which cannot be easily or wholly subsumed under Jung's religious visions or Freud's deeply sorrowful analytical stance. Yet we can hardly help but feel, in this ultimate edifice of new unity, that Freud's analysis of dreams and any deep experience of Unity Temple must in some sense coincide, since each has a kind of final result: the illumination of the individual human spirit and its release into the ultimate family, the community of mankind. Above all, what seemed closed, like the human mind or this building on the outside, is opened—what seemed dark, is light.

About that community of light in the twentieth century I cannot forebear to say one quick word as epilogue. Wright's buildings have sometimes been deprecated because they seem to serve primarily a restricted middle class. Freud has been criticized on similar grounds. Yet some of the finest Social-Democratic public housing built in Europe during this century owed a good deal to Wright's earlier work. One thinks first of the housing in Amsterdam during and just after World War I, where the most important architect was Michael de Klerk. De Klerk achieved his own condensation of symbols out of a Dutch
past, like the spire in his Public Utility Housing of 1918–21, but the strong horizontal 11.19
continuities that bring the heavy brick work into motion would have been unthinkable without the influence of Wright. They swing the building out from its old symbols to a new horizontal velocity along the railroad tracks. So in this community housing destined largely for railroad workers—who, in the European way, were proudly bound up both in their trade and their working-class solidarity—de Klerk indeed designed the whole group like a train of cars in motion, pulled along smartly by a powerfully chugging locomotive at

11.19 OPPOSITE, TOP LEFT: Michael de Klerk. Public Utility Society Housing, Eigen Haard Estate extension, Amsterdam, 1917–21. Exterior

11.20 OPPOSITE, TOP RIGHT: Frank Lloyd Wright. Gale House, Oak Park, Illinois, 1909. Exterior. From *Frank Lloyd Wright: Ausgeführte Bauten* (Berlin, 1911)

11.21 OPPOSITE, BOTTOM: Karl Ehn. Karl-Marx-Hof, Vienna, 1927–30. Exterior

the other end. Wright never allowed himself such overt representation of recognizable images in building form, but the feel of the whole as of much of Amsterdam is like that of
his expansive, heavy, horizontally dynamic Midway Gardens of 1914 (now gone). Or take 12.32
Wright's projection of flat-planed volumetric balconies, as on the Gale House. These had 11.20
a profound effect in Holland. It is not too much to say that de Klerk quotes them at one remove in another of his housing projects, of 1921. Then that motif is expanded enormously in scale and lifted on great arches reminiscent of those of Richardson and Wright, and it becomes the monumental embodiment of Social-Democratic solidarity and defiance in the unmatched low-cost public housing that was built in Vienna between 1919 and 1934.

The Heiligenstadt Houses of 1927, called, loyally and provocatively, the Karl- 11.21
Marx-Hof, culminated that development. There the great images were drawn up in battle line to face the main street on one side and the urban railroad station on the other. They were the symbols of left-wing Vienna set out for all their friends and enemies to see. Beyond them north and south along the Heiligenstadt Strasse stretched spacious enclosed courtyards, long and wide, protected by narrow iron-grated entrances from the hostile forces outside. In those courtyards the aura of Wright is very strong—long balconies, interwoven planes. But the great flag-bearing insignia have got to be, I think, among the most moving of twentieth-century shapes, certainly among the most emphatically powerful. Fireplaces, chimneys, and balconies, not to mention Egyptian temples, Roman triumphal arches, and Gothic cathedral facades, are condensed into one body with outstretched arms to make the mother of all forms. It is remarkably like an enormous image of the great Stone Age Mother herself, as we can still see her today warding off anxiety from her own breast-shaped houses, the trulli of Apulia.

Can Karl Ehn and his associated architects who built the Karl-Marx-Hof have consciously had such images in mind? Probably not. One supposes that Jung would have liked to think that, at the least, some unconscious folk-memory guided their hands in their need for a magical sign to ward off the danger that already threatened these houses from the political right wing. Can Freud, who was explicitly no Marxist, have paid any attention to what went on here, and can he have recognized this most majestic of symbols for what it was? One guesses not, in this instance as well—and there is no expression whatsoever of interest in these houses to be found in Freud's biography—though Freud's own apartment on the Berggasse, as we mentioned earlier, was packed with archaeological objects embodying related themes.

Can Ehn, in the larger sense, have been affected by Freud's work, or do we come at the end to another historical parallel, this time a poignant and rather ironic one? Ironic because the community houses of Vienna, the homes of that working class with which psychoanalysis from that day to this has failed to establish contact, were in sober fact Freud's protection and that of his house; they were the fortresses of that left wing which was, by the mid-thirties, the only serious bulwark that remained between Austria and the aggression of the National Socialists in Germany. And when those houses were stormed by Dolfuss and the Heimwehr in 1934, that bulwark was swept away, and the

Nazis entered Vienna in the Anschluss of 1937. Freud, "the Jewish witch doctor," was forced to flee. He died in exile in London in 1939. Four of his sisters were not able to get out and were exterminated in the Final Solution.

Now, of course, we can see the Karl-Marx-Hof and the other community houses at peace under Austria's present Social-Democratic government, and occupied once more as they were intended to be. The Secession Building is also still there, rather playfully fulfilling its function in a typically Viennese way. Closer to home, Unity Temple, unlike the Larkin Building and so many other lost and irreplaceable masterpieces of American architecture, is still with us. But the process whereby it, like all great works of art, came to form will always remain one of the sacramental mysteries of our humanity. Freud above all recognized the inexhaustible ambiguity of art and even resented it a little, I think, and clearly held its link with the mind's secrets in the greatest reverence and awe. Wright tells us something about that as he draws up Unity Temple in his study. He writes:

> In all artists it is the same.
>
> Now comes to brood—to suffer doubt and burn with eagerness. To test bearings—and prove assumed ground by putting all together in definite scale on paper. . . .
>
> Yes, and what a poor creature, after all, creation comes singing through. . . .
>
> Night labor at the draughting board is best for intense creation. It may continue uninterrupted.
>
> Meantime, reflections are passing in the mind. . . . the "fine thing" is reality. [Freud would have said the same.]
>
> Reality is spirit . . . essence brooding just behind aspect!
>
> Seize it! And . . . after all, reality *is* supergeometric, casting a spell or a "charm" over every geometry. . . .
>
> Yes, it seems to me, that is what it means to be an artist . . . to seize this essence brooding just behind aspect. These questionings arising each with its train of thought by the way, as at work.
>
> It is morning!

Notes

1 But Wright was always ready to remodel, as his own house and studio amply show. So he both came to decisions rapidly and as rapidly produced new forms. His confidence and energy were dauntless.

2 They were both Nietzschean: Wright openly (why not, it was another art), Freud protesting innocence (it was the same art). Many artists, philosophers, and critics were clearly involved with these ideas around 1900. Nancy Olsen, in her as yet unpublished essay on the use of words in Cubist paintings, "Cubism, Freud, and the Image of Wit," points out, for example, that Freud's book of 1905 on jokes, though proposing the same phases in their (for him) largely unconscious production, also owes something to Bergson's book of 1900 on the same topic. But, we must now go further, I think, to recognize that the very act of abstraction itself was Freudian, in terms of Freud's analysis of form-making, even though abstraction in modern art was not appreciated by Freud himself.

3 "Condensation" and "displacement," for example, are the major critical facts that link the Parthenon and Chartres and most distinguish them among the other temples and cathedrals of their series.

4 Here I use the definition of the unconscious as "repressed" which Freud used when he wrote *The Interpretation of Dreams*. Later he added another type of unconscious which he called the "original," claiming, as Jung did, that it contained old folk memories.

5 As I tried to show some years ago in my book on his work, Wright turns to a quite open use of Pre-Columbian, especially Maya, forms after 1915 and condenses and displaces them into something very much his own by the early twenties. From the late thirties on Wright seems to quote from ancient non-Hellenic Mediterranean sources directly and with minimal revision of the model. Does this signal at once a renewed and increasingly more conscious interest in religious symbolism and a slackening of creative energy in the last decade or so of his life? It may be relevant to note that while Wright never seems to have shown any special interest in Freud or Jung he came in his later years increasingly under the spell, woven mainly by Olgivanna Wright, of the mystical and pedagogically oriented system of Gurdjieff, ultimately related to the Anthroposophy of Rudolf Steiner. It is possible here to think of a mind, once Freudian in its rigor, turned somewhat less realistic and self-critical by its increasingly exotic surroundings.

6 Wright's father clearly deserves more credit for Wright's character than he has normally received. He gave Wright his love of music and his essential "temperament," and when he left home he took up his lonely life in what can only be described as a manly way, without complaint or recrimination of any kind.

7 Wright claims that he played with the Froebel gifts after he was brought to his father's pastorate near Boston "at the age of three." But since the move to Boston took place in 1874 such was clearly impossible. Of course, Wright's mother may well have introduced him to Froebel long before 1876. Wright's association of his education with the Centennial may well represent one of his significant "displacements" of the type Hines discovered.

8 The tapping of the dream structure involved in the modern release of the self seems a much likelier source than the totally unrelated theories of Einstein (as cited by Giedion, for example) for the appearance of such elements in Wright and Cubism. Clearly, abstract art can be the most personal of all arts, since it is the most purely self-referential and, as we have already shown, can be the closest to "unconscious" motivations.

"Architecture, Sculpture, and Painting: Environment, Act, and Illusion." In *Collaboration: Artists and Architects,* ed. Barbaralee Diamonstein. Exh. cat. New York: Whitney Laboratory of Design, Watson-Guptill Publications, 1981.

12

Of all the essays in this book, this one best reveals Scully in his role as teacher and lecturer. "Architecture, Sculpture, and Painting: Environment, Act, and Illusion" is an intense and evocative study of the interrelationship of the three major art forms throughout the history of the Western tradition from ancient Egypt to the present. It grows out of the introductory course on the history of art that Scully began teaching at Yale in the late 1940s and, in the form presented here, became assigned reading for that course in the 1980s and 1990s. It expresses Scully's totalizing vision of art—meaning painting, sculpture, *and* architecture—as an integral and unifying framework for life and his understanding of the dialectic of empathy and association that informs the human experience of art.

But this essay is far from being simply an art-historical account of how the different arts have interacted over time. It was commissioned as the centerpiece of a catalogue for a highly polemical exhibition generated by the disillusionment with modernism and the revival of interest in the academic tradition that had gained wide publicity with the Museum of Modern Art's show of drawings from the Ecole des Beaux-Arts in the fall and early winter of 1975–76. The exhibition *Collaboration: Artists and Architects* was organized by Barbaralee Diamonstein in celebration of the centennial of the Architectural League of New York, opening at the New-York Historical Society in March 1981 before traveling to venues in thirteen other cities over the next two and a half years. Instead of illustrating past achievements, as the Brooklyn Museum's show *The American Renaissance* had done less

Architecture, Sculpture, and Painting: Environment, Act, and Illusion

It is a mistake to base judgments about architecture upon criteria which are concerned with architecture alone. To do so is to assess the present state of architecture and to chart out courses for its future on grounds which are in fact too narrow, because architecture is not an isolated art. It is only part of one large human art, indeed of what must be regarded as the fundamental art, which is the shaping of the physical environment and of living in it. All the physical arts (a better term than "visual arts") are aimed toward the fulfillment of those two complementary needs. They are thus one art, of which the functions of the major parts may roughly be articulated as follows: through the art of architecture human beings create an environment for themselves; they shape a space. Through the art of sculpture human beings populate that environment, that space, with their own creatures, embodiments of their own perception of the quality of being alive, which is above all the quality of being potentially able to gesture or to act. Through the art of painting human beings create the illusion of every conceivable kind of environment and of every kind of action in relation to those environments. Painting is the art which,

than two years previously, Diamonstein invited contemporary architects of the likes of Frank Gehry, Michael Graves, Richard Meier, Cesar Pelli, and Robert Stern to ask artists of their own choosing to develop a project together (those five chose Richard Serra, Lennart Anderson, Frank Stella, William Bailey, and Robert Graham, respectively). From the curatorial point of view, although certainly not for some of the architects and artists involved, the concept of collaboration carried an explicit reference to the Beaux-Arts system of education, of which it was a crucial component, and to the turn-of-the-century City Beautiful, to which it had given its essential character. The catalogue essays by Diamonstein, Paul Goldberger, Jonathan Barnett, and Scully all attest to this.

Scully deals specifically with the issue of collaboration only as part of a larger discourse on the relationships between the arts, clearly historicizing it as the product of a particular moment in time and using it as a pretext for other, more pressing concerns. His main objective is to define what he considers to be the inherent purpose, or "mode of being," of each of the three main visual arts—he argues that architecture shapes the space of the environment, sculpture embodies the human act, and painting imagines illusory worlds—and to show how the dominance of one art form in any given period influences the way the others are conceived and deployed. Although appearing at first to buy into the modernist argument for a delimiting, medium-based critique, which was popularized in the 1950s and 1960s in the art criticism of Clement Greenberg, Scully was not interested in preserving distinctions but rather in multiplying potentialities through the process of cross-fertilization. Greek architecture is powerful *because* it is sculptural, Baroque *because* it is pictorial. In this adaptation of what Henri Focillon referred to as "the law of technical primacy," Scully reveals his debt to the latter's *Life of Forms* and, through that, to the romantic philosophy of art of Hegel and Hugo.

Whereas earlier eras had benefited from the synthesis of the arts enforced and held in balance by the unquestioned dominance of either painting, sculpture, or architecture, the idea of a studied and self-conscious collaboration between artists and architects

as Josef Albers, the incomparable teacher of abstract art, put it, "makes us see what isn't there." All the arts of illusion, from television to holography, are therefore encompassed by it. It is the freest of all the arts, the most able to explore the character of imagined environments and of new modes of action. Often in history, once painting has discovered its way, it has been the first of the arts to indicate the route that the other arts, especially architecture, were soon to travel.

We therefore cannot think about the present and future of architecture without thinking about all the other arts as well. All the great modern architects, those most concerned with creating their own imagined environment, have known this and have reacted to it in one way or another. Wright always had the other arts in mind, and he consistently

developed toward the end of the nineteenth century as a critical tool in the academic reaction against an unwelcome blurring of boundaries combined with a growing autonomy of the arts. Scully gives serious consideration to this return to the classical tradition and places special value on the contribution of the American Renaissance to modern culture. So much so that, by contrast, the individually enforced order of the spaces created by the modern masters—Frank Lloyd Wright, Mies van der Rohe, and Le Corbusier—is seen as ultimately an egotistical gesture incapable of providing the basis for a meaningful and broad-reaching environmental art. How to use the legacy of academic classicism thus becomes the fundamental question for contemporary architecture and the key to its future. The line from Louis Kahn to Aldo Rossi and Robert Venturi is, in Scully's view, the one to follow, although it does not appear to offer any basis for a return to true collaboration of the arts. For this reason, Scully asks whether one should follow a more strictly historicist line, like that proposed by Allan Greenberg, which would at least allow for the adoption of a common language of form. It is obvious, however, that Scully is uneasy with the idea and, for the moment, maintains the need to remain distanced and ironic in relation to the past. But his willingness to question himself on this issue in print is impressive, especially as the answer is ultimately left in abeyance.

tried to subjugate them to, or to weave them into, one architectural system. Le Corbusier, on the other hand, tried to employ the freer methods of painting and sculpture in the making of architectural form. Mies tried to create his luminous, weightless environments with the presence of sculpture and, secondarily, of painting always the essential criterion in his mind. Right now, in 1981, with the relaxation of the special grip upon our imaginations which these architects exercised and with the catastrophe to the environment as a whole which the modern movement brought about now plain to our eyes, architects and critics are faced with several fundamental questions relative to the future of their art. One of those questions relates to the problem of tradition. How far, for example, can tradition be called to our aid at present? Can we, more specifically, revive the academic tradition of classical form? Can we, as Allan Greenberg and others would like to do, employ Renaissance and Baroque design once more—straight and without parody—and create an environment with it? If we consider that question in purely architectural terms, we find that there is no logical way in which it can be answered in the negative. Questions of economy, of constructional methods, of program and technology, once analyzed, in fact create no barrier whatever to its accomplishment. Even ornament is possible, however we may wish it. We are left with the uneasy feeling, which we ascribe to a holdover of modern prejudice in us, that there must somehow be more than adaptation of the past

open to us. There must be something new. Despite our revulsion against the International Style's destruction of our cities through its hatred of tradition, we still instinctively tend to recoil from a straight revival of the classical past. The nineteenth-century vernacular is another matter. It has been revived in the work of the most progressive architects and is wholly alive once more. Function, structure, and propriety indicate its use in many cases, especially in domestic architecture, and the inevitable rise of considerations relative to energy will only confirm its revival. But classical architecture, correctly assembled at urban scale, with the full panoply of ornamental detail and of sculpture and painting of the kind that is appropriate to it—can that be? Collaborative problems, aiming toward a positive solution to that question, were the yearly gala events of Beaux-Arts architectural education. I remember that they continued on at Yale for a long while under the modern regime of the late forties and early fifties. Teams of architects, painters, and sculptors got together. By that time, though, nobody knew what to do, because nobody knew any longer what his special role was meant to be—what his part of the art was supposed to contribute. So everything came out as arty blobs, prehistoric caverns without the animals or the cosmic signs. If we are to have classical architecture, we must start with the premise that we must have collaborative problems once again. If so, we must first decide what the
arts are and what they do. There is no better place to start than on the Campidoglio in 12.1
Rome, where Michelangelo pushed his buildings back at a diagonal to show that architecture is, supremely, space and then placed the Roman equestrian statue of Marcus Aurelius in it to act out, through its gesture, the creation of that space by human action. There could be no clearer demonstration of architecture as environment and of sculpture as act. Between the two the world is shaped for human behavior and is made to describe and encourage it.

Architecture, therefore, is an affair not primarily of individual buildings but of the entire constructed environment from farms to cities. Its first component is the natural world, in Rome almost entirely covered over but heaving up just the same in the seven hills and culminating on the summit of the Capitoline. That component we experience physically, that is, empathetically, as it lifts and subsides, and associationally, as our cultural coding directs us. We experience it in itself and in terms of its human connections. If we know the history of Rome, the experience of the Capitoline is almost unbearably poignant, as, after centuries of deprivation, the Renaissance symbolically takes over the center of Rome's civic power once more. If we don't know our history, it all means less. Thus we experience even nature most fully the more we know, from geological information to historical fact. The same is much more intensely the case with human constructions, because in them we are dealing directly with human intentions as well. We must experience them in relation to nature and in relation to each other. On the Campidoglio we feel the buildings pushed back; we feel the statue push them and then ride up into the volume of space between them. This is empathy. Is it culturally coded? Probably so, but surely more broadly than associationism. So we feel the domes rise. We know they are churches. In an American context they would more likely be government buildings. Each affects us

Michelangelo and others. Piazza del Campidoglio, Rome, sixteenth century and later. Aerial view, looking north-west 12.1

differently. We are squeezed between the palazzi down below, can read the floor levels and sense the restricted scale and so, by contrast, the great bloom of space on the summit of the hill. We will always feel this physically long after the history of Rome is forgotten and its original cultural meaning obscured. Empathy may therefore be regarded as the most essential fact of our experience of a work of art. Other meanings, involving association, may pour in and out of it as the culture of the viewer changes. Such meanings are always multiple anyway and are not limited by the artist's intentions, of which the work of art is never the simple sum. A system of linguistic analysis, like that in vogue among the present crop of semiologists, which reduces the physical arts to the conveying of information through signs, is thus faulty, because it is secondary and partial. It ignores the major vehicle of meaning, which is physical experience. But the two modes are also inextricably interwoven. There is no form which is void of associations, just as there can be no meaning without form. Hence knowledge and experience reinforce each other.

So with sculpture. Marcus Aurelius looms over us. We sense him above us, in a dominant position. His body straddles the horse, his weight solidly balanced upon its back. His arm stretches over us in the gesture of command that Michelangelo turns into

the act of building. In the sixteenth century it was thought that he was Constantine, hence probably blessing. Seen as that, the effect is subtly different. But more than this—and a Greek invention—the figure assaults the place. The act, to embody the concept of human freedom, must sometimes attack or resist the environment. So one of Claes Oldenburg's first colossal projects was for a reef of concrete locked into the four corners of an intersection to block two busy streets in New York. Marcus Aurelius rides forward into the void. He is not space. In these ways, through these arts, human beings learn how to be human, how to experience and to read the environment, how to shape it, and what it is like to act in it and against it, if necessary. Buildings themselves will, of course, combine the two functions in varying degrees. The more a building is expressed as a simple container of space the less sculptural it will be, but then its details may become active, then perhaps the whole massing. The classic vernacular generally combined simple volume with sculptural details; late modern buildings, to the detriment of the environment in urban situations, tended toward spectacularly sculptural massing. So the Farnese Palace defines its square, but also, especially in the gesture of its cornice
by Michelangelo, acts sculpturally upon it, while Nôtre-Dame-de-Ronchamp alights 4.10
upon the summit of its hill like a winged victory, a sculpturally active being, gesturing to the whole horizon.

Painting works with the same human problems. If we take as example a
Renaissance painting, to keep the forms more or less similar, we find Piero constructing 12.2
an environment with what his generation regarded as "divine perspective" and placing in it portentous figures who are framed by it. They recede into its depths like frightening visions and loom forward as giants toward the frontal plane. We are moved by painting's freedom, by its power to combine act and environment in a way more intensely visionary and potentially active than can normally be achieved by architecture and sculpture. Piero's is a panel painting, free of architecture. In many cases the painting is a mural adjusted to its architectural setting, like Caravaggio's *Calling of St. Matthew*, where the light source in the painting, the essential element in its definition of space and action, coincides with the source of light of the chapel in which it is placed. Still, leaving such adjustments aside, we find painting evolving from Piero's use of sculptural figures in an architecturally constructed setting to Caravaggio's whole mastery of optical illusion in light. So painting, by its very nature, pursues a course aimed toward being able to create whatever it likes. But sculpture, like architecture, is not primarily illusion. It is primarily "real." It stands in real space, natural and/or manmade. To make sculpture thus resembles, recalls, or suggests an act of primitive creation. The sculptor is godlike. Dare he
take on that role? Picasso shows him sleepless, his heavy hand on the architectural 12.3
frame, the mountains of the earth far beyond, while before him his creatures, standing on a base of mountains made by him, mount each other in copulation or conflict, alive, active, and generating energy. The sculptor has created not life but something more than an image of life, certainly not a "representation" or even a "sign" of life. He has embodied life, and his creature becomes mysteriously more real than other creatures. This is the case with Picasso's goat, to which he tethers a living goat. The eye asks: which is real?

ABOVE, LEFT: Piero della Francesca. *The Flagellation of Christ,* c. 1455–60 12.2

ABOVE, RIGHT: Pablo Picasso. *The Sculptor's Studio,* number 18, 1933 12.3

This is sculpture's ancient aura, its magic. It is real, more real perhaps than we are. It surrounds the house. So the essence of the experience of sculpture is physical, involving an awe for life and a deep sense of physical being, a love for it, a fear of it. Sculpture is therefore essentially body. It invades space. It is not required to re-create the image of a living creature to do that. Oldenburg's *Lipstick* invaded Beinecke Plaza at Yale and confronted the columns of the Memorial there with its sad little thing hanging down. Like Chaplin: big space, stern authorities, poor little fellow. Hence the tracks; they suggest that it wandered in like a toy, stopped, abashed. Moved to Morse College, the *Lipstick* stood up, secure in its sympathetic entourage of closely protective towers. Not "representing" any creature, it is yet a creature; it behaves like one. Any sculpture which doesn't, and which regards its mission as primarily the modeling of space—and we shall note some of that kind later on—had better, and without prejudice regarding its quality, be called "architecture" in order to keep the operating potentialities of each art clear.

It is a big thing to set these creatures out in the world. Each culture has approached this potent act in different ways. Egypt, as always, has the whole problem worked out so clearly and, according to its principles, so satisfyingly, that only the creatively destructive Greek mania for heroic and disruptive action was able to overthrow it. First: there are no sacred mountains in Egypt. They were made, rising over the Valley of the Nile. The pyra-
16.6 mids at Giza are also sun's rays, serving the cult of Ra, like the pyramidia of his obelisks, as if the shafts were buried in the ground. They create a new environment, changing this world, harnessing the sun, making everything all right forever. So their Pharaohs sit in the Valley temples below them in complete confidence. They seek the immobility of the block of stone out of which just enough is carved away to reveal them sitting there. Their eyes are open forever; the hawk of Egypt, the unwinking bird, directs their eyes, like those of the Sphinx above them, toward the sun. They are transfixed by its rays. So, in this case, they are alive forever precisely because, though minimally articulated for movement,

12.4 ABOVE, LEFT: *Mycerinus and His Queen*, from Giza, Egypt, c. 2470 B.C.

12.5 ABOVE, RIGHT: Palace, Knossos, Crete, second millennium B.C. Central court, looking toward Mt. Jouctas

they do not move. They do not wink in the sun. So they as bodies are always ready, literally, to house the Pharaoh and to fix him in the eternal life of his god, the sun.

Equally in standing statues. Potentially active, they choose not to act but instead 12.4
to assume their timeless, ritual roles: sister-wife who supports husband-brother Pharaoh, his headdress flat-planed, sharp-edged, and aggressive, hers soft-contoured and rounded, her body a stalk, his a trunk rising in a broad V, while his legs subside downward from the knee in enormously heavy masses, the whole compression of his weighty body flowing downward into great feet spreading out on the earth. She embraces the trunk like a vine. The empathetic experiences and the associational references are infinitely rich in what may at first seem to be very simple forms.

If the Egyptians had the problems of human life worked out in a way that encouraged the embodiment of life in monumental immobility, the Bronze Age Minoans did not. Their sacred mountains were natural ones like Mount Jouctas, seen down the
length of the court of the royal palace at Knossos. The manmade form is a longitudinally 12.5
extended hollow, sited so as to receive the sculptural force of the mountain, whose horns came charging down the court when the bull dance took place within it. The dancers seized those horns and let themselves be launched into space when the bull tossed his head. That act embraced nature's power and was shaped by it exactly as the court itself was. Action was everything but was generated by nature's energy; it did not oppose nature's force. It is probably for those reasons that Minoan civilization does not seem to have produced monumental sculpture. The permanent immobility of Egypt was of no use to this cult, wherein the fluid movements of the dance as a whole could most easily be embodied in groupings of small bronze, terra-cotta, or ivory figurines. At the same time, nature was all; she was not challenged; so no counter force, either architectural or sculptural, was brought to bear to balance her forms.

Temple of Hera II, Paestum, c. 450 B.C., looking east 12.6

12.6 It was the Greeks who did this. The Greek temple stands up as a clearly man-made form, shaped to confront the sacred landscape. Inside, it houses the image of its divinity. Outside, it makes the character of that being physically manifest in empathetically human terms. In this case it is Hera at Paestum, goddess who holds the land for men as their fair share, hence heavy and massive, weighing solidly on the ground, balancing the hill beyond as a man-conceived, manmade being. All previous sacred architecture, like that of Egypt, had fundamentally imitated natural forms, so calling the power of nature to themselves. Not the Greek temple. Its forms are all abstract, obviously man-imagined, but at the same time its peripteral colonnade suggests the bodies of standing human beings. It thus introduces a new element into nature: isolated man, who challenges the natural order with his own embodiments of heroic action and unquenchable desire. So each archaic and classic temple, before the formula dries up, is a physical body
16.8 with an appropriate kind of force. Athena at Paestum is taut, vertical, and aspiring, embodying not the rich fertility of man and earth like Hera but the competitive action of the polis upon it. Each temple is therefore sculpture, because it is basically an active body, masking with its colonnades every indication that it contains a box of space within

12.7 *Kleobis and Biton*, Delphi, c. 580 B.C.

it. Sculpture is indeed the dominant art of the Greek archaic period. Kleobis and Biton, in 12.7
myth also servants of Hera, are like her columns, solid as oxen, bulging with compressed power. Their legs are articulated actively as muscular springs for action. They are athletes like the Minoan jumpers but are now tragic heroes: monumental sculpture, man-sized in scale. They stand in the sacred precincts as potentially active beings, like the temple. It is all one art.

The bodies of the temples also support figural sculpture. From the earliest period these figures were used as an enhancement of the temple's own physical power. At Corcyra the Gorgon crowned the pediment, culminating the building's force and projecting it menacingly outward. Therefore she and her attendant offspring and guardian felines are cut as fully in the round as possible. They are almost entirely freestanding, unlike Egyptian architectural relief which repeated the plane of the wall or floated within it. Egyptian "decoration," flat and bright whether it was painting or painted relief, thus modified its host mass by turning its planes into signs. But Greek "decoration" articulated its host body by increasing its active articulation. So the Greek figures, hotly painted, thundered with individual action on the pediment, roughly adjusted to its shape but at first without any dramatic unity among themselves. In the metopes it was the same. Here the heroes stood forth, quintessential figural concentrations of the temple's own heroic stance. Hercules, subduing nature's monsters, was always foremost among them.

In these ways the Greek temple, which was the foundation of the Western tradition of collaboration between the arts, was in fact the result of the dominance of one art,

sculpture, and of an extraordinarily powerful and single-minded view of the sacred building as a single body, the intrinsically unified embodiment of aggressive sculptural power. For these reasons, archaic painting is sculptural as well. Most of it which remains is on vases. They, too, are actively physical forms, bursting with hearty life. Their taut geometry, as in all Greek art, is used to firm up the activity of the form. They are of the same family as the columns and the kouroi, and the figures painted on them are like the sculpture in the pediments and metopes. They are solid, defined by clear lines and planes, not shadowed by atmosphere but carved out of the black pigment or built up in red and white paint. They are isolated and heroic too, neither environmental nor spatial. Upon the swelling chests of the vases the male heroes smite their enemies, monster or Amazon. All this of course was entirely the opposite of what painting was to become when it freed itself from sculpture's "reality" and discovered its own gift for illusion. The shift to the red figure style in Greek vases was the first step in that process. The figure was no longer engraved but drawn with a pen or a brush on the natural surface of the vase and now gave off light against the polished black pigment around it, leaping forward off the surface, where before if most of the vase was to be made black, a metope frame had to be cut for its own black body to stand out against the terra-cotta ground. Then, with Polygnotus and the other great painters of the fifth century, painting became monumental, intellectually and emotionally complicated and expressive, achieving tragic stature and undoubtedly
5.1 affecting sculpture, as in the pediments of the new Temple of Zeus at Olympia. The figures are now fitted into their frame like paintings and are clearly meant to be seen from below with an adjustment to perspective angle. Most of all, they now embody not only physical being but also states of mind, reflecting the individual soul, by stance and expression, in exactly the way for which Polygnotus was famous. The great *Iliupersis* of Polygnotus at Delphi was conjecturally restored by Robert in 1893 from Pausanias's extensive description of it in the second century A.D. Looking at its major themes, the horse rolling over, the dead warrior, the seated figures with children in their arms, the great beast that overlooks the scene, we cannot fail to observe that all the figures of
5.4 Picasso's *Guernica* of 1937 are to be found there. It was clearly Picasso's primary model—a fact which has inexplicably escaped comment by his historians—a model reformed into pedimental shape and fused into violent action by another contemporary work of Greek art, the west pediment at Olympia. The draped arm of the central figure there, whether Apollo or Peirithous, is even echoed in the arm of Picasso's woman rushing in from our right toward the center of the *Guernica*. So Greek painting's first moment of monumental dominance eventually affected the creation of one of painting's foremost monuments in the twentieth century. What Greek painting itself accomplished is
12.8 reflected for us at some remove by Roman frescoes, like those from Boscoreale in the Metropolitan Museum of Art. A convincing and realistic perspective is created, based on the fact that we focus only on one percent of the space directly before us but are optically aware of everything within a full 180 degree arc of vision. The Greco-Roman painter thus wraps a wide wall around us or, in smaller, more vertical spaces, will lead us on a walk, looking down at a garden bench, up at a pergola. He will sometimes cut, by

12.8 ABOVE, LEFT: Wall paintings from villa at Boscoreale, first century A.D. Metropolitan Museum of Art, New York

12.9 ABOVE, RIGHT: Acropolis, Lindos, Rhodes, fourth–second centuries B.C. Reconstruction, model, 1960

illusion, what seem to be small windows in his walls, to show us an extensive landscape, often seen from above and far off. In such landscapes he paints those sacred features which had originally been worshipped at their full scale, and as he brings them into the optical illusion of a perspective system he dematerializes architecture into an optical play of light as well. He now creates the whole environment and endows it with a nostalgic, Theocritean glow.

Some of the old awe is past; nature itself is being shaped. Hence architecture
too becomes environmental; the temple loses a good deal of its old muscular bulk, while 12.9
its attendant propylaia and stoas open out into enclosing, space-making frames of slender columns. The architect even touches up, like a painter, the sacred landscape features to make them more conical, more optically appropriate. This is the illusionistic world of the Hellenistic and Imperial periods. But it transforms itself into the Christian Middle Ages by turning its optical gifts to a new transcendent focus, not on the sun-struck shapes of this world but on the hypnotic dazzle of the next. Mosaic, an ancient art, now especially serves these desires and rivets our attention on the splendors of a heavenly light. It replaces sculpture, climbs up on the walls and adjusts itself to their curvature, shaping an environment of weightless splendor and hieratic dreams. "Decoration," to touch again on that theme, dematerializes the architectural plane. This all culminates in
Hagia Sophia, where, unlike the Parthenon (but the same divinity, Wisdom, directs both 12.10
programs), the point of the building is not to blaze as a victorious sculptural body in the landscape under the light of day, but to create a vast interior environment within which human beings can find psychic shelter. All pressures and weights are transcended in the dazzle of the mosaic and in the magically floating canopy of the golden dome, heaven's symbol. The exterior of Hagia Sophia is simply a shell to contain this space; it makes a great bridge to heaven, surmounted by the dome, but it is not itself solidly figural, like the temple, but hollow, thus environmental, in its effect. For all these reasons figural sculpture, that so intensely pagan, bodily art, progressively dwindles away in this transcendent pictorial environment, eventually to come under actual iconoclastic prohibition for a considerable length of time.

Where and how does monumental figural sculpture come back? It does so in Romanesque Western Europe and in ways which suggest that it was generated by the
12.11 architectural environment itself. The Romanesque church is as much a dominant environmental shelter as Hagia Sophia, but, though painted, it is not weightless but solidly structural and massive. Its small windows are cut deeply into heavy walls, whose weight is carried by compound piers which are profoundly sculptural, almost figural, ponderously deploying their masses outward from their thick inner blocks to fat, round colonnettes resting heavily upon the pavement. Right at the capitals, where the structure's dramatic transferal of weight can be most felt, there the figural sculpture appears, men and monsters squirming into active life as if generated by the compressive heat of the stone. The figures are thus primarily an outgrowth of the environment and conform to its architectural shape. As decoration, they bring the mass to life. They do not challenge it. They don't even really populate it; they are of it. Elsewhere, over doorways, where the structural facts of the environment require only a thin slab of stone, because the weight is being taken by the arch above it, the figures again appear. Now, though, they are flattened laterally to conform to the character of that thin plane. They burn with excited linear fires and offer up their emotion to the environment, scorching along the surface of the stone.

BELOW, LEFT: Isidoros of Tralles and Anthemios of Miletus, Hagia Sophia, Istanbul, 532–37. Interior. From Gaspare Fossati, *Aya Sofia Constantinople* (London, 1852) 12.10

BELOW, TOP RIGHT: Sainte-Madeleine, Vézelay, c. 1104–32. Nave 12.11

BELOW, BOTTOM RIGHT: Cathedral of Notre-Dame, Chartres, 1145–1220. West portals 12.12

One of the very first things that the architecture which can be identified as
Gothic did was to pull those figures forward from their plane into a solid three dimensions. 12.12
Instantly, as at Chartres, they became grave and calm, belonging in the environment but not dominated by it—creating a truce, a peace. Down below, the figures turn into statue columns, vertical and stiff, wholly obeying the architecture's law but again forward of its plane and sweet-faced in human contentment and dignity. Now they are a self-respecting population, a delegation of gentle beings sent to greet us on arrival. Inside they all disappear in a new kind of transcendent light, grander and more mysterious, more purely come from heaven even than that reflected off the mosaics of the East. It is the light of stained glass, for which in large measure the whole Gothic edifice was raised. In it figures swim like droplets of color, their narrative function subordinate to the overall, environmental color screen. Soon they become larger and the glass clearer; they begin to exercise their power as figures upon the environment. An early example of that is the famous Virgin of the Belle Verrière who comes floating in with the sun in the south ambulatory of the choir at Chartres. She is a creature of light, and as she is seen from the crossing under the arches of the transept, she balances the Black Virgin who holds the dark north ambulatory, seen at exactly the same angle on the other side, from the same climactic point in front of the choir. Down below in the crypt sits the Vierge sous Terre, the third of the triad.

It is out of the light of the Belle Verrière that the late medieval painting of
northern Europe essentially derives. Van Eyck's droplets of oil capture the light within 12.13
them. The solid physical body which Italian painters like Giotto had achieved a hundred years before is turned magical by this interior light. The perspective is hypnotic, magical itself. Van Eyck seems perfectly clear about this: he brings the Virgin as a giant down from the now wholly clear glass windows and has her fill the vessel of the church—illusionistically, as only painting could achieve it. He shows us the mystery of the Mass, ultimate sacrifice of the Lamb, and he makes us grasp it visually with methods which recall those of Greece and Rome. We focus on the critical, bright spot in the center, while out around it, as White has shown, swells a barrel of figures exactly shaped to fill the oval frame of our vision. We take in the whole without strain, on a ground plane tipped up to contain and to let us perceive it all, including great cities in the distance, as magically clear as the flowers in the grass before us.

We see it all, but we are not in it; it is indeed a visionary world. What the Italian
Renaissance does above all is to pull us into the painting space, to make us walk into it 12.2
and among its noble sculptural figures, set like columns at our eye level, standing on the same ground plane as we. As they deploy back into space, the landscape that marches with them becomes misty in a perspective illusion now atmospheric as well as linear. Perhaps for the first time in painting (since we do not really know what all the lost Greeks did) a relation between figure and landscape is set up which is as solid and physically persuasive as that achieved by the Greek temple in its landscape. A new heroic confrontation is thus achieved. But that relationship is, by definition, not an easy one. It is hard to set the heroic act free and still have it fit into an environment. There is a strong contradiction

FAR LEFT: Jan van Eyck. *Madonna in a Church,* c. mid-1430s 12.13

NEAR LEFT: Donatello. *Saint George,* Or San Michele, Florence, c. 1415–17. Bronze copy of original marble 12.14

in modes of being involved. Pollaiuolo shows us that the optics are demanding. The viewer must look left and right to take it all in—unlike Van Eyck's focus which holds us steady—while the figures seem to loom over the landscape behind them. The difficulty is not so much technical as conceptual. How can the free act, which the Greeks opposed in a tragic balance with the environment, be made to fit into it? Fate and free will, how reconciled? This was an especially difficult question because the Renaissance was above all the freeing of European man to act on his own without the old environment to sustain him. Its very first sculpture shows this. That is, the Gothic statue column had slowly gained the power to act—to move, group, and converse—but only within and respecting the frame of architectural environment. The whole beautiful development from Reims to Sluter shows this. The final achievement is dramatic, not revolutionary. But a contrast between St. Theodore on the south porch of Chartres and Donatello's St. George in his shallow niche
12.14 at Or San Michele shows the change. St. Theodore, though he carries his weight on his own feet, is bound up with the environment, supported and canopied by it. The twist of the column below him is continued by his baldric to bind him into place. His strength is in his faith, his submission. Donatello's St. George is alone, pushed forward out of his shallow niche. He is nervous, taut, and aggressive, a creature of will and anxiety, already a modern man, liberated from the environment and from trust in it, free and alone to act as he can in the world. This is why the Renaissance begins (if we may employ such a term) precisely with sculpture, indeed with those figures by Donatello of the first two decades of the fifteenth century. It begins with the act.

A new environment soon follows. Brunelleschi, disappointed sculptor, creates it. It is based on the new perspective, which Manetti tells us that Brunelleschi invented, and

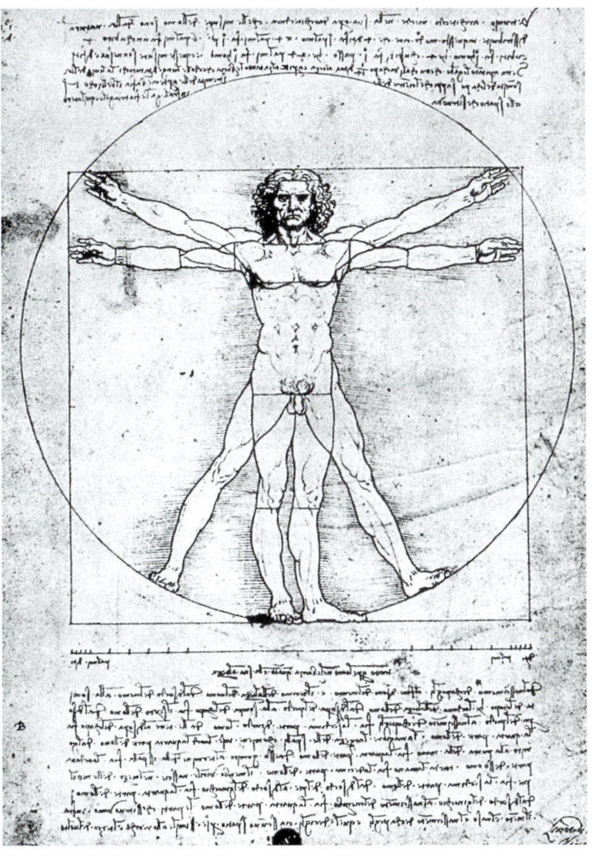

12.15 ABOVE, LEFT: Leonardo da Vinci. *Vitruvian Man of Perfect Proportions*, c. 1490

12.16 ABOVE, RIGHT: Filippo Brunelleschi. San Lorenzo, Florence, 1421–60s. Nave

upon the Vitruvian figure, undoubtedly reflecting Pythagorean and perhaps Platonic idealism, of the *Man of Perfect Proportions* who fits into the primary shapes of the universe, the 12.15
circle and the square. Brunelleschi's architecture is like Leonardo's drawing of that figure. 12.16
The environmental shapes of circle and square, of cube and sphere, are spatial, not sculptural. They are drawn tight as wire, stretched into thin frames and canopies by the overwhelming desire to make space, not mass. The observer, the human being, is the active sculptural figure; the architecture is pure, perfect volumes of space. But this system of space-making is so exact and complete that there is no place for sculpture in it, and not much really for painting either. Here an intense conflict is apparent, between the idea of liberated action in sculpture and of the perfect environment in architecture. How can they be brought together? Ideally, only in painting, where the sculptural figures can be fitted through illusion into the perspective box. Here the West settles, and has continued to do so since that time, for free investigation rather than for contentment, for an imagined future rather than present ease. In this way the magnificent dominance of Renaissance painting over the other arts begins to take shape. In the largest sense it continues right up to the present day. The conjunction of environment and act is made only with enormous tension and difficulty, as we have already noted, so that it remains an engrossing, profoundly intellectual and emotional problem, endowing Baroque and modern painting with

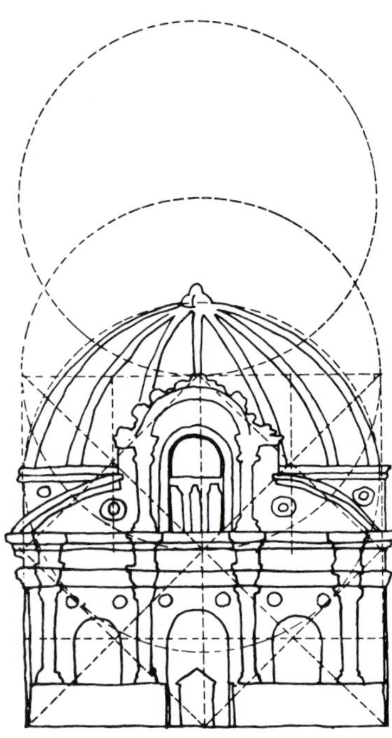

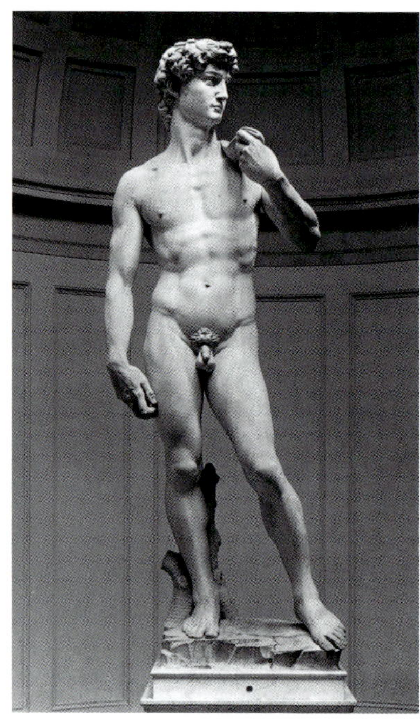

ABOVE, LEFT: Leon Battista Alberti. San Francesco, Rimini, c. 1450. Theoretical analysis of facade by C. Ragghianti 12.17

ABOVE, CENTER: Michelangelo. *David,* 1501–4 12.18

ABOVE, RIGHT: Michelangelo. *Rondanini Pietà,* c. 1555–64 12.19

that quality of inexhaustibility and discovery which it may only be at the very edge of losing right now. But so far as sculpture is concerned, there is clearly no place for it in the new Renaissance scheme of things. There is really no place for it on church facades, where concern is for an expression of the perfect harmony of circle and square. San Lorenzo never gets a facade, thus remaining a purely spatial perspective box. Michelangelo projected one for it: circles and squares. The first concerted project for a new Renaissance
12.17 church exterior was in fact Alberti's for Rimini—circle, cube, and sphere, at once purely conceptual and heavy with Roman gravity. All the solids were in a sense a decoration; they brought drawing into mass. Palladio perfected the type. Sculpture, where present, is so placed and confined as to seem purposefully inhibited and repressed.

If so, what of the act? Michelangelo poses that question early in his career. The
12.18 *David* is a giant ready for action. The hand swells with the immanence of the cast stone; the profile is determined. The whole young body is trained down, lean and hard. It is ready. But then, as so many observers have noted, when we move to the side everything changes. The body becomes a pliant stalk without force, supporting a head too large for it. The face expresses doubt, perhaps fear, perhaps sympathy. There is in any event uneasiness about the character of action, a sense, guilt-ridden and very non-Greek, of action's ambiguous justifications. Is action worthwhile? This means: is it worthwhile making sculpture? Michelangelo's enormous compassion wars with his superhuman vitality over this ambiguity all his life. The struggle itself endows his sculpture with its special life-in-depth, far beyond anything Greek, and with its eternal restlessness. Physical, passionate, yearning in and through the flesh, it is also rent with soul, with abnegation and sorrow. Is it worthwhile to emerge from the stone? So much pain. Is it

worth it to be born? Finally, at the very end of his life, indeed as he is dying,
Michelangelo seems to say, no, it is not worth it—to sink back into the arms of the
mother is all. With his last strength he lops off the heroic arm and shoulder of the Christ
in the *Rondanini Pietà*, and as the forms fall back and subside, he scrapes—one can feel 12.19
his life waning—scratches with his clawed chisel on the surface of the stone, roughen-
ing the forms, turning the faces back into formlessness and decay, like Monet's painted
veil across his dead wife's face. But as the shapes fall back they assume a prehistoric
form; a carved tusk, like an ivory, and this, gathering itself, arches up and over like a
wave about to break, the arc rising as Michelangelo dies, so left at the edge of its ultimate action forever.

In the end, Renaissance sculpture can thus be said to disappear at the hands of its
greatest sculptor, because of the paradox that action poses for the thinking mind. The
act cannot challenge the environment forever. Eventually it merges with it. This is
exactly what it does in Baroque architecture and sculpture. Just as Baroque painting
conquers illusion wholly and thus controls a total environment, so Baroque architecture
and sculpture merge into a pictorial drama. It is modeled in light like painting and is
framed and directed as upon a stage. Bernini's Cornaro Chapel is all that. The donors 12.20
watch from the box, like Rembrandt's syndics attending, while the play goes on. St.
Theresa's ecstasy, spot-lit, is echoed in the pediment above her which bursts open with
release. The facade of Borromini's San Carlo alle Quattro Fontane justifies its name by 12.21
environmentally controlling the crossing of its streets, while the gestures of the figures in
its niches seem to direct the undulations of its facade and to project them upward to the
culminating painted oval in the center. Contrast should be made with Palladio's
Redentore, where the gestures of the sculptural figures, active enough in themselves, are
squelched by the tight niches and sat on by the heavy pediments above them. At San
Carlo the niches open up, the pediment breaks, the environment consents to the act so
that in fact there is no confrontation between these two opposites anymore but only a
rhythmic oneness, the famous Baroque principle of unity at work. But that very union
robs the act of its intensity. The heavy price that is paid for it, therefore, is the loss of
sculpture's special, primitive aura, in which it invades the environment, may threaten it
or us, may be somehow dangerous and therefore peculiarly alive. Now we know that it is
theater and so not ultimately serious—and marvelous theater, like that back and forth
play, eventually illuminated at night, between sculpture and architecture in the Piazza
Navona. Here the Italian seventeenth century's greatest architect and sculptor come
together and thus demonstrate the Baroque's special strength in architecture and sculpture as well as its severest limitations. It is play, in which sculpture, though endlessly
delightful, in fact merges into the environment and its special dangerous presence is
lost. In that sense, decoration is all.

This again is the reason why painting—with the exception of a couple of generations which are dominated by the French classic garden—remains the dominant art. Only
Vaux, Versailles, and Chantilly can so merge the act into a total architectural environment. 16.12, 16.16

Painting's dominance, which may be said to have created the English landscape garden itself, finally culminates in the nineteenth century. So Constable can lead us into his world and can merge us with it precisely because painting has now become the wholly environmental art into which the act can be inextricably woven. Sculpture, on the other hand, tends, despite its various Neoclassic reactions, to become increasingly pictorial right up to the later years of the nineteenth century, and it is no accident that it was the Baroque world of dramatic unity which was revived at Chicago in 1893. The old synthesis still held because the sculpture was still eminently, indeed increasingly, pictorial, the figures disembodied into brushstrokes of light and dissolving into the background like those in the illusionistic frescoes of Rome. That development was also sociologically exact, since it was the fundamental objective of the nineteenth-century middle class—and had indeed been a Roman objective as well—to discourage anarchic acts and to create a safe, integrated environment. This is the environment into which we are optically drawn by the greatest painter of the age, Monet, as he merges figures and places into one veil of color, unifying all. It is the very height of painting's capacity to draw us into the magical spaces of dreams. Looking into the little ponds with their water lilies and finding the whole sky reflected in them, we sink into the depths and into the clouds as well.

ABOVE, LEFT: Gianlorenzo Bernini. Cornaro Chapel, Santa Maria della Vittoria, Rome, 1645–52 12.20

ABOVE, CENTER: Francesco Borromini. San Carlo alle Quattro Fontane, Rome, begun 1665. Facade 12.21

ABOVE, RIGHT: McKim, Mead and White. Boston Public Library, 1888–95. Main staircase, with murals by Pierre Puvis de Chavannes 12.22

At a fundamental level, this merger with nature may be said to have been the most advanced state of the arts around 1890. It was in accord with nineteenth-century scientism and with its belief in continuous process, and its most obvious architectural union occurred in Art Nouveau and, even more splendidly, in the related work of Antoni Gaudí. The academic reaction of the nineties can be regarded as having been directed in large part against that very merger. It has always been the academic's intention to have things clear and categorized, and a thinned-out and rationalized classicizing form has, over the past several centuries, generally served as the academic language of the visual arts. It was founded on the Baroque synthesis but shared little of the Italian Baroque's intensity. Its background was primarily French and was ultimately grounded in the classicism of Poussin. That tradition had indeed been kept functional by the pedagogic continuity of the French Academy. There can be no doubt that with the nineteenth-century reorganization of the Beaux-Arts some clear thinking took place about the relationship between the arts and—again the archetypal Beaux-Arts program—their collaboration in the shaping of the environment. This seems especially true in America, perhaps because the concept of a new Renaissance was so consciously and enthusiastically embraced here. It had, moreover, a splendid beginning: with Richardson and La Farge at Trinity Church in Boston, where the forms were by no means classical and the achievement was far more than academic. The whole interior is one warm glow—what Hitchcock called a "mist" of living color—to which the great western stained glass windows by La Farge contribute the noblest share and set a grand scale of united tone. La Farge's figural panels around the church, in which he was assisted by Saint-Gaudens, are of a similar gentle grandeur. One feels that the best of the century is here. As was soon to be the case in Chicago, the environment is indeed all; the vast colored volume of space is deeply pictorial, but the ambient is firm and monumental. A sculptural solemnity, in that sense truly Romanesque, and absent in Chicago, shapes the whole.

Out of this beginning, by the 1890s, came other achievements in collaboration by architects who had in part been trained by Richardson. None was of his pure genius, but, like him, they were all imbued with the academic system and knew how to employ it. So McKim, Mead and White set up their Boston Public Library on Copley Square across from Trinity in the rational manner of Labrouste at the Bibliothèque Ste. Geneviève, though they cannot help softening and archaeologizing his taut, spare forms. But like him they lead us through the ground floor to a stair that rises at the rear of the building to attain the main reading rooms of the upper floor. Where Labrouste used a copy of Raphael's *School of Athens* on the rear wall, McKim, Mead and White open theirs more widely to light and direct us upward to the climax in enlightenment by means of the
murals of Puvis de Chavannes. These are classicizing and, like the building, not the most 12.22
intense of forms, but they are dynamically adjusted to the architectural frame and so flow up the stairs and float toward the empyrean of the top landing.

That association of basically classical academic figures with essentially classical academic architecture went on to produce some of fresco painting's greatest triumphs in the twentieth century. The system was able to transform the airy fantasies of Puvis de Chavannes into the tumultuous proletarian crowds of Diego Rivera, whose revolutionary figures boil out of the walls along the stairway and around the courtyard of Mexico's National Palace. They do not fit into the architecture but swamp it; they occupy the government building like a revolutionary army. The whole vast achievement of the Mexican collaboration among the arts was possible because it had this program. It was aimed toward a revolutionary end; it was trying to arouse, teach, and triumph. Giotto returns, since now a story must be told movingly and clearly, and the broad, blunt figures, endlessly eloquent in their gestures, can be turned to a Mexican purpose with Aztec sculptural power. Orozco is different; his forms attack the environment with fire and reform it in their flames. He and Rivera are thus poles apart, and this itself shows the vitality of their common tradition, since they were after all working in an old and disciplined mural system which they were able to infuse with the bite of new objectives and beliefs. During that curious period of the recent past when the stylistic movement toward abstraction was considered more significant than matters of quality and meaning, or was regarded as synonymous with them, the Mexican muralists were generally undervalued, though not, it must be noted, in Mexico. It should now be obvious that they were giants, their quality absolute; they blew an old world apart with their uniquely pictorial union of sculptural and environmental aggression.

The painters of the American scene who painted murals under the auspices of various public agencies during the thirties were directly inspired to a mural art by the example of the Mexicans, as was the decision of the New Deal administration to commission them. But with the exception of Shahn who painted as a pure Social Democrat at Roosevelt, New Jersey, and elsewhere, they were generally less certain than the Mexicans about what the social meanings and objectives of their murals were to be. In the end, despite considerable levels of satire and of bitter social concern in their easel works, they tended in their public frescoes to construct a hymn of praise for the continent, especially for the Middle West, and for the human beings, larger than life, who framed it or had shaped its history. So their murals, though heroic in intention, tended also to be elegiac or descriptive. Hence they were never as aggressive as those of the Mexicans: they did not attack the environment but eulogized it and so never achieved the power that could blast old frameworks and suggest new ones. They are weaker than the Mexicans but have also been seriously undervalued nonetheless. Benton is splendidly resourceful in space and incident at Indiana University and the Missouri State Capitol, Curry epic in Topeka; while Grant Wood, whom even the most recent student of the American scene characterizes as not a very good painter, is in fact the gravest and noblest of them all when seen on the broad stretches of wall which he respects so intensely or in his studies for them. He is not Giottoesque like Rivera but of the Quattrocento, recalling Piero and Uccello. His figures are sculpturally conceived, enthroned in clear stages of space.

Traditional sculptural character was therefore a primary ingredient in the most effective of all the figural mural series from the 1890s to 1940. (We saw earlier that much the same was true of the *Guernica* of 1937.) What of sculpture itself and its relation to architecture during those years? At first, as in Chicago, it retained its power to act effectively, though in the continuing neo-Baroque accord with the environment. For example, Grand Central Station by Reed and Stem, and Warren and Wetmore, embodied the rush of the trains below it and of the automobile traffic around it by setting off Mercury's rush forward against the point marker of the New York Central office tower far back across the open space. The sense of flight and freedom is compelling—

or was so until Pan Am (much maligned surely, but deservedly so) brutally blocked the view.

Everywhere during the generation of the 1880s to about 1910, sculptors like Saint-Gaudens knew how to populate the environment and to bring it alive with their embodiments of action. Farragut steams forward against the current, damning the torpedoes in Central Park. We empathetically stand with him; by association we share his danger. Sherman on horseback comes clip-clopping down Park Avenue, sawing on the reins, head bare, brow bent back as with one of his migraines, the fruit of awareness. Victory strides before him. He rides like War, Famine, Pestilence, and Death behind her.
Most of all, Colonel Shaw marches with his black troops down Beacon Street. It is all 12.23
there as Robert Lowell said it in his ode "For the Union Dead":

12.23 Augustus Saint-Gaudens. *Robert Gould Shaw Memorial*, Boston, 1884–97

Their monument sticks like a fishbone
in the city's throat.
Its Colonel is as lean
as a compass-needle.

He has an angry wrenlike vigilance,
a greyhound's gentle tautness;
he seems to wince at pleasure,
and suffocate for privacy.

. . . .
when he leads his black soldiers to death,
he cannot bend his back.

It is probably to be expected that the most desperate experience in American history before 1917, the Civil War, should have triggered its most consistent and significant sculptural response. At the head of the Mall in Washington, Grant, motionless in the saddle, guards the Capitol; its dome, under construction all through the war, rises behind him. He stares down the long vista toward the Potomac, still as an animal, dangerous as Hell, his slouch hat pulled over his eyes. To left and right field artillery is coming to his support, the horses reeling, the guns bouncing behind them. Down the long axis, far off,
his back to the Potomac, America's major cult figure broods, as real a presence to us as 12.24
Zeus was to Pheidias at Olympia. Like that Zeus he is set back in the shadows of a temple's cella, illuminated only through the open door and by whatever artificial light (cressets perhaps then, an electric bulb now—it doesn't make any difference) seemed necessary to reveal his being. But to terminate the axis more firmly, this temple is turned
so as to present its broad side to the Mall, and through it Lincoln looks out toward the 12.25
obelisk of the Washington Monument and, in the far distance, toward his necessary instrument, the great general in front of the dome. How large a part association plays in

ABOVE, LEFT: Henry Bacon. Lincoln Memorial, Washington, D.C., 1912–22. Interior, with statue by Daniel Chester French 12.24

ABOVE, RIGHT: Lincoln Memorial. Aerial view 12.25

the experience of public monuments can be tested in people of my generation by recalling our reaction to these forms before and after the Kennedy funerals. It is true that a change in critical stance has also occurred over that period. We now appreciate classicizing academic art as once we did not. But much more than that is the overlay of images which have soaked these monuments in blood and sorrow: John Kennedy's noble caisson passing around the Lincoln Memorial in solemn cortege and crossing the bridge to Arlington, and there, finally and unbearably, the flag taken off the coffin and folded in neat quick folds and placed in the widow's hands. Even more: Robert Kennedy's funeral, when the train with his body, delayed after tragic accidents along the line from New York, sent the hearse late to the Lincoln Memorial in darkness and rain, while those from the Poor People's encampment, who had waited for it all day, stretched out their hands toward it in front of the colonnade with the image behind them until the hearse picked up speed and moved away to show us at last on our television screens, not the Irish Guards in formation as at John's interment, but the open grave in the rain and the dead man's son, the first of the pallbearers, staggering up the slope toward it, his face twisted in unspeakable pain. Now we see the monuments of Washington, Greek and Roman as they are, in the full dimension of their cultural reference and can say with them, "The Gracchi are dead, Tribunes of the people. Now comes night." And the night came.

What happened to that academic vocabulary of forms, that articulation of architectural frame and sculptural and pictorial presence? The answer is that it eventually lost its distinction between those parts, and the several components eventually merged into one, as the most "advanced" arts, so we noted above, had already tended to do long before. A
12.26 comparison between the triumphal arch at the World's Columbian Exposition of 1893
12.27 and the main entrance to Bertram Goodhue's Nebraska State Capitol of 1922–27 makes
that plain. In the latter building the sculpture wholly merges with architecture and grows out of it. The mass becomes more potent, but considerable articulation (which means

intellectual and emotional qualification) is lost. We are in the world of the Art Deco skyscrapers whose originally more or less classic language had been simplified, primitivized, 12.27
and, from the classical point of view, barbarized over the decades. These qualities indeed shape Art Deco's power. Architecture, sculpture, and painting are all pressed back, flattened together and stripped, marvelously drawn between what were then called the modern and the traditional modes. Rockefeller Center has its life in this living tension, this electric vitality; it intensifies environmental and active forces in one compressed union. Though matchless, it has its limitations, some of them perhaps conceptual. It is too bad that the lobby of the RCA Building no longer can show Rivera's mural above its elevators; it was destroyed because of its Marxist iconography. The present set is spatially spectacular but sloppy and essentially meaningless. In that vein, the lobby of the incomparable Chrysler Building is surely the most integrated, with the long ghost of the building itself riding in overhead above the entrance, while the figural sections of the ceiling coincide with the marble panels on the walls and the abstract sections with the banks of wall lights. Art Deco's jazzy conversion of old rhetorical traditions into decorative exercises—delightful but (without prejudice) superficial—thus works perfectly to celebrate the triangularity of this space with its diagonal patterns. Art Deco *is* decorative. It is not tragic drama, and while it has been deservedly revalued in recent years, it is useful to realize that this is why, in its own day, both traditionalists and pure modernists despised it.

The "advanced" arts, of which I spoke earlier, had already primitivized themselves by the beginning of the century, but they had done so in an attempt to intensify meaning. For this reason they became sculptural rather than pictorial, casting out much

12.26 NEAR RIGHT: Charles Atwood. Triumphal Arch, Court of Honor, World's Columbian Exposition, Chicago, 1893

12.27 FAR RIGHT: Bertram Goodhue. State Capitol, Lincoln, Nebraska, 1922–32. Exterior

ABOVE, LEFT: Pablo Picasso. *Nude with Raised Arms*, 1907 12.28

ABOVE, RIGHT: Pablo Picasso. *Painter with a Model, Knitting* (illustration for *Le Chef d'oeuvre inconnu* by Honoré de Balzac), 1931 12.29

of painting's power of illusion to get back to sculpture's archaic reality. So Cézanne wants his forms to seem sculpturally touchable, in contrast with Monet's optical shimmer; and Maillol contrasted with MacMonnies shows the difference in sculpture.
12.28 Maillol's bather is structurally solid, really planted in space. Picasso picks her up, adapts her pose, merges her with African sculpture, which was, from his point of view, more primitive yet and full of the magical power that Western sculpture had given up long before. He builds his *Demoiselles d'Avignon*, his proto-Cubist synthesis of sculpture and painting, out of these elements. The faces turn into masks. Disquieting presences begin to appear. Sculpture too takes on this quality. Lipchitz's *Figure* of 1930 has the power to project threat. It is not a projection of ourselves into space but a being which convinces us that it may not wish us well. Sculpture now regains its old aura, its menace. Cubism itself, as the *Demoiselles d'Avignon* had already suggested, was in large measure sculptural painting, purposefully giving up Monet's and even Cézanne's coloristic splendors in order to sweep stern vertical figures together in the center of the canvas; out of some cosmic chaos they take on body before us. Their appearance suggested several roads for sculpture and painting to travel. One of these was certainly toward abstraction. Picasso himself shows us that painting can now do anything; there are literally no boundaries to
12.29 transference and illusion. His painter is not an ancient hero wrestling with living creatures, like his sculptor, but a sweaty shaved-head who draws proto-Pollocks or a geometric abstraction who leaves a Greek profile on the canvas. With sculpture, existing in real space, the situation was necessarily more limited. If it became abstract but wanted to remain figurally active—in which there was no essential contradiction—the experience of it necessarily had to become more fully empathetic because it was generally less associational. One had to feel with these forms as with a structural creature, integral to itself. This is the way most of us in my generation learned to read meaning in art. An abstract sculptor, like Brancusi, might well add the associational element

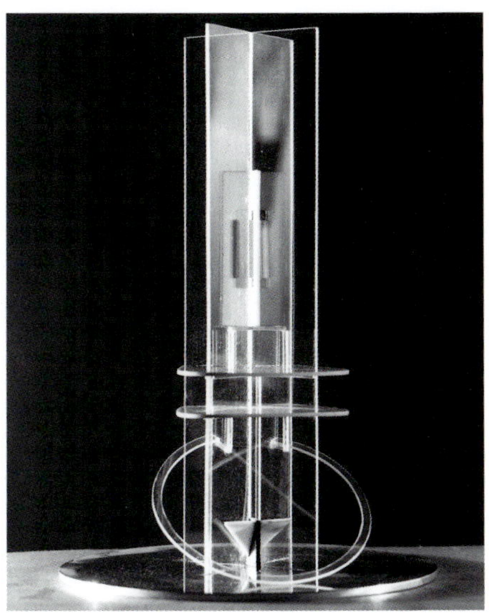

12.30 ABOVE, LEFT: Naum Gabo. *Project for a Glass Fountain*, c. 1925

12.31 ABOVE, RIGHT: Pablo Picasso. *Man with Sheep*, 1944

through a title, such as *Bird at Rest* or *Bird in Space*. The former piece of sculpture does indeed physically subside downward, and the latter does indeed physically rise and gather to leap gleamingly upward. But the names held, and their enhancement of the meaning is an indication of how empathy and association are indeed inextricably interwoven in our experience of form.

But in the movement toward abstraction some sculpture lost its figural, active quality and became environmental, thus indistinguishable from architecture and, in that
definition, adding nothing to it. Abstract painting such as Mondrian's was also environ- 2.7
mental. Indeed, it played a considerable part in creating the environment shaped by the
International Style, in which Constructivist sculpture like Gabo's *Project for a Glass* 12.30
Fountain also takes on an architectural character and loses the special sculptural stance. This is precisely why Picasso, the father of pictorial abstraction, never let his sculpture approach too close to that state. His figures are alive; he would be Greek if he could, but the pluralistic torment of the modern age is upon him. He loves and creates the animals,
but his animal bearer, unlike its ancestor from the archaic Acropolis, must struggle to 12.31
hold the beast. The two are not locked together in a common physicality; the placid fellowship is lost. The animal is terrified; it knows that the man is a stranger in its world.

The question of how architecture and sculpture and, secondarily, painting should relate to each other was thus raised anew by modern art. It is worthwhile to look briefly at the way the three major architects of the Abstract period (as it might be called) handle that relationship. For Wright, developing out of his Froebel training as the first great architectural abstractionist, the environment was everything and all the arts were made to
contribute to it. So his early houses were interwoven spatial constructions exactly scaled 1.23
to their inhabitants. The space-defining moldings were big and insistent, crossing just above head height; they at once defined a close sense of shelter and led the eye outward

to horizontally continuous space. All the furniture was scaled to the architecture. The interior was to create a perfect environment for the raising of children, disciplined, ordered, sheltering, and expansive. The effect was of great peace so long as the inhabitants accepted the environment's gentle but pervasive laws. There was no room for rebellion, therefore normally no space for sculpture. It is true that Wright loved to give his favorite clients a plaster model of the Nike of Samothrace, about four feet high. Hence this domesticated Victory sometimes sailed into Wright's spaces, but it hardly dominated them; instead it tended to make them look bigger by its diminished scale. Wright also sometimes employed the sculptor Richard Bock to execute pieces of sculpture that he himself had designed. Their most significant collaboration in Wright's early work (aside from the Froebel babies with their cosmic balls of yarn that crowned the
11.5 piers of the Larkin Building) was in the Susan L. Dana House. There they set a penis-
11.6 shaped figure, entitled *The Flower in the Crannied Wall*, directly behind the abstractly
contracting and expanding entrance archway. The column within the female image is an ancient symbol of marriage and fertility. It occurs in those Maltese mother-goddess temples that Wright was later to recall in some of the round buildings of his last decades. Its most expressive use is by Giotto at Padua, when Joachim, learning in exile that Anna will bear a child, rushes back to Jerusalem and meets her at the Golden Gate. The glowing arch of the gate emits columnar forms which culminate in the cone of Joachim and Anna holding each other. The environment is literally packed with active life: an ultimate image of the objectives of the physical arts.

Wright's and Bock's most elaborate work occurred at Midway Gardens. There
12.32 the columnar figures, suggestive already of Cubist influence, are totally adjusted to the
architectural shapes of the environment and submissive to them. The order is expansive and total, like an image of continental, integrated America. Everything is bound up in the stretching and interweaving of the forms, sweeping and continuous. One senses that it is in fact a uniquely American vision—to be contrasted with Giotto's contained world—of the kind in which the Abstract Expressionist painters, Jackson Pollock in particular, were later to participate, wherein all separate shapes are caught up in the swing of the vast, unifying spatial rhythms. So Wright's work is essentially all environment, subordinating all acts except the aura of the architect's own, and there is literally no place for painting or sculpture to operate freely within it. How could it have been otherwise in this compelling image of a nineteenth-century America determined to homogenize itself and to achieve a new, bigger, and persuasive order?

Mies van der Rohe inherits from Wright that sense of a total environment, flowing from part to part. But Mies eases off the pressure, thins out and simplifies the forms.
12.33 He leads us in the Barcelona Pavilion—the cult shrine of that aspect of the modern
movement—to a classic sculptural figure whose gesture seems to be setting the enclosing planes out in space, so creating the environment by its own act. In this way it recalls the Marcus Aurelius on the Campidoglio. The human act makes the world. This is why Mies would never use abstract or environmental sculpture in his spaces, but instead always employed traditionally figural shapes. His architecture is the abstract, flowing

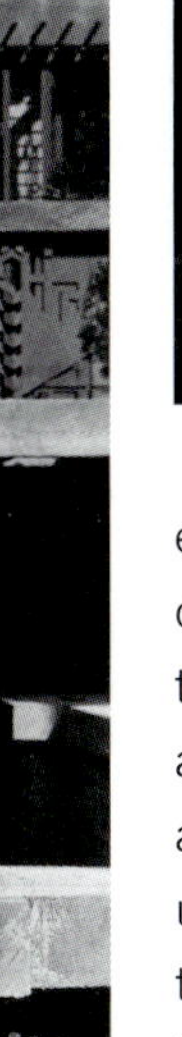

environment, his sculpture the bodily act. Finally, in his late work, Mies settles for a less 12.34
dynamic but equally grand conception, in which the solid figures are set in vast space, totally undirected and unrestrained, nobly free in a great volume of air. The structure, as at Houston and elsewhere, may be kept wholly outside the space in order not to intrude any compressive sense upon the liberating spatial experience. Painting, too, may hang untrammeled in those volumes, but its presence is not so keenly felt by Mies as is that of the sculpture; it is the midspace solid that he loves and the weightless planes that define the environment around it.

From the very beginning, of course, Le Corbusier's buildings were studied in pictorial and sculptural terms, which is one good reason why their appeal has been so strong
and pervasive. Some of the early houses stood on legs, taut like insects but vertically 4.8
stretched like people. The interior spaces were tumultuous, their shapes brought to life by
rhythmically interactive elements from Le Corbusier's Purist painting itself. Their call is 13.2
to action; they do not primarily seek to protect or to shelter a family; they are not Freudian and Oedipal like Wright's early houses, but rather *anti-Oedipe*, already schizophrenic.[1] They encourage many contradictory and rather youthfully activist modes of action, not one paternal order. In his late work Le Corbusier gathers those objectives all up into big sculptural forms. The Modular stands on its primitively muscular legs and gestures
upward; so does the Unité d'Habitation at Marseilles. So do the piers of the High Court at 5.3, 8.16
Chandigarh. Like the columns of the Temple of Athena at Paestum, they leap continuously upward with no horizontal cornice to limit their energy. Both buildings embody, in the face of a vast landscape, humanity's triumphant civic enthusiasm, what Sophocles called "the feelings that make the town."

These heroic gestures, too, seem to me to be echoed in the Abstract Expressionist painting of those same years, especially in that of Franz Kline. It was an existentialist decade, which means, in art at least, an idealistic one. Indeed, all the Abstract period was essentially idealist, not realist, in its objectives and methods. So the three architects we have considered essentially wanted to do it all themselves and to create their own new pattern of act and environment, and they all bent reality to the shape of their overweening Idea. It is true that Wright in his own way as an American had the strongest realist component in him, while Le Corbusier was the most idealist and Mies was the closest to academic classicism. But they all set up total orders, so that the kind

12.32 ABOVE, LEFT: Frank Lloyd Wright. Midway Gardens, Chicago, 1913–14. Interior. Figure of Contemplative "Spindle"

12.33 ABOVE, CENTER: Ludwig Mies van der Rohe. German (Barcelona) Pavilion, International Exposition, Barcelona, 1928–29. Interior court, with sculptural figure by Georg Kolbe

12.34 ABOVE, RIGHT: Ludwig Mies van der Rohe. Cullinan Wing, Museum of Fine Arts, Houston, 1954–58. Interior

of collaboration between sculpture and architecture which created, for example, monumental Washington, would not have been possible under their sway. They tended to wipe out all acts other than their own or the kind they envisaged, and they permitted few associations that fell outside their system. Among them, though in widely varying degrees, in which Wright now seems much the least reductionist, they destroyed the existing architectural environment and left a pitifully reduced urbanistic language, indeed an urbanistic nightmare, in their wake.

One might infer from these unhappy developments that what was needed was to bring back an authentic academic order, perhaps the old academic system of the Beaux-Arts. That had at least belonged to a tradition which had shown itself capable of building cities and in which, as a corollary, a place had been worked out for painting and sculpture to operate fairly freely. It happens that there is one great transitional figure, Louis I. Kahn, who did in fact take the first difficult steps toward the re-creation of such an order—much of which took shape, pointedly enough, in his designs for museums. Trained in the Beaux-Arts and separated from it by the dogmas of the modern movement, he found his way back to it, step by step and largely unconsciously, after an agonizing struggle of many years. Kahn was at the same time as idealist as his older rivals and in many ways even more abstract than they. Like them, he was convinced that he had to reinvent order from the beginning, and his first mature building, the Yale Art Gallery, does go far toward persuad-
12.35 ing us that it is a truly primitive beginning. The insistent tetrahedrons of the concrete pseudo-space frame demand to be read as a rude but inescapable law of things. Under them, painting and sculpture take on an intensely valuable but rather threatened life. Their very being constitutes a challenge to the demanding environment which is at the same time operating according to systems, unlike those of Wright, from which it leaves them exempt. A primitively articulated academic system is thus set up. Something hard and true about the separate roles of actions and environment is being said. But finally, in his last years, as at the Kimbell Museum in Forth Worth and the British Art Center in New Haven, Kahn shapes the environment around its essential element, which is light, through which its volume and all bodies within it are wholly, gently, silently revealed. The effect is of permanence and peace and, in comparison with the earlier building, of a kind of death.

Again, though Kahn thought that he was beginning, he was in fact seeking out the kernel of what he had been taught in his youth: the academic, more or less classical tradition of the Beaux-Arts. So in the end it is the first of modern Beaux-Arts buildings,
17.34, 17.33 Labrouste's Bibliothèque Ste. Geneviève, which is his final model. His British Art Center, like Mies's buildings at IIT, is articulated fundamentally according to Labrouste's system, with a skeleton structure and in-filling panels. But Kahn's building is more physical than Mies's, more traditional, more solid in weight and mass. Kahn wanted those qualities above everything else, and he had begun to find them in the beautiful concrete planes and frames of the scholars' studies in his Salk Center, with the wooden panels set within them and no visible sign of glass. Finally, by wrapping Roman ruins

12.35 RIGHT, TOP: Louis I. Kahn. Yale University Art Gallery, New Haven, Connecticut, 1951–53. Interior

12.36 RIGHT, BOTTOM: Louis I. Kahn. Indian Institute of Management, Ahmedabad, India, 1962–74. Exterior

around buildings, Kahn was able to arrive at the pure voids in solid walls of Ahmedabad 12.36
and Dhaka, articulated by what he called his "brick order," that too derived from Rome. Scalelessness is sought, hence timelessness, escape from the particularities of function, permanent immobility, and, once again, the silence.

This is Kahn's final order. It is an academic classicism reduced and reconstructed at a primitive and static level. A fundamental question of this architectural generation has been how that new beginning could be carried further. Here it is interesting to observe how it has had two related but very different effects. In Europe, with Aldo
Rossi and, secondarily, the other Neorationalists, it was its pure solid, immobile being 10.1, 10.2
that was felt, and these qualities often are the foundation of Rossi's haunting work,

ABOVE, LEFT: Aldo Rossi. Teatro del Mondo, Venice, 1979. Aerial view 12.37

ABOVE, TOP RIGHT: Venturi and Rauch. Trubek and Wislocki Houses, Nantucket, Massachusetts, 1970–72. Exterior 12.38

ABOVE, BOTTOM RIGHT: Venturi and Rauch. Fire Station No. 4, Columbus, Indiana, 1965–68. Exterior 12.39

touched, as Kahn himself was, by de Chirico's nostalgic and disquieting spirit and by its progeny in Fascism's heavy, static, disoriented forms. The world is haunted by the associations they invoke, but they are being revived with new intentions, curiously innocent, linked in Rossi to the very roots of Italian tradition, in which death indeed balances life, and its city crowns the hill across from the city of the living or crowds close up to its gates. In that city are presences real but void of action. So in Rossi's cemetery projects the forms are all sculptural but wholly immobile. The silence is wholly that of death. But
12.37 in his Teatro del Mondo, riding its barge around the Venetian lagoon, the image is alive, like a wingless Shalako bird, high-shouldered, top-heavy, slightly goofy, and benevolent, a good-hearted clown kachina led into town.

In America, by contrast, the most important effect of Kahn's work has generally been very different from that exhibited by the Neorationalists: it has been toward action rather than immobility, realism rather than idealism, irony rather than sorrow. Venturi's project for a monument in Princeton Memorial Park takes Kahn's abstract shapes at Dhaka and
15.14 turns them into a being, caught in a deep cry. His Guild House takes Kahn's "ruins wrapped around buildings" and transforms them into a false front on Main Street that can gesture like a sign. The gesture is not tragic and heroic like those of Le Corbusier,

but joyful, ebullient, and ironically self-deprecating. Association is invoked by calling
the abstract sculpture which crowns the facade a television aerial, which it is not in fact.
This special union of what seem the commonest kinds of forms (dumb and dull, Venturi
calls them) with extraordinary sculptural presence in both empathetic and associational
terms is an indication of where Venturi's special importance lies: he brings back traditional and vernacular architecture and endows it with contemporary communicative
power. His spaces are simple; he concentrates with extraordinary humanist perception
on the governing symbol, like the curiously active chimney in his famous house project 15.2
of 1959. The sculptural corollary is to be found, I think, in the magically real figures of
Duane Hanson, where simple, dumb, absolute imitation produces people with the terrible quality of being both alive and dead. They cross some line to be with us. Which is the
sculptor, which the work? People who come to watch join the group. It is Pop art's prime
achievement that it has made sculpture popular. Once more, it populates.

The same is true of Venturi's Trubek and Wislocki Houses, dumb cottages as 12.38
imminent as gods. They are real, and they act. They are pure vernacular Shingle Style
and lonely beings as well, standing up, turning toward each other in the fogs off the sea.
(Now, Rossi's theater recalls them.) Out of another common vernacular, that of the strip,
Venturi's firehouse at Columbus, Indiana, calls to us from the side of the road. The envi- 12.39
ronment comes alive with the endless complicated actions of people in situations or with
their simple presence. Magic Realist painting is similar. The everyday environment is
fraught with being, sometimes with irony, sometimes with love. Painting, sculpture, and
architecture here all seem to share a renewed sense of common life. Nothing can be bor-
ing because all is living. One is tempted to feel that if there is any real hope for the future
it lies in our perception of that.

Venturi, to go further, seems always to have understood the dual realities of environment and act. His Roosevelt Memorial entry is environmental sculpture, a great 12.40
earthwork. In this it not only invokes the gardens and the fortifications of the classic tradition in which Venturi was trained but also prefigures the earth sculptures, like those of
Heizer, of the decade which was to follow. Venturi can also challenge the environment
with forms that seem to menace it, like his unexploded shell for Fairmount Parkway, not
explicitly ironic like Oldenburg's great toilet floats for London but intrusive like them,
inserting another order of being into the urban scene. By contrast, environment and act
are unified in Venturi's project for the town center of Thousand Oaks, California, sweeping 12.41
along the freeway and lifting up its flag, like those on the Karl-Marx-Hof in Vienna, to be 11.21
seen not by nearby pedestrians but by drivers closing in at suicidal rates of speed. So the
graphics of the older project, an essential component of its emotional effect, are enlarged
to highway scale and change their sense as we draw up to them and read only part of their
sign. This is indeed sculpture, architecture, and painting all together.

In complementary action to the two kinds of physical being—that of creatures
and that of places—comes painting's world of illusion where all can be brought together
through optical means. Venturi showed how that resource could function in his competition for the National Football Hall of Fame. All its forms are in accord with existing 15.15

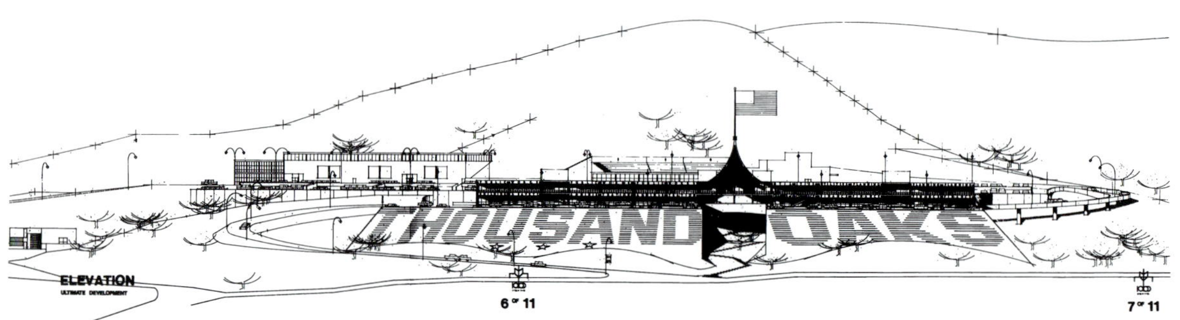

ABOVE, TOP: Robert Venturi with John Rauch, George E. Patton, and Nicholas Gianopulos. Franklin Delano Roosevelt Memorial project, 1960. Perspective 12.40

ABOVE, BOTTOM: Venturi and Rauch. Thousand Oaks Civic Center project, Thousand Oaks, California, 1969. Elevation 12.41

reality, and all are transformed. The cars come up and park in great waves. Above them a tremendous electronic signboard, like the screen of a drive-in theater, presents memorable plays, relives historic situations; the backs run and are tackled like giant constellations across the face of the night. Piano and Rogers originally intended such a screen on the plaza facade of the Centre Pompidou and cited this project as their proto-
12.42 type. Inside, the fixed exhibits were to have been supplemented by movie projection through which the boundaries of the space are dissolved. Soon lasers could have conjured up three-dimensional holographs of solid figures in the middle of the air. In this way painting joins architecture and sculpture at the height of its contemporary freedom to "make us see what isn't there," and the fact of collaboration—not the old ideal of it but the present fact of it—is achieved. As the Romans opened out the whole wall through perspective long ago and as nineteenth-century scenic wallpaper made the most spectacular topographies of the globe readily available through mass production, so now illusions invade our space and pull us into theirs. The dweller in the ten-foot room of a conceivable future might walk one day in the gardens of Vaux-le-Vicomte and descend the next to the Colorado in the depths of its canyon or travel for many days in arduous stages across the Sahara or struggle with the wheel of a clipper ship through a long, bad passage round the Horn. There will always be those of us who are suspicious of such ease of electronic creation, but the history of art shows us that the human mind can deal with whatever the techniques of its art can fabricate for it. From the moment the bosses of the cave ceiling at Altamira were transformed through painting into bison, the doors to all other worlds have been open. Only power is essential, whether from the shoulder or the turbine. If the latter should fail, art might well fall back again to the pine board we whittle in our hands. And not much would be lost. A universe could be shaped and populated with that as well, though in another way.

12.42 Venturi and Rauch. National Football Hall of Fame project, Piscataway, New Jersey, 1967. Interior perspective

To return to more immediate questions: a number of contemporary architects other than Venturi have shown themselves to be aware of the issues of act and environment and of their implications for architectural form. Moore, for example, believes in the primacy of the physical experience of architecture, which he calls the "haptic," and he designs houses which are buoyant frames for human action, especially in the vertical dimension. He has confidence in the ability of human beings to decide things for themselves and is unfailingly amused by the results. He goes on television to induce the citizens of wherever he may be to make specific suggestions about whatever urban project he is involved with according to their own concept of what they want to do in a place, and his designs for public spaces take special cognizance of such interrelationships, seen through the model of play. They convey a great deal by making it all seem a playful assemblage, like the Piazza d'Italia in New Orleans. So columns, entablatures, and inscriptions can be 12.43
piled up in ways widely acceptable because it all appears to be harmless fun. Water gushes forth, cascades, and leaps in sparkling sheets, uniting everything. Like the Baroque which Moore knows so well, the conflict between will to order and will to anarchy is glossed over. The issue doesn't seem important because everything really is decoration once again.

Charles Moore. Piazza d'Italia, New Orleans, 1978–79. Perspective 12.43

In Graves the issue is joined with deep seriousness. His house projects are intensely environmental. Indeed, they stretch out across the landscape and hollow out grottoes and bosquets in a perhaps mythical forest. They are also intensely sculptural in that their massively active elements may often seem to be attacking the general architectural order. This is a supremely mannerist condition, and it is a fundamental reason why colossal Mannerist rustication, rather than the flowing profiles of the Baroque, seems to possess a special appeal for many architects now. Of all those architects Graves is the boldest and strongest. Like Giulio Romano, he may make his keystones seem to fall, his doorways split, his facades crumble. Decoration revolts; it attacks the building. The architectural environment is under assault by Titanic sculptural forces. Finally, though, the whole is still largely pictorial, because so much is in fact taking place upon a single plane, illusionistically endowed with depth. Sculpture's primitive force is marvelously evoked, as in a Mannerist grotto, but the mood, as there, is a romantic one,
12.44 richly melancholy. Now, Graves's project for the Portland Public Service Building in Portland, Oregon, so cruelly savaged by the criticism of local architects, moves out into a grander realm of mannerist intransigence, involving powerful architectural decoration with figural sculpture at enormous scale. There are surely many problems of suitability and relationship as yet unresolved in this stupendous assemblage, but for all that it is a great, indeed an epoch-making work, strange and courageous, and it very much deserves to be built as Graves designed it.

Stern, too, as in his project for Best Products, seems aware of the issue. He clearly tries to bring it back as close as he yet dares to its classic context and vocabulary. In this we come again to that question which has been one of the minor themes of the argument. How far back can we go? One of the criteria, perhaps, might be fitness, the old classical "propriety." And in this category, like almost all the other entries in the Best's exhibition, Stern's project may be said to fail. Because of the very richness of its admirable iconography it is literally top-heavy, trying to say too much for the program; it
15.21 has too much sign for the building. This is what Venturi apparently understood in the

12.44 ABOVE, LEFT: Michael Graves. Portland Public Service Building, Portland, Oregon, 1980–82. Elevation

12.45 ABOVE, RIGHT: Allan Greenberg. Brant House, Greenwich, Connecticut, 1979–83. Elevation

same program; sometimes wallpaper, properly scaled, is just right and enough, and more classic in "decorum" than pediments, stoas, or Palladian windows.

It may indeed be taken as true that things never happen as we expect them to or give us quite the ideal that we hoped for. This is because we can only imagine the reality with which we are familiar and can rarely recognize the new reality when it arrives. Our conceptual screens, through which our minds filter all phenomena, have to change first. That is, I think, one reason at least why it is worthwhile to write about art: to struggle with that process. It is the fundamental human problem of growth, which involves how to break our own preexisting models of reality in order to be able to ask the new questions out of which knowledge can grow. We have, for example, been able to think our way back to an appreciation of Beaux-Arts architecture and its collaborative achievement, and beyond that to the fundamental question of ornament as a whole. Is that the end of our search? How
lovely it might be if Greenberg's dream of the return to the classic tradition, straight, 12.45
noble, unparodied, could be realized. Will it ever be? What sculpture will adorn or challenge it? What painting? Though no less real an image of human action than those shaped by the Greeks, could a tourist by Duane Hanson really stand in a pediment, peering out across the parkway? Could Baeder paint it? Perhaps. But if not, we should ask ourselves why not. And the answer seems to be that there might well be some sort of consciousness lacking, something real about things as we feel them to be in Hanson, Baeder, Heizer, and Venturi which is not there. Some irony perhaps but most of all some comment. So Venturi comments about the historical styles when he employs them: turns them into cutouts, or changes their scale, or blows out the color. He parodies them, as of course do Moore, Graves, and Stern, which to Greenberg is a deplorable thing. But for all the distortions and through them, Venturi shows us what the issues are: how the act is embodied in a building, though it remains environment. Once again, correctness is not

Venturi and Rauch. Flint House, Greenville, Delaware, 1978–80. West (rear) elevation 12.46

enough, if it ever was. But propriety and decorum still play the critical parts, so that a
12.46 screen of Greek columns by Venturi takes on the touchingly wistful presence of the American Greek Revival (big act, little building) and is then flattened out and stretched in accordance with the volumetric space and thin wall structure of the Shingle Style vernacular itself. The comment is double and in the end, to revive a ghastly term, functionally right. Act and environment are in the tension of life.

There can be no doubt that the historicism of the modern movement, which said that we could not do this or that because our times would not let us, must be rejected. Existentialism taught us once and for all that we are the times. We make them; we are responsible for them. We cannot hide from that necessity for action and choice in the arms of the zeitgeist. But we do in fact feel things in certain ways. Artists of course will always see things afresh and will inevitably surprise us and so change our feelings. The classical sculptor who will place Apollo on a classical pediment may be honing his chisel at this moment. Another Poussin may be assiduously reading Ovid, Livy, and the Bible and sharpening his pencil. Still, one doesn't really think so. The academic synthesis no longer responds to the depth, breadth, and critical awareness of our consciousness. Nor, as the postmodernists so correctly insist, should we expect to have only one style of art or one synthesis of styles. Instead we will probably have as many styles of art as we have of life, most of them contradictory of each other. The word "style" will be devalued, as it probably ought to be. We have already liberated ourselves from that concept through our wreck of the International Style. The feeling is of a new freedom but not of a new salvation. There will be no new, soul-saving synthesis. We must get used to the fact that we have lost our souls and, as Picasso so instinctively seems to say, are now forced to find our way back to fellowship with our mutilated brothers, the animals. No, the soul as an item of distinction is finished, but there will be the physical arts, taking shape out of whatever programs and materials they can find. We should face the fact that they are now our cult. We will always have to shape our environment in one way or another with them, preferably, in future, with solar and other nondestructive sources of power. We will be required to populate that environment and to act in certain ways. We will surely seek to explore new modes of being through the pictorial imagination which is the very stuff of our dreams. The questions so laid bare will always be relevant to us and will provoke all our arts. They may be arts of agony, derision, or sorrow. We ask ourselves if they will be able to collaborate with each other or will tear us with their autonomous frenzies. That will depend on us, because we are not dominated, as some of our mentors may have seemed to think in the past, by an overwhelming inevitability in human history or in the forms of art. We are what we make ourselves. The art of the future will be what we have become.

It is reasonable to take a pessimistic view of the outcome. A critic can hardly fail to do so. But experience shows that the artist is incurably optimistic. He composes if necessary out of disaster and decay. He has little to do with the good or the desirable, with ethical structures or ideologies. He knows with a fierce physical certainty that, as Oscar Wilde put it, "The aesthetic reaction has nothing to do with the intellect, or the emotions." It bursts free. In its service the artist twists everything to his own ends, which are ruthless ones. He *will* make forms, no matter what, and out of our worst defeats fashion other dreams, worlds, and populations to come.

Note 1 Gilles Deleuze and Félix Guattari, *Anti-Oedipus: Capitalism and Schizophrenia*, trans. Robert Hurley (New York: Viking Press, 1977). These Marxist psychiatrists seek to substitute a synthesis of Marx and Nietzsche for Freud. They dislike the family, viewing it, as Freud did, as the root of present ills but, unlike Freud, are prepared to abolish it and, in their view, to release humanity to the schizophrenia of multiple modes of behavior. Their view is independently shared by Jencks as a postmodern desideratum.

NEIL LEVINE

"Le Corbusier, 1922–1965." In *Cité Frugès and Other Buildings and Projects, 1923–1927*. Vol. 2 of *The Le Corbusier Archive*, ed. H. Allen Brooks. New York and London: Garland; Paris: Fondation Le Corbusier, 1983 (originally unillustrated).

The 1980s gave rise to a spate of multivolume publications of the collected drawings of the major figures of modern architecture. Frank Lloyd Wright's work was published between 1984 and 1988, Mies van der Rohe's between 1986 and 1992, Louis Kahn's in 1987, Walter Gropius's in 1990 and 1991, and Alvar Aalto's in 1994. All but the first of these were produced by the Garland Publishing Company under the general editorship of Alexander Tzonis. The initial, and most extensive, venture in that series was the thirty-two-volume edition of Le Corbusier's drawings, edited by H. Allen Brooks, which appeared between 1982 and 1985. It was also the only one of these encyclopedic catalogues for which a group of outside experts was asked to contribute introductory essays. Some of the authors, like André Wogenscky and Jerzy Soltan, had worked for the architect; others, like Stanislaus von Moos and Tim Benton, had devoted a good part of their scholarly efforts to the study of his work; still others, like Reyner Banham, Alan Colquhoun, Kenneth Frampton, and Manfredo Tafuri, were known for their writings on the architect within the broader context of the history of the modern movement. Of all the contributors, Scully was no doubt the person least associated with the legacy of Le Corbusier and certainly the scholar who had come to be most critical of his work and its impact on the urban environment.

Brooks—who was a graduate student in architectural history at Yale in the early 1950s, when Le Corbusier's postwar buildings were beginning to exert a decisive influence on Scully's thought (see "Modern Architecture: Toward a Redefinition of Style," chap. 4)—chose

13

Le Corbusier, 1922–1965

VINCENT SCULLY

This is a daunting moment to be asked to write a critical assessment of Le Corbusier's mature work. The research of so many talented scholars at the Fondation Le Corbusier and elsewhere over the past decade has turned up such a richness of new and highly specific information about Le Corbusier that an older critic like myself, who has not directly participated in that research, cannot help but fear that his historical perspective, not to mention his critical instincts, may well be contradicted at any moment by newly discovered and unexpected facts. At the same time, the universal questioning of the principles and forms of modern architecture now taking place—in which this writer has been involved for some twenty years—also forces us to look at Le Corbusier's work in several new lights. One cannot write about it now quite as one could in 1961. His urbanism, for example, cannot help but be judged as faulty in conception and highly destructive in practice, especially as we have seen it more or less universally carried out in American redevelopment and the French "New Towns," not to mention at Chandigarh itself, at Brasilia, and elsewhere.

Scully to do the broad survey of the architect's career from the time he began practicing in Paris until his death in 1965. Brooks saw this as a pendant to his own contribution, which presented the much less well-known work that Charles-Edouard Jeanneret had done in his native Switzerland prior to taking up residence in France and the nom de plume he would use for the rest of his life. Scully used the occasion to try to define and elucidate what lay at the heart of Le Corbusier's art and how that art should ultimately be assessed in the context of the entire history of Western architecture. Critical to any final judgment would be the problem of Le Corbusier's urbanism and the postwar architecture that was its direct outgrowth. In this regard, the essay represents a review and a reappraisal of Scully's own attitude toward Le Corbusier as that had changed over the course of a quarter of a century.

In his writings of the 1950s and very early 1960s, Scully focused almost entirely on Le Corbusier's architecture rather than his urbanism; certainly it was the architecture of the postwar years that elicited his greatest enthusiasm and interest. The Unité d'Habitation at Marseilles, the Chapel at Ronchamp, the Maisons Jaoul just outside Paris, and the High Court and Assembly Building at Chandigarh all had a powerful sculptural presence that rejected the lightness and impermanence of the International Style of the 1920s and portended a return to a traditional massiveness and weightiness that Scully saw as Hellenic in derivation, humanist in meaning, and existentialist in contemporary expressive terms. The urban implications, however, soon appeared to be disastrous for the traditional

This major and inescapable fact, touching architecture's primary reason for being, which is to shape the human environment as a whole, tends to cast a shadow over other considerations and even over our view of Le Corbusier's individual buildings themselves. And even these, which are so much more lively and varied than his urbanistic framework, now invite questions that many of us would not have posed two decades ago. Does, for example, the elimination of almost all directly associational and most purely plastic detail that his buildings of the twenties shared with those of De Stijl, Gropius, Mies, and so many others constitute in fact a serious reduction rather than a liberation of architecture's vocabulary? Does the so-called modern movement, or rather that specific part of modern architecture that Hitchcock and Johnson called the International Style, represent, despite the many acknowledged masterpieces that it produced, a temporary and, as seen at this moment in time, almost inconceivable aberration in the general development of architectural tradition and of modern architecture as a whole? Does not such reductiveness, if it should indeed be regarded as that, represent a romantic primitivism that is hard to square with the complex urbanistic traditions that have in fact formed modern cities and, indeed, all types of contemporary buildings? Logically, at least, that reductiveness cannot be regarded as having much to do with the various technocratic arguments with which Le Corbusier, like his contemporaries, so often defended his forms. Here, though, Le Corbusier's view was from first to last markedly different from perimeter-block, street-ordered city (see "The Death of the Street," chap. 7, and "Doldrums in the Suburbs," chap. 8), which led Scully, like many others, not only to castigate Le Corbusier's entire urbanist project but to question in new ways the overall significance of his architecture. Many of those who wanted to keep the flame alive followed the line laid out by Colin Rowe: a deemphasis of Le Corbusier's recent work, as well as his urban designs in general, in favor of his canonic compositions of the 1920s as the basis for a modern pedagogy to replace the defunct Beaux-Arts system. Scully, however, never bought into this position. The essay written for *The Le Corbusier Archive* shows him grappling with what had turned into a love-hate relationship without avoiding any of the unwelcome evidence.

Scully posits Le Corbusier primarily as an artist and only secondarily as an architect. His background, and later avocation, as a painter becomes fundamental to the understanding of his work. The loss of vision in one eye in 1918, resulting from a detached retina, explains his lifelong preoccupation with relating what is seen to what is known, and with translating two-dimensional shapes into three-dimensional space. Le Corbusier's uniqueness lies in his ability to invent forms as a painter would, freely, as pure gesture. The gestures give the buildings a figural quality that causes us to read them in imagistic terms. The playful and ironic overlapping of images gives the works their quintessentially modern stamp. In the postwar period, however, when the forms become aggressively sculptural and massive, they take on a primitive, uncouth character that has all the power—both positive

that of his Northern European colleagues. It was always visual, never emotionally reductive, as theirs often was. For him, architecture was a "play of forms under the light," an art to "touch my heart." The question that must be asked, therefore, is what was the character of that vision, of that emotion, and of the forms they brought into being?

Physiological answers to such questions are as inadequate as psychoanalytical ones. The brain is total in its grasp of phenomena, of their purely visual no less than of their technical sides. It is always arranging matter, taming the intractable. Its conceptual structures direct how we see, and its intentions guide our hands, which, as Le Corbusier always insisted, are also its teachers. One cannot reduce the workings of that complex organism to the promptings of one condition or to the exploitation of, or reaction to, one peculiarity. Yet we cannot help but be especially interested in Le Corbusier's way of seeing in view of the fact that his mature style of the twenties, different in fundamental visual ways from everything he had done before, began with the loss of sight in his left eye. That loss was exactly contemporary with his first painting in oil, the famous
13.1 white cube, *La Cheminée*, of 1918, and, according to Le Corbusier, was caused by his nighttime work on the large sketch for it. Referring to himself in the third person, as he so often rather disquietingly tended to do, he later wrote: "L-C lost the use of his left eye when doing this drawing at night: separation of the retina."[1]

While eye specialists will tell us that the retina cannot be separated in quite this way and though Le Corbusier had suffered from eye trouble since childhood, still the

and negative—of the heroic and the tragic. Scully bemoans the loss of civility such an architecture implies for the future of the city but finds it impossible to deny its artistic impact ("We would not give those gestures up, but neither would we permit them to destroy the town"). In the end, Scully refuses to reduce the problem to one or another acceptable alternative and allows this sense of ambiguity to define the architect's place in history. Le Corbusier, the most influential architect since Imhotep, becomes the very symbol of modernism, the Faustian hero, the anti-Christ who must destroy all before he can create—and whose creations follow the rules he alone has devised.

fact remains that his retina did separate at this time, while he was working on his "cube." It left him permanently blind in that eye, since no surgical procedure to deal with that condition was developed until the 1920s, and the operation must be done at once. Le Corbusier therefore operated with monocular vision throughout the rest of his life. A person in that state will never think about it and will function perfectly normally until all at once a staircase will flatten out before him or he will reach for something handed to him suddenly and miss it by a foot. Instantly, he will think the stairs back into perspective or adjust his hand. In other words, like all of us, he thinks in three dimensions but must keep thinking, even if unconsciously, all the time. This can enormously sharpen his faculty of seeing and heighten his excitement in it; he lives inside the drama of a world opening and closing around him. He "sees" all planes as flat with linear edges, but he "thinks" them into depth and rounded contours.[2] His hand helps him, too, as it tests the plasticity of objects. Le Corbusier's Purism, which insists on graspable shapes with definite edges, as well as his passionate outburst at Vassar against Caravaggio's chiaroscuro, ought to be recalled here. Similarly, his very preoccupation with painting, beginning, so he tells us, with *La Cheminée*, of which he says, "This first picture is a key to an understanding of his approach to plastic art: mass in space: space," now becomes wholly comprehensible. "Mass" and "space" were what he had to find visual equivalents for, to make himself see them. And thereafter, so he tells us, he painted every single

ABOVE, LEFT: Charles-Edouard Jeanneret (Le Corbusier). *La Cheminée,* 1918 13.1

ABOVE, RIGHT: Le Corbusier. Ozenfant House, Paris, 1922. Interior, studio 13.2

morning of his life, beginning each day by mastering its visual phenomena, out of which most of the supremely pictorial shapes of his architecture, beginning with its governing cube, were to come into being.

One might object that flat planes and linear edges, for example, had already begun to characterize the early phases of the International Style before Le Corbusier's first works of that kind appeared. One thinks especially of Rietveld and van Doesburg, whose isometrics of 1920 are strikingly monocular, flipping back and forth as they do between two and three dimensions. There is no doubt that the vision was already being shaped by other people—and for various reasons, preoccupation with the flat plane of a canvas probably foremost among them—but it was Le Corbusier, in 1922, who suddenly exploited that new vision architecturally and endowed it with the special dramatic aura
13.2 that was to enable it to dominate the architectural world. The interior of his Ozenfant House literally explodes into space; all the old details of the great European tradition, which had qualified edges and modified changes of plane, are burned away in the whiteness of the light. All planes are as thin as paper, all frames are as taut as lines. High up in space, one plane curves alone, modeling the white light. Whatever the mechanism by which the architect was seeing, he was clearly doing so with an excitement about flatness, thinness, light, and an elimination of detail that had never before been so passionately felt by any architect. He was exploiting his own way of seeing with a fierce and liberating joy. According to that way, the space could not go flowing out on the horizontal, as Mies's space of the twenties was soon to do. It needed a clearly conceptual frame of reference close by on all sides: hence the hollow vertical cube, against which all advances and recessions in depth can be judged, can be "ranged." The cube of air also serves another of the determinants of Le Corbusier's design: its Platonism, which had been much in evidence in Ozenfant as well. That side of classicism, which is at once late antique, medieval, and Renaissance, was joined in Le Corbusier by his love for Greek temples, in which he had read the hardness, linearity, and heroic activism that also characterize the Ozenfant interior. All the materials of his earlier maturity were thus gathered

together in this house for an artist, glorifying the romantic creator and setting him free as the self-appointed shaper of the modern world. It was the ideal program for Le Corbusier to begin with, far more so than his house at Vaucresson of about the same time.

The Maison La Roche, of 1923, was in the same vein. Late in life Le Corbusier was to call it his "house of thunder." In it the visual excitement became daring and vertiginous. The edges of the planes in the great hall dance forward and back within their defining volume; the long wall of the gallery curves; the ramp dives down; the ceiling of the top floor of the hall bends our heads, as if we had optically misjudged its position. We are not quite sure where anything is; we walk with the alertness of hunters through a strange and challenging environment, beset by Le Corbusier's thunderous forms. It is perfect that the Fondation Le Corbusier is housed here.

To be sure, there are many other lines of approach to Le Corbusier's work of this period. From a more largely schematic point of view, we might start with his Ideal City of 9.5
1922, that same fateful year when he laid out for the first time the overwhelming Neoplatonic vision that was eventually to shape so many of the new cities of the twentieth century and to destroy too many of the old. Like a Futurist, he hailed the automobile and the airplane and heroized the capitalist "manager." In these enthusiasms he echoed the proto-Fascist aesthetics of the period, as his general air of athleticism also did. But the major outlines of his plan, with its radiating avenues, is right in the French classical tradition, stemming from Versailles and here especially recalling L'Enfant's Washington. Three building types are proposed for it, and they progressively attack the density of its fabric. The first is a traditional quadrangular housing type, which still respects the street. The second is a long linear building *à redents*, which resembles the fencelike château of Versailles itself, defining not a street but a vast garden. Finally, cruciform skyscrapers tower in superblocks of *jardins anglais* and wholly destroy all previous kinds of urban definition.

To begin with, Le Corbusier designed only the first type, proposing *immeubles-villas* on a wildly luxurious scale. It was not realistic housing, like the quadrangles of Amsterdam or Vienna of the same period; it remained "ideal," visionary, divorced from serious social concerns but reflecting a tenacious middle-class belief in the reform of society through art. Its apartment unit became the basic weapon of Le Corbusier's assault upon the architectural world, the vehicle of his visual propaganda. From it he built his Pavillon de l'Esprit Nouveau of 1925 and extracted his Citrohan House type, 4.8
recalling the Aegean megaron in form, which he refined from 1922 onward and built at Stuttgart in 1927. By that time, he had it standing on its *pilotis* legs, so that the whole body of the building became taut, thin, light, and energetic. It was very Greek in a triple sense, suggesting at once a hero's house, a Platonic form, and a sculptural body. Inside, here as in the Pavillon, Le Corbusier's springy staircases bounded up through the high spaces. It was after all the liberation of life that he wished to embody in his *machine à habiter*—and a peculiarly youthful life at that. The settings do not suggest the raising of families, despite Le Corbusier's numerous references to the "family hearth." Wright's domestic interiors of the early twentieth century really do make us think of the heavily

interwoven "family romances" of Freud, with which they share a sense of dominant parental authority most of all, but Le Corbusier's suggest liberation from authority and freedom of choice, like that of the *anti-Oedipe* schizophrenic mode that was later to be proposed by Deleuze and Guattari. We are not intended to relax under the comforting direction of continuous horizontal planes; we climb up, we come out on the roof, we look out, at least in theory, over Paris. Le Corbusier's strange and epoch-making linear drawings, traced over drafted originals (the line wavers at the edges of perception), beautifully convey the intended effect of advance and recession within high volumes of space. Even the smallest spaces are torn apart by shamelessly exaggerated perspectives and the dramatized interaction of unusual shapes. "Ce n'est pas très pratique, mais c'est original," said a friend to Cook about his house at Boulogne-sur-Seine, where the great living room is all challenge and tumult, from which one ascends to the roof garden, overlooking
18.2 the Bois. It is adult play, not least in the Stein Villa at Garches, where we are led to an entrance facade as thin as something only drawn, not constructed. It is pure *disegno*, where an aesthetic at once optical in method and Neoplatonic in implication has accomplished what none of the endless generations of European architects seeking the ideal had previously been able to do: it has abolished mass, modeling, and contour, has indeed conquered matter and achieved the status of pure idea. Behind that magic screen every kind of spatial wonder lies waiting to deploy, because the Dom-ino system of *pilotis* and slab has liberated the plan, too, from structural matter. Other aspects of Le Corbusier's classicism, whether Palladian or Greek, now seem much less significant than this Neoplatonic dematerialization, which might be seen as the very climax of Renaissance theory and which was clearly the essence of Le Corbusier's art of the twenties and of the International Style as a whole once he had put his stamp on it.

These unimaginably original syntheses of eye and mind culminated of course in
18.7 the Villa Savoye, which is the most optically complex and the most perfectly Neoplatonic of all the houses. It is as labyrinthine as a brain; the experience is literally "cerebral," contained as it is within a thin shell lifted above the ground. That shell creates a pure environment devoid of mass, a purely Neoplatonic drawing of square and circle, like
12.15 those of the Renaissance *Man of Perfect Proportions* that the inhabiting human body stretches to fill. It is led to do so by movement through spaces that are partly enclosed and partly open, penetrated by the diagonal of the ramp but always enframed. One is inside a wholly realized hollow object, the image of a world. Standing on its legs, the building is a kind of creature too, but much less so than the Citrohan type, because it is not directional. Rich in ambiguities, it seems at times tethered rather than supported by its columns, lifting above the grass, offering us a panorama of passage over the land. It is also the richest in ship imagery of all of Le Corbusier's buildings of this period. How wonderful, too, that a work of such complex and wholly gratuitous art could be seen as the result of a systematic process of design, involving the famous "Five Points" of *pilotis, toit jardin, plan libre, façade libre, fenêtre à échelle humaine (en longueur).* By the late twenties Le Corbusier was describing those points as the necessary criteria, the sine qua non, of the new architecture. Having done so, he instantly discarded them.

By 1930 he was already building the de Mandrot House with its bearing walls of rough masonry, and in the immediately succeeding years he proposed or built several other houses of a similar preindustrial solidity and peasant cast—one of them for Chile and brazenly ripped off by Antonin Raymond in Japan. ("Les grands esprits se rencontrent," was Le Corbusier's comment.) Academics of my generation can vividly remember students of the late 1940s condemning Le Corbusier for what they regarded as this total betrayal of the machine age and the machine aesthetic, indeed of everything in which he had professed to believe before. Their mistake, encouraged of course by his own polemic, lay in regarding him as primarily a conceptual artist and a prescriptive prophet. He was those things in part, and often pretended to be them wholly, but he was in fact an instinctive artist before everything else.[3] And he was an artist of a special kind: not primarily an architect in the traditional way, who knew about how to build and to get along with preexisting buildings and with the complexity of urban conditions, but an artist, architect by choice, who was driven to seek out the beginnings of things. His ultimate concern was with the essence of illusion, with fantasy, myth, and disguise. Hence the machine aesthetic, though enormously liberating for a while, was clearly a reductive one. It was finally not enough for him, indeed could not be. He had to explore, go deeper, out of which a profoundly heroic primitivism was eventually to arise. Even his preoccupation with total planning was an aberration of his will to make everything his own individual art. By the early thirties it led him toward the "Four Routes" of his linear city, radiating across
Eurasia and culminating in godlike gestures like the highway megastructures for Algiers 13.3
and South America. Looking at them today one feels once again the wild thrill of a wholly arbitrary but magnificent vision at landscape scale. Precisely because of all this Le Corbusier was destructive of the real urban environment, which was infinitely more complex than he was willing to face or, indeed, competent to control.

His loyalty, unswervingly given, was to his own vision, his primal search. It might of course be argued that he was in some sense forced inward during the thirties, first by his loss of large public commissions such as the League of Nations of 1927 and the Palace of the Soviets of 1931 and secondly by the general rise of antimodern totalitarianism in Europe. Whatever the case, once cut off from the big world, he was somehow directed, like so many other modern men in a similar situation, toward primitive experience. Surrealism played a part in it; his de Beistegui roof garden of 1931, with its fireplace and its grass, was a wholly surreal environment. Surrealism and the primitive lent some of their flavor to his own apartment at the Porte Molitor: rough party wall, camp chairs challenging *sièges à grand confort* in lively conversations, curving stairs with masklike chair backs up above. There he mounted an exhibition of what he described as "art *called* primitive," in which he showed a cast of the *Athenian Calf Bearer* barbarously polychromed. This conjunction of archaic Greek sculpture with primitive feeling was to be central to many of his later, heroically conceived forms. In 1935 he wholly reversed
the Five Points and thrust a weekend house underground, with heavy concrete vaults and 13.4
grass on the roof. A blown-up photograph of one of the Ionian *korai* from the Acropolis of Athens floated in its skylight, looking more Oriental than ever and indeed suggesting the

Khmer sculpture that Malraux was dramatizing during this time in his romantically savage novel *La Voie royale*. France *outre-mer*, colonial France tied to Africa and Asia by links of affection and violence, France that regards itself as having a special flair for such things: all that is suggested in this elegant cavern, this ironic grotto half underground. One says ironic because there remains a kind of intelligent distance, especially apparent in the furniture, a marvelously active collection of the popular, the primitive, the high tech, and the *en série*. During these same years the work of Frank Lloyd Wright was also exhibiting an exotic and consciously primitive character, in this case a profoundly Amerindian one. Wright seems very straight and serious with such forms. With Le Corbusier there is more comment and a marvelous pictorialization. A sense of ironic play still persists, and everything is still linear and taut.

Directly after World War II, however, the tone changed. The war was a disillusioning period for Le Corbusier. His revered "managers" had turned out badly; his Villa Savoye was brutalized and used as a barn. Perhaps in part for that reason he became a
13.5 "Brutalist" himself. His Maisons Jaoul picked up the theme of the weekend house and endowed it with a truly awesome mass. As if in some sorrowful anger the thin factory sash and the stuccoed walls of the earlier work are ruthlessly cast aside. The machine-age materials and images, upon which Le Corbusier had once so insisted, are buried under an avalanche of brick and concrete. The effect of weight is as exaggerated as that of lightness was before. It is as if Le Corbusier is *inventing* mass, perhaps to convince himself that it can really exist. Americans may be reminded of some of Frank Furness's dramatically compressive masses, equally primitive in their power though suggestive of the archaic machinery of their time. In the Maisons Jaoul enormously scaled concrete lintels are carried on thick bearing walls of brick but are so hefty themselves that they can span voids and still carry further masonry stories. The interior space is rigidly controlled by the span of the Catalan vaults between the lintels, thus setting up long dark tunnels that, though sometimes opened to a second story, are totally different from the high, bright interiors of the twenties. One is now in a cavernous darkness lit by isolated shafts of light. The theme of "liberation" is entirely given up; the aim now seems to be permanence, solidity, and some emotional connection with chthonic forces.

No reversal could be more complete or, so it appears at this moment in time, more tragic. That difficult word can be used here in a double sense. The environment created by the Maisons Jaoul does seem to possess the dark mythic grandeur of the ancient tragic mode, but the houses also have consequences that may be described as tragic insofar as the Brutalism and the late modernism they triggered did indeed turn out to be the ultimate destruction of the old urban fabric through their exaggeratedly anti-contextual and aggressive design. It is true, as we have noted, that Le Corbusier's urbanism had always been destructive of the traditional city, but until the Brutalist, late modern period, that urbanism had remained theoretical, largely unrealized. Only now in the Brutalist decades of the fifties and sixties did the overall urbanistic scheme begin to take hold. But leaving that aside and thinking only in terms of the relationship of new buildings to old ones in existing cities, it seems obvious that the Ozenfant House, for

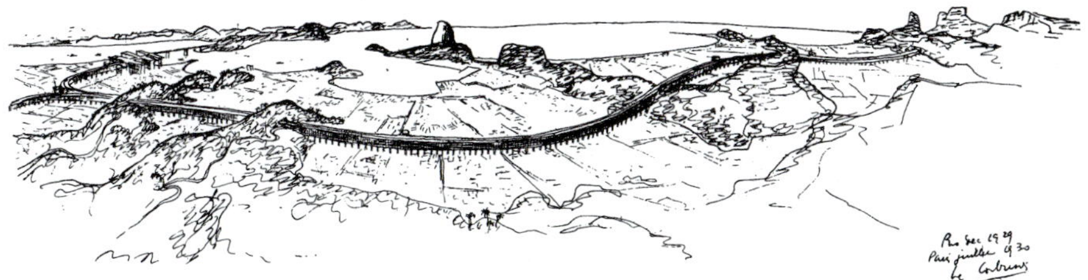

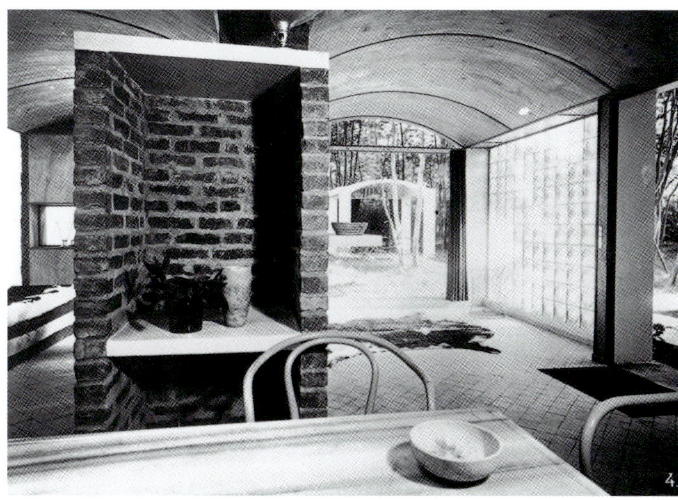

13.3 ABOVE, TOP: Le Corbusier. Urbanization of Rio de Janeiro project, 1929–30. Aerial perspective

13.4 ABOVE, BOTTOM LEFT: Le Corbusier. Weekend House, La Celle-Saint-Cloud, France, 1935. Interior

13.5 ABOVE, BOTTOM RIGHT: Le Corbusier. Maisons Jaoul, Neuilly-sur-Seine, France, 1952–55. Exterior

example, got along very well with the other houses on its little street. Even with its original saw-toothed roof, it was basically a simple block enclosed by flat walls, just as they were, and if it employed a different system of surface decoration, that hardly mattered very much in any basic contextual sense. It was still the urban tradition of the house block, which at once kept the architectural order of the city and could be decorated as one liked, so creating a certain variety within the larger order. All that continued to hold pretty well even through the period of the Gothic Revival, which did in fact represent what turned out to be a minor assault upon it. But with the Brutalist followers of the Maisons Jaoul all that changed; true barbarians invaded the town. Their scale tended to become so great, their *béton brut* so uncouth, their massing so structurally exhibitionist and assertive that there could be little question of the new buildings getting along with the old. The civility of the town was violated. At the time, thinking of the Neoplatonic thinness of the twenties, I described Brutalism as a reinvestment of European architecture with its traditional physicality. Now I think that judgment was dead wrong; the new physicality was not traditional, but primitivistic. The thin, planar, weightless forms of the twenties were not in themselves destructive of the urban tradition at all, so long as they remained, as they could have done, only one of many substyles within its palazzo-block mode. But the Brutalism initiated by Le Corbusier in the Maisons Jaoul would have none of that. It was a true declaration of hatred for the laws of the city (perhaps, as has been suggested, for bourgeois society as a whole), certainly for all contextual groupings across the generations and indeed for everything invented before it. Now buildings really began to stand on their heads and reinvent the wheel and blow things apart. Only now did modern architecture truly begin to destroy the town.[4]

Yet how complex it all is, and how it pulls at our instincts, because the Maisons Jaoul are magnificent as well, sculptural presences somber and splendid, freighted with ancient signals, heavily masked. They are brutal, but they are also heroic, mythic antagonists not only of the soft life of the town but of nature as well. In that direction, though with some interesting exceptions, almost all of Le Corbusier's architecture now moved.
5.3 The mighty *unité* at Marseilles took his earlier apartment blocks, especially his Swiss Pavilion of 1932, and transformed them into a unified sculptural figure, manipulating *pilotis* and *brise-soleils* so that it became a muscular giant standing on its legs. Its mus-
12.6 cularity strongly suggests that of the Temple of Hera II at Paestum, which Le Corbusier had published several times and which he regarded as an archaic building. Hence the archaically aggressive figure in the Modulor of 1948 set the sculptural shape of the trend. The rough concrete, too, played an essential part. With it other aspects of the eye-mind relationship come again into play. The experience is now markedly tactile. The mind knows through the hand's modeling of matter. It escapes from optical illusion into a physical "reality" like that of primitive sculpture. This is exactly the opposite of the method and effects of the twenties except for the mighty fact that, because of his years of mornings painting in the studio, where he had been working with such shapes ever since the twenties themselves, Le Corbusier was always able to endow the primitivistic forms with a distinctly optical wit. They move through and past each other in unexpected combinations. They are "pictorialized" and "ironicized," even while they are lumbering like prehistoric monsters into our world. Because of this and because of their powerful abstraction, their images remain multiple. The *unité* is a giant, a temple, an aircraft carrier. Its *pilotis* are the legs of a colossus, a bomber's tires; the shapes on its roof are
13.6 maritime, a medieval city, a dirigible's hangar. The roof is a mountaintop itself. The schematic organization of the building as a whole is amazing enough, with its interlocking apartment units, double-height living areas charged with rudely modeled peasant furniture by Charlotte Perriand, and long slots of bedrooms from which each occupant, *insonorisé* from the neighbors, looks out at only the largest of Mediterranean realities, the mountains and the sea. Theoretically there should have been a fleet of *unités* maneuvering in the plain. Where is the old city now, when citizens inhabit not urban quadrangles, evoking palaces as, say, in the Social-Democratic housing of the twenties in Vienna, or even neutral slabs suggesting a well-behaved proletariat allowed a look at the grass, as in the *Siedlungen* of Berlin from the same period, but a kind of ship, touching chords of

identification not with civilization but with teams, crews, war bands, cults. It is exhilarating; one feels the pull toward it and the destructiveness in it, the impatience and the violence. There is a splendid photograph of the *unité* at Nantes that best captures the feeling. The giant, harsh, savagely painted vessel plunges into, wipes out, the town.

We are in the realm of basic Mediterranean religion and myth, not of the Enlightenment, as if once the machine aesthetic was given up, everything in between having been contemptuously abandoned, only the primordial could remain. At Marseilles a concrete play mountain on the roof echoes the shapes of the mountains on the horizon. So at Sainte-Baume Le Corbusier had hoped to build a pilgrimage center for one of the three Marys within and under a sacred mountain with a lifting peak like a prow. Frustrated in these hopes, he built the prow into the pilgrimage church of Nôtre-Dame-du-Haut at 4.10
Ronchamp, which was another sanctuary of the goddess on a mountaintop. It hardly seems necessary to try to talk here about all the things that Ronchamp is: a bell ringing in what Le Corbusier called its *acoustique paysagiste*, an airplane taking off out of Hadrian's Villa and the sanctuaries of Sardinia, the cavern under the airfoil, wrapped in earth, piercing the sky, the mass collapsing, rising. The images are innumerable and overlapping. In the end it would seem once again to be the decades of painting that made it possible for Le Corbusier to model such eccentric and active shapes as architects had hardly imagined before. There is nothing like them, not only in their asymmetry but also and especially in their lack of dominance by any of the systems—spatial, structural—whereby even the most apparently fantastic of architects, such as Gaudí, had consistently ordered their forms. It is pure gesture, the space as well as the mass, modeled by the painter's/sculptor's hand. One is reminded of the Action Painting and the Abstract Expressionism of the same decade, especially that of Franz Kline. Like such painting, Le Corbusier's buildings are experienced in primarily physical, empathetic terms, and whatever associations they may suggest remain shifting and cloudy. They are no less powerful for that. In the end, at Ronchamp it is, I think, the bell we most experience, as its movement swings from the hooded presence to the left of the doorway and rushes around the rear of the building in one great curve to burst outward on the end toward the exterior altar, its pulpit swinging in it like a clapper before the curved sounding board of the wall behind it, the whole splitting as with one great booming note at the lifted prow.

Firminy is less than this but still more personal, an elemental goddess-cone. La 13.7
Tourette is again a drama of hill and horizon. It lifts off the slope; its cloister does not touch the earth but is raised with a couple of tormented shapes at ambiguous levels above the ground. Much has been rightly made of Le Corbusier's debt to the Cistercian monastery of Le Thoronet for some of these forms, but the differences are striking, too. There is no rest at La Tourette, only an uncompromising hardness, modified by light. Even more than Ronchamp it seems the very essence of religion and of monasticism in particular—not ethics or good intentions or a vague reverence, but terror, discipline, passion, devotion, and sorrow. The stern high box of the church, like the crudest shaping of rough matter into the least inflected of shapes, is burst apart beside the high altar by piercing shafts from the "cannons of light," detonating the multiple altars with fierce

reds and blues. Outside, the monks' cells, almost exactly like the bedrooms in the *unité* at Marseilles, are lifted to the horizon like one massive concrete beam. We sense that this, in contrast to the artist's house with which he began, is now Le Corbusier's ideal program: ascetic and majestic, personal and communal in a single, basic sense, stressing in the end a tragic and very Hellenic relationship between men and the natural world.

What can we say of Chandigarh at this moment in time? It is in many ways such an awful city, such a demonstration of how not to build a new city, especially in a searing climate. It has at the same time so much nobility and grandeur, and such brutal workmanship, which is ascribed, rather slanderously, to untrained local labor but which arises in truth out of the most European of hungers for a lost primitive state. It is in every way the projection of European attitudes, myths, and problems upon a non-European culture and environment. Kahn's Dhaka lies in partial ruin not so far away; it is another Western dream of timeless order, there of the circle and the square once more. But Chandigarh, like Le Corbusier's other late works, has passed beyond the Platonism of
4.9 his youth. Now its Titanic gestures (one cannot call them Olympian) deploy before the greatest mountains of all, far greater and more terrible than those of Greece. Can those Hellenic gestures sustain themselves in such a place, far away from the Aegean homeland, farther than Alexander's soldiers were on the Indus plain? In the first photo-
8.16 graphs of the High Court at Chandigarh a sentry stood at attention before the piers. Empathetically we identified with them and him and recognized the human act of law that makes the city, raised, like that embodied in the Temple of Athena at Paestum, before the mountain's face.

Then Le Corbusier himself blew it all apart with his wonderful, powerfully visual irony: the piers were painted various heavy reds, blues, and greens. The Indians took over and erected a Lally-columned shelter all across the face of the monumental *brise-soleil* and replaced the soldier with pots of straggly flowers. ("Venturi's mother's geraniums," a student called them almost fifteen years ago.) The image is in fact a telling one in view of what has happened between the early sixties and today. The heroic, primitivistic image Le Corbusier's late work embodied has fallen into disrepute. The civil virtues of cities and of the long-standing classical and vernacular traditions that have made cities now seem much more germane to architecture and to human life as a whole than do a few tragic gestures, however archetypal and grand. We would not give those gestures up, but neither would we permit them to destroy the town. Even those architects and critics, not a few, who remain obsessed with Le Corbusier tend universally to reject his late work in favor of his light, bright, fundamentally more civil buildings and projects of the twenties.

It is also true, as John White has pointed out, that Le Corbusier showed several flashes of a very different sensibility in his late years, different alike from those that directed his early and most of his late work. It was a sensibility toward skeletal construction in steel, which he had never really exploited before. His Roq et Rob structural scheme was one example, his Heidi Weber Pavilion in Zurich another. Even his Carpenter Center at Harvard departed from the *béton brut* that his followers were religiously

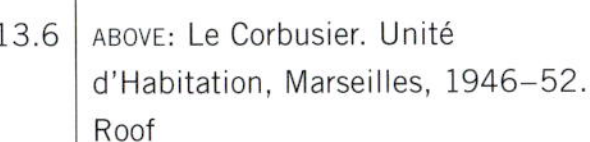

13.6 ABOVE: Le Corbusier. Unité d'Habitation, Marseilles, 1946–52. Roof

13.7 RIGHT: Le Corbusier. Monastery of La Tourette, Eveux-sur-l'Arbresle, France, 1953–60. Exterior

exploiting in Cambridge. It is a light box (and balloon) of smooth concrete, and though it breaks up the urban order right enough, it does so in a disarmingly charming manner.

It is clear that Le Corbusier would have continued to change. How can he then be assessed? There was never an architect like him, never one really so free, like some strange amateur. In that he was also a prodigious destroyer, an anti-Christ burning the world. Nor was there ever after Imhotep another architect so influential—it is not too soon to say, so immortal—who was so responsible for changing the environment as a whole and having it built up around his own cosmic schemes. Certainly there was never one, not even Michelangelo, who after all worked within the classical tradition, who was so anarchically personal, indeed so "divinely" creative, in his work. At the same time he persistently called for routinely applicable, objective standards. He was the most modern of men, a complex structure not yet wholly understood, therefore seeming contradictory to us, hard to pin down. In the end he seems to contend only with the angels, in the age-less contests of myth, and his death in the Mediterranean was of that kind.

Notes

1 Le Corbusier, *Creation Is a Patient Search* (New York: Praeger, 1960), 55. So far as I know, Le Corbusier never published this fact anywhere else, and Francesco Passanti tells me that it is never mentioned in his correspondence.

2 Those for whom monocular vision can be corrected by a contact lens, as Le Corbusier's could not be (and, as it happens, this writer's—who claims no other kinship with Le Corbusier—can be), can testify to the enormous, sometimes dizzying changes in perception that result, especially in terms of spatial interval and the chiaroscuro of contours.

3 Why not, after all, give up the so-called machine aesthetic, no less arbitrary than any other, unless its stripping of architectural form had some essential human meaning: as an image of social leveling, for example, perhaps even as one vehicle of social revolution? But Le Corbusier did not see it that way. "Architecture *or* Revolution" was his motto. Many architects and critics of the former persuasion remain intransigent to this day. They "see" politically—"morally," they might say, incorrectly—not aesthetically; Le Corbusier was the reverse.

4 The work of Mies and his followers may be taken as the great exception to this development of the fifties and sixties. In its reductiveness, however, it at least tended toward a similar end.

NEIL LEVINE

Introduction to *The Louis I. Kahn Archive: Personal Drawings. The Completely Illustrated Catalogue of the Drawings in the Louis I. Kahn Collection, University of Pennsylvania and Pennsylvania Historical and Museum Commission.* 7 vols. New York and London: Garland, 1987 (originally unillustrated).

Scully met Louis Kahn in 1947 when Kahn was hired by the Yale School of Art and Architecture as Visiting Critic in Design. Subsequently promoted to Chief Critic, Kahn taught at Yale through the 1950s, during which time he and Scully developed a friendship that lasted until the architect's death in 1974. When Kahn arrived in New Haven, he was little known, having built nothing of great note. The commission for the Yale University Art Gallery (1951–53), which he owed to his former partner George Howe, who had become chairman of the Department of Architecture at the university, was Kahn's first high-profile job. After that came the bathhouse for the Trenton Jewish Community Center (1955), the Richards Medical Research Building at the University of Pennsylvania (1957–65), the First Unitarian Church in Rochester (1959–69), and the Salk Institute for Biological Studies at La Jolla (1959–65). Scully published a short piece on the Yale Art Gallery in the French journal *Muséum* in 1956 but, more important, included Kahn as a major figure in the evolution of contemporary architecture in a series of articles beginning in 1954 with "Archetype and Order in Recent American Architecture" (see chap. 3) and culminating in 1962 with "Wright, International Style, and Kahn" (an abridged version of "Frank Lloyd Wright and Twentieth-Century Style"; see chap. 6), in which Kahn's work was viewed as opening the next phase in the history of modern architecture. That same year Scully published the first book on Kahn, in Braziller's Makers of Contemporary Architecture series, a book that established him as the main interpreter of Kahn's work for a generation and more of students and professionals.

14

Introduction to *The Louis I. Kahn Archive: Personal Drawings*

VINCENT SCULLY

In 1983 Philip Johnson, by then the best-known architect in the United States, publicly voiced the opinion that Louis I. Kahn would eventually be rated only a minor figure in the history of twentieth-century architecture. I believe that Johnson was wrong and that Kahn will continue to be regarded as a very major figure indeed, and one of a very special kind. It is true that he will never attain the curiously titanic stature which has already been accorded those architects, primarily Wright, Mies, and Le Corbusier, who in various ways did most to shape that kind of modernism which dominated a good part of the century and came to be called the International Style. They, along with the polemicist Loos and the pedagogue Gropius, brought the old world crashing down. They stormed Olympus, overthrew its pediments and columns, proscribed its classic language, banned history, derided tradition, and remade architecture according to the iconoclastic and often contradictory principles of formal reductionism, social leveling, and personal caprice. The historians Giedion and Pevsner also come into the story, as does, with Hitchcock, Johnson himself. In general, a heavy Germanic hand was laid upon history, criticism, and the

When the 1962 Kahn book appeared, the Rochester Church was not yet completed and the Salk Institute was just beginning construction; the fully mature work, like the National Assembly complex in Dhaka, Bangladesh (1962–83), the Indian Institute of Management at Ahmedabad (1962–74), the Library at Phillips Exeter Academy (1965–72), the Kimbell Art Museum at Fort Worth (1966–72), and the Yale Center for British Art (1969–74) were far off in the distance. Although Scully was urged more than once by Braziller to do a second, enlarged edition of the book, he never did so, and his thoughts on Kahn's later development remain disappointingly dispersed in a number of journal articles and introductions to exhibition catalogues published between 1964 and 1978. The invitation to write the introduction to the seven-volume catalogue of the personal drawings in the Kahn Archive acquired by the Commonwealth of Pennsylvania and housed in the Furness Building of the University of Pennsylvania gave Scully the opportunity to reflect on the entirety of Kahn's career and formulate the kind of synthesis that had eluded him so far.

Despite the fact that almost nothing for which Kahn would eventually be esteemed was yet visible, or in many ways even imaginable, Scully claimed in his 1962 book that Kahn was "unquestionably first in professional importance among living American architects" and that his ability to begin entirely "afresh" and reformulate a new basis for architecture at the most fundamental level of structure, space, and order already placed him in the rarefied company of Wright and Le Corbusier. But what set Kahn apart from "the Late

teaching of architecture, ending the dominance of the French in that field. In the United States the fall of the Ecole des Beaux-Arts resulted in the gutting of some fine architectural libraries in many schools of architecture and, in one extremely relevant instance, it is rumored, in a literal burning of the books. The International Style was, in the end, more than a little totalitarian in its conceptual structure.

Kahn's role in all this was multiple. He was both victim and avenger: victim because modernism brutally separated him from the classicism in which he had been educated and that was natural to him; avenger because his work, as it were despite itself, eventually moved toward the restoration of classicism and indicated a number of other ways in which the International Style itself might be transformed and modern architecture as a whole richly complicated, leavened, and extended. Trained in the Beaux-Arts under Paul Cret, Kahn emerged from architectural school in the late twenties into a world which the Germans were just beginning to dominate, and he accepted their principles so wholeheartedly that it took him more than twenty years to find himself again. Abandoning his classical language, he embraced the modernist dictum that everything had to be reinvented from the ground up and probably, though illogically, repeatedly reinvented in every new program. Everything, at least, had to be wholly "original" every time. This was common modernist theology, but it was normally honored in the breach, since each of the great revolutionaries clearly had his own "style," which was supposed to show a consistent "development" from job to job. Here each modern architect was in fact a romantic,

Baroque of the International Style," as Scully described the devolution of the modern movement in the 1950s, and what ultimately determined Kahn's unique path, was his strong early training in the classical Beaux-Arts system and an increasing predisposition to allow its principles and directives to return to the fore after having been forcibly repressed in the years of high modernism. Where this would lead was something Scully was not yet ready to predict. A crucial question, he realized, would turn on the role history would play in Kahn's future work, for his Beaux-Arts schooling had taught him "to regard the buildings of the past as friends rather than enemies, friends from whom one was expected . . . to borrow freely." How could one sustain the modernist pressure for originality in this situation? And if Form is the immaterial and abstract foundation of the accommodating process of Design, as Kahn believed, "is Form, 'dream-inspired,' really Memory at the last?" Scully asked. The relatively short introduction to the catalogue of Kahn drawings offers some answers to these questions, although Scully's final and more developed thoughts on the subject would have to wait until the publication in 1992 of "Louis I. Kahn and the Ruins of Rome" (see chap. 17).

Scully's analysis of Kahn's career in the essay that follows builds directly on the arguments of his earlier book and really deviates only in terms of its final assessment of the historical significance of Kahn's work. The Beaux-Arts training, its repression, and its ultimate return (though "concealed" and unacknowledged) define the ground against which

acting out a Faustian role in reshaping himself and the world and creating a new language of his own. Kahn gave himself up wholly to that idea. He truly believed in origins, or, as he chose to call them, Beginnings. The primitivism that was a persistent leitmotif in modernism, and that had come by the forties to dominate Le Corbusier's work, took on a new kind of life in Kahn's design, in which every structural element eventually came to be reinvented, every assemblage reassembled, every joint remade. From this the major strength of Kahn's architecture was to derive. Its solemn quiet was the result of its palpable structural order and the dignity of its connections, as if the whole had settled into some permanent repose, elemental and natural to itself.

Historically, it seems clear enough that Kahn could not begin to grow as an architect until he found his own "primitive" sources, his personal Beginnings. His work of the thirties and forties was frustrated and inhibited by that lack. By the late forties, though, his innate classicism was beginning to find its way back up to the surface of his mind. He talked incessantly about Order and sought it everywhere. In the modernist sense, however, it had to be an invented Order, a new Beginning; it could not be the "Orders" themselves. During 1951–52 a happy set of circumstances brought all the necessary elements
12.35 together in the Yale Art Gallery, Kahn's first important commission. Here the pyramids of Giza, of which Kahn had just done some magnificent pastels in situ, suggested one of the most basic of Platonic shapes as a Beginning; the tetrahedronal space frames of Buckminster Fuller (an old friend of Kahn's and the special hero of Anne Tyng, Kahn's

the figures of modernist invention and originality carry out their transformative role. The result, obsessively expressed in the physicality and materiality of the structural detailing of the buildings, is a powerful tension between classicism and modernism that opens new avenues for architecture. Scully isolates the dialectic of Form and Design, first articulated in the Rochester Church, as not only the key to Kahn's methodology but also the most clear and intelligent way to understand how history and memory play their part in the creative process. But although Form is now seen as unequivocally a product of the historical consciousness, Kahn's unwillingness to admit any explicit reference to history, as a consequence of his adherence to modernist dicta, tends to undermine and limit the full potentiality of his breakthrough. Unlike in 1962, when everything was still a question, and when Kahn was apparently completely on his own, his influence could now be seen in architects as different as Aldo Rossi, Robert Venturi, Charles Moore, and Allan Greenberg—and their articulation and elaboration of ideas of symbolism, classicism, and typology made Kahn's own work, by contrast, seem less rich and less fulfilling than it might have been. Certainly, Scully's own growing awareness of the perceived shortcomings of modernism played an important part in this judgment. Be that as it may, Kahn was no longer to be ranked with the revolutionary figures of Wright, Mies, and Le Corbusier, architects who overthrew a system and put an entirely new one in its place. Rather, Kahn represented a transformational force that revealed what could be made out of a rigorous regard for history, modernist and premodernist alike.

closest collaborator at that time) provided a modern instance, and a structural one, while the open loft spaces which seemed proper to the program offered the ideal pretext for the monumental tetrahedronal concrete slab that Kahn finally brought forth. It was the first of his great shapes, and it set the pattern for those to come, combining as it did a primitive Beginning with a classicizing Order and a structural justification. It does not really matter here if, as the associated engineer pointed out, the structure is not what it seems. The thing *looks* structural, primitive, and repetitively ordered all at once. It has a solemn weight. Its presence remains awesome, and it is still one of the most telling of modern works to be seen anywhere.

By 1955, in the little Trenton Bathhouse, Kahn had combined his pyramid with 6.6, 6.7
its complementary ideal shapes, the circle and the square. He was filling out his Platonic repertoire and finding his way back to a more complete classical vocabulary. At the same time, Trenton's cross-axial plan, defined by hollow piers, closely recalled that of St. Front at Périgueux. Here Kahn seems to have been relearning what he had been taught: that human order is a cultural construction and its archetypes are therefore to be found in human history. He was relearning his early lessons, though he was not admitting that heretical fact to anyone, certainly not to his associates, probably not at this time to himself. But he was on that road. His pyramids and tetrahedrons flared up into the splendid
space-frame precast skyscraper project of 1957, again worked out with Anne Tyng, and 9.1
that vision transformed itself into San Gimignano's vertical towers to house the Richards

17.12 Medical Laboratories of 1959. It is the systematic assemblage of precast structural elements which most endows that building with its special dignity. Its medieval towers are also extremely moving; they are towers of pain, built upon the bodies of sacrificed animals. But, despite Kahn's functional justifications for them, they do not really work very well. The articulation of functions and services from which Kahn derived their forms is not noticeably efficient in practice. There is no sun protection; the occupants paste up silver foil where necessary.

Kahn was all too aware of these problems, and he set out to solve them. In that sense, his work was the apogee of modernism. It was trying to "solve" problems of function and structure afresh, as if they had never occurred to anyone before. If questions of symbol beyond those of functional propriety were in Kahn's mind, they were not enunciated by him and, as in most modernist works, were at first only distantly embodied in the buildings themselves. The mayor of Leningrad was right enough in 1965 when he sug-
17.14 gested that Kahn's Unitarian Church in Rochester did not "look like a church." Yet it was the first of Kahn's buildings in which all the forms were fresh inventions, growing directly out of Kahn's own analysis of structure and function. The latter category, too, was especially enriched by Kahn's newly developed preoccupation with natural light: how to introduce it into the building; how to direct it, as to the books in the laps of readers ensconced in the window seats; how to cut down glare or let it bloom, as in the wonderful central meeting hall. The light, as here, is valued as a determinant of architectural form; it suggests shapes or, it might be more accurate to say, it helps suggest ways to modify and particularize those forms which the mind has already chosen for the program.

17.13 Kahn identified that process of development as one of Form and Design, and his description of it remains the most cogent analysis of how new shapes come into being that any contemporary architect, perhaps since the young Frank Lloyd Wright, has made. It is a curious but very useful amalgam of Platonic idealism and pragmatic realism. Faced with an architectural program, the mind, according to Kahn, selects from the forms it has already stored away the one which seems to suit the situation best. Then, through Design, the architect bombards that chosen Form with the particulars of the program until it deforms in response to them. If, however, the original Form was the right one, the whole thing, however modified by Design, will still hold together in the end. If the Form was the wrong one, it will be stretched too far for coherence and a new Form must be chosen, so that the whole process can start over. Kahn's Form at Rochester, selected in response to his judgment that the classrooms, the library, the kitchen, and so on should all cluster around a central meeting hall, turned out to be very close to that archetype of the idealist tradition, the circle in the square, which was described by Vitruvius and drawn so often during the Middle Ages and the Renaissance. Those essential shapes were eloquently deformed at Rochester, but they eventually held, and the beautiful final plan resulted. Kahn notes that the congregation had originally preferred a kind of binuclear scheme with the classrooms and the meeting hall as distinct blocks
11.16 connected by a corridor, as in Wright's Unity Temple. Here, though, that Form fell apart because all the smaller rooms "wanted" to get closer to the meeting hall.

Kahn's statement of method was especially important in the early sixties because it acknowledged human history as the instigator of the aesthetic process—which, by definition, has to be true, in the sense that all human making is culturally based. So the classical philosophers identified Mnemosyne, Memory, as the mother of the Muses. And Kahn's formulation was classic all through. It specifically cast out the empirical flow diagrams of Bauhaus pedagogy, which tried to deal with everything tabula rasa, and it recognized the fact that the human mind is stored with forms out of its cultural heritage and thinks in those forms, modifying them only in degree in response to the changes of external reality. Kahn appreciated the profound cultural rhythm involved in this when he noted that it was all a movement from the Immaterial to the Material and back again.

In any event, the experience of designing the church at Rochester seems to have brought Kahn to a confident maturity and confirmed him in his method of design. This entailed the breaking of the mental barrier which the International Style had set up between the present and the past—in this case literally between Kahn and his own past. Kahn's recognition of Forms in the mind is a corollary of that liberation. Suddenly the past he had loved and in which he had been steeped at the University of Pennsylvania came flooding back to him: Rome most of all. The sites he had visited in 1950–51 and afterward with, or under the influence of, the great classicist Frank E. Brown, of the American Academy in Rome, now offered up their forms to him. The House of Augustus on the Palatine and the work of Rabirius, Trajan's Market, Hadrian's Villa, Ostia, all suggested those Forms out of which the grandeurs of the Salk Institute for Biological 17.17, 17.19
Research, the Indian School of Management at Ahmedabad, and the capitol at Dhaka 12.36, 17.22
took shape. Every one of those groups of buildings was, in one way or another, a Roman ruin—a ruin which specifically triumphed over the International Style by the subordination of glass or its total elimination.

It is true that Kahn subjected those ruins to startlingly Piranesian deformations in order to accommodate contemporary requirements, but their forms suggest functional use much less than they seem to embody a kind of unchanging monumentality. Those in India and Pakistan especially take on the character of hollow shells, pierced with vast harmonies of circles and triangles at a curiously detached, rather cosmic scale not quite that of mankind. In part for that reason, from Salk to Dhaka, the buildings became progressively more timeless—much more literally hard to date—and at last utterly still. They were much more Platonically ideal and abstract than anything produced by the International Style. They seem pure immaterial music, but their solemn brick and concrete masses are at the same time aggressively material too. Indeed, out of that Roman union of concrete and brick came Kahn's special delight, his Brick Order, a marvelous "misreading" of the Roman relieving arch over a wooden lintel as he had seen it used in the brick and concrete warehouses of Ostia. From Ostia too came the Temple of Jupiter Optimus Maximus Capitolinus as it rose above the Forum—its podium stairs of white marble, its wall eroded into roofless vertical masses marked by relieving arches—to be deformed and reformed
into Dhaka's capitol building itself. The little Thermopolium at Ostia, aggrandized by 17.27, 17.23

Piranesi's vision in those etchings of Roman ruins Kahn had collected since boyhood,
17.22 became the mysterious crypto-portici running under Dhaka and Ahmedabad alike, while
17.25 the "basilica" of Trajan's Market adjacent to his forum at Rome was echoed in Ahmeda-
17.26 bad's largest hall.

Behind Kahn's desk in his crowded, totally unstylish office in Philadelphia, Piranesi's fantastic map of the Campus Martius filled most of the wall. Shape after shape in Kahn's work derived from it. Kahn was once more in the full flood of Roman grandeur and had become in some ways the most Roman architect since McKim, Mead and White in their greatest days. From one thing, however, he held back: from all Roman decoration and detail. He was still determined to be abstract and to reinvent all the architectural elements, and he did not intend to employ any kind of decorative embellishment he could not justify to himself as a built thing. Surely integrity of construction had become his ultimate criterion, and as we have noted, he deformed all his Roman Forms in accordance with it. At the same time, the International Style impress was still there, not only in the Platonic idealism of the work—which Kahn shared with the young Le Corbusier, if not with the older—but also in Kahn's refusal to acknowledge publicly, and usually even to himself, that he was in fact closely adapting Roman forms. He was still caught in the romantic myth the International Style had adopted; he had to be the Inventor, the Faustian creator of everything. That state of mind tended to solidify in Kahn as he became an object of increasing adulation to students in his later years and began to settle into a guru's role. Like the successors of Augustus he was especially swayed by the adoration of the East, paid to him in overwhelming measure by his students from Asia.

Other stresses were involved. Denise Scott Brown has suggested that Kahn began to open up to direct formal suggestions from history only when Robert Venturi, who had been trained in the Beaux-Arts at Princeton, came to work in his office in the mid-fifties. Certainly the relationship between Kahn and Venturi, his greatest student, was, like that between Sullivan and Wright, never a simple or easy one. Moreover, the direction that Venturi soon took in his work, toward symbol and association, was foreign territory to Kahn. It is never mentioned by him, though on several occasions he later specifically derided the evidence of it in Venturi's work. A blindness toward such architectural resources was one of the limitations Kahn shared with all the architects and almost all the critics of his generation. He himself was involved solely with the physical experience of physical form: with empathy, though he did not call it that. Out of that preconception, along with his special sense of static presence and permanence, derives the similarity between his work and the philosophy of Heidegger, which he apparently never read but with which, as Norberg-Schulz has shown, he would have been in complete sympathy—at least up to a point. That point was marked by the special strain of mysticism which was in him somewhere and which J. Kieffer especially has had some success in identifying with Jewish mystical traditions. The most telling of these instances is
17.8, 17.9 Kahn's obvious adaptation of the Tree of the Sefiroth for the plan of his Mikveh Israel
Synagogue.[1] Such relationships to Kabbalist shapes and ideas, in which the concept of Silence plays an enormous part, were never mentioned by Kahn, so far as I know, even to

his oldest friends, but he tended to keep his relationships compartmentalized in any event and, like the great conspirator every artist is, to cover his tracks from one cell to the other. So he may well have discussed the matter with someone as yet unknown.

We ask ourselves if Kahn's work would have been stronger and more complete if he had not been under the stresses of secrecy and concealment or had never fallen under the spell of the International Style at all but had continued to grow along with the modern classicism in which he had been trained by Cret. I think the answer to that question, however interesting the alternative it suggests, has to be in the negative. Kahn probably needed his stresses. It was in his nature to want to reinvent the wheel, and he was obliged by the mythology of the modern quest to lose and find his way. The wonderful tensions which shape his work would hardly have existed otherwise or have so solemnly resolved themselves in the end into such pregnant Silence. Every detail in Kahn's late buildings convinces us that he had thought it through from the beginning, lived his life through it, and finally assembled it with everything else into a hard-won
calm. The Kimbell Museum in Fort Worth is the equivalent of the half-round Roman 17.30
vault and light, fixed forever. The library at Exeter is the circle in the square, under, as 17.32
Alex Gorlin has shown, the compass of the Mason laying out the world. The project for the Inner Harbor at Baltimore is the ultimate concrete frame, shaping a visionary landscape of the sublime.

In a way, the British Art Center at Yale, Kahn's last completed work, is the most 17.33
touching, if not the most primordially powerful, of all the late projects, because here Kahn turned to glass, that unsympathetic, breakable, International-Style material he had tried to cast out before. Now he handles it with rare eloquence, so detailing its framing that it is almost totally reflective, exploding in sheets of light across the face of the dull stainless steel panels with which it is associated and mirroring the grand Beaux-Arts
decoration of the old Art Gallery by Egerton Swartwout across the way. With glass Kahn 17.35
turned also to Mies van der Rohe, whose rectangular loft spaces he had employed in his own Yale Art Gallery of twenty years earlier, at the very beginning of his mature career.
Now, in the British Art Center, it is Mies in the tradition of Labrouste whom he invokes, 17.34
as he employs a skeleton frame with infilling panels. Heavier than the work of Mies, Kahn's building evokes that modern classicism, initiated by Labrouste, which was once called the Néo-Grec, but it is still wholly devoid of even the leanest decorative embellishment, the smallest classical detail. It is still all Kahn, primitive Kahn of the Beginning, all solid structure and pure spatial volumes, all solemn assemblage of materials at silent joints, everything at once obsessively perfect and just at the edge of savage crudeness, but all Silence and Light, with no gestures at all except for that of the giant stair tower looming in the vast Great Hall. It is a wonderful place to be in, lit by an even light at once white and gentle in spaces calm, generous, and strongly framed, while its windows focus the stretch of university buildings across the street with the hyperclarity of some magical lens.

In such spaces it is possible to feel that the young Italian architects upon whom Kahn exerted such an important influence in the sixties and early seventies are probably

15.14 closer to him in spirit than are those Americans such as Venturi and Moore who were also decisively affected by him. The forms of Mario Botta and some others derive directly from his and exploit the same kind of monumental geometry that he favored. But the
10.1, 10.2 curiously timeless, haunted buildings and projects of Aldo Rossi, despite Rossi's critical reservations about Kahn as an architect, are in some fundamental ways the closest of all. They embody much the same kind of static, archetypal order. They, too, avoid gestures in favor of utter quiet and, perhaps most of all, are derived directly from those enduring classic and vernacular traditions from which Kahn drew so much of his strength. Those traditions are touched for both architects by the haunting sorrows of twentieth-century
17.5 experience. Kahn drew from Mussolini's Forum in 1950 in a way that recalls de Chirico's paintings, just as Rossi's work constantly reminds us of Mussolini's EUR, where de Chirico's spirit is felt everywhere. De Chirico is as present in the disorienting hollow brick circles of Dhaka as he is in the windowless, roofless palazzo of the cemetery at Modena. It is the essential Italian urban type with, as it were, everything inflammable burned away: the vision of a metaphysical city where nothing changes. Where, however, Kahn sought originality from his study of the type, Rossi seeks the type itself. He is thus able to abandon the iconoclastic strivings of modernism, and especially of late modernism, for whose individualistic antics he feels a cold contempt, and to link all his individual works to the traditional concept of the city as a whole, in which individual buildings play the role of their type in defining the architectural environment. Rossi is thus freed, as Kahn was not, to employ the classical orders, in part because he recognizes how well the classical types were worked out to enhance, indeed to celebrate, the urban situation.

The inveterate idealism of the Europeans is also related to Kahn's own persistently idealist bent, which he shared with the International Style architects of his generation. Moreover, before his death, Kahn had already tacitly condemned the direction taken by Venturi and Moore, with its fundamentally realist approach, not to mention its dynamic of movement, its ambiguity, and its wit. Venturi and Moore, like Rossi, have also liberated themselves to incorporate classical and other historical elements in their work, although never, unlike Allan Greenberg, for example, without subjecting them to considerable contemporary comment. And it was most of all Venturi's embrace of association and representation in architecture that offended the modernist abstraction which played such an essential part in Kahn's approach. Venturi, closest to Kahn, was also furthest from him in this, since it was he who first incorporated symbolic gestures into his architecture in a way that was totally foreign to Kahn's purely empathetic stance. Venturi's conceptual leap marked a radical shift in architectural theory and design, one that left Kahn, along with almost everyone else at the time, on one side of a chasm with Venturi on the other. In the solitary instance where Kahn may be felt to have been consciously attempting to incorporate both representation and symbolism into a facade in a way reminiscent of Venturi—in the theater at Fort Wayne, that is—the results approach caricature.

This is not to say that symbolism is absent from Kahn's work. It most emphatically is not. True enough, symbolic content is embodied in every form, which cannot be perceived by human beings as devoid of such qualities, but with Kahn the symbolism,

though always veiled in abstraction, can be very strong indeed, and it grew stronger as time went on, as in the dark towers of the Richards Center, a village of research and a castle of animal agony; in the fellows' studies at Salk, stretching out eagerly to peer into the distance; in the passionate, subcontinental excess of Ahmedabad, the stark parody of an
English collegiate quadrangle; in Dhaka's crashing cymbals of power, deafening with cir- 17.28
cular clangor in the vast concrete labyrinth about its Assembly Hall; in Exeter's enormous 17.32
concrete circles, enclosed within their protecting brick square and thundering out over the hundreds of human beings reading in and around them.

The signs and symbols are certainly there in Kahn's buildings, all emphatically embodied in solid matter. They are intrinsic to the structural forms, which is their greatest strength, and now, some twelve years after Kahn's death, it seems clear that they will endure. Here Kahn, trying so earnestly to express the character of human institutions in abstract form, may even be said to have set Venturi on his more consciously symbolic course, however much each may otherwise have owed to the other. It is sad that the apparent lack of comprehension was there at the end. It has since been exploited by modernist critics who would like to use Kahn as a stick to beat "postmodernism" with, although they tended to ignore his work when he was alive. Kahn's own intransigence, though, is not to be wondered at, because the way he followed was a hard one. It left its impress upon him and pitilessly shaped his life.

Its character can be traced in his drawings, some of which seem hewn out of solid rock, smashing their way toward the mind's vision through the most obdurate of materials. All the drawings testify in one way or another to Kahn's endless search for personal originality and architectural order all at once, so that many of them seem to be pulled in several directions as they attempt to do many different things. From his great travel sketches, the watercolors of the late twenties and the pastels of the early fifties, through which the whole of his career can be prophetically read, right down through every category of study to the quickest sketches done in the office, Kahn's drawings seem to be trying to shape new and difficult visions and to articulate their structure. In consequence, few of them, even those of old buildings, are overly graceful or obviously pictorial or even picturesque. They are normally angular, harsh, impatient, intransigently pursuing the Quest through which Kahn transformed the modern movement into something new, which is now being explored by the greatest architects on both sides of the Atlantic. Perhaps it would be truer to say around the world.

One or two of those architects have developed qualities of a kind Kahn did not possess. None, however, builds with quite such marvelous structural connections or such rigorously classical assemblage. None has come close to Kahn's physical power. If God is in the details, as Mies van der Rohe once claimed, Jehovah in his Silence is there in Kahn's. It is hard to see him as a minor figure. He is much more resonant with awe and terror than any of those who sit on Olympus now.

Note 1 As published in a wood engraving by Leonhard Beck on the title page of Gikaitilla, *Portae lucis* (Augsburg, 1516). Kieffer's work has so far been published privately as *Louis I. Kahn and the Ritual of Architecture* (1981).

NEIL LEVINE

"Robert Venturi's Gentle Architecture." In *The Architecture of Robert Venturi,* ed. Christopher Mead. Albuquerque: University of New Mexico Press, 1989.

Of all the architects Scully has written about, none has become as closely linked with his name as Robert Venturi. Scully was the first major critic or historian to single out Venturi for praise, and he wrote the introduction to the book of architectural theory that brought Venturi to public as well as broad professional notice in 1966. Only two years after the architect had completed his first project—the interior renovation of the James B. Duke House for the Institute of Fine Arts in New York—Scully chose Venturi as one of six young architects for the annual "New Talent USA" issue of *Art in America* that came out in early 1961 (the five others were Edward Larabee Barnes, Ulrich Franzen, Romaldo Giurgola, John Johansen, and Paolo Soleri). Scully's choices were particularly prescient. The year before, by contrast, Henry-Russell Hitchcock had selected Howard Barnstone and John Black Lee; and, in 1962, Ada Louise Huxtable picked Gunnar Birkerts, Craig Ellwood, Mark Hampton, and Tasso Katselas. In the essay reprinted here, Scully notes that it was the neo–Shingle Style Beach House project of 1959, illustrated in the *Art in America* article, that had initially made him aware of Venturi and that it was Robert Stern, when he was an architecture student at Yale a few years later, who encouraged him to look at Venturi's work.

At Stern's urging, Scully visited the Guild House, in Philadelphia (1960–66), while it was in construction, as well as the recently completed house the architect built for his mother, Vanna Venturi, in Chestnut Hill (1959–64). When Arthur Drexler decided to have the Museum of Modern Art publish Venturi's *Complexity and Contradiction in Architecture*

15

Robert Venturi's Gentle Architecture

VINCENT SCULLY

Thinking about the work of Robert Venturi, and I have thought about it a good deal over the past twenty years, it struck me this time that he is a little like Franklin Roosevelt. Roosevelt saved the capitalist system in America—pretty much from itself—and was hated for it by all capitalists; Venturi saved modern architecture from itself and has been hated for it by almost all modern architects. I think the reason is this: modern architecture simply could not, would not, deal with the complexities of the city. Its urbanism, like its architecture, was abstract. So it destroyed the city, casting out everything that had been laboriously developed over the centuries to make the city worth living in.

Le Corbusier is the best example. Once he had eliminated all of traditional urbanism, which he did by the early twenties, he soon grew weary, by the early thirties at least, of the machine aesthetic with which he had replaced it. He found that he had nowhere to go except back to the primitive, the primordial—precisely because he had written out of history all of the centuries of civilized development in architecture that combine to make a city. Le Corbusier's late work embodied a primitive, sculptural force,

as "the first in a series of occasional papers concerned with the theoretical background of modern architecture"—a decision that would mark a new era in the discourse of contemporary architecture—Venturi asked Scully (whose second wife, Marian, was editing the rather unwieldy manuscript) to write the introduction. In his opening paragraphs Scully dramatically described the book's argument as unfolding "like a curtain slowly lifting from the eyes" and compared it, in terms of significance, to Le Corbusier's *Vers une architecture* of 1923. Venturi more modestly characterized his effort as a "gentle manifesto" for a "nonstraightforward architecture," using historical references from an extremely broad range of sources to suggest ways of bringing the "richness and ambiguity of modern experience" into an architectural orthodoxy that had become severely constrained by its own "puritanically" exclusionary beliefs.

The introduction to *Complexity and Contradiction*, which was read by many as throwing down the gauntlet, equated Venturi's ideas with the paradigm shift that had set the modern movement in motion in the 1920s. And just as that one had opposed the eclecticism of the Beaux-Arts, this one opposed the purism of the modern. Scully pointed the reader to Venturi's antiheroic stance, especially in regard to the urban environment; to the ironic, accommodating aspects of a design process based on the particularities of human use and meaning rather than the abstractions of structural expression; and to the scenographic and humanistic possibilities of an architecture in touch with vernacular and mass-culture traditions. He noted that Venturi, while avoiding his former employer "Kahn's structural preoccupations in favor of a more flexibly function-directed method," should nevertheless be seen as completing "that renewed connection with the whole of our past which Kahn's mature work had begun."

Over the years, Scully continued to champion Venturi's work as opening a new, more humane, and more culturally responsive phase in the evolution of modern architecture. The accommodation of his buildings to preexisting conditions was now seen as the basis for the development of contextualism, a fundamental factor in the reorientation of urbanism in the 1970s and 1980s. The role of decoration, of social commentary, and of spatial imagination in planning also came in for greater consideration. In the text of the brochure accompanying the 1971 exhibition of Venturi's work at the Whitney Museum, Scully introduced two new themes that would remain key to his later writings on the subject: 1) that Venturi's architecture represented a rejection of idealism and an embrace of realism; and 2) that the communicative intention of his work was conveyed by a semiology

and its proper setting could only be that of antique religion itself: the natural world. It was surely a very great, though limited, image. The High Court Building of 1951–56 at 8.16
Chandigarh, with the continuous upward thrust of its piers, past any lintel, makes us feel empathetically the vertical stance of the soldier who stands before it. The forms are like those of a Greek temple, since both embody a challenge to the natural world. But when this primordial, primitive giant left the landscape and lumbered into our cities in the 1950s and 1960s, it laid waste to the urban landscape, flailing about with Neanderthalic

of symbolism and sign. Finally, the climactic section on Venturi in *The Shingle Style Today, or, The Historian's Revenge* (1974) made use of Harold Bloom's study *The Anxiety of Influence* in concert with the Freudian concept of "condensation" to account for the architect's capacity to reuse and remake history.

"Robert Venturi's Gentle Architecture" is Scully's most complete overview to date of the architect's career. It was first presented as the keynote lecture in a symposium organized by Christopher Mead at the University of New Mexico Art Museum in October 1985 on the occasion of the exhibition *Venturi, Rauch and Scott Brown: A Generation of Architecture* that emanated from the Krannert Art Museum at the University of Illinois at Urbana-Champaign (other speakers in the symposium included Tom Beeby, Stephen Kieran, David Van Zanten, and myself). The title of Scully's piece, taken from Venturi's 1966 "manifesto," is meant to convey the fundamental qualities of reasonableness, modesty, caring, and civility that Scully believes underlie all of Venturi's work and are ultimately its most significant aspect. The architecture's contextualism—its respect for and ability to "get along" with what has preceded it—is, as Scully often noted in the past, crucial in this regard. But here Scully adds Venturi's concern for type, as revealed in the interplay between the classical and vernacular traditions, as a fuller explanation for the unique success of his designs. Neither literal in his references to the past—as some of his progeny are—nor aggressively unwilling to acknowledge its influence—as his modernist forbears were—Venturi occupies in Scully's heartfelt summation a truly liberal, and therefore quite fragile, middle ground. He remains halfway between modernism and historicist postmodernism, the putative savior of the modern movement—a prophet without honor in his own country.

roarings. Kallman, McKinnell and Knowles's Boston City Hall of 1962–69 is a very good example of the late modern, so-called Brutalist buildings that despised, trampled upon, destroyed the scale of the city and, most of all, cut through the complex web of urbanistic adjustments from which a city is made.

Venturi, it seems to me, was the first to begin reversing all of that. He mitigated the abstraction of modern architecture and made it contextual once more. His buildings were prepared to get along with the other buildings in the city, to take up their roles in a gentle comedy of citizenship rather than in a melodrama of pseudoheroic aggression. Venturi's architecture is therefore involved with healing, but it remains a modern archi-
15.1 tecture. The taut, continuous, thin wall of Gordon Wu Hall of 1980–83 at Princeton University, with the columnar structure visible behind the glass, creates a wholly modern gesture. It could be of no other age. Venturi shapes a contemporary architecture that is more wholly modern than that of the International Style because it can also engage in a dialogue with the architecture of the past. This seems to be the first fact about Venturi.

Another seems to be that Venturi, of all the architects I have known, has worked most through the principle of condensation. Sigmund Freud first stated this principle in the modern age when he described how what he called the "dream work" brought "dream thoughts" into "dream content." The first stage in that process was the condensation of

15.1 Venturi, Rauch and Scott Brown. Gordon Wu Hall, Princeton University, Princeton, New Jersey, 1980–83. Exterior

opposites to form a "new unity." That aesthetic idea is originally Scholastic, since Scholastic philosophy employed the word *concordantia*, the reconciliation of opposites, to define what Freud meant by condensation.

We can watch Venturi work this way in his pioneering project of 1959 for a
Beach House—the one through which most of us became aware of his existence. He 15.2
began with McKim, Mead and White's Low House of 1887, which was first published by 18.5
Henry-Russell Hitchcock in *Rhode Island Architecture* (1939) and which had by the 1950s become a key monument in American historiography. Having written *The International Style* (1932) with Philip Johnson, Hitchcock had instinctively turned back to look at the historical alternatives to the International Style, especially the American architecture of the later nineteenth century. The Low House, with its vast, frontal gable, became the archetypal image of that way of building. For me, working on my doctoral dissertation in the late 1940s, this was the building that first engaged my interest and, indeed, launched me into a work that emerged in part as *The Shingle Style* (1955). And it was this building that caught Venturi's eye in 1959. He took over the frontal gable but thrust an enormous chimney up through it. That chimney represents a condensation of
the Low House with the house of Middlefield designed in 1908 by Sir Edwin Lutyens. 18.6
Lutyens was without question the greatest British architect of the early twentieth century, but he has been despised by the modernists because his architecture remained representational. Venturi used Lutyens to adapt the roof organization of his project, but he blew up the chimney in scale. It is now single and mighty, rising up behind the dunes

Robert Venturi. Beach House project, New Jersey shore, 1959. Model 15.2

to mark the position of the house, confronting the sea like a medieval tower. I remember how I resented that extravagant gesture when I first saw the project. I said to myself: "How dare he wave that thing in my face. Let him keep it to himself." When Charles Moore first did his own study after Venturi's project, in his project of 1961 for the Jenkins House, he ripped out the chimney and designed the house without it.

It was Robert Stern—at that time a student of mine at Yale University—who induced me to go look at Venturi's work. That is the lucky thing about teaching: it provides us with young people who force us to grow in the only way that we can grow, by bursting the framework of preconceptions within which we live. As we get older and our symbolic life lies more and more inside our by now ossified previous experiences, that act of liberation becomes increasingly difficult. It becomes harder and harder for us to break free. Therefore, the teacher is the most fortunate of men, so long as he allows himself to be taught, and it is clear that a decisive conceptual transformation was required for people of my generation to be able to appreciate Venturi's importance.

18.1 Venturi's first important project to be built was his mother's house, the Vanna Venturi House of 1961–64. Disarmingly simple after the spatial antics of late modernism, its plan, like that of the Beach House project, is based on a symbolic conception rather than upon one that is purely spatially abstract. It is centered on the idea of the chimney, the hearth, from which—and you can feel it—the space is pulled. The space is distended from that hearth as the mass of the chimney rises up to split the house. Here

the principle of condensation becomes an extremely complex and interesting one. With
the chimney rising through the gable, the general *parti* derives from that of the Beach
House. Now, however, the living room is half-vaulted, and that semicircle is picked up in 18.3
the tacked-on arch of the facade; now, the whole house is rising and being split through
the middle.

This conception has a distinguished genealogy. It begins with the Chandler 1.17
House of 1885–86 in Tuxedo Park, New York, by Bruce Price, where a gable shelters a little, half-round Palladian window at the top and two bays on the first floor. Then, in the
same year, Price built the Kent House—also in Tuxedo Park—where he brought the gable 1.14
around to the front and placed in it a rather larger half-round window. The facade of the
Kent House is, in fact, symmetrical, but the view published in *The Builder* in 1886 makes
it look as if the walled terrace were asymmetrically placed. This caught the eye of Frank
Lloyd Wright when he built his own house in Oak Park in 1889. Wright was, without ques- 1.16
tion, the greatest American condenser of architectural opposites before Venturi; at any
rate, he decisively condensed the two houses by Price—bringing them together and presenting his own "new unity," his clear Platonic triangle of frontal gable. That triangle is a
pure, abstract, geometric shape, but in terms of our cultural associations, it also says
"house," as a child might draw one. Wright distrusted such associations, insofar as they
were historical, and soon eliminated the gable from his work.

Venturi returned to it. The associational factor itself now becomes central to
Venturi's conceptual structure, endowing it with dimensions of meaning that were inac-
cessible to his friend, mentor, and boss, Louis I. Kahn, for whom he worked in the
1950s. Just up the road from Venturi's house for his mother is Kahn's Esherick House of 15.3
1959–61, from which all associational elements that might suggest "house" have been
rigorously eliminated. It is the pure abstraction of the International Style in which Kahn,
in his own way, deeply believed. The building is divided into two boxes, filled with light,
essentially scaleless, marvelously static. But in Venturi's house the gable rises, opens,
lifts. It is at once more sculpturally active and more like a house than are Kahn's flat-
roofed boxes.

Venturi thus exploits and interweaves the two ways whereby we experience all
works of art: physically and through association. They affect us empathetically, through
our bodies, and associationally, through everything we know from our cultural coding.
Venturi also exploits here the ancient tradition of Platonic order embodied in the essential shapes of triangle, circle, and square. The human figure fitted in the circle and the 12.15
square constitutes the most obsessive image of Western architectural theory. It derives
from a passage in Vitruvius, which surely has much older, probably Pythagorean, sources
behind it. The circle and the square become the basis for Gothic and Renaissance architecture alike and, as ideally dematerialized by Le Corbusier, for the International Style as
well. Venturi uses them as the cosmic emblem of his little house. He centers the square 18.1
void, broken at the top, and around it he draws his circle, broken upward as well and
extended by projection into the earth. The scale becomes enormous, and in the center of
it all Venturi's mother sits in a kitchen chair with a pot of geraniums at her feet. The

ABOVE, LEFT: Louis I. Kahn. Esherick House, Chestnut Hill, Pennsylvania, 1959–61. Exterior 15.3

ABOVE, CENTER: El Lissitzky. *Beat the Whites with the Red Wedge,* 1919 15.4

ABOVE, RIGHT: Aldo Rossi. *The Cabanas of Elba,* 1973 15.5

naked male hero, Leonardo da Vinci's emperor of the universe, has been superceded by a feminist image—one not shrill but wry and quiet. Aggression gives way to affection. The associational references encompass most of human history.

It can come as no surprise that Venturi has played a critical part in the liberation of women in architecture, not only in his relationship with his partner and wife, Denise Scott Brown, but in all his attitudes to women as students and as members of his staff. He has wholly abandoned the heroic, macho stance characteristic of so many architects in the recent past and has incorporated more civilized principles into the life of his firm and into his architecture.

Along with that has come a larger liberation for men and women alike: a liberation from the romantic conception of the architect as the perennial inventor of the wheel. Modernism, and late modernism in particular, was rent to incoherence by the insistence of its practitioners upon "originality," not only because it gave rise to every kind of schizoid behavior in the concealment of sources even from the self, but also and more seriously because of the primitive assault upon the urban fabric to which the search for originality gave rise. This is the major source of the hatred with which the architectural profession fell upon Venturi: he took its most satisfying, its most childish myth away. But in doing so, Venturi profoundly rationalized and civilized the profession. Rational discourse, though rare, now became possible as it replaced the crude, shouted slogans of the recent past. Even disagreement could be imagined. When asked about some students at Princeton University who had criticized his work, Venturi said in effect, "Sure, why not. It's only architecture, not religion."

At the same time, Venturi has revived modernism in its essential aspects. He goes back beyond the Bauhaus to the most intense moments of modernism when it really wanted to say something, to change the world politically as in every other way. For Venturi, the political dimension is there only by analogy, but much the same excitement, the physical liveliness, the desire to communicate, is present. El Lissitzky's revolutionary poster of 1919, *Beat the Whites with the Red Wedge*, can be compared to Venturi's 15.4 house in its use of a broken circle and its explosive, sharp-edged forms. And though Venturi did not use words in this project, as El Lissitzky does in his poster, he was soon to do so.

But, in house architecture especially, Venturi was also about to look more closely at tradition. His mother's house is very modernist in the sense that it looks abstract, indeed like a model; Venturi abandons in it the shingles that Wright had used. In the Trubek and Wislocki Houses of 1970–71 on Nantucket Island, however, he turns more 12.38 directly to the Shingle Style, with which, of course, he had been deeply involved since his Beach House project. For Venturi, the two houses are also like the Greek temples at Selinus, Sicily, as they turn slightly in toward each other above the sea. Like Greek temples, they are also types—here simple, more or less transformed, vernacular types. The Wislocki House on the right is, particularly, the essence of shack and of vertical standing body. Those two qualities have similarly been appreciated by Aldo Rossi who, without contact with Venturi, has employed exactly the same shapes. In Rossi's drawing, *The Cabanas of Elba* of 1975, they are like little people, active and proud, rather hectic in their 15.5 competition with each other, each staring with the cyclopean eye of a circular window in its gable.

The Wislocki House is like that: we feel it standing; we sense a person. It, too, has eyes—made with the crossed mullions in the square windows. A crossed mullion prevents the window from becoming a pure void—it winks and keeps to the surface. It also has, hauntingly back in behind it somewhere, the empathetic association of the Cross itself. Rossi uses it that way with great effect in his Elementary School of 1972–76 at Fagnano Olona, and elsewhere, as in the Teatro del Mondo of 1979. What a lovely little 12.37 building the Teatro del Mondo is, balancing itself on its barge like a top-heavy Shalako; it has all the curious innocence of a primitive type, as does the Wislocki House.

In any event, it is clear that Rossi and Venturi alike are dealing with vernacular and classical traditions in very lively ways. If we start with Wright's Hillside Home School of 1887 at Spring Green, Wisconsin, built two years before Wright's own house, we find a perfect Froebel triangle, a classical gable shape with a half-round window in it. Below the triangle is a bay, and in the bay is a big, overscaled, cross-mullioned, vernacular window. This can be compared to one of Rossi's most famous architectural studies, surely done without knowledge of Wright's work, where we look through a window out on the city, with our coffeepot echoed out there in the buildings, and we see facing us Rossi's fountain of 1965 for his City Hall Square at Segrate: a little cylinder which supports a perfect triangle. The open windows employ Wright's thin, cross-axis mullions. Both Wright and Rossi use the same archetypal forms, at once vernacular and classical in their history.

In the Trubek House, Venturi takes Wright's bay but chamfers only one side of it. He retains the half-round window in the gable's face but moves the vernacular window, with its cross mullions, around to the side and explodes its scale. The house does not simply "face"—it pivots and breathes. The power in all this depends upon the existence

ABOVE, LEFT: Robert A. M. Stern. Wiseman House, Montauk, New York, 1966–67. Exterior 15.6

ABOVE, RIGHT: Robert A. M. Stern. Mercer House, East Hampton, New York, 1973–75. Exterior 15.7

of the type itself, just as it did in Greek temples. That is how real individuality is made manifest—it can only be felt in comparison with a norm. So the Trubek and Wislocki Houses become lively animals, like the cabanas in Rossi's drawing; they are two active creatures, with porches like beaks, one thin, one fat, both about to jump as they perch above the sea.

Venturi's movement toward traditional architecture, especially toward the Shingle Style, has been very important for subsequent American work. Robert Stern was Venturi's first imitator, as he was one of his first critical supporters. In terms of artistic influence, it is interesting that Stern snuck up on Venturi from the rear when he adapted
15.6, 18.4 the back of the Vanna Venturi House for the front of his Wiseman House of 1966–67. He stretched the forms and turned the little flattened arch into a big arch and the slit in the wall into a crevasse. It is all very tormented. Stern was still trying to be original in a late modernist way. He was therefore trying to change his source as much as he could.

15.7 In the Mercer House of 1973, Stern turned, as had Venturi, to the Shingle Style itself, specifically to a house of 1880–81 by Arthur Little, called Shingleside. This had been an important house in its time; it was published in the English *Building News* in 1882 and clearly had some effect in England upon people like C. F. A. Voysey. Stern's house may not look much like Shingleside, but it does have its rounded bay, its porches with their high posts, and its play of the curved against the flat surface. It is all there but, oh, how deformed. Then Stern began to learn something that architects at that time most needed to learn, which was that the closer one gets to the type, to the tradition, the stronger the building is going to be—especially where it counts: in those relationships of everything to everything else out of which the whole human settlement is made. So Stern went on to work his way back to the type, again to the Low House and to Venturi's own beginning in the Beach House project of 1959. But Stern, along with Allan Greenberg in his somewhat different way, has been much more literal than Venturi in his movement toward tradition. He has most of all tried to learn how to build and to detail in a traditional

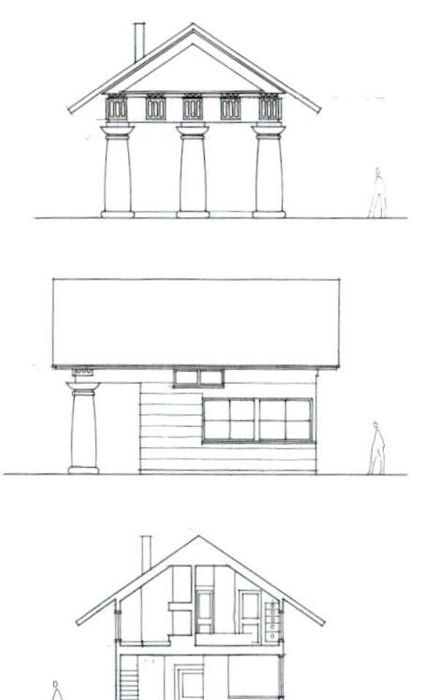

15.8 ABOVE, LEFT: Venturi and Rauch. Coxe and Hayden Houses, Block Island, Rhode Island, 1979–82. Exterior

15.9 ABOVE, RIGHT: Venturi and Rauch. Basic Tuscan Doric House, from Eclectic House Series project, 1977–78. Front elevation, side elevation, and section

way. "God is in the details," Mies van der Rohe once said, and Stern has learned how to put it all together with those details that have always been right there in the lumber yard but which modernist architects would not use. Stern would like to learn how to do traditional architecture without, as he says, "caricature."

But not Venturi. He is caught, right now, between the modernists who will not forgive him and the postmodernists who feel that he does not go far enough. Venturi will never make a building without a comment, without something in it that can only be of now. It is not a sense of the zeitgeist which directs him—not a feeling of being limited by the present, but rather of being liberated by it to comment as he desires. In this, what power he has. None of the others, the literalists, has that power, but Venturi directs it always toward a contextual end.

Venturi's Coxe and Hayden Houses of 1979–82 on Block Island show that. How 15.8
stark they are as they look out toward the sea. One is tight and closed, but in the other, the wall of the whole bottom floor is ripped out and glazed. They are presences; they have an emotional content, special to themselves. But they are also Block Island to the life.

Having identified the gable type, Venturi obviously believed that he could do whatever he wanted with it as the context suggested. That leap of the imagination is also anti–International Style. One of the many contradictory ideas of the International Style was its conviction that there could be only one correct solution to any problem. Architecture was a matter of solutions—you solved the puzzle, like Miss Marple. Probably nothing so half-baked has ever stunted architectural thought as this conviction, or been so wholly false to the way the mind works, or to the ways in which art occurs. Nevertheless, this was the bottom line of academic criticism. That, for example, is why Michael Graves was hated so much by the "modern" architects when he won the competition of 1980 for the Portland Building in Portland, Oregon. They, like their counterparts now in New York who are attacking his proposed addition to Marcel Breuer's Whitney Museum, were annoyed by drawings in which Graves showed many different "solutions,"

Venturi and Rauch. Brant House, Greenwich, Connecticut, 1970–73. Exterior 15.10

all more or less equally valid, each absolutely different, as all works of art are different. I am sure that Graves was emboldened to do that in part by Venturi's earlier example.

On the other hand, when Venturi gets into the tension between forms, which is a consequence of working with and changing the past, he always seems to realize that he is dealing with one basic issue which, in Western civilization, and perhaps especially in America, has been the interaction between the vernacular and the classical traditions. Thomas Jefferson understood that interaction perfectly, and his buildings—like Monticello of 1768–1809—are eloquent explorations of the ways in which big, over-scaled classical elements can hold a vernacular structure, including the special demands of the program, together. From this struggle comes a wonderful vitality. When Jefferson got around to the side of Monticello, he did what he would not do at the front: he let windows break, gasping, through the classical entablature. In his little project for a Greek Revival
15.9 house, the "Basic Tuscan Doric" from the Eclectic House Series project of 1978, Venturi says exactly the same thing. Here is his comment on the great American Dream, a pure temple that is adjusted to ourselves. The colossal columns step forward, but little windows pop out at the side, up in the entablature, so that the rooms behind them can breathe. That tension, most eloquently embodied here, is a living one.

Venturi has sometimes been called a tool of the capitalist system by European
15.10 critics, and the Brant House of 1970–73 in Greenwich, Connecticut, was indeed designed for a capitalist who made a lot of money out of paper. The house is very green, like new money. Venturi makes this capitalist enter through the garage, which Venturi calls "a beautiful garage," to reach a beautiful formal staircase. The client did not like it very much and finally decided to expand it and not enter through the garage. So in 1977–78, Venturi prepared an addition to the house that remains one of his grandest and most sophisticated designs. A bit reminiscent of Lutyens and having the true ease of an English country house, it found no favor with the client.

15.11 ABOVE, LEFT: Venturi and Rauch. (Second) Brant House project ("Mount Vernon"), 1978–79. Front elevation

15.12 ABOVE, RIGHT: Venturi and Rauch. (Second) Brant House project. Plan

The client wanted something that linked him more solidly to the great American tradition, especially the part of it that was related to horses; so he got Allan Greenberg to design a Mount Vernon on an adjoining piece of property in Greenwich. 12.45 Greenberg made a very big Mount Vernon, one which is grander and heavier and more regular than the original and which has many more and richer classical details. The client made him take off the cupola; that hurt the building a good deal. Philip Johnson supported the client's desire to stand the building on a terrace—which cuts off the base of the columns from the approach and hurts the building even more.

All of this infuriated Venturi. For him, the touching and important thing about George Washington's Mount Vernon of 1740–87 was that it, like Jefferson's architecture, was all tangled up with being just a farmhouse and wanting to possess a classical stance. One problem came in wanting to center the pediment over the door, which is not quite in the center, with the result that the windows are off, as is the cupola. In his Mount Vernon project of 1979 for Greenwich, Venturi said, "Well, we'll center the pedi- 15.11 ment right under the cupola and center the windows under that," but then the door slides off—way off. On the other side, he lets the windows peek-a-boo behind the columns. And he works out a really witty plan where the Palladian wings are all pulled 15.12 together into a sort of ranch house. All has been changed and subverted. Venturi remains a great planner; it is the root of all his work. His design is clearly more witty than Greenberg's, and more lively. Can we say that he makes the idea of Mount Vernon more palatable, more reasonable, more fun in terms of modern life? Surely Greenberg's Mount Vernon, for all its many solid qualities, is a rather inflated affair; Venturi's is endearing, as is the original in its own way.

In general, the comments introduced by Venturi into his buildings have a sweetness and a gentleness about them that no other architect touches today. The Flint 15.13 House of 1978 stands for his work. It overlooks a cornfield. On the ground floor is a solid row of wonderfully mullioned windows, while up above a much bigger window in the gable is masked by an open arch. The arch is not arbitrary; it conceals the enormous change of scale that is taking place in the upper window. Behind the windows on the

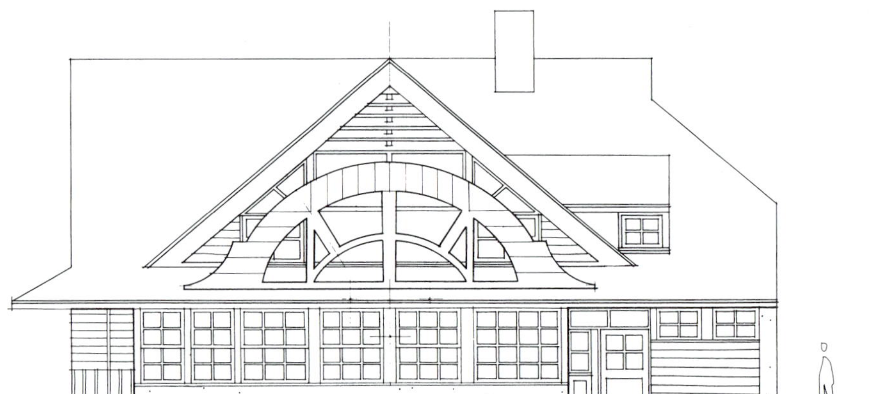

15.13 Venturi and Rauch. Flint House, Greenville, Delaware, 1978–80. East (front) elevation

ground floor is a long, tiled room, a hall full of light. It is as simple as can be—a big farmhouse room in which, in fact, some of Venturi's own furniture would go very well. Here again Venturi has been a pioneer in the extension of modern design. His furniture, like his architecture, is simple and full of life, and it combines empathetic and associational characteristics. In his chairs, for example, Venturi combines the modern, molded plywood of Alvar Aalto with profiles and patterns that are directly reminiscent of specific period styles. Perhaps the most effective is his version of the Queen Anne style, since it reflects at once the most sculptural, the most comfortable, and the most intensely American of chairs. Covered with a pattern that Venturi calls "grandmother's tablecloth," it begins to radiate the "sweetness and light" that Mark Girouard ascribed to the Queen Anne style in his book *Sweetness and Light: The 'Queen Anne' Movement, 1860–1900* (1977).

Above the hall, lighted by the window that is masked from the outside, a music room fills the gable of the house. Its decoration says "music," with the wonder of a child—all cut out and painted. It is a good deal like the chairs—flat and cookie-cut and with a special, lyrical, almost childlike freshness.

12.46 The other side of the house is screened by great Doric columns cut flat. Curiously enough, their unusual forms are the result of an extremely rational process. It would seem that Venturi first wanted to have big, round, Greek Revival columns. Then he changed his mind, apparently because true columns would have done two things: taken up too much space and broken up the basic unity of the house, which is that of a wall—the thin shell of the American house—that encloses a space. Moreover, by flattening the columns he could make them much broader, so that they become at once more monumental and more like a wall. They no longer fight with the containment of the house volume as a whole. This columned facade should be seen from the woods directly behind the house. The columns are seen from below as they rise up and pull out from the vernacular shell. It is Jefferson all over again: the common structure and the classical dream.

Venturi's bigger buildings are all studies in similar condensations, and they are
15.14 all specifically contextual as well. We start with the Guild House of 1960–63 in Philadel-

15.14 Venturi and Rauch (with Cope and Lippincott). Guild House, Philadelphia, 1960–66. Main facade

phia, and Louis Kahn's "Brick Order." That "Order" represented a purposeful misread- 12.36
ing by Kahn of the Roman relieving arch over its wood lintel as he had been shown it by Frank Brown at Ostia and elsewhere. Kahn turned it around to make the horizontal lintel a concrete tension member which holds the arch together. It is highly structural, very taut, very tense. Venturi adapted that "Order" in the Guild House, but he in turn misread it all in order to gesture with the brick surface past the structural frame. Venturi separated the two, and that is what makes the gesture of the surface so eloquent: we can sense its separation from the frame as it moves across the frame. Kahn's effects are structural, Venturi's dramatic.

This is the kind of difference that Kahn could never forgive in Venturi because it instantly subverts Kahn's hard-won, agonized structuralism and turns it into a gesture of humanistically conceived dramatic power. Venturi thus moves toward what the 1960s would call a "semiotic" architecture. From the beginning, he is the architect of the sign in every sense of the word. The facade of the Guild House is pure sign since it overrides though by no means denies the structural considerations. Again, we cannot help but feel that this was the kind of thing that encouraged Graves to clad the structure of his
Portland Building with a totally independent surface. 12.44

The Guild House also seems to show a knowledge of the great housing projects, especially those by Michael de Klerk, which were built in Amsterdam in the teens and
11.19 twenties but which the International Style had ignored. In Michael de Klerk's third Eigen Haard Housing Estate of 1917–20, there is a big column on the street and a lower zone of a different color, like a water line, as if de Klerk were celebrating the return of the tide or suggesting a ship's plimsoll line. The complex is also like a train, with the Post Office the engine, but it invokes the ship image as well. Venturi takes the column and makes it black, and then, with the crenellated brick above, goes beyond de Klerk to the paintings of Vermeer. He invokes only a few of the innumerable connections that the human brain makes between the inexhaustible cultural items with which it is furnished. His work resonates with memory as it calls up centuries of time, including the immediate past.

15.4 El Lissitzky also reappears, and now Venturi's white and red planes are joined by words. How the planning authority in Philadelphia hated Venturi's sign: they wanted "Guild House" to appear in little gilt letters about the size of a brick. Venturi instead achieves a scale that is at once nobly Roman and brashly modern. He revives modernism's passion from the days before the Bauhaus denatured it, took out the words, eliminated the exuberance, and turned it into what the Museum of Modern Art was so destructively to call "Good Design"—modern art with the sting taken out. Venturi's sign is not political but aesthetic. Nevertheless, it breaks through the gentrification of modernism and taps the revolutionary sources of modernism's life.

Most of all, the Guild House is a great frontal gesture, one which reminds us of other great buildings of the 1920s and 1930s, which the International Style had totally ignored. Even the Marxist critics, perhaps they in particular, had refused to honor Karl
11.21 Ehn's Karl-Marx-Hof of 1927–28 in Vienna, that ultimate fortress of *Rote Wien* which fell before the assault of the right wing in 1934. Everything about it expresses solidarity, defiance, triumphal communal living. Its meaning is expressly political. Venturi had no such program to fulfill and so, instead, made an ironic gesture that invokes a painful memory. The facade of the Guild House does not rush up to lift the flags of Vienna and the Socialist Party. It rises to what Venturi called a television aerial. In fact, it was not a television aerial; that essential piece of equipment is in reality a messy little thing hidden behind the chimney. This is an abstract piece of sculpture. Everyone would have applauded if Venturi had said: "This is by the great Hungarian abstract sculptor so-and-so; it is called 'Man's Hope' and represents the triumphal union of art and architecture." But Venturi *called* it a television aerial and the critics went mad with rage. References to the old folks watching television were not regarded by them as genteel. Something about jogging would have been okay, one supposes, or perhaps a representation of Ivan Ilyich in extremis. Louis Kahn told the mayor of New Haven that he would not trust an architect who put a television aerial on top of his building. He and the other critics were speaking out of the ideal stance that modernism affected; Venturi was trying to deal with the real, and with the compassion that only irony can handle. He is wholly an artist, and his primary concern is to increase the aesthetic intensity of everyone's reaction to his building. And he did; where there might have been apathy or pro forma approbation, there was at

least concern. The aerial was later removed and the building misses it badly, but it was part of a decade of research by Venturi into how the reaction of human beings to architecture might be intensified and enriched.

The very basis of that reaction is physical empathy turned loose to perceive the power of everyday things around us. I remember how moved I was when I first saw the Guild House, with its big, square windows. The power was there, as it is in Rossi's work. It is the power of the vernacular and the contextual—heightened and geometricized. Those windows and the brick wall and the little stringcourse all derive from the way every old building used to be built, but they are now made more conscious, stronger. "Main Street [is] almost all right," Venturi said in *Complexity and Contradiction in Architecture* (1966). "Almost." It can be made better, yet it is a viable architectural structure that is not to be outraged or destroyed. Louis Kahn, by contrast, inhabited an ideal world. His buildings on
the Indian subcontinent, his Government Center in Dhaka, Bangladesh, begun in 1962, 17.27
are perfect in this regard. There they are, timeless, scaleless, structural beings of wonderful silence, with a monumentality that transcends function or place. But Venturi's rather similar forms stand right there on the street. Clarified and ennobled, they signify the presence of dignified human beings in the American mainstream.

The most intense and enduring hatred toward Venturi developed when he wrote, with Denise Scott Brown and Steven Izenour, *Learning from Las Vegas* (1972) and designed his architecture of the signboard: an architecture to attract our attention from our automobiles, an architecture to be seen from the fast-moving street. Critics like Kenneth Frampton, who has a deep and obsessive dislike of Venturi, called this kind of architecture "cynical populism." For Frampton, populism means, basically, American. It also means something not of the European avant-garde; something vulgar, which somehow plays into the hands of American capitalism by imitating the signs of the strip.

Venturi is neither populist nor cynic. The facade of his Fire Station No. 4 of 12.39
1965–67, for example, when compared with the signs of Las Vegas, is not at all like them. It is abstracted and clarified: it is modern architecture strengthening something "almost all right." It is modern architecture that, like Konstantin Melnikov's Constructivist Soviet Pavilion of 1924–25, wants to project information, to shout that this is the mighty Engine Number 4, which is ready to explode through the doorway to do battle with the flames. The white brick of the Fire Station cuts across the functional areas (the windows of which are all different according to the needs of the rooms) to rush up to the big number 4, grand in scale and triumphantly projected. Frampton has nothing against the Soviet Pavilion; why should he against this? There is nothing cynical or even capitalist about a fire station. In fact, Venturi's building was designed well before he did his study of Las Vegas. That research came after he had perceived its possibilities through works like this.

Venturi's most important project in this regard may well be his project of 1967
for the Football Hall of Fame, which he called a "Bill-Ding-Board." The automobiles were 15.15
intended to drive up and park in great waves. In front of them, beyond a wonderfully classic *parterre d'eau*, Venturi raised the great billboard facade, which would electronically

Venturi and Rauch. National Football Hall of Fame project, Piscataway, New Jersey, 1967. Model 15.15

and rather improbably show Princeton beating Pennsylvania. Behind it, reached through a low, spreading arch at the base of this semiotic marvel, were the exhibition halls where,
12.42 among other things, lasers would conjure up figures out of thin air, three-dimensional images hurtling through space. There can be little doubt that the art of illusion, the art of the television screen and of electronic fantasy, will play a considerable role in the architecture of the future, much as painting and sculpture did in the architecture of the past. In any case, Venturi's billboard became the model for what Piano and Rogers intended to build at the Pompidou Center in Paris (1977). They hoped to complete the building with a great electronic screen, like Venturi's, but it was cut out of the budget. It could only have added to the wonderful vitality of the plaza in front of it, and might have proved more durable than the exposed science-fiction structure of the building, which now seems to be well on the way to falling apart.

12.41 Venturi's project of 1969 for the Thousand Oaks Civic Center in California, a competition he did not win, is also a vast sign. One first glimpses it from afar on the freeway; coming closer but still far away, one sees that it says "THOUSAND OAKS" at a great scale. A colossal American flag, supported on the famous false front of the American western town, crowns the complex. Venturi clearly understands how we see
15.16 things on the American freeway, in American space. Closer yet, the sign says "SAND OAK" and looms overhead.

One cannot talk properly about Venturi without spending a good deal of time on things he was never able to build, competitions he did not win. The Franklin D. Roosevelt Memorial project of 1960 for Washington, D.C., was one of the first—a superb landscape space. Then, much later in his career, the Westway Development project of 1980–84 for New York City (I never thought I'd be rooting for a throughway)—a noble
15.17 urban park. Or the Brighton Beach Housing competition of 1968 for Brooklyn, New York, where he projected a splendid series of apartments, all of which had a view of the

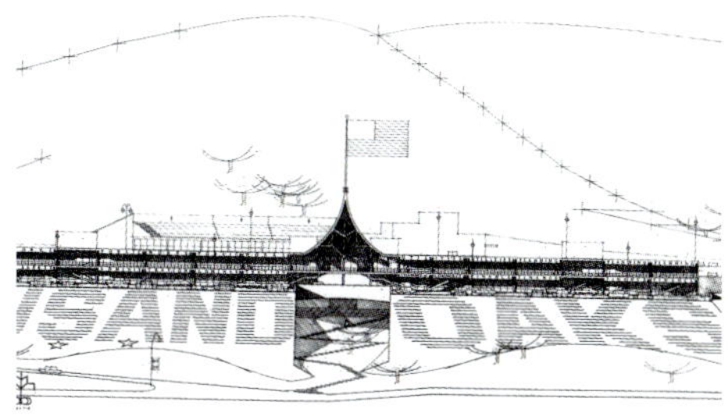

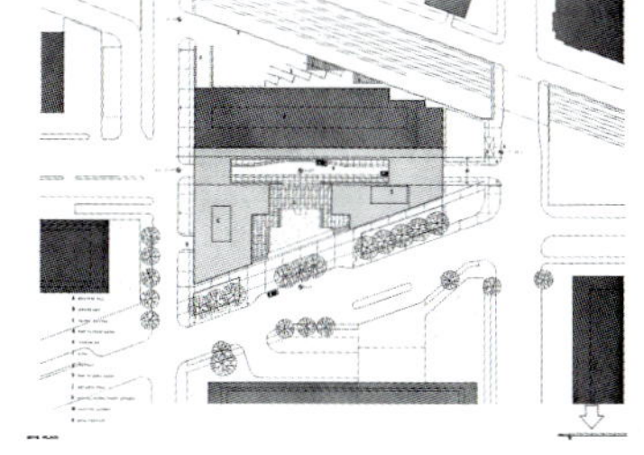

15.16 ABOVE, TOP LEFT: Venturi and Rauch. Thousand Oaks Civic Center project, Thousand Oaks, California, 1969. Elevation detail

15.17 ABOVE, TOP RIGHT: Venturi and Rauch. Brighton Beach Housing project, Brooklyn, 1967–68. Model

15.18 ABOVE, BOTTOM LEFT: Venturi and Rauch (with Caudill Rowlett Scott). Transportation Square Office Building project, Washington, D.C., 1967. Perspectives toward Capitol and east along Interior Way

15.19 ABOVE, BOTTOM CENTER: Venturi and Rauch (with Caudill Rowlett Scott). Transportation Square Office Building project. Plan

15.20 ABOVE, BOTTOM RIGHT: Venturi and Rauch. Mathematics Building project, Yale University, New Haven, Connecticut, 1969. Perspective

water—as did the old apartments on the street behind the project. The winning entry by Wells and Koetter was a pastiche after Le Corbusier, Kahn, and Giurgola. It blocked everybody's view with tormented shapes and finally could not be built. But the jury was profoundly swayed by Philip Johnson's negative opinion, when he said, in effect: "Why, Venturi's project looks like any old apartment building you see around New York." Two years later, when he wanted to build on Welfare Island, Johnson had decided that "I want my building to look like any old building around New York," because, being quick on the uptake, he had come to know by that time what the score really was.

Or again, Venturi's Transportation Square Office Building project of 1967, was 15.18, 15.19
blocked by the Washington Fine Arts Commission, headed by Gordon Bunshaft, after it had won first prize in the competition. The important building in that project was, of course, the big one with the dome on it at the end of Maryland Avenue, and there was also a preexisting office building across the street. Venturi's building responded to those two buildings, at once complementing its neighbor and directing attention down the avenue toward the Capitol. Behind its front plane, a lively shopping street was to have been concealed—Main Street brought into context. The commission refused to approve the design. Venturi cited Alvar Aalto as a precedent, and the setback of his design is in fact a lot like Aalto's National Pensions Institution Building of 1952–56 in Helsinki, Finland. Bunshaft reportedly said: "It's an insult that you should mention Alvar Aalto's name, Venturi. You're not worthy to mention Alvar Aalto's name in this context. What we're gonna have here is a building that stands in the center of space with space all around it." So Venturi, to save the developer's money, designed what Bunshaft demanded, but he kidded him a little, maybe, by giving him a pattern on the pavement that was the same as the pattern on the building. Bunshaft's committee did not like that either. Finally, Venturi came in with one they would accept—each project, of course,

somewhat less good than the first—but it was too late to build it and the developer had to withdraw for financial reasons; here was another project that Venturi did not get.

15.20 Another example is the Mathematics Building project of 1969 for Yale University, with which Venturi won an enormous competition as the unanimous choice of a large and varied jury led by Kevin Roche. This, too, was a contextual triumph on its street. Opening like a great gate up Prospect Street, it would have looked up the hill toward the science complex on the summit and marked the entrance to the humanities below. The building is shaped in a wonderful, gentle curve, very simple and strong, with the library marked by a monumental cross-mullioned window that opens generously up the street. Venturi won, but then the donor died, the building costs rose, and it was never built.

These disappointments make it especially appropriate that Venturi's alma mater backs him so strongly now. The president of Princeton University has become his
15.1 most enthusiastic supporter since he built Gordon Wu Hall. I have since been saddened by Robert Stern's negative remarks about this building. He calls it "sly" (in a strange television series called *Pride of Place*) when it is in fact strong and decisive, splendid with its older Tudor neighbors, and powerful in its commentary on the relationship between skeletal and bearing-wall forms. The stretch of surface, the expansion joints brought down through phantom keystones which are themselves spread nonstructurally across the wall, all emphasize the dynamic tensions which can be felt to exist in a cladding wall that must, for fundamental architectural reasons, play a civic and intelligent role in a university's special kind of urban context. The abstracted Tudor gateway further emphasizes those relationships. Here is Venturi's inveterate contextuality, foreign to the egos of most architects: the preexisting buildings on the site shape his, which then improves them.

Venturi has often lost projects for the very worst of all reasons—for P.R. reasons. He does not sell himself as well as many architects do. When it comes to the sharkskin-suited phase, with the illuminated models, he really is an anti-hero and just cannot do it. He comes across as being too off-hand, as if he were not trying hard enough. It is really a question of taste and propriety. When, for example, the Best Products competition to decorate its outlets on the strip came up, Venturi was not in the
15.21 competition. But he had, in 1977, designed one of the buildings, for Oxford Valley, Pennsylvania. All he did was put a kind of flowered wallpaper on it. I remember one of those noncritics in one of those awful pseudo-European periodicals saying, in effect: "Here's an example of a great opportunity lost. Venturi might have done something like the others, like Stern and Graves, and he just didn't rise to the occasion." The others rose all right. Robert Stern did a project with which I should be pleased because he called it "The Earth, the Temple and the Goods." But still, the mind asks: "Why all those scary columns, that Sicilian pediment? It's only Best Products, after all." Michael Graves produced a vast stoa, with solemn columns enclosing a majestic forum. Again the mind asks why. What these projects lack is the old classical virtue of decorum, of propriety. The program simply could not support such whoop-de-do without embarrassment. It is ridiculous to try to turn Best Products into a monstrous temple or a colonnaded

15.21 RIGHT, TOP: Venturi and Rauch. Best Products Showroom, Oxford Valley Mall, Langhorne, Pennsylvania, 1977. Exterior

15.22 RIGHT, BOTTOM: Venturi and Rauch. Institute for Scientific Information, Philadelphia, 1977–79. Exterior

garden. All you can properly do is wallpaper it. And how beautiful Venturi's building is, how the pattern so easily takes off, far beyond Stern's gestures, to rise out of the earth and slide up to the sky. Its virtues are in the end classical ones.

The same is true for a computer building, Venturi's Institute for Scientific 15.22
Information of 1978 in Philadelphia. The facade, seen alone, looks like a computer printout, as if Venturi were being either cute or too off-hand. But when seen in the context of its street, which is made up of long, modernist horizontals, the facade enriches the whole environment of the street and enforces its intrinsic order—and it does so without trying to be anything it really is not. It is another act of propriety. Venturi knows beyond all else when to hold back. Almost no other living architect has the perception, or the modesty, to be able to do that. And here the context was International Style.

Most architects today design only surfaces; it is a tradition that goes back to
Louis Sullivan's skyscrapers. One of Venturi's surfaces is on the Lewis Thomas Labora- 15.23
tory for Molecular Biology of 1983–85 at Princeton University. The first reaction of everyone who has seen it is to hate it. This is the building which aroused the distaste of the Princeton students to whom I referred earlier. Here is an architect who is still able to

ABOVE: Venturi, Rauch and Scott Brown. Lewis Thomas Laboratory for Molecular Biology, Princeton University, Princeton, New Jersey, 1983–85. Elevation 15.23

LEFT: Venturi, Rauch and Scott Brown. Khulafa Street Building project, Baghdad, 1981. Model 15.24

shock us after all these years, who pushes our perceptions to the limit so that we almost always pull back at first. (Nothing attests more to Venturi's unerring instinct for life than this.) Look at how dense that surface is, how passionately dense as Venturi keeps the mullioned windows small, almost solid. Then he stretches a fat, round ogive over the entrance without any supporting column. This has guts to it. Everything that is strong will always, like the outrageous chimney of the Beach House project, make us angry at first. We have to protect our little worlds, do we not?

I have been hard on the International Style in this talk, but Venturi's project of
15.24 1981 for the Khulafa Street Building in Baghdad is in the International Style, a building to be built out of cast-in-place concrete with just a little lacy stuff to make it Islamic. It is pretty good and could shape a good Iraqi street. In fact, the president of Iraq loved Venturi's work, and if the war with Iran had not intervened, a good deal of it would probably have been built. Venturi's astonishing project of 1983 for the State Mosque in Baghdad was the major casualty. Though it did not win the competition, it was liked best
15.25 by the president. There is a most astoundingly grave gesture on the inside, where the infinity of God is carried on vast beams made up of open and visually weightless arches—below the springing of those arches, all the columns have been removed. It is as "modern" as the reaction of the Bauhaus designer who wanted to span the Johnson Wax

15.25 Venturi, Rauch and Scott Brown (with Ali Mousawi). State Mosque of Iraq project, Baghdad, 1982–83. Interior perspective

Building with a single beam—except that in Venturi's mosque every column is somehow present, a ghostly company miraculously phantomized. At the same time, there is gentleness everywhere. All the surfaces are decorated and show care, even love. This is the commodity with which Venturi deals. For a man who has rejected heroic pretensions and turned architects toward a more civil role, Venturi is surprisingly complete. From his chairs to his mosque, from the Guild House to the Trubek and Wislocki Houses and Gordon Wu Hall, not to mention Times Square and Westway, Venturi touches the core of modesty and intelligence in all of us and endows the rather frightening monster of modern America with a curious sweetness of heart.

NEIL LEVINE

"Architecture: The Natural and the Manmade." In *Denatured Visions: Landscape and Culture in the Twentieth Century,* ed. Stuart Wrede and William Howard Adams. New York: The Museum of Modern Art, 1991.

Although Scully is known primarily as a historian and critic of modern architecture, his main areas of research from the mid-1950s through the early 1980s were, first, ancient Greece, then the pueblos of the American Southwest, and, finally, the classical garden of seventeenth-century France. The theme underlying all these projects was the relationship between architecture and the natural environment, which became the subject of Scully's synoptic book *Architecture: The Natural and the Manmade,* published by St. Martin's Press in 1991. The grand historical synthesis of that work is epitomized in the essay of the same title reprinted here.

It was in the early 1980s that Scully first brought this large body of material together in lecture form. Its initial appearance in print came as a six-part series in the monthly column "Architecture in Context" that he contributed to *Architectural Digest* (September 1984–February 1985). This version is based on the lecture he presented in the symposium "Landscape and Architecture in the Twentieth Century," held at New York's Museum of Modern Art in the fall of 1988. A general reawakening of interest in landscape architecture—signaled, in part, by the creation in 1981 of the *Journal of Garden History*—occurred in the mid- to late 1970s on the heels of the movement in art toward site-specific sculpture and Earthworks that accompanied the growing concern for ecological issues. The MoMA symposium was organized by the museum's director of the Department of Architecture and Design, Stuart Wrede (a former student of Scully's), and the landscape

16

Architecture: The Natural and the Manmade

VINCENT SCULLY

The way human beings see themselves in relation to nature is fundamental to all cultures; thus the first fact of architecture is the natural world, the second is the relationship of human structures to the topography of the world, and the third is the relationship of all these structures to each other, comprising the human community as a whole. The question of the relationship of the manmade to the natural world is especially germane today for many reasons. The most obvious and surely the most important one is the threat to the existence of the natural environment itself that many kinds of human structures now pose. The second, perhaps less cataclysmic but closely related, is the general failure of canonical "modern" architecture to work out any set of relationships to nature that are special to itself. Modernism cast aside the lessons of the French classical tradition of garden design and urbanism with which earlier twentieth-century masters, like Sir Edwin Lutyens, were able to do so much and settled, generally, for watered-down versions of other relationships, such as those worked out in the English Romantic garden or in the architecture of ancient religions: in the case of Frank Lloyd Wright's late work, for example, that of Pre-Columbian America; in Le Corbusier's, that of Greece.

historian William Howard Adams to examine the changing attitudes toward the "long-ignored subject" of the relationship between architecture and nature and to survey the most recent scholarship in the field. The organizers' premise was that "the aesthetics of the twentieth century . . . were fundamentally hostile to nature" and that "the modern movement had, on the whole, led to a divorce between architecture and nature." In the results published three years later in the volume *Denatured Visions: Landscape and Culture in the Twentieth Century*, they acknowledged that the symposium "was a confirmation of our original sense of crisis."

Scully was one of the five featured speakers at the two-day event who were asked to present broad overviews of the subject by placing it in historical perspective. John Dixon Hunt discussed the landscape garden since the Renaissance as a cultural construct; Robert Rosenblum surveyed the attitude of twentieth-century painters toward the depiction of nature; Kenneth Frampton examined the field of modern landscape design since the turn of the century; and Leo Marx spoke of the significance of the ideology of space in American intellectual history. All four talks generally ended on a rather negative note, describing modern culture as having become increasingly alienated from nature. Scully, whose talk opened the series and encompassed the largest chronological as well as geographical scope, was no different in this regard. On the other hand, he, as someone who had been at the forefront of the new landscape discourse—and profoundly committed to a contextualist approach to architecture—suggested that the very study of the past reveals the more positive "need to revive our traditions and begin again."

"Architecture: The Natural and the Manmade" looks at the history of building in the West as an aspect of man's conceptual and physical shaping of the landscape. The lens through which that history is seen is professedly a twentieth-century one. In their rejection of the recent past in favor of more primitive models, Frank Lloyd Wright and Le Corbusier are assumed to represent the two fundamentally opposed attitudes toward nature that

These two ways of relating to nature—the Pre-Columbian and the Greek—are in fact primordial opposites. In the first, manmade monumental structures imitate the shapes of nature: in the second, they contrast with them. Yet it is more accurate historically to say that the first approach seems to have been worldwide and to have characterized the way most human beings originally thought of the earth-man relationship, while the second was almost literally invented by Greece and has dominated world architecture, especially that of Europe, almost ever since. It is at once the glory of the modern age and its problem.

We who inhabit the American continent are especially fortunate to have a living culture which espouses the old way still active among us. I refer of course to the Pueblo people of the Southwest, in whom the ancient, non-Greek rituals and way of relating to nature are still wholly in force and can be read in their architecture. We also possess the great monuments of Mesoamerican civilization, where the operation of basically the same principle can still be seen. That principle is mimetic; it begins with imitation. At

originally determined how building and landscape interact. The first, characteristic of pre- or non-Greek cultures, is a mimetic, subservient one, in which the natural features of the landscape are echoed and made manifest in the architecture. The second, of Greek invention and characteristic of all those cultures deriving from the Hellenic tradition, is an abstract, confrontational one, in which the manmade building and the natural landscape are set in contrast to one another. In both, a belief in the sacredness of the natural environment informed and gave mythic power and meaning to the architectural whole. While the mimetic approach remained essentially unchanged over time and across cultures, the confrontational one slowly evolved in relation to the historical transformations of Western Europe until the seventeenth century, when a radical extension of its methodology took hold in the France of Louis XIV in response to the construction of the modern nation-state. The new symbiotic relation between building and landscape established itself at a regional and territorial scale that allowed it to serve, until the beginning of the twentieth century, as a successful model for a modern urbanism structured on the ideal order of nature. Although Scully acknowledges that it would be impossible simply to reengage with that tradition mindless of the other lessons to be learned from history, the prominence he gives to the planning of the French classical garden in the schema presented here attests to his growing support for the neotraditionalist New Urbanism that his former students Andres Duany and Elizabeth Plater-Zyberk had been proposing since the early 1980s.

Teotihuacán, surely the greatest religious center this continent has ever known, the so-
16.1 called Temple of the Moon lies at the end of the main ceremonial axis of the site, the Avenue of the Dead, and echoes with its shape the pyramidal form of the mountain that rises behind it. That mountain, called Tenan, "Our Lady of Stone," is running with springs; in order to help draw the water out of it, its pyramidal geometry is intensified in the temple into which strong horizontal lines of fracture, like the faults through which underground water seeps, are introduced. Human beings are part of nature, building nature's shapes, but they must assist the idle gods in their work: hence, human sacrifice, whereby men feed the natural machine with their blood. Exactly so is the mountain echoed and its hydraulic structure intensified.

16.2 The water goddess from Teotihuacán, now in Mexico City, can also show us that precisely this was intended. A great mass weighs down upon her head. It is notched in the center, exactly like the mountain above the temple. Its weight compresses her body, which compacts itself into horizontal lines of fracture, while water is squeezed out of her hands. The more or less *tablero* construction of her skirt is like that of the Temple of Quetzalcoatl at Teotihuacán. There the water from the earth and the water from the sky are squeezed out of the mountain, gushing forth in feathered serpent heads like so many fountains. The god of agriculture, the plumed serpent, the great divinity of the Americas, is thus drawn by human art out of nature's forms.

16.1 TOP LEFT: Temple of the Moon, Teotihuacán, before third century A.D. View down Avenue of the Dead

16.2 TOP RIGHT: Water Goddess, from Teotihuacán, before third century A.D.

16.3 BELOW, LEFT: Taos pueblo and Taos Mountain, New Mexico

16.4 BELOW, RIGHT: Temple I (Tomb of Ah Cacao), Tikal, C. A.D. 600–900

The same is true in any modern pueblo, most spectacularly and traditionally at Taos. Here the set-back profiles of the magnificent North House at once echo the horned 16.3
and stepped profiles of sacred Taos Mountain beyond it and abstract them into man-made cubes making a basically pyramidal form. Magically, it draws a life-giving stream out of the mountain and, from the side, stands five stories straight up to touch the sky. It is the Pueblo sky-altar, whose serrated profiles echo and abstract the shapes of the clouds. The same divinity is being evoked here as at Teotihuacán.

The ritual dances of the Pueblos still complete those relationships today. At Tesuque, a Tewa pueblo south of Taos, the profiles of the house of the governor pick up those of Lake Peak, the Sacred Mountain of the East, while the facade of the church, an intrusive European element, is shorn of its Hispanic towers so that it can repeat the conical profile of Old Baldy beyond it. In these ways the long horizontal profiles of the Sangre de Cristo range are reflected in the architectural forms and are further invoked by the long lines of dancers who pound the earth the whole day through, drawing the power of nature down into the pueblo, beating it into the plaza's dust.

From Teotihuacán to Taos and Tesuque—as from the Aztec's great Tenochtitlán to the Hopi towns—the major principle of imitation and intensification is everywhere the same. But at Tikal, in the classic Maya area, it might at first appear that the principle 16.4

does not apply. No mountains are visible. The temple bases are springy and high. Is a more man-centered principle at work, such as historians have always wished to discern in Maya art? Certainly the tall figure of Temple I suggests that of a standing, richly caparisoned priest-king, exactly like the king, Ah Cacao, buried within it. The shorter, squatter Temple II that faces it suggests the figure of Ah Cacao's queen, Lady Twelve Macaw, who is carved on its lintels and whose memorial it is. The royal couple is clearly there, king and queen facing each other. Yet the more general principle is at work as well, adjusted to the character of this site. The base of Temple I leaps high above the rain forest, as it once did above the houses of its town. The temple on the summit is built of concrete throughout, so that, unlike the temples of Mexico, it has survived the ages. Its interior is small and dank. When we climb up the steep stair to it in the heat we are greeted in the doorway by a wet rain breath, the very essence of its companion clouds, whose profiles its rich roof-comb amply enhances. It is one of the first skyscrapers of the Americas, literally scraping the clouds for rain.

Here the ziggurats of Mesopotamia come to mind. They, too, were manmade mountains, standing in the center of their cities, sacred mountains built down in the river basin where no mountains are. So they echo nothing. Hence their display is freer. They push out their masses, complicate the rhythmic variation of their setbacks, and in every way dramatize the heroic tread of the priest-king, like Gilgamesh, who mounted them as a conqueror and represented his people to the dangerous and capricious gods in the temple at the top. In the end, the only immortality Gilgamesh could count on was embodied in structures like these, and in the good, well-fired bricks out of which he built his city's walls.

At Sakkara in Egypt, at just about the same time, plenty of influence from Mesopotamia can be seen, including the manmade stepped mountain itself. There, however, the king did not climb the pyramid but was buried below it, and its massive presence was intended to ensure his immortality and to signal it from afar. Yet when the
16.5 pyramid is viewed from within the temenos at Sakkara at the place where a wall of cobras, recalling the serpents of Quetzalcoatl, is obviously positioned to focus a straight axial view of it, nothing whatever about it suggests three dimensions, as do the profiles of the Pre-Columbian temples and those of Mesopotamia as well. Our minds supply no other sides to it beyond the one we see. It becomes a stairway climbing away into the sky. In this it already exhibits a special Egyptian character, wherein the pyramid, the sacred mountain, will be adjusted to evoke not primarily the power of the earth but that of the
16.6 sky. That principle is completely exemplified at Giza. There the true pyramids slant their faces away from the viewer and disappear at a point in the sky. Nor, seeing the corner of a pyramid, do we supply it mentally with its two other sides, but with one only: we reduce it to a tetrahedron. Moreover, the pyramids at Giza were all sheathed in blazing white limestone, shining dazzlingly in the sky, as they were seen from the river valley below them. For all their actual mass, they were visually pure light—the light of Re, the sun, into whose boat the pharaohs were thus magically introduced by them. They were a battery in echelon, deployed high on a shelf of desert above the west bank of the Nile, the

16.5 ABOVE, LEFT: Pyramid complex of Zoser, Sakkara, c. 2600 B.C.

16.6 ABOVE, RIGHT: Pyramids of Chefren, Cheops, and Mycerinus, Giza, c. 2530–2460 B.C. Aerial view

side of sunset and death. They look east toward the morning sun; the Sphinx is the gunner. He wears his pharaoh's face. Multiple stone images of that pharaoh sat enthroned in the valley temple just below him. In them the king's head was held steady by the hawk, Horus, who alone could stare into the eye of the sun. So the Sphinx looks eastward unblinking, charging the whole great mechanism by focusing forever on the arising blinding brightness.

In these ways, Egypt and Mesopotamia built their own sacred mountains but employed their energies in wholly different directions. In Crete, during the same period of the third and second millennia B.C., we find a situation more like that which prevailed in the Americas. Once again the sacred mountains are right there in nature, and human architecture found a way to adjust to them based on much the same mimetic principle. In
Crete, it is true, there is much less direct imitation of the natural form: emphasis is placed 12.5
instead on the central courtyard, placed so as to be axially directed toward the sacred mountain and to receive its force. At Knossos, we are led to a stairway at the north end of the long court, beyond which rises Mount Jouctas, the home of the goddess of the earth, whose headdress is at once conical and horned, as is this mountain presence itself. It lies on the axis of the main south propylon of the palace, in the range of buildings behind which the throne room was placed. Here the king, perhaps bull-masked as Poseidon, received the earthquake tremors of the place seated on his quivering bucket-seated throne, draining the power of the goddess into the palace through his own body. At
Phaistos, where there was apparently no throne room, the axis of the court itself is directly 16.7
on the mountain and is celebrated by the unique engaged columns that flank the doorway from the court on that side. Here the bull dance, like those of the American Pueblos, took place under the mountain's own sanctifying horns, and both the natural form and the human ritual evoking it were visible to spectators who gathered on the flat roofs exactly as they do in the pueblos today. Indeed, the courtyards of Knossos and Puye above Santa Clara are almost exactly the same in conformation and mountain orientation, and the

ABOVE, LEFT: Palace, Phaistos, Crete, c. 1500 B.C. Central court, looking toward Mt. Ida 16.7

ABOVE, RIGHT: Temple of Athena, Paestum, c. 510 B.C. 16.8

darkly looming buffalo dancers of the latter strongly recall the charging bull in relief above the northern entrance of the former.

In later Greek myth the conical shape of Mount Jouctas suggested the shape of the Mycenaean tholos tomb (and may indeed have inspired the building of that shape in the first place), so that Mount Jouctas came to be identified as the place where the Cretan Zeus was buried, while Mount Ida above Phaistos, opening as it does into a wide set of horns, became the mountain where Zeus was born.

Enter the Greeks, who took over Knossos and Phaistos by 1400 B.C. Although they clearly reverenced the goddess of the earth and wanted to live under her protection, they were driven by other passions and traditions as well. Their gods were to be wholly in the shape of mankind and would eventually embody all the characteristics of human thought and behavior that could be realistically imagined by human beings. Therefore the Greek temple, once fully developed, cast off the age-old imitation of natural forms in favor of the evocation of the human presence in landscape. The latter was still sacred, too, normally marked as such by the same horned and conical mountain forms. Thus the box of the cella of the temple was enclosed by a peripteral colonnade suggesting the vertically standing bodies of human beings. Each column is like a Greek hoplite, a self-contained, impenetrable geometric figure densely massed with other such figures in a human phalanx so that the power of all is made to act as one. The temple becomes one
12.6 body. The Doric Temple of Hera at Paestum, to take a well-preserved example, is built not only to bring the conical hill inland into the goddess's view from the cella across her altar, but also, as seen in the landscape, to contrast with the conical hill, so presenting the viewer with two images, the new, humanly conceived image of Hera and the traditional landscape form. This becomes the essential structure of classical Greek thought: fate and free will, nature and man, in tragic confrontation and ultimate harmony. Hence, each Greek temple is different from every other temple, since each embodies the special character of its particular divinity. Yet the temples had to be enough alike so that absolute differences of character could be perceived in their forms, as is possible only
16.8 with creatures of the same species. So the Temple of Athena at Paestum is set on a slight rise and must be seen from below. Its columns are more slender than those of Hera and their point of entasis is high rather than low; therefore they are read as lifting briskly rather than as weighing heavily on the ground, like those of Hera's temple. Moreover, and

16.9 Sanctuary of Zeus, Olympia, 457 B.C. View from Temple of Zeus to Mt. Kronos

uniquely among Greek temples, the high pediment of Athena's temple never had a horizontal cornice, so that the whole body of the building lifts like Athena, the embodiment of the action of the polis, flourishing her aegis in defiance of the landscape forms. For the Greeks, from the very beginning, the hard edges of the city were a dangerous assault on nature, requiring the protection of the gods but certain to infuriate some among them.

At the same time, the columns of temples of Apollo of the same period have no entasis whatever. At Corinth they simply stand immovable, the phalanx of the Greek male god confronting nature's wildest natural forms. That defiance culminated at Delphi, under the Horns of the Phaedriades, where the columns of Apollo's temple (the present ones are Hellenistic, but they, like those of the archaic period, are equally without entasis) stood out in triumph above the abyss of the Pleistos shining bright before the horns.

In the classic period of the mid-fifth century, the Greeks looked in two directions: back, at Olympia, to the time of kings and heroes, and forward, on the Acropolis at Athens, to democracy and empire. At Olympia the theme is law and limit, at Athens the breaking of limits and the victory of the human political system over everything—even, by implication, over nature itself. At Olympia, the site of the Sanctuary of Zeus is domi- 16.9
nated, perhaps better to say protected, by a gentle conical hill that rises above the sacred grove and was the backdrop for all the activities, especially those of the Olympic Games, which took place below it. Pindar tells us that Herakles named it the Hill of Kronos, where the dead god, the father of Zeus, was buried. Like Mount Jouctas, it was a tholos cone, and before it the manmade temple of the living god took its stand. The first Temple of Zeus, close under the flank of the hill, was renamed the Temple of Hera after the building of the second; and the Pelopion, the shrine of the human king of the Peloponnesos, lay between them, enclosed in a space formed by them and the hill. It is the place of the Olympic truce. The human crimes that threatened that truce are explored in the pediments of Zeus's temple, while Herakles goes about his labors in its metopes, humanizing the land, and the seated Zeus of Pheidias looms inside. Beyond that, everything about the site is calm, gentle, deeply quiet. To the deep roar of the crowd it must always have offered a commanding silence.

At Athens, everything is different. The Parthenon blazes on the top of a fortress 16.10
hill, a disquieting condensation of Doric and Ionic modes. Matchless, a wholly new unity, it rises in its sacred landscape but, like imperial Athens itself, it seems to lift free of

Acropolis, Athens, fifth century B.C. 16.10
Distant view, looking east

earth and all the old ways. On the Acropolis one constantly hears people saying, "I can't take it in." The temple swells laterally like an Ionic temple but is still held to a Doric body. It looms, awesome, silently bursting to be free. Its sculptures bring the old antagonisms between men and nature into harmony. In the pediments nature consents to Athena's triumph; and the gods, in human form, become mountainous themselves. Political man is the measure of all. The Parthenon, still new, represents, literally, the victory of Western civilization over everything and was from the beginning the definitive embodiment of European hubris and pride. From this moment, one feels, the order of nature was everywhere endangered by the power of mankind.

Rome was different; she sought, primarily, not to win but to rule. The major topographical feature with which she first dealt was the chain of mountains that forms Italy's spine. Whereas Greece is shaped by bowls of small plains encircled by mountains, and its temples rise up in the center of the spaces so formed, Roman sacred sites are on
16.11 mountain slopes, looking out toward the coastal plains. The Temple of Fortune at Praeneste is the archetypal sacred site, the most important in Italy. Fortuna Primigenia was at once the offspring and the nurse of Jupiter. Her waters nourished the land and were in fact led through the terraces of her temple down from the mountain to quicken the crops in the rich agricultural lands below. This recalls Teotihuacán; and at Praeneste profoundly pre-Greek forms do take shape once more, a suggestion of the ziggurat most of all. Yet Rome could hardly have identified those dreary piles of rubble far off in Mesopotamia for what they once had been. The form at Praeneste grows primarily out of the hill but was crowned with a sparkling Hellenistic colonnade, like that of the open altar of Zeus at Pergamon, but curved into a hemicycle, containing and shaping the space. We mount the ramps, turn up the central stair, climb to the hemicycle, and, turning within its embrace, look out over what seems to be the whole world of land and sea,

of which we feel ourselves the commander. The columns spread out left and right from our body like the legion deploying. We recall that, unlike the Greek phalanx, which, like the Greek temple, formed a solid mass, the legion could fight in open order and often won its battles by enveloping the enemy in its wings. Moreover, the Latin *templum* means not a building but a sacred space. Exactly so did Rome come to envelop the space of the Mediterranean world entire, and she built an exact image of that empire in the Pantheon. There the thick wall of Roman provinces surrounds "Our Sea," while the sun shines down from above and illuminates the planets standing in their niches around the walls. Why go outside? It is all here; the world enclosed, ordered, and made ideal by Rome. But it is the cosmos, too; stepping into the shaft of sun we are blinded by it and the walls around us disappear. We stand in the velvet blackness of interplanetary space. The Pantheon is, I suspect, the biggest space ever made by mankind, even bigger than those constructed later, as at San Vitale, when Christian Rome learned how to make the containing walls dissolve in a dazzle of light.

In this way, Rome set the major building program for the Middle Ages, whose concern was the creation of ideal interior spaces, not the experience of the natural world
outside. Again, a late Roman monument shaped that internal world most fully: Hagia 12.10
Sophia embodies the ideal order of the universe in the Pythagorean union of the circle and the square. It reflects the famous passage in Vitruvius wherein he hails the fact that the human body seems to fit easily into these ideal shapes. Scores of medieval and
Renaissance drawings illustrating that idea culminate in Leonardo's famous example. 12.15
The human image is sculptural and heroic, but the ideal shapes are drawn thin as wire, remaining pure Idea, untrammeled by matter. In this way the interior of Hagia Sophia avoids any indication of weight, and the circle of the dome, apparently unsupported, is made to float over the square as if "suspended on a golden chain." Where is nature now? The universe is perfected here. The great Gothic cathedrals of Western Europe pursue similar aims, drawing the worshipper down the nave to the crossing, beyond which the gateway to heaven, the facade of the choir, rushes upward, and the circular rose windows of the transept arms spin up as well, transcending gravity at the very edges of our arc of vision and lifting us into the Pythagorean, finally Neoplatonic, harmony of the spheres.

When Western mankind finally goes outside again, so to speak, Praeneste becomes the model. Bramante introduced it into the Vatican gardens at the very moment he was rebuilding the ancient basilica. Its vast new dome, the ideal interior space, was balanced out in open nature by the ramps and hemicycle of the primary sacred site of pagan Rome: Fortuna's sacred mountain. Praeneste continued to be the fundamental model for most of the gardens of the sixteenth century: the Villa d'Este is the foremost example. It, too, lies on a slope of the Apennines, opening out to the Latin plain. In antiquity it may well have had two shrines of Hercules, one above the other, at least nearby, and may itself have looked a good deal like Praeneste at that time as well. Again, the point is water, Pindar's "best of all things," and the wonder of the Villa d'Este is how its waters, actually pumped from below, are made to seem as if bursting with a daemonic abundance out of the sacred slope itself, beyond which, in fact, the ancient pagan

ABOVE, LEFT: Sanctuary of Fortuna Primigenia, Praeneste (Palestrina), c. 80 B.C. 16.11

ABOVE, RIGHT: André Le Nôtre, Louis Le Vau, and Charles Le Brun. Château of Vaux-le-Vicomte, 1656–61. Aerial view from north 16.12

waters of Tivoli's grottoes still roar like Poseidon underground. In this way the Villa d'Este and the other important gardens of the sixteenth century, such as that of the Villa Lante at Bagnaia, all invoked the ancient sacred sites, embellished them, and keyed up their violence and awe in ways that are surely the very basis of modern romanticism. The earth is seen as wild, dangerous, filled with at least the passions of the gods. The English Romantic garden of the eighteenth century was a gentled, softened, Anglicized product of similar intentions, and its roots lay in Italy.

The French classic gardens of the seventeenth century are an entirely different matter. True enough, some of the earliest examples, like that at Saint-Germain-en-Laye, the ancient seat of the kings overlooking Paris, seem to derive directly from the Villa d'Este and are set on a slope. But when Nicolas Fouquet brought André Le Nôtre, Louis
16.12 Le Vau, and Charles Le Brun together at Vaux-le-Vicomte an entirely new type of garden emerged. Le Nôtre planted the site with trees—the forest that ennobled Fouquet—and then made the flat parterres appear to be pushing the trees back, exploding as they do out in space forward and aft of the château. Only the building itself has weight; therefore it is planted on an island within a moat, so that its weight will not seem to rest on the ground. That primary element, the flat surface of the earth, is kept paper-thin: the water of the *bassins* seems to slide through just below its taut surface. We are drawn into the château, only two rooms deep, and immediately propelled through the elliptical room behind the entrance out to the garden on the other side. There the view is all velocity: the evergreen hedges of the geometric parterres of Italy are cut down tight so as not to impede the rapid movement of the eye, and the *broderie* leaps out across the thin plane of the ground. The effect is not of the imposition of an order upon the earth,
16.13 as the English were to say it was, but of a vast release, not only of the human spirit, which is liberated into space, but also of some great order within the earth itself, now made visible, freed.

The garden treatises written during the seventeenth century by Boyceau de la Barauderie, the Mollets, and others, are all very clear on the basic point of how and why this new topographical countenance was made. One starts with geometry, they say, but then the art of landscape architecture requires a knowledge of scale—*échelle*—in order to

16.13 RIGHT: André Le Nôtre, Louis Le Vau, and Charles Le Brun. Château of Vaux-le-Vicomte. Aerial view from south

16.14 BELOW: Gianlorenzo Bernini. *Louis XIV*, 1665

transfer the geometric figures to the surface of the earth at the proper size. That process, they say, is called *pourtraiture*: and it is indeed a portraying, on the one hand of the client himself, like Nanteuil's touching portrait of Fouquet of just these years, and on the other, of the inner geometric framework of the earth itself, now brought forward in the only way such ideal order can be portrayed, as pure drawing upon its surface, free of all mass.

Louis XIV instantly saw all the possibilities inherent in this system. Imprisoning Fouquet, he brought the magic trio of collaborators to his father's hunting lodge at Versailles and built there a portrait of his new France: centralized, with straight new roads and long canals, and most of all at continental scale, extending, in Descartes's term, "indefinitely" beyond the horizon. The portrait is also of himself, as Vaux's was of
Fouquet. Bernini alone of Louis's portraitists captures his aspiration in these years. He is 16.14
the Sun King, young, carried on a cloud, like those that float across the great open flat land of Versailles and the fields of France.

The sacred mountain is no more. The king is everywhere over France; his eyes are made to shine with light looking out to vast distances. His hair is water and fire, like

LEFT: André Le Nôtre, Louis Le Vau, Charles Le Brun, and Jules Hardouin-Mansart. Château of Versailles, begun 1662. Parterre du Sud and Pièce d'Eau des Suisses 16.15

BELOW: André Le Nôtre, Louis Le Vau, Charles Le Brun, and Jules Hardouin-Mansart. Château of Versailles. Aerial view 16.16

OPPOSITE: Arc de Triomphe de l'Etoile and surrounding streets, Paris. Aerial view 16.17

the fountains that tell his story in transparent silver screens. Most of all, in the flat
parterres, drawn tight as wire and clothed in his livery, the king himself achieves the 16.15
Neoplatonic dream: he is the individual at the center. The diagonals of his body's action 16.16
project out across the circles and the squares and his will becomes more than regional, shaping the land of France in celestial *étoiles* and so, like the medieval kings before him, linking the kingdom to a cosmic order.

Versailles was the first image of the modern nation-state at continental scale. Its plan thus became not only the model for the gardens, never very satisfactorily carried out, that were built by princelings of Europe, soon to pass away, but also for Washington, the ceremonial center of the first emergent republic of modern times, the very soul of American political aspiration, and the most wholly classical of modern capitals. The best of modern urbanism everywhere derives from Versailles: modern Paris, the consummate
work of art of modern times, most of all. There the fabric of the modern city is cut to the 16.17
shapes of Versailles. In the end, Paris is a garden, too. Its streets are *allées* defined by building masses like clumps of trees, with the mansards rounding them over at the top. It embodies a classicism blending north and south, and, like the Gothic cathedral, it is at last suggestive of the shapes of nature itself. No other urban scheme at great scale has improved upon its achievement or come near it. Peter Cook, the inventor of Archigram's science-fiction city, once said a true and touching thing: "Archigram is all right," he said, "so long as you still have Paris."

Inconceivable, therefore, the horror of the French New Towns where only the Catalan Ricardo Bofill seems to understand what Paris means. Nevertheless, Paris always carried the seeds of its own destruction, as all strong forms seem to do, since the plan of Versailles, perhaps as filtered through Washington, became Le Corbusier's model

9.5 for his Ideal City of 1922. In it, however, the classical garden is destroyed. The boulevards are bereft of their trees and rush through an urban wasteland. The traditional street is progressively obliterated from the perimeter of the plan to the center, where only flat-topped skyscrapers stand in the superblocks as the automobiles speed by, like predators taking over the world. This vision became the model for the urbanism of the International Style, was there to complement the love of the automobile and the dislike of urban complexity that characterized American redevelopment in the 1960s, and is now the very image of all too large a part of our world. In recent years it has even begun to eat away at Paris itself.

In return, though, the classic garden, that of Versailles in particular, has helped shape the contemporary reaction to the cataclysmic planning of the International Style by healing the wounds it has inflicted on our cities and knitting up the urban fabric once
10.3 again. Leon Krier's monumental drawing for La Villette, in Paris, is one of the first documents of that classical revival. It filled in the city blocks, disciplined the automobile, and seems in every way to have been based upon an aerial photograph of Versailles.

Classical France offers much more than this. Le Nôtre's *étoiles* at Versailles were matched by Vauban's *étoiles* along the Rhine. Louis XIV expanded the frontiers of Continental France exactly as he expanded the campaigns of building at Versailles. He
16.18 reached the Rhine, the Alps, and held the Pyrenees. And Vauban built his forts in echelon, in depth behind the frontiers everywhere; they were reflections of the same art that shaped the gardens, projecting as they did long lines of flat-trajectory cannon fire to the horizon. As such, their outerworks, the *dehors*, kept expanding too. It always seemed advisable to have another *demi-lune*, *ravelin*, and *glacis* out there in space. Where can the Self stop in its defense against the Other?

Like the gardens, the fortifications became earth sculptures at ever-expanding scale. They held the frontiers from Flanders to Alsace and the borders of Andorra. When, therefore, the French built their railroads all at once in the 1840s, all of France became one great *étoile*, with long straight axes radiating from Paris to the frontiers, each railroad running to one of Vauban's citadels. Here is Ideal France, as every French schoolchild knows her, almost a pure geometric figure, but locked into the topography of Europe: centralized, organized, complete. Her shape belongs to Louis, made by his gardens and his forts. Colonial-minded historians of the nineteenth century criticized him for indulging these preoccupations while France's colonies fell. But was he wrong? All the colonies of Europe are gone, but France retains the viable continental mass with which Louis endowed her. The threat to the frontiers, too, was not an illusory one. In the most recent invasion from the north, the traditional enemy from across the Rhine fell afoul of Vauban's flooded canals and *demi-lunes* at Gravelines and Bergues. Finally, French infantry, dug in at Bergues, kept them out of Dunkirk for a week, and the army got away. Right there, stumbling over Vauban's forts, Hitler lost his war.

Our reaction to that story reflects, I suppose, an identification with the nation-state and, especially, an aesthetic admiration for the first and most beautiful of them all—modern France—shaped as she is on the same principles from Versailles and Paris to the mountains and the sea. Clearly, such identification cannot be enough any longer, and it surely reflects one of the climactic victories of the human aggression against nature that is so splendidly embodied in the Parthenon.

We would seem to require broader and simpler modes of identification, based not upon political life, if that is possible for mankind, but upon the very fact of life itself. In a way, Taos is that, where all are one: man and mountain, snake, eagle, and cloud. Each is real, and worthy of respect as living: all are divine. Yet we cannot entirely cast aside that shining vision of the gods as human which was the Greeks' double-edged gift to mankind. We are torn two ways, but one thing is clear: in the modern age, and especially with that architecture we have most identified as "modern," we have on the whole shaped the earth badly. We need to revive our traditions and begin again.

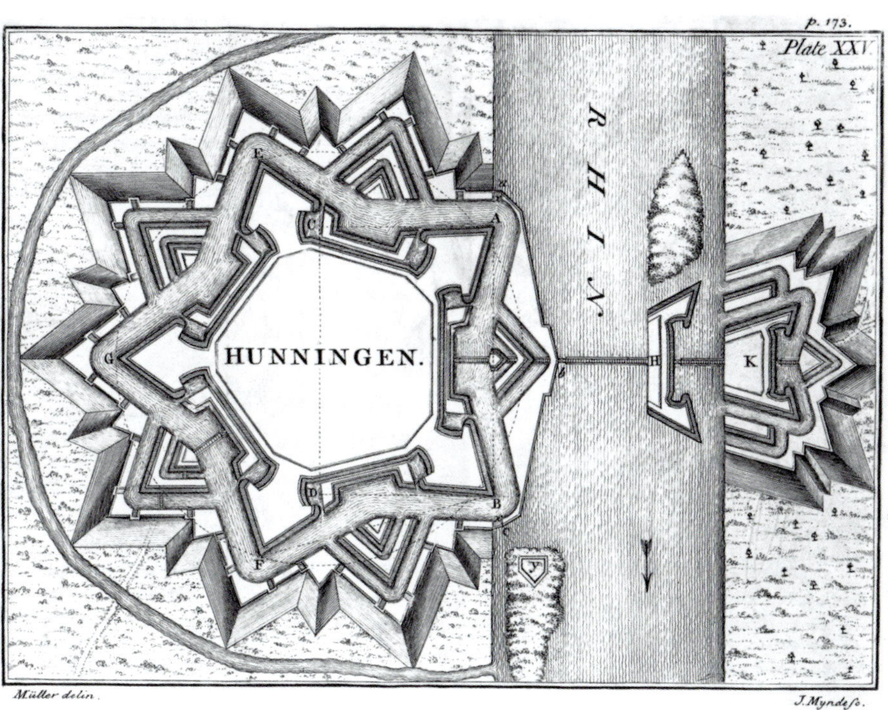

16.18 Sébastien Le Prestre de Vauban. Fortifications, Huninque, France, late seventeenth century. Plan. From John Muller, *A Treatise Containing the Elementary Part of Fortification, Regular and Irregular* (London, 1774)

NEIL LEVINE

"Louis I. Kahn and the Ruins of Rome." *MoMA: The Members Quarterly of the Museum of Modern Art,* no. 12 (Summer 1992): 1–13.

By the time of his death in 1974, after no more than fifteen years of mature work, Louis Kahn had established himself—through buildings like the Salk Institute for Biological Studies (1959–65), the National Assembly complex in Dhaka (1962–83), and the Kimbell Art Museum (1966–72)—as the most significant and influential architect in the world. Publications, which had until then been limited mainly to articles in professional journals, now began to proliferate. Romaldo Giurgola and Jaimini Mehta's monograph, *Louis I. Kahn* (1975), was the first complete survey of the architect's career. It was soon followed by Heinz Ronner, Sharad Jhaveri, and Alessandro Vasella's *Louis I. Kahn: Complete Work, 1935–1974* (1977). Books by August Komendant (1975), the engineer who worked closely with Kahn, and Alexandra Tyng (1984), Kahn's daughter, dealt with the subjects of structure and philosophy. The drawings in the Louis I. Kahn Archive, housed at the University of Pennsylvania, were published in 1987, with an introduction by Scully (see chap. 14). Kahn's writings and lectures were published by Richard Wurman in 1986 and, in a more authoritative edition, by Alessandra Latour in 1991. An exhibition in 1978 of Kahn's previously little-known paintings and drawings, done mainly as travel sketches, was accompanied by a catalogue with an essay by Scully. Jan Hochstim's more comprehensive *Paintings and Sketches of Louis I. Kahn* (also with an essay by Scully) came out in 1991.

The year 1991 was the pivotal one in this initial review and assessment of the architect's career. The culminating event was the opening that fall, at the Philadelphia

17

Louis I. Kahn and the Ruins of Rome

VINCENT SCULLY

Louis I. Kahn was about the best thing that happened to most of us who were privileged to know him over the years. Historically, Kahn's work turned out to be a hinge: Robert Venturi, who was close to Kahn, and European architects who owe a lot to Kahn, like Aldo Rossi, have brought about what is, in my opinion, the most important development in architecture in the second half of the twentieth century. That is the revival of the classical and vernacular traditions of architecture and their reincorporation into the mainstream of modern architecture. Along with that has come historic preservation, a powerful popular movement, and the only major development in contemporary architecture which has been led by the people—with the participation of a very few architects, such as Venturi, Rossi, and Leon Krier—rather than by professionals.

These are all things that Kahn really didn't care a rap about. He had no desire to restore the traditions of architecture. He didn't have much interest in preservation. His city plans, which people are writing about now, are largely exercises in formal fantasy, rather than seriously considered plans. He was a modern architect in every way; that is to say, he wanted to invent, to "reinvent the wheel" in every project. He was deter-

Museum of Art, of the first major retrospective of Kahn's work, organized by the Museum of Contemporary Art of Los Angeles and co-curated by the architectural historian David Brownlee and the architect-historian David De Long (both members of the faculty of the University of Pennsylvania). *Louis I. Kahn: In the Realm of Architecture* was seen in a stunning installation designed by Arato Isozaki—based on Kahn's unbuilt project for the Mikveh Israel Synagogue (1961–72)—in Paris's Centre Georges Pompidou (spring 1992), New York's Museum of Modern Art (summer 1992), the Gunma Museum of Modern Art in Japan (fall 1992), Los Angeles's MoCA (spring 1993), and the Kimbell Art Museum in Fort Worth (summer–fall 1993), before closing at Peter Eisenman's Wexner Center for the Arts at Ohio State University (winter 1993–94). The scholarly catalogue, written mainly by Brownlee and De Long and published in 1991, presented a massive amount of new material in what was, in effect, the first major art-historical account of Kahn's work since Scully's book of 1962.

Scully, who was described by MoCA's Director, Richard Koshalek, as an "inspiration" and a "guiding spirit" of the exhibition, wrote a brief introduction to the catalogue in which he situated Kahn in the larger context of the development of modern architecture. Likening him to Moses leading his people to the Promised Land he would never, however, be able to enter himself, Scully described Kahn as taking architecture beyond the conventions of the late International Style "to a much solider modernism, . . . in which the revival of the vernacular and classical traditions . . . would eventually come to play a central role." The key to the success of his "lonely quest," according to Scully, was Kahn's discovery "late in

17.1 Theo van Doesburg and Cornelis van Eesteren. Private House project, 1923. Axonometric

mined not to use readily identifiable historical forms in his buildings, and he continues to be hailed as a prophet and a hero by those architects who consider themselves moderns in the canonical sense, who don't want anything to do with the revival of tradition.

These architects want to continue to invent, want the freedom to invent that the painter has always had, which the architect took over from the abstract painting that developed in the first decades of this century. Kahn's work is like the work of those new-modernists only in its abstraction, and in his determination to invent. Their approach can be represented by Theo van Doesburg's 1923 study, which is all graphic design: the 17.1

life [of] how to transform the ruins of ancient Rome into modern buildings." It was an idea Scully had adumbrated as early as 1962 on the basis of the preliminary designs for the Salk Institute but, with the physical evidence of the architect's travel sketches along with the significant body of work that issued from the incipient Romantic-Classicism of the project for Jonas Salk, he could now document the trajectory and explain the rich meaning of Kahn's mature work.

The three-page catalogue introduction served as an outline for a lecture that eventually became the essay reprinted here. "Louis I. Kahn and the Ruins of Rome" was given at the Design Center in Washington, D.C., in late April 1992 and then again at the Museum of Modern Art in New York when the Kahn exhibition traveled there in mid-June. It fully develops the thesis of Kahn's reawakening to the value of ancient architecture as an answer to his search for order. Providing the most complete account he has yet to give of Kahn's evolution, Scully details the importance of his residency at the American Academy in Rome in 1950–51, his contact with the archaeologist Frank Brown, and the travel sketches he did that year. He shows how the architect gradually internalized his perceptions, combining them with a classical geometry grounded in structural rationalism and filtering them through the expressive lens of Piranesi's imaginary vision to create an architectural world alien from many of the characteristic features of modernism yet deeply ingrained in its moral and ethical imperatives.

house is not drawn in perspective, the way one sees buildings, but in axonometric projection, to make it look like a Cubist painting. It is a composition that seems absolutely free because there's no up, no down, no weight, no static, no masses. It's an abstract, free invention, with constant movement of compositional planes.

This is absolutely the opposite of how Kahn worked, because what Kahn did was
12.36 *build*, construct, as in his Indian Institute of Management at Ahmedabad (1962–74). He would never design anything the shape of which didn't derive from its structural character. This is how he began to make architecture anew. Instead of an architecture that is an affair of constantly shifting aesthetics and choices, all of them very free, architecture became again an affair of masses, of solids, of the weight of bricks, of horizontal ties holding arches together. You feel them thrumming with tension—at least Kahn wants it to look that way.

Kahn provided a kind of primitive new beginning for architecture, which is what he always said he was after, by starting with *building*: the basic, primitive, architectural fact of building. This is what makes architecture different, fundamentally, from all of the other arts. Through illusion, painting can embody all kinds of acts and environments; sculpture populates space with gesture and with movement; architecture is the construction of an environment and of volumes of space made in a structural way. Kahn's buildings have that par excellence.

17.2 ABOVE, LEFT: Mellor, Meigs and Howe. Newbold Estate, Laverock, Pennsylvania, 1921–24. Exterior

17.3 ABOVE, CENTER: Louis I. Kahn. *Street Scene with a Church Tower, Italy,* 1928–29

17.4 ABOVE, RIGHT: Louis I. Kahn. *Bay Houses, Amalfi Coast, Italy,* 1928–29

Kahn's mature work is illuminated by a consideration of his early experience as
an architect. For example, a house of 1924 by George Howe, with whom Kahn worked in 17.2
the early 1940s, displays the subordination of glass and the ruinlike voids within heavy
masonry that are characteristic of Kahn's late projects. In a sense, this is the architecture that he grew up with. On a trip to Europe in 1928–29, four years after Kahn
graduated from the University of Pennsylvania, he drew at Assisi, with a soft, flat car- 17.3
penter's pencil, an architecture of mass, of pure void, and devoid of glass. When he did
watercolors like figure 17.4 on that same trip, down near Positano, it's basically the 17.4
same primitive architecture of solid masonry masses that have pure dark voids, without
glass, punched into them.

The "high style" architecture in which Kahn was trained by Paul Cret at the University of Pennsylvania was called "modern classic" or "stripped modern" in its time, and Cret, more than anybody else, created it. His Folger Library and Federal Reserve buildings in Washington, D.C., major commissions in Cret's office during the time Kahn worked for him in 1929–30, are good examples. They're much like that vernacular architecture that Kahn had sketched in Europe, in the sense that they're heavy, massive, and symmetrical. What you feel is the mass and the void, and glass plays very little part in the design. It's a traditional classicism simplified under the pressure of modernism, but still retaining a monumental symmetry, and employing permanent materials, beautifully assembled. No sooner was Kahn trained in this approach, however, than Le Corbusier's
Villa Savoye (1929–31) burst upon the architectural profession. Suddenly one could no 18.7
longer look at buildings that were symmetrical, massive, heavy; one could no longer use the classical order in which Kahn had been trained, because now architecture had to be thin, taut, light, asymmetrical, stretched out to pure idea.

Modern classic architecture began to be used not only in the United States, where it made some of our best buildings in the thirties, but also by the totalitarian nations. The Fascists used it, as in Rome in the mid-thirties, and the Nazis used it, as at Nuremberg. So, politically, you couldn't touch it. Modern criticism has tended to portray

ABOVE, LEFT: Louis I. Kahn. *Rome, 1951,* 1951 17.5

ABOVE, RIGHT: Louis I. Kahn. *Piazza del Campo, No. 1,* 1951 17.6

the style as an architecture of repression, maintaining that fundamental canard to this day. Kahn separated himself as well as he could from modern classicism through the thirties and on into the forties by taking up the new, light architecture of glass and thin Lally columns, a way of building to which he was fundamentally unsympathetic.

When he came to Yale in 1947, it was clear that here was a man who'd lost an *order* and was looking for it everywhere. What that order was nobody knew. He didn't know himself, but he constantly talked about it—not about flow diagrams and flow patterns, the kind of thing they were then talking about at Harvard, but about order, especially the order of crystals. It was as if he, like a lot of people in architecture and art history in the late forties, wanted to get outside art, to something that would sanction art. It was as if art had worn itself out. Kahn felt there had to be some kind of scientific basis for his work. It was a curious time in our lives, when we lost confidence in the things that we live by. I don't think he knew a lot about crystallography—the rest of us knew nothing—but he was looking for an order that would develop like the order of crystals.

At about this time Kahn's old friend and partner, George Howe, managed to get him an appointment as Fellow at the American Academy in Rome, where he was from 1950 to 1951. When he returned to Italy, he no longer used watercolor. By the forties watercolor had been banished because it belonged to the bad old decadent Beaux-Arts days, but he got as close to it as he could in a simpler medium: he took up pastels, and he began to do great ones. Among the first was one of a forum—not the Roman Forum,
17.5 not Trajan's Forum, but a forum in the architecture he'd been trained in: Mussolini's Foro Italico. The only thing Kahn added was a building to the right to cast an ominous shadow. That, of course, is in the tradition of de Chirico, who, as a young Italian in Paris in the teens, homesick for Italy, painted its haunted squares, its new industrialism, chimneys, trains, statues on plinths. That is what Mussolini wanted to build: a haunting image of Italian tradition. And the Fascists were sometimes able to do just that, as in the

17.7 Louis I. Kahn. National Assembly complex (Sher-e-Banglanagar), Dhaka, Bangladesh, 1962–83. Exterior of hostels

EUR, site of the Esposizione Universale di Roma, which was supposed to open in around 1942, except that Mussolini was otherwise engaged. It is now one of the most popular places to live in Rome. The EUR has a de Chirico–like perspective that finally leads to a building without glass, like a great ruin, which is the House of Italian Culture, all arches, pure void, open air, standing out against the sky.

Kahn then traveled, and he went to the squares of Italy, probably the greatest
urban spaces that mankind has ever created. In his pastel of the Piazza del Campo in 17.6
Siena, he gets rid of everything that establishes scale, such as doors, people, and kiosks, making it mysterious by wiping that all out in one great red swash. This elimination of elements that tell you how big things are became fundamental in Kahn's mature architecture,
as at Dhaka. Looking at the exterior of the hostels there, how can we tell that it's a housing 17.7
group that has several floors within it? There's no way to tell. Instead, it is one strange, timeless shape—beyond function, beyond the changes that function always implies, reflecting in the water almost the same composition Kahn created in his pastel of Siena.

In that same year, 1950–51, he traveled outside Italy, and he went to Greece. When he drew in pastel the great Temple of Apollo at Corinth, however, he made it and the background orange. The pastel doesn't show us the wonderful white light of Greece because he wasn't looking for that. He found what he was looking for, apparently, in Egypt, where you do see that warm terracotta color, as in his pastel of columns at Karnak,
which suggests the massing of his later Mikveh Israel Synagogue project. 17.8

A great deal has been written about Kahn's relation to Jewish mysticism. His widow Esther Kahn says that he wasn't a practicing Jew, and he rarely talked about Judaism, but there's no doubt that when the chips were down, he would turn to it. When he came to make the proposal for the Mikveh Israel project for Philadelphia, which would have been, I think, the most important monument of synagogue architecture in the modern day, he found the shape of his synagogue in a Jewish tradition, the Kabbalah, drawing directly, as Anselm Kiefer has since done, on medieval and Renaissance texts illustrating
the tree of the Sefiroth. The cylinders indicated by the circles on the plan are hollow, and 17.9
can contain, if necessary, the quorum of ten men; a thousand congregants may be seated in the main space.

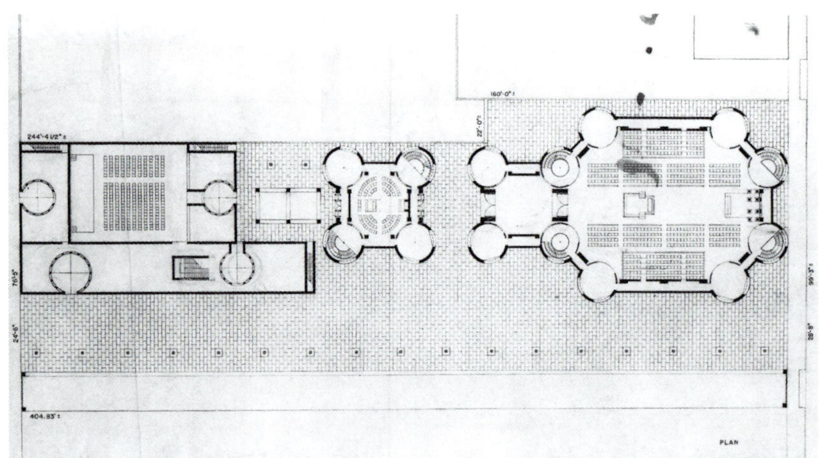

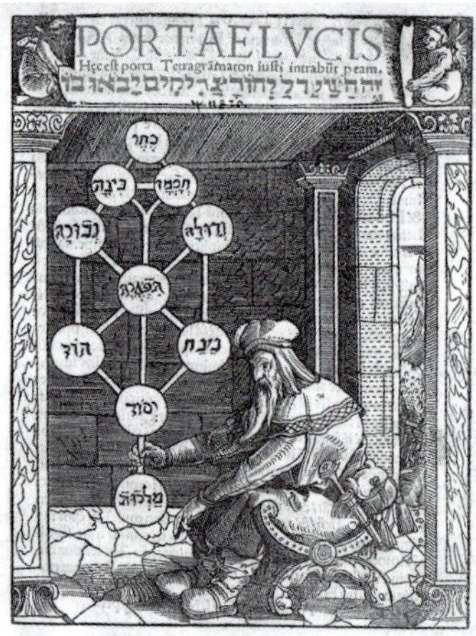

ABOVE, LEFT: Louis I. Kahn. Mikveh Israel Synagogue project, Philadelphia, 1961–72. Plan 17.8

ABOVE, RIGHT: Tree of Sefiroth. From Paulus Ricius, *Portae lucis,* 1516 17.9

When Kahn traveled in Egypt, he had to have a document or stamp on his passport that said he was an Episcopalian, or something of that sort, because Egypt was still at war with Israel. They weren't allowing Jews to travel there. But in the end, Egypt seems to have unlocked Kahn's Jewishness, and at last he came to the most important
17.10 place of all for him, to the pyramids at Giza, and made what I think are his greatest pastels. Kahn saw the pyramids as embodying divinity, and as creatures of light. Indeed, he saw them dissolving in light: the great four-sided mass of the pyramid disappears in the drawing into reflections that make you think that maybe it has only three sides, or only one, facing forward. He also wrote a poem while he was there, calling Giza "The Sanctuary of Art, of Silence and Light." He couldn't have used two words more descriptive of the divinity, especially in Jewish literature, than "silence" and "light." The very fact of silence, in a good deal of medieval Jewish and Christian theology, is the clearest indication of the presence of God, while light, of course, is practically the most important word in the beginning verses of Genesis.

While he was in Egypt Kahn received, again through George Howe, his first important commission, for the Yale University Art Gallery. The pyramids, as he looked at them, had turned into tetrahedrons, and then into planes, some light and some dark, and he worked out the idea that the pyramids could in fact be carriers of light. He combined with this idea the concept of the space frame advocated by his most important collaborator of that time, Anne Tyng, and the tetrahedronal forms of Buckminster Fuller. Fuller had come to Yale when the Art Gallery was being designed, and talked and talked. He also built a cardboard dome over the architecture school at Yale, which slowly rotted in
12.35 the sun. Kahn condensed the pyramids with the space frame and created his incomparable slab. It isn't, of course, a space frame. You can see that it is made up of braced beams. The effect, however, is of a great articulated canopy—indeed, of a kind of crystalline order. If at any time Kahn came close to communicating a sense of the order of crystals, perhaps it was here.

The importance of Kahn's achievement at the time it appeared can be grasped if we look at one of Mies van der Rohe's climactic spaces of the fifties, such as Houston's

Museum of Fine Arts, where the structure is all outside the space. Inside, the space is dematerialized, if one can use that term, the masses are weightless planes that are far away, and the sculpture appears as discrete bodies in a void. When Mies himself organized an exhibition for that space, he selected classical sculpture because he wanted the solid human figure in this Constructivist world. Humanity is thus placed in a Neoplatonic idea of perfect space, without any matter, any mass. That is the great quality of Miesian space. 12.34

Kahn is just the opposite. All at once matter is present, challenging space. You feel that invincible Western tradition of physicality in architecture. Indeed, the Yale Art Gallery was regarded in its day as a monument of the New Brutalism, which in fact committed so many crimes. Through the primitive, overweening masses of its buildings, modernism finally destroyed our cities. But this building by Kahn was different. It seemed to embody a law, a system, not a brutal gesture. Nevertheless, Kahn contained the Yale Art Gallery within a Miesian envelope. That rectangular volume was not chosen by Kahn but by Howe, before Kahn came back from Egypt, and Kahn exploited it. A gallery director later installed continuous wall planes, like those in the Museum of Modern Art, and Kahn never got over that. He said he learned not to make a big, uninflected space like this again, because people could change it so easily. In addition, he didn't know how to design an entrance, or rather, *wouldn't* design one not suggested by structure, so he just set it back, and you slide into the building at the side. Kahn's refusal to design anything he can't intrinsically build continues right through his career. What's inside the Yale Art Gallery, of course, is what he loves, and what haunted him: the pyramids. The staircase is especially wonderful; you look up the staircase and the black 17.11
shadow of a pyramid floats there, weightless, pure shadow, pure light—silence and light—overhead.

Finally, in 1955, when he was coming close to leaving us at Yale, Kahn built actual pyramids for the bathhouse he designed to be part of a Jewish community center 6.6, 6.7
near Trenton. They are four-sided, and you feel, even more than in the art gallery, I think,

17.10 BELOW, LEFT: Louis I. Kahn. *Pyramid Studies, Egypt,* 1951

17.11 BELOW, RIGHT: Louis I. Kahn. Yale University Art Gallery, New Haven, Connecticut, 1951–53. Stairwell ceiling

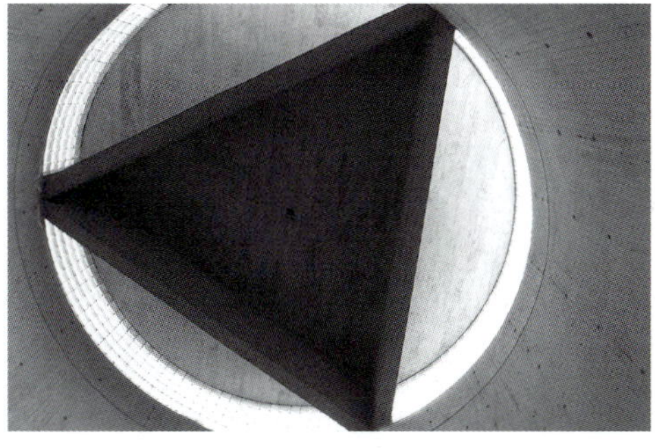

the great silence of the structure and the profound poetry of the light that he experienced before the pyramids of Egypt. In Trenton, he came also to other basic shapes that have pervaded Western architectural aesthetics since the days of Vitruvius and before, the square and the circle. There are five squares, and in the middle he has a circle. The four squares outside are capped with pyramids.

12.15 The well-known image by Leonardo of the *Man of Perfect Proportions* is only one of hundreds of such drawings derived from the passage in Vitruvius where he says, more or less, that it's wonderful that the human body is proportioned so that it can fit into the perfect shapes of the square and the circle. This idea, probably Pythagorean, obsessed the Middle Ages and was taken up by Neoplatonism during the Renaissance. It suggested the basic image upon which Gothic and Renaissance architecture alike are based. Implicit in it is the idea that there exists a fundamental order that you can find only in drawing, that is, in the domain of conception; if gross matter intervenes, you get farther away from the idea of an underlying order of the universe as a whole. The forms thus drawn are taut as piano wire: the circle and the square. Kahn's embrace of this idea connects him with the richest part of the classical tradition, its theoretical center, from which are derived the great architectural images of the order of the world—for example, the new France and the cosmic order as embodied in the great French classic gardens of the seventeenth century. This is a central theme of history that Kahn, once taught by Cret and other French Beaux-Arts architects, was now able, in a sense, to reclaim.

More than that, Kahn returned to a plan type, also traditionally French and Beaux-Arts, the concept of served and serving spaces. Structures are articulated by small spaces, which, acting as corridors, lavatories, or whatever, serve large spaces. This is how he articulated the cross-axial plan of the bathhouse at Trenton. We get the feeling that he

Louis I. Kahn. Alfred Newton Richards Medical Research Building, University of Pennsylvania, Philadelphia, 1957–60 (*left*); Biology Building addition, 1961–65 (*right*). Exterior 17.12

was really seeing for the first time all the things he'd been trained to look at in his youth, as illustrated in the books of Eugène-Emmanuel Viollet-le-Duc and Auguste Choisy. In the plan of Saint-Front, at Périgueux, for example, there are five squares, each with a circle in the middle—a dome on pendentives—and they are articulated by piers grouped in fours, making small spaces in exactly the same places Kahn has them in his plan.

That plan broke Kahn loose from the Miesian envelope within which everybody, including himself, had been designing. It freed him to articulate a building, to study its function—"what it wanted to be," as he'd say—and make a very special, new organism of it. The result was the articulated plan of his Alfred Newton Richards Medical Research 17.12
Building at the University of Pennsylvania (1957–65). Some of the small spaces on the peripheries of the squares seen here are staircases, and some house the ducts that remove noxious air from the laboratories. Kahn shows that these towers are non-structural by stepping them in, or by cutting a triangle at the bottom of those housing staircases. The whole structure is articulated around great precast concrete columns. All these elements suggest that the building has wholly developed out of function and structure, as if it were entirely contemporary and had no antecedent, as if it really grew out of a pragmatic analysis of how it wanted to be.

As Kahn studied the laboratory's towers, other forms haunted him: the towers of San Gimignano that he had painted in watercolor on his trip to Italy in the 1920s. Those are solid masonry masses, based firmly on the ground. They are all much the same and they group in a way that seems strangely appropriate for the Richards laboratory, which is, if I may say so, a place of hard work and a tower of pain. The normal image of a laboratory is of an aseptic place, beyond morality. This building has the sense of human beings, working in the community of a shared profession, ruthlessly doing things that are hard and tragic.

Still, those towers look structural; they dominate the columns and were criticized for that. The actual structure, when you see it, is very beautiful, though: the tense interlocking of the precast elements, the dry joints, the reduction of the spandrels in section as they approach a corner. You sense that Kahn is *building*. He said that when he began to imagine that the crane was like his arm, and the big precast elements were like bricks he could carry in his hand, "then I could feel what I was doing."

Kahn, returning to what he'd been taught, recalled in the Richards complex the great drawings by Auguste Choisy in his *Histoire de l'architecture* of 1899, which was Kahn's text. Choisy loved worm's-eye perspectives of dry structures like Greek temples, put together piece by piece, locked together without mortar, and that's what Kahn was able to re-create here. However, in terms of function, which was supposed to be the other modern determinant of the design, nothing really works very well. The squares are too small to contain the laboratories. Pieces of equipment have to be put out in the corridors. There's no sun protection; people put silver paper up in the windows. So when he came to add the Biology Building, Kahn not only fiddled with the structure, but also put in library carrels at the top to make a cornice. He studied how people would sit, and how the little low windows would cast light on a book, while the big window above illuminated

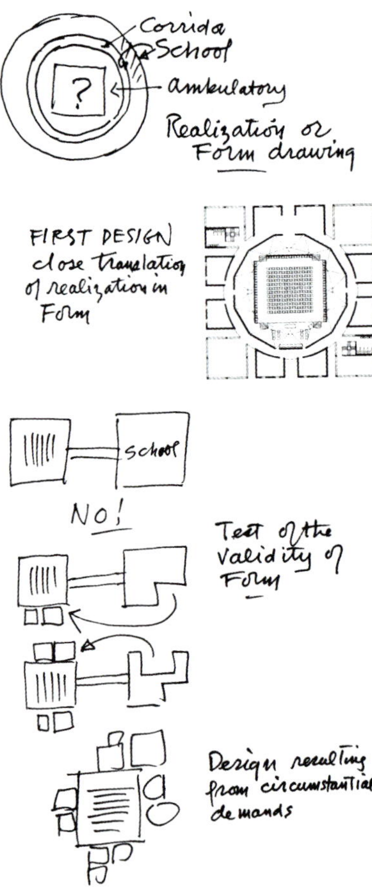

Louis I. Kahn. First Unitarian Church and School, Rochester, New York, 1959–69. Form and Design drawing 17.13

the space as a whole without glare. Though the library was taken out of the project before the building was constructed, the carrels were retained, as a device to terminate the towers—a gross dereliction of method from Kahn's own point of view.

For this reason, Kahn began to ask himself, How do I use the forms that populate my mind; how do I actually form my work? When he came to Rochester to build the
17.13 First Unitarian Church and School, we can see the answer taking shape. He begins by saying, When you get a new program, a form suggests itself. Here that form was basically a circle within a square, representing a central meeting hall with a kindergarten, a library, and other functions grouped closely around it because, Kahn explained, all of those functions occasionally want to use the large space.

Having established that form, Kahn then bombards it with the specific demands of the program—his approach is really Neoplatonism and realism combined. As he does this, he says, the plan will deform, and this is what happened as the Rochester plan developed. If it doesn't deform too much, he says, that means that the original form idea was the right one to use. If you choose the wrong form in the beginning (as Kahn said the clients themselves did), and bombard it with specific demands, it will deform too much, and you can't build it.

At Rochester, as the ideal geometry of Kahn's circle-within-a-square form distorted, an eloquent plan developed in which the entrance space is larger, the library big, 17.15
the kitchen long, and classrooms moderate in size. From that point on we can trace everything about the building through its reception of light. We feel that he has expressed function and structure like an absolute modernist, and that the plan is also absolutely abstract—that he's achieved, in a sense, the modern ideal.

The windows are set back, to protect from glare, he said, so we hardly see the 17.14
glass in the exterior wall, which becomes very plastic and solid. Up above, four great monitors rise to light the central space, whose bony structure is one of his greatest. You
can really feel the silence he talked about, thrumming as with the presence of divinity, 17.16
when the cinder block is washed silver by the light that floods down upon it, while the heavy, heavy slab is lifted overhead. This space joins that of the Yale Art Gallery as one of Kahn's early essays in the sublime, into whose vast silences all his late work was to move.

17.14 RIGHT: Louis I. Kahn. First Unitarian Church. Exterior

17.15 BELOW, LEFT: Louis I. Kahn. First Unitarian Church. Plan

17.16 BELOW, RIGHT: Louis I. Kahn. First Unitarian Church. Interior of auditorium

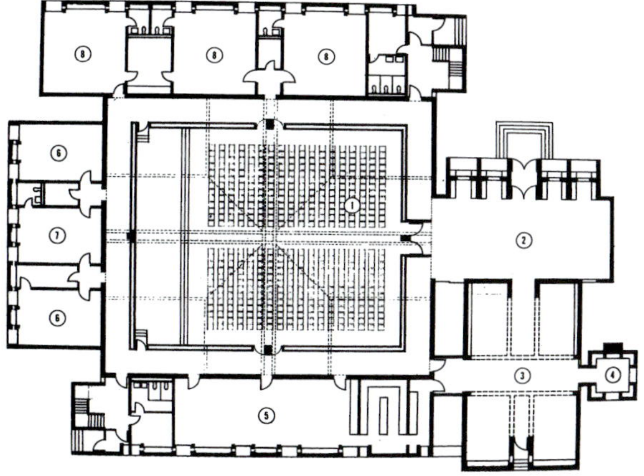

In 1965, I accompanied Kahn to the Soviet Union, where his work was included in an exhibition of American architecture in Leningrad. He walked around with the mayor of the city, who was inspecting the show, and they came to this Rochester building. The mayor said that it didn't look like a church, which by Russian standards was true enough. Kahn instantly replied, "That's why it was chosen for exhibition in the Soviet Union." The translator wouldn't translate it, but all the Russians laughed anyway, indicating they understood perfectly well what we were saying. And, of course, it doesn't look like a church. It has the abstraction Kahn insisted upon, and, more than this, the glass is subordinated. The way Kahn liked to look at the building, and the way it was first published, was in elevational views where the glass in the walls is far enough back to be in shadow, and the glass in the monitors above doesn't show at all, so that it looks as if it's all mass.

Kahn's real turning toward the ruins of antiquity started with his first project for the Salk Institute for Biological Studies in La Jolla. There he had a big Vierendeel truss that spanned the laboratories, leaving the work space open and flexible. In his first
17.17 schemes for the scholars' studies adjoining the laboratories, Kahn produced a plan which consisted of a square with a fanning pattern opening out from the center. He'd seen that pattern in the so-called Domus Augustana, on the Palatine Hill in Rome—part of the Flavian palace—probably built by the great architect Rabirius. It is a nymphaeum—once full of water flowing and rising, so that its energies were projected into the air—in which there is a wonderful fanlike pattern opening out to half-circular segments on all four sides.

Kahn had rediscovered the ruins of Rome when he went there in 1950, under the influence of the greatest Romanist that those who knew him are likely to know, Frank E. Brown of Yale University and the American Academy in Rome. Brown wrote one of the shortest and, I think, one of the best books about Roman architecture. He led us all to Rome; he led Kahn to the ruins. Earlier historians, and even the Beaux-Arts architects who used Roman forms, wrote about Rome as if it had just a utilitarian architecture, an engineer's architecture; it wasn't pure and glowing like that of Greece. Brown made us see that it was a poetry of space, of light and water. He led us to Hadrian's Villa, the Flavian palace, Trajan's Market, and Ostia. Kahn went to all those places, alone and with Brown, looked at them hard, and drew them.

BELOW, LEFT: Louis I. Kahn. Salk Institute for Biological Studies, La Jolla, California, 1959–65. Axonometric of preliminary scheme for laboratories and scholars' studies 17.17

BELOW, RIGHT: Louis I. Kahn. Salk Institute for Biological Studies. Central courtyard, facing west 17.18

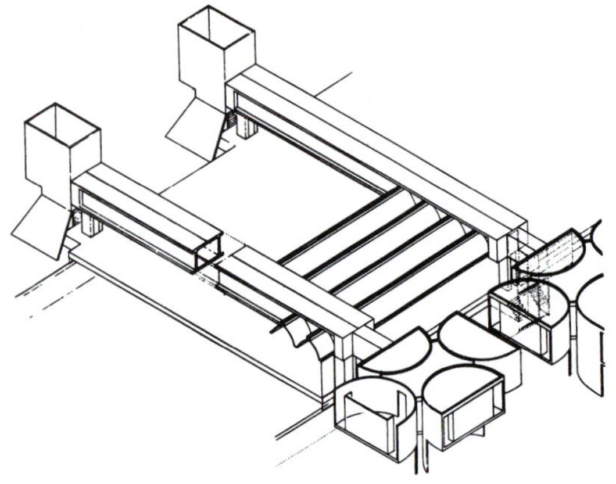

17.19 Louis I. Kahn. Salk Institute for Biological Studies. Community Center project. Model

Eventually, Kahn eliminated the fanlike pattern because he wanted to establish a view towards the sea from the scholars' studies, and so he articulated the buildings in accordance with that intention. In addition, glass is once again almost completely subordinated. The words that people most use to describe the Salk Institute are "Acropolis" and "marble"; the milky concrete is so beautifully formed that the sense is of being in a perfect, classic world. That impression is heightened by the fact that right out there off the coast is one of the favorite places for hang-gliding in Southern California, so every once in a while Icarus glides across the scene. 17.18

Kahn originally intended to bring trees into the central courtyard, but the architect Luis Barragan, as Kahn acknowledged, told him to leave it open. Kahn also projected housing and a community center that would have been on the bluff above the Pacific. In that community center, he proposed a very strange thing: a series of rooms, some of which were square and some cylindrical. They all had walls of glass. They were to be protected from glare by thin concrete walls, circular ones around the square rooms, and square ones around the circular rooms. He called this "wrapping ruins around buildings." 17.19

This is the first really complete proposal for something in three dimensions that resembles Roman ruins as Kahn saw them. But it's more than that. A student of Brown's at the Academy, who was an engineer, went to the forum baths at Ostia and proved (to everyone's satisfaction, anyway) that their orientation was such, and the power of the hypocaust, which distributed heat to the baths, was such, that these wonderful rooms—some rectangular, some cylindrical, opening with columns—probably never had glass. The Romans had plenty of glass, but here they probably didn't use it. That helped sanction the whole thing for Kahn: They didn't use it, I won't use it. He saw how wonderful it would be to have the dark void in the pure ruin, to have the opening in the curving wall, to have the round arches and the flat lintels, and the typical keyhole arch that we find all over Hadrian's Villa. Kahn used all those forms.

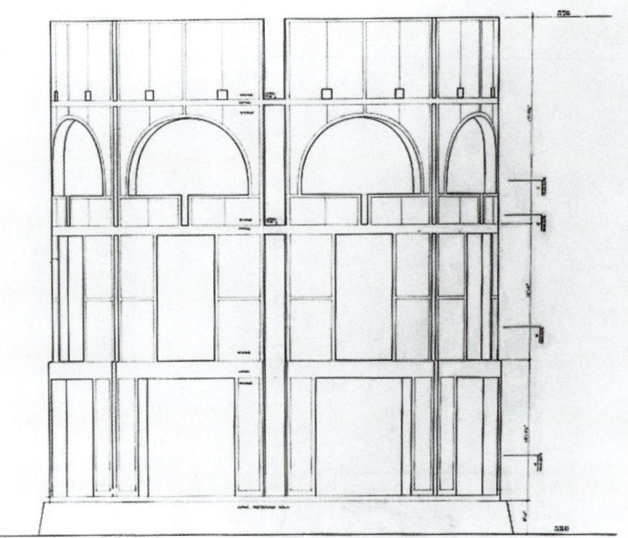

Louis I. Kahn. Salk Institute for Biological Studies. Community Center project. Elevation 17.20

17.20 A drawing Kahn made for this project seemed to me, when I saw it in 1962 as I was writing a book about Kahn, the greatest drawing in modern architecture that I'd seen. It expressed *romanitas*, the gravity of Rome, the bigness of Rome—what Brown called the authority of Rome. Notice, however, that unlike Roman ruins, Kahn's drawing shows thin walls, a bit like those of Corbusier or of Pier Luigi Nervi, taut with their own bending. And indeed, Kahn always keeps the wall as thin as he can. Everybody said, Well, Loony Lou: he's wrapping ruins around a building. Nobody can do that. It's like having to build two rooms each time. It's ridiculous.

Of course, Kahn had the last laugh, because just after this he received the commissions for his great projects on the subcontinent of India, where he didn't have to have glass in most instances, and those great primitive shapes began to appear. In his Indian
12.36 Institute of Management, in Ahmedabad, Kahn even created an order again, his lost order. It was a structural order, derived from a misprision, a conscious misreading, of Roman brick and concrete construction, with lintels over openings, as at Ostia. In this kind of Roman construction, of course with very thick walls, the mason laid a section of brick on both sides, filled it with concrete, and let it set. He then capped it, built up a scaffold if necessary, climbed up, and did it again. Over an opening, often with a wooden lintel, he built an arch between the sections of wall to divert the heavy concrete from the lintel until the concrete set.

Kahn took this procedure and turned it around. He made the lintel concrete (which the restored lintels at Ostia are), and it is the lintel that seems to hold the arch together as a tie. Everything reverses the ancient method. The concrete tie is a taut element that dramatizes the presumed thrust of the arch, and you can feel it hum like a bowstring. Corbusier, late in his life, also turned to a kind of primitive mass in his buildings, but his masses are in a way more like primitivized Greek temples, sculptural bodies

17.21 ABOVE, TOP LEFT: Giovanni Battista Piranesi. *The So-Called Villa of Maecenas at Tivoli*, from *Vedute di Roma*, after 1748

17.22 ABOVE, TOP RIGHT: Louis I. Kahn. National Assembly complex. Crypto-portici

17.23 ABOVE, BOTTOM LEFT: Thermopolium (tavern), Ostia Antica, second century. Interior

17.24 ABOVE, BOTTOM RIGHT: Louis I. Kahn. National Assembly complex. Outpatient Clinic, loggia

in whose gesture we feel a modern violence. Kahn's aren't like that; we don't read the human body in Kahn. His approach is Roman: we read the environing space and the structure, which is self-contained. Therefore, its presence never tires; its gesture, if any, is always potential, mysterious. Structure, not sculpture: fundamentally, that is how the primitivized classic in Kahn is different from that in Le Corbusier.

All of Kahn's sources are present in his Indian Institute of Management. Kahn said he needed the brace across the arches there because of earthquake problems, but of
course the model is Piranesi. Giovanni Battista Piranesi was one of Kahn's great loves, 17.21
and he bought every book by Piranesi that he could find. Kahn didn't read a lot—*pace* those who talk about his philosophy and so on. He looked at the pictures, like most architects, and he loved Piranesi, who was really the inventor of what Kahn was doing. Piranesi is one of the first great Romantic-Classic architects, those who began the modern age by going to the ruins of Rome. What the Romantic-Classic movement wanted was the sublime, which was, in that aesthetic, different from the beautiful: it was crude and frightening, awesome and dangerous. The Piranesi of the great Roman ruins, with light
coming down from above, is matched in Kahn's great Roman crypto-portici, the under- 17.22
ground passages that he built at Ahmedabad and at Sher-e-Bangla Nagar, the Capitol of Bangladesh, Dhaka. He's building Piranesi: the sublime, the ruin. It's true that Kahn concealed his sources—he won't use columns and entablatures, for example, because that would be a giveaway—so now he can be deified by the modernists as inventing it all out of his head. But it really is coming out of the ruins of Rome—rebuilt, in the marvelous

FAR LEFT: "Basilica" (Main market hall), Trajan's Market, Rome, C. A.D. 100–112. Interior 17.25

NEAR LEFT: Louis I. Kahn. Indian Institute of Management, Ahmedabad, India, 1962–74. Interior 17.26

BELOW: Louis I. Kahn. National Assembly complex. Assembly Building, exterior 17.27

illogicality of art, on the Indian subcontinent. In the wonderful spaces within the loggia 17.24
of the clinic at Dhaka, the visitor doesn't really need to conjure up Piranesi: it's almost
purely Kahn and the ruins of Ostia—here of the Thermopolium, the tavern, near the 17.23
House of Diana.

Kahn's use of the ruin is not only visual, it is also conceptual, structural, and
systematic. For example, Trajan's Market in Rome, above his forum, offers some of the 17.25
greatest brick and concrete construction, such as the impressive cross-vault lighting of
the long tunnel vault over the nave of the central basilica. Kahn re-created that effect in
a simpler structure of brick arches. He doesn't need a cross-vault because he has a rein- 17.26
forced concrete slab, so that he can do it in the flat. He simplifies and clarifies the basilica's basic *parti*—the architectural concept realized by the structure—according to how he can build it most simply.

Again, in the Temple of Jupiter Optimus Maximus that rises above the forum at
Ostia, there is a marble staircase and two frontal planes that are a product of erosion, as
well as walls containing relieving arches of different shapes. It's not that far from all those
elements to those of the great central council building at Dhaka. At the same time, every 17.27
one of the shapes in its plan, some square, some cylindrical, can be found in Piranesi's
fantastical reconstruction of the Campus Martius in Rome, which always hung behind
Kahn's desk in his office in Philadelphia. Kahn used those shapes as he had intended to
do at Mikveh Israel, as containers of light, their thin walls cut through with circles and
tall pyramids, while big circles light the great council chamber in the center. What 17.28
Kahn wanted was mystery, a sense of majestic and ambiguous scale, of function transcending into awe. It is totally, as it were, outside time—has escaped time as a ruin
does—containing within it, as always, the sublime. We are reminded of Piranesi's
Carceri, the terrible stairs going up into space, seen through the enormous circles, vertigi- 17.29
nous and awesome.

Many of Kahn's later buildings in America are like those Roman projects, which found such a natural, full outlet on the subcontinent. In the Kimbell Art Museum in Fort

17.28 NEAR RIGHT: Louis I. Kahn. National Assembly complex. Assembly Building, interior

17.29 FAR RIGHT: Giovanni Battista Piranesi. *Prison with a Doorway Surmounted by a Colossal Wheel-shaped Opening*, from *Invenzioni Capric di Carceri*, c. 1745

17.30 OPPOSITE, TOP: Louis I. Kahn. Kimbell Art Museum, Fort Worth, Texas, 1966–72. Exterior

17.31 OPPOSITE, BOTTOM: Louis I. Kahn. Library, Phillips Exeter Academy, Exeter, New Hampshire, 1965–72. Exterior

Worth (1966–72), he employed the Roman round-headed arch, but deformed it so that,
in his view, the ceilings would distribute the indirect light better. The running arches of
the porticos on the outside are actually very close to an element at Hadrian's Villa. At the
Kimbell, glass is again strikingly subordinated, so that Kahn is always close to his 17.30
Romantic-Classic roots, to the ruin, deformed only a little. The same thing is true of his
Library at Phillips Exeter Academy (1965–72), in Exeter, New Hampshire, which he 17.31
won't allow to come together at the corners as a completed building. This can be compared with the facades at Hadrian's Villa and also with Ahmedabad, where Kahn set
some panes of glass far back in the window opening. At Exeter he wants us to see the
building as a brick and concrete ruin with the glass where he absolutely has to have it,
shoved into the ruin without ceremony. Beyond that, he wants us to perceive the square
of the exterior with the vast concrete circle inside it. It's a diagrammatic realization of 17.32
the Neoplatonic order indestructible within the ruin.

So far Kahn was wholly Romantic-Classic, but in the Yale Center for British Art 17.33
(1969–74), effectively his last building before his death, he almost completely changed. Here, in his analysis of how to use classicism, and how to make a modern building fronting a street, it is as if Kahn jumped almost a hundred years, from Piranesi
in 1745 to Henri Labrouste's Bibliothèque Sainte-Geneviève of 1843–50 in Paris, 17.34

17.32 BELOW: Louis I. Kahn. Library, Phillips Exeter Academy. Interior, central space

ABOVE, LEFT: Louis I. Kahn. Yale Center for British Art, Yale University, New Haven, Connecticut, 1969–74. Exterior 17.33

ABOVE, RIGHT: Henri Labrouste. Bibliothèque Sainte-Geneviève, Paris, 1843–50. Exterior 17.34

which is unquestionably the most copied building of the nineteenth and twentieth centuries. Labrouste asked himself, How would the Greeks have built with columns if they had to contain space, too? It was not enough just to put the columns in front of the wall, as in the classicizing or Romantic-Classic buildings of earlier generations. How do you make *sense* of it, how rationalize it, most of all how condense the opposites of column and wall to make a new unity?

Labrouste's answer was a system consisting of a lower zone (the ground floor's exterior); a stringcourse; and a columned arcade, expressing the upper story, partially filled with panels, some glass and some solid. That's the theme out of which H. H. Richardson built the Marshall Field warehouse in Chicago and Sullivan built the Guaranty Building in Buffalo. The skyscrapers all come out of it in one way or another. It's a basic modern type, and Kahn used it in New Haven. He's got the frame, he has the infilling panels of stainless steel, which has such a matte finish that it looks like slate, and the panels of glass. Mies, in part through his nineteenth-century German predecessor, Karl Friedrich Schinkel, used the same system, for example at the Illinois Institute of Technology. But Kahn's frame, unlike that of Mies, expresses weight and compression. The lintels weigh heavily on the piers; the joint is point-loaded, static, Greek, silent.

The outside of the Yale Center conveys no sense whatever of a ruin, as his first projects for it had done. But inside there are still sublime effects, as in the big cylinder housing of the stair, which doesn't quite reach the beams spanning the library court, so that it's like a monster in the space. And in the top floor, the light still floods down from above, illuminating the silence. Most of all, however, the magic is in the glass, which Kahn had avoided and tried to subordinate all his life. Now the glass comes alive as an incandescent, reflective material. On the exterior, he presents it cleanly and without detailing, and the stainless steel panels are so matte in finish that the glass surface explodes with light. Standing across from the building, near the corner of High and
17.35 Chapel Streets, one sees, as if illustrating the Cartesian perception that the angle of reflection is the same as the angle of sight, that the building is reflecting all the buildings across from it. One sees first of all the wonderful old Art Gallery by Egerton Swartwout of 1926–28. A little farther on it reflects Kahn's own art gallery of 1951–53. Then, down at the end of the street, it reflects Paul Rudolph's Art and Architecture

17.35 Chapel Street, New Haven, Connecticut. View north: Swartwout's Art Gallery, Kahn's Art Gallery, and Rudolph's Art and Architecture Building. These buildings face Kahn's Yale Center for British Art (not pictured)

Building of 1958–63. However much that building may be criticized, nobody can fault its siting: where Kahn's building is a cut-off box, Rudolph's opens in a great gesture to embrace it from across York Street, so concluding the impressive movement of Yale's art and architecture buildings down Chapel Street.

We can see how right Kahn had been to adorn his earlier art gallery with stringcourses. They carry the eye down the street. As in the older building, Kahn still doesn't "design" an entrance in his new one. There he decided, when the students and the city demanded that there be shops on the ground level, that he would leave the end bays open. The visitor just slides in and then enters the great court.

Perhaps, though, Kahn almost embraces the principle of contextuality in the new building. He is, after all, right across the street from his own earlier building. He has treated the street as a community space, and he has in large measure carried on that dialogue between the generations which the older buildings embody. That is what architecture primarily is, after all, and what makes the city as a whole. One wonders whether Kahn would have gone further in that essential direction if he had survived. But it is moving to know that this last building of his looks across to his old art gallery, where he struggled with the pyramids, wrestling like Jacob with the angel, all night long, when the first great architects of Western civilization reached out to him and set him on his way.

NEIL LEVINE

"Everybody Needs Everything." In *Mother's House: The Evolution of Vanna Venturi's House in Chestnut Hill*, ed. Frederic Schwartz. New York: Rizzoli, 1992.

This is the only essay in this book that takes a single building as its subject and the analysis of the design process as its object. By 1991, when "Everybody Needs Everything" was written—and when Robert Venturi was finally awarded the Pritzker Prize—the small house that Venturi began to design for his mother in 1959 and eventually built in the Philadelphia suburb of Chestnut Hill in 1963–64 had become the iconic figure of postmodernism. It was as celebrated a domestic design as Le Corbusier's Villa Savoye or Frank Lloyd Wright's Fallingwater, "the biggest small building of the second half of the twentieth century," as Scully himself remarked in his opening sentence. But despite the house's significance, little was known of its protracted and complex design history until the publication of *Mother's House: The Evolution of Vanna Venturi's House in Chestnut Hill*, which included all one hundred fourteen known drawings and six study models plus a preface by Aldo Rossi, an introduction by the book's editor (Frederic Schwartz), Venturi's description from 1966 in *Complexity and Contradiction* as well as his commentary "25 Years Later," and the main essay by Scully.

As Schwartz notes in his introduction, Vanna Venturi purchased the three-quarter-acre lot and commissioned the house from her son shortly after the death of her husband in 1959. Robert Venturi—who was to live with his mother in the house until 1967, when he married Denise Scott Brown, a colleague in the architecture school at the University of Pennsylvania—was then thirty-four years old. He had received his master's

18

Everybody Needs Everything

VINCENT SCULLY

> First Russian student, on the Vanna Venturi House: "Who needs it?"
> Second student: "Everybody needs everything."
> Leningrad, 1965

18.1 Robert Venturi's little house for Vanna Venturi, designed 1959–63 and built in 1963–64, has turned out to be the biggest small building of the second half of the twentieth century. It has been big in its effects, in its initiation not only of the vernacular and classical revivals of the past thirty years, but also of the abstractly theoretical architecture of the same period. It is also big in itself, in the archetypal order of its form. Its facade is a diagram of that order. And even if only its facade were known, or if in fact there were no building behind it, that diagram would still have a telling effect because it is a perfect drawing, weightless as pure line and transcending material, of Neoplatonic order imposed upon or growing out of human life: hence the asymmetrical windows of various sizes, but all functions of the square, which slide across it. These do not destroy but underscore and enliven the essential and purely geometric shapes of the facade: the triangle, the circle,

Venturi and Short. Vanna Venturi House, Chestnut Hill, Pennsylvania, 1959–64. Front facade 18.1

degree from Princeton in 1950, worked for Eero Saarinen from 1951 to 1953, been at the American Academy in Rome in 1954–56 on a Rome Prize Fellowship, and worked nine months in the office of Louis Kahn on his return in 1956. When he began designing his mother's house, he was associated with the well-established Philadelphia firm of Cope and Lippincott but soon opened his own office with William Short in 1960. Vanna Venturi apparently set no strict deadline for her son, and it was thus up to him to decide when the design was fully resolved. Schwartz relates the five-year running joke among students at Penn: when someone asked "What does Venturi do all the time?" the answer was "He designs his mother's house." Due to this long, drawn-out process, the Vanna Venturi House was not the first of Venturi's projects to be completed, although it was the first, and still the most influential, of his designs to be built.

Between July 1959, when the earliest rendered drawings are dated, and May 1963, when the construction drawings were completed, the house went through six separate schemes, some of them having two or even three variants. In the 1965 double-issue of *Perspecta* that was edited by Robert Stern, a very limited selection of images of schemes II–V (four views of models and eleven drawings) was illustrated in addition to photographs and drawings of the building as built. The complete collection of drawings and models, however, languished in the archives of the architect's office until 1981, when Frederic Schwartz (then director of the New York office of Venturi, Rauch and Scott Brown) was working on an

exhibition of the firm's drawings for the Max Protetch Gallery in Manhattan, when he came across them and had the idea to publish the entire set. Before that could happen, however, some were sold in 1983 to the Deutsches Architekturmuseum at Frankfurt am Main, and Heinrich Klotz published eleven of the drawings of the final design along with one elevation of scheme IIIA (misidentified as the 1959 Beach House project) in his *Revision der Moderne: Postmoderne Architektur, 1960–1980* (1984), a catalogue of the Frankfurt museum's collection of contemporary architectural drawings. Four years later, New York's Museum of Modern Art acquired the six models.

With its wealth of previously unpublished material, the Schwartz book came as a revelation. Rossi spoke in his preface of "the moving experience of following the young architect's design and the repeated variations." "Looking at the galleys of this book," he said, "I feel as though I have rediscovered an interest in architecture which I had gradually been losing." Even Scully, who had known Venturi for many years and had visited the house soon after its completion, says he had no idea of all the transformations the design had gone through before being shown the material on which he was to base his essay. Scully had always assumed, as he had often written, that the Vanna Venturi House evolved directly from the architect's 1959 Beach House project. The newly available drawings made him realize the story was more complex, and much more interesting. "Everybody Needs Everything" is a fascinating, intense, at times humorous investigation of the twin challenges

and the square, here in fact a near-square, all drawn taut as wire. They are indeed handled as line drawing on paper. Who would guess that the wall they shape is in fact built of plastered cinder block? It is carefully made to look like a cutout cardboard model of a curious color, associated with no material. All the modernist cant, rooted in nineteenth-century materialism, about the "expression of materials," is not simply honored in the breach, which was often the modernist way, but overtly cast aside, much as Le Corbusier had done in the early 1920s.

18.2 The entrance facade of Le Corbusier's Stein Villa at Garches, for example, is treated as pure screen, linear and weightless but perforated at its upper level to reveal the shapes of a bathroom swelling outrageously behind it. Like Le Corbusier, Venturi is stretching the European aesthetic of the ideal to its uttermost limits, or reducing it to its essentials, which reside in the line drawing of perfect geometric shapes. Venturi's facade is not transparent like Le Corbusier's, but it goes further than his in focusing upon the most pervasive and essential Neoplatonic image of all, which is that of the human figure
12.15 placed in the center of the circle and the square. It is the Vitruvian vision, drawn hundreds of times throughout the Middle Ages and the Renaissance and no less essential to the development of Gothic architecture than it was to that of the Renaissance. Venturi taps directly into that ideal power, and in a rather baroque or perhaps a modern way he makes it more dynamic. The central opening looks square but is in fact rectangular. It is

of artistic influence and critical writing. On the one hand, there is Venturi's struggle with his mentor Louis Kahn, an adversarial relationship that Scully likens to the one between Frank Lloyd Wright and Louis Sullivan, in which the influence must be understood to run both ways. On the other, there is the struggle of the art historian to see as the artist did and to find the precise words to translate the physical process of form-making into verbal equivalents. The drawings, not as objects of connoisseurly concern but rather as indices of ideational content, become the nearly autonomous and transparent actors in a dramatic narrative that seems to take place halfway between Scully's mentor Henri Focillon's "life of forms" and what Louis Kahn would describe as their "existence-will." No essay by Scully is as exemplary as this one of the author's extraordinary ability to convey to others how architecture becomes meaningful.

18.2 Le Corbusier. Stein Villa, Garches, France, 1926–28. Front facade

a pure void, emerging directly from the ground upon whose plane the human figure rests while the circle bursts apart around it, seeming to explode outward from the human being in the center and, by extension, arcing down into the earth as well. The image becomes even more embracing; the figure at its center more powerful.

And here Venturi works his great switch. All previous embodiments of human centrality in this diagram had been of the heroic male figure, an athletic, aggressive being who fits into but basically dominates the essential shapes of the world. But here it is Vanna Venturi, seated in her kitchen chair with a pot of geraniums beside her. She is tiny, but the space detonates around her. Directly above her head the gable splits to release her energy beyond the circle and the square to the empyrean. Here the rich balance of opposites, or complementaries, which was to shape all of Venturi's later work, achieved its first and still its most compelling image. Contrasted with the traditional male figure, Vanna Venturi is at once antiheroic and feminist in meaning. She is stronger than he: at rest, she breaks the mold. It was this combination of subversive attitudes that caused so many architects of the 1960s to hate Robert Venturi so earnestly. He was striking at their heroic image of themselves as godlike creators, an idea fundamentally ridiculous in itself and dangerous to architecture but one which was deeply rooted in romanticism and which later modernism had done everything to encourage. The fact that Vanna Venturi was Robert Venturi's mother fueled the fires. Everybody knew all about mothers in 1960. It was risky for a male to admit that he had ever had one. The truth is that the macho pretensions of architects have always rested upon rather shaky foundations in the modern period. Such could easily be read in the early sixties in their destructive urbanism and Brutalist constructions alike. Modernism had trapped them in an unreal and untenable mythology from which they needed release very badly. Venturi went to the heart of the matter with his gentle feminist image, a harbinger of healthier things to come.

Behind Vanna Venturi the void of the square opens to a further subversion of the ideal order of the facade, much as Le Corbusier had done in his bathroom at the Stein Villa. So Venturi shows us an interior as if in tumult behind the frontal plane, with a false stair rising to infinity above the second floor, like the ladder of Jacob's dream mounting to heaven. Below that apparition the entrance void opens to the right to show us the hidden front door, beyond which the interior spaces are all easily and asymmetri-
18.3 cally adjusted to each other. How easy indeed it all seems: the curved wall on entry, the chair rail leading us along, the coved ceiling over the dining table recalling the exterior circle, the fireplace pushed over by the staircase and inflected back toward the main space, the stair itself contracted and expanded, making the most of its opportunities for drama, the bedroom "under the eaves," the boy's room (again driving the critics crazy),
18.4 the stair to heaven, finally the little parapeted balcony at the rear, where everything is the reverse of the front. A wide flat arch stretches across and contains the volume of the house in contrast to the detached split gable of the other side. Here we are even allowed to see that the building embraces three dimensions. There is a moderately scaled chimney in the middle; it had been made to look like a flat plane, simply part of the facade, on the entrance side. Still, the walls remain thin; the little porch by the dining room denies the house a closed corner at that point, and that International Style reference is enhanced by the pipe railing of the basement stair.

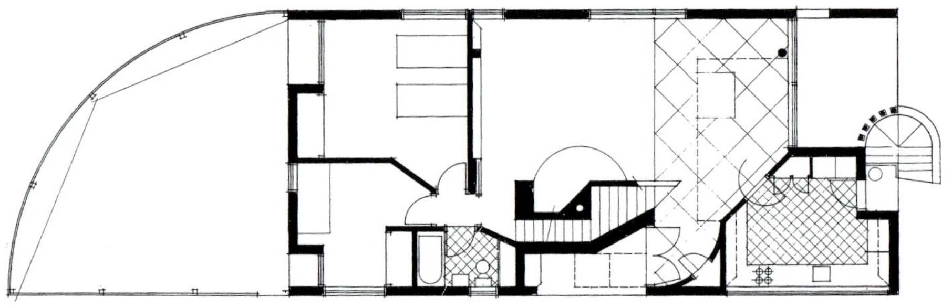

Venturi and Short. Vanna Venturi House. Final presentation drawing, 8 December 1962. First-floor plan 18.3

18.4 Venturi and Short. Vanna Venturi House. Rear facade

Surely there was never a building so in love with the complexities and contra-
dictions of architecture and with its own immediate architectural past, with modernism.
As Philip Johnson's Glass House was in one distinct way the ultimate modern building— 19.2
reduced, that is, to a frame for the individual in nature—so Venturi's was the other
distinctly modern statement, one totally affected by the complexity of the modern condition and the availability of historical data and therefore wanting to try everything with
which the contemporary human brain is stored. That complexity is what makes the genesis of its design so interesting, more interesting at the moment than its effects, which
are, as noted above, well known.

The ancestry of the Vanna Venturi House once seemed clear enough. First came
Venturi's great project for a Beach House of 1959 with its vast shingled, frontal gable 15.2
derived from that of McKim, Mead and White's Low House of 1887, and its outrageous 18.5
chimney, adapted from those of Sir Edwin Lutyens at Middlefield of 1908, and with more 18.6
than a touch of the Villa Savoye of 1929–31 in its thin skin, horizontal voids, and *pilotis*. 18.7
From the Beach House it seemed a direct step to the frontal gable of the Vanna Venturi
House, with its echoes of Frank Lloyd Wright's own house of 1889, even in the neo- 1.16
Vitruvian half circle pasted on the facade. Moreover, Robert Stern had published a few
early studies of the Vanna Venturi design in his unique *Perspecta 9/10* of 1965 (pp.
38–39) and, while these differed in plan from the final version, exhibiting as they did
squarish, separate rooms of a kind Venturi has always acknowledged as Louis I. Kahn's,
they were otherwise of a type stressing the relationship to the Beach House, to its chimney and gable. So both of Venturi's important early designs seemed to be direct spin-offs
from the climactic years of the Shingle Style of the 1880s, with only moderate indications of influence from the work of Kahn, in whose office Venturi was employed for nine

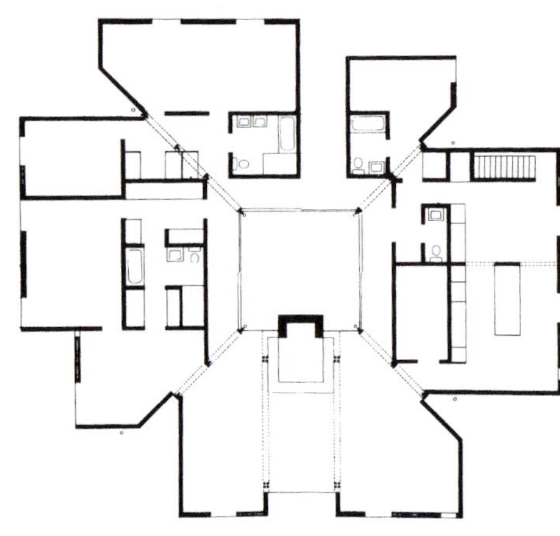

ABOVE, TOP LEFT: McKim, Mead and White. Low House, Bristol, Rhode Island, 1886–87. Exterior 18.5

ABOVE, TOP RIGHT: Sir Edwin Lutyens. Middlefield, Great Shelford, Cambridgeshire, 1908. Exterior 18.6

ABOVE, BOTTOM LEFT: Le Corbusier, Villa Savoye, Poissy, France, 1928–31. Exterior 18.7

ABOVE, BOTTOM RIGHT: Louis I. Kahn. Goldenberg House project, Rydal, Pennsylvania, 1959. Plan 18.8

highly fraught months, beginning in September 1956. Perhaps there was also some
18.8 reflection of the plan of Kahn's Goldenberg House project of 1959 in the Beach House
and some sanction for its monumental shingled gable in Kahn's powerful pyramidal roofs
6.6 at Trenton of 1955. But the Vanna Venturi House itself seemed wholly foreign to Kahn's
work, and its gable, traditionally expressive of "house," indeed stands in firm contrast to
15.3 the abstract, flat-roofed boxes of Kahn's Esherick House, of 1959–61, just up the road.
But now that Venturi has released the relevant drawings for publication—a long series beginning, it would seem, in 1959—it becomes apparent that the design for the Vanna Venturi House did not at all begin as a simple progression from the Beach House project. It is obvious, on the contrary, that Venturi started with some elements that were his own and some that were Kahn's and wrestled with that mixture through years of drawings. These leave a record of the struggle of antagonists loving and fearing each other, coming out only toward the last with something that was almost wholly new, and Venturi's own, with accreted experiences purged away or fused into his own being. In the process, curiously, Venturi seems to have passed through stations on the road through Kahn's work, and his own, where many less driven individuals were come to rest—Giurgola, Botta, and many others as well. Beyond that, the sequence of drawings recalls Wright's relationship to Sullivan from 1887 to 1893, deeply emotional on both sides, ending in the rejection of

the younger man by the older, in which the forms original to the apprentice and to the master are not always easy to define.

The sequence begins with a group of drawings from Venturi's archives which
illustrate a masonry project of concrete block and heavy concrete lintels. On the ground
floor, one thinks as much of the late Le Corbusier as of Kahn, but up above the design
bursts into a welter of roof shapes expressive of elaborate schemes for encapsulating dis- 18.9
crete interior spaces and lighting them from above. They seem typical of Kahn at his
most obsessed. Yet when we look at the date we must pause because the urge to light
spaces from above, indeed to design in section, comes to Kahn only later and is most
beautifully developed in his later museums. Venturi himself believes that the sectional
preoccupation and the overhead lighting are his own and derive from his personal experience of the oculi and thermal windows of Rome. Above everything else in this first
project, Venturi's own obsessive chimney looms. It is clearly the architect's central love
at the moment, his image of his own individuality—which he seems determined at this
point to make more macho than that of his colleagues. (One can hardly help but recall
Melville's story *I and My Chimney*, about a man who defends the central chimney mass
of his colonial house from his wife and daughters, who are convinced it is structurally
faulty, as well as terribly in the way, and want to tear it down.) Hence the chimney is the
single feature of this design that is shared with the Beach House project. The section
shows high, coved spaces, light monitors, and skyscraper flues. Even what we have come 18.10
to think of as Kahn's "ruins wrapped around buildings," which first appear in his work in
the first design for the U.S. Consulate in Luanda, Angola, of 1959–62, are there in the
section to set up a deep spatial layering for the main facades. But again there is a critical question of date here. Kahn's ruins don't stand free of his enclosing walls until his
project for the Salk Community Center of 1961–62; Venturi's drawings of this first Vanna 17.19
Venturi project are earlier than that, so that Venturi's layering would seem to be entirely

18.9 Venturi and Short. Vanna Venturi House, Scheme I, July 1959. Rear elevation

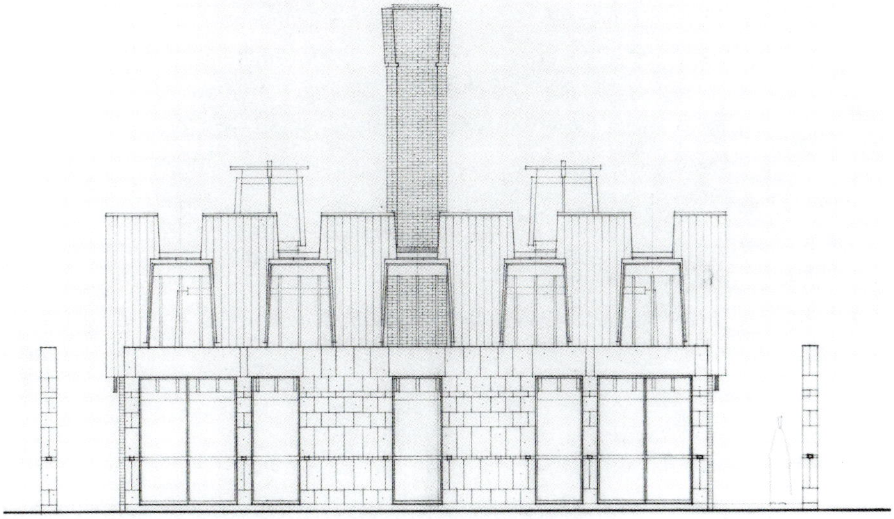

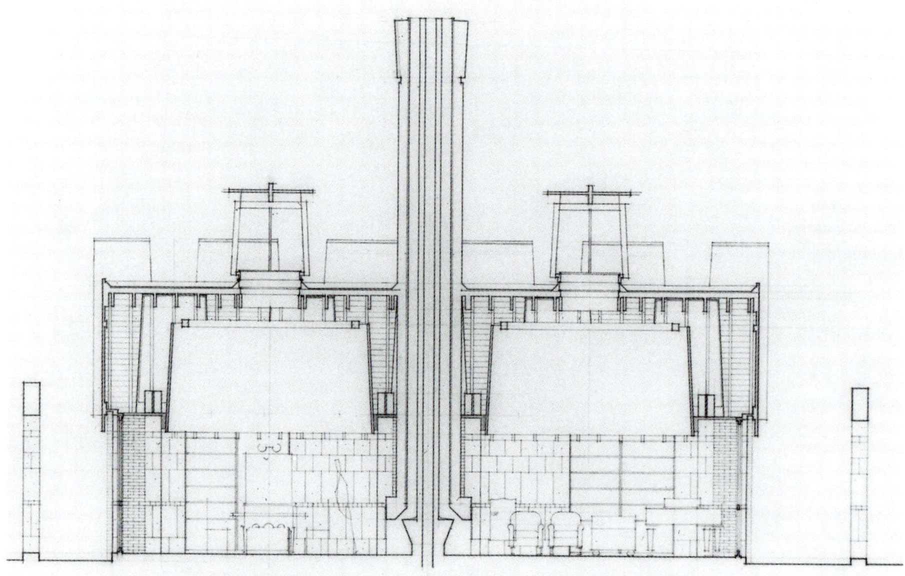

18.10 Venturi and Short. Vanna Venturi House, Scheme I, July 1959. Section

his own, not derivative from Kahn's. It clearly predates Kahn's in any event. Venturi himself traces it back to his earliest projects and ascribes it, again, to Rome, specifically to Brasini's Forestry Building at the EUR of 1942, now demolished. Moreover, Stern's *Perspecta 9/10* (pp. 50–51) also published a project for a "House at Chestnut Hill" (known also as the Pearson House) by Venturi, dated 1957, where the layering of ruins far out in space was already conspicuously present. Its plan, though strung out, also
18.11 resembles that of some of the early plans of the Vanna Venturi project published by Stern, but what is apparently the first plan for that project, never before published, now
18.12 comes as something of a shocker. It is pure Kahn, and the Kahn of the Fleischer project of 1959, not of the much less characteristic Goldenberg House, which Venturi himself, however, specifically identifies as Kahn's as well. Curiously, Venturi vividly remembers the Goldenberg plan but not the Fleischer one. But the Vanna Venturi plan, like the Fleischer, is rigidly cubical, stiff, and basically symmetrical; each space is a discrete structure, while out beyond the main facade the ruins rather dementedly stand. Then it
18.13 is shown on the site, slightly canted off the major axes of road and lot, thus arbitrarily avoiding its natural placement as all the other early site plans were also to do.

Side elevations follow and begin to be reworked on their own. A slanted roof slips in and all the forms begin to simplify somewhat below it. The layered walls disappear. The section is stronger and clearer; the chimney still rides high, but then the whole mass is cut into again, cut down, lowered, and made more modest. But now something
18.14 new intrudes. One quadrant of the building is cut into in plan on a savage diagonal, one that Venturi credits, like the plan of his Beach House, to Kahn's Goldenberg plan. Wall ends begin to chamfer and zip; Giurgola, in part Botta, are suggested. The layering goes wild. The plan is studied interminably. The fireplaces become ever more complex

18.11 RIGHT: Venturi and Short. Vanna Venturi House, Scheme I, July 1959. First-floor plan

18.12 BELOW, LEFT: Louis I. Kahn. Fleischer House project, Elkins Park, Pennsylvania, 1959. Plan

18.13 BELOW, RIGHT: Venturi and Short. Vanna Venturi House, Scheme I, July 1959. Plot plan

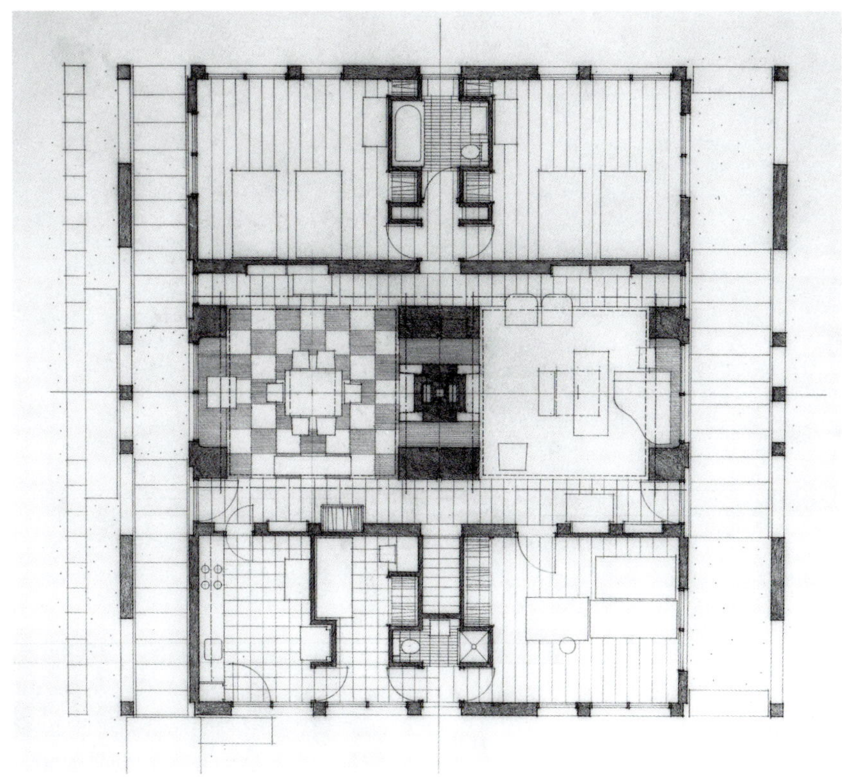

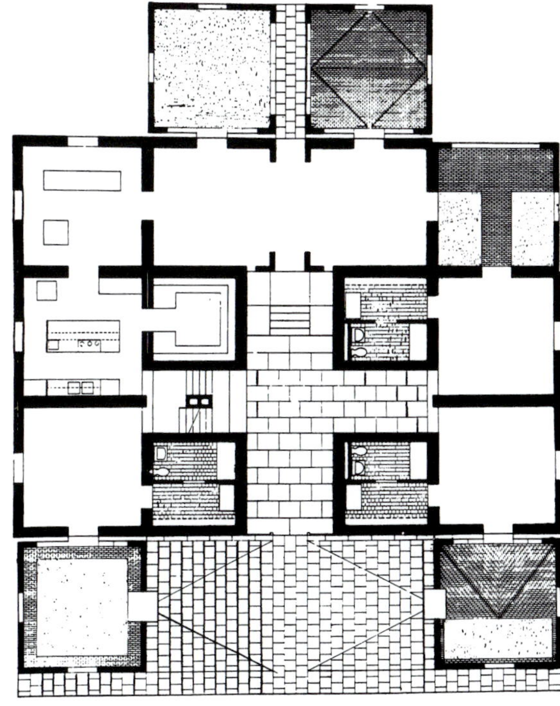

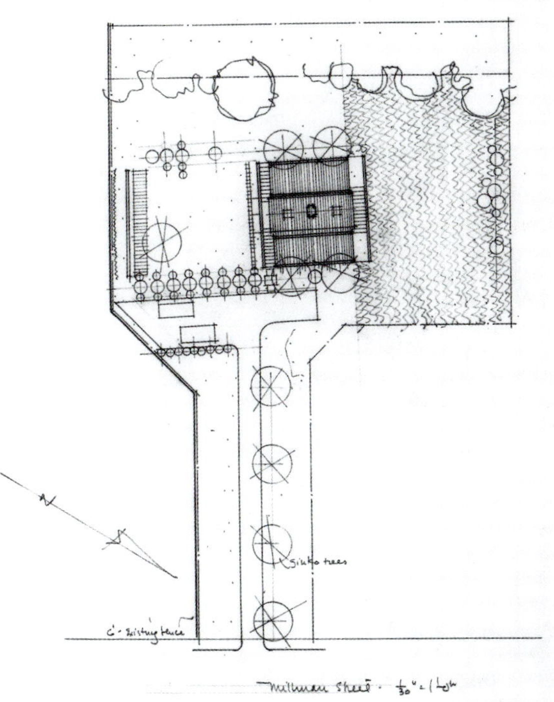

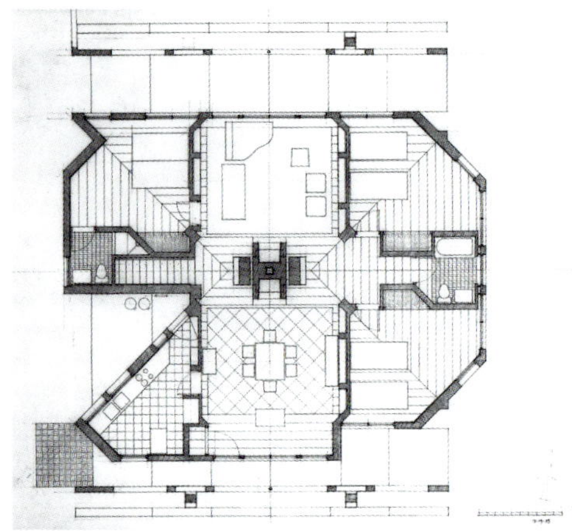

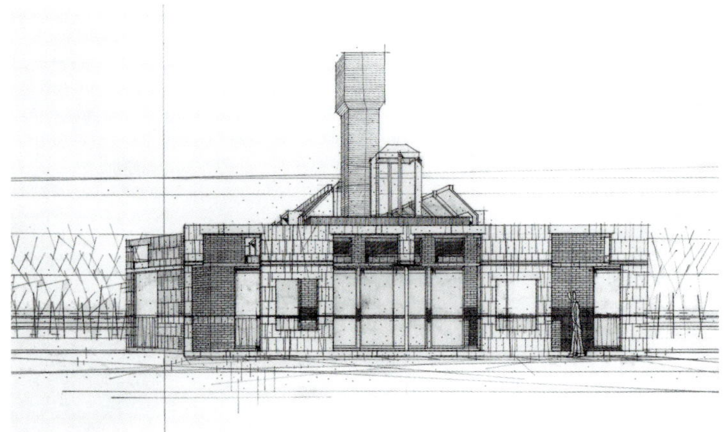

monuments in the center: they are grottoes, caverns, towers. The structure is always of
block masonry, solid, structurally demanding, shaping very separate spaces that are
18.15 essentially dominated by it. The screening walls reappear and various complicated moni-
18.16 tors proliferate above. The block pattern of the masonry walls remains of major concern,
as do the medieval flues and the canted placement on the lot. The thing continues to
18.17 rotate on the lot. It begins to want to sprout an enclosed court; this was to remain a preoccupation almost to the last. It also appeared in Venturi's eloquent scheme for the
Millard Meiss House of 1962, which was produced when the sequence of design here had
just been completed, and which suggests the earlier Kahn-like plans and especially those
of the project of 1957 published by Stern.

The study plans for the Vanna Venturi House are endless. Slowly they begin to
compact, to simplify, and to become less symmetrical; the zips and zaps tend to turn into
18.18 projected planes of wall. Then the Beach House chimney reappears in its original form,
bursting up the center much as its precursors had done. The flues are room size. Soon,
18.19 however, the chimney thins out and leaps much higher, as if in the paroxysm of approach-

ABOVE, LEFT: Venturi and Short. Vanna Venturi House, Scheme IIA, 19 July 1959. First-floor plan 18.14

ABOVE, RIGHT: Venturi and Short. Vanna Venturi House, Scheme IIB, 31 August 1959. Perspective from southwest 18.15

BELOW, LEFT: Venturi and Short. Vanna Venturi House, Scheme IIC. Section 18.16

BELOW, RIGHT: Venturi and Short. Vanna Venturi House, Scheme IIIA. Plot plan 18.17

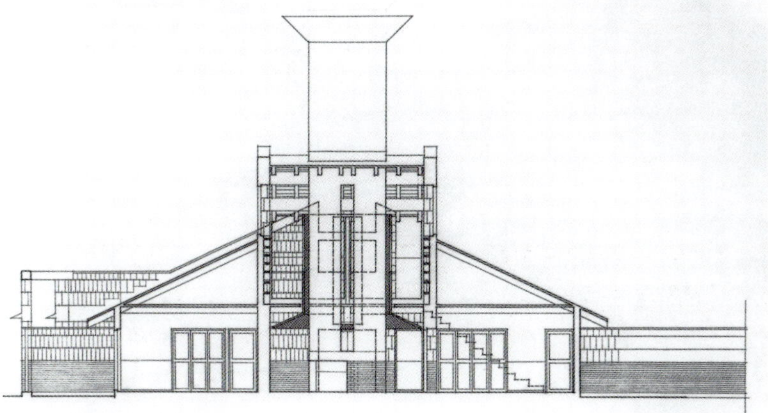

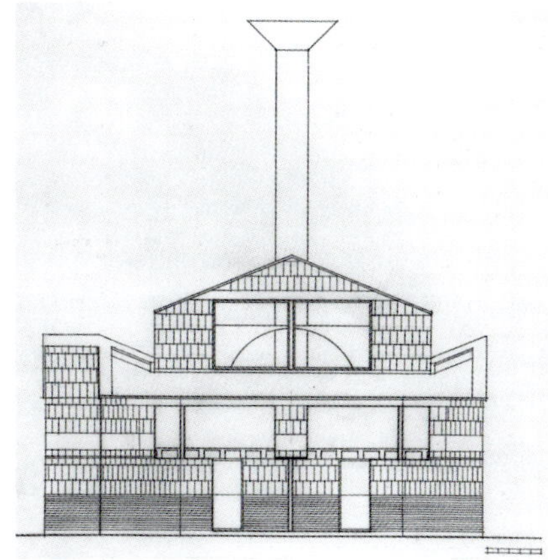

18.18 ABOVE, LEFT: Venturi and Short. Vanna Venturi House, Scheme IIIB. Section

18.19 ABOVE, RIGHT: Venturi and Short. Vanna Venturi House, Scheme IIIA. Front elevation

ing death, and for the first time (at least in this numbered sequence, where some drawings may well have ended up out of strictly chronological order in Venturi's archives) a half-round window appears, enormous in scale. This, of course, had been a central feature of Wright's house, and of numerous gables by Jefferson before him. Palladio had used it on the entrance facades of several villas, where its derivation was from the high windows of Roman baths. Kahn probably got it directly from Hadrian's Villa or from one of the other Roman ruins so essential to his later work, to which he was led in 1950–51 by the great classicist of the American Academy in Rome, the late Frank E. Brown. The round arch in strikingly Roman guise was indeed the major space maker and room shaper of Kahn's Fleischer project, arching up in four planes to model a separate canopied vol- 18.20
ume over each room. By 1960 it had also played a decisive part in Venturi's design for Guild House as well. And the facade of that building clearly owed a direct debt to Kahn's 15.14
Luanda project and to the project for the Salk Community Center, in which the outer layer of "ruin" is at once integrated with the building and expressed as a freestanding plane, pierced by a half-round opening. Yet that thermal window was Venturi's, too, part of his own direct legacy from Rome.

It would seem that the arched windows attracted Venturi as the natural opposite of the chimney—spatial rather than sculptural, sheltering rather than aggressive. Otherwise, for a while the designs are all Low House but the gables remain masonry block. 18.21
The chimney continues to jump up and down but begins to become rather ghostly in effect, drawn in thin outline as if about to disappear. It is obviously beginning to lose its symbolic hold on Venturi, perhaps without his own full awareness of the change, because all of a sudden, though still elaborate, the fireplaces are no longer in the center; they are pushed toward one side and the plan is enormously simplified. Clearly the idea of a second 18.22
floor has begun to come into play. Hence the monitor structure for the first-floor rooms can no longer be maintained, and the thrust of the chimney must concomitantly dwindle.

Venturi fiddles with these new ideas. In section, the design begins for the first 18.23
time to resemble the final project a little. The fireplace is leaning. The round arch is lifting as a big window; it is killing off the chimney at last. A containing void, now rather

simply conceived, is winning out over thrusting mass and monumental structure—which
18.24 is still, however, of masonry blocks. But there a shift now occurs. The lintels are bigger; there is less insistence on the block, at least in some drawings. A stair is seen in profile through a window, and a chopped-off three quarters of a circle, like some used by Venturi later, is experimented with. The block is still there, but the volume is stretching, so that the lintels seem to be stretching too, as if beginning to feel the lateral spatial pressure to which the lintel as finally built on the facade so tautly responds. The windows, as well, are close to the final examples; they are turning square and getting cross-mullioned. It is all thinning out, becoming much less structurally obsessive. When will he get rid of the blocks, we ask.

BELOW, TOP: Louis I. Kahn. Fleischer House project. Model 18.20

BELOW, CENTER LEFT: Venturi and Short. Vanna Venturi House, Scheme IIIB. Side elevation 18.21

BELOW, CENTER RIGHT: Venturi and Short. Vanna Venturi House, Scheme IVB. Model 18.22

BELOW, BOTTOM LEFT: Venturi and Short. Vanna Venturi House, Scheme IVB. Section 18.23

BELOW, BOTTOM RIGHT: Venturi and Short. Vanna Venturi House, Scheme IVB. Side elevation 18.24

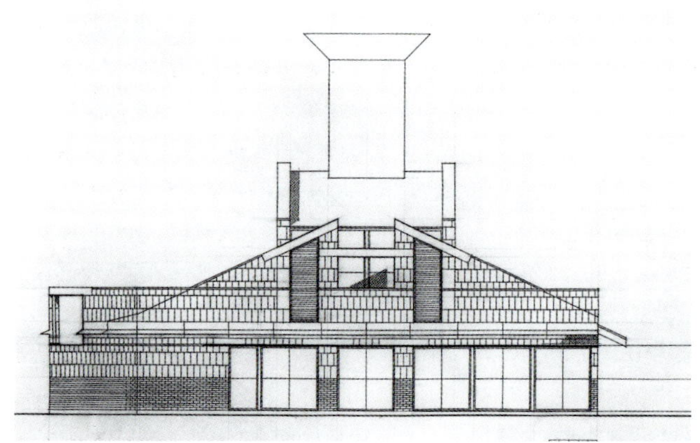

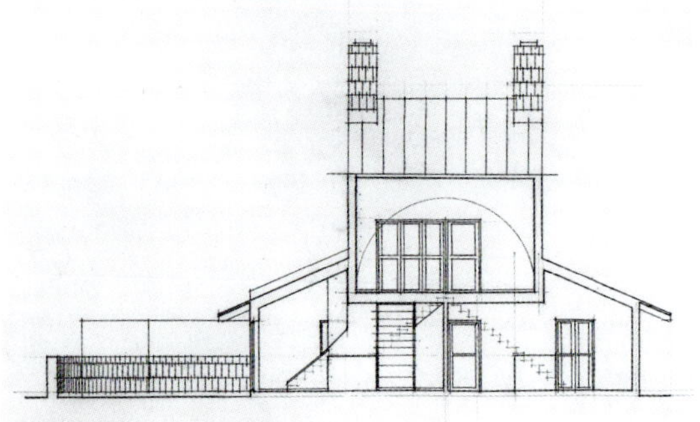

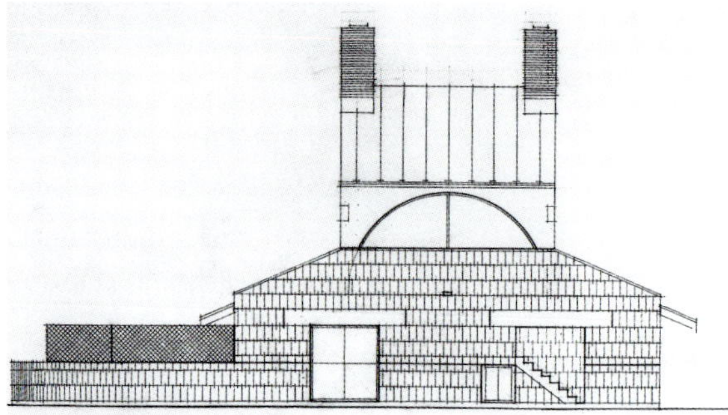

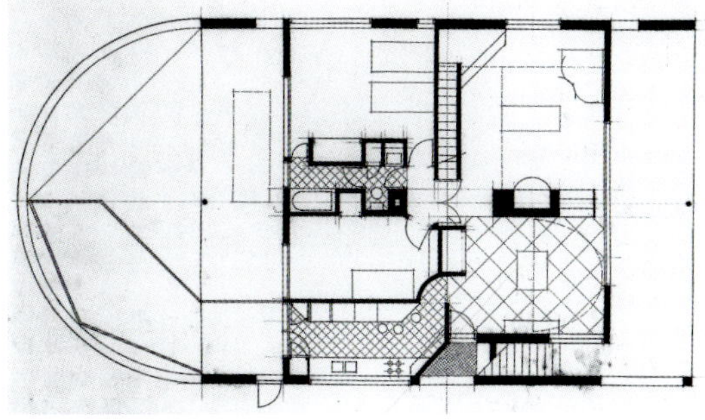

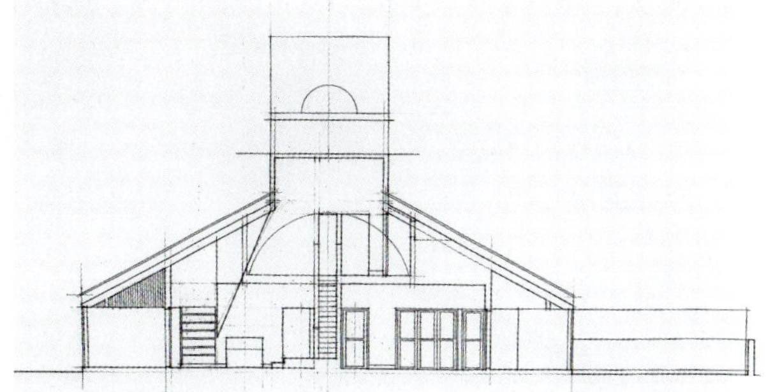

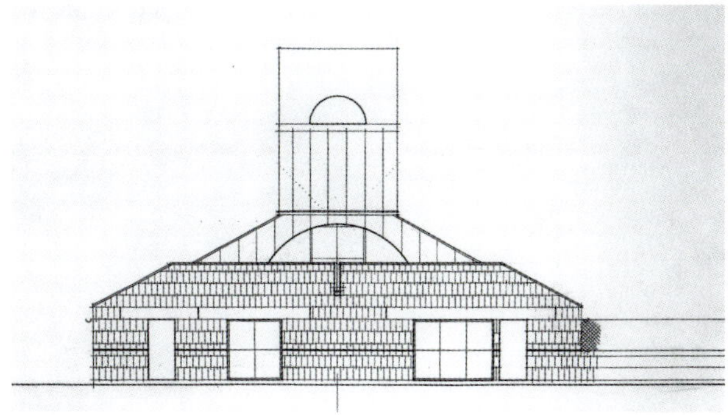

18.25 ABOVE, LEFT: Venturi and Short. Vanna Venturi House, Scheme V, 12 June 1962. First-floor plan

18.26 ABOVE, RIGHT: Venturi and Short. Vanna Venturi House, Scheme V, 12 June 1962. Section

18.27 RIGHT: Venturi and Short. Vanna Venturi House, Scheme V, 12 June 1962. Rear elevation

The plan itself is rushing rapidly toward the final version. The Lutyens-like void 18.25
before the entrance door appears, along with Lutyens's typical curved walls avoiding edges within. One room is tiled; there is an upstairs eyrie with bath, all much more modest than the earlier upstairs bedrooms. Clearly, budgetary limitations, the young architect's best friends, are beginning to play a part. They, or his own classical sense of decorum, which he was to develop so effectively later, are helping Venturi enormously here. Grandiose ideas and ancient obsessions are fading. We are getting down to the
wire. "Do this plan all over," says one drawing. The sections are close to final realization. 18.26
There is a true spatial economy and unity that the earlier versions lacked. There is no duplication; everything acts with maximum valence, rising now not to the aggressive
sculptural mass of a chimney but to the arched window of the upper room. Then the rear 18.27
elevation is fixed; the essentials are almost there; they only need to be proportioned. But there is still the block, and the whole thing continues to roll drunkenly on the site. This version is studied further in plan and elevation.

Finally, a decisive shift in emphasis occurs: from now on, no masonry block is drawn. It is still there as structure, apparently, but is now stuccoed over, and the elevations are studied as line and volume. The drawings are now uniformly gentle; the time for aggressive assertion seems past. The solids are indicated only minimally, as if simply to define spaces, but the symbolic clarity of their shapes is stronger than ever, as is their archetypal geometry. It is as if Venturi had worked his way through all the inessential sturm und drang of late modernism to come out at last into a reasonable, peaceful pool of space and symbol, spiritually simple, certain, and strong, needing to pump no iron.

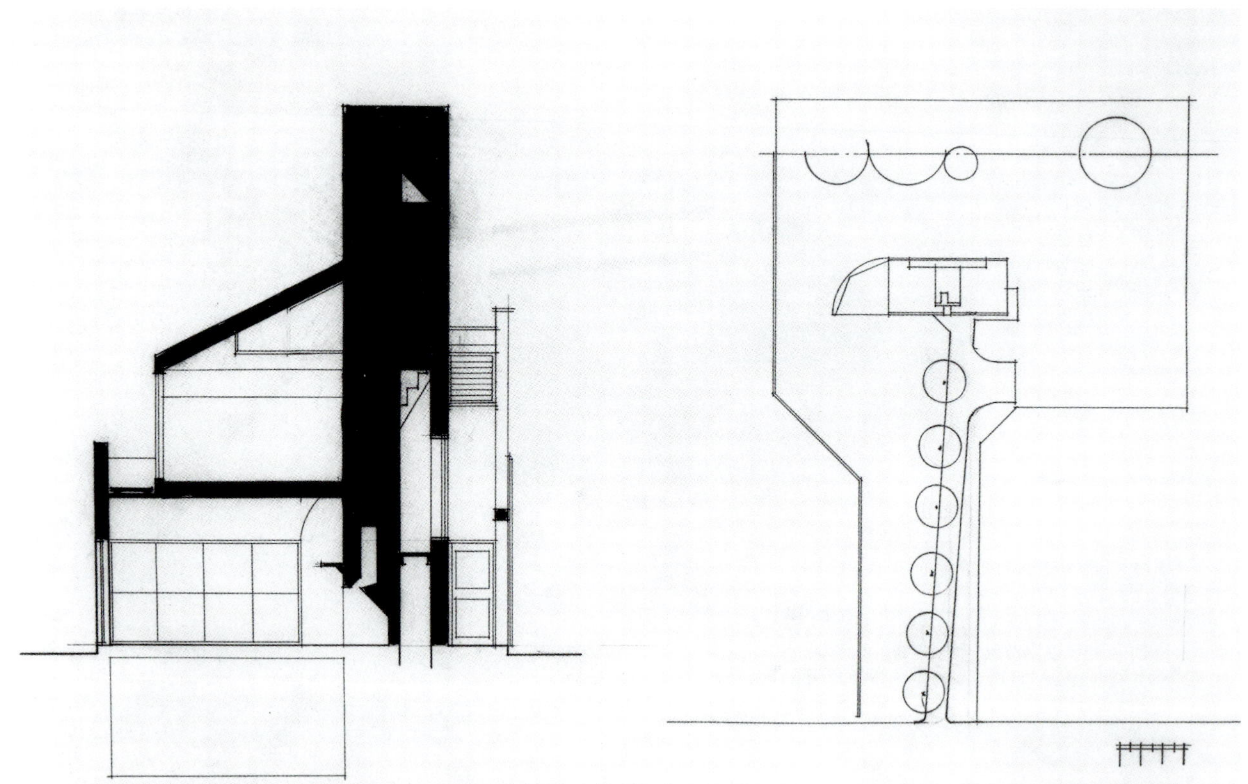

Venturi and Short. Vanna Venturi 18.28
House, Scheme VI, 8 December
1962. Section and plot plan

18.28 With the section drawing we are fundamentally there. The design is almost
fixed; most of all, perhaps, the house has now come to rest on the lot, facing the
entrance drive—though oh-so-correctly kept off the central axis—and lining up with the
18.29 orthogonals of the ground shape. The plan is almost ready, too; the major spaces are in
place, but their peculiarly genial flow from one to the other has not yet been worked out.
So Venturi tries loosening up the kitchen, and then moves on in that rhythm to unite the
18.3 whole thing; working with circles to resonate off the entrance arc, the stair coming alive,
the two bedrooms adjusting to the circulation and each other. It is all turning into his
own kind of planning, flexible and resourceful, imprisoned in no geometric scheme. It
now seems to owe nothing essential to Kahn, though surely something to Aalto and
Lutyens and to the young Le Corbusier as well, and it was to take on a special kind of
casual force in Venturi's later work.

The final scheme is solidly dimensioned at last, but Venturi jumps to modify the
18.30 living room wall. The upstairs room takes on its definitive shape and establishes its relationship to the ghost stair and to the window-of-appearances behind the facade. Sections
and elevations, mainly pure line, now try to work out the final relationships between the
chimney and the roof. Then it is done, and we get all the neatly dimensioned drawings.
How moving it is to witness the dénouement of the process, to this point highly personal,
when the architect sits down to make it all materially real and, most of all, to communicate it clearly to the builder. Even the thin structure of the fence shaping the courtyard on
the side is drawn, but will never be constructed. The facade is studied in three drawings

18.29 TOP: Venturi and Short. Vanna Venturi House, Scheme VI. First-floor plan, study

18.30 CENTER: Venturi and Short. Vanna Venturi House, Scheme VI, 8 December 1962. Second-floor plan

18.31 BOTTOM: Venturi and Short. Vanna Venturi House, Scheme VI. Front elevation, study

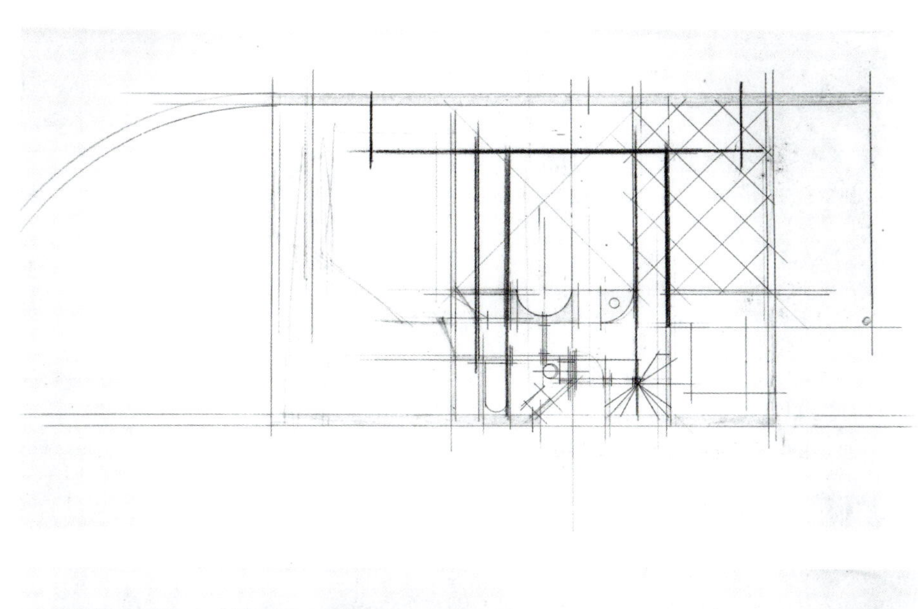

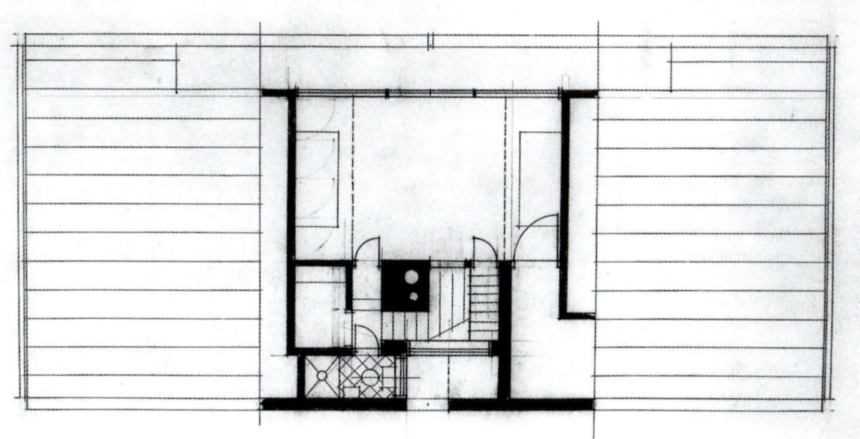

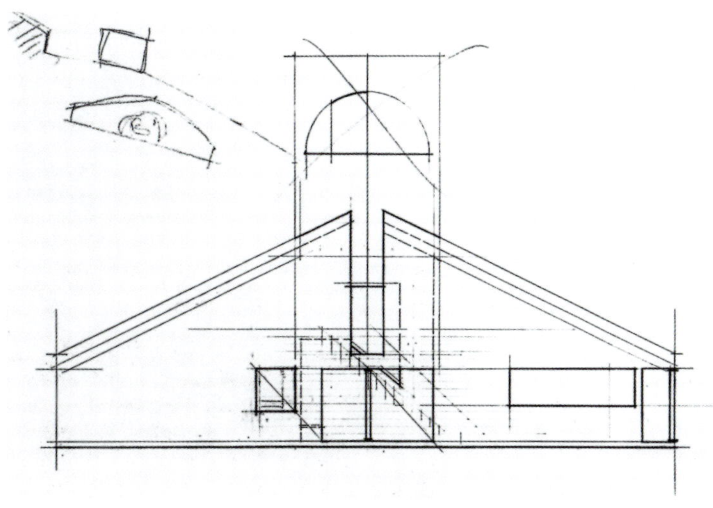

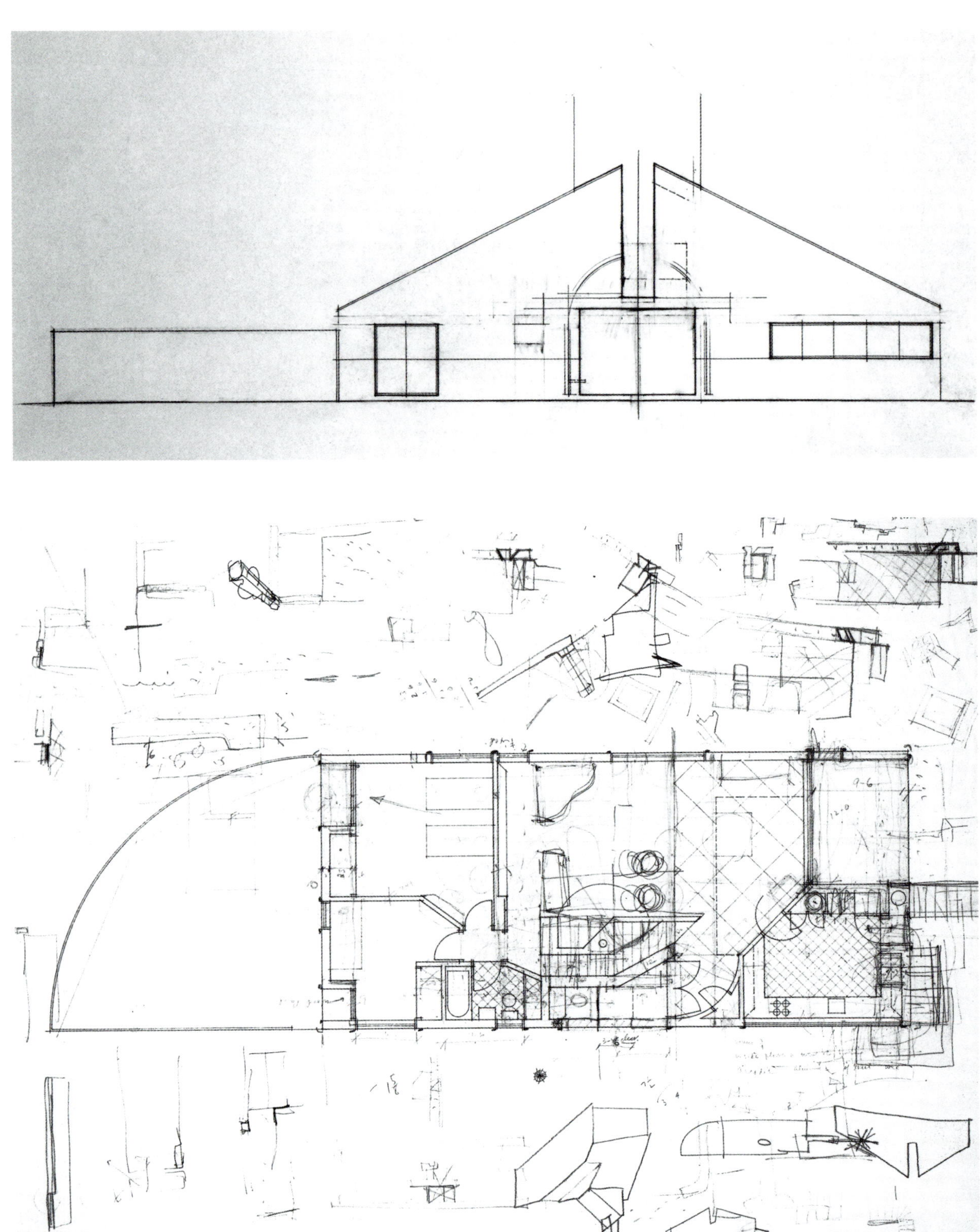

18.32 OPPOSITE, TOP: Venturi and Short. Vanna Venturi House, Scheme VI. Front elevation, study

18.33 OPPOSITE, BOTTOM: Venturi and Short. Vanna Venturi House, Scheme VI. First-floor plan, study with sketches of massing

that were rather naughtily sold, with others, to the Deutsches Architekturmuseum in
Frankfurt. The first has a rectangular central opening, pronouncedly horizontal with a col- 18.31
umn stuck in it. The other two both study the application of an arched strip to the facade 18.32
over the opening and seem to eliminate the column. The arch springs from what appears to be pilasters framing the opening, which is itself now approaching a square shape. No drawing which has yet surfaced quite prepares us for the finished entrance facade, where the fragment of the circle—the descendant of Vitruvius and Palladio and forebear of a thousand similar appliqués—leaps free of the near-square below it to suggest the whole Neoplatonic circle wheeling around it at last. When this process, a passionate and many-layered one, was complete, it had involved the most difficult but often most essential of creative acts, which is the elimination of the very heart of the original intention as the work of art grows. The story has been told so often that it need hardly be assigned a source:

> There was a great king with a young wife whom he loved to distraction. She died. He gathered the finest craftsmen in the world to build a beautiful sarcophagus for her, and he placed it in the center of his biggest mosque. Soon the architectural setting came to seem unworthy of the sarcophagus and its contents, and the king had the mosque rebuilt, larger, finer, grander, more splendid than before. He studied it for years. It was still not right. He rebuilt it once more, distilling it to pure space and air, pure light, blue, white, and gold. Again he studied it, long and hard, this time for many years. Something was still wrong. Finally he knew what it was. He called his vizier to him and pointed to the sarcophagus and said, "Take that thing away."

Venturi's abandonment of what could not conceivably be abandoned was less terrible, perhaps, but no less critical to him. And it was triple: he gave up, most of all, his very insignia, his conceit, the chimney, which was in large measure his self-love, and next the building blocks, and of course the ruins as deep layering, which, however, he most brilliantly incorporated, along with everything else, into the magisterial facade, which may have owed something critical to Luanda and Salk. Whatever the case, it was the ancestor of all the layerings of planes in space that were to play an important part in Venturi's later work and became, in turn, obsessive in that of hundreds of other architects.

A host of afterthoughts, regrets, and nervous qualifications seem to come flood- 18.33
ing in at the very last, with some tiny sketches of the massing. Most touching is a lovely, 18.34
spare line drawing of the facade partly effaced by a heavy sketch of what may be a study for the fenestration of the living room but which looks for all the world like the Villa Savoye. Where really can the truth be said to lie (the pun creates itself) and how can it be wholly told? Memories are treacherous in the oceanic flux of such endeavors, and words are another medium yet, reaching out with difficulty to translate the visual myth and evoke the material surface of the dream, most of all, of the mysterious physical process itself. But the words are there, most especially Kahn's as he asks in the drafting

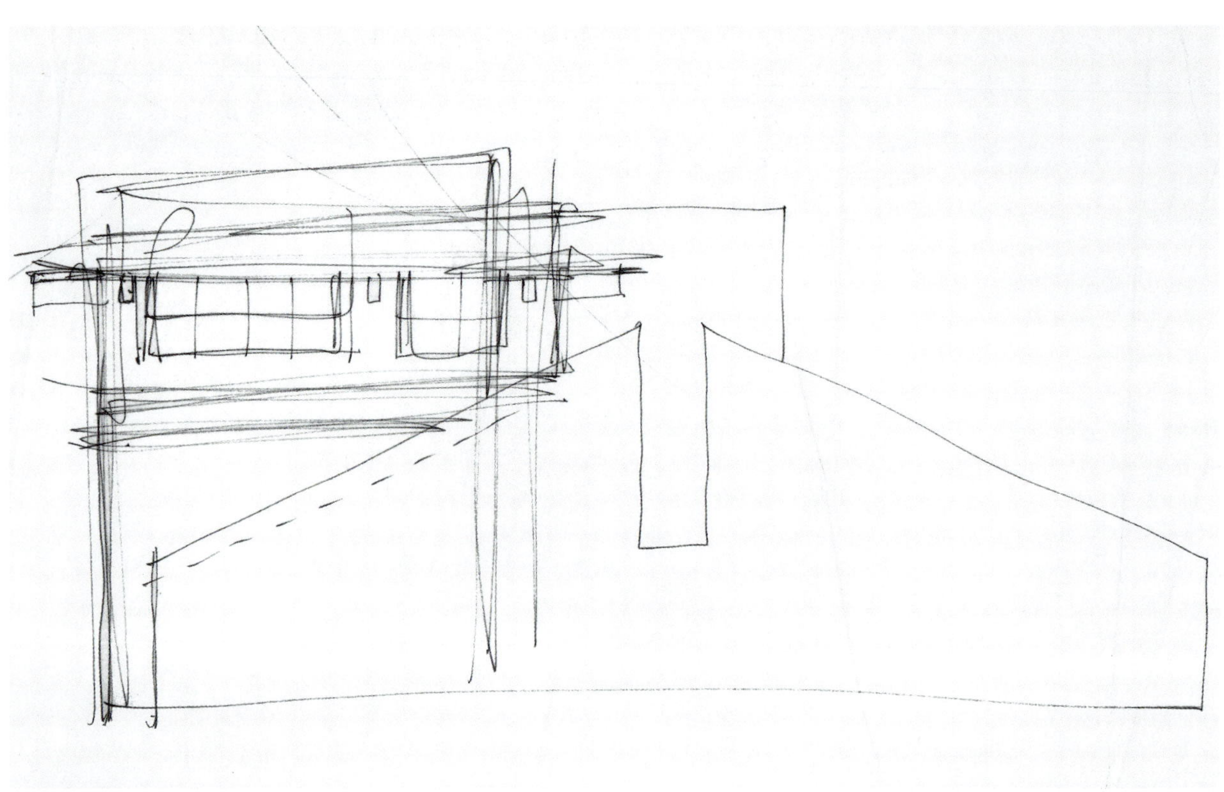

Venturi and Short. Vanna Venturi House, Scheme VI. Front elevation, study 18.34

room what the building "wants to be," perhaps only vaguely guessing himself what he may mean.

Therefore, Venturi often brought his drawings for the Vanna Venturi House to Kahn's office after he had left Kahn's employ. Colleagues apparently made some models for him, and their memory, perhaps faulty, is that Kahn didn't seem to like the scheme very much. Perhaps he couldn't bring himself to do so or to tell them that he did. Others remember him as advising Vanna Venturi to go ahead and build. At any rate, Venturi was clearly doing things that were constitutionally unsympathetic to Kahn. Yet he had without question already learned a lot from Venturi, who, trained as he had been by the last indomitable corporal's guard of the French Beaux-Arts at Princeton, had never been subjected to the Germanic iconoclasm of modernism's most intolerant and limiting school —to which Kahn, at least in his professional life during the 1930s and 1940s, had most destructively been exposed.

So Kahn himself was eventually liberated by Venturi to recall his own past, no less than that of humanity as a whole, and to build upon it. Those elements of design, mostly Roman, which are early in Venturi and late in Kahn, attest to that. Kahn, on the other hand, presented the young architect with a number of specific forms, most especially that diagonal in plan which he himself was almost never to use. But the relationship was much deeper, more painful, and much more important than that. Kahn indeed gave

Venturi everything, a bit as Louis Sullivan had given the young Frank Lloyd Wright so long before, by engaging the younger man in his own grim struggle to define himself and to be. And Venturi, alone of all the fine architects who worked with Kahn and learned from him, accepted that challenge wholly, even if it had to mean, as it always seems to, the loss of the master's dearly desired love at last. So Venturi broke through, but alone, to an enhanced identity and another land. So Jacob wrestled with the angel at the passage of Penuel, who said to him:

> "Let me go, for the day breaketh."
> And he said, "I will not let thee go, except thou bless me."
> And he said, "Thy name shall be called no more Jacob,
> but Israel: for as a prince thou hast power with God and
> with men, and hath prevailed."

NEIL LEVINE

"The Architecture of Community." In *The New Urbanism: Toward an Architecture of Community,* by Peter Katz. New York: McGraw-Hill, 1994.

As the leading critical voice for a return to "the classical and vernacular traditions," Scully became a strong advocate of the New Urbanism in the early 1990s, and its neotraditional, community-oriented principles have remained a major theme of his writings up to the present. The movement, which owed much to Scully's own early criticism of modern urbanism (see "The Death of the Street," chap. 7), had its immediate origins in the mid- to late 1970s in the work of Aldo Rossi, Robert Venturi, Robert Stern, and Leon Krier, and its first and still most prominent realization in the creation of the Florida resort town of Seaside, planned by Scully's former students Andres Duany and Elizabeth Plater-Zyberk beginning in 1979.

The design of Seaside and its critical reception are central to the discourse about urban renewal and suburban sprawl that emerged in the 1990s and to which Scully's text "The Architecture of Community" is addressed. After considerable time spent refining the plan and establishing the urban and architectural codes that would ensure the desired pedestrian scale, coherent streetscape, building typologies, neighborhood orientation, and generous public spaces of the future town, the construction of Seaside progressed at a slow though steady pace through the early 1980s. The first articles in professional journals appeared in 1984–85. Public awareness was significantly increased by the exhibition of drawings of the town organized by David Mohney, coauthor (with Keller Easterling) of the first book on Seaside (Princeton Architectural Press, 1991). It opened at the Urban Center

19

The Architecture of Community

VINCENT SCULLY

The architects who are published in this book believe that the principles shaping their work, among them the establishment of public space, pedestrian scale, and neighborhood identity, are as applicable to center city as to suburban conditions. This may well be true, and there are one or two urban projects to suggest it, but it is a fact that the most characteristic situation with which most of this work deals is a suburban one. In view of the fact, too, that there are a number of active contemporary strategies for the healing of center city that are not mentioned in this volume—the historic preservation of neighborhoods and their inhabitants is one example among many—the book's title, *The New Urbanism*, cannot help but seem overly comprehensive.

The New Suburbanism might be a truer label, because the *new* theme that links these projects is the redesign of that vast area in which most Americans now live, sprawled between the metropolitan center, which is emptying out, and the open countryside, which is rapidly being devoured. The major issue surely has to do with reshaping that sprawl of automobile suburbia into communities that make sense, and *Toward an Architecture of Community*, the book's subtitle, is what this book is primarily about. In

Gallery in New York in the fall of 1985, under the sponsorship of the Architectural League of New York, before traveling to a number of other venues throughout the United States. As more and more buildings went up and the shape of the town became clearer, articles proliferated in the architectural journals as well as in the popular press. Significant coverage in *Time*, *Newsweek*, and *Smithsonian*, for instance, served to make Seaside the paradigmatic example of the New Urbanism. In inverse relation to the growing popularity of Seaside was the negative reaction of the academic and professional elites, who focused on the upper-middle-class demographics of the resort town and the "nostalgic" character of its architecture. The two sides were joined in "Seaside and the Real World: A Debate on American Urbanism" that was held in New York in April 1993 and published four months later in the first issue of the programmatically Neomodernist journal *ANY*.

Scully visited Seaside in the spring of 1990 after receiving an honorary degree from the University of Miami. The first of his publications about the town appeared in the *New York Times* in January 1991. In the same year, he contributed an article entitled "Seaside and New Haven" to the book *Andres Duany and Elizabeth Plater-Zyberk: Towns and Town-Making Principles* (edited by Alex Krieger and William Lennertz), which was produced in connection with the exhibition of the architects' work at Harvard's Graduate School of Design the previous fall. Scully's growing involvement with the town-planning movement spearheaded by his former students and, by then, his current employers and colleagues at the University of Miami made him the obvious choice to give the opening lecture at the First Congress for the New Urbanism (CNU), which took place in Alexandria, Virginia, in October 1993, under the leadership of Duany and Plater-Zyberk. The Congress was meant to bring together for the first time practitioners and others from around the country who were engaged with "the movement to reform American urbanism." Its name was specifically designed to echo the modernist, Corbusier/Giedion–dominated Congrès Internationaux

that sense, it has to do with architecture at its proper scale and put to its proper use, which is the shaping of the human environment within the natural world, the building of the human community entire.

All human culture is intended to protect human beings from nature in one way or another and to mitigate the effect upon them of nature's immutable laws. Architecture is one of humanity's major strategies in that endeavor. It shelters human beings and reassures them. Its purpose is to mediate between the individual and the natural world by creating the physical reality of the human community, by which the individual is linked to the rest of humanity and nature is in part kept out, in part framed, tamed, and itself humanized. So architecture constructs its own model of reality within nature's implacable order. It is within that model that human beings live; they need it badly, and if it breaks down they may well become insane.

That is exactly what is happening today, and not only in America, but the pattern, as so often in contemporary history, can be perceived most clearly here. This is so,

d'Architecture Moderne (CIAM) that had established the criteria for the urbanism of the postwar years that the CNU was hoping to counteract. The theme of the first meeting was "The Neighborhood, the District, and the Corridor." In addition to Scully, Duany, and Plater-Zyberk, speakers and presenters included Jonathan Barnett, Peter Calthorpe, Robert Fishman, James Kunstler, Barbara Littenberg, David Mohney, Elizabeth Moule, Steven Peterson, Stefanos Polyzoides, and Daniel Solomon. Scully's talk, entitled "An Urbanism for Our Time," was in part based on the essay reprinted here, which had been written just a few months prior to the meeting.

"The Architecture of Community" was initially published in 1994 in Peter Katz's *The New Urbanism: Toward an Architecture of Community*, the first major compendium of projects embodying the new ideas (the book's subtitle was suggested by Scully, who would have preferred the entire movement to be known as the Architecture of Community rather than the New Urbanism). Short essays by Calthorpe ("The Region"), Duany and Plater-Zyberk ("The Neighborhood, the District and the Corridor"), and Moule and Polyzoides ("The Street, the Block and the Building"), plus a historical overview by Todd W. Bressi precede the survey of twenty-four projects, the first ten of which are grouped under the rubric "Establishing the Urban Pattern" in new towns and suburban areas and the remainder under "Reconstructing the Urban Fabric." Scully's text, which was supposed to have been the foreword but was instead turned into an afterword by Katz because of its overly critical tone, was

in part, because Americans have in fact destroyed so many kinds of communities during the past generation. The process began directly after World War II, when the remaining trolley tracks, the very lifeline of town and suburb alike, were apparently bought and torn up by the automobile interests. Public transit had been declining since 1914 in any event as the number of automobiles rose. The redevelopment of the 1960s completed the destruction and showed the true shape of the holocaust. The automobile was, and remains, the agent of chaos, the breaker of the city, and redevelopment tore most American towns apart to allow it free passage through their centers, which were supposed to be revitalized by affluent suburban shoppers thereby. Instead the reverse took place: the automobile created the suburban shopping mall, which sucked the life out of the old city centers everywhere. This is ironic enough, because the existing center-city communities had themselves been destroyed by redevelopment in order to bring the largely mythical suburbanite shoppers in. To follow I-95 and its various connectors from New England to Florida is to watch that evil process at work from Oak Street in New Haven to Overtown in Miami, at the very end of the road. Their communities physically torn apart, and given no opportunity to form new ones, many of the inhabitants of center city began to lose their minds, as who would not. Many of them were African-Americans from the rural South who had been lured to the big cities to work in war plants during World War II; then the factories moved away with perfect cynicism, seek-

meant to provide a framework for understanding the intentions and accomplishments of the movement as a whole. Almost as if to prove the strength of its aims and, even more, the potential embodied in the initial results at Seaside, his essay begins and ends by pointing out certain general weaknesses in the work so far: its suburban rather than truly urban focus, its lack of provision of housing for the poor, and the equivocation of some of its leaders, especially Duany and Plater-Zyberk, over the necessity of classical and vernacular forms to the success of the designs. None of this, however, diminishes in his eyes the real achievement of Seaside, which is the creation not necessarily of a community but of an image or symbol of community, serving as a model for something that modern architecture had proved itself constitutionally and ideologically incapable of producing. The creation of codes that link the two-dimensional urban plan to the three-dimensional architectural forms is analogized to the way laws in society mediate relations between the individual and the group. In this, Duany and Plater-Zyberk are seen as reclaiming for architecture the larger, though perhaps more self-effacing, role it had traditionally played to the benefit of the community.

ing even cheaper labor back in the South once more; then, in financial panic, the big cities redeveloped themselves in the manner already described and there its people were, out of work under the Piranesian piers of the freeway, in a surreal wasteland with homes, churches, stores, and most of all the orienting street grid of the city, all shot to hell.

By contrast, the suburbs, closed off from the urban population by what Frank Lloyd Wright once called "the iron hand of realty," seemed like Paradise, but they were spawning their own neuroses too, fed by endless hours on the road and no connection with much of anything when one got where one was going. Soon fear came to play its part. It rode behind the locked doors of the automobiles and was eminently justified, whether by the nut on the highway, or the sniper on the overpass, or by what happened if the wrong exit was taken off the connector.

Whatever other factors have been involved in this disintegration of community, it is still the automobile—and how much we all love it—which has done the job. It has not only obliterated the community's physical structure but has also made us feel that the community's psychic protection is unnecessary, and that what the car seems to offer in terms of individual freedom is enough. It is a device of deep illusion and may be said to have rendered all of society insane. Indeed, the years to come will soon show us whether the automobile and what we have thought of as civilization can coexist.

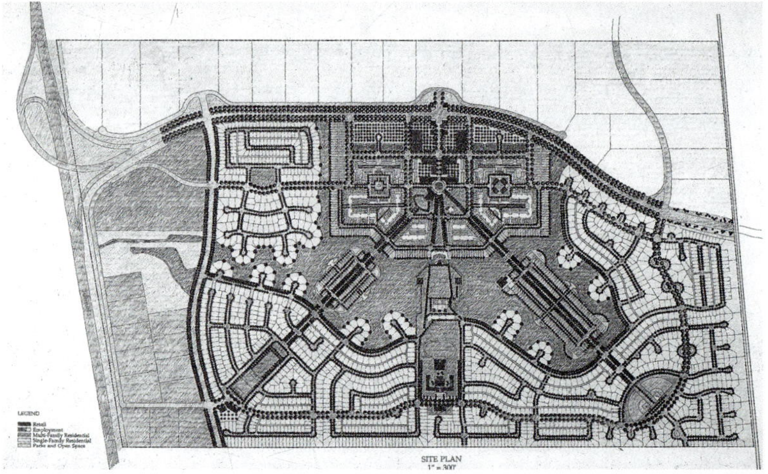

LEFT: Peter Calthorpe. Laguna West, California, 1990. Master plan 19.1

ABOVE: Philip Johnson. Glass House (Johnson House), New Canaan, Connecticut, 1946–49. Exterior 19.2

Some of us were writing and teaching all this in the 1960s—even then the eventual effects on American society were predictable enough—and some younger people were apparently listening. Peter Calthorpe, a student at Yale in the 1970s, seems to
19.1 have been one of them. His "transit-oriented development," as assembled at Laguna West, is an attempt to regroup the suburb into a density which makes public transit feasible. It is shaped by avenues that radiate, like those of Versailles, from a center of public buildings and spaces, among them a "village green." One thinks of the seventeenth-century grid plan of New Haven, Connecticut, with the great Green in the center. As the grid moved west to shape most of the cities of the continent, the Green, the public space, tended to disappear under the pressure of private greed. Calthorpe now tries to bring it back, reflecting the attempt by many organizations over the past thirty years to preserve or restore public space. One recalls the fight under Margaret Flint of the New Haven Trust for Historic Preservation to preserve the scale and amenity of New Haven's Green itself in 1967. Indeed, the combats of that year—when New Haven's post office and city hall were saved from redevelopment and after which, by extension, the brutal demolition of low-income neighborhoods was brought to a halt by Senator Lowell Weicker—might be regarded as the true beginning of the contemporary preservation movement, through which, for the first time in the modern period, a popular mass movement has discovered the means and the political clout to force architects and civic officials alike to do what the informed public wants them to do.

That movement, now boldly led by the National Trust for Historic Preservation, does seem to reflect the yearning to rebuild community which is felt by most Americans today. It now seems obvious to almost everybody—as it did once before, in the 1870s, when the Colonial Revival began—that community is what America has most conspicuously lost, and community is precisely what the canonical modern architecture and planning of the middle years of this century were totally unable to provide. This was so for many reasons; foremost among them was the fact that the modern architects of the heroic period (Wright, Le Corbusier, Mies van der Rohe, Gropius, and their followers) all despised the traditional city—the finest achievement of Western architecture, put together piece by piece over the centuries—and were determined to replace it with their own personal, utopian, idiosyncratic schemes. Le Corbusier's Ville Radieuse was the most influential of them all; and it furnished the basic model for American redevelopment itself. Even the social structures involved were eerily the same: both were "cités d'affaires," cities of business, from which the poor were to be excluded. The German modernists had advanced equally catastrophic ideas, based upon their concept of the "zeitgeist," the "spirit of the age," that did not allow anything which had been done before to be done again or even to be preserved. So Hilbersheimer proposed his endless miles of high-rise slabs, his landscapes of hell, out of which the mass housing of the 1950s took shape, much of it to be dynamited as wholly unlivable hardly more than twenty years later.

In all these cataclysmic proposals for the city there was a true hatred for the world as it was socially constituted, but there was also something else, a consuming contempt for it on aesthetic grounds. The modern architects of the International Style had largely taken abstract painting as their model, and they came to want to be as free from all constraints as those painters were, free from everything which had always shaped and limited architecture before, in part from statics itself (forms must float) and from roofs, windows, trim, and so on, but most of all from the restraints of the urban situation as a whole: from the city, from the community. Their buildings were to be free of zoning laws, and from the need to define the street, and from all respect for whatever already existed on
and around the site. They were to be free—like Lever House or the Pan Am Building or the 7.2, 7.3
Whitney Museum or even the Guggenheim Museum—to rip the old urbanism apart or to outrage it, or, perhaps most truly, to use its order, while it lasted, as a background before which they could cavort. Most of all they had to be abstract; they could not under any circumstances be inflected toward their surroundings by classical or vernacular details or stylistic references of any kind. Such would have constituted an immoral act. Here was another madness to complement the others. It is still prevalent today among many architects who, baffled by the complexity of reality, still insist that architecture is a purely self-referential game, having to do with formal invention, linked madly enough with linguistics, or literature, but not at all with the city or with human living on any sane terms. Such architects claim to reflect the chaos of modern life and to celebrate it. Some of them pretend to worship the automobile, and the "space-time continuum," like Marinetti before them idolizing violence, speed, war, and Fascism in the end. "Whom Zeus wishes to destroy," said Aeschylus more or less, "he hastens on with madness."

Yet it should be said that there is hardly an architect or critic living today who has not been drawn to modern architecture during his life and does not love thousands of modern works of art. But the urban issue has to be faced. The International Style built many beautiful buildings, but its urbanistic theory and practice destroyed the city. It wrote bad law. Its theme in the end was individuality; hence its purest creations were
suburban villas, like the Villa Savoye and Philip Johnson's Glass House. These cele- 18.7, 19.2
brated the individual free from history and time. One could not make a community out of them. In the Glass House especially the individual human being seems wholly liberated

from the entire human community. The secret is technology, a chancy thing; plugged into its heating and lighting devices the existential mortal man can dispense with everything else that once stood between nature and himself. He enjoys the sensation of being wholly alone in the world. His architecture cannot, will not, deal with community issues.

So Neomodern architecture, in its present "Deconstructivist" phase, though
popular in the schools—why not, it offers the ideal academic vocabulary, easy to teach as
a graphic exercise and compromised and complicated by nothing that exists outside the
academic halls—has been failing for a long time in the larger world of the built environment itself. Here it is clear that the most important development of the past three decades
or more has been the revival of the classical and vernacular traditions of architecture,
which have always dealt with questions of community and environment, and their reintegration into the mainstream of modern architecture. That development in fact began in
the late 1940s with an historical appreciation of the American domestic architecture of
the nineteenth century—which I tried to call the Stick and Shingle Styles—and it first
15.2 took new shape in the present with Robert Venturi's shingled Beach House of 1959.
18.1 Venturi then went on, in the Vanna Venturi House of the early 1960s, to reassess the early
buildings of Frank Lloyd Wright, which had themselves grown directly out of the Shingle
Style of the 1880s, and he worked his way wholly back into the Shingle Style itself, as in
12.38 the Trubek and Wislocki Houses of 1970. Here Venturi rediscovered a basic vernacular
type, very close indeed to the types "remembered" (as he put it) by Aldo Rossi in Italy very
15.6, 15.7 soon thereafter. Many other architects then followed that lead, Robert A. M. Stern foremost in time among them. Stern soon learned to abandon his compulsion to invent—his
early houses, though based on Shingle Style models, are proto-Deconstructivist in form—
in favor of trying to learn how to design traditional buildings well, and to group them in
ways that make sense. The point became not style but type and, by extension, context.
Here again Robert Venturi's work led the way. Wu Hall in Princeton, the Institute for
Scientific Information in Philadelphia, and the Sainsbury Wing of the National Gallery in
London, all inflect what are otherwise clearly modern buildings toward the particular
15.1 "styles" which preexist on each site: Tudorish in Princeton, International Style in
15.22 Philadelphia, classical on Trafalgar Square. Each new building thus enhances and com-
pletes the existing place on its own terms. The city is healed rather than outraged—poignantly so in London, where the site had actually been blitzed and where early schemes to build upon it lent credence to Prince Charles's remark that modern architecture had done more damage to England than the Luftwaffe. Now the architect gives up his semi-divine pretension to be Destroyer and Creator and to invent new styles like new religions, and aspires instead to the more humane and realistic role of healer, of physician. Venturi was surely encouraged in this new pragmatism by the work of his wife Denise Scott Brown in neighborhood design and advocacy planning. So, with Venturi, the architect abandons the iconoclasm of much of the modern movement in favor of the idea that he belongs to a long and continuous architectural tradition, through which cities in the past have on the whole been built correctly and in reasonable accordance with human needs.

Out of this view, which is in fact the natural culmination of the vernacular and classical revival, the work of Andres Duany and Elizabeth Plater-Zyberk derives. It completes the revival by dealing with the town as a whole. It reclaims for architecture, and for 19.3, 19.4 architects, a whole realm of environmental shaping that has been usurped in recent generations by hosts of supposed experts, many of whom, like those of the truly sinister departments of transportation everywhere, have played major roles in tearing the environment to bits and encouraging its most cancerous aberrations. With these two young architects, and with their students and colleagues at the University of Miami, architecture regains its traditional stature as the means by which cities are made.

I have written elsewhere how, as architecture students at Yale in the early 1970s, Duany and Plater-Zyberk led my seminar into New Haven's vernacular neighborhoods and showed us all not only how intelligently the individual buildings were put together but also how well they were related to each other to make an urban environment—how effectively the lots worked, and the porches related to the street, and the sidewalks with their fences and their rows of trees bound the whole fabric together, and how street parking was better than parking lots and the automobile could be disciplined, and how, most of all, it could all be done again—and fundamentally had to be done again as all of a piece if it was going to be done right—from the turned posts and the frontal gables to the picket fences, the sidewalks, and the trees. Everything that the International Style had hated, everything that the "zeitgeist" had so Germanically consigned to death, came alive again. For me, marinated in modernism, it was the revelation of a new life in everything. There was no reason whatever why the best of everything had to be consigned to the past. Everything was available to be used again; now, as always in architecture, there were models to go by, types to employ.

So it is important to remember that for Duany and Plater-Zyberk the plan as such did not come first. First came the buildings, the architectural vernacular, because it was after all the buildings which had brought the old New Haven grid up into three dimensions to shape a place. Duany and Plater-Zyberk's critics have never really understood this. It is again a question of types which, with their qualifying details and decoration, have shown themselves capable of shaping civilized places and of fitting together in groups to make towns. Leon Krier was also instrumental in helping us see 10.3 this, and he became one of Duany and Plater-Zyberk's most important mentors and was to build a beautiful house at Seaside.

Terms like "historicism" are not relevant here—the zeitgeist mentality is "historicist," not this one—but ancillary concepts like those relative to symbol are relevant indeed, and no excuse need be made for that fact. Human beings experience all works of visual art in two different but inextricably interrelated ways: empathetically and by association. We feel them both in our bodies and in terms of whatever our culture has taught us. Modernism at its purest fundamentally wanted to eliminate the cultural signs if possible—hence abstraction. It was Venturi himself who, in his epoch-making *Complexity and Contradiction in Architecture* (1966) and his *Learning from Las Vegas* (1972), first brought an awareness of the centrality of symbolism back to architecture, and he was

ABOVE: Andres Duany and Elizabeth Plater-Zyberk (master planners). Seaside, Florida, begun 1979–82. General view 19.3

LEFT: Andres Duany and Elizabeth Plater-Zyberk. Seaside. Master plan 19.4

the first to use semiotics as an architectural tool. It was he who introduced literary criticism itself, especially Empson's theory of ambiguity, into the contemporary architectural dialogue. Faced with this, the Neomodernists would like to divert it by replacing the relevant primary architectural symbols—those having to do with nature, place, and community—with secondary and diversionary ones having to do with linguistics or whatever else may be dredged up out of the riot of sign systems in the human mind.

Not Duany and Plater-Zyberk. Their eyes are on the reality of things as they are. That is why Seaside is so moving. Whatever it may be in fact—a resort community, a modern-day Chautauqua—it has beyond that succeeded, more fully than any other work of architecture in our time has done, in creating an image of community, a symbol of human culture's place in nature's vastness. It does this in terms of the densely three-dimensional organization of its building types as they group together, almost huddle together, on the shore of Florida's Panhandle, pressed close up to the gleaming white sand, the green and blue sea, and the wild skies of the Gulf of Mexico. Therefore, Seaside is not an affair of plan only, not only of two-dimensional geometry, as all too many planned communities in this century have tended to become. True enough, Seaside's plan as such has a distinguished ancestry. It owes a direct debt not only to Versailles and to the whole French classic planning tradition, out of which Washington no less than modern Paris took its shape, but also to the fine American planning profession that flourished before Gropius came to Harvard in the 1930s and destroyed it at its heart. One thinks here especially of John Nolen's work of the 1920s in Florida, so well illustrated by John Hancock in Jean-François Lejeune's brilliant publication *The New City: Foundations* (1991). All the planning shapes at Seaside are in Nolen's plans for Venice and 19.5
Clewiston, both in Florida: the grid, the broad hemicycles, the diagonal avenues. And Nolen was of course not alone in his time. Planners of the teens and twenties like

19.5 John Nolen. Venice, Florida, 1926. Master plan

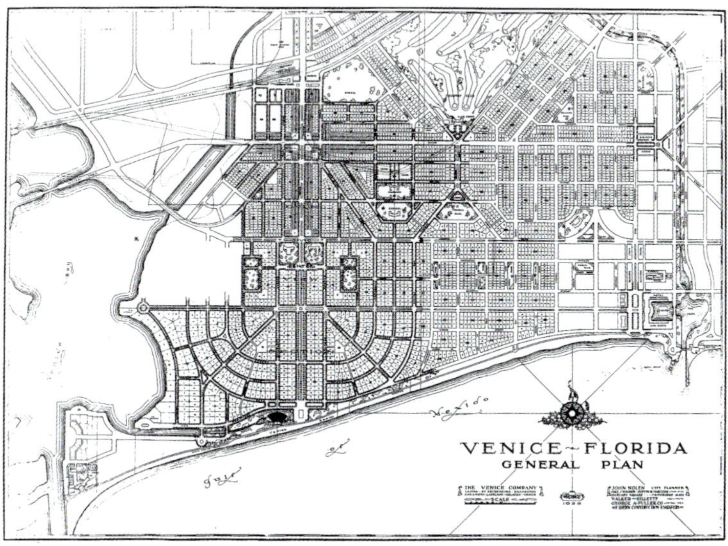

Frederick Law Olmsted Jr., Frank Williams, Arthur Shurtleff, Arthur Comey, George and James Ford, every one of them with at least one degree from Harvard, also come to mind, as do many others. It is true that one weakness of these planners, a somewhat Jeffersonian preoccupation from early in the century onward with what they called the "congestion" of the cities, was to play into the hands of the modernist iconoclasts and the automobile freaks after World War II. Otherwise, the New Urbanism, so-called, is in large part a revival of the classical and vernacular planning tradition as it existed before International-Style modernism perverted its methods and objectives.

But Duany and Plater-Zyberk differ from Nolen—and so Seaside from Venice—in one fundamental aspect: they write a code that controls the buildings as well as the plan. They therefore ensure that the three-dimensional reality of the town will fulfill the concept adumbrated in its plat—without themselves having to design every building in it. Hence they encourage many other architects and builders to work, as they can do freely enough, within the overall guidelines. Nolen could not normally exert that much control. So his streets are often ill-defined, his axes climaxed by gas stations, the whole inadequately shaped and contained. Calthorpe so far has been in something of the same fix.

But Duany and Plater-Zyberk had learned not only from Nolen but also from George Merrick, the developer of Coral Gables, upon which he worked most directly from 1921 to 1926, when the hurricane of that year wiped him out but failed to kill his town. Merrick is one of the true heroes of American architecture, and an unlikely one. He was a Florida real estate man of the bad old days of the boom when so many of Florida's lots were resold two or three times in one day and were in fact under water. But not those of Coral Gables, which also has an unusual plan, involving a perimeter of tightly gridded streets that contains and protects a free-flowing English garden within it—its shapes probably suggested by its several golf courses—and all fundamentally at automobile scale: the automobile scale of the 1920s, that is, the scale of "motoring," which is what Coral Gables, though it once had a fine public transportation system, was fundamentally intended for. We can't really blame Merrick for his beautiful renderings of fine boulevards with a few dignified town cars proceeding along them. Who could have foreseen the explosion of the species that was to come? But what Duany and Plater-Zyberk and Robert Davis learned from Coral Gables was not only the general lesson that a fine coherent small city could be made out of suburban elements but also the specific lesson that it took a draconian building code to do it. That's what Merrick had, a code that shaped first the beginnings of a Spanish or, perhaps better, a Mediterranean Revival town and then introduced little villages into it that were French or Chinese or South African Cape Dutch or Southern Colonial—all perfectly delightful, especially the Chinese.

With the hurricane of 1926, Merrick went bankrupt and lost control, and the houses, especially after World War II, became more typically suburban—squashed down, spread out, less urbane, and less naturally groupable—while the lots became much bigger, so that a certain structure, or scale, was lost. But much of the code held, and a fundamental urban order continued to be maintained. In the end that order was furnished largely by the trees. They shape the streets and cover them over against the sun

19.6 Walter Chatham. Row houses, Seaside, 1991. Exterior

and are the major architectural elements that make the place special and unified in every way, and disguise the worst of the houses.

Seaside's structure does not derive from its trees. The windy Gulf Coast is not sympathetic to them, and the "jungle" will grow up only to the height that is protected by the houses, but the principle of shaping the streets three-dimensionally is written into the code. Streets are as narrow as possible—automobiles can get through them perfectly well but their scale remains pedestrian—and they are closely defined by picket fences and front porches and by building masses brought tightly up to them. There are no carports and few garages. The cars survive well enough and the street facade retains its integrity. So the important place-maker is the code. It is not "fussy" or "escapist" but essential, and at Seaside it may not have been written strictly enough.

It is curious that the houses there which have been most published in the architectural press—though not in the popular press, which understands the issues better—are those which most stridently challenge the code, as if originality were architecture's main virtue and subversion of community its greatest good. The houses by
Walter Chatham at Seaside are the most conspicuous in this regard. Each destroys a 19.6
type; his own intrudes what looks like a primitivistic cabin, something appropriate to a glade in the Everglades, into a civilized street of humanly scaled windows, flat trim, and delicate porches, and so barbarizes it, while his row houses at the town's urban core do the two things no row house can do without destroying the group: interrupting the cornice line and dividing the individual house volume vertically down the middle. Yet Robert Davis encourages Chatham (whom everybody likes anyway) and continues to give

him buildings to do, perhaps valuing his intransigence as an image of the therapeutic license within the general order—or simply because it is invariably published. To go further, it would be salutary to see what a really fine architect like Frank Gehry—his work almost Deconstructivist but much too genial, accomplished, and untheoretical for that—might be able to do within the code at Seaside. Gehry has shown not only that he knows how to inflect his apparently anarchic buildings toward the places they are intended for but also that he understands and loves American wood frame construction. He might well find a way to reinterpret the tradition and retain civility in ways that Chatham, for example, has not yet been able to do.

Distressing, though, is the tendency of Duany and Plater-Zyberk, when addressing Neomodernists, to suggest that they employ the vernacular in their projects only because it is popular with their clients. This buffoonery, genial enough, nevertheless leaves them open to the charge of "pandering" to the public which their opponents are not slow to advance. But the pandering in this case, as in that of Chatham, is to the architectural magazines and the professional club. It makes a joke of everything Duany and Plater-Zyberk have come to stand for, and it denies the historical facts of their rise. That they should seem to need the approval of professional coteries they have far outclassed may be taken as an aberration of success and an indication of the tight hold (like that of the Marine Corps or the Catholic Church) which the architectural profession exerts on anyone who has ever belonged to it. In any case, another generation—some collaborators, others trained by Duany and Plater-Zyberk, others affiliated with them at the

19.7 OPPOSITE AND ABOVE: Ambrogio Lorenzetti. *Allegory of Good Government,* Palazzo Pubblico, Siena, Italy, 1338–40

University of Miami and therefore much more liberated than they—will surely carry on the work. Some names that come to mind, and there may surely be others (many mentioned elsewhere in this book), are: Jorge Hernandez, Teofilo Victoria, Maria de la Guardia, Jorge, Mari, and Luis Trelles, Rocco Ceo, Rafael Portuondo, Geoffrey Ferrell, Charles Barrett, Victor Dover, Joseph Kohl, Jaime Correa, Mark Schimmenti, Eric Valle, Scott Merrill, Jean-François Lejeune, Ramon Trias, Maralys Nepomechie, Gary Greenan, Dan Williams, Monica Ponce de Leon, Richard McLaughlin, Armando Montero, Thorn Grafton, Suzanne Martinson, Rolando Llanes, Sonia Chao, Maria Nardi, Frank Martinez, Ernesto Buch, Douglas Duany, Dennis Hector, Joanna Lombard, Thomas Spain, Roberto Behar, and Rosario Marquardt, whose rapt and noble paintings have helped to set a Mediterranean impress on the school.

It is true that Seaside seems so deceptively ad hoc that it can take a good deal of disruption. Could Kentlands? Probably not so much. But the point is clear. All human communities involve an intense interplay between the individual and the law. Without the law there is no peace in the community and no freedom for the individual to live without fear. Architecture is the perfect image of that state of affairs. Ambrogio
Lorenzetti showed it to us in Siena, in his *Allegory of Good Government*. There is the 19.7
country all rounded and rich in vineyards and grain. There is the city wall cutting into it, behind which the hard-edged buildings of the town jostle each other and shape public spaces where the citizens dance together. A figure of Security floats above the gate and guards it. Alongside this great scene an allegory of the town government is painted on

the wall. The Commune sits enthroned, a majestic figure surrounded by virtues. Below him all the citizens of the town are gathered, each dressed in his characteristic costume and all grasping a golden cord which depends from the Commune itself. The cord is the law which binds them together and which they hold voluntarily because it makes them free. In the center of the scene the figure of Peace reclines at her ease.

Seaside, which in fact resembles Lorenzetti's densely towered town more than a little—as does Battery Park City at another scale—embodies this necessary duality well. It is interesting in that regard to compare its houses and their groupings with those at Laguna West, where Calthorpe has pointed out that he was not able to control the architectural situation so completely. It is even more interesting to visit the towns along the Gulf near Seaside which imitate it. The picket fences are there, and they help quite a lot, as do the gazebos and the vernacular architecture as well. But the roads are all too wide, the lots usually too big; the density is not really present, so that the automobile still seems to be in command and the pressure of the communal law is not really applied. Therefore, these derivations from Seaside are all less convincing as places. They should not be despised for that, because their movement is in the right direction, but the point remains luminous: architecture is fundamentally a matter not of individual buildings but of the shaping of community, and that, as in Paris, Uruk, or Siena, is done by the law.

Still, one cannot help but hope that the lessons of Seaside and of the other new towns now taking shape can be applied to the problem of housing for the poor. That is where community is most needed and where it has been most disastrously destroyed. Center city would truly have to be broken down into its intrinsic neighborhoods if this were to take place within it. Sadly, it would all have been much easier to do before redevelopment, when the basic structure of the neighborhoods was still there, than it is today. But, whatever the size of the city as a whole, the "five-minute walk" would have to govern distances and the scale of the buildings themselves should respond to the basically low-rise, suburban-sized environment that, for any number of reasons, most Americans seem to want. It is therefore a real question whether "center city" as we know it can *ever* be shaped into the kind of place most Americans want to live in.

19.8 The Clinton neighborhood illustrated in this volume is surely a measurable improvement in that regard over the usual development of Manhattan's blocks, but the scale is still enormous, much larger than that of Vienna's great Gemeindebauten of the period 1919–34, which it otherwise somewhat recalls. It is very urbane, with reasonable public spaces. But in America, unlike Europe, only the rich have normally chosen to live in high-rise apartments. The poor have almost always aspired to what they have been told every American family rates: a single-family house in the suburbs. Ideally they want Seaside. And since we are no longer modern architects who act upon what we think people ought to have rather than what they want, we should try to figure out how they can get it. The building type itself should present no problem, especially if its basic visual qualities and its sense of personal identification can be captured in a narrower, higher, perhaps even multifamily type. In fact, some of Duany and Plater-Zyberk's basic models, and those of Melanie Taylor and Robert Orr at Seaside, were the two- and three-family

19.8 RIGHT: Steven Peterson and Barbara Littenberg. Clinton Neighborhood project, New York, 1986. Axonometric

19.9 BELOW: Robert A. M. Stern. Subway Suburb project, Bronx, 1976. Aerial perspective

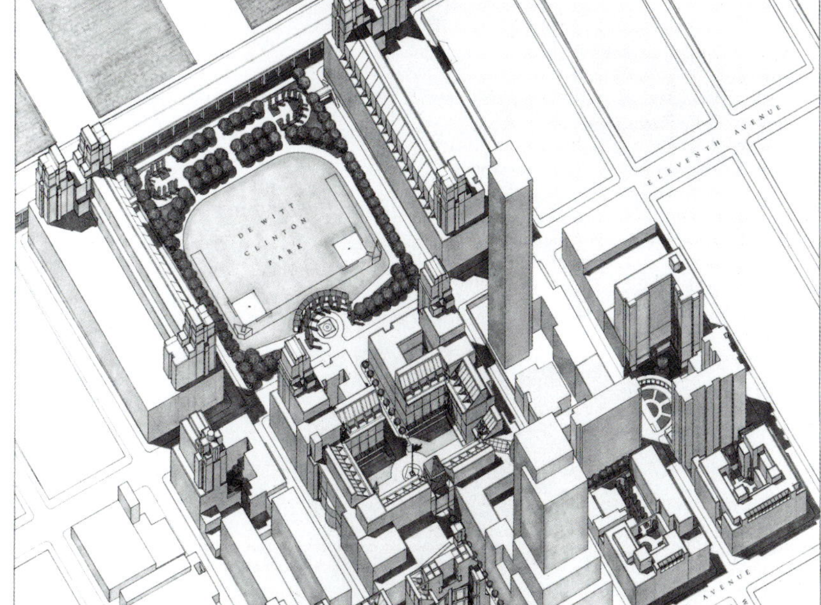

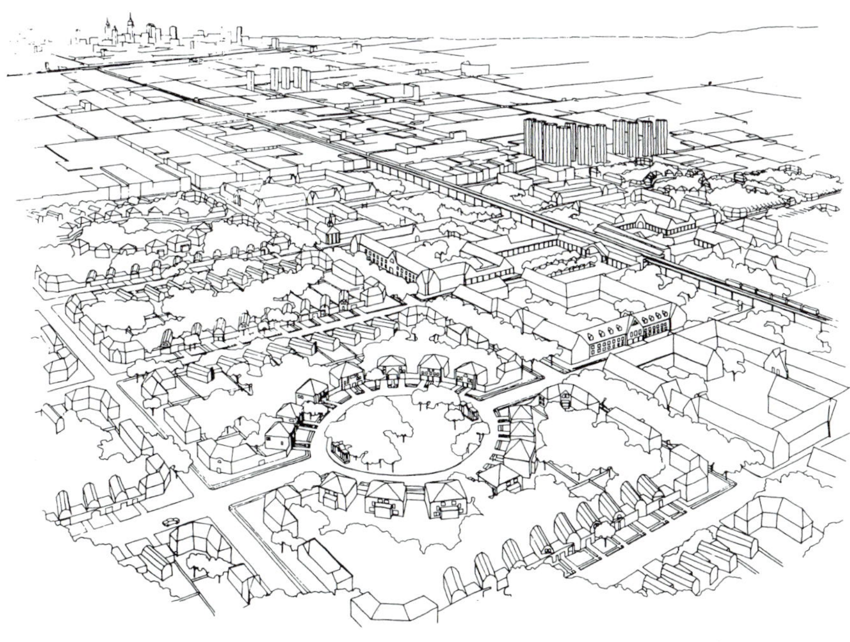

11.2 wooden houses of New Haven's modest neighborhoods, a good three stories tall with porches, bay windows, and high frontal gables, a nineteenth-century blue-collar Stick-and-Shingle structure that defined city streets with a compelling presence and some density but at a moderate scale.

Here, too, a half-forgotten contemporary project comes to mind: Robert Stern's
19.9 Subway Suburb of 1976. Stern proposed that the city services from subways to sewage that still existed in the South Bronx, above which the city lay burned, wasted, and unwanted, should be utilized to create what amounted to a suburban community of single and double houses laid out according to the existing street pattern. Some of the details Stern employed, and perhaps the house types themselves, were not close enough to their superior vernacular prototypes to be convincing today, but the idea was there. HUD later built a few single-family houses in the area that were snapped up at once despite their lack of psychological and physical support from a community group, and similar houses elsewhere can be seen standing in otherwise tragically trashed ghettoes all over the northeast, meticulously groomed behind their chain-link fences. There is reason to believe, therefore, that the Seaside type and related vernacular models, easy and economical to construct, might well be adapted for many urban situations. Such is already being done in dribs and drabs by Habitat for Humanity. But could it be funded as a mass program at urban scale?

Seaside, Kentlands, and Laguna West could be built by developers because there was money to be made out of them. Will it ever be possible to make money by building communities for the poor? Ways may yet be found to do so; some combination of private investment with intelligent government subsidies at all levels may do the trick. The federal government itself once spent so much money on redevelopment, at a time when the architectural profession hardly knew what to do with the city, that we may hope it will reorder its priorities and begin to spend some now when the profession is better prepared to spend it wisely.

Urban organizations like Chicago's Center for Neighborhood Technology, of which Michael Freedberg is Director of Community Planning, are watching the work of Duany and Plater-Zyberk and Calthorpe and the others very carefully to see if there is anything in it they can use. In Chicago they sit, of course, at the heart of a wonderful urban-suburban order of the recent past, with the Loop, the community of work, and Oak Park, the community of home, perfectly connected by the elevated suburban train. But that order too is breaking down, with work moving centrifugally to Chicago's periphery so that the existing east-west transit serves it perfectly no longer. In the long run a version of Calthorpe's "TODs" might be of relevance here.

To say that there is much hope in this or any other present model would be overstating the case. But there is a lot of determination. One drowns in the urban situation but works with what one has. It would be sad if Seaside, for one, were not to inspire imitations far from the Gulf. Seaside itself sometimes seems to be sinking under the weight of its own success. Everybody in the country appears to be coming to look at it, smothering it, ironically enough, in automobiles during the summer. The only thing that can save it, says Duany, is more Seasides, plenty of them, and this is surely true in the largest social sense. The town of Windsor, for example, by Duany and Plater-Zyberk, with two polo fields, is aimed at as rich a clientele as exists. It offers large "estate" houses around a golf course and others along the shore. In the center, however, is a tightly gridded town, and that is where every client so far has wanted to be. So the rich, who can choose, choose community, or at least its image. How much more must the poor, who must depend upon it for their lives, want community? If Seaside and the others cannot in the end offer viable models for that, they will remain entirely beautiful but rather sad. Perhaps they will in fact do so, because human beings are moved to act by symbols, and the symbol is there. When the great winds rise up out of the Gulf—and the storm clouds roll in thundering upon the little lighted town with its towered houses—then a truth is felt, involving the majesty of nature and, however partial, the brotherhood of mankind.

"America at the Millennium: Architecture and Community." In *The Pritzker Architecture Prize 1998: Celebrating the Twentieth Anniversary of the Prize: Presented to Renzo Piano.* Los Angeles: Hyatt Foundation, Jensen & Walker, 1999 (originally appeared untitled and unillustrated).

Scully's belief that the New Urbanism represents the single most important development in the architecture of the final two decades of the twentieth century led him to reevaluate many of his earlier views and to reformulate his understanding of the history of modern architecture in its terms. The argument of "The Architecture of Community" (see chap. 19) was elaborated and expanded in the twenty-fourth annual Jefferson Lecture in the Humanities, a highly prestigious event sponsored by the National Endowment for the Humanities. Scully gave the talk at the Kennedy Center for the Performing Arts in Washington, D.C., in May 1995. It was later presented as the Raoul Wallenberg Lecture at the University of Michigan and published by its College of Architecture and Urban Planning in early 1996. Condensed into a trenchant twenty-minute talk, it was delivered at the White House in June 1998 as part of the Millennium series at the White House, showcasing American creativity and innovation in the arts, humanities, and sciences. Both for its special venue and its concision of expression, it is this version that has been chosen for inclusion here.

Scully's invitation to lecture came from the White House Millennium Council as a result of the decision of President and Mrs. Clinton to host the twentieth annual Pritzker Architecture Prize award dinner. The Pritzker Prize—often referred to as the "Nobel of architecture" (other recipients have included James Stirling, I. M. Pei, Richard Meier, Kenzo Tange, Frank Gehry, Aldo Rossi, Robert Venturi, Tadao Ando, and Rafael Moneo)—was

20

America at the Millennium: Architecture and Community

Thank you, Carter. Mr. President, Mrs. Clinton, ladies and gentlemen. I'd like to express my affection for Jay and Cindy Pritzker. But, being here at the White House, has rendered me nearly speechless. I find it very difficult to say anything at all in this daunting setting. I'd never realized before, never having been here, that Jefferson is directly behind us. Right on axis. Right down there. You can see the light on it. He's looking right at us in this direction. And Mrs. Clinton has told me that he happens to be exactly where he is because of Franklin Roosevelt who wanted to be able to look directly out of his bedroom window at him. I think we're fortunate today that we once again have a President and a First Lady who are able to take up that view in fellowship.

This award of the Pritzker Prize to Renzo Piano is an especially happy one because it reminds us of the warm ties in architecture that have always existed between Italy and the United States.

They began, of course, well before Jefferson. But they're best seen in his work where Monticello rides its little mountain in the Piedmont of Virginia under the Blue

awarded in 1998 to Renzo Piano. The jury, chaired by J. Carter Brown, who was also Chairman of the Commission of Fine Arts, thought the nation's capital city to be a particularly appropriate site for the twentieth ceremony since the first, when Philip Johnson was the recipient, had been held at Washington's Dumbarton Oaks in 1979. Normally the ceremony simply included speeches by representatives of the Pritzker interests and the host institution as well as by the winning architect. Because the White House wanted to use the event to highlight the more general significance of architecture within the context of millennium events, it was decided to invite a speaker from outside the Pritzker group to broaden the discussion and add another perspective. Although it is clear that Scully's advocacy of the New Urbanism was a major reason the White House chose to invite him (indeed, he was specifically asked to speak on that subject and not on Piano's work), it may not have been all that clear to them how much his perspective on what to value in architecture would differ from, and even subvert, the aesthetic and ideological premises of the Pritzker jury and laureate.

While noting Piano's "roots in the classic Italian philosophy and tradition" along with his "unerring sensitivity for site [and] context," the Pritzker jury commended him for being "always restless and inventive," for persevering "with unrelenting experimentation." Piano, in his acceptance speech, compared the architect to a scientist, like Galileo, "exploring the unknown," living "on the frontier," "experimenting and taking risks," "groping in the dark, abandoning points of reference, facing the unknown"—even "insolently and stubbornly," if need be. Nothing could be further from the antiheroic stance of the architect that Scully had first defended in Venturi and, through the work of New Urbanists like Andres Duany and Elizabeth Plater-Zyberk, he had ultimately come to see as the need not only to respect but to follow explicitly the examples of tradition and convention. "America at the Millennium: Architecture and Community" presents this case in such a forthright way that Hillary Clinton felt impelled, in her comments following it, to characterize the talk as "eloquent and forceful, but quite subversive," adding, in its defense, that she was "very grateful for that."

After observing, with some reservation, "how much the individual, highly idiosyncratic architect is admired throughout the world today," Scully begins his talk, in

Ridge, and is modeled on Palladio's Villa Rotonda rising among the foothills of the Alps. Those ties have been strengthened over the centuries, especially by the American Academy in Rome, where hundreds of American architects and other artists have learned their trade or refreshed themselves at the incomparable Italian fountain—among them, John Russell Pope, Louis I. Kahn, Robert Venturi, Frank Gehry, Michael Graves, Richard Meier. Those well known names, like that of Renzo Piano himself, suggest how much the individual, highly idiosyncratic architect is admired throughout the world today, but honoring them also reminds us that architecture is a communal art, having to do with the whole manmade environment, the human city entire, rather than only

deference to the occasion, by praising both Piano and previous Pritzker prizewinner Gehry for the ways in which their buildings relate to the existing urban landscape. But this is only to point to the larger issue of thinking about the city as a whole and the necessary balance between freedom and order, or between the individual and the law, that allows the city to become a place of community. In America, the classical tradition, beginning with Jefferson, is invoked as the touchstone that, after more than half a century of denial, has been perceived once again, with the New Urbanism, as the basis for an architecture that transcends the individual will to form. To lay out this scenario at such an occasion as directly as he did, no matter how much it might have been expected, was very courageous and says much about Scully's moral conviction and sense of purpose. The strong plea in the end for the government to take up once again the classic liberal role of providing housing for the poor may have seemed far removed from the Pritzker Prize's criteria for architectural excellence, but clearly was meant, in the context of the White House, to speak to a higher purpose. Hillary Clinton thanked Scully not only for his subversiveness but also for his "impassioned plea on behalf of architecture that represents our aspirations, as human beings, as citizens to build and live in communities" and for "pointing out . . . that individuals need one another, they need the law, they need a sense of community to feel not only that they belong, but that they have a purpose, and that architecture and the environment . . . are major ways in which individuals see reflected their own meaning and identity."

the individual buildings in it. The questions arising from that condition have a political as well as a purely artistic relevance; they touch on fundamental issues such as the relation of freedom to order, of innovation to stability, most of all of the individual to the law. Renzo Piano has shown himself to be well aware of those issues. His National Center for Science and Technology respects the solid structure of traditional Amsterdam and is placed at its very edge where it can lift up to give a view from its roof terrace back across the beautiful city and also reach out and away like one of Holland's proud old ships set-
20.1 ting sail for the Indies. On the other hand, at his earlier Pompidou Center, done with Richard Rogers, Piano exploits the block structure of Paris, and echoes it in the cubic mass of his own building. But he contrasts dramatically with it in his details, and old and new together shape a lively city square full of urban theater. Piano's building needs Paris, and uses it.

But what can we say about that side of American mythology which despises the city, as Frank Lloyd Wright in his later years at least pretended to do? He would, as at Taliesin West, echo the forms of the natural environment, but not those of city buildings, as in the Guggenheim. But he cannot escape those buildings. Without them, his spiraling shapes would lose their force and, indeed, their uniqueness. Imagine those buildings gone and all Guggenheims down the street. It would be the strip, and everything would be lost. So Wright, too, needed the city's order.

20.1 RIGHT: Renzo Piano and Richard Rogers. Pompidou Center, Paris, 1971–77. Exterior

20.2 BELOW: Frank Gehry. Guggenheim Museum Bilbao, Spain, 1991–97. Exterior

Frank Gehry understands all that perfectly well, and has built his new Guggenheim in Bilbao outside the grid of the town, sited to be framed by its dark, strongly 20.2
defined streets. Beyond them it billows up like a shining cloud and directly reproduces the shapes of the high conical hills in whose bowl the city is set. On the other side, the building is a ship; it has sailed boldly up the river, and rammed into the main highway bridge, buckling under the impact, and lunging at passersby like a monster fish with silver scales. Here, however playful, is contextual design, wherein the building respects the structure of the city and complements it, calling to its natural surroundings as well.

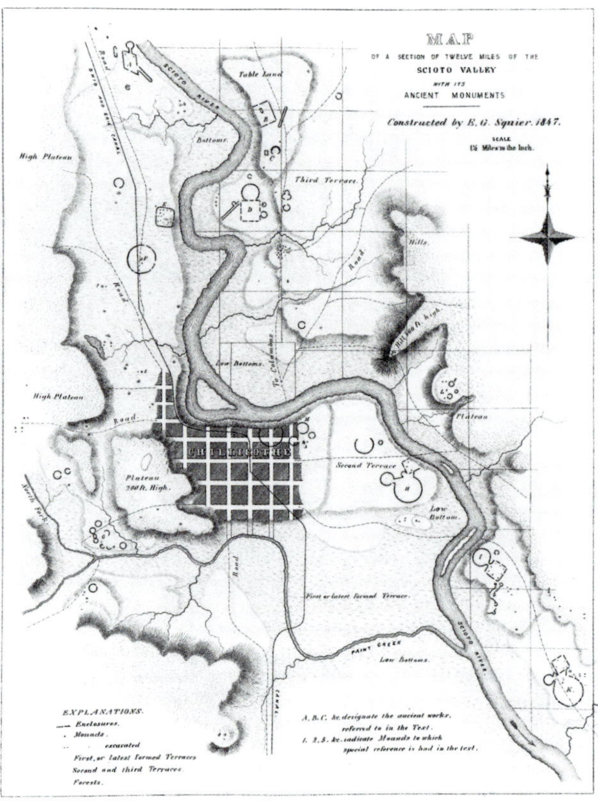

Gehry's freely sculptural, computer-translated work is admired as peculiarly American and is emulated, if not very well, by young architects all over the world, but few of them understand or care about the urban frame in relation to which it has to be seen. That urbanism is fundamentally classical in derivation, and again, it was Thomas
20.3 Jefferson who brought it to the brand new United States. The first state capitol, that in Richmond of 1785, is a classical temple conceived by Jefferson as rising over the city above the James. Its model was a Roman temple but the image it creates is more fundamental than that. It is of the Greek city-state, of the Parthenon, rising above Athens, embodying the passionate aspiration of Greek Democracy for political power. So from the beginning the idea of the city as a whole, however modest in size, is central to Jefferson's perception of classicism. Monticello itself is conceived as a little city, dropping its circular road system over the slopes of the hill in a pattern that recalls the ideal hilltop towns of Italian Renaissance design that Jefferson knew from his architectural treatises. He calls the University of Virginia "an academical village," drawing together a community of professors, students, and books, all embodied in columns of different sizes and intended to open out across space as Jefferson said education itself should do: "indefinitely," which was his word, through life and beyond the horizon. And as the United
20.4 States itself moved "indefinitely" westward, it was Jefferson's grid plan that centuriated

ABOVE, LEFT: Thomas Jefferson. State Capitol, Richmond, Virginia, begun 1785 20.3

ABOVE, RIGHT: Chillicothe, Ohio, and surrounding area. Map by E.G. Squier, 1847. From E. G. Squier and E. H. Davis, *Ancient Monuments of the Mississippi Valley* (Washington, D.C., 1848) 20.4

the landscape and shaped its new kind of civilization. Here the hard, square grid of Chillicothe in Ohio contrasts with the soft rounded shapes of the Indian mounds that Jefferson loved equally well.

And when he maneuvers the northern senators into agreeing on the Potomac at Goose Creek (which he loved to call the "Tyber") as the site for the nation's capital, Jefferson proposed a modest little grid plan for it, set north of the creek and looking down the river toward Alexandria. Indeed, the grid was the only one of the many elements of classical planning of which Jefferson wholly approved. He distrusted, as symbols of absolutism, the long axes, the hemicycles, and the radiating avenues of Versailles, but it was those elements, united with the grid, that shaped Pierre L'Enfant's plan for the much larger Washington which the first president approved and Jefferson loyally helped build up during his years in office. At that time, the city stopped at the bank of the river where the Washington Monument came to rise, and while it was in that state, modern Paris with its leafy boulevards took form, and in a joint enthusiasm for Paris and Washington together, the American Institute of Architects met here in 1900, and out of that came the McMillan Commission and the filling in of the Potomac and the addition of the long
reflecting pool like the Grand Bassin at Versailles and the building of the Lincoln and 12.25
Jefferson Memorials and the Bridge to Arlington. Then that plan, loaded with the major images of American political life, created hundreds and hundreds of beautiful new towns and extensions of old towns all over the United States, culminating by the time of the
Depression in the work of planners like John Nolen in Venice, Florida, of 1926. Even poor 19.5
old New Haven had a project connecting its nine colonial squares and their Green with the new railroad station by Cass Gilbert, which was another tree-lined boulevard extending, not destroying, the integrity of the city.

But then the Depression came, and war, and a generation of Americans grew up who had apparently forgotten what a town was, or how a city was built, and who were obsessed by enthusiasm for the free passage of the automobile at the expense of all other values. We were told that this was the way it had to be done by hero-architects like Le Corbusier, and hero-administrators like Robert Moses put it heroically, savagely, into practice, and the Bronx was destroyed, and I-95 and its connectors came to New Haven and smashed through between the railroad station and the old town, destroying everything in their path. And I-95 went on down the East Coast, reaming out the centers of cities, scattering neighborhoods, mostly those of black Americans, all the way to Miami, where as its last act it obliterated Overtown, an African-American community of long standing, where Cab Calloway had delighted to sing.

We also tore down some irreplaceable buildings during that inconceivable period. Penn Station in New York was the most tragic example. All that great space with all its public dignity and grandeur, was cut down to the level of the rat-like burrows that were, perhaps, all we deserved. But that demolition of 1963 gave rise to New York's powerful preservation law of 1965, while in 1966 the National Register of Historic Places was instituted, and the National Trust for Historic Preservation began to grow in popular strength and in concern for communities with every passing year.

And when we set out to resist the destructive aspects of redevelopment in New Haven in the 1960s we rediscovered two ancient principles: first, that the traditional plan counts and stabilizes the city. The Green was everything to us, and when its integrity was threatened, as by an ill-conceived project for a government center, the people rose to arms and were soon supported by their elected representatives. Secondly, we came to perceive something that had been forgotten in the arrogance of high modernism: that once upon a time buildings and cities had been designed to get along with buildings from previous generations, so creating places that outlast individual human lives—as King Gilgamesh of Uruk had discovered in his own city more than four thousand years before. So when Cass Gilbert of the Woolworth Building designed New Haven's Free Public Library in 1908, he shaped it to respect the churches on the Green, built a hundred years earlier. Here the principle of context was seen as more important than style or invention, and was intended to make the whole Green a little better on its own terms. Fortunately, for all of us, a young architect, Robert Venturi—whose eyes had been opened by Rome—
15.14 had begun to design in just that way once again. His Guild House of the early 1960s intends not to stand out as an invention, but to blend with its neighborhood, so strengthening the street and exhibiting that respect for the rest of the community which was embodied as well in the major, and peculiarly American, social movements of that time. I refer, of course, to the black liberation, women's liberation, and gay liberation that have profoundly affected the way Americans think about who belongs to the community and what its structure should be.

The next step was the revival of traditional town planning as a whole. Here the first important response was that of 1976 by Robert Stern to the tragedy of the South Bronx. Stern proposed that the beginnings of a traditional American town, the kind of place where most Americans of all economic levels had always wanted to live, should be laid out in that destroyed area where nobody wanted to live and the land was worth nothing but the infrastructure of subways, water, and power was buried in the ground. Upon
19.9 these services, Stern laid out the traditional grid and the Green. He eliminated those high-rise slabs that had destroyed neighborhood cultures everywhere and were soon to be demolished all over the country. Some were, in fact, blown up. Stern chose instead something as close as possible to the single-family house of American tradition as it had been adapted for dense urban use during the nineteenth century, as in the two- and
11.2 three-family houses of New Haven and other cities. They are set on narrow lots and their high frontal gables dignify the street, as do their generous porches, grass plots, sidewalks, and branching elms—all making an urban structure of a scale hard to beat. Andres Duany, a refugee from Cuba, worked for Stern at this time, and while he and his wife, Elizabeth Plater-Zyberk, a refugee from Poland, were students at Yale, they learned from these houses, and out of that beginning, with the sponsorship of the idealistic
19.3, 19.4 developer, Robert Davis, came their town of Seaside on Florida's Panhandle, begun in 1979, and the first of their many new towns and neighborhoods. There all the elements of the classic plan as employed by Nolen again came into play: the grid, the hemicycles, and the radiating avenues, and the town was built up employing the vernacular architec-

ture of Florida's Gulf Coast, the Redneck Riviera. The federal presence, the post office, is right there where it should be, in the center of the town, designed by Robert Davis himself out of the classical books of architecture that Jefferson himself had used. The automobile is not excluded from the town, but is disciplined by it, like all its citizens. There are no gates. The coast road runs right through, the traffic has to slow up as the town crowds in upon it. And when a car turns into a street, it finds that the corners are not cut back for it—as departments of transportation all too often insist they must be. Instead, it is forced to stop and to turn slowly, exactly as an automobile should move in the town. The streets are narrow. By code, the houses must be built close up to them so that a sense of community is always physically palpable. The new developments up and down the Gulf Coast that are doing their best to imitate Seaside, as they all are doing, mostly fail on this point so that everything is too far apart and the feeling of community is lost. The code has to be strict, but there is none for public buildings; we can easily well imagine a building by Gehry or Piano at the end of any of these streets, and someday soon one will surely rise in that hemicycle where now a tent contrasts with the other forms and is framed by them. The code makes possible the ordered town *and* the special monument. The individual needs the law.

Such codes created the great cities of Europe. The public gesture of Siena's town hall seems to push back the facades of the buildings that shape the wonderful Campo of that city precisely because those facades were prevented by law from having any kind of projection that would encroach upon the public space. And the best general description we have of the city as a product of law is a fresco inside that town hall called
the *Allegory of Good Government*, or the *Ideal Republican City in Its Landscape*. It shows 19.7
the city all hard-edged, with people dancing in the street, set in a Tuscan landscape gentle and soft, where the farmers are reaping the wheat. Everything works together through Good Government, with the figure of Security presiding over the gate. Next to this scene is another in which the town sits enthroned; he holds a cord that is voluntarily grasped by all the citizens in their special costumes, affirming that each one of them gives up a little personal freedom in order to live in peace with everybody else. So Hesiod wrote long ago that the animals all eat each other, but to mankind, Zeus gives *Dike*, Justice, so that we can live together in towns.

At this level of town-making we are, I think, almost there, close to creating that peaceful image of a human community again. And not only for the rich. The Nehemiah neighborhood in Cleveland is one of many urban areas reclaimed by the practitioners of the New Urbanism. The intentions are the same, the humanity equal to that of Seaside.
An aerial photograph of Cleveland recalls Robert Stern's touching perspective of his 20.5
Subway Suburb, with the towers of Manhattan in the distance. We are that close, I think, to dealing with the awesome problems of center city; perhaps by the magical year 2000 we'll be able to do so.

But we have little reason to congratulate ourselves today, especially when we think of the many beautiful neighborhoods that were built in manufacturing centers up and down the eastern seaboard and elsewhere by the federal government as wartime

LEFT: Andres Duany and Elizabeth Plater-Zyberk (master planners). Central Neighborhood (Nehemiah), Cleveland. Aerial view 20.5

BELOW: Hepburn and Parker, with R. Clipston Sturgif. Crane Development, near Seaside Park, Bridgeport, Connecticut, begun 1918. Perspective 20.6

emergency housing during the First World War. Seven housing groups were built in
Bridgeport, Connecticut, now a beleaguered community much burnt out and struggling
to survive. Within it, each of those communities is still in very good condition, obviously
loved as a place where people want to be. The one that was intended for the lowest-paid
workers in the factories is the most beautiful of them all. It's closest to Long Island Sound
and is therefore called, hauntingly, Seaside Park. It was designed under the general guid- 20.6
ance of John Nolen by some of the best architects in the United States according to those
traditional principles with which we've become familiar. The image of the single-family
house is present everywhere, though subdivided in various ways to meet the narrow
budget. But the identity is always there, the good door, the bay window.

Directly after the war, a congressional investigation concluded that the federal government should get out of the housing field, calling it too "socialistic" and, it said, "un-American," and it specifically chided the architects of Seaside Park for, I quote, "undue elegance in design."

Directly across the street from Seaside Park is a housing project of the late 1930s which scrupulously avoids that fault. Now it is a set of barracks, floating in asphalt, and was, for a long while, the center of drug distribution in that part of the city. So much for those who claim that environment has no measurable effect upon human beings. Clearly, the poor need Seaside Park's kind of neighborhood more than any other people do. And we have denied it to them for a long time. What they ask is no different from what everyone else in the United States seems to want: a dignified place to live, a supporting community, the protection of the law. Once we did all this right in the United States, and with the help of the Almighty, we'll do it again.

Bibliography of Vincent Scully's Writings

1948 "Architecture as a Science: Is the Scientific Method Applicable to Architectural Design?" *Yale Scientific Magazine* 22 (May 1948): 4–6, 18, 20, 22, 24, 26.

1951 "One-Room House Gives Up Privacy and Slick Finishes, Gains Spaciousness and Flexibility." *Architectural Forum* 94 (June 1951): 162–64.

1952 With Antoinette F. Downing. *The Architectural Heritage of Newport, Rhode Island, 1640–1915.* Cambridge, Mass.: Harvard University Press, 1952. *A second revised edition, with new introduction to part four, was published by Bramhall House (New York) in 1967; this edition was reprinted by American Legacy Press (New York) in 1982; and by C. Potter (New York) in 1987.*

"Michelangelo's Fortification Drawings: A Study in the Reflex Diagonal." *Perspecta: The Yale Architectural Journal* 1 (Summer 1952): 38–45. *This article is the abridged version of what later appeared in* Actes du XVIIème Congrès International d'Histoire de l'Art (Amsterdam, 23–31 Juillet 1952) *(The Hague: Imprimerie Nationale des Pays-Bas, 1955).*

1953 With Philip Johnson, Pietro Belluschi, Louis Kahn, and Paul Weiss. "On the Responsibility of the Architect: Discussion." *Perspecta: The Yale Architectural Journal* 2 (1953): 45–57.

Review of *Early American Architecture from the First Colonial Settlements to the National Period*, by Hugh Morrison. *Journal of the Society of Architectural Historians* 12 (May 1953): 29–30.

"Romantic-Rationalism and the Expression of Structure in Wood: Downing, Wheeler, Gardner, and the 'Stick Style,' 1840–1876." *Art Bulletin* 35 (June 1953): 121–42. *Later republished as the introduction to* The Shingle Style and the Stick Style: Architectural Theory and Design from Downing to the Origins of Wright, 2nd rev. ed. *(New Haven, Conn., and London: Yale University Press, 1971).*

"Somber and Archaic: Expressive Tension." *Yale Daily News* (special supplement, "The New Art Gallery and Design Center: Dedication Issue"), 6 November 1953, 10.

1954 "American Villas: Inventiveness in the American Suburb from Downing to Wright." *Architectural Review* 115 (March 1954): 168–79.

"Archetype and Order in Recent American Architecture." *Art in America* 42 (December 1954): 250–61.

"Mackintosh and Art Nouveau." Review of *Charles Rennie Mackintosh and the Modern Movement*, by Thomas Howarth. *Architectural Record* 115 (March 1954): 46, 48, 332.

Review of *Power in Buildings: An Artist's View of Contemporary Architecture,* by Hugh Ferriss. *Art in America* 42 (October 1954): 232.

"Wright vs. the International Style." *Art News* 53 (March 1954): 32–35, 64–66. *Letters to the editor regarding this article and Scully's reply were published as "The Wright-International Style Controversy,"* Art News *53 (September 1954): 48–49.*

1955 *The Shingle Style: Architectural Theory and Design from Richardson to the Origins of Wright.* New Haven, Conn., and London: Yale University Press, 1955. *Later republished in expanded form as* The Shingle Style and the Stick Style: Architectural Theory and Design from Downing to the Origins of Wright, *2nd rev. ed. (New Haven, Conn., and London: Yale University Press, 1971).*

"Invention and Architecture in Victorian England." Review of *Early Victorian Architecture in Britain*, by Henry-Russell Hitchcock. *Architectural Record* 117 (March 1955): 46, 48, 336.

"Michelangelo's Fortification Drawings: A Study in the Reflex Diagonal." *Actes du XVIIème Congrès International d'Histoire de l'Art (Amsterdam, 23–31 Juillet 1952).* The Hague: Imprimerie Nationale des Pays-Bas, 1955. *This article is the complete version of what had previously appeared in* Perspecta: The Yale Architectural Journal *1 (Summer 1952): 38–45.*

1956 "Architecture and Ancestor Worship." Review of *An American Architecture*, by Frank Lloyd Wright, *Walter Gropius: Work and Teamwork*, by Sigfried Giedion, and *Italy Builds*, by G. E. Kidder Smith. *Art News* 54 (February 1956): 26, 56–57.

"Bramante's Great Space." Review of *The Cortile del Belvedere*, by James S. Ackerman. *Architectural Record* 119 (March 1956): 62, 66, 384, 388, 392, 396.

"Le Musée des beaux-arts de l'Université Yale New Haven / Art Gallery and Design Center, Yale University, New Haven." *Muséum* ("L'Architecture contemporaine et les musées contemporaines") 9 (1956): 101–13.

1957 "Modern Architecture: Toward a Redefinition of Style." *Perspecta: The Yale Architectural Journal* 4 (1957): 4–10. *Later republished in* Reflections on Art: A Source Book of Writings by Artists, Critics, and Philosophers, ed. Susanne K. Langer *(Baltimore: Johns Hopkins University Press, 1958); and as "Modern Architecture," in "Redefinitions of Style: A Symposium,"* College Art Journal *17 (Winter 1958): 140–59.*

1958 "Modern Architecture." In "Redefinitions of Style: A Symposium." *College Art Journal* 17 (Winter 1958): 140–59. *This article is a reprint, with minor changes, of "Modern Architecture: Toward a Redefinition of Style,"* Perspecta: The Yale Architectural Journal *4 (1957): 4–10.*

"Modern Architecture: Toward a Redefinition of Style." In *Reflections on Art: A Source Book of Writings by Artists, Critics, and Philosophers*, ed. Susanne K. Langer. Baltimore: Johns Hopkins University Press, 1958. *This article had previously appeared in* Perspecta: The Yale Architectural Journal *4 (1957): 4–10.*

"The Nature of the Classical in Art." *Yale French Studies* ("Contemporary Art" Issue), nos. 19–20 (Spring 1957–Winter 1958): 107–24.

1959 "Louis Sullivan's Architectural Ornament: A Brief Note Concerning Humanist Design in the Age of Force." *Perspecta: The Yale Architectural Journal* 5 (1959): 73–80.

"A Scholarly and Solid History of Architecture Since 1800." Review of *Architecture: Nineteenth and Twentieth Centuries*, by Henry-Russell Hitchcock. *Architectural Record* 125 (January 1959): 60.

1960 *Frank Lloyd Wright*. Masters of World Architecture Series. New York: George Braziller, 1960.

"Architecture of the Twentieth Century." In *Arts of the United States: A Pictorial Survey*, ed. William H. Pierson Jr. and Martha Davidson. New York: McGraw-Hill, 1960.

"Modern Architecture at Yale." *Yale Banner* (1960): 207–24.

"The Precisionist Strain in American Architecture." *Art in America* 48 (Fall 1960): 46–53.

1961 *Modern Architecture: The Architecture of Democracy*. The Great Ages of World Architecture Series. New York: George Braziller, 1961. *A second revised edition, with new preface and new part three, "Twelve Years After: The Age of Irony," was published by George Braziller in 1974.*

"A Critique—Environment and Act." In "Architecture—Fitting and Befitting." *Architectural Forum* 114 (June 1961): 86–87.

"The Heritage of Wright." *Zodiac* 8 (1961): 8–13.

1962 *The Earth, the Temple, and the Gods: Greek Sacred Architecture*. New Haven, Conn., and London: Yale University Press, 1962. *A second revised edition, with new preface, was published by Praeger (New York) in 1969; a third revised edition, with new preface, was published by Yale University Press in 1979.*

Louis I. Kahn. Makers of Contemporary Architecture Series. New York: George Braziller, 1962.

"L'Ironie en architecture." *Revue d'esthétique* 15 (July–December 1962): 245–53.

"Wright, International Style, and Kahn." *Arts* 36 (March 1962): 67–71. *This article is the abridged version of what later appeared as "Frank Lloyd Wright and Twentieth-Century Style," in* Problems of the Nineteenth and Twentieth Centuries, *vol. 4 of* Studies in Western Art: Acts of the Twentieth International Congress of the History of Art *(Princeton: Princeton University Press, 1963).*

1963 "The Athens Hilton: A Study in Vandalism." *Architectural Forum* 119 (July 1963): 100–103.

"The Death of the Street." *Perspecta: The Yale Architectural Journal* 8 (1963): 91–96.

"Frank Lloyd Wright and Twentieth-Century Style." In *Problems of the Nineteenth and Twentieth Centuries.* Vol. 4 of *Studies in Western Art: Acts of the Twentieth International Congress of the History of Art.* Princeton: Princeton University Press, 1963. *This article is the complete version of what had previously appeared as "Wright, International Style, and Kahn,"* Arts *36 (March 1962): 67–71.*

"Kleanthes and the Duchess of Piacenza." *Journal of the Society of Architectural Historians* 22 (October 1963): 139–54.

"A Note on the Work of Paul Rudolph." In *The Work of Paul Rudolph, Architect.* New Haven, Conn.: Yale University Art Gallery, 1963.

1964 "Architecture and Man at Yale." *Hokusai-Kentiku* 31 (November 1964): 74–80. *This article had previously appeared in* Saturday Review, *23 May 1964, 26–29.*

"Architecture and Man at Yale." *Saturday Review,* 23 May 1964, 26–29. *Later republished in* Hokusai-Kentiku *31 (November 1964): 74–80.*

"Art and Architecture Building, Yale University." *Architectural Review* 135 (May 1964): 324–32.

"Capitals of Klopedi." *Architectural Review* 135 (February 1964): 129–34.

"The Earth, the Temple, and the Gods: Greek Sacred Architecture. Addenda." *Journal of the Society of Architectural Historians* 23 (May 1964): 89–99.

"If This Is Architecture, God Help Us." *Life* 57 (31 July 1964): 9.

"Light, Form, and Power: New Work of Louis Kahn." *Architectural Forum* 121 (August–September 1964): 162–70.

"New British Buildings." *Architectural Design* 34 (June 1964): 266–67.

"Reply to Homer G. Thompson's Review of *The Earth, the Temple, and the Gods: Greek Sacred Architecture.*" *Art Bulletin* 46 (March 1964): 119–20.

"Reply to Norman Mailer." In "Mailer vs. Scully." *Architectural Forum* 120 (April 1964): 96–97.

"Total Environment." Review of *The Italian Landscape*, by Ivor de Wolfe. *Architectural Review* 135 (May 1964): 317.

1965 "Doldrums in the Suburbs." *Journal of the Society of Architectural Historians* 24 (March 1965): 36–47. *Later republished in* Perspecta: The Yale Architectural Journal *9/10 (1965): 281–90.*

"Doldrums in the Suburbs." *Perspecta: The Yale Architectural Journal* 9/10 (1965): 281–90. *This article had previously appeared in* Journal of the Society of Architectural Historians *24 (March 1965): 36–47.*

"His Ideas Are Woven into the Ages." *Life* 59 (24 September 1965): 123–24.

Introduction to *The Work of Louis I. Kahn.* Exh. cat. San Diego: La Jolla Museum of Art, 1965.

"Louis I. Kahn: Form, Design, and the Human City." *Show* 5 (May 1965): 22–28.

"Palace of the Past: Frederic Church's Olana at Hudson, N.Y." *Progressive Architecture* 46 (May 1965): 184–89.

"Prologue: Wood in Architecture." *Journal of the Royal Architectural Institute of Canada* 42 (December 1965): 37.

1966 "America's Architectural Nightmare: The Motorized Megalopolis." *Holiday* 39 (March 1966): 94–95, 142–43. *Later republished in* Zodiac *17 (1967): 162–67.*

Introduction to *Complexity and Contradiction in Architecture*, by Robert Venturi. The Museum of Modern Art Papers on Architecture. New York: The Museum of Modern Art; Chicago: Graham Foundation for Advanced Studies in the Fine Arts, 1966.

1967 With Antoinette F. Downing. *The Architectural Heritage of Newport, Rhode Island, 1640–1915.* 2nd rev. ed. New York: Bramhall House, 1967. *The first edition was published by Harvard University Press (Cambridge, Mass.) in 1952. The second revised edition contained a new introduction to part four: "Nineteenth-Century Resort Architecture." Later reprinted by American Legacy Press (New York) in 1982; and by C. Potter (New York) in 1987.*

Arquitectura actual. Cordoba, Argentina: Instituto Inter-Universitario de Historia de la Arquitectura, 1967.

"America's Architectural Nightmare: The Motorized Megalopolis." *Zodiac* 17 (1967): 162–67. *This article had previously appeared in* Holiday *39 (March 1966): 94–95, 142–43.*

"His Themes Were Sun, Air, Space." Review of *Creation Is a Patient Search*, by Le Corbusier, *The Radiant City*, by Le Corbusier, and *Le Corbusier: 1910–1965*, ed. Willy Boesiger and Hans Girsberger. *New York Times Book Review*, 19 November 1967, sec. 7, pp. 8, 10.

"Recent Works by Louis Kahn." *Zodiac* 17 (1967): 58–118.

"The Threat and the Promise of Urban Redevelopment in New Haven." *Zodiac* 17 (1967): 171–75.

1968 Letter to the Review Editor. *American Institute of Planners Journal* 34 (March 1968): 127.

"Transcript: Vincent Scully's Remarks, Nov. 25." *Novum Organum*, 3 December 1968, 1–2.

1969 *American Architecture and Urbanism.* New York: Praeger, 1969. *A second revised edition, with new preface, was published by H. Holt (New York) in 1988.*

The Earth, the Temple, and the Gods: Greek Sacred Architecture. 2nd rev. ed. New York: Praeger, 1969. *With new preface. The first edition was published by Yale University Press (New Haven, Conn., and London) in 1962; the third revised edition, with new preface, was published by Yale University Press in 1979.*

"Oldenburg's Realism." *Novum Organum*, 15 May 1969, 1.

"RIBA Discourse 1969: A Search for Principle between Two Wars." *RIBA Journal: The Journal of the Royal Institute of British Architects* 76 (June 1969): 240–47.

1970 "American Houses: Thomas Jefferson to Frank Lloyd Wright." In *The Rise of an American Architecture*, ed. Edgar Kaufmann Jr. New York: Praeger, 1970.

"Becton Belongs in Goo-Goo Land." *Yale Daily News*, 26 February 1970, 3.

1971 *Pueblo Architecture of the Southwest: A Photographic Essay.* Photographs by William Current. Austin: University of Texas Press, 1971.

The Shingle Style and the Stick Style: Architectural Theory and Design from Downing to the Origins of Wright. 2nd rev. ed. New Haven, Conn., and London: Yale University Press, 1971. *With new preface and introduction, the latter having previously appeared as "Romantic-Rationalism and the Expression of Structure in Wood: Downing, Wheeler, Gardner, and the 'Stick Style,' 1840–1876,"* Art Bulletin *35 (June 1953): 121–42. A shorter version of the book's text had previously appeared as* The Shingle Style: Architectural Theory and Design from Richardson to the Origins of Wright *(New Haven, Conn., and London: Yale University Press, 1955).*

Introduction to *The Work of Venturi and Rauch: Architects and Planners.* Exh. cat. New York: Whitney Museum of American Art, 1971. *Later republished in "Zur Arbeit von Venturi & Rauch/A Propos de Venturi & Rauch,"* Werk-Archithèse *64 (July–August 1977): 4–10.*

Review of *Model City,* by Fred Powledge. *New York Times Book Review,* 24 January 1971, sec. 7, pp. 8, 10.

1972 "In Praise of Women: The Mescalero Puberty Ceremony." *Art in America* 60 (July–August 1972): 70–77.

"Men and Nature in Pueblo Architecture." In *American Indian Art: Form and Tradition.* Exh. cat. Minneapolis: Walker Art Center, 1972.

1973 Foreword to *Conversations with Architects,* by John W. Cook and Heinrich Klotz. New York: Praeger, 1973.

1974 *Modern Architecture: The Architecture of Democracy.* The Great Ages of World Architecture Series. 2nd rev. ed. New York: George Braziller, 1974. *With new preface and new part three, "Twelve Years After: The Age of Irony." The first edition was published by George Braziller in 1961.*

The Shingle Style Today: or, The Historian's Revenge. New York: George Braziller, 1974. *Excerpts from this book later appeared in* A+U: A Monthly Journal of World Architecture and Urbanism, *no. 52 (April 1975): 97–106.*

"Education and Inspiration." *Architecture d'Aujourd'hui* 173 (May–June 1974): vi. *Later republished as "Louis I. Kahn (1901–1974): Education and Inspiration,"* Yale University Art Gallery Bulletin *35 (Summer 1974): 6–7.*

"Ingalls Rink: It's a Bird, It's a Plane, It's . . ." *Yale-Harvard Hockey 1974* (program), 23 February 1974, 5.

"Lipstick (Ascending), on Caterpillar Track, Gift to Yale University, Claes Oldenburg." *Yale Revue,* 16 October 1974, 14–15.

"Louis I. Kahn (1901–1974): Education and Inspiration." *Yale University Art Gallery Bulletin* 35 (Summer 1974): 6–7. *This article had previously appeared as "Education and Inspiration,"* Architecture d'Aujourd'hui *173 (May–June 1974): vi.*

"Thruway and Crystal Palace: The Symbolic Design of Roche and Dinkeloo." *Architectural Forum* 140 (March 1974): 18–25.

1975 *Pueblo: Mountain, Village, Dance.* New York: Viking Press, 1975. *A second revised edition, with new preface and postscript, was published by University of Chicago Press in 1989.*

Foreword to *The New Jerusalem: Planning and Politics*, by Arthur Kutcher. Cambridge, Mass.: MIT Press, 1975.

"The Shingle Style Today: or, The Historian's Revenge." *A+U: A Monthly Journal of World Architecture and Urbanism*, no. 52 (April 1975): 97–106. *This article contains excerpts from the book of the same title published by George Braziller (New York) in 1974.*

"Works of Louis Kahn and His Method." *A+U: A Monthly Journal of World Architecture and Urbanism* (special issue: "Louis I. Kahn: Sono zenbo," published as volume two of a boxed set) (1973–75): 287–300. *This special issue was also published as a single volume in 1975.*

1976 "The Yale Mathematics Building: Some Remarks on Siting." *Oppositions: A Journal for Ideas and Criticism in Architecture*, no. 6 (Fall 1976): 22–23. *Later republished as "Das Gebäude der mathematischen Fakultät an der Yale University—Bemerkungen zu seiner Lage/Le Mathematics Building de Yale. Quelques remarques sur sa situation,"* Werk-Archithèse *64 (July–August 1977): 38–39.*

1977 "The Case for Preservation." *New York Times*, 2 October 1977, sec. 23, p. 18, Connecticut Edition.

"Das Gebäude der mathematischen Fakultät an der Yale University—Bemerkungen zu seiner Lage/Le Mathematics Building de Yale. Quelques remarques sur sa situation." *Werk-Archithèse* 64 (July–August 1977): 38–39. *This article had previously appeared as "The Yale Mathematics Building: Some Remarks on Siting,"* Oppositions: A Journal for Ideas and Criticism in Architecture, *no. 6 (Fall 1976): 22–23.*

Introduction to *The Villa Badoer at Fratta Polesine*, by Lionello Puppi. London: Architectural Press, 1977.

Note to *Complexity and Contradiction in Architecture*, by Robert Venturi. 2nd ed. New York: The Museum of Modern Art; Chicago: Graham Foundation for Advanced Studies in the Fine Arts, 1977. *Later republished in "Zur Arbeit von Venturi & Rauch/A Propos de Venturi & Rauch,"* Werk-Archithèse *64 (July–August 1977): 4–10.*

Remarks in "Forum: The Beaux-Arts Exhibition," ed. William Ellis. *Oppositions: A Journal for Ideas and Criticism in Architecture,* no. 8 (Spring 1977): 167–68.

"Yale Center for British Art." *Architectural Record* 161 (June 1977): 95–104.

"Zur Arbeit von Venturi & Rauch/A Propos de Venturi & Rauch." *Werk-Archithèse* 64 (July–August 1977): 4–10. *Material in this article had previously appeared in the introduction to* The Work of Venturi and Rauch: Architects and Planners, *exh. cat. (New York: Whitney Museum of American Art, 1971); and in the note to* Complexity and Contradiction in Architecture, *by Robert Venturi, 2nd ed. (New York: The Museum of Modern Art; Chicago: Graham Foundation for Advanced Studies in the Fine Arts, 1977).*

1978 Introduction to *Diners*, by John Baeder. New York: H. N. Abrams, 1978.

Introduction to *The Travel Sketches of Louis I. Kahn*. Exh. cat. Philadelphia: Pennsylvania Academy of the Fine Arts, 1978.

1979 *The Earth, the Temple, and the Gods: Greek Sacred Architecture*. 3rd rev. ed. New Haven, Conn., and London: Yale University Press, 1979. *With new preface. The first edition was published by Yale University Press in 1962; the second revised edition was published by Praeger (New York) in 1969.*

"Can Less Be More?" *Newsweek,* 19 November 1979, 142.

Foreword to *The Architecture of John F. Staub: Houston and the South*, by Howard Barnstone. Austin: University of Texas Press, 1979.

Foreword to *The Decorative Designs of Frank Lloyd Wright*, by David A. Hanks. New York: E. P. Dutton, 1979.

Foreword to *Philip Johnson: Writings*. New York: Oxford University Press, 1979.

"On the Michael Graves Monograph." Review of *Michael Graves*, ed. David Dunster. *Architectural Design* 49, no. 10–11 (October–November 1979): 278.

1980 "Frank Lloyd Wright and the Stuff of Dreams." *Perspecta: The Yale Architectural Journal* 16 (1980): 8–31.

"How Things Got to Be the Way They Are Now." In *Architecture 1980: The Presence of the Past. Venice Biennale*, ed. Gabriella Borsano. New York: Rizzoli, 1980.

"The Tribune Competition 1922/1980." In *Late Entries to the Chicago Tribune Tower Competition*. Vol. 2 of *Chicago Tribune Tower Competition,* ed. Stanley Tigerman. New York: Rizzoli, 1980.

"Where Is Modern Architecture Going?" *G A (Global Architecture) Document* 1 (Summer 1980): 6–11.

1981 "Architecture, Sculpture, and Painting: Environment, Act, and Illusion." In *Collaboration: Artists and Architects*, ed. Barbaralee Diamonstein. Exh. cat. New York: Whitney Laboratory of Design, Watson-Guptill Publications, 1981.

Introduction to *Three Centuries of Notable American Architects*, ed. Joseph J. Thorndike Jr. New York: Charles Scribner's Sons and American Heritage, 1981.

"Marcel Breuer: 1902–1981." *Skyline* (October 1981): 11.

"Postscript: Ideology in Form." In *Aldo Rossi: A Scientific Autobiography*, by Aldo Rossi. Opposition Books. Cambridge, Mass.: MIT Press, 1981.

"Robert A. M. Stern: *Perspecta* to Post-Modernism." *Architectural Design* 51 (December 1981): 98–99.

"The Shingle Style Revival." *House Beautiful* 125 (August 1981): 76–77, 98–99.

"The Star in Stern: Sightings and Orientation." In *Robert Stern*, ed. David Dunster. London: Architectural Design and Academy Editions, 1981.

1982 With Antoinette F. Downing. *The Architectural Heritage of Newport, Rhode Island, 1640–1915*. 2nd rev. ed. New York: Bramhall House, 1967. Reprint, New York: American Legacy Press, 1982. *The first edition was published by Harvard University Press (Cambridge, Mass.) in 1952; the second revised edition was later reprinted by C. Potter (New York) in 1987.*

Wesleyan Photographs. Photographs by Philip Trager. Middletown, Conn.: Wesleyan University Press, 1982.

"Henry-Russell Hitchcock and the New Tradition." Introduction to *In Search of Modern Architecture: A Tribute to Henry-Russell Hitchcock*, ed. Helen Searing. New York: Architectural History Foundation; Cambridge, Mass.: MIT Press, 1982.

"The Humana Competition." In *A Tower for Louisville: The Humana Competition*, ed. Peter Arnell and Ted Bickford. New York: Rizzoli, 1982.

Introduction to *The Temples of Greece*. Photographs by Mary Peck. New York: [privately printed], 1982.

"Michael Graves' Allusive Architecture: The Problem of Mass." In *Michael Graves: Buildings and Projects, 1966–1981*, ed. Karen Vogel Wheeler, Peter Arnell, and Ted Bickford. New York: Rizzoli, 1982.

1983 "Architecture: Gwathmey Siegel and Associates." *Architectural Digest* 40 (December 1983): 120–31, 178, 80.

Introduction to *Prehistoric Pottery of the Southwest*. Exh. cat. New York: Whitney Museum of American Art, 1983.

"Le Corbusier, 1922–1965." In *Cité Frugès and Other Buildings and Projects, 1923–1927*. Vol. 2 of *The Le Corbusier Archive*, ed. H. Allen Brooks. New York and London: Garland; Paris: Fondation Le Corbusier, 1983. *Later republished in* Le Corbusier, *ed. H. Allen Brooks (Princeton: Princeton University Press, 1987).*

Preface to *Pasanella and Klein: Interventi pubblici e privati nel settore della residenza*, by Alessandra Latour. Rome: Edizioni Kappa, 1983.

1984 "Architecture in Context—America's Eminent Architectural Historian Begins a New Column with the Intriguing Question: Does MoMA Always Know Best?" *Architectural Digest* 41 (August 1984): 134, 138, 140, 142.

"Architecture in Context—In the First of a Series on 'The Natural and the Man-Made,' Vincent Scully Looks at the Spiritual Harmonies of Pre-Columbian and Pueblo Architecture." *Architectural Digest* 41 (September 1984): 52, 58–59, 64.

"Architecture in Context—Continuing His Series on 'The Natural and the Man-Made,' Vincent Scully Lauds the Ziggurat, Temple and Pyramid." *Architectural Digest* 41 (October 1984): 66, 72, 78, 82.

"Architecture in Context—Vincent Scully Traces the Progression from Minoan Palaces—Ruled by Nature—to Archaic Greek Temples—Glorifying Man." *Architectural Digest* 41 (November 1984): 216, 222, 227.

"Architecture in Context—Two Classical Sites Reflect the Polarities of Ancient Greek Thought: One Law-Abiding, the Other Ruthless and Expansive." *Architectural Digest* 41 (December 1984): 214, 218, 222.

"Architecture: Margaret McCurry, Stanley Tigerman." *Architectural Digest* 41 (April 1984): 156–63, 194–95.

"Architecture: Robert A. M. Stern." *Architectural Digest* 41 (June 1984): 136–41, 164, 166.

"Between Wright and Louis Kahn." In *Carlo Scarpa: The Complete Works*, ed. Francesco Dal Co and Giuseppe Mazzariol. Milan: Electa; New York: Rizzoli, 1984/1985.

1985 "Architecture in Context—Following the Precedent of Roman Architecture, Renaissance Villas Reflect Man's Hard-Won Victory over Nature." *Architectural Digest* 41 (February 1985): 150, 152, 156, 158, 160.

"Architecture in Context—Framing Nature, Greek Temples Defined the Environment and Inspired the Architecture of Ancient Rome." *Architectural Digest* 41 (January 1985): 148, 150, 152, 154, 156.

"Architecture: Venturi, Rauch and Scott Brown." *Architectural Digest* 41 (March 1985): 184–91, 234, 236.

"Buildings without Souls." *New York Times Magazine*, 8 September 1985, sec. 6, pp. 42–43, 62–66, 109–11, 116.

"The End of the Century Finds a Poet." Introduction to *Aldo Rossi: Buildings and Projects*, ed. Peter Arnell and Ted Bickford. New York: Rizzoli, 1985.

"Epoch Architecture—From Times Square to Red Square." Review of *New York 1900*, by Robert A. M. Stern et al., and *Gold in Azure*, by William Craft Brumfield. *Architectural Digest* 42 (December 1985): 206, 210, 214, 218.

"The Seal: An Existential Odyssey at Branford Harbor." *Architectural Digest* 42 (October 1985): 30, 34–35, 38.

1986 *The Villas of Palladio.* Photographs by Philip Trager. Boston: Little, Brown, 1986. *Portions of this text had previously appeared in "Palladio in Context: The Classical and Vernacular Traditions,"* Close-up *16 (Spring 1986): 37–43.*

"American Architecture: The Real and the Ideal." In *American Architecture: Innovation and Tradition*, ed. David G. De Long, Helen Searing, and Robert A. M. Stern. New York: Rizzoli, 1986.

"Architecture: Philip Johnson. The Glass House Revisited." *Architectural Digest* 43 (November 1986): 116–25, 220. *Later republished in* Philip Johnson: The Glass House, *ed. David Whitney and Jeffrey Kipnis (New York: Pantheon Books, 1993).*

"Architecture: Robert A. M. Stern." *Architectural Digest* 43 (March 1986): 108–15.

Foreword to *Studies and Executed Buildings by Frank Lloyd Wright.* New York: Rizzoli, 1986. *This book is a translation of Frank Lloyd Wright,* Ausgefürte Bauten und Entwürfe von Frank Lloyd Wright *(Berlin: Ernst Wasmuth, 1910).*

"Frank Lloyd Wright and Philip Johnson at Yale." *Architectural Digest* 43 (November 1986): 90, 94.

"Louis I. Kahn in the Soviet Union." *Architectural Digest* 43 (May 1986): 62, 66, 71.

"Mies—The Centennial Exhibition." *Architectural Digest* 43 (October 1986): 76, 80, 84, 86.

"Palladio in Context: The Classical and Vernacular Traditions." *Close-up* 16 (Spring 1986): 37–43. *Later republished in* The Villas of Palladio, *photographs by Philip Trager (Boston: Little, Brown, 1986).*

"Unity Temple and the A & A." *Perspecta: The Yale Architectural Journal* 22 (1986): 108–11.

1987 With Antoinette F. Downing. *The Architectural Heritage of Newport, Rhode Island, 1640–1915.* 2nd rev. ed. New York: Bramhall House, 1967. Reprint, New York: C. Potter, 1987. *The first edition was published by Harvard University Press (Cambridge, Mass.) in 1952.*

"Architecture: David Sellers." *Architectural Digest* 44 (June 1987): 146–51, 220, 222.

"Charles Moore at Williams." *Architectural Digest* 44 (December 1987): 66, 70–71, 74, 78.

Introduction to *The Louis I. Kahn Archive: Personal Drawings. The Completely Illustrated Catalogue of the Drawings in the Louis I. Kahn Collection, University of Pennsylvania and Pennsylvania Historical and Museum Commission.* 7 vols. New York and London: Garland, 1987. *Later republished as "Jehová en el Olimpio: Louis Kahn y el final del Movimiento Moderno."* A & V: Monografías de Arquitectura y Vivienda, *no. 44 (November–December 1993): 6–15; English trans. 97–100.*

"Le Corbusier, 1922–1965." In *Le Corbusier*, ed. H. Allen Brooks. Princeton: Princeton University Press, 1987. *This article had previously appeared in* Cité Frugès and Other Buildings and Projects, 1923–1927, *vol. 2 of* The Le Corbusier Archive, *ed. H. Allen Brooks (New York and London: Garland; Paris: Foundation Le Corbusier, 1983.*

"The Meyer May House in Context." In *The Meyer May House, Grand Rapids, Michigan.* Grand Rapids, Mich.: Steelcase, 1987. *Later republished as "Das Meyer May House in seiner Umgebung: Exzellente Restaurierung eines 'Prairie House' von F. L. Wright in Grand Rapids, Michigan."* Architektur, Innenarchitektur, Technischer Ausbau *98 (January–February 1990): 44–50.*

"Robert A. M. Stern: New Spaces in an East Hampton Shingle-Style Cottage." *Architectural Digest* 44 (September 1987): 26–31.

"The Shape of Ourselves: Robert Venturi's Chairs." *Architectural Digest* 44 (April 1987): 62, 68, 73.

1988 *American Architecture and Urbanism.* 2nd rev. ed. New York: H. Holt, 1988. *With new preface. The first edition was published by Praeger (New York) in 1969.*

New World Visions of Household Gods and Sacred Places: American Art and the Metropolitan Museum of Art, 1650–1914. Boston: Little, Brown, 1988.

"Aldo Rossi: Architect of Love and Memory." *Architectural Digest* 45 (October 1988): 148, 150, 153.

"California Dreamers: How Charles and Henry Greene Changed the Look of America." *Art and Antiques* 11 (September 1988): 98–103.

"The Failure of the Hero Architect." *Metropolitan Home* 20 (November 1988): 81–83, 200.

Foreword to *Domino's Mansion: Thomas Monaghan, Gunnar Birkerts and the Spirit of Frank Lloyd Wright*, by Gordon Pritchard Bugbee. Troy, Mich.: Planning Research Organization for a Better Environment Press, 1988.

Introduction to *Hugh Newell Jacobsen, Architect*, ed. Massimo Vignelli. Washington, D.C.: The American Institute of Architects Press, 1988.

Introduction to *The Nature of Frank Lloyd Wright*, ed. Carol R. Bolon et al. Chicago: University of Chicago Press, 1988.

"Ricardo Bofill: Vincent Scully Assesses the Radical Classicism of the Spanish Architect's Housing Projects." *Architectural Digest* 45 (April 1988): 59–61.

"Winslow Homer and the Waters." *Architectural Digest* 45 (April 1988): 204, 210, 214.

1989 *The Architecture of the American Summer: The Flowering of the Shingle Style.* New York: Rizzoli, 1989.

Pueblo: Mountain, Village, Dance. 2nd rev. ed. Chicago: University of Chicago Press, 1989. *With new preface and postscript. The first edition was published by Viking Press (New York) in 1975.*

"Architecture: Frank Furness. A Stick Style Curiosity on the Jersey Coast." *Architectural Digest* 46 (March 1989): 34, 38, 42.

Foreword to *American Classicist: The Architecture of Philip Trammell Shutze*, by Elizabeth Meredith Dowling. New York: Rizzoli, 1989.

"Robert Venturi's Gentle Architecture." In *The Architecture of Robert Venturi*, ed. Christopher Mead. Albuquerque: University of New Mexico Press, 1989.

"Theory and Delight: Wexner Center for the Visual Arts." *Progressive Architecture* 70 (October 1989): 86–87. *Later republished as "Teoría y deleite: Las abstracciones de Eisenman,"* Arquitectura Viva, *no. 11 (March–April 1990): 27–31.*

1990 With Rudolph F. Zallinger, Leo J. Hickey, and John H. Ostrom. *The Great Dinosaur Mural at Yale: The Age of Reptiles.* New York: H. N. Abrams, 1990.

"Animal Spirits." *Progressive Architecture* 71 (October 1990): 90–91.

"The Automobile Is a Destroyer." *Connecticut Preservation News* 13 (September–October 1990): 4.

"The Blacksmith." *Yale Alumni Magazine* 54 (November 1990): 32–33.

"Das Meyer May House in seiner Umgebung: Exzellente Restaurierung eines 'Prairie House' von F. L. Wright in Grand Rapids, Michigan." *Architektur, Innenarchitektur, Technischer Ausbau* 98 (January–February 1990): 44–50. *This article had previously appeared as "The Meyer May House in Context," in* The Meyer May House, Grand Rapids, Michigan *(Grand Rapids, Mich.: Steelcase, 1987).*

"Michael Graves." *Architectural Design* ("Post-Modernism on Trial" Issue) 60, no. 88 (1990): 44–59.

"Shingle-Minded Pursuits: A Massachusetts Town Is Rediscovering Its Legacy of Master Builders." *House and Garden* 162 (November 1990): 57–66.

"Teoría y deleite: Las abstracciones de Eisenman." *Arquitectura Viva*, no. 11 (March–April 1990): 27–31. *This article had previously appeared as "Theory and Delight: Wexner Center for the Visual Arts,"* Progressive Architecture *70 (October 1989): 86–87.*

1991 *Architecture: The Natural and the Manmade.* New York: St. Martin's Press, 1991.

"Architecture: The Natural and the Manmade." In *Denatured Visions: Landscape and Culture in the Twentieth Century*, ed. Stuart Wrede and William Howard Adams. New York: The Museum of Modern Art, 1991. *Later republished in revised forms as "Architecture: The Natural and the Manmade," Stated Meeting Report,* Bulletin of the American Academy of Arts and Sciences *46 (November 1992): 30–53; as "Mankind and the Earth in America and Europe," in* The Ancient Americas: Art from Sacred Landscapes*, ed. Richard F. Townsend, exh. cat. (Chicago: The Art Institute of Chicago, 1992); as "Arquitectura y naturaleza: El hombre y la tierra en América y Europa,"* Saber Ver *11 (July–August 1993): 36–75; and as "Architecture: The Natural and the Manmade," in* The Encyclopedia of the Environment*, ed. Ruth A. Eblen and William R. Eblen (Boston and New York: Houghton Mifflin, 1994).*

"Back to the Future, With a Detour through Miami." *New York Times*, 27 January 1991, sec. 2, p. 32.

Introduction to *Louis I. Kahn: In the Realm of Architecture*, by David B. Brownlee and David G. De Long. Exh. cat. Los Angeles: The Museum of Contemporary Art; New York: Rizzoli, 1991.

Introduction to *The Paintings and Sketches of Louis I. Kahn*, by Jan Hochstim. New York: Rizzoli, 1991.

"Marvelous Fountainheads. Louis I. Kahn: Travel Drawings." *Lotus International*, no. 68 (1991): 49–63.

"Seaside and New Haven." In *Andres Duany and Elizabeth Plater-Zyberk: Towns and Town-Making*, ed. Alex Krieger and William Lennertz. New York: Rizzoli; Cambridge, Mass.: Harvard University Graduate School of Design, 1991.

"Something New under the Sun: Ca'Ziff." *Metropolitan Home* 23 (June 1991): 49–57, 94.

"The Terrible Art of Designing a War Memorial." *New York Times*, 14 July 1991, sec. 2, p. 28. *Later republished as "Un Art redoutable: Concevoir un mémorial de guerre," trans. Françoise Hamon, Françoise Levaillant, and Joel Perrin,* Histoire de l'art *27 (October 1994): 93–95.*

"The Work of a Lone Hero." *The Pennsylvania Gazette: Alumni Magazine of the University of Pennsylvania* 90 (December 1991): 29–31.

1992 "Architecture: The Natural and the Manmade." Stated Meeting Report. *Bulletin of the American Academy of Arts and Sciences* 46 (November 1992): 30–53. *This article is a revised version of "Architecture: The Natural and the Manmade," in* Denatured Visions: Landscape and Culture in the Twentieth Century*, ed. Stuart Wrede and William Howard Adams (New York: The Museum of Modern Art, 1991).*

"Everybody Needs Everything." In *Mother's House: The Evolution of Vanna Venturi's House in Chestnut Hill*, ed. Frederic Schwartz. New York: Rizzoli, 1992.

Introduction to *French Royal Gardens: The Designs of André Le Nôtre.* Photographs by Jeannie Baubion-Mackler. New York: Rizzoli, 1992.

Introduction to *Robert A. M. Stern: Buildings and Projects, 1987–1992*, ed. Elizabeth Kraft. New York: Rizzoli, 1992.

"Louis I. Kahn and the Ruins of Rome." *MoMA: The Members Quarterly of the Museum of Modern Art*, no. 12 (Summer 1992): 1–13. *Later republished in* Engineering and Science *56 (Winter 1993): 2–13.*

"Mankind and the Earth in America and Europe." In *The Ancient Americas: Art from Sacred Landscapes*, ed. Richard F. Townsend. Exh. cat. Chicago: The Art Institute of Chicago, 1992. *This article is a revised version of "Architecture: The Natural and the Manmade," in* Denatured Visions: Landscape and Culture in the Twentieth Century, *ed. Stuart Wrede and William Howard Adams (New York: The Museum of Modern Art, 1991). This article was later republished as "Arquitectura y naturaleza: El hombre y la tierra en América y Europa,"* Saber Ver *11 (July–August 1993): 36–75.*

"Style and Context." *Yale Review* 80 (April 1992): 17–25.

1993 "Arquitectura y naturaleza: El hombre y la tierra en América y Europa." *Saber Ver* 11 (July–August 1993): 36–75. *This article had previously appeared as "Mankind and the Earth in America and Europe," in* The Ancient Americas: Art from Sacred Landscapes, *ed. Richard F. Townsend, exh. cat. (Chicago: The Art Institute of Chicago, 1992).*

Foreword to *Graham Gund Architects*. Washington, D.C.: American Institute of Architects, 1993.

Foreword to *Modern Architecture: Romanticism and Reintegration*, by Henry-Russell Hitchcock. New York: Payson and Clarke, 1929. Reprint, New York: Da Capo Press, 1993. *Scully's foreword appeared only in the reprint edition.*

"Jehová en el Olimpio: Louis Kahn y el final del Movimiento Moderno." *A & V: Monografías de Arquitectura y Vivienda*, no. 44 (November–December 1993): 6–15; English trans. 97–100. *This article had previously appeared as the introduction to* The Louis I. Kahn Archive: Personal Drawings. The Completely Illustrated Catalogue of the Drawings in the Louis I. Kahn Collection, University of Pennsylvania and Pennsylvania Historical Museum Commission, *7 vols. (New York and London: Garland, 1987).*

"Louis I. Kahn and the Ruins of Rome." *Engineering and Science* 56 (Winter 1993): 2–13. *This article had previously appeared in* MoMA: The Members Quarterly of the Museum of Modern Art, *no. 12 (Summer 1992): 1–13.*

"Philip Johnson: The Glass House Revisited." In *Philip Johnson: The Glass House,* ed. David Whitney and Jeffrey Kipnis. New York: Pantheon Books, 1993. *This article had previously appeared as "Architecture: Philip Johnson. The Glass House Revisited,"* Architectural Digest *43 (November 1986): 116–25, 220.*

"A Virtual Landmark." *Progressive Architecture* 74 (September 1993): 80.

1994 "The Architecture of Community." In *The New Urbanism: Toward an Architecture of Community*, by Peter Katz. New York: McGraw-Hill, 1994. *Later republished in* Projetto *3 (June 1998): 38–49.*

"Architecture: The Natural and the Manmade." In *The Encyclopedia of the Environment*, ed. Ruth A. Eblen and William R. Eblen. Boston and New York: Houghton Mifflin, 1994. *This is a revised version of the article that had previously appeared in* Denatured Visions: Landscape and Culture in the Twentieth Century, *ed. Stuart Wrede and William Howard Adams (New York: The Museum of Modern Art, 1991).*

"Un Art redoutable: Concevoir un mémorial de guerre." Trans. Françoise Hamon, Françoise Levaillant, and Joel Perrin. *Histoire de l'art* 27 (October 1994): 93–95. *This article had previously appeared as "The Terrible Art of Designing a War Memorial,* New York Times, *14 July 1991, sec. 2, p. 28.*

"The Lipstick at Yale: A Memoir (1989)." In *Large Scale Projects*, by Claes Oldenburg and Coosje van Bruggen. New York: Monacelli Press, 1994.

"Urban Architecture Awakens from a Bad Dream." *City Journal* 4 (Autumn 1994): 75–80.

1996 "The Architecture of Community." 1996 Raoul Wallenberg Lecture. Ann Arbor: University of Michigan, College of Architecture and Planning, 1996. *Later republished in revised and abridged form as "America at the Millennium: Architecture and Community," in* The Pritzker Architecture Prize 1998: Celebrating the Twentieth Anniversary of the Prize: Presented to Renzo Piano *(Los Angeles: Hyatt Foundation, Jensen & Walker, 1999).*

With Jorge Hernandez, Catherine Lynn, and Teofilo Victoria. *Between Two Towers: The Drawings of the School of Miami*. New York: Monacelli Press, 1996.

"Charles Barrett: Architetto classico." *A & C International*, no. 5 (September–December 1996): 14–17.

Foreword to *Building a Dream: The Art of Disney Architecture*, by Beth Dunlop. New York: H. N. Abrams, 1996.

Foreword to *Centerbrook: Volume 2*, by Andrea Oppenheimer Dean. Rockport, Mass.: Rockport Publishers, 1996.

Introduction to *Philip Johnson dall'International Style al Decostruttivismo*, by Alba Cappellieri. Naples: CLEAN, 1996.

"Philip Johnson: Classicism, Revolution, and Existential Change." *ANY (Architecture New York)* (special issue), no. 90 (1996): 58.

1997 "A Dream of Coral Gables." In *Coral Gables: An American Garden City*, ed. Roberto M. Behar and Maurice G. Culot. University of Miami School of Architecture, Institut Français d'Architecture. Paris: Éditions Norma, 1997.

"Jonathan Weinberg Moralist." In *Jonathan Weinberg: Paintings and Prints*. Exh. cat. New York: Cortland Jessup Gallery, 1997.

"The Mall That May Ruin Coral Gables." *Forum: The Magazine of the Florida Humanities Council* 20 (Summer 1997): 7–9.

"A New Modern Eclectic." In *Alexander Gorlin: Buildings and Projects*. New York: Rizzoli, 1997.

1998 "The Architecture of Community." *Projetto* 3 (June 1998): 38–49. *This article had previously appeared in* The New Urbanism: Toward an Architecture of Community, *by Peter Katz (New York: McGraw-Hill, 1994).*

"The Architecture of Yale and New Haven: Built on Change and Mutual Respect." *Yale Daily News*, 6 November 1998, B1–B2.

"The Banque Bruxelles Lambert (Suisse), Geneva Context." In *Bank and Architecture: Banque Bruxelles Lambert-Geneva; Mario Botta-Architect.* Geneva: Banque Bruxelles Lambert; Milan: Electa, 1998.

"A Lesson on Louis I. Kahn." *Area: Rivista Internazionale di architettura e arti del progetto* 39 (July–August 1998): 82–85.

"Vietnam Veterans Memorial." In *Maya Lin.* Milan: Electa; Rome: American Academy in Rome, 1998.

"The View from Above." Review of *Bird's Eye Views: Historic Lithographs of American Cities*, by John W. Reps. *Preservation: The Magazine of the National Trust for Historic Preservation* 50 (November–December 1998): 87–88.

1999 "America at the Millennium: Architecture and Community." In *The Pritzker Architecture Prize 1998: Celebrating the Twentieth Anniversary of the Prize: Presented to Renzo Piano.* Los Angeles: Hyatt Foundation, Jensen & Walker, 1999. *Although the title "America at the Millennium: Architecture and Community" did not appear in the Pritzker publication, it was the title given by Scully to the original lecture. This is a revised and abridged version of the article that had previously appeared as "The Architecture of Community," 1996 Raoul Wallenberg Lecture (Ann Arbor: University of Michigan, College of Architecture and Planning, 1996).*

"Best Town Square." *New York Times Magazine,* 18 April 1999, sec. 6, p. 118.

Foreword to *Shepley Bulfinch Richardson and Abbott: Past to Present*, by Julia Heskel. Boston: Shepley Bulfinch Richardson and Abbott, 1999.

"Tomorrow's Ruins Today." *New York Times Magazine*, 5 December 1999, sec. 6, pp. 38, 42.

2000 "The American City in A.D. 2025." *Brookings Review* 18 (Summer 2000): 4–5.

"On Cesar Pelli." In *Cesar Pelli: Building Designs, 1965–2000.* New Haven, Conn.: Yale University School of Architecture, 2000.

Foreword to *Density by Design: New Directions in Residential Development*, by Steven Fader. Washington D.C.: Urban Land Institute, 2000.

"Yale, New Haven, and the Buildings for the Arts." *Yale University Art Gallery Bulletin* (2000): 21–25.

2001 "On New Blue." In *New Blue: Recent Work of Graduates of Yale School of Architecture, 1978–1998.* New Haven, Conn.: Yale University School of Architecture, 2001.

Index

Page numbers in *italics* refer to illustrations.

D

E

H

I

S

T

U

V

W

Y

Z

Text and Photography Credits

Permission to reproduce the essays in this volume is provided by the publishers as listed on the opening page of each chapter. Additional text credits are as follows:

ART IN AMERICA, December 1954, Brant Publications, Inc. (chap. 3)

© 2003 Artists Rights Society (ARS), New York/ADAGP, Paris/FLC (chap.13)

© 1954, ARTnews LLC. Reprinted courtesy of the publisher (chap. 2)

Reproduced by permission of The McGraw-Hill Companies (chap. 19)

Reprinted by permission. © 1991 The Museum of Modern Art, New York (chap. 16); © 1992 The Museum of Modern Art, New York (chap. 17)

Copyright © 1963 by Princeton University Press. Reprinted by permission of Princeton University Press (chap. 6)

Copyright © 2003. Reproduced by permission of Routledge, Inc., part of The Taylor & Francis Group (chap. 14)

The photographers and the sources of visual material other than those indicated in the captions are as follows (numerals refer to figures). Every effort has been made to credit the photographers and the sources; if there are errors or omissions, please contact Princeton University Press so that corrections can be made in any subsequent edition.

Alinari/Art Resource, New York (12.1, 12.2, 12.14, 12.16, 12.18, 12.19); and Scala/Art Resource, New York (19.7)

Art Resource, New York (4.4)

Artistic Houses: Being a Series of Interior Views of a Number of the Most Beautiful and Celebrated Homes in the United States, with a Description of the Art Treasures Contained Therein (New York: D. Appleton, 1883–84), facing 106 (11.1)

© 2002 Artists Rights Society (ARS), New York/ADAGP, Paris/FLC (4.8, 4.9, 9.5, 13.1, 13.3)

© 2002 Artists Rights Society (ARS), New York/Beeldrecht, Amsterdam: (17.1); The Museum of Modern Art, New York, Acquired through the Lillie P. Bliss Bequest, oil on canvas, 53 1/2 x 24 1/4 in. (135.9 x 61.6 cm), Photograph © 2002 The Museum of Modern Art, New York (6.4)

© 2002 Artists Rights Society (ARS), New York/VG Bild-Kunst, Bonn: (15.4); Yale University Art Gallery, New Haven, Connecticut, Gift of the Collection Societe Anonyme (8.8)

James Bailey, "Louis Kahn in India: An Old Order on a New Scale," *Architectural Forum* 125 (July–August 1966): 44 (17.26)

Sylvester Baxter, "The Government's Housing at Bridgeport, Connecticut," *Architectural Record* 45 (February 1919): 135 (20.6)

Courtesy of the Busch-Reisinger Museum, Harvard University Art Museums, Cambridge, Massachusetts, Gift of Walter Gropius, Photo: Photographic Services, © President and Fellows of Harvard College, Harvard University (2.1)

Photograph courtesy Calthorpe Associates, Berkeley, California (19.1)

© Collection Centre Canadien d'Architecture/Canadian Centre for Architecture, Montreal, Photo: Henry Fuermann (1.23)

Photograph © by Richard Cheek for the Preservation Society of Newport County, Rhode Island (1.26)

Chicago Historical Society, Photo: Bill Hedrich, Hedrich-Blessing (HB-04414-E3) (2.11)

Division of Rare and Manuscript Collections, Cornell University Library, Ithaca, New York (19.5)

Photograph courtesy Duany Plater-Zyberk & Company (19.4); property of U.S.H.U.D., shows the Central Neighborhood, Cleveland, designed by Duany Plater-Zyberk & Company (20.5)

Photograph copyright © Pedro E. Guerrero (4.7, 8.14)

Jan Hochstim, *The Paintings and Sketches of Louis I. Kahn* (New York: Rizzoli, 1991), 63 (17.3)

By permission of the Houghton Library, Harvard University, Cambridge, Massachusetts (16.18); Department of Printing and Graphic Arts, Houghton Library, Harvard College Library, Typ 520.16.425 (17.9)

Reproduced by permission of The Huntington Library, San Marino, California. Photo: Harwell Hamilton Harris Papers, The Alexander Architectural Archive, The General Libraries, The University of Texas at Austin (8.2)

IBM Corporate Archives (8.17)

Courtesy Johnson Wax (11.18)

Louis I. Kahn, *The Work of Louis I. Kahn: La Jolla Museum of Art* (San Diego: Federal Printing Co., 1965), n.p. (17.16)

Copyright 1977 Louis I. Kahn Collection, University of Pennsylvania and Pennsylvania Historical and Museum Commission (6.6, 6.8, 9.1, 17.5, 17.8, 17.12, 17.20, 18.8, 18.12, 18.20); Photo: George Pohl (17.19)

By permission of Sue Ann Kahn (17.4, 17.6, 17.10)

Kevin Roche, John Dinkeloo, and Associates (9.6)

Michael Marsland/Yale University, New Haven, Connecticut (9.2, 9.3, 17.11)

Rare Books and Special Materials Collection, Media Union Library, University of Michigan, Ann Arbor, Photo: Henry Fuermann (11.9, 11.14)

Arthur Ingersoll Meigs, *An American Country House, the Property of Arthur E. Newbold, Jr., Esq., Laverock, Pa.* (New York: The Architectural Book Publishing Co., 1925), 9 (17.2)

All Rights Reserved, The Metropolitan Museum of Art, New York, Rogers Fund, 1903, 03.14.13 (12.8)

The Mies van der Rohe Archive, The Museum of Modern Art, New York, Gift of the architect, ink on illustration board, 30 x 40 in. (76.2 x 101.6 cm), © 2002 The Museum of Modern Art, New York (2.3)

Photograph Courtesy The Mies van der Rohe Archive, The Museum of Modern Art, New York (2.5, 8.21, 12.33)

MIT Museum, Cambridge, Massachusetts (8.22)

Nancy Mitford, *The Sun King* (New York: Harper and Row, 1966), facing 120 (16.15)

Elizabeth B. Mock, *If You Want to Build a House* (New York: Museum of Modern Art, 1946), 36 (8.9)

© 1989 Thomas S. Monaghan, Henry Fuermann Collection. Photograph used by permission, Ave Maria University (11.17, 12.32)

© 2002 Mondrian/Holtzman Trust/Artists Rights Society (ARS), New York. Photo: Giraudon/Art Resource, New York (2.7); Peggy Guggenheim Collection, Venice, The Solomon R. Guggenheim Foundation, New York, Photograph © The Solomon R. Guggenheim Foundation, photo: David Heald (4.5)

Michael Moran (19.3, 19.6)

Grant Mudford (17.32)

Courtesy, Museum of Fine Arts, Boston, Reproduced with permission, © 2000 Museum of Fine Arts, Boston, All Rights Reserved: Gift of Mary Louisa Boit, Julia Overing Boit, Jane Hubbard Boit, and Florence D. Boit in memory of their father, Edward Darley Boit, 19.124, oil on canvas, 87 3/8 x 87 5/8 in. (221.9 x 222.6 cm) (1.25); Harvard University, Museum of Fine Arts Expedition, 11.1738, 54 5/8 x 22 3/8 x 21 1/4 in. (139 x 57 x 54 cm) (12.4)

The Museum of Modern Art, New York, Gift of The Howard Gilman Foundation, graphite and color pencil on tracing paper, 21 3/4 x 38 3/4 in. (55.2 x 98.4 cm), Digital Image © 2002 The Museum of Modern Art, New York (10.1)

Photograph © Hans Namuth, Ltd. (15.6)

The Newport Historical Society, Newport, Rhode Island, Photograph by Wm. King Covell, Covell Collection: neg. 103 (1.22); neg. 104 (1.24)

Office for Metropolitan Architecture, Rotterdam, Netherlands (10.5)

Peterson/Littenberg Architects (19.8)

© 2002 Estate of Pablo Picasso/Artists Rights Society (ARS), New York: (12.28, 12.29); Giraudon/Art Resource, New York (5.4); National Gallery of Canada, Ottawa, Purchased 1957 (12.3); Gift of R. Sturgis and Marion B. F. Ingersoll, Philadelphia Museum of Art (12.31)

Photograph © Robert A.M. Stern Architects (15.7, 19.9)

Photograph © Cervin Robinson, All Rights Reserved (4.3, 6.3)

Jan Rowan, "Wanting to Be," *Progressive Architecture* 42 (April 1961): 134 (17.13)

Vincent Scully, "Archetype and Order in Recent American Architecture," *Art in America* 42 (December 1954): 252 (3.1)

———, "Architecture, Sculpture, and Painting: Environment, Act, and Illusion," in *Collaboration: Artists and Architects,* ed. Barbaralee Diamonstein, exh. cat. (New York: Whitney Laboratory of Design, Watson-Guptill Publications, 1981), 29 (12.17), 51 (12.43)

———, "Doldrums in the Suburbs," *Journal of the Society of Architectural Historians* 24 (March 1965): 37 (8.4), 38 (8.5, 8.6), 39 (8.7), 40 (8.10), 43 (8.16)

———, "Frank Lloyd Wright and the Stuff of Dreams," *Perspecta: The Yale Architectural Journal* 16 (1980): 12 (11.2)

———, "Robert Venturi's Gentle Architecture," in *The Architecture of Robert Venturi,* ed. Christopher Mead (Albuquerque: University of New Mexico Press, 1989) 15 (15.5)

E. G. Squier and E. H. Davis, *Ancient Monuments of the Mississippi Valley: Comprising the Results of Extensive Original Surveys and Explorations* (Washington, D.C.: Smithsonian Institution, 1848), facing 3 (20.4)

John Calvin Stevens and Albert Winslow Cobb, *Examples of American Domestic Architecture* (New York: W. T. Comstock, 1889), plate XXXVIII (1.10)

Tate Gallery, London/Art Resource, New York (1.27)

Photograph courtesy Venturi, Scott Brown, and Associates (12.40–12.42, 12.46, 15.1, 15.2, 15.9, 15.11–15.13, 15.16–15.21, 15.23–15.25, 18.3, 18.4, 18.9–18.11, 18.13–18.19, 18.21–18.34); Photo: Tom Bernard (15.8, 15.22); Photo: Tom Crane (10.4); Photo: George Pohl (15.15); Photograph © Cervin Robinson (15.10); Photo: William Watkins (15.14)

Ernst Wasmuth, *Ausgeführte Bauten und Entwürfe von Frank Lloyd Wright* (Berlin, 1910), plate IL (2.2)

World's Columbian Exposition. Official Views of the World's Columbian Exposition, issued by the Department of Photography, C. D. Arnold and H. G. Higinbotham, official photographers (Chicago: Chicago Photo-Gravure Co., 1893), plate 13 (12.26)

Frank Lloyd Wright, *The Early Work* (New York: Horizon, 1968), 64 (11.20)

Courtesy The Frank Lloyd Wright Archives, Scottsdale, Arizona (6.1, 11.10)

The drawings of Frank Lloyd Wright are copyright © 2001 The Frank Lloyd Wright Foundation, Scottsdale, Arizona (11.16)

© 2002 Frank Lloyd Wright Foundation, Scottsdale, Arizona./Artists Rights Society (ARS), New York (2.2, 2.4, 2.6, 2.10, 2.12, 6.2, 6.5)

Yale University Art Gallery, New Haven, Connecticut, Gift of the Collection Societe Anonyme (12.30)

Designed by Scott Santoro / Worksight

Typeset in Minion and Trade Gothic by Sam Potts

Printed on 115 gsm Nippon Paper Matt Art

Printed and bound by South China Printing, Hong Kong